"P.S. BURN AFTER READING"

The Kellock-Taschereau Commission and Soviet Espionage in Canada

PATRONS OF THE SOCIETY

Professor Constance Backhouse

Chernos, Flaherty, Svonkin, LLP

Gowling WLG

Hull & Hull LLP

Mr. Wayne Kerr

The Law Foundation of Ontario

McCarthy Tetrault

Osler, Hoskin & Harcourt LLP

Pape Chaudhury

Paliare Roland Rosenberg Rothstein LLP

The Hon. Robert Sharpe

Torys LLP

WeirFoulds LLP

The Osgoode Society is supported by a grant from
The Law Foundation of Ontario

The Law Foundation of Ontario
Advancing access to justice

The Society also thanks The Law Society of Ontario
for its continuing support.

REINHOLD KRAMER AND TOM MITCHELL

"P.S. Burn After Reading"

The Kellock-Taschereau Commission and Soviet Espionage in Canada

Published for the Osgoode Society for Canadian Legal History by
University of Toronto Press
Toronto Buffalo London

Toronto Buffalo London
utppublishing.com
Printed and bound by CPI Group (UK) Ltd, Croydon, CR0 4YY

ISBN 978-1-0498-0466-8 (cloth)   ISBN 978-1-0498-0468-2 (EPUB)
ISBN 978-1- 0498-0467-5 (PDF)

Library and Archives Canada Cataloguing in Publication

Title: "P.S. burn after reading" : the Kellock-Taschereau Commission and Soviet espionage in Canada / Reinhold Kramer and Tom Mitchell.
Other titles: Kellock-Taschereau Commission and Soviet espionage in Canada
Names: Kramer, Reinhold, 1959– author | Mitchell, Tom, 1949– author
Series: Osgoode Society for Canadian Legal History series.
Description: Series statement: Osgoode Society for Canadian Legal History series | Includes bibliographical references and index.
Identifiers: Canadiana (print) 20260175250 | Canadiana (ebook) 20260175269 | ISBN 9781049804668 (cloth) | ISBN 9781049804675 (PDF) | ISBN 9781049804682 (EPUB)
Subjects: LCSH: Canada. Royal Commission to Investigate the Facts Relating to and the Circumstances Surrounding the Communication by Public Officials and Other Persons in Positions of Trust of Secret and Confidential Information to Agents of a Foreign Power. | LCSH: Gouzenko Affair, Canada, 1945–1946. | LCSH: Espionage, Soviet – Canada. | LCSH: Spies – Canada. | LCSH: Intelligence service – Canada. | LCSH: Canada – Politics and government – 1945–1980. | CSH: Canada – Politics and government – 1935–1957.
Classification: LCC FC583.G6 K73 2026 | DDC 327.1247/071 – dc23

Cover design: John Beadle
Cover image: Envato

The manufacturer's authorised representative in the EU for product safety is Mare Nostrum Group B.V., Doelen 72, 4831 GR Breda, The Netherlands.
Email: gpsr@mare-nostrum.co.uk.

We wish to acknowledge the land on which the University of Toronto Press operates. This land is the traditional territory of the Wendat, the Anishnaabeg, the Haudenosaunee, the Métis, and the Mississaugas of the Credit First Nation.

This book has been published with the help of a grant from the Federation for the Humanities and Social Sciences, through the Awards to Scholarly Publications Program, using funds provided by the Social Sciences and Humanities Research Council of Canada.

University of Toronto Press acknowledges the financial support of the Government of Canada, the Canada Council for the Arts, and the Ontario Arts Council, an agency of the Government of Ontario, for its publishing activities.

Canada Council for the Arts   Conseil des Arts du Canada

ONTARIO ARTS COUNCIL
CONSEIL DES ARTS DE L'ONTARIO
an Ontario government agency
un organisme du gouvernement de l'Ontario

Funded by the Government of Canada   Financé par le gouvernement du Canada   Canada

To Rhett, Brody, Wynn, and Sid, twenty-first-century Canadians

To Rita

Contents

Foreword ix

Acknowledgments xi

Introduction 3

1 The Gouzenko Question 7

2 Read / Varcoe Redux 27

3 PC 411 39

4 PC 6444 49

5 Before the Royal Commission I 60

6 Moscow Speaks 92

7 Accountability Crisis 99

8 The First Interim Report 107

9 Before the Royal Commission II 116

10 In the House of Commons 169

11 Before the Royal Commission III 185

12 Loose Ends 231

13 The Final Report 256

Epilogue 273

Note on Sources 281

Notes 285

Index 453

Foreword

In September 1945, Soviet cipher clerk Igor Gouzenko defected to Canada, and revealed that Canadians were spying on their own country. How would the Canadian government respond to such shocking news? *"P.S. Burn After Reading"* shows how, in one of the first clashes of the Cold War, Canada used the Kellock-Taschereau Commission – sometimes appropriately, sometimes inappropriately, the authors argue – to thwart these homegrown agents and defend Canada's national security. From the precociously intelligent Doukhobor Emma Woikin ("Nora") – having lost her husband to suicide, lonely as a cipher clerk in Ottawa, and befriended by Soviet Maj. Vsevolod Sokolov – to the cagey Harvard MBA Eric Adams, who stood at the centre of Canada's war financing, *"P.S. Burn After Reading"* examines the Canadian spies and Canada's counter-strikes against them through legal machinations. Mitchell and Kramer show that, despite some human rights missteps, the Canadian government was correct about guilt in almost all the cases. This deeply researched account brings forward new and crucial details about all aspects of the Gouzenko affair, including the legal proceedings, showing in the process that Gouzenko's stolen cache remains the West's first and most revealing glimpse into the secret world of Soviet military intelligence.

The purpose of the Osgoode Society for Canadian Legal History is to encourage research and writing in the history of Canadian law. The Society, which was incorporated in 1979 and is registered as a charity, was founded at the initiative of the Honourable R. Roy McMurtry, formerly attorney general for Ontario and chief justice of the province, and officials of the then Law Society of Upper Canada. The Society seeks to stimulate the study of legal history in Canada by supporting researchers, collecting oral histories, and publishing volumes that contribute to legal-historical scholarship in Canada. This year's books bring the total published since 1981 to 135, in all fields of Canadian legal history – the courts, the judiciary, and the legal profession, as well as the history of crime and punishment, women and law, law and economy, the legal treatment of Indigenous peoples and ethnic minorities, and famous cases and significant trials in all areas of the law.

Current directors of the Osgoode Society for Canadian Legal History are Constance Backhouse, Heidi Bohaker, Brendan Brammall, Bevan Brooksbank, Shantona Chaudhury, Paul Davis, Doug Downey, Linda Silver Dranoff, Matthew Gourlay, Timothy Hill, Ian Hull, Mahmud Jamal, Jennifer King, Waleed Malik, Dana Peebles, Linda Plumpton, Paul Schabas, Robert Sharpe, Jonathan Silver, Lorne Sossin, Michael Tulloch, Peter Wardle, and John Wilkinson.

Paul B. Schabas
President

Professor Emeritus Jim Phillips
Editor-in-Chief

Acknowledgments

We thank Lee Oliver and everyone at the National Archives (Kew) for their work digitizing the wide range of records that we have used for this book. At Library Archives Canada, Gilles Bertrand, Quinn Robinson, Alexandra-Maude Daley-Proulx, Astrée Ève Thériault, Dylan Roy, and Margaret Couper responded to our questions about archival records held there. Anik Laflèche went miles to locate the original version of PC 1945–5991 and, along with Ariane Gauthier, guided us through the Mackenzie King diaries. David Neilson at the Privy Council (Ottawa) furnished a copy of the 1981 order-in-council that released the Kellock-Taschereau transcripts to the public. Percy Miller at Canadian Research Knowledge Network provided details about the posting of Kellock-Taschereau inquiry transcripts, exhibits, and related documents on the database Canadiana Héritage.

We thank Greg Kealey for his criticisms and suggestions on the first draft of our book and for pointing us to Tim Sayle's *Canada Declassified* and the work of Australian historian Philip Deery. John Rice translated and explained Alan Nunn May's account of the 1945 atomic bomb test, while Andrew Pernal and Yelena Kondrashina translated portions of Mikhail Milstein's autobiography. Philip V. Girard suggested several corrections to our text and responded to our questions about personnel at the federal Justice Department, Bryan Palmer about the versions and breadth of Third International Marxism, Jim Bronskill and Steve Hewitt about Operation Feather Bed, David Borys about spies in World War II Canadian Army Civilian Affairs operations, and Kevin Riehle, Tyler Wentzell, V.M. Zubok, Allan Levine, and Jim Naylor about various other issues. Cameron Harvey ended our search for photographs of E.K. Williams. Terry Crowley shared his research on Alex Skelton and Janet Turner, while Wayne Chan brought his expertise on codes to assist us with the interpretation of MI6 cables crossing the Atlantic.

Joel Kropf did research for us at Library Archives Canada, and Bill Morrison offered his customary wisdom and encouragement.

At the Brandon University Library, Heather E. Tornblom did marvellous work securing texts, especially unpublished sessional papers, and the *Fitzpatrick Commentary on the Australian Royal Commission on Espionage* (1955). Sarah Kienas helped us secure access to the only copy of Mikhail Milstein's autobiography in North America and, with Robert Kowaluk at Inter-Library Loan, a variety of other essential texts. Rainer Schira provided biographical details on Douglas How. We thank Stacey Lee for her suggestions on index construction and her industry in repairing the microfilm reader. Jillian Lougheed assisted with the location of hard-to-find items and Chris Hurst responded to questions about the existence and availability of esoteric journals. University archivist Christy Henry provided Tom Mitchell with a conducive workplace and insightful suggestions on the initial draft of the manuscript.

We also received help from individuals in distant places: Monica Smart at the Provincial Archives of New Brunswick helped with the Douglas How fonds; Linda White at the Memorial University Archives with *National Affairs Monthly*; and Stuart Hay, Manitoba Legislative Library, with the writings of E.K. Williams. Information came from Alan Doyle at the University of British Columbia about Agatha Chapman, and from Jean-Philippe Lepage at the Ottawa Public Library about "Turners" in Ottawa c. 1945.

At the University of Toronto Press, we thank the two readers who offered useful suggestions, and thank Terry Teskey for her copyediting work. We also thank Len Husband for his vote of confidence in our manuscript and his skill navigating it through the approval and production channels. Tom Mitchell thanks Bonnie Mitchell for her patience and support with another "project." Reinhold Kramer thanks Rita for her help, as always, with everything.

"P.S. BURN AFTER READING"

The Kellock-Taschereau Commission and Soviet Espionage in Canada

Introduction

On 6 August 1945, President Harry Truman announced that the US had dropped an atomic bomb on Hiroshima.[1] Truman's secretary of war, Henry Stimson, described the ghastly destruction and then immediately called for an international regime to ensure that atomic energy would be used only for "the well-being of the world"[2] – although he knew that a second bomb would be dropped on Nagasaki in three days. Truman's announcement sent an ominous jolt, a new *x*-factor into the post-war world order in the process of being born.

At the same time, in Ottawa, cipher clerk Igor Gouzenko, who worked for spymasters in the Chief Intelligence Directorate of the General Staff of the Soviet Army (GRU), was planning to defect, carefully earmarking documents and files that would disclose the inner workings of Soviet military intelligence in Canada and implicate more than a dozen Canadians in Soviet spying. Already in the previous year, he had run afoul of Colonel Mikhail Milstein, a GRU deputy director in North America on an inspection tour of GRU stations.[3] Upon his return to Moscow, Milstein reported his concerns to GRU chief Lt. Gen. Ivan Ilichev, who, while he made light of Milstein's worries, nevertheless ordered Gouzenko to return to Russia. Gouzenko's boss, Col. Nikolai Zabotin, stalled the return, but in spring 1945 Milstein repeated his concerns, and Ilichev's replacement, the very cruel and very successful Col.-Gen. Fyodor Kuznetsov, reissued the order.[4] By late August, in the wake of Truman's announcement and as Gouzenko wavered about when to defect, the GRU in Moscow cabled Zabotin, ordering Canadian collaborators to dig for the specifics about the atomic bomb: "technological process, drawings, calculations."[5]

Finally, on 5 September 1945, laden with GRU operational files (including some that he had been ordered to destroy), Gouzenko made his move.[6] A day earlier, on the other side of the world, Konstantin

Soviet defector Igor Gouzenko, twenty-six-year-old Red Army lieutenant and cypher clerk (Library Archives Canada, RG 33/62, Royal Commission to Investigate the Communication of Secret and Confidential Information to Agents of a Foreign Power, fonds/ e002280291-001)

Volkov, an NKVD lieutenant in Istanbul, had contacted the British consulate there with a similar plan to defect and to turn over (for a high price) intelligence to MI6. Gouzenko knew nothing of this. What followed in the days after Gouzenko's defection was initially almost a black comedy as, one after another, the *Ottawa Journal*'s night staff, the RCMP, the city police, and senior aides to Prime Minister Mackenzie King all turned Gouzenko away. The Canadians might be forgiven for failing to grasp the significance of this young Red Army officer's pleas for asylum, delivered in limited English with a heavy Russian accent. He grew more and more agitated. Meanwhile in Europe, British double agent Kim Philby heard about Volkov, and Soviet assassins were dispatched to retrieve him. Volkov would eventually be taken to NKVD headquarters in Lubyanka Square, interrogated, and executed alongside his wife.[7] Gouzenko was saved from Volkov's fate when Canadian External Affairs officers began to grasp Gouzenko's importance and told the RCMP to take him and his family into protective custody.

The RCMP quickly discovered that Gouzenko carried an explosive story. His revelations about Soviet intelligence penetration shocked authorities in Ottawa, London, and Washington,[8] and pointed to the existence of similar spy networks elsewhere.[9] Meanwhile, in Moscow, Soviet intelligence chiefs were beside themselves, fearing the exposure of their agents in Canada, Britain, and the US.[10]

Some historians of the Cold War have ignored the Gouzenko affair, leaving spy stories behind in favour of the much larger geopolitical struggles between the Soviet Union and the West in central Europe and the Far East, finding, even before the end of World War II, the beginnings of the Cold War in policies such as Stalin's secret police kidnapping the leaders of the Polish resistance and sending them to Moscow for show trials.[11] American historian Amy Knight, on the other hand, treats the Gouzenko affair and its arrival in public as a pivotal event: the first volley of the Cold War. We intend to place a history of the Kellock-Taschereau Royal Commission at the centre of the security and political crisis initiated by Gouzenko. The existing literature on Kellock-Taschereau falls generally into studies concerned with World War II–era civil liberties and with the emerging Cold War. Canadian commentators have privileged the coercive aspects of the commission that led both to the Canadian civil rights movement[12] and to a resurgent anti-Communism that World War II's Grand Alliance had put on pause.[13] In contrast, we seek to provide a foundational Canadian chapter in the new security and intelligence history that has emerged since the 1990s. This is an international literature made possible by the opening of archival collections principally including British (MI5 and MI6), American (Venona decrypts), and Soviet (KGB) archives. The archives of the GRU have remained sealed, so that Gouzenko's stolen cache, at the centre of our narrative, remains the West's only glimpse into that body of records.[14]

Our story concerns why and how the Kellock-Taschereau Commission emerged as the Canadian liberal state's chosen instrument to address the crisis, how the inquiry conducted its business, and what it disclosed about Soviet spying in Canada. According to British authorities, the Kellock-Taschereau *Final Report* would become "the most widely circulated document of its kind ever issued by a commonwealth government."[15] A detailed exploration of what the testimonies and the *Final Report* revealed about Soviet spying has not yet been attempted. We intend an institutional history, but one that connects with the biographies of those investigated, and with the national and international politics that brought the inquiry into existence and through which its findings reverberated. The Gouzenko crisis was *sui generis* in the history of Canadian intelligence and security, exploding out of nowhere, since Canada had done nothing to precipitate it and initially even resisted Gouzenko's offer of information about Canadian and British citizens spying for the Soviet Union. That Mackenzie King eventually created a separate personal diary devoted exclusively to the Gouzenko affair provides one measure of its singularity.[16] Confronted with the revelations and recognizing the need for instruments far beyond those available to a normal police investigation, King's inner circle took months to come up with – reluctantly – a strategy to address the intelligence, security, diplomatic, and legal features of the crisis. Amy Knight called the King response "an unrelenting witchhunt,"[17] but that's inaccurate, even though the liberal state did stretch the limits of legality to defend the security of Canada. Innocence before the law isn't the same thing as innocence – if it were, there would have been no need for a #MeToo movement. The Canadian state's 1946 weapon of choice: a coercive, truth-seeking inquiry ranging far beyond any prior Canadian inquiry,[18] strengthened by the powers of the War Measures Act and later justified by the Lockean doctrine of *salus populi suprema lex esto* (the safety of the people must be the supreme law).[19] Canada's response to the crisis gave political and security leaders in the West an unprecedented view of Moscow-directed GRU spying in the West, of native Communist organizations as in-place recruitment fields for domestic agents, and of the tradecraft involved in cultivating, recruiting, and managing the contributors to Soviet espionage. The way in which the state faced up to its obligations to safeguard the nation against security threats presents a complex story, both legally and morally.

1
The Gouzenko Question

5–30 September 1945

After Gouzenko's misadventures on September 5th and 6th, Under-Secretary of State for External Affairs Norman Robertson eventually, on the 7th, ordered the RCMP to take him and his family into protective custody and to secure his cache of contraband Soviet documents.[1] At the time of his defection and despite his civilian cover, Igor Gouzenko was a lieutenant in the Red Army,[2] a carefully selected and trained operative in the GRU, which had been reconstructed and renamed after Stalin's late 1930s purge decimated the upper ranks of its military intelligence predecessor.[3] Gouzenko claimed that ideology made him defect – he could now "see what a free people can do."[4] But his motives were likely more mixed. A "charwoman" had reported to the NKVD (Soviet internal security) that Gouzenko had left a confidential document among scraps of paper lying around the cipher room, prompting his imminent (and anxiety-inducing) recall to Moscow.[5]

Also anxious were members of Mackenzie King's inner circle, and especially King himself. Gouzenko had made Canada, perhaps for the first time in its history, the focus of an international crisis just as a new international order was being forged, and King feared that a wrong move could throw a wrench into post-war relations between the West and the Soviet Union. Shortly before Hiroshima, the Potsdam Conference had created the Council of Foreign Ministers (including the US, Britain, and the Soviet Union among others), and now its London meeting to set the terms for the post-war order was only days away. King might be forgiven for wishing that Gouzenko and his stolen documents would melt quietly back into the Russian embassy.[6] A shroud of secrecy descended over the affair. Only a small group of high-level officials including Robertson, his deputy Hume Wrong (assistant under-secretary in External Affairs), Charles Rivett-Carnac of the RCMP Intelligence Branch,[7] British High Commissioner to Canada Malcolm MacDonald,[8] and his deputy Stephen Holmes[9] met to advise King on policy. Because the Gouzenko documents were stowed each night in an empty Corby whiskey box in Robertson's office, this group became the "Corby Committee,"[10] and Gouzenko was given the code name "Corby." The circle was kept "as narrow as possible."[11] Although a select group of political and security leaders in Britain and the US were briefed, among Canadian cabinet members only Minister of Justice Louis St. Laurent knew about Gouzenko from the beginning. C.D. Howe and Acting Prime Minister J.L. Ilsley were brought into the circle a month later, but most cabinet members were kept in the dark until the defection was leaked to an American journalist in February 1946.[12]

A few days into the crisis Norman Robertson, to coordinate with Britain and the US, added British Undersecretary of State for Foreign Affairs Sir Alexander Cadogan to the small circle,[13] telling him that Russian agents had gained access to "secret telegrams exchanged between our two governments."[14] At a time when British security services didn't have a single agent hidden among the Soviets, and knew almost nothing about Soviet intelligence, Gouzenko suddenly gave the British their first real post-war view into Soviet spying.[15] At the same time, Malcolm MacDonald also contacted Cadogan and, without naming British atomic scientist Alan Nunn May directly, warned Cadogan that Gouzenko would be identifying a British scientist in Canada as a Soviet spy.[16] Mackenzie King, who was not only prime minister but also minister of foreign affairs, took some comfort from this: it wasn't just Canada that was guilty of security lapses.[17] The Canadians made sure to impress upon the British the shared blame. Norman Robertson reminded MacDonald that the "vetting of United Kingdom scientists sent to Canada on project was responsibility of British government and if these leakages on further investigation prove as serious as they appear at moment then H.M.G. will be liable to criticism by United States Government."[18]

Fearing that Nunn May would return to England and then flee on to Moscow, Robertson on 10 September "strongly advised the passing of a special O. in C. [order-in-council] very secretly which would re-enact certain clauses of the *Defence of Canada Regulations,*" to have Nunn May watched, to arrest him if necessary, and "to see that he did not get away with papers."[19] King agreed and signed for the creation of PC 5991. Ministers J.L. Ilsley (Finance), C.D. Howe (Munitions and Reconstruction), and Douglas Abbott (Defence) also signed, though they were told "only enough ... to justify their signing." PC 5991 was

Rt. Hon. W.L. Mackenzie King signs a loan agreement with the United Kingdom, 6 May 1946. Behind King stands British High Commissioner Rt. Hon. Malcolm MacDonald. Behind MacDonald is Canada's under-secretary of state for external affairs, Norman Robertson. (Library and Archives Canada, WLM King – PA-112258)

meant to stop Nunn May from giving out secret information, either verbally or in documents, to restrict his movements, and if necessary to detain him. But the panicky nature of the government's action was evident in the order-in-council. The detention provision was clear, but the other clauses flared in broad, obfuscatory language, allowing the prime minister or minister of justice, for the safety of the state, to make orders "(a) prohibiting or restricting the possession or use by that person of any specified articles; (b) imposing upon him such restrictions as may be specified in the order in respect of his employment or business, in respect of his movements or place of residence, in respect of his association or communication with other persons, or in respect of his activities in relation to the dissemination of news or the propagation of opinions."[20]

The next day King and St. Laurent fine-tuned their work. Using PC 5991, they directed the RCMP to "maintain a close supervision over, and ... intercept communications with A.N. May by telephone, by telegraph, by post, or otherwise." Second, they directed the RCMP to arrest, detain, and interrogate Nunn May and search his belongings at whatever time and under whatever conditions the minister of justice would decide. But there is no evidence that Nunn May's telephone was tapped or that his mail was opened. The orders and related directives were stored in the "vault of the Clerk of the Council."[21] They were never used.

The circle of those who knew about the Gouzenko revelations was small, and yet, now that London had joined, the circle suddenly grew large enough to include a Soviet agent. What neither King nor Robertson knew was that in addition to the British scientist Nunn May, the Kremlin had a double agent – Kim Philby – high up in MI6. Communication between Ottawa and London was routed through British Security Coordination's HYDRA, a secure communications network for British intelligence,[22] yet Philby was always present on his MI6 perch to pass every Gouzenko development on to the Soviets. Philby, who had worked for Soviet intelligence since 1934 and for MI6 since early in the war, was put in charge of Section IX, Soviet and Communist counter-intelligence in 1945.[23] On 11 September Guy Liddell, MI5 director of B Division (counter-espionage) since 1940,[24] noted in his diary that Philby had shown him a series of telegrams that implicated Nunn May. Liddell, unaware of Philby's true stance, emphasized that "the whole thing of course is wrapped up in about 4 layers of cotton-wool as it concerns the atomic bomb."[25]

Despite the protective cotton wool, within a week Philby had already given the Soviets early news of Gouzenko's defection via fellow Soviet agent Guy Burgess and his NKVD controller Boris Kreshin.[26] At the same time, Philby was composing "cautious and soothing" memoranda for MI6 chief Stewart Menzies to use in briefing Prime Minister Clement Attlee.[27] By 17 September 1945, "Victor" (Lt. General P.M. Fitin, chief of NKVD foreign intelligence[28]) in Moscow confirmed to "Bob" (Kreshin) that "Stanley's [Kim Philby's] data about the events in Canada in the 'Neighbours' [GRU's] sphere of activity ... does correspond to the facts."[29] As Washington, London, and Ottawa debated how to address the Gouzenko question, Philby kept Moscow up to date, but he did so with extra vigilance.[30] On 18 September, Fitin moved to shore up security around his important British agents. He considered ending Krotov's responsibility for meetings with agents, because of "S's information about the disruption of our work ... and the intensification of counter-measures against us." Krotov would remain in charge of "Stanley" and "Hicks" [Guy Burgess], but he shouldn't increase meetings with them "under any circumstances."[31] Three days later, Krotov was instructed that "in view of the NEIGHBOURS ... affair in CANADA and the circumstances which have arisen at your end [London] as a result of this," he was to transfer control of "Hicks" to an unidentified control and to cut meetings down "to once a month." "Hicks" and "Stanley" should concentrate on "passing us material dealing only with large fundamental issues,"[32] and agents should carry no documents to meetings.[33] Fitin added a further caution: "If, however, you notice that, as a consequence of local circumstances, greater attention is being paid to you and to our workers by the COMPETITORS [MI5], you may break off contact temporarily with the sources." During such a lull, Fitin suggested, "Try to create a pretext ... Meet [your agents] more by neutral methods of contact, go to theatres, cinemas, etc. Warn all our comrades to make a thorough check when going out to a meeting and, if surveillance is observed, not to try, under any circumstances, to evade the surveillance and meet the agent regardless."[34] A month later, Fitin gave similar instructions to "VADIM," Anatoly Gromov (or Gorsky), who served the NKVD under cover as first secretary of the Soviet embassy in Washington.[35] While we have discovered no direct evidence of Moscow warning GRU and NKVD handlers in Canada to restrict contact with their Canadian agents, Emma Woikin disclosed that "she was warned early in October to cease work as there might be trouble."[36]

Although Mackenzie King wouldn't live long enough to see Philby unmasked in 1963, the very existence of double agents such as Philby could partially justify the approach that King would eventually be convinced to take. The simultaneous arrests, the refusal of *habeas corpus*, the incommunicado, all these procedures so problematic for civil rights were one of the few ways of dealing with a hostile power whose clandestine networks shrouded in obscure nomenclature could foil regular police procedure. Although World War II was over, a new emergency, one created by a former ally early in the war and hidden from the West by the machinations of Soviet tradecraft, had arrived without Western leaders recognizing it.

British agents – MI6's Peter Dwyer (from Washington), British Security Coordination Jean-Paul Evans (from New York), and in mid-September MI5's Roger Hollis (from England) – quickly made their way to Ottawa,[37] and over the next five months various approaches were floated inside the magic circle ... only to go nowhere. Charles Rivett-Carnac, along with his superior at the RCMP, Commissioner Stuart Wood, wanted to publicize the Gouzenko revelations immediately, because (in King's summation) "to expose the whole thing might cause our people to cut away from the Russian influence altogether."[38] Unlike the Nazi, the Fascist, or the "usually recognizable" enemy alien, Wood said, "Your 'Red' has the protection of citizenship, his foreign master is not officially an enemy and, unless he blunders into the open and provides proof of his guilt, he is much more difficult to suppress." In particular, Wood worried about "fifth column activity" carried on under the cover of organizations that pretended to be loyal to the Constitution.[39] With the RCMP's very creation (out of the NWMP) in 1920 and its responsibility for domestic security closely tied to post–World War I labour radicalism, that force would remain preoccupied with the threat of Communist subversion even when the threat had abated. The content of the "Special Branch lectures" in 1951 – which included lectures titled "World Communism Since 1947," "Communist Infiltration into Government Departments," "Subversive Activities in Trade Unions," and "Communist Fronts in Canada" – indicates how the Gouzenko affair galvanized the force.[40] Late in September, Commissioner Wood lobbied St. Laurent. Although Wood gave lip service to the primacy of diplomatic considerations, he insisted that publicizing the Gouzenko affair would weaken Soviet attempts at "world domination." "If the public was to be informed of the widespread activities of the Soviet Union and its agents," he wrote, "this would form a most active deterrent to the growth of Communism."[41] At the same time, Wood knew that detention of the suspects would "cause an immediate outcry from their supporters and a campaign in the party press," as he would warn St. Laurent in October. A "speedy" trial would be necessary, yet legal counsel would need time to work through Gouzenko's complex evidence. And the involvement of Labor-Progressive (i.e., Communist) MP Fred Rose from Montreal meant that lawyers would need to handle the cases carefully.[42]

St. Laurent wasn't a tough sell, since he shared Wood's fervent anti-Communism.[43] Under the Defence of Canada Regulations, the Canadian Communist Party had been declared an illegal organization, and from the moment St. Laurent became minister of justice in December 1941, he resisted any softening of that stance. It was an article of faith for him that Canadian Communists would be willing to use force to overthrow the government.[44]

Wood wanted St. Laurent to engage a lawyer with "wide experience in conspiracy prosecutions,"[45] someone like Montreal criminal lawyer Gérald Fauteux KC, a leading prosecutor who had recently worked for the Department of Justice on wartime internments.[46] Royal courts, especially the Star Chamber, had developed the notion of conspiracy as a criminal offence, and governments had used the doctrine of conspiracy

Minister of Justice Rt. Hon. Louis St. Laurent, who authorized the use of PC 6444 (Library and Archives Canada, Louis St. Laurent- PA-4316498/ e010969219)

as a way of responding both to straightforward criminal cases and to possible treasonous challenges to the state. Gradually, common law courts too adopted the doctrine.[47] The threat of prosecution against imagined or actual criminal conspiracies served as a bulwark against organized labour in the nineteenth century.[48] In 1919, Winnipeg's Citizens' Committee ran a successful private prosecution for seditious conspiracy against the leaders of the Winnipeg General Strike.[49] If the King government couldn't come up with direct evidence of offences against the Official Secrets Act, conspiracy charges against the suspects might open an alternate route to convictions, and St. Laurent approved Wood's recommendation of Fauteux.[50]

Wood urged prosecutions wherever there was enough evidence.[51] But US president Harry Truman demurred, since immediate arrests might undermine his attempts to negotiate an international agreement on the atomic bomb, and Wood's approach was initially disregarded.[52] Recognizing the need for diplomatic unity, Mackenzie King prepared to talk in person with Truman and with British prime minister Clement Attlee.[53] The British wanted to arrest Nunn May in coordination with arrests of the Canadian suspects but, in Washington at the end of September, King agreed with Truman that no action be taken until all three nations could settle on a coordinated procedure. Arrests wouldn't come until over four months later, when Wood's narrative, embraced by St. Laurent, would influence the appointment and conduct of the Kellock-Taschereau Commission.

3–31 October 1945

Nunn May's actions in London were also scotching arrest plans. Since 1943 Nunn May had been in Montreal, working with the National Research Council (NRC) on nuclear weapons.[54] As Gouzenko revealed, Nunn May, through Col. Zabotin, had given the Soviets "valuable information about atomic research" and samples of uranium-233 and -235 (enriched).[55] Gouzenko showed Canadian authorities the scheme for Nunn May to return to England in mid-September and to meet a Soviet agent near the British Museum on 7 October. Such a meeting could open the door to May's arrest under Britain's Official Secrets Act.

However, an arrest would also act as an immediate red flag to Soviet agents in Canada, so MI5's Guy Liddell wanted "synchronized" arrests of Nunn May and the Canadian suspects. Liddell told Roger Hollis, the MI5 agent recently arrived in Ottawa, to coordinate with the RCMP,[56] and by early October they had a British/Canadian agreement on how to proceed after the arrests.[57] John Read,[58] legal advisor to the Department of Foreign Affairs, and Frederick Percy Varcoe,[59] deputy minister of justice, devised (after discussions with St. Laurent, Hume Wrong, and the RCMP) what we will call the "Read/Varcoe" plan, whose final incarnation would be the Kellock-Taschereau Commission.[60] RCMP commissioner Wood disclosed the details to FBI director J. Edgar Hoover: when British authorities were ready to arrest Nunn May, Canada would use the War Measures Act to detain those named by Gouzenko, and wherever evidence warranted it, to lay charges under the Official Secrets Act.[61] The "remaining suspects" would be interrogated and their residences searched. Wood's wording implied that the "remaining suspects" would face a traditional police investigation, and that a formal inquiry about Soviet espionage would "follow" police actions.[62]

But Hume Wrong gave a different account on 6 October: "Except in three or four instances, there are grave doubts as to whether prosecution would result in convictions by reason of necessity for complying with the strict rules of evidence."[63] Despite the documentary record that Gouzenko had bagged, his evidence still amounted to "hearsay," making criminal prosecutions of the Canadian GRU collaborators problematic. Because the Russian documents used code names and because Gouzenko could not provide direct evidence against anyone other than Soviet officials (who stood beyond the reach of Canadian law), his evidence would be useful only if Canadian authorities could find direct evidence of offences against the Official Secrets Act or of participation in a GRU conspiracy.[64] Although Gouzenko, as cipher clerk, accurately tallied the information that the Canadian suspects had handed over to the Soviet Union and although he proved to be a reliable witness, he could really only testify about what GRU chief Zabotin or other Soviet spies had said. To accept Gouzenko's "testimony" would amount to accepting the unsworn words of Zabotin, who could not be cross-examined.[65] All this was compounded because Gouzenko, as an officer in the GRU, was technically a co-conspirator with the Canadian spies. Since he could face death if the RCMP turned him over to the Soviets, Gouzenko would have reason to make himself indispensable to Canadian authorities, even if it meant inventing a few accusations.

Wrong's evidentiary concerns were well founded. Much later, when the cases went to trial, defence lawyers fiercely objected, and judges cautioned juries. For example, in Matt Nightingale's case, which rested entirely on Gouzenko's testimony, the judge warned the jury against accepting the "unsupported" evidence of an "accomplice" (i.e., Gouzenko).[66] But there was a way around the problem. If the Crown could give "independent proof" that a criminal conspiracy existed "and that an accused was party to that agreement," hearsay evidence would be admissible.[67] In his 6 October telegraph to Robertson, Wrong explained that a plan of action had been developed that addressed the problem of taking immediate action "against persons concerned," and that offered a possible solution to the evidentiary challenges.

The Read / Varcoe plan, Wrong explained, could solve the problem of hearsay evidence.[68] As early as 2 October, Wrong told Robertson that the Department of Justice was "rather wedded" to the idea of a royal commission as the best means of "exposing the facts and getting on the record evidence that would not be admissible in court proceedings."[69] The plan would start with an order-in-council allowing St. Laurent to detain suspects indefinitely and to appoint a royal commission to interrogate them. Unlike British royal commissions, which had been de-toothed in the seventeenth century, the Canadian Inquiries Act of 1846 reinstated the Crown's abilities to confer on Canadian inquiries coercive powers – such as compelling witnesses to testify.[70] Since commissioners would not "be bound by strict rules of evidence," they would be better equipped to pry information out of the suspects.[71] Later on, some of this information might just resurface in prosecutions under criminal code. In other words, either confessions or evidence of a conspiracy would turn Gouzenko's "hearsay" accounts into evidence.[72] The commissioner could recommend a suspect's immediate release or, conversely, tell the Crown that continued detention was "necessary to the safety and interests of the state."[73] By implication, the suspect could then be charged under the Official Secrets Act or the Criminal Code.

Wrong's account suggests that the Read/Varcoe plan was drawn loosely from the recently disbanded Defence of Canada's Regulations, which permitted the state to detain anyone reasonably suspected of attempting to give information to the enemy. The Regulations required that the minister of justice appoint an advisory committee (rather than a royal commissioner) to determine the fate of detainees.[74] However, the new plan moved aggressively beyond the Regulations. The Regulations did not contemplate interrogation of detainees, whereas under Read/Varcoe the commissioner could loosen the definition of what constituted evidence, just as Wrong implied, to permit hearsay. Moreover, while the Regulations had their own penalties and were not linked procedurally to the Criminal Code, Read/Varcoe explicitly contemplated "later prosecutions."[75] Read and Varcoe knew that witnesses without lawyers (to explain the protections available under Article 5 of the Canada Evidence Act) would be vulnerable to self-incrimination.[76] Under the Defence of Canada Regulations, a detained person could "make objections against the order either in person or by counsel, solicitor or agent; and it shall be the duty of the Minister [of Justice] ... to secure that every such person is informed of his right to make objections."[77] In contrast, the Read/Varcoe proposal's use of the federal Inquiries Act seemed designed to prevent suspects from objecting to their detention and from requesting legal counsel. Only if charges were made against a witness was the commissioner obliged to let the witness (under Article 12) retain a lawyer, but by that time the witness would have already incriminated themself.[78]

A few months later, E.K. Williams would make these unstated features of the Read/Varcoe plan explicit and prominent in his "Top Secret" 7 December recommendation to Mackenzie King, but King was already sympathetic to the approach by 7 October. While he was in Britain conferring with Prime Minister Attlee, King noted in his diary that "the wise course for Canada to take would be to appoint a Royal Commission and summon before it all those whose names we have."[79]

But Read/Varcoe became an immediate casualty of the King government's contingent handling of the crisis. On 6 October ministers J.L. Ilsley (finance and acting prime minister while King was in London), C.D. Howe (munitions and reconstruction), and Douglas Abbott (defence),[80] along with St. Laurent, employed the War Measures Act – still unrescinded – to approve PC 6444,[81] which empowered the "Acting Prime Minister or Minister of Justice" to direct the arrest, detention, and interrogation of anyone suspected of "communicating secret and confidential information to an agent of a foreign power or otherwise acting in a manner prejudicial to the public safety or the safety of the state."

This repeated the vital provision of the 10 September order-in-council for Nunn May's arrest (PC 5991) taken from the Defence of Canada Regulations, that those so detained were in legal custody, but now the government cast the net wider.[82] Far beyond the powers of either the Defence of Canada Regulations or the Inquiries Act, PC 6444 let the ministers authorize the RCMP to search the detained person's premises and seize anything that might give evidence of secrets being passed to a foreign power.[83] No committee, just St. Laurent himself, stood as gatekeeper: "The Minister of Justice if satisfied that the detention of any person so detained is no longer necessary for the public safety or the safety of the State may make an order releasing him."[84]

Conveniently, given the secrecy required in handling the Gouzenko crisis, no statute required that PC 6444 be made public. Since 1939 the King government had consistently tabled in Parliament all orders-in-council relating to the war, a practice eventually formalized in 1947 through PC 4876 (Statutory Orders and Regulations Order), which required that all orders and regulations "having general effect or imposing a penalty" be published fortnightly in the *Canada Gazette*.[85] However, in 1945 only Illsley, St. Laurent, Howe, and others on the Gouzenko file knew that PC 6444 existed. Not until 14 March 1946 would Mackenzie King reveal the order to the House of Commons.

PC 6444 contained no provisions for a royal commission. The idea for a non-royal commission variant of the Read/Varcoe plan was the product of the immediate contingencies confronting the government in early October with the possible arrest of Nunn May. The approval of PC 6444 reflected action taken in haste without due regard to any endgame strategy. The problem with only a police interrogation under PC 6444 was that detainees weren't legally obligated to answer questions. But in front of a royal commission, witnesses must answer all questions. Two veteran RCMP interrogators, detective inspectors Clifford Harvison and M.F.E. Anthony, were summoned to wait in Ottawa – Harvison from Winnipeg, Anthony from Vancouver[86] – but to what end? No one, not even Nunn May, was arrested.

The delay was Britain's. MI5 had readied itself for Nunn May's planned encounter with his Soviet handler near the British Museum: "One man was to see May in at Tottenham Court Road end, Hunter and Burt established in the pub with one watcher, and a car with one watcher would be stationed down Montagu St. near a callbox with which we arranged communications. Tommy Harris would drive through the area in a car a few minutes before 7 and a few minutes before 8 in order to cover the possibility that the meeting had been arranged according to Summer Time [*sic*]."[87] Yet the meeting never took place. Kim Philby had alerted Moscow about Gouzenko's revelations, and the GRU, in turn, warned its agents against any contact with Nunn May. For weeks and weeks, MI5 kept up its surveillance of Great Russell Street and Museum Street in the evenings, but Nunn May never appeared.[88] In 1951, when Philby came under strong suspicion, he (affecting, of course, to speak from the British point of view) called the Volkov assassination "a total failure," but insisted that the Nunn May case was "an almost unqualified success."[89] Not true, but as MI5's Evelyn McBurney pointed out, Nunn May couldn't expose Philby. Volkov could.[90]

Nunn May's no-show in 1945 put Canadian arrests on hold too. The suspects remained at liberty, under surveillance, and Harvison and Anthony sat in Ottawa through the fall, studying the Soviet archives provided by Gouzenko, waiting for the hammer to fall.[91] In December, they were sent back to Vancouver and Winnipeg to await instructions. PC 6444 was never employed for the purpose it was created, and its later use in different circumstances would prove problematic.

Shuffling through PC 5991, the Read / Varcoe plan, and PC 6444, the government overlooked a more legally and politically expedient route. The World War I precedent *Re George Edwin Gray* (1918) had cleared the way for the government to modify legislation via orders-in-council. *Re Gray* tested Borden's order-in-council PC 919, approved under the War Measures Act to eliminate exemptions set out in the Military Service Act and to penalize anyone who didn't report for military duty when called up. Gray, who didn't report, was arrested and jailed by the military. He applied for *habeas corpus* on the grounds that PC 919 was *ultra vires*, because it should not be able to amend a statute passed by Parliament.[92] In a 4:2 decision, the Supreme Court rejected Gray's application and declared PC 919 constitutional.[93] The majority argued that Parliament had the power (and the intention) through section 6 of the War Measures Act to confer wide powers on the executive to amend existing legislation through orders-in-council (such as PC 919) and even allow the executive (through the Military Service Act) to suspend *habeas corpus*. St. Laurent was certainly aware of the *Re Gray* precedent since he had relied on it in a 1943 case in which chemical manufacturers had challenged St. Laurent's ability to regulate, under the War Measures Act, the production and sale of some chemicals. Relying on *Re Gray*, the Supreme Court had unanimously affirmed the legality of St. Laurent's action.[94]

The King government could have used the door opened by *Re Gray* to resurrect aspects of the British Official Secrets Act in Canada's Official Secrets Act (the OSA, a statute that carried the imprimatur of Parliament): the power to detain suspects in custody, the power to require them to answer questions (by police or by inquiry), and the power to penalize non-cooperators through orders-in-council approved with the War Measures Act. Legal challenges to the state's modification (via orders-in-council) of the OSA would have been blocked by *Re Gray*. OSA provisions for legal detentions could have blocked *habeas corpus* challenges, and similar provisions could have blocked challenges to the Royal Commission interrogations. (Time would show that PC 6444 made the King government's Gouzenko strategy vulnerable to several of these challenges.) Had Mackenzie King privately shown the amended OSA to Conservative leader John Bracken and CCF leader M.J. Coldwell and explained to them why the War Measures Act was still needed, the government could have denied the existence of any "secret" orders when the time came to rescind the War Measures Act. (PC 5991, never employed, would have to be rescinded.) Of course, the amendments to the OSA would lapse with the revocation of the War Measures Act, but the King government held the authority to extend the War Measures Act until the Gouzenko crisis could be resolved. In 1923, the Judicial Committee of the Privy Council had ruled that only the federal government held the authority to decide when to rescind a War Measures Act.[95] Hindsight is always 20/20, but it seems arguable that in ignoring this option the King government demonstrated a surprising poverty of strategic imagination and legal acumen.

Alongside the failure to devise an effective strategy, there was still the problem of aligning all three governments behind immediate arrests, and there were practical problems as well. Canadian officials thought that Nunn May, a British subject working for the British government in Canada, should be arrested under British statutes. The British, however, wanted him prosecuted under a Canadian statute. The policy tensions evident in Wood's counsel to St. Laurent were mirrored in Britain where Foreign Secretary Ernest Bevin wanted Nunn May handled aggressively, while Prime Minister Attlee worried about the political and diplomatic repercussions of such actions. And even MI5 couldn't push in an unqualified way for arrests. As Guy Liddell advised the RCMP, MI5 had no legal basis to arrest Nunn May unless Canadian authorities could supply direct evidence against him.[96] Since Nunn May, with his involvement in the atomic bomb, was the biggest fish, it wouldn't make sense to start arresting suspects while ignoring him. The Canadian position was also complicated because Mackenzie King insisted on a united action with England and the US: he didn't want Canada to face the wrath of the Russian bear alone. Ultimately, Canada *would* act independently, and the success of that independent action would, if anything, contribute to a greater sense of Canadian competence in counter-espionage. But in October 1945 that independent action was still months away.

The day after Nunn May failed to meet his Soviet handler, British security officials – MI5's Sir John Stephenson, Roger Hollis, and their boss Guy Liddell – and Foreign Office functionaries – Alexander Clutterbuck, Neville Butler, and T.E. Bromley – all met with Norman Robertson in London. They agreed to push Attlee, Mackenzie King, and ultimately Truman to formulate a clear policy on whether arrests should be made publicly or the suspects investigated without publicity.[97] The push to secure a decision from the leaders succeeded. With the prospect of a nuclear treaty on the table, Attlee and King decided on 21 October to hold off the arrests: they still wanted the suspects interrogated, but privately. King still harboured the fantasy that if only he could have a little chat with Stalin, they could solve the problem amicably.[98]

For very good reasons, the King / Attlee quiet approach was stillborn. The RCMP quickly concluded that it "was impossible to obey,"[99] and British Foreign Secretary Bevin cited the main objections. First, the RCMP did not have "the resources required for the simultaneous interrogation of eighteen or twenty suspects." They needed detentions "for a week or more," which "would cause considerable comment and anxiety among [the suspects'] families and co-workers and publicity could hardly be avoided." Any attempt to interrogate two or three suspects on a given day would immediately result in messages to "the head of the Communist Party in Canada who would warn the other suspects and cause them to destroy any remaining evidence and they would then be useless to the police." The police work would be successful only if "all the suspects were interrogated at the same time and held until interrogation is complete." Bevin wrote, "we are dealing too tenderly with these people," and he wanted to end their activities, but he could not see any way to handle the crisis without publicity.[100]

Malcolm MacDonald, meanwhile, foresaw very different problems with the King / Attlee directive. "I venture to suggest," he told Sir Alexander Cadogan, "that if Russians do by now definitely know (as seems at least possible) that we are aware of the details of espionage organization, they will think us weak and afraid if we do not take definite diplomatic as well as police action." He believed that the Russians would learn immediately of any interrogations of those exposed by Gouzenko and draw two conclusions: "First, our failure at the same time to either take some diplomatic action with them or to give publicity to proceedings will convince them that we feared them. Second, if they are preparing some counter offensive (e. g. an espionage trial of their own in

Moscow), they might open this at once, and so prejudice the chance of our exploiting present situation to our advantage."[101]

For Attlee and King, these problems were secondary to maintaining workable diplomatic relations with Russia, especially given the future meetings with the Russians about the atomic problem. At the end of October, Attlee and King decided that because of the difficulty of interrogating all the Canadian suspects simultaneously, no action at all would be taken.

1–28 November 1945

Frustrated, the RCMP's Stuart Wood noted that two months had passed since Gouzenko's defection, yet the agents he had exposed were "still permitted to function."[102] Wood sent St. Laurent a detailed sixty-seven-page RCMP report, "Soviet Espionage in Canada,"[103] illustrating the volume of traffic and the nature of the information supplied by the suspects.[104] Soviet agents remained in position at the Bank of Canada, the Department of Defence, the NRC, the Department of External Affairs, the Department of Munitions and Supply, and the Office of the UK High Commissioner. From New York, William Stephenson wrote to Menzies, "Although we have indications that whole network has been warned we cannot be sure that they are not continuing to operate." He cited the example of the Los Angeles–based Soviet agent who had been operating on a Canadian passport belonging to Ignacy Witczak. Gouzenko exposed the fake "Ignacy Witczak" but, Stephenson explained, the agent was "warned and he is now on run." In New York, "Witczak" shook FBI surveillance in a Turkish bath and later surfaced in Chicago.[105] Witczak and members of Col. Zabotin's network ran about unchecked, "since instructions are that no action be taken which might precipitate matters." Delaying arrests increased "chances of Russians getting in first with a trumped-up charge and of agents over here perfecting their cover stories and destroying any incriminating evidence." Stephenson also feared that the Gouzenko story was already on the street.[106]

Mid-November in Washington, British officials, including MacDonald and Roger Hollis, again met secretly with the Canadians to come up with a new joint-action plan. It was the Canadians Norman Robertson and Hume Wrong who, drawing heavily on Read/Varcoe, tugged the others away from the Attlee/King quiet approach. The "Washington plan" was still intended to avoid damaging diplomatic relations with the USSR, so it emphasized interrogations, but it also included arrests and prosecutions of "identified agents" in Canada with "supporting

RCMP commissioner Stuart Wood, who led the police investigation (Library and Archives Canada / Royal Canadian Mounted Police fonds – Commissioner Stuart Wood / e008406888)

action in UK and USA" – which meant the arrest of Nunn May. Soviet diplomats who acted as spies would be expelled. For its process, Canada would appoint a judge, "acting as a Royal Commissioner and authorized to sit in camera."[107] All this would start on Monday, 26 November, with King announcing the spy revelations in the House of Commons.[108]

Kim Philby quickly passed the details of the Washington plan on to the Soviets:

> 1. Beginning 26 November (the precise date to be determined) persons who are mentioned in the Canadian case in Canada and "May" will be detained for questioning. 2. King and Attlee feel that the detention of a large number of people will reveal this fact. After all, they don't want relations between Britain and the USSR to deteriorate. Therefore they are trying to control such openness. On the day the suspects are detained King will announce that the Canadian authorities have uncovered a major intel. network; many of the suspects work at Canadian govt. agencies, and all of the trails lead to the Sov. Embassy in Canada ... Canadian authorities will invite the Soviet ambassador in Canada and notify him that Zabotin and his entire staff, which was involved in intel. work, are "personae non gratae." They have decided not to demand that the Sov. ambassador himself be recalled. King in his announcement will appeal to public opinion not to use this case to set off an explosion of anti-Sov. propaganda. At the same time King may send a personal message to Cde. Stalin regarding this matter. 3. The persons on whom there is evidence they engaged in intel. work will be convicted. A royal commissioner will be appointed for the judicial hearings. This case may be heard behind closed doors ... 4. According to Butler's report, the Americans are currently investigating another Soviet intel. organization in the US. Therefore they don't want to take any actions regarding the Canadian case since this could harm their new investigation ... 5. Truman reacted favorably to the actions that King and Attlee proposed ... 6. The "Hotel's" [MI6, Philby's organization] station chief in the US, Stephenson, reported to the "Hotel" that FBI chief Hoover said that Truman was poorly prepared on this matter when he met with Attlee and King. Hoover is sure that the actions against the Zabotin network will cause harm to the Americans' new investigation in the US.[109]

Philby also summarized the FBI investigation triggered by the defection (unknown in Canada) of American NKVD operative Elizabeth Bentley in early November 1945: "The FBI assumes that this network is controlled by the NKVD. So far, they have succeeded in identifying 30 Soviet agents, whose names the FBI has not yet conveyed to Stephenson. 'S' expects that the position taken after the 14 November talks between Truman, Attlee and King may change the actions of the Canadians and the British. If the Federal Bureau of Investigation carries out the new investigation quickly and successfully, the Americans will be able to take actions simultaneously against the persons who are mentioned in the Canadian case and are in the US."[110]

Yet the 25th and 26th came and went. This time it was the Americans who balked. As Philby correctly noted, the FBI was preoccupied with its own spy investigations.[111] Communist Party of the USA member Elizabeth Bentley exposed a network of some forty Soviet spies, more than Philby thought, who had penetrated the American government.[112] She had been an NKVD agent and courier from 1938 to 1944, and her revelations turned out to be on a par with Gouzenko's in importance.[113] At the same time and in the wake of the failed Council of Foreign Ministers conference of September 1945, Secretary of State James Byrnes was planning a new initiative to mend fences with Moscow.[114] The Americans were thus "reluctant to throw any pebble that would disturb United States–Russian relations."[115] Finally, on the evening of 27 November, US under-secretary of state Dean Acheson, speaking for Truman, told the Canadian ambassador Lester Pearson that the US was ready for whatever action Canada might take, but wouldn't promise a joint action.[116] King, probably insulted by the Americans' lukewarm response, balked at confronting Russian power alone.

On 24 November 1945, the people's commissar of state security of the USSR (NKVD), V. Merkulov, had brought these developments to the attention of Joseph Stalin, summarizing Philby's Gouzenko information, including accounts of Nunn May and of a Soviet agent code-named "Elli" in the British security service. Merkulov explained how, because of Gouzenko, "Amer. counterintelligence (the FBI) has lately intensified surveillance of employees of Soviet offices in the US and is actively investigating members of the Amer. Com. Party suspected by the FBI of cooperating with Sov. intel." Merkulov broke the news of Elizabeth Bentley's defection and conveyed Philby's report that the FBI now knew that Soviet agents had "penetrated deep into Amer. government agencies." Merkulov therefore "issued a directive to the stations of the NKGB [a new acronym for the NKVD] in the US to cut off contact immediately with all of the persons Bentley knows about through our work, to warn agents about Bentley's betrayal and to instruct them regarding their line of behavior and necessary precautionary measures."[117]

A few days later Philby, via his London handlers, updated Stalin on Canada: "Mackenzie King cannot bring himself to implement the steps in the Canadian case that were laid out by him and Attlee. The British keep putting pressure on him. King is waiting for actions in the US."[118] Philby even gave Stalin a copy of the "text of Mackenzie King's statement that he will make on the day the agents of the GRU's Canadian station are arrested."[119]

1–3 December 1945

In Ottawa in early December, King reverted again to the quiet option. If the Americans didn't want to hold up their end, he would let the Washington plan gather dust and keep everything in-house, turning to the Inquiries Act Part II (Departmental Inquiries). Although the Inquiries Act held potentially powerful weapons of interrogation, an in-house "departmental" inquiry would have blunted those weapons. Originating as An Act to authorize making certain investigations under oath (1880), Part II authorized commissioners to issue subpoenas and to compel the testimony of government employees. But King's idea of no arrests "except where confessions may be forthcoming" would have allowed the suspects to return home each night and to coordinate their stories, weakening the inquiry, perhaps even allowing suspects to be exfiltrated to Moscow.[120] Resurrecting his earlier delusions about a diplomatic solution, King planned to tell the Soviet ambassador that Ottawa demanded the recall of Zabotin and everyone implicated in spying. This would hardly step beyond the conventional choreography of peacetime diplomacy: Ottawa would demand an end to Soviet spying; Moscow would deny the charges but accept the expulsions; little publicity; little rancour; little accomplished.

The RCMP's Stuart Wood instantly perceived the weakness of the arrest strategy and objected.[121] Wood lectured St. Laurent on what would happen if King tried his stick-and-carrot charm on the Soviets: "Immediately after Mr. King's interview with the ambassador, the network of agents implicated, if not already warned, will be cautioned and will then be in a concrete position to prepare themselves for any investigation or inquiry which may follow." The ensuing publicity would be "uncontrollable" and, most damningly, interrogations wouldn't stop "the activities of such key men in the network as [Communist organizer] Sam Carr and [Labor-Progressive MP] Fred Rose who should be the primary targets of any action." A return to the Washington plan, with many arrests and closed-door hearings, would provide better investigative tools.[122]

Wood was undoubtedly happy that, like all the plans contemplated from the outset of the Gouzenko crisis, King's went nowhere. Before King could ask for a meeting with Russian ambassador Georgy Zarubin, the Russians, one step ahead, announced his almost-immediate departure and asked King to meet with Zarubin. It turned out to be a non-event, an exchange of diplomatic pleasantries and mutual calls for closer political, economic, and cultural relations between Canada and the Soviet Union.[123] Faced with a departing ambassador and resistance from his own security officials, King shelved his initiative. This back-and-forth on the best strategy to deal with the spying shows how unsure the historical actors were about the best way forward. There was nothing inevitable about the form that the royal commission would ultimately take, and it would only arrive in the tension between nations, in the urgency of dealing with the spies, and in the participants' difficult choices. After all of the legal, political, and diplomatic efforts, Canada's response to the Gouzenko crisis amounted to very little. But Mackenzie King knew that with spies still in place, and the Gouzenko story circulating in London, Washington, and Moscow, inaction was not an option. What would his next move be?

2
Read / Varcoe Redux

4–28 December 1945

After the Nunn May no-show in London, the influence of the Justice Department ebbed. Norman Robertson, Hume Wrong, and Mackenzie King took charge. The never-implemented Washington plan had emphasized security and policing via a royal commission and prosecutions, alongside a press initiative against the Soviet Union. But the Justice Department's advice that prosecutions probably wouldn't lead to convictions influenced King's alternative plan: quiet diplomacy via a limited number of "departmental" inquiries rather than a federal royal commission.[1] The Justice Department told King that courts would only admit Gouzenko's hearsay evidence if the Crown could prove that a conspiracy existed,[2] but King decided to test that advice, and ordered St. Laurent to get an "immediate outside legal opinion."[3] In response, St. Laurent summoned E.K. Williams, a Winnipeg commercial lawyer and the current president of the Canadian Bar Association, to Ottawa. Maybe King only wanted legal advice, but Williams gave him much more: a restated and amplified version of the Read / Varcoe proposal.

Williams, an Ontario native born in 1889, had arrived in Manitoba as a twenty-one-year-old. He joined the bar and rose to prominence.[4] Through the Canadian Bar Association, he maintained a long-standing professional relationship with St. Laurent and, astutely, also cultivated King by praising King's father, an Osgoode Hall lecturer under whom Williams had studied. Williams even sent King a commonplace book (owned by Williams's brother-in-law) containing a copy of a letter to King's famous grandfather, William Lyon Mackenzie. By December 1945, St. Laurent and King were already considering whether to appoint Williams, a former Conservative, as Manitoba Chief Justice.[5]

Counsel to the commissioners
Winnipeg lawyer E.K. Williams
(University of Manitoba Archives, UM_
pc018_A81-012_018_10674_008_0001)

Williams's native tongue was a combination of common-law discourse (transmitted through Blackstone[6]), Anglicanism, and fierce anti-Communism. If history were to avoid falling into "a futile tragedy of blood," it must reach for "the Kingdom of God."[7] In 1934, he warned the graduating class of United College (now the University of Winnipeg) against "following new leaders and strange gods." The church, not labour unions, would be the "salvation of workers" and of everyone else.[8] Earlier, Williams, as a twenty-nine-year-old lawyer, had rallied the anti-labour Citizens' Committee of 1000 against the Winnipeg General Strike. Not only did he help prosecute the strike leaders, but credible reports also indicate that on 21 June 1919, "Bloody Saturday," the slightly built five-foot-seven-inch Williams, who eschewed physical exercise of any kind, "rode with the troops that swept down Main Street in the wake of the mounted police" assault on Winnipeg's working class.[9] During World War II, at the Winnipeg Board of Trade, he railed against Canadian "Quislings" and wanted them named. "Who are they?" he asked, and then answered, "The obvious ones are the Communists. They have been disloyal to Canada from the start of the war to June 22, 1940 [when the Communist Party was banned]. They have no place in this country. We should place the mark of beasts on them and put them where they belong."[10]

Here, Williams echoed John Locke who, in his *Second Treatise on Government* (1689), argued that men who declare enmity against the state place themselves outside of legal protections: "such men are not under the ties of the commonlaw of reason, have no rule except that of force and violence, and so may be treated as beasts of prey – dangerous creatures that will certainly destroy me if I fall into their power."[11] Of course, notions of parliamentary supremacy and the obligation of the state to defend itself underlay wartime jurisprudence generally, and allowed state security to trump civil liberties. In many litigations, the argument surfaced that courts must step aside when the state needed to protect itself. In short, "freedom must be abridged to protect freedom."[12] The European war had ended in the spring, the Far East war in early August of 1945, but in October PC 6444 declared a new existential threat to Canada's security. The same note sounded in Williams's report to the Department of Justice.[13]

Williams brought extensive experience about just how an executive inquiry could wield state power. He had served as counsel for Winnipeg lawyer and former Conservative candidate C.P. Fullerton when the Perdue Commission (1915) investigated Fullerton's charges that T.C. Norris's Liberal government had come to power in Manitoba via a corrupt agreement with the former Conservative government. The Perdue Commission grew out of an original inquiry (1915), under Chief Justice T.B. Mathers, investigating the corruption associated with the construction of Manitoba's new legislative building, and led to criminal charges against former premier Roblin, two cabinet members, and the contractor Thomas Kelly, all of whom were subpoenaed to testify before the inquiry. Williams watched how, despite unprecedented legal challenges brought by Kelly's lawyer, the Manitoba Court of Appeal affirmed the commission's constitutional propriety and legal authority, including its power to compel testimony.[14] This appeal judgment, cited multiple times in subsequent challenges, bolstered Canadian executive inquiries as instruments of state power.[15] Eyes on this weapon, Williams, alongside other members of Winnipeg's Citizens' Committee of 1000, had asked, unsuccessfully, for a federal inquiry to bring labour radicalism to heel in 1919.

Encountering Gouzenko's revelations, Williams soon understood both their significance and their legal shortcomings. He wanted every lead traced before making anything public, but, of course, the RCMP Criminal Investigation Branch's exhaustive report "Soviet Espionage in Canada" had already been there, done that. Gouzenko had been "questioned and cross-questioned" about reports composed by Russian officials, telegrams, and notes that disclosed the names, code names, and activities of agents recruited in Canada. The RCMP concluded that Gouzenko's "information ... has been found amazingly accurate."[16] Officers had even studied handwriting samples and the paper upon which the documents were composed. Despite their Soviet provenance and ownership, Williams believed that the documents would be *admissible* in court or in front of a royal commission.[17] Although their reception in court would turn out to be conditional, he was right about their reception by a royal commission. While technically hearsay, these documents could force witnesses to prove their innocence.

So far, so good. But Williams doubted the documents' legal value for criminal prosecutions of Canadians. Yes, they made compelling evidence against the Russians – "those in whose custody they were and those who brought them into existence" – but Canadian courts held no jurisdiction over Russian diplomats. In Williams's opinion, because the documents included materials in the handwriting of only four Canadians, the documents would be considered *direct* evidence only against those four: Gordon Lunan (code-named "Back"), employed by Canadian Wartime Information Board as editor of "Canadian Affairs"; Durnford Smith ("Badeau"), a researcher affiliated with the NRC; Emma Woikin ("Nora"), a cipher clerk in the Department of External Affairs; and Harold Gerson ("Gray"), working in the Department of Munitions and Supply. As for the others, the Crown needed evidence of a conspiracy in order to make the hearsay evidence stick. Williams told King that the evidence probably wouldn't stand for criminal prosecutions, and he didn't want to prosecute even the four strongest cases yet. His advice repeated Justice Department advice from September 1945, but Williams went into greater detail. The Soviets' use of code names and "cut-outs" (go-betweens) made prosecutions difficult.[18] How could the Crown prove a conspiracy when Gouzenko knew "none of the individuals in question" personally? The code names came "from his employers and, without some other link, would not be admissible."[19]

Entries in Mackenzie King's diary make it clear that, from December on, Williams became an integral member of the magic circle – the "Corby" Committee – and it was his endgame strategy, rooted in the Read / Varcoe proposal of late September, that came to dominate. Williams had a policing and security agenda that extended beyond punishing spies. By combining a police investigation with a royal commission, he wanted to till the ground for prosecuting Communists and Communist sympathizers both in the criminal courts and in the court of public opinion. A traditional police investigation probably wouldn't produce confessions or incriminating testimony, but "The Commission," Williams stressed, "has full control over its own procedure and the way in which it will handle all matters coming before it. It may, and in this case should, sit in camera. It need not be bound by the ordinary rules of evidence if it considers it desirable to disregard them. It need not permit counsel to appear for those to be interrogated by or before it." In short, it could be secret, accept hearsay evidence, and deny legal counsel to the suspects. To give the commission legitimacy, Williams proposed that two (unnamed) "Judges of the Supreme Court of Canada" be appointed. He seems to have understood that to meet the threat of Soviet subversion he was recommending that the Canadian state trample on centuries of common law norms, but in his view "the vital nature of the matters to be dealt with fully justify [*sic*] the procedure recommended."[20]

In time, the commission would be condemned as a Star Chamber proceeding, but Williams wasn't treading on entirely new ground. In a watershed 1846 moment, Canadian royal commissions broke away from their British cousins. From time immemorial, the British Crown had appointed inquiries with coercive powers, but during the British constitutional and civil strife of the seventeenth century Parliament had nullified a wide range of prerogative powers, particularly via the Petition of Right (1628), the Act for the Abolition of the Star Chamber (1641), and the Bill of Rights (1689). These statutes spelled out common-law protections against the Crown's power to compel witnesses to appear at inquiries, to force testimony under oath, and to produce any required documents. The Crown could still appoint "commissions to inquire only,"[21] but in the eighteenth century Parliamentary select committees dramatically diminished the importance of royal commissions. Yet, by the early nineteenth century, the growing need for objective social and economic data for legislative action prompted a dramatic revival of royal commissions.[22] Ninety-one were appointed between 1831 and 1844.[23]

These royal commissions soon became subjects of legal controversy: how much coercive power should the Crown have?[24] In 1835 the British Crown – effectively the British cabinet – appointed a royal commission on municipal corporations to deal with Britain's many rotten boroughs, and gave it "full power and authority" to call witnesses, "to administer an oath or oaths to any person," and to demand any "charters, rolls, records, orders, deeds, books, papers, or other writings."[25] But when the commission approached a large and important trade guild – the Merchant Tailors' Company – to demand its records, the Merchant Tailors objected that "by common law, which is the right of the subject, no man can be compelled to disclose any matter that may expose himself to peril, except in the due course of justice."[26] This stance that the Crown could no longer demand such things gained formal acceptance seventeen years later when law officers of the Crown acknowledged that commissions couldn't be granted "compulsory powers."[27] By the 1850s, coercive British royal commissions were a thing of the past.

In the Province of Canada, a flood of false claims for damages after the rebellion in Lower Canada led to the Inquiries Act in 1846, when a royal commission was needed to investigate whether requests for reimbursement were legitimate.[28] Prior to 1846, the Crown in Canada (as in Britain) could appoint an inquiry through prerogative rather than statutory authority. However, after 1846 and in Canada alone, the Inquiries Act returned some of the Crown's long-extinct prerogative powers, granting commissioners the power to force all witnesses to testify and to turn over any requested documents.[29] The Act was supposed to be temporary, ending in 1847 or 1848, but the coercive powers proved invaluable, and as a result the new Inquiries Act (re-enacted by Canada's Parliament in 1868) revived inquisitional powers denied to the British Crown.[30]

In Britain, legislation to grant coercive powers to Crown-appointed inquiries was considered and rejected. In 1910 The Balfour Committee, reviewing royal commission procedures, obliquely passed judgment on Canadian coercive inquiries. It concluded that granting the Crown authority to confer power on inquiries to require testimony on oath and to demand documents would be "a grave departure from present constitutional practice, and from our experience of Royal Commission work we know of nothing which would warrant so serious a change." Only "a special Act of Parliament" could alter that.[31] Eventually, in 1921 (after an MP alleged that officials in the Ministry of Munitions had destroyed certain contract papers), the British Parliament did pass the Tribunals of Inquiry (Evidence) Act that empowered the state to give an inquiry's leader coercive powers, but only after both Houses of Parliament passed a resolution declaring that an inquiry's subject matter was of urgent public importance.[32]

Over in Canada, the 1846 Inquiries Act was challenged, but unsuccessfully. The first legal challenge came in 1863, questioning the jurisdiction and the use of hearsay evidence during a commission headed by lawyers Richard Lafrenaye and Marcus Doherty. The terms of reference for that commission read like a criminal indictment and the proceedings sound like a preliminary hearing into criminal charges:[33] allegedly, three clerks, including Charles Schiller, "had embezzled ... Government monies" and "committed perjury."[34] Schiller's lawyer argued that the commission had "invaded the precincts of criminal jurisdiction … [that] the proceedings … were in the highest degree illegal, and subversive of the liberty of the subject," and that the commission had received hearsay evidence that in "an ordinary trial, the accused could attack."[35] As it would be for the commission arising from Gouzenko, the central question was "Is this a trial or an inquiry?" Although Justice Monk of the Quebec Superior Court initially sympathized, he nevertheless concluded that the charges formed a "proper subject matter" of investigation for the commission, that the commissioners had "acted legally" under the 1846 legislation, and that they hadn't usurped the powers of any criminal court.[36] Against arguments that the state had invaded the terrain of the courts, Monk's decision provided the template for subsequent rulings.

Yet the Inquiries Act also protected witnesses against self-incrimination: "no witness shall be compelled to answer any question, by his answer to which he might render himself liable to a criminal prosecution."[37] This protection would be removed in 1889 when the Boodle Commission struggled to investigate civic corruption in Quebec City, after a railway company paid massive kickbacks to members of Premier Honoré Mercier's Liberal government. Faced with potential criminal charges, witnesses refused to testify on the grounds that their testimony might be self-incriminating. In December 1888 the attorney general of Quebec and the inquiry's commissioner tried to break the impasse by asking John Thompson, the federal minister of justice, to give the witnesses a pre-emptive general pardon. Thompson refused,[38] so the investigation was adjourned indefinitely. But the matter did not end there. Instead, Thompson crafted An Act to make further provision respecting inquiries concerning Public Matters (1889),[39] which made all witnesses before federal or provincial inquiries compellable, irrespective of whether their testimony might be self-incriminating.[40] A partial defence remained: evidence so taken would not be admissible in a criminal trial (unless a witness gave false evidence).[41] A fuller statement was added by Thompson in 1893 as the Canada Evidence Act, under which the Kellock-Taschereau Commission would operate. Section 5 made all witnesses in criminal trials, civil proceedings, and commissions of inquiry compellable:[42]

> No person shall be excused from answering questions upon the ground that the answer to such question may tend to criminate him, or may tend to establish his liability to a civil proceeding at the instance of the Crown or of any other person: provided, however, that no evidence so given shall be used or receivable in evidence against such person in any criminal proceeding thereafter instituted against him other than a prosecution for perjury in giving such evidence.[43]

If a witness wanted their answer not to be used in a criminal proceeding, did they have to *specifically object* to answering the question in order to secure the protection? Discord in the courts on this question resulted in an 1898 amendment. To avoid self-incrimination, witnesses had to register an objection *each time* an incriminating question came up.[44] How many witnesses before a federal inquiry would, in the absence of legal counsel, be familiar with such complexities of the Canada Evidence Act?

In 1890 a contractor, Arthur Godson, took a different tack, challenging whether an inquiry under the Ontario Municipal Act contravened natural justice. A County Court judge had been appointed to investigate whether contractors had obtained payments from the city unlawfully. In *Arthur W. Godson and The Corporation of the City of Toronto*, Godson, not named in the inquiry's terms of reference, objected. Because the inquiry called a lot of businesspeople, including himself, as witnesses, this implication of guilt could harm his standing in the business community. He insisted that specific charges against him be formulated for investigation. He secured an injunction, only to have the Ontario Court of Appeal strike it down, finding that neither the inquiry's terms of reference nor its conduct was judicial, but were confined to investigative and reporting functions. The majority of the Supreme Court of Canada agreed. Chief Justice W.J. Ritchie, speaking for the majority, concluded that the commissioner "was not acting judicially in holding this inquiry."[45] Dissenting, Justice John Gwynne objected that to take evidence against someone without a formal charge or complaint was to subvert natural justice,[46] because anyone who may be "injuriously affected in his pecuniary interests, his reputation and business prospects by the judgment ... must be entitled to have the inquiry conducted in a judicial manner."[47]

Gwynne was an outlier. By the 1930s, commissions of inquiry were increasingly cast as *administrative* as opposed to *judicial* tribunals.[48] In 1934 D.M. Gordon, a "pioneer of Canadian administrative law scholarship,"[49] observed that a "judicial tribunal looks for some law to guide it" while "an administrative tribunal," with absolute procedural discretion, is (in its domain) "a law unto itself."[50] The independence of Canadian executive inquiries circa 1945 was spelled out in detail in *Re Ashby* (1934), where the Ontario Appeal Court, relying on Gordon, affirmed that "an administrative tribunal ... possesses a complete, absolute and unfettered discretion and, having no fixed standards to follow, it is guided by its own ideas of policy and expediency."[51] Without a body of administrative law to delimit them, inquiries were quite free – as long as they stuck to the subject.

Alongside these changes, the power to deny legal counsel to commission witnesses had always been assumed. It first appeared explicitly in the federal Inquiries Act in 1912, when Robert Borden's government amended the legislation to confirm the power of commissioners to use lawyers and experts. The Liberal opposition cried foul and demanded the same for witnesses. As a result, the revised Inquiries Act of 1912 included a new section 12 that provided that "commissioners *may* allow any person whose conduct is being investigated under this Act, and *shall allow* any person against whom any charge is made in the course of such investigation, to be represented by council" (our emphasis). Nevertheless, as long as commissioners avoided levelling a charge at a witness, the right to a lawyer could be denied. This authority to decide when to grant legal counsel, combined with the requirement that witnesses must answer questions put to them, gave Canadian commissioners of inquiry more investigative authority than their counterparts in British parliamentary or American congressional inquiries.

Reflecting back on *Godson v. Toronto*, Robert Howe found an inherent conflict in the wish to give commissions of inquiry as wide a latitude as possible and the wish to safeguard individual rights.[52] Howe, writing in the 1970s, called the problem of when, how, or if the rules of natural justice applied in these commissions "one of the most troublesome problems in the whole of administrative law."[53] Even now, with the post-Charter development of a mature body of Canadian administrative law, little has changed.[54]

E.K. Williams understood that the power to compel testimony, combined with the power to deny legal counsel, would allow commissioners to ferret incriminating evidence out of the Gouzenko suspects. Confessions of guilt or testimony that incriminated others would solve the "hearsay evidence" problem and open the door to criminal prosecutions. His orchestration promised a truth-seeking process, though it would also place the suspects in a kind of Kafkaesque theatre. He imagined the "detention of ten or fifteen people, all taken into custody at the same time and held in a place where they could not be communicated with and, in fact, in a place which would be unknown to their families and friends." He thought that the lapse between Gouzenko's defection and the arrests, far from hamstringing the state, might even play to its advantage: "If those whose conduct is to be investigated are now taken into custody and, after a lapse of some days[,] interrogated, the results would probably be better after a period of relaxation from fear of proceedings than if they had been taken into custody at once." "Prearranged stories" would have fallen from memory and the shock of arrest might even unsettle some suspects to the point of "deciding to tell what they know or at least part of it."[55]

Through this gauntlet of sudden arrest, incommunicado confinement, repeated interrogation, no legal representation, and denial of *habeas corpus*, Williams anticipated that "confessions may be obtained in some cases, statements will be obtained in practically all ... and counsel for the Commission should cross-examine on them."[56] Williams thereby linked PC 6444, an executive inquiry, the Official Secrets Act, the conspiracy provisions of the Criminal Code, and criminal proceedings. Left unstated was that his proposal amounted to an unprecedented assault on the judicial safeguards inherent in Canadian citizenship. But he certainly knew that some people would object, that the detentions "would undoubtedly be a matter of public comment." Indeed, after the Kellock-Taschereau's procedures became public months later, the Mackenzie King government did not escape charges that it was employing totalitarian methods. In the event, King and others would (as Williams had in his 1942 anti-Communist speech to the Board of Trade) turn to Locke's argument about wartime policy, defending governmental actions as the right of a person to destroy another who threatens them with destruction. Such language, directed at Roman Catholics in the Stuart era,[57] was later secularized by Locke when he referred to those who lay "the foundation for overturning the constitution and structure of any just government" as "the common enemy."[58] Even leading Russophiles, such as Escott Reid in the Department of External Affairs, had been shaken by the Gouzenko crisis and by Kremlin machinations at the UN and in Eastern Europe. "The Communists today are the Papists of the last half of the seventeenth century," Reid argued. "You have citizens who give an allegiance elsewhere and your normal system of justice and individual rights breaks down."[59] Here were Locke's "beasts of prey": defendants who wanted all the protections afforded by a democratic system, but who conspired to undermine that very system, even violently so.

In December 1945, Williams merely suggested that King prepare a statement "to let the public know something of what was being done."[60] Although Williams paid lip-service to foreign policy implications and the need to "ensure that the United Nations Organization should function as satisfactory and smoothly as possible," he nevertheless judged these considerations as secondary to the "vitally serious matter" of Soviet espionage.[61] As had the RCMP's Stuart Wood, Williams dismissed the idea of a departmental inquiry, which, despite coercive powers to compel testimony and secure documents,[62] wouldn't have the scope or the weight of a royal commission.[63]

Initially, Williams hoped that the Americans would harmonize their "special secret Senate Committee" investigating Soviet espionage with the Canadian royal commission, allowing the two legal teams to exchange notes. He knew that the US Senate's coercive powers would be weaker than a Canadian commission's, yet he expected the Americans to find alternative ways to get "statements or confessions which could be placed before the Senate Committee."[64] The Canadian government could grant the Americans time to prepare a joint investigation, but the wait should not go past 15 January.

Like previous efforts to bring the Americans on board, the plan failed, and by the end of December Mackenzie King was ready to act.[65] Williams's tactics became King's. The soon-to-be retired King, conscious of the need to protect his political legacy, warmed to Williams's political cost-benefit analysis and picked Supreme Court judges Robert Taschereau and Roy Kellock to head the commission of inquiry. Taschereau hailed from a distinguished Québécois family, his grandfather having served on Canada's original Supreme Court and his father having spent sixteen years as premier of Quebec (1920–36). Taschereau graduated from the Quebec Seminary and Laval University, and by 1940, at age forty-three, he was appointed to the Supreme Court. During the war, he had served on tribunals created under the Defence of Canada Regulations to hear appeals from individuals detained under the Regulations.[66] His would be the sole dissenting vote when, in 1957, the Supreme Court declared Quebec's anti-Communist "padlock law" unconstitutional.[67] In 1963 he would become Chief Justice. Kellock, a graduate of Osgoode Hall in 1920, specialized in labour arbitration. He was appointed to the Ontario Court of Appeal in 1942 and two years later to the Supreme Court, where he spent fourteen years. Like Taschereau, he had served on the Defense of Canada Regulations tribunals.[68] He was also no stranger to commissions of inquiry: in the previous year, he had been appointed to investigate the May 1945 Halifax riot of returned Canadian soldiers.[69] When he died, in 1975, the *Globe and Mail* would praise him as "much admired for his work on the Kellock-Taschereau Royal Commission."[70]

Later, when called upon to justify the coercive aspects of the Kellock-Taschereau proceedings, King would cite E.K. Williams's report, Williams's status in the Canadian legal community, and the participation of Supreme Court judges Robert Taschereau and Roy Kellock as evidence that the government had acted prudently. However, despite bringing in unimpeachable chairs and celebrating the utility of royal commissions, Williams neglected to canvas the legal vulnerabilities of inquiries carried on under statutory authority. Canadian

Royal commissioner and Supreme Court justice Roy Kellock (Library Archives Canada, Justice R.L. Kellock – PA-047343)

inquiries brought unwilling witnesses before them with a subpoena or a bench warrant. Williams contemplated the use of an order-in-council approved with the authority of the War Measures Act as the instrument to prod the recalcitrant before the commissioners. Later, *habeas corpus* proceedings brought by those detained under PC 6444 would reveal vulnerabilities in Williams's proposal. He might have offered King a more secure foundation for his endgame against Soviet espionage through amendments to the 1939 Official Secrets Act, but he chose the path already mapped out by King's Justice Department.

3
PC 411

4 January–5 February 1946

In early January, Minister of Justice St. Laurent and Hume Wrong from External Affairs sailed to the opening session of the UN General Assembly in London, and on 22 January they met with British Foreign Secretary Bevin, US Secretary of State Byrnes, Sir Alexander Cadogan, and Sir John Stephenson (MI5) of the Dominions Office. The British agreed not to oppose Mackenzie King's decision to implement the September Read/Varcoe plan of arrests.[1] On 1 February, a Friday, Malcolm MacDonald telegraphed Cadogan that King wanted to bring the hammer down immediately, and that he was "keeping Williams ... in Ottawa for this purpose."[2] But before King could act, American journalist Drew Pearson shocked listeners of his Sunday NBC radio broadcast *Drew Pearson Comments* with a bombshell that decisively ended all the back-and-forth. Pearson revealed King's message to President Truman: a Soviet agent in Canada had suddenly exposed Russian spy networks in Canada and the US.[3]

No one knows who leaked the story to Pearson, or why. Possibilities include Truman's chief of staff Admiral Leahy or MI6's William Stephenson, acting in collusion with J. Edgar Hoover.[4] Amy Knight points a finger directly at Hoover, since Pearson's disclosures gave the FBI "a climate in which to launch their spy hunt more aggressively."[5] Dennis Molinaro, citing MI5 archival documents (though no smoking gun), argues that the British government and its security services were likely responsible.[6]

Mackenzie King was apparently sanguine. Always on the lookout for omens (such as the position of the hands on a clock), he considered the breaking news to be a "good thing ... it gives us a special reason for starting immediately with our inquiry." Naturally, he felt somewhat apprehensive: "What may grow out of the inquiry … I cannot say, … but there can be little doubt that a heavy responsibility now rests on our shoulders, and that it will grow into one of the major sensations of the day."[7] Within twenty-four hours, a report on Gouzenko winged its way to cabinet, and by Tuesday, acting through Crown prerogative and the federal Inquiries Act, cabinet approved PC 411, creating the inquiry headed by Kellock and Taschereau and granting it coercive investigative powers.[8]

Augmenting October's secret PC 6444, which allowed St. Laurent to detain anybody suspected of passing on secret information to a foreign power, PC 411 reached back to the 1846 Inquiries Act and, more immediately, to the Read / Varcoe proposal. In December, with the Gouzenko matter percolating, Parliament had approved the National Emergency Transitional Powers Act (TPA).[9] This legislation set 1 January 1946 as the date for the proclamation invoking the War Measures Act to be rescinded,[10] but it allowed orders-in-council approved under the War Measures Act (and not cancelled) to remain in force – so PC 6444 (and PC 5991) remained available.[11] Justice Minister St. Laurent had assured the Commons that no secret orders existed that would survive via the TPA. Later he would insist to Parliament that PC 6444 (and PC 5991) had slipped his mind,[12] though it's hard to imagine that others aware of PC 6444 and PC 5991 – including Mackenzie King, J.L. Ilsley, C.D. Howe, and Douglas Abbott – neglected to remind and correct St. Laurent.

Williams had contemplated using PC 6444 in his 7 December report.[13] Via this "special order," the government could detain suspects "in lawful custody" and interrogate them prior to their appearance before the commission. In fact, the plan couldn't proceed without PC 6444, since only through the order could the government arrest, detain, and interrogate while (by the minister's order) ostensibly overriding *habeas corpus*.[14] On 5 February Mackenzie King (who in public studiously avoided the word "arrests" and instead spoke of "detention" or "taking into custody") confided to his private diary that he had "suggested having the Commission appointed at once, to take evidence in secret wherever Corby [Gouzenko] may be. Then *make the arrests* necessary of our own people and defer to that moment my having a word with the Russian Ambassador."[15]

It might not have been apparent to casual observers that Kellock-Taschereau Commission procedures were more "judicialized" and coercive than most royal commissions, but even those observers might have noticed that the commission looked an awful lot like the preliminary hearing for an expected criminal prosecution. PC 411 began, "Secret and confidential information has been communicated directly or indirectly by public officials and other persons in positions of trust to the agents of a Foreign Power to the prejudice of the safety and interests of Canada."[16] Sounding like an indictment, this language was lifted directly from the Official Secrets Act's reference to actions "prejudicial to the safety or interests of the state."[17] The commissioners were directed to "inquire into and report upon *which* public officials and other persons in positions of trust or otherwise have communicated, directly or indirectly, secret and confidential information ... to the agents of a Foreign Power" (our emphasis). The Justice Department planned to refer any offences to the provincial attorneys general in Ontario and Quebec, and indeed, in the months afterward, when Kellock and Taschereau found evidence of conspiracy and offences against the Official Secrets Act, criminal proceedings followed.[18]

Gouzenko had *heard* conversations of GRU officers; he had *read* the secret documentary records (notes, telegrams, reports, dossiers) at the centre of GRU operations; but none of this was admissible evidence. The Crown needed direct evidence that the suspects had visited a "prohibited location," prepared a document "directly or indirectly useful to a foreign power," or communicated information – code words, sketches, passwords, documents – to a foreign agent.[19] Alternatively, the Crown could try to prove that the suspects had an agreement – a conspiracy – to offend the Official Secrets Act. In his 7 December report, Williams had made it clear that he wanted to use Gouzenko's hearsay evidence. He expected it to generate testimony – ideally confessions – implicating the suspects in a conspiracy. For the most part, the inquiry did fulfil his expectations. Confessions of guilt could, if made without the witness's objection, be admitted as evidence in a subsequent criminal trial: Gordon Lunan, Emma Woikin, Kathleen Willsher, Edward (Ned) Mazerall, and Raymond Boyer would all be convicted on their confessions. Despite this, there was no guarantee that witnesses who implicated others before the inquiry would repeat their testimony in a courtroom. Lunan would implicate several suspects during the inquiry, only to refuse to testify in subsequent criminal trials. As a result, charges would be dismissed against David Shugar and Israel Halperin, because the Crown couldn't produce direct evidence in the form of Lunan's testimony. Even if the Crown were to call the commission stenographer to testify that Lunan had incriminated Shugar and Halperin during the inquiry, the defence couldn't cross-examine Lunan, thereby technically making his words – "the stenographer said that Lunan said ..." – hearsay evidence. Carleton County Court judge A. Gordon McDougall would find that Gouzenko's documents were inadmissible as evidence of conspiracy: "Such evidence ... could be accepted only when the accused person had first been linked with other conspirators."[20]

Future criminal trials aside, the Kellock-Taschereau Commission was not just a substitute for a traditional police inquiry, but the instrument of choice to address threats to the security of the liberal state. If the state really was under attack, the Lockean response would be to abrogate some of the rights of those contributing to the threat. The inquiry would furnish an account of the origins and history of Soviet spying in Canada, the focus of the spying, Russian recruitment of Canadian agents and strategies to handle them, the motivation of those who betrayed their oaths of loyalty to Canada, the reach of Soviet networks in the Canada and beyond, and the role of the Communist Party as an in-place source of Canadian spies. Not only could such an account help update security arrangements and cleanse the country of subversives, but it would also place the Soviet Union's and the Canadian Communist Party's subversion on the public record.

To achieve these purposes, Williams, a careful student of the controversial 1915 inquiries, massaged PC 411 to avoid legal challenges. The commission's terms of reference let Kellock and Taschereau "adopt such procedure and method as they may deem expedient" and allowed them to "alter or change the same from time to time." In instrumental terms, the commissioners could proceed in camera, require testimony, and deny lawyers to the witnesses. Commissioners were explicitly directed to create a verbatim record in shorthand, a record clearly designed for future criminal trials. The record would be received by the state as correct without being "read over to or signed by the person examined."[21] In addition, Kellock and Taschereau were instructed to provide "interim reports to the Governor in Council on any matter ... together with the evidence then before them and their findings thereon." Although orders made under the Transitional Powers Act must be reported to Parliament within fifteen days if Parliament was in session, PC 411 was created through Crown prerogative powers, not through the Transitional Powers Act, so King had no obligation to report the order-in-council until he was prepared to tell the world about the Gouzenko crisis.[22] Malcolm MacDonald, who provided accurate commentary on the Gouzenko affair to Cadogan in London, reported that a primary reason for secrecy was to allow the commissioners "to complete Corby's examination without any risk of Russian attempts to dispose of him physically or start propaganda which might prejudice position whilst he is giving evidence."[23] That was true, but only part of the picture.

5–13 February 1946

Long before Drew Pearson's salvo, preparations for the inquiry had begun, preparations reflected in how quickly Kellock and Taschereau leapt to their work. The day of their appointment, they began examining Gouzenko's stolen documents and documents arising out of the RCMP's months-long investigation.[24] For each Gouzenko suspect, RCMP dossiers specified their family origin, religious affiliation, education, professional and occupational history, political affiliations, links to Communists, and evidence against the suspect.[25] Zabotin's handwritten notes from the Russian embassy safe were translated, detailing the origins of Soviet espionage in Canada circa 1942–43, including the roles of Raymond Boyer ("Professor"), Sergei M. Koudriavtsev ("Leon"),[26] Maj. Vsevolod Sokolov ("Davie"), Sam Carr ("Sam"), Pavel Mikhailov ("Molier"), Fred Rose ("Fred"), and Harold Gerson ("Gray").[27] There was the seven-page "Record of Materials Sent to the Address of the Director," known as "Grant's Mailing List," a detailed list of materials sent on 5 January 1945 to GRU headquarters by Zabotin ("Grant"), as well as confidential correspondence from Canada's Department of Foreign Affairs, correspondence that had found its way to the Soviet embassy. Throughout the Gouzenko trove lay the names of Canadians, those who had been targeted for recruitment alongside those who had agreed to work for the GRU, their code names, and their espionage activities. Once Kellock and Taschereau read through these documents, they planned to interrogate Gouzenko in secret for three days, followed by testimony from heads of departments in which the suspects worked. With this foundation established, the "second stage" would consist of interrogating the suspects.[28]

Kellock, Taschereau, and their supporting cast met on 13 February in the Justice Building.[29] All in attendance were sworn to secrecy, as would be subsequent participants. Nevertheless, the commissioners would soon reveal that the secrecy oath could be waived in any prosecution arising from the inquiry.[30] Lawyers for the commission were E.K. Williams, Gérald Fauteux, and D.W. Mundell.[31] E.L. Featherstone and W.W. Buskard, who produced a verbatim record of the proceedings, would later be called as witnesses in criminal trials to affirm the authenticity of testimonies at the commission.[32] And there were special guests with no official role: Inspector John Leopold, the RCMP specialist in Communist subversion who had investigated Gouzenko's allegations, "assisted" the inquiry;[33] Arnold Smith, a hardliner in the debates on handling Soviet Russia, represented External Affairs and would later draft important sections of *The Report of the Royal Commission* (hereafter called the *Final Report*).[34]

The inquiry began with star witness Igor Gouzenko describing Zabotin's office as spy central. In 1941, prior to the opening of the Soviet diplomatic mission, Maj. Vsevolod Sokolov ("Davy" or "Davie") had arrived in Ottawa, supposedly just a civilian inspector, checking the war-materiel work in Canadian factories as part of the Canadian Mutual Aid Program to the USSR after it entered the war against Nazi Germany. Sokolov began constructing a spy network of agents that would eventually encompass Montreal, Ottawa, and Toronto, organized through the Communist Party's Sam Carr, Labor-Progressive MP Fred Rose, Sokolov's wife, and others.[35] When the first Soviet legation came, Sergei M. Koudriavtsev ("Leon"), nominally the "First Secretary," took over as the network's director for a while.[36] Then Military Attaché Col. Zabotin arrived and established more direct relations between the Russian embassy and its Canadian agents. Under strict orders not to implicate himself directly in spying, Zabotin relied on staff members to handle the agents:[37] Lt. Col. Petr Motinov ("Lamont"), Lt. Pavel N. Angelov ("Baxter"), and Lt. Col. Vassili Rogov (variously "Brent" and "Jan"), all nominally assistant military attachés; Capt. Georgi ("Chester") Gourshkov, the chauffeur; Nikolay Zheveinov, nominally a TASS (Telegraph Agency of the Soviet Union) news correspondent but actually a GRU operative; and, not least, Sergei Gousev ("Henri"), the embassy doorman, who may have been a member of the dreaded NKVD, Stalin's secret police who spied on the spies.[38] Although most of the Soviet spies belonged to the GRU (military intelligence), Gouzenko's testimony suggested a distinct NKVD network as well in Canada.

Gouzenko described his role as a cipher clerk who communicated highly sensitive information between the Russian embassy and GRU headquarters in Moscow.[39] In the weeks before his defection, he had carefully selected and lifted the best files showing the operations of Soviet spy rings in Canada,[40] and even pointing beyond to rings in London and Washington.

He had kept precoded and decoded telegrams between Ottawa and Moscow,[41] as well as torn bits of blue paper, notes that Zabotin had given him to destroy.[42] In his testimony, he explicated the spy lingo in the translated telegrams. "The center" meant GRU headquarters,[43] while "the corporation" referred to all "Communist parties abroad," including the Canadian Communist Party;[44] any member thus became a "corporator."[45] The "Comintern" referred of course to the "Communist International," which, according to Gouzenko, not only directed the activities of Communist parties worldwide[46] but also maintained

Col. Nicolai Zabotin, Russian military attaché (*top right*), with James A. Northey, president of the Canadian Aid to Russia Fund (*top left*), and actor Paul Robeson (*seated*), 25 September 1944 (Toronto Star Photographic Archive, Toronto Public Library)

files on "every Communist in the whole world."[47] Following the dissolution of the Comintern in 1943, the records of the Third Communist International were deposited with the Institute of Marxism-Leninism in Moscow and closed, except to the most politically powerful.[48]

Most importantly, over the course of his three-day testimony, Gouzenko implicated more than a dozen Canadians as spies. Undergirding his testimony was "Grant's Mailing List," prepared by Motinov with the assistance of Gourshkov's wife.[49] The first items in the list (numbers 105–107) were credited to "Green," a construction draftsman at a Montreal locomotive works, but Gouzenko didn't know his real identity.[50] Gouzenko's knowledge was limited to overheard conversations or to whichever of Zabotin's files he had managed to access.[51] Nevertheless, those snatches of conversation did expose many real names. The item "Conversations with professor on the decisions of the secret session of Parliament" (number 108), credited to "Debouz," referred to MP Fred Rose's report on McGill professor Raymond Boyer, whose name Gouzenko had caught when Zabotin and Motinov were discussing the atomic bomb.[52] According to "Grant's Mailing List," two letters from Canada's ambassador in Moscow Dana Wilgress to Mackenzie King had somehow crept into GRU headquarters (numbers 109–10 on Grant's list).[53] Gouzenko said that the code-named source, "Ellie" (or "Elli"), was Kay [Kathleen] Willsher, the secretary of the British high commissioner in Canada.[54] Contracts, correspondence, and reports related to munitions (numbers 111–73) came from "Foster" – the code name for Scotland Benning, who worked in the Department of Munitions and Supplies and the Department of Economic Planning[55]– while a forty-six-page booklet of biographical notes on members of the Canadian government (number 174) was credited, uncamouflaged, to "Sam" – Sam Carr the national organizer of the Communist Party of Canada.[56] Later, he became "Frank." "Nora," a cipher clerk like Gouzenko but in the Canadian Ministry of Foreign Affairs, had given Zabotin Foreign Affairs telegrams, forms, and photographs.[57] Gouzenko identified her as Emma Woikin.[58] Other contributors were "Gray," identified as Harold Gerson from the Department of Statistics in Munitions and Supply,[59] and "Ernst," identified as GRU agent Eric Adams,[60] who had provided over two dozen documents, including correspondence with private companies, reports on munitions, and a description of a new waterproofing invention.[61]

The "Frank" file contained a reference to Matt Nightingale ("Leader"), a "Squadron Leader in the Air Force" working for Bell Telephone,[62] and a note from Sam Carr to David Shugar ("Prometheus"), "a specialist in anti-submarine protection" who worked at Naval Headquarters.[63]

Another file, entitled "Back," detailed meetings between Lt. Col. Rogov[64] and Gordon Lunan ("Back").[65] It contained the document "Scheme of the Group 'Research,'" translated from Rogov's Russian into English and directing Lunan on how to create a network of informers.[66] In his inquiry testimony, Lunan would reveal the names of more spies: Israel Halperin ("Bacon"), identified by Gouzenko as possibly a mathematician working for the NRC; Durnford Smith ("Badeau"), a radio engineer at the NRC; and Ned Mazerall ("Bagley"), also at the NRC.[67] The file on "Badeau" detailed some of the tasks given to Smith.[68] Rogov, as Zabotin's intermediary, was both the principal handler of the Lunan circle and their paymaster: the records revealed that Rogov had distributed money to Lunan, Halperin, Smith, and Mazerall.[69] Like Nunn May, most of those implicated by Gouzenko were highly educated. Some – Boyer, Smith, and Mazerall – were with the NRC; others held senior administrative or advisory positions: Lunan, Halperin, Adams, Benning, Gerson, and Shugar. Two – Nightingale and Fred Poland – had served in the RCAF. Woikin was the only suspect who hadn't attended university.

The Russians treated the espionage material as highly sensitive. Gouzenko explained how Zabotin kept it in an envelope addressed to "The Director," marked "Top Secret," and sealed with five seals. This package was then placed in a second envelope and addressed "Personal – Secret, to the secretary." Then into a third envelope, again with five seals, and addressed "To the People's Commissary on Foreign Affairs, not to be opened by anyone but Novikov." Who was Novikov? No one. "Novikov," the Russian equivalent of English's anonymous "Smith," simply signalled that the parcel contained intelligence work. Finally, the parcel, sheltered by diplomatic immunity in a diplomatic bag and chaperoned by a pair of armed NKVD couriers, made its way by steamer to Moscow.[70]

Gouzenko's first appearance before the commission (he would appear a second time, later on) concluded with a "political statement" in which he explained the political rationale behind his defection. In his original statement two days after his defection he had, clearly with some rhetorical help from the RCMP interrogators, celebrated the liberal state, a narrative that no doubt gave ideological support to some of the more authoritarian aspects of PC 411. In front of the inquiry in February, he affirmed that his original statement should be entered into the commission records as part of his testimony:

> Having arrived in Canada two years ago I was surprised during the first days by the complete freedom of the individual which exists in Canada

> but does not exist in Russia. The false representations about the democratic countries which are increasingly propagated in Russia, were dissipated daily ... To many Soviet people abroad it is clear that the Communist Party in democratic countries has changed long ago from a political party into an agency net of the Soviet Government, into a fifth column in these countries to meet a war, into an instrument in the hands of the Soviet Government for creating artificial unrest, provocations, etc., etc. ... I am glad that I found the strength within myself to take this step and to warn Canada and other democratic countries of the danger which hangs over them.[71]

Even the GRU's Col. Milstein, of all people, would post a similar assessment of the West in his memoirs: "I, brought up on certain communist dogmas, even to myself found it difficult and fearful to admit that the United States is a wonderful country, and Americans are mostly good simple people, hard workers ... Residents of [New York] were not limited in walks, did not eat on cards, did not freeze in unheated dwellings, did not even imagine what it means to live in communal apartments."[72] Despite other, more selfish motives that no doubt also lay behind his defection, Gouzenko, like Milstein, had gained a genuine respect for the taken-for-granted democratic character of life in the West. Nunn May's atomic information was potentially earth-shattering, literally so, but to focus only on atomic secrets is to ignore the incipient state of Soviet spy networks in 1945 and to miss the much wider, future-oriented strategic objectives of Soviet spying. One question will likely never be answered: what security and intelligence gems did Zabotin deliver to Moscow before Gouzenko announced "last call"? And Moscow's infiltration of the Canadian state had just begun. It is not hard to imagine how the security of Canada and the West would have been profoundly compromised if Gouzenko had met the same fate as Konstantin Volkov.

4
PC 6444

9–16 February 1946

Although commissions of inquiry are intended to be objective arm's-length investigations,[1] the independence of the Kellock-Taschereau Commission was compromised from the outset, not only because of its highly political nature, but also because of Mackenzie King's own personal and political investment. He read the events as something like a pinnacle of his prime-ministership. In grandiose terms he told his diary, "I cannot interpret these events and how all of this has come direct to my doorstep in any way other than in the play of world forces and unseen forces beyond that I have been somehow singled out as an instrument on the part of unseen forces to bring about the exposure that has now taken place. There has never been anything in the world's history more complete than what we will reveal of the Russian method to control the continent as a result of Corby fleeing to the Department of Justice and the course then taken, which has been taken under direction of my office."[2] Testimony transcripts became King's daily reading. On the one hand, he interpreted Gouzenko's defection as "a case of a man's soul and conscience being aroused," turning him into "a true world patriot." On the other hand, King also gave a more occult credit to "unseen forces granting protection that was essential to preserve [Gouzenko's] life and to enable the documents which he brought forth to be disclosed."[3]

Surprisingly, Drew Pearson's original bombshell on NBC radio about Russian spying attracted no immediate press reaction in Canada or Britain.[4] However, almost a week later, on 9 February, the *Ottawa Citizen* finally picked up the story. In Malcolm MacDonald's summary and insider account, "a Russian agent in Canada had surrendered," but US Secretary of State Byrnes had "side-stepped press conference questions" about whether Canada had advised the US of a spy ring operating in Canada and the US. During his next show on the 10th, Pearson, responding to a listener's criticism that he was "baiting Soviet Russia," doubled down: "Within three weeks Canada will stage one of the most dramatic trials in history. I predict that certain Canadian officials who gave information to Soviet [*sic*] will be brought into open trial where entire world can judge accuracy of my revelation last Sunday."[5]

All of this was too much for the Kellock-Taschereau Commission. On the day the inquiry formally opened to take Gouzenko's testimony, the "Royal Commissioners" (again in MacDonald's words) "suddenly decided to-day to prevent any further damage by leaks from Drew Pearson by taking action before his next Sunday broadcast." They would end Gouzenko's testimony by Saturday afternoon, and just after dawn on Sunday the RCMP would knock on the doors of Woikin, Mazerall, Smith, Halperin, Benning, Adams, Gerson, Nightingale, Poland, Shugar, Willsher, and Boyer.[6] The government would briefly acknowledge the arrests, but names and reasons would be kept secret "in hope that this will enable RCMP to interrogate for 2 or 3 days without outside demands forcing legal representation."[7] During the interrogations, the inquiry would momentarily pause; then, on 20 or 21 February, the suspects would begin to appear before the commission. "This stage," MacDonald expected, "will most likely not be in camera." Almost immediately, the plan was amended, with the arrests moved forward to Friday in case any suspects intended to leave Ottawa for the weekend.[8]

Putting the plan into action wasn't easy. When E.K. Williams asked St. Laurent to use PC 6444 to arrest the suspects and to place them before the inquiry for interrogation, St. Laurent balked. Later he would tell Parliament that he protested, wanting to avoid using his authority without some "judicial authority to make me feel that I should exercise those powers."[9] Pressed by Williams to trigger PC 6444 or face the consequences of failing to do so, St. Laurent demanded political cover. Cover materialized. The inquiry lawyers sent him a letter affirming that the commissioners supported them in asking St. Laurent to detain the suspects via PC 6444.[10]

For St. Laurent's benefit, Williams, Kellock, and Taschereau staged a bit of theatre. On the second day of Gouzenko's testimony, Williams interrupted the proceedings. He told the commissioners to "make the application which we have in mind,"[11] and a carefully orchestrated dialogue followed. Taschereau asked Williams to confirm that "all the names that you have just mentioned are names of persons who were mentioned yesterday in the evidence, and that … [it was] your desire and the desire of the other counsel that a letter be sent to the

Right Honourable Mr. St. Laurent ... to detain these persons for *interrogation by the Mounted Police*"[12] (our emphasis). Williams said yes, and Taschereau, speaking also for Kellock, announced the prearranged conclusion: "We have come to the conclusion that we should accept your advice and that such a request should be sent to the Minister of Justice." With no mention of Drew Pearson, Taschereau listed the commissioners' reasons. First, he cited "the extremely serious nature of the disclosures so far made and indicated by the evidence." Second, "the full extent of the ramifications of the disloyal practices and the persons engaged therein may be even greater than is already known and may be continuing." Finally, Taschereau cautioned that "the matter appears to be so serious from the national standpoint that ... the course you advise should be pursued in these exceptional circumstances." Kellock's closing comment, in which he agreed "with Brother Taschereau," underlined the constructed nature of the exchange: "We had an intimation yesterday that such an application would be made, and we have both had an opportunity of giving it very careful consideration."[13]

On the basis of the "evidence already submitted," its seriousness "from a national standpoint," and the commissioners' agreement, Williams and Fauteux petitioned St. Laurent "that you should be requested to exercise the powers conferred upon you by P.C. 6444, 6th October, 1945 and to issue Orders for interrogation and, for that purpose, detention of the following persons," namely Halperin, Shugar, Nightingale, Poland, Mazerall, Smith, Boyer, Benning, Gerson, Adams, Woikin, and Lunan.[14]

PC 6444, because it relied on the authority of the War Measures Act, exposed King's Gouzenko policy to dangers from which the Official Secrets Act, a parliamentary statute, would have been immune. On a close reading, the only powers provided by PC 6444 and not available under the OSA related to the conditions of detention. OSA 11 (1) (2) allowed for detentions of spies and contained robust search and seizure provisions, so, given the evidence, legal challenges to the suspects' detentions under the OSA would likely have failed. OSA 13(1) also allowed for in-camera court proceedings. Once the suspects were in custody, a royal commission could subpoena them. But an individual detained under the OSA could not be held incommunicado and denied access to family and to legal counsel.

The nature of the Gouzenko crisis justified overriding some civil liberties affecting those implicated in Soviet spying: without the false security of hindsight, the actors in the drama couldn't know whether Gouzenko's revelations, highly significant in themselves, were the sum of Soviet spying in Canada or merely the tip of an iceberg. And there would eventually be the cautionary tale of Kim Philby to show how much damage, in terms of human lives and state secrets, a mole could do if they stayed underground. The advantage of holding the suspects incommunicado – no lawyers, no access to family, no communication with the world beyond the RCMP barracks – was that they couldn't coordinate their stories and thereby evade the prisoner's dilemma of not knowing how much the other suspects were talking. However, perhaps more troubling is the thought of what a Canadian government with illiberal tendencies might do with such a precedent.

In their *Final Report*, Kellock and Taschereau would refer to the Inquiries Act as the "law governing the inquiry."[15] That wasn't quite correct: the legal and discursive framework governing the Kellock-Taschereau Commission was a wartime constitutionalism that permitted the government, in the name of state security, to temporarily set aside common law limits on state power. Ironically, St. Laurent didn't actually need to issue new orders, since back on 7 October he had already signed orders of detention for each suspect. As a result of Nunn May's informed prudence, he wasn't arrested in London, and no Canadian domino-arrests followed either ... but the orders remained.[16] On the eve of the February arrests, King confided to his diary that they would provoke "some questioning," but he took shelter in the seriousness of the matter: "I think there will be a disposition by Parliament to agree that the right course ... has been taken as the evidence is so strong."[17] For King, the issues had leapt well beyond domestic politics. "We have now entered upon a situation of world significance," he thought, correctly so.[18] Later, when (as St. Laurent anticipated) the press and the opposition called the arrests illiberal, he and the commissioners would defend the use of PC 6444 with reasons of state and with Locke's "the safety of the people must be the supreme law."[19]

At 7 a.m. on Friday, 15 February, the RCMP descended on the suspects. A "report" from the Civil Liberties Association of Ottawa described the RCMP entering homes and seizing persons without showing search or arrest warrants.[20] Indeed, the October orders had authorized the RCMP to enter at any time any premises used by the suspects, to search anybody there, and to seize anything that might be evidence of espionage.[21] Originally, the RCMP had planned a 3 a.m. raid, but King, likely sensing Gestapo-like tactics incompatible with Liberal values, nixed the idea.[22] The suspects were transported to a barracks at Rockcliffe, outside Ottawa, and held there, uncharged, and incommunicado.[23] Malcolm MacDonald gave a report similar to the CLA's, adding that the suspects were "under heavy guard with building covered by searchlights during night. They are having all necessary comforts, good food, books, and magazines."[24]

Not every detention went as planned. When the RCMP showed up at the Montreal home of Eric Adams, he was nowhere to be found. He had flown to Saskatchewan on business for the Development Bank. When the RCMP arrested him in Prince Albert, a telegram from his wife Sally was waiting, sent several hours after the RCMP appeared at his Montreal home: "HELEN's baby is dying."[25] Under questioning, Adams's wife indirectly admitted the obvious: that the telegram was a coded warning. Although contradicting Adams's later claims of innocence, coded warnings and code names would later save him from jail during his criminal trial.[26]

Arresting Kathleen Willsher, a British citizen working in Canada, and Gordon Lunan, a Canadian temporarily working in London, presented technical challenges.[27] The British High Commission authorized Willsher's arrest,[28] relying on the fact that by British Order-in-Council 1860, approved 17 March 1941, employees of the British government in Canada were subject to the Canadian Official Secrets Act.[29] British officials instructed the RCMP on hospitality etiquette for British prisoners, telling the Canadians to "give Willsher every proper comfort, facility, and consideration whilst she is detained."[30] Lunan, meanwhile, was placed under surveillance, as Hume Wrong and Norman Robertson strategized about whether to make a military arrest (since Lunan was still in the army[31]) or to recall him to Canada on a manufactured pretext (such as to join a board re-examining of wartime food prices[32]). Wrong worried that Lunan had made direct contact with the Soviet embassy in London,[33] but in the end Lunan flew back to Canada and was arrested at Dorval Airport.[34]

At 4 p.m., a few hours after the arrests, King summoned Nikolai Belokhvostikov, the Russian charge d'affaires, to the Prime Minister's Office. He arrived, the seriousness of the situation underscored by the fact that NKVD chief Vitali Pavlov accompanied him,[35] and King presented them with a press release, "carefully prepared in combination with St. Laurent and Williams,"[36] announcing that Canadian secret information had been leaked to the staff "of a foreign mission in Ottawa" and that Supreme Court justices had been appointed to a royal commission to investigate.[37] Belokhvostikov responded with "all motions of surprise, distress etc. and left saying he must consult with his government."[38] One hour later King released the statement to the press.

16–20 February

King's press release stepped gingerly through the PC 6444 minefield, emphasizing the serious circumstances confronting Canada, contemplating "prosecutions ... in cases in which the evidence warrants it," and declaring the investigation *sub judice*: there would be no discussion of the matter until its completion before the courts. But the Liberals would soon be driven to forget this declaration.[39] Despite the silence or perhaps because of it, press reaction "gathered great force," according to Malcolm MacDonald, "and all large papers throughout Dominion devoted much space to it with violent headlines." The silence around the detainees invited wild speculation, and some Toronto journalists placed the number at fifty. Details of the inside story began leaking out, with the *Ottawa Morning Journal* introducing the name "Ivor Gosenko" [*sic*] to the world for the first time.[40] King complained that someone "on the inside" was leaking information.[41] Twenty-four hours on, MacDonald reflected on the broader problem of managing the story: the lack of official information, he thought, led to "every kind of sensationalism," and worse, speculation was pumping up the "atomic aspect" of the story.[42]

While Moscow maintained an ominous public silence, newspapers in Paris, London, Washington, and Moscow featured the Canadian spy story on the front page, already signalling an incipient Cold War. In October 1945, George Orwell's commentary "You and the Atomic Bomb" in Britain's *Tribune* had inaugurated this way of speaking. He imagined a condition in which nuclear weapons would imprison the world in a "peace that is no peace," dominated by a few powerful nuclear states that were "at once unconquerable and in a permanent state of 'cold war' with their neighbours."[43] In France, the *Paris Press* trumpeted, "A-T-ON VOLÉ LE SECRET DE LA BOMBE ATOMIQUE," and the *France-Soir*'s "SCANDALE ATOMIQUE EN CANADA" speculated about the Soviet embassy's involvement, while *Ce Soir*, a Communist paper, carried only a "small item" with "no reference to the Soviet Embassy."[44] In London, the mass circulation *Daily Mail* and *Daily Express* carried large headlines, "CANADA ORDERS ATOMIC BOMB INQUIRY ON LEAKAGE" and "ATOMIC SECRETS TOLD – OFFICERS HELD." All British reports identified the Soviet embassy.[45] Popular press reports brandished "many lurid details in the [suspense novelist E. Phillips] Oppenheim manner,"[46] while the "respectable press" trod more "gingerly," although the *Telegraph* did carry the front-page headline "Mr. King accuses Russia."[47]

Canadian High Commissioner in London Vincent Massey, who passed these press reactions to Mackenzie King, remarked on a split along ideological lines. Left-wing papers such as *Reynolds News*[48] and the *Daily Herald*[49] downplayed the spying and spoke of "shrill rumours." The *Daily Worker* even more stridently proclaimed, "Anti-Soviet

Campaign Gets Going." The *Express*[50] broadened the grounds of debate by quoting some British scientists who believed that the spy crisis "would never have happened if the United States had been willing to divulge atomic secrets."[51] This wishful narrative, which depended on a very benign interpretation of Stalin, also appeared in the "left liberal" *News Chronicle* and the *Glasgow Herald*. The *Herald* quoted a Labour MP who decried the "witch hunt" in Canada, while the *Chronicle*, more plausibly, expected that until the science behind the atomic bomb was shared, "every country in the world will neglect no opportunity to find out about it." Since *The Daily Worker* was "pressing hard" on the witch-hunt-as-diversion narrative, Massey wanted "an authoritative statement" from Canada to silence "prejudiced and erratic sources."[52] Although many of the weeklies ignored the Gouzenko story, the exception was the *New Statesman*, edited by Russophile Kingsley Martin,[53] which "not unexpectedly" said that "all Governments employ spies, and this incident is the inevitable result of the refusal to share atomic secrets."[54]

This public airing of the Gouzenko affair in the British press apparently prompted Kim Philby of MI6 to compose an anodyne summary for British officials, including the directors of intelligence in the armed services. Roger Hollis, head of MI5's F Division responsible for counter-subversion,[55] strongly objected. Because Canadian matters were the responsibility of MI5, Hollis insisted that Philby had no business authoring the report. Writing to Sir Stewart Menzie, head of MI6, Hollis noted serious gaps in Philby's account: Philby had ignored the specific intelligence that the GRU had sought in Canada and had failed to mention the Communist Party's role in recruiting agents.[56]

From Washington, Ambassador Lester Pearson and his press analysts[57] summarized the US reaction. King's announcement was front-page news everywhere, and although American journalists quickly intuited that Russia must be the unnamed "foreign power," the government's reluctance to give details lent a "spy thriller" quality to the news stories. How serious were the leaks? The *Chicago Daily News* quoted scientists at the University of Chicago who naively "doubted the possibility of a serious leak of atomic information," because no more than "a dozen entirely trustworthy" Canadians were privy to the secrets.[58]

On the one hand, American newspapers began wide speculation about the failure of Washington to act against spy threats in the US. FBI director J. Edgar Hoover even used the *New York Journal-American* as a stalking horse to prod President Truman into action. The *Journal-American* reported that someone named "Chevchenko"[59] was at the centre of the Canadian story, but also that "a certain Alfred Adamson,[60] a Russian spy reputed to be the ringleader of the plotters in Canada, had eluded the FBI and escaped from his hotel in New York some weeks ago." Unlike Canada's coming down refreshingly hard on "disloyal citizens and foreign spies," sluggish America sat on its hands "despite a mountain of evidence against Adamson."[61] Only much later would "Adamson" be revealed as a fiction. In a similar vein, Drew Pearson's hyperbolic, unsourced stories about Russian spy rings involving "1,700 people ... in Canada and the United States" warned that the FBI "had let spies slip through their fingers for fear of upsetting the diplomatic applecart with Russia."[62] A less alarmist but still exaggerated Canadian AP story, widely disseminated in the US, claimed that high-level "Government employees" were implicated in Soviet spying and that the Russians were "building a large spy service in Canada."[63] Nevertheless, like the *Journal-American*, papers such as the *Cincinnati Enquirer* credited Canada for taking action.[64] American politicians quoted in the stories tended to be "non-committal," and, as Lester Pearson cautioned Norman Robertson, they unintentionally deepened "the sinister implications of the news by their silence and gravity." Senator Henry Styles Bridges (later a leading McCarthyite[65]) demanded an FBI inquiry.[66]

On the other hand, some journalists to the left of centre either downplayed the Canadian revelations or called attention to the moral double standard in relation to spying. The Mutual Broadcasting System's veteran broadcaster Cedric Foster, who during the war had been the voice of "News Out of Europe Tonight,"[67] observed that Americans shouldn't be too perturbed "since there have always been spies."[68] Bill Cunningham, a *Boston Herald* columnist and MBS commentator,[69] took the controversy to be the product of "artful propaganda" on the part of a "tired Britain" against an "expanding" Russia. He counselled his listeners not to be "deflected by scare heads [*sic*] from Ottawa."[70] Whereas UP syndicated columnist Marquis Childs[71] stoked fears about a hidden American fifth column loyal to Communist Russia,[72] *PM*, a NewYork–based left-liberal (pro-labour and anti-fascist) tabloid,[73] accused Childs of "setting one group of Americans against another under the guise of patriotism." Instead, *PM* considered that the real danger ran the other way: "the tom-toms were beating and the witch-hunt about to begin."[74]

Some commentators sensed an immense geopolitical drama waiting in the wings. Leif Eid, Washington bureau chief of NBC News,[75] believed that the Canadian spy story "presaged a struggle between Communism and Capitalism."[76] Others already predicted "Russian Communism" and "Democratic Capitalism" would face off "in the next world war."[77] Historian and journalist Lothrop Stoddard, a hyperbolic anti-Communist,[78] interpreted the reports from Canada "as the first unearthing of the world-wide scope of Russian designs long suspected."[79] He cited "Exercise Muskox," a joint military exercise of Americans and Canadians traversing the Arctic on snowmobile to establish a presence there.[80] Not unexpectedly, much of this incipient Cold War commentary swirled around the atomic bomb. Drew Pearson told his Sunday-night audience that the Russians wanted the bomb, and he offered disquieting details of a Russian agent, apprehended near Seattle, who "carried the atomic bomb plans and samples of the metal from which the bombs were made."[81] Pearson foresaw a showdown and, without any evidence, asserted that "Operation Muskox" had been undertaken "on knowledge that the Russian had made a detailed survey of the waterways in Alaska and Canada."[82] In an 18 February UP story, Major General Leslie Groves, leader of the Manhattan Project, insisted that the US "had lost more security on the bomb during the past four weeks than during the entire wartime development period."[83] The next day, US Secretary of State Byrnes responded, disputing such claims and insisting that "the secret 'know-how' of the atomic bomb" was still in "exclusive" American possession, that even its British and Canadian partners hadn't been given the full details.[84] Brynes claimed, tendentiously, that the Canadian "spy plot" had "no ramifications" in the US, and he didn't foresee any American arrests. More honestly, he also rejected assertions by journalists that known Soviet agents had been allowed to leave the US.[85] Not everyone was convinced.[86]

Those leaning left, including some members of Truman's administration, saw the atomic issue and the morality of spying generally in hazier moral terms. Joseph E. Davies, the veteran diplomat and former US ambassador to Moscow, tended to idealize Communism, taking Stalin's words and even the show trials at face value.[87] Davies observed that "if we refused atomic information to the Russians, our fighting allies, they had a 'moral right' to try to get them by espionage."[88] While the *Philadelphia Inquirer* criticized Davies, arguing that the atomic bomb wasn't a threat to Russia, that American "goodwill and fairness … was everywhere apparent, and blocked only by determined Russian imperialism and mistrust,"[89] the *Daily Worker* (Moscow's surrogate in the American public sphere) saw a "sinister conspiracy of 'war-minded imperialists' in Ottawa, Washington and London" trying to obstruct the Soviet Union's international "fight for democracy."[90] *Times-Herald* columnist John O'Donnell added "his word of derision for the naive Washingtonians who affect to be surprised that such unethical methods are in use by the United States government behind its mask of hypocritical internationalism."[91] Even conservative columnist David

Lawrence[92] deplored in *The World* the "holier than thou" attitude taken by some Americans towards Soviet espionage, especially since the US was "plainly preparing to set up a world-wide spy system on its own behalf."[93]

Canada certainly felt the international roiling of the media and, less than a week after King's shock wave, pressure to discard the policy of silence.[94] Pressure mounted, especially after 20 February when Moscow broadcast its indignation: the Gouzenko inquiry was nothing more than a British-inspired, Canadian-activated, anti-Soviet campaign, and the supposed uncovering of GRU agents in Canada was a ruse crafted to embarrass Moscow. The diplomatic friction around the creation of the UN must have set Britain and Canada off. Of course, such claims were pure fiction. Kim Philby had kept the Soviets well informed about Gouzenko from the beginning, and, while publicly keeping silent, internally the Soviets were already flaying their "diplomatic" corps for Gouzenko's sins and for the laxness that allowed him to abscond with secret documents. Soon Zabotin, his wife, and son would all be sent to prison for Zabotin's laxness. Back in 1944, Col. Mikhail Milstein had arrived in North America as a GRU operative to check on Soviet employees. Luckily for him, he had verbally reported his doubts about Gouzenko, about Gouzenko's unusual living arrangements away from the embassy apartments, and about Gouzenko's access to the embassy safe where secret documents were kept. Nevertheless, after Gouzenko's defection, Milstein was summoned to "the gloomy and terrible building on Lubyanka Square" – Beria's headquarters – to be grilled.[95] As for Gouzenko himself, a special section "X" in the Soviet administration, headed by a man known only as "The Stutterer," considered "all possible ways of punishing Gouzenko," including the possibility of, to use Soviet intelligence lingo, "organizing a 'wedding,'" but Stalin forbade any killing, since he wanted to maintain the PR value of the Soviet Union's victory over the Nazis.[96]

Moscow's affected outrage about Gouzenko now deepened the question of what, after the defeat of Nazi Germany, should happen to the marriage-of-necessity between the West and the Soviet Union. In 1939 Moscow had dismissed the war as an imperialist adventure. In 1942, after the German invasion of Russia, it suddenly became the Great Patriotic War. Moscow's relations with its wartime allies were always riven with ambivalence: from Moscow's perspective, the reluctance of the Allies to open a second front in Europe until nine million Soviet soldiers had been sacrificed hardly inspired confidence that the West had anything but its own interests in mind. At the same time, London and Washington never forgot that Lenin, Trotsky, and the original

Bolsheviks were intent on world revolution,[97] although Stalin's turn to "Socialism in One Country" in the late 1920s repudiated this commitment. Nevertheless, undergirding the February 1946 war of words was Stalin's expectation of an inevitable conflict with capitalism and Truman's incipient policy of containment, so the Gouzenko disclosures, even within a few days of becoming public, were already catalyzing Cold War ideologies.[98]

5
Before the Royal Commission I

16 February–3 March RCMP Preliminaries

Before Moscow expressed its outrage, as the world was still debating King's shocking press release, Commissioners Kellock and Taschereau questioned Gouzenko, the RCMP officers who had interrogated him, and Department of External Affairs staff who had stonewalled the Soviet embassy's search for Gouzenko. At the same time the RCMP, led by detective inspectors Clifford Harvison and M.F.E. Anthony, were grilling the espionage suspects.

Originally, the Read/Varcoe plan had contemplated interrogations by a royal commissioner, not by RCMP officers, but E.K. Williams had scotched that. He calculated that sudden arrests and incommunicado detentions would add psychological pressure and weaken the suspects into confessions. During a police interrogation, the arrested person had no legal obligation to say a single word, and any statement must be made voluntarily, a principle affirmed in 1914 and reaffirmed by Justice Kellock himself in a 1949 decision. Any other kind of statement simply wouldn't be admissible.[1] Of course, *voluntary* confessions or testimony directly incriminating others (though open to legal challenges) could till the ground nicely for the commission.[2] According to Harvison, the suspects were told they had been implicated in Soviet spying, but that they had the right to refuse to answer questions.[3] Nevertheless, he must have known that the conditions of incarceration could undermine later claims that the suspects' testimony was fully voluntary.

It's clear from Malcolm MacDonald's detailed summaries that the RCMP gave interview transcripts and progress reports to the politicians. MacDonald reported that the two accused women, Emma Woikin and Kathleen Willsher, offered little resistance. Woikin confessed, admitting that she gave information and documents to the Soviets and received at least one "present" of fifty dollars, but she refused to name her contact (who, MacDonald suspected, was Mrs. Sokolov, wife of Maj. Vsevolod Sokolov). Of great interest to MacDonald, as British high commissioner, was Woikin's revelation that "she was warned early in October to cease work as there might be trouble." Even though MacDonald had no idea about the Kim Philby–depth of Russian intelligence penetration, he correctly deduced that such warnings explained why "Primrose" (atomic scientist Alan Nunn May) didn't contact the Russians in London, despite his plans to do so.[4]

Kathleen Willsher wrote two confessions. She had first been approached for information by Fred Rose, and MacDonald believed her claim that she didn't know that her data were going to the Soviets: "She does admit discussions with [Eric] Adams in general terms and says that on occasions he made notes. This, she states, was to help cause of Labor-Progressive Party and we are inclined to believe this." She wouldn't admit giving Adams documents, but she did accept "expenses" of twenty-five dollars for a trip to Montreal. MacDonald commented ironically, "She is ingenuously prepared to return this money now."[5] After further interrogations, she admitted answering Adams's questions, but he wanted more than she knew about activities of MI6. She said that she gave Adams details of a 3 November letter from Canada's ambassador in Moscow, Dana Wilgress, to Mackenzie King, although this would later seem questionable. "She salves her conscience," MacDonald said, "by drawing a fine distinction between passing of information verbally and in writing and still refuses to admit to latter."[6] She told Adams about financial arrangements between Britain and Canada, and implicated Agatha Chapman, who arranged some of Willsher's contacts with Adams. "Willsher," MacDonald summarized, "still attempts unconvincingly to explain away these and earlier admissions as innocent results of discussion groups to which she belonged."[7]

The men's responses were more varied, running from outright denials and demands for legal representation to guarded admissions, with many shades in between. Matt Nightingale initially looked pliable to his interrogators. On 18 February they expected that he was "likely to sing shortly as he came through his interview badly and asked for writing materials later."[8] The next day, commenting on Nightingale's written statement to the RCMP, MacDonald observed that "at first glance it appears to be most guarded document with few half admissions designed to give impression that writer may have talked indiscreetly in company which he did not realize was undesirable."[9] Nightingale had met GRU operative Lt. Col. Vassili Rogov – whom he knew as "Jan" – on the Ottawa–Montreal train and "thought 'Jan' might give him work in Europe on telephone construction." Rogov visited Nightingale's apartment and met him at least once on a street corner at night-time. MacDonald concluded that "Nightingale knew very well what was going on but that for reasons of their own Russians did not finally make any serious use of him. He may be capitalizing on this and feel free to make admissions."[10]

Gordon Lunan, meanwhile, denied any wrongdoing, but "unfortunately for him," MacDonald said, "he colours easily under shock. He did so when his cover name was quoted to him and when shown Photostat of his first instruction from Grant [Zabotin]." With the evidence overwhelming against him,[11] Lunan crumpled and gave a full confession within six days of his arrest. More importantly, he implicated Smith, Mazerall, and Halperin, linking them to the Soviet embassy,[12] and, since it was Fred Rose who recruited him, he also implicated the Canadian Communist Party directly in Soviet espionage,[13] confirming the Gouzenko documents.[14]

Ned (Edward) Mazerall was somewhat less forthcoming and, like Nightingale, wrote a guarded confession, admitting that Fred Rose approached him too, that his cover name was "Bagley," and that he had worked for Lunan. MacDonald said, "[Mazerall] has minimized importance of how much information he gave. He has implicated no one else and only mentioned Lunan with reluctance ... He is an impracticable idealist."[15] As the interrogations wore on, MacDonald noticed, "Mazerall's nerves and his memory are improving simultaneously. He has recalled considerable details of communist cell to which he belonged."[16]

Fred Poland, as soon as he was arrested, was "vociferously demanding legal representation ... [He] told his wife that, if he were not heard of in three days, she could look for him in mines of Siberia."[17] After a couple of days, he gave "a written statement on Lunan as house companion if true [*sic*], it is well put together and covers Lunan's habits, telephone calls etc." More suspiciously, papers seized from Poland showed that he had contacted NKVD chief Vitali Pavlov on at least six occasions, leading MacDonald to wonder whether Poland was an "NKVD man," and whether that, rather than innocence, explained his cooperation on the subject of the GRU-run Lunan.[18] Ultimately, there would be significant doubts about whether Poland was a spy. MacDonald admitted, "Poland has explained appearance Pavlov's name among his papers reasonably. He originally met him at Embassy reception for the press. He has also written to his wife, who is particularly active on his behalf, not to attempt at present to interfere in situation."[19] Poland may have felt that Gouzenko had nothing on him and therefore wanted to keep the fuss to a minimum. Later, when his interrogation dragged on, his wife would file for *habeas corpus*. The RCMP interrogator was undecided as to Poland's guilt.

The day after the arrests, MacDonald had said that "the most affected so far is Durnforth [actually Durnford] Smith who is clearly very frightened and shows signs of breaking." Commenting on Smith's initial denials, MacDonald explained, "Smith flatly denies any knowledge of affair nor will he admit to recognizing Photostat of his own handwriting. He suggested it was probably a forgery. He is however in bad nervous shape and his guard reports that he was physically sick after his first interview. He will probably confess later."[20] Despite these expectations, Smith didn't break. He was interrogated "exhaustively" and became "acutely apprehensive" but, MacDonald conceded, "every approach produces only denial. In view evidence against him, it is most likely he will not be further interrogated as it will almost certainly prove profitless."[21] Even after Mazerall implicated Smith, exposing Smith's suggestion that the two "work[ed] together on photographing documents," Smith would admit nothing.[22]

"The tough ones," MacDonald judged, "will be Shugar, who declared whole proceedings ridiculous," and "Adams, who refused even to admit date of his birth without lawyer." Since Adams responded to every question with "no comment," someone joked that he should be offered a job: "he might be used to answer press inquiries at RCMP H.Q., otherwise, he is of no value."[23] Other hard nuts included Boyer, "Halperin who is shaken but slippery," and "Gerson who is entirely confident."[24] Except for Boyer, MacDonald was right. Gerson, though initially confident, "was severely shaken" when he "was shown photostats of his own handwriting" in the espionage documents,[25] and the next day he asked "how many years imprisonment" he would likely receive."[26] When the stenographer wasn't present, Gerson indirectly admitted his own culpability, but in the end he balked at a full confession: "morally," he said, he could not "bring himself to incriminate this person and that person."[27] Shugar, after nine days of non-cooperation, finally "admitted to having been questioned by Sam Carr on R.D.X. and on location of various Canadian laboratories." After he answered some questions "in general terms," MacDonald hoped that he would become a useful witness,[28] but that didn't happen. On 1 March, Shugar went "on hunger strike no doubt to urge further [unreadable][29] for his press campaign."[30]

Like Shugar, Scot Benning proved cagey in his answers, an approach that would ultimately serve him well legally. Already in his preliminary interview, MacDonald described him as "comparatively assured and RCMP interrogator has impression that he was warned and that he may have shrewd idea of how much we know. When confronted with some evidence he took line that someone else must have had access to documents attributed to him and pointed out that many of them would not come his way in course of his work. In letter written last night to wife, which looks as if it was partly designed to be read by RCMP (as indeed it was), he appears as innocent but willing victim of circumstance."[31]

Raymond Boyer, unlike the other hard nuts, did crack, and Harvison brought him "to point of complete confession." Boyer admitted knowing Zabotin and Sokolov, although it was, again, MP Fred Rose, not someone from the embassy, who was the connection. MacDonald revealed that "Boyer gave ROSE the R.D.X. formula knowing that it was to be passed on to Russia … His explanation is exactly same as Primrose's [Nunn May's] appears to be – that he believed these activities to be for general good … Harvison … is satisfied that Boyer was motivated by what appeared to him at time to be sincere reasons." Lunan, Mazerall, and Willsher were all motivated by ideology too, in MacDonald's opinion, not by "financial bait." For this reason, he wanted the "fullest educative publicity" for the Gouzenko case, particularly to deter "susceptible fellow-travellers."[32] As time went on, Boyer would become even more cooperative and turn away from the Communist Party.[33]

Emma Woikin ("Nora"), 22 February

Although some of the suspects would have to wait weeks for the inquiry's call, the commissioners, piggybacking on RCMP interrogation reports and buttressed by PC 6444, began their questioning within a week of the arrests. Those who confessed or incriminated others moved to the front of the line. Woikin, Willsher, Mazerall, and Lunan appeared before the inquiry within days of their detention, while the hard cases were sent back to Rockcliffe to meditate on their sins.

On 22 February, after seven days in detention, Emma Woikin was summoned before the Kellock-Taschereau Commission to be interrogated by Gérald Fauteux. Woikin was twenty-five years old. MacDonald described her as "a pathetic case," a person whose difficult life made her easy prey for the Russians: "Conscious of her origins and vaguely believing she might assist political system, under which she was led to believe poverty did not exist, she agreed to work for them." Born in Blaine Lake in north-central Saskatchewan to Russian Doukhobors,[34] Woikin was precociously intelligent and had skipped a couple of grades in school.[35] She had married at sixteen, but her only child died

Emma Woikin, with her attorney J.P. Erichsen-Brown (*right*) and brother (*left*), leaves an Ottawa courtroom, 21 March 1946 (Toronto Star Photographic Archive, Toronto Public Library)

at birth in 1939 and her husband, suffering from depression, committed suicide in 1942. Alone, she eventually completed a clerical course, and although she didn't want to leave Saskatchewan, where her only friends lived, her score on a civil service examination got her a job in the Passport Office in Ottawa and then as a cipher clerk in the Department of External Affairs.[36] Still, her self-esteem was low. In a letter home, she wrote about her loneliness and her few acquaintances: "I wonder often why they like me and then I know it's because they don't know me, right?"[37] Gouzenko testified that she was the agent code-named "Nora"[38] and that he had overheard Col. "Milstein, Sokolov, and Col. Zabotin" discussing "how to develop her."[39] They agreed that Sokolov would become "more friendly with her, invite her to visit him."[40]

The process of recruiting and developing Canadian agents was of keen interest to the inquiry. Most recruits had an ideological vulnerability rooted in a naive view of life in the Soviet Union, but Woikin's motivation was more personal. She testified that she met Sokolov and his wife in May 1944 at a dinner prior to a concert by Montreal's Glinka Choir under the auspices of the Federation of Russian Canadians. Woikin subsequently visited the Sokolovs for dinner a few times, and in early summer 1944, Sokolov put the question to her: would she agree to share information from External Affairs? A few days later, by telephone, she said yes.

Woikin was the only suspect who didn't have a prior association with Communism, and Fauteux wanted to know why she agreed to spy. Clearly, the friendship offered by Mrs. Sokolov must have played a role, and the possibility of an infatuation with Maj. Sokolov has also been suggested.[41] But to Sokolov, Woikin had "said that she liked Russia, that she wanted to help Russia."[42] To Fauteux, she expanded, "Perhaps it is because I have a feeling of love for that country. Perhaps it is because we think that there is – we may be wrong or we may be right, but there is hope for the poor or something." Because of her former poverty, her difficult life, and likely her Named Doukhobor distrust of the state,[43] Woikin understandably also had some ambivalence towards Canada. On her National Registration form, completed in 1940, she declared that she owed allegiance to no country, yet when she applied for a position in External Affairs in 1943, she affirmed that she was "a British subject of Russian origin." In the spring of 1944, she told External Affairs that she wanted to serve in Russia. Why? Fauteux asked. She didn't really know: "Maybe it was just from the kind of life I had, maybe – just that I look to that country for security and I would like to live there." She added, "There was a time when I was quite poor, I guess, and my baby died because we had no medical care and nobody seemed to care. My husband was sick and to such a stage where nobody seemed to intervene at all."[44] However, June Callwood's biography of Woikin shows that, clearly, she did receive medical care. Dr. J.J. Perverseff, worried about a breech birth, urged Woikin to go to St. Paul's Hospital in Saskatoon. She did. But even so, the umbilical cord asphyxiated the baby at birth and, in the callous procedures that reigned at the time, she wasn't even allowed to see the dead baby. Her husband, Bill, suffering from severe migraines and depression, long refused medical attention before his suicide three years later.[45] If, despite her heavily edited memories, her private suffering was a motive, there were other, less emotionally charged motives too. Woikin testified that when Maj. Sokolov offered to pay for her cooperation she declined, yet when Mrs. Sokolov, unannounced, gave her an envelope containing fifty dollars, Woikin kept the money.

After Woikin agreed to spy for Maj. Sokolov, she told him that she could perhaps be of greater assistance by leaving External Affairs and getting a position in "the Commercial Counsellor's office." Sokolov, however, shut that idea down, saying, "You can help Russia much better if you remain where you are."[46] Since she ciphered outgoing messages and deciphered those incoming for External Affairs,[47] Woikin had sworn an oath of secrecy,[48] but among Gouzenko's Soviet embassy documents were handwritten summaries of External Affairs telegrams, summaries that Zabotin told Gouzenko came from "Nora." These secret telegrams, from London to Ottawa, explained the British government's concerns about developments in Central and Eastern Europe in late August 1945. Zabotin had the information translated into Russian and telegraphed to Moscow on 5 September 1945, Gouzenko's last day in the Soviet embassy.[49] Woikin had been directly involved in deciphering two of these summarized telegrams and had easy access to the rest, according to Stanislas Daley, her supervisor at External Affairs. Compared against the original telegrams, "Nora's" summaries proved to be near-replicas,[50] and when Woikin was shown the documents in her own handwriting, she confessed. Deciphering messages or reading those deciphered by others, she had memorized the contents and written them out later at home. "About three" times during the summer of 1945, she had made reproductions in this manner and passed them on (through others) to Maj. Sokolov.[51] Woikin also disclosed aspects of GRU tradecraft. She had no direct contact with a Russian handler but would initially meet Mrs. Sokolov on a street or in a theatre or shop to pass on the summaries. Subsequently, she was told to go into the bathroom of a dentist's office on Laurier Avenue and to leave her scripts under the toilet tank cover. Once the script was safely secreted, she would contact the Sokolovs to confirm that it had been picked up.[52]

Woikin acknowledged that it would be against Canadian interests to give the material, marked "Secret" or "Top Secret," to the Soviets.[53] Her claim that she had given the GRU material only in the summer of 1945 was contradicted by Zabotin's 5 January 1945 mailing list, where "Nora" was credited with "copies" of ten telegrams, eleven photographs, and three "forms."[54] Many of these telegrams (in secret cipher[55]) were to Mackenzie King from British secretary of state for Dominion affairs Christopher Addison (Prime Minister Clement Attlee's ally and confidant in the newly elected Labour government),[56] addressing the post-war turmoil and Russian intervention in what would become the Eastern Bloc – Bulgaria, Hungary, Romania – as well as issues in Austria, Yugoslavia, and Spain. After the Russians thrust the German army out of Eastern Europe, newspapers began to report Russia's systematic plans to seize power and establish Communist regimes.[57] Moscow's political machinations and troubling attacks on the autonomy of the Eastern countries would later be seen as the beginning of what Churchill would call the descent of the Iron Curtain.[58]

It's possible that Sokolov specifically asked her for information on the situation in Eastern Europe. In Bulgaria, the defeat of German forces led to a coalition government composed of a "patriotic front" of Bulgarian political parties. However, Communists had taken charge of the Ministries of Justice and the Interior, and by the spring of 1945 the *Globe and Mail* reported that "public life" in the country was "under complete Communist sway." Opponents of the new order – some one to two thousand politicians, journalists, and academics – had been "sentenced to death and executed." In addition to these "official executions," the Communists killed some fifteen to twenty thousand people in political assassinations on the premise that any opposition to Communist control, including from the leftist Bulgarian Agrarian National Union, should be treated as fascist. A similar process was evident in Romania, where an "official program" of political repression targeted the "Iron Guard," while "violent attacks" were also directed at opponents of the Communists and at adherents of the National Peasants' Party.[59]

From Moscow's perspective, these Eastern developments flowed naturally from the 1944 Anglo-Soviet agreement that after Germany's defeat Europe would be reordered according to "spheres of interest." Of course, the policy never authorized the Great Powers to *impose* governments on the liberated regions. Although some historians have argued that a liberal understanding of the agreement ended with the defeat of Germany,[60] the Big Three's "Declaration on Liberated Europe" at Yalta (in February 1945) had promised broadly based interim governments, rights of freedom of speech and assembly, and democratic elections.[61] Russia immediately defied those constraints. With Churchill losing the election to Clement Atlee and Labour, it therefore remained to be seen just how Britain and the US would respond. In late 1944, leading figures in the British Foreign Office had been ready to "write off southeastern Europe" to ensure good relations with Moscow. However, by the spring of 1945, soon-to-be undersecretary of state for the Foreign Office Sir Orme Sargent, was calling for a "showdown" with the Soviet Union.[62] Woikin's summaries could give Moscow up-to-the-minute insider information about how the West was reacting to Soviet manipulations in the East.

In mid-June, the Soviet news agency TASS reported that Bulgaria would hold elections on 26 August 1945.[63] Many observers saw this as an attempt to legitimize the new Soviet-backed Bulgarian government through an undemocratic "election."[64] Just what did Moscow have in mind for the region? The Council of Ministers, created at Potsdam to oversee post-war reconstruction, would be pursuing such issues in London in mid-September. On 24 August, Addison sent Mackenzie King Britain's concerns and told him that Russia kept avoiding a discussion of "the problem of Bulgaria, Yugoslavia, Hungary and Romania." Addison worried that the planned elections in these countries would "only result in a totalitarian system ... under the supervision of the Russians." Yet Addison's greater fear was that arguing with Russia about Eastern Europe would "endanger our relations."[65] Insider information that the British prioritized the relationship with Russia above rigged elections would have been useful news in Moscow.

In Hungary Addison, through London's "political representative" Alvary Gascoigne,[66] reported on municipal elections set for 7 October 1945. General Béla Miklós had been elected leader of an interim Hungarian government-in-exile in 1944,[67] but, Addison disclosed, the Russians were hurrying up the elections: "[Miklós] is afraid to oppose too strenuously as he may be forced to resign and may be replaced by the Extreme Leftists." The British considered the elections a trial balloon: "If the outcome will be favorable to the leftists, they and the Russians will rush a general election soon after."[68] Addison was only marginally more optimistic about Austria and Yugoslavia. Because half of Austria was occupied by Britain, the US, and France, he thought that democracy had a chance, but he worried that "Russians imported from Moscow ... will be in the lead" of the formation of any government. He also told King, "There is not much hope for Yugoslavia having a Democratic Government," since "Tito" (Josip Broz) was ignoring the British-inspired Tito–Šubašić Agreements.[69] Nevertheless, London thought that it was "too early to step in."[70] What he meant by "stepping in" he didn't reveal: most likely it would have been to support Tito's partisans.[71] In Woikin's 24 August summary, Addison reported (from the British ambassador in Belgrade) "fairly serious fighting between Yugoslav armies and Cetnecka ... to the east of Banjaluka," where the ambassador thought General Dragoljub "Draža" Mihailovic might be.[72] Mihailović led the "Cetnecka" or "Chetniks," a monarchist, largely Serbian nationalist force, against Tito's Communist partisans in a battle for control of Yugoslavia.[73] Here Addison worried about a rift between Britain and the US, since the Americans had never endorsed British policy on Yugoslavia.[74] Clashing interests could widen divisions, but, said Addison, "We have to try to prevent that."[75] Although it's unlikely that Woikin's information held any military value, Yugoslavia was a subject of considerable interest to the Soviets,[76] who would certainly want to know if they could exploit any US/Britain disagreements there. In the event, Yugoslavia ended up with a Communist government, but not one subservient to Moscow.[77]

Woikin had also summarized a 28 August telegram in which Addison turned to relations with Franco's Spain. At Potsdam the Soviets, angling for a Communist government in Spain, had urged action against Franco as a collaborator with Germany and Italy; however, Britain and the US would go no further that to deny Spain membership in the new United Nations.[78] The Soviet ambassador to Britain, Feodor Gusev, therefore ridiculed British Foreign Secretary Bevin, saying that "Britain was carrying out the agreements of the Potsdam, especially in regard to Spain." This was an ironic dig at the Anglo-American insistence that states must be free to decide their own destiny. Gusev noted that from the content of "Bevin's speech of August 20th Franco could well see that no action was intended against him." In the speech, Bevin had stated "that Britain would welcome a change of Government in Spain, but would not countenance any action that would bring on civil war." Bevin fired the ironies back at Gusev, asking, in relation to the Potsdam agreements, "Was not the Soviet Union asking [Britain] to overstep them?" "To this Gusev made no reply."[79] In the case of Spain, Woikin's summaries wouldn't have been helpful, not only because the Soviets already knew Addison's information but also because, unlike in Eastern Europe, Soviet hands were tied in Spain.

More potentially damaging was the possibility (raised by Commissioner Kellock and agreed to by Woikin's superior, Stanislas Daley) that Woikin might have unwittingly given the Soviets a key to the Canadian cipher code. If the Soviets were tracking messages from the Canadian embassy in Moscow and if she had summarized a telegram sent from that embassy, the Soviets could have broken the Canadian code.[80] However, contra Kellock, there is no evidence that Woikin's summaries played any such role. We know (in the inverse situation) that Gouzenko's documentary cache didn't allow the West to break any Soviet codes: "Gouzenko's information helped Western cryptanalysts understand Soviet communications procedures but did not directly contribute to the Venona breakthrough. He brought out GRU messages that identified Soviet assets, but no codebooks or one-time pads."[81]

Nevertheless, espionage doesn't always rely on the value of this or that piece of intelligence, or even in the windfall of cracking the enemy's code – just as important is the accumulation of knowledge about the priorities of the enemy and even of friends. Taken as a whole, Woikin's summaries let the Soviets gauge the strength of British and American opposition to Soviet East Bloc policy. In fact, the RCMP's Gouzenko analyses reported that some of Woikin's contributions had been useful enough to be "called to the attention of Marshal Stalin."[82]

According to Amy Knight, "Woikin was more a victim than a spy."[83] By basing the argument on an appeal to pity and diminishing the value of the intelligence that she gathered, Knight implies that spying is defensible if one's life is difficult and if the information is available through other channels. Yet Woikin didn't diminish her own culpability. When Fauteux asked her to give any "excuse or justification ... for conveying secret information to a foreign power," she responded, "There is not much I can say."[84] In January 1946, in the weeks before her detention, Woikin had gone to the Russian embassy and applied to become a Russian citizen. Although she denied that any specific events nudged her to try to emigrate to Russia,[85] the timing of the request – in the months after the Soviets cut off contact and just before the Gouzenko affair became public knowledge – does make one wonder whether she feared arrest. On 28 February, Woikin was recalled before the inquiry and told that because she had admitted giving secrets to a foreign power, she was now entitled to a lawyer. She declined the offer.[86] Two days later she was released under PC 6444 but immediately taken into custody under the Criminal Code to face conspiracy charges and offences against the Official Secrets Act. At her trial on 10 April 1945, she pled guilty and was sentenced to two years and six months in Kingston Penitentiary.[87]

Kathleen Willsher ("Elli"), 25 February

Unlike Woikin, Kathleen Willsher, assistant registrar at the British High Commission, had only passed on information verbally, never creating documents for her spymasters. She had given Eric Adams information that he passed on to the Soviets, but denied that she was the source for dispatches from Canada's ambassador in the Soviet Union, Dana Wilgress, to Mackenzie King, or notes related to policy conferences involving the Canadian and British governments. She had gone to Montreal to give Adams information, trips partly arranged by Agatha Chapman, yet Willsher denied that she was serving the Soviets. She merely wanted to assist the Labor-Progressive Party (LPP).

Such a distinction was either naive or disingenuous. The Canadian Communist Party, declared an illegal organization under the Defence of Canada Regulations in 1940, simply reformed itself in 1943 as the LPP, and it served as a Soviet outpost. In August 1945 Leon Mayrand, a veteran Canadian diplomat stationed in Moscow, observed that Soviet claims that the Comintern had been dissolved in 1943 were false. Its centre of operations had simply been shifted from Moscow to locations abroad, including Paris.[88] Moscow controlled most western Communist parties and, as Mayrand showed, spying was an important facet of that control.[89] Relying on Comintern records, Alexander Trapsky argued that "local parties never deviated from strict Stalinist discipline or from adherence to Soviet state interests."[90] Taking the opposing view and focusing on Britain, Andrew Thorpe claimed that there was no "solid, unbreakable chain of command from Stalin's office … to the most minor CPGB member."[91] If Thorpe's rather narrow claim can be sustained only via hyperbolic wording ("solid, unbreakable"), it remains a fact that British, American, Australian, and Canadian Communist leaders – notably LPP leaders Fred Rose and Sam Carr – uniformly assisted in Soviet spying.[92]

To counter spying, the Official Secrets Act cast a broad net. An accused person's actions didn't need to directly harm the safety or interests of the state: a conviction could happen "if, from the circumstances of the case, or his conduct, or his known character as proved, it appears that his purpose was a purpose prejudicial to the safety or interests of the State." The clause could invite broad fishing expeditions about an individual's education, politics, personal relationships, professional affiliations, and reading habits. Yet alongside the potentially McCarthyite pressure of such investigating, it was nevertheless important to unearth the reasons why a government employee would divulge state secrets. At the same time, a nefarious motive need not be present, according to the act: if an accused not "acting under lawful authority" possessed "any sketch, plan, model, article, note, document or information" deemed secret, that document would be considered "to have been made … for a purpose prejudicial to the safety or interests of the State," unless the accused could prove otherwise.[93] Such problematic reverse-onus clauses were intended precisely for cases such as those of Willsher and the other suspects: legally, one could not argue that in passing on secret information one was motivated by some higher purpose, whether it was to assist the LPP or to bring about a utopian form of government.

Willsher had graduated from the London School of Economics in 1926, and four years later the British High Commissioner's office in Canada hired her as a clerk-typist. Her interest in socialism had begun with Britain's Labour Party, but by 1933, after attending "some Anglo-Russian cultural meetings in London" where she viewed films and listened to idealized accounts of contemporary Soviet Russia,[94] her interests grew more "Communistic." She wasn't alone. After Hitler's rise to power, Moscow and the Comintern took a less confrontational approach to non-Communist leftist groups and encouraged a popular front against fascism.[95] Although Labour leadership resisted collaboration with the British Communist Party, many influential voices encouraged collaboration. At the London School of Economics, Harold Laski, "a brilliant teacher who exercised a profound influence on several generations of students," stood as "the most articulate proponent of a British Popular Front.[96]

Willsher testified that she considered herself a member of the Canadian Communist Party when she joined a Communist study group in 1936, a watershed year for her. She took her membership in the study group, with a monthly contribution, and attended until 1939. When the Canadian Communist Party was proscribed, her affiliation lapsed, and for three years, she said, "We had no groups." But in 1942 she was again invited to Eric Adams's group at the apartment of Agatha Chapman, who, like Adams, worked at the Bank of Canada as a research economist. Economics was the group's focus, and an "interest in Communistic writings and teachings" became the qualification for membership. "We discussed socialist literature," Willsher said, "Marxist literature."[97] Adams seemed to be in charge, and among the attendees was Scot Benning, who worked for the Department of Munitions and Supply. Until Adams left for Montreal in 1944, the group met "about every three weeks" for about "an hour and a half,"[98] reviving Willsher's affiliation with the Communist Party.[99]

Such study groups linked the LPP to the Soviets, and became a place to cultivate GRU agents, especially those who exhibited a certain kind of altruism. Historians drawing on the KGB archives in Moscow and the Venona files in the US have described how Communist parties in the West, with their clandestine culture, supplied Soviet intelligence with candidates to build spy networks.[100] And more than espionage was at play: through the popular front tactic, Moscow sought not just spies but loyal (and often covert) adherents in leadership roles throughout civil societies in the West. Canada's LPP placed "all-class unity" at the centre of its public policy,[101] yet its sudden policy reversals – 1928 (Class Against Class), 1934 (Popular Front Against Fascism), 1939 (Popular Front Against War, Conscription and the Imperialist Regime), 1942 (A Common Front For Victory) – show that the Canadian Communist Party jumped whenever Moscow said "jump." Philip Deery has convincingly insisted that Western Communist parties and the threat they posed must be placed at the centre of a new Cold War history.[102]

Already in 1935, Willsher had been cultivated. It was MP Fred Rose who recruited her at the study group. Fauteux asked her, "Is he the first one who suggested to you that you could contribute to the promotion of the Soviet government by giving him … information of value which passed through your hands in ... the High Commissioner's office?" Willsher objected, "He didn't say 'Soviet government.' He said the Canadian party, the Canadian Communist Party."[103] Did Willsher concur, Kellock probed, that what Rose wanted was "an improper thing ... to do?" She replied, "Well, I did, but I felt that I should contrive to contribute something towards the helping of this policy, because I was interested in it. I found it very difficult, and yet I felt I should try to help." Kellock wondered if she felt "that there was a higher law," arising out of her "political convictions." She agreed, "Yes. It was a struggle."[104] After a month of wavering, Willsher decided to give Rose information from the High Commissioner's office,[105] and subsequently, whenever anything came up that she thought might interest him, she made a mental note and passed it on to him.[106]

Willsher also implicated Eric Adams.[107] Between 1942 or 1943 and September 1945, she complied with his requests for information, either at study group meetings or in Adams's car after he moved to Montreal. Agatha Chapman give Willsher a heads-up about where and when Adams's car would appear.[108] By 1944 Willsher had become assistant registrar at the British High Commissioner's office, responsible for incoming and outgoing letters and telegrams. While secret documents did not pass through her hands (because they were not registered), she nevertheless had access to them.[109] Fauteux questioned her about her readiness to meet Adams's requests: "Do you mean, Miss Willsher, that by becoming a member of the Communist Party you are expected to do what you are asked to do regardless of any obligation you may have in any other direction; is that what you mean?" Willsher assented, "That is the sort of thing, yes."[110] At the time, the Communist Party wanted details about the war effort, and Willsher complied.[111]

Inquiry lawyers were particularly interested in Willsher's possible role in the Soviet acquisition of notes concerning negotiations between Ottawa and London related to Allied financial and military planning. In late November and early December 1944, John Maynard Keynes had led a delegation to Ottawa to finish negotiating Canada's role in the post-war renewal of the British economy.[112] The records of these meetings were marked "Top Secret,"[113] but Willsher testified that Adams wanted to know the financial proposals, and that she gave him whatever details she could remember about "loans or gifts to be made by Canada to Great Britain."[114] Official and "Top Secret" reports on these negotiations were typed up by both British and Canadian participants, but the notes mentioned in Zabotin's list were handwritten and weren't marked as "secret." They were almost certainly composed by Adams ("Ernst") based on conversations with Willsher, with Adams then relaying the information to Moscow[115] – while Willsher assumed that the information was merely going to the executive of the Canadian Communist Party.[116] In Zabotin's mailing list, "Ellie" (Willsher) also received credit for two late-1944 letters sent by Wilgress to Mackenzie King that included discussion of financial credits to ensure trade between the USSR and Britain. She never saw the letters, she said,[117] but did see some details of the contents, which she shared with Adams.[118] As we will see in Adams's testimony, it again seems likely that he, not Willsher, passed the letters on to Zabotin.

Fauteux asked about Willsher's state of mind during the spying. She agreed that she had concealed her Communist affiliations from the Office of the High Commissioner. Like other Communists (unless they worked on a newspaper or on the party's national executive), she followed the tradecraft playbook and avoided buying Communist books publicly, but had a proxy pick them up for her.[119] Like Kellock, Fauteux pushed her to explain her moral understanding of the relationship between her political affiliation and the state:

FAUTEUX: "Being called upon to make a decision as between your master and the country you were working for, on the one hand, and the Communist Party, on the other hand, you told us that you decided in favour of the Communist Party?

WILLSHER: "Yes."

FAUTEUX: "Because you felt that you owed loyalty to the Communist Party first?

WILLSHER: "Yes."

She said that she understood the Official Secrets Act, the penalties for contravening it, and the impropriety of her actions[120] – in fact, she melodramatically overestimated the act's penalties, saying, "I know I can be shot quite easily, if necessary."[121] But she excused herself via the qualification preached in "popular front" circles: "I do not think the Communist Party is necessarily against the interests of Canada and that is why I did not feel – I thought it was in the interests of all in many respects, particularly during the war … The Communist party does not work against the interests of Canada."[122]

On the morning of 28 February, when Willsher was recalled before the commissioners and advised as per section 12 of the Inquiries Act that because a charge could be made against her, she could now have access to a lawyer,[123] she only vaguely understood what that meant: "Where do I get counsel? Is it expensive?"[124] Unlike some of the men who stonewalled the commission, she was unsure of her rights as she tried to speculate about how lawyers might help her: "They would know the fine legal points of the investigation, the terms under which it was drawn up. That may make no difference; I do not know those points."[125] Asked if she wanted counsel to represent her, she said, "I do not think there is any reason that I should."[126] Two months later, she pled guilty to a one charge of violating the Official Secrets Act and was sentenced to three years in a penitentiary.[127]

Ned Mazerall ("Bagley"), 27 February

Thirty-year-old Edward (Ned) Mazerall was an electrical engineer from the University of New Brunswick who had worked for Westinghouse and the CBC before arriving at the NRC in 1942 "to help in the development of radar equipment."[128] Like other NRC employees, he swore three oaths – "the Oath of Allegiance, the Oath of Office and the Oath of Secrecy."[129] Beginning in 1941, he had attended Communist Party study groups. Bob Edmonds, a CBC announcer who later worked at the newly created National Film Board, befriended Mazerall, and as Mazerall explained, "He was gradually acquainting me with his own philosophy, and asked me to come to some of these meetings," mainly for "the study of Marxist philosophy."[130] Shortly after Fred Rose was elected in 1943, Agatha Chapman invited him to her home to analyse "the difference in the stand taken by the Labor-Progressive Party and the CCF." It was Rose who, according to Gouzenko, identified Mazerall as someone whom Lunan should cultivate and draw into the Soviet espionage net.[131]

In 1946, after twelve days of detention at Rockcliffe, Mazerall appeared before the inquiry. Gouzenko had identified him as the NRC employee code-named "Bagley."[132] In a "guarded confession" to the RCMP, Mazerall had admitted his code name, described Communist Party study groups that he attended, and spoken of meeting with Gordon Lunan, Fred Rose, and Durnford Smith.[133] Since a witness before an inquiry was required to answer questions, Mazerall, with a bit of prodding from Fauteux, agreed that the study group he had joined could be described as "a cell of the Communist Party."[134] Membership centred on vocations: "[the organizers] tried to keep people together who had things in common."[135] Despite attending Communist study groups for several years, and despite paying a dollar a month (the equivalent of $20 per month in 2026) to Chapman in support of the Labor-Progressive Party,[136] Mazerall didn't consider himself a Communist. Yet he qualified this statement in a way that negated it: "Well, it was a sort of tacit consent, you might say, but there was no official Party, and no official membership."[137] In June 1945, Lunan asked Mazerall to lunch, and eventually showed Mazerall his cards: "He asked me if I would supply him with information."

FAUTEUX: "For whom?"
MAZERALL: "For the Soviet Union."[138]

In July, Mazerall brought Lunan two reports. One was a "long term proposal by Dr. McKinley for future civil aids to air navigation." The other was a report Mazerall had written for McKinley on "a distance indicator for civil aids to navigation, short range."[139] Lunan was not authorized to receive such a report, Mazerall admitted, and he knew that the report would be sent to the Soviets.[140] Fauteux quoted from Lunan's GRU report: "I had a very successful meeting with Bagley and he agreed to participate to the furthest of his ability ... He is interested in the work and immediately promised to be of assistance. I gave him a full quota of tasks, and he promised reports on his work and on various other aspects of the general work at his place."[141] However, Mazerall said that he never followed through, except for the two reports.[142] The evidence in Lunan's reports to Rogov, and Rogov's summaries about the "Research Group," suggests that Mazerall was telling the truth.[143]

Later, Mazerall implicated an NRC colleague, testifying that Durnford Smith discussed Lunan's requests and "wanted to know whether we could get together and procure our information, pool it." Mazerall declined the offer.[144] He also testified that David Shugar and Scot Benning, the latter apparently a Labor-Progressive functionary of some kind, attended the study group meetings.[145] Mazerall declared that he had received no money from Lunan, and that an offer of money would have sunk his involvement: "the slightest suggestion of it would have discouraged it as far as I was concerned entirely ... I would have told him to get out of the car, and I would have driven away ... it is one thing to do things because you think you can do some good by it, but it is another thing to do it from a purely monetary point of view."[146]

What motivated Mazerall? A line that Lunan used on him was the general idea of scientific cooperation, as Mazerall explained: "It was more that as scientists we were pooling information, and I actually asked him if we could hope to find this reciprocal." Kellock's follow-up question subtly highlighted Mazerall's naivety about such hoped-for reciprocity:

KELLOCK: "Did you ever have that experience?"
MAZERALL: "I did not. No."[147]

Like that of many Communists and fellow-travellers, Mazerall's deeper motivation, spurred on by his reading and his circles of discussion, lay in the utopian hopes that he thought the Soviets incarnated: "I felt that they stood first and foremost for peace, and that if they had their way there would not be any wars. Not only that, but I must say that I am a socialist, and that there was a government which was a socialist government and if left entirely to themselves could prove socialism could work." In Mazerall's assessment, Western critiques of the Soviet experiment were mistaken: "the Soviet Union is not the vicious place it has been painted."[148]

Canadian critiques of the period had indeed found viciousness in the Soviet Union. Ontario Conservative Party leader George Drew, after a 1937 trip to the Soviet Union, dismissed claims about the freedom of the Russian masses as "a myth." He told the *Globe and Mail* that in the Russian countryside and small towns, the population was "mostly in bare feet and tattered rags." He had "never before seen whole masses of people literally on the verge of starvation" and found it hard to believe that "such ghastly destitution still existed anywhere in the world." There were "wholesale executions … almost daily." He described a report in *Pravda* setting out a list of twenty-four engineers shot without trial for "Trotskyism, sabotage and anti-Russianism." Stalin, supposedly the "Father of the Russian People," had "shot or imprisoned, every one of his old associates. No one knows whose turn will be next." It made "the reign of Ivan the Terrible seem like one of the happy periods of Russian life."[149] Although some anti-Communist rhetoric ran through Drew's account, this did not negate the reality of Stalin's Great Purge of 1937–8, which saw 681,692 Russians executed.[150]

The groupthink fostered by the study groups must also have influenced Mazerall, at least initially. When Kellock invited Mazerall to distinguish between a "socialist" and a "communist," he couldn't. Nevertheless, he said, "I would like to see this country as a socialist country, because I think under those circumstances everyone would have a better chance of living and enjoying life."[151] At some point, he had grown disillusioned with the study groups. Expecting friendliness and democracy, he found that "there were some of the members who seemed to feel that it was more of a militant organization." He complained, "In the homes in which we held the meetings there were numerous interesting books around, and I felt on occasion I would like to pick one up to look at it only to have one of the members tell me to put the book down and come to order." Such high-handedness galled Mazerall, so he began to make excuses to avoid meetings. And yet, although he didn't like the group, he still valued "the things that they stood for."[152]

After Mazerall's day before the inquiry, Malcolm MacDonald observed, "Like Woikin and Willsher, though more deeply involved, he is again the honourable fellow-traveller." MacDonald blamed Lunan for making "fullest use" of the "politically naive" Mazerall, who sought to fulfill a higher duty.[153] But MacDonald concluded ominously that the "case against him will stand in court."[154] When Mazerall was recalled before the inquiry, he was offered a lawyer, purposely too late as usual, and an opportunity to bring in further evidence. Mazerall responded with a brief narrative: "When I was questioned by the Inspector of the Royal Canadian Mounted Police, my natural reaction was to deny my part in it. He showed me headlines in the papers at the time which indicated to me that it was vastly more important than I had suspected. I regret my part in it. He told me that I could show my further good faith in this and indicate my regret by admitting my part in it. I have done that." Only Lunan could have given evidence against him but, Mazerall said, "I thought it would be better if I told the truth to the best of my ability."[155] He didn't think that a lawyer could do much for him.

After Mazerall's testimony at the inquiry ended and he faced criminal charges, his lawyer, Royden Hughes, would argue that Mazerall had been "persecuted."[156] If that's a bit exaggerated, it's true that Mazerall hadn't been informed that he was likely to be charged, hadn't been offered a lawyer, and hadn't been given the protections of the Canada Evidence Act. How important was Mazerall's material? Later, the commissioners would opine, "The fact that these reports were shortly thereafter presented to the Third Commonwealth and Empire Conference on Radio for Civil Aviation should be considered as an extenuating circumstance in Mazerall's favour."[157] But this support did not save him from criminal prosecution following the inquiry. On 22 May 1946, Ontario High Court Justice A.C. McRuer found Mazerall guilty of conspiracy to offend the Official Secrets Act and sentenced him to four years in the penitentiary. His appeal was dismissed.[158]

Gordon Lunan ("Back"), 27 February

A linchpin during the Kellock-Taschereau Commission and for subsequent prosecutions, the operative who could implicate Mazerall, Durnford Smith, Israel Halperin, Fred Rose and, through Rose, the Communist Party of Canada in Russian spying was Gordon Lunan. His testimony was vital, because he had been in direct contact with the Russian embassy and he was predicted to be the last cooperative witness.[159] He would indeed cooperate, reluctantly, yet he also took note of the evidence and would step no farther than corroborating what the state already knew.[160] Even so, what he said was highly damaging to himself and to several others.

Lunan was born in Kirkaldy, Scotland, and arrived in Canada in 1938, a twenty-four-year-old full of ambition. He wanted to write, and found employment with advertising agencies in Montreal, before joining the Canadian army in January 1943. By the summer of 1945, he had been promoted to captain, was married with one child, and worked in Ottawa as editor of *Canadian Affairs* at the Canadian Information Service (formerly the Wartime Information Board).[161]

After being detained, Lunan denied any wrongdoing, but once he saw the RCMP's evidence against him he agreed to cooperate. His recruitment by the Russians had begun with a teaser. On a train between Ottawa and Montreal, Fred Rose, whom Lunan had known since 1943, asked him about his work and future plans. Rose then said that Lunan should meet "an interesting person." Some days later, on Lunan's desk at the Canadian Information Service, an envelope materialized, concealing a typewritten invitation to a meeting at a quiet, mostly residential spot near St Alban's Church in Ottawa, and code words to exchange with the person there. Lunan immediately knew that the message came from Rose. Perhaps it was linked, Lunan speculated, to his writing aspirations. Fauteux doubted that: "Is it customary for writers to arrange for interviews through anonymous notes and so on?" No, Lunan conceded, but when Fauteux tried to probe Lunan's state of mind at the time, Lunan balked. Of course, questions related to state of mind – *mens rea*, the guilty mind, without which even a very harmful act might not be culpable – are central to criminal prosecutions. Although the Official Secrets Act made a person's "known character" a ground for conviction, a way of showing that the defendant's purposes were damaging to the interests of the state, this facet of the act had never been tested in court, so no one had any idea where judgments would fall in the event of such charges. Later, at the suspects' criminal trials and appeals, judges took a narrower line on "known character" (for example, in the Henry Harris case[162]), subverting the legislation's aggressive effect by finding that the government couldn't have intended a broad interpretation that verged on guilt by association. At the inquiry, however, the commissioners, hoping to use the suspects' associations as evidence of conspiracy, probed Lunan's state of mind, his telephone directory, and his address book,[163] laden with names of other suspects. But Lunan would only offer a single neutral motive for going to the mysterious meeting: "curiosity."[164]

After dark, at the corner of King Edward and Daly in early March 1945,[165] Lunan met a man whose strong Russian accent made him very difficult to understand. "Jan" (GRU operative Lt. Col. Vassili Rogov) asked Lunan to write commentaries on Canadian politics. At the end of the meeting, "Jan" handed Lunan an envelope and they agreed to meet again.[166] During the Kellock-Taschereau Commission hearings, Lunan was presented with a copy of a message that Gouzenko had retrieved from the safe in the Russian embassy: "The scheme of your group will be approximately much as it is shown below." In a sketch, "Jan" appeared at the apex, followed by "G. Lunan (Back) -nickname." Under Lunan, the diagram fanned out to three people: "Isidor [*sic*] Halperin nickname- (Bacon)," "Doruforth [*sic*] Smith (Badeau) -nickname," and "Ned Mazerall (Bagley) -Nickname." Below the diagram was written, "You will know me (as Jan) but nobody else." There followed, in Russian-inflected English, a list of tasks for Lunan to pursue with each man. "Badeau" (Smith) was asked for reconnaissance on the NRC: "What kind of work is his department engaged in and what departments it is in contact with (by work)." "Bagley" (Mazerall) was asked "to give the models of developed radio-sets, its photographs, technical (data) facts and for what purpose it is intended." Every three months, he should "write the reports in which to characterize the work of radio department, to inform about the forthcoming tasks and what new kinds of the models are going to be developed" – in other words the developments in microwave radar that Mazerall and Smith were working on. "Bacon" (Halperin) was asked to "give the organization and characters of Valcartier Explosives establishment's direction" and to write a report on the organization's work. Such early tasks were designed to draw the targets into GRU work. Gouzenko exposed not a mature functioning network, but one under development, with the Soviets casting a wide net for the future. Evidently, Moscow hoped that Halperin might unearth atomic bomb secrets, an assignment only hinted at, "If possible to pass on the prescription (formulas) of explosives and its samples."[167]

According to Alexander Foote, who worked as a Soviet agent in Switzerland during World War II,[168] it was unusual for the Soviets to host a spy ring directly in an embassy, with a supposed diplomat such as Rogov running agents. More common was the Swiss set-up, where a private legal resident directed the Soviet network.[169] Ideally, the "resident director" would be a non-Russian of foreign nationality, not liable to military service, and capable of operating even if the target country were at war with the Soviet Union. This *rezidentura* reported directly to Moscow, independent of official Soviet representation in the host country.[170] Nevertheless, the Canadian-style embassy spy system was used both in Australia and in Britain, where the GRU's Yuri Modin, a young commercial attaché, handled John

Cairncross, Anthony Blunt, and Kim Philby, the most famous Soviet agent of the era.[171]

Tradecraft had to be explained to the rookie spies. Rogov's "scheme" for his "research group" directed that all documents passed to Lunan by Halperin, Smith, and Mazerall bear the "nicknames" conferred by Rogov. Whenever submissions couldn't be handed over "irrevocably," they would be photographed and returned. For his personal reference, Rogov created an annotated record, a score card for the research group.[172] He emphasized secrecy to Lunan: "I beg you to instruct every man separately about conspiracy in our work." If Lunan had any doubts that he was being asked to spy, the sentence typed across the bottom of the page would have erased them: "After studying burn it."[173]

In his testimony, Lunan said that he was "very disturbed" by Rogov's message and did not act on it for several weeks.[174] Then, on 28 March 1945, the day of the planned meeting with Rogov, Lunan sat down at his typewriter in Canadian Information Services and wrote a three-page report, addressed to "Dear Mother and Father," summarizing his efforts to recruit Halperin, Mazerall, and Smith. He said, "neither Bacon, Bagley nor Badeau are well known to me either personally or politically, nor I to them."[175] The political motivation of the three was crucial, of course, because their work would require, as Lunan put it, "close cooperation with Russia … and sympathy with the Communist Party program."[176] Fauteux, channelling the Gilbert and Sullivan song (in which "every boy and every gal / That's born into the world alive / Is either a little Liberal / Or else a little Conservative!"), suggested, "you were not looking for a little Liberal or a little Conservative, you were looking for someone sympathetic to the Communist party." Lunan agreed.[177] He and Smith had met previously through the "Quebec Committee for Allied Victory,"[178] a committee linked to the Communist Party,[179] yet Smith still proved wary, and Lunan reported to Rogov that "progress" had been "held up" because Smith was checking Lunan's "credentials."[180] Halperin, on the other hand, was both "enthusiastic" and "politically experienced," so Lunan approached him directly.[181]

Questions of security also slowed Lunan down. He didn't want to approach the three recruits "point blank with all the tasks." He told Rogov, "They already feel the need for maintaining a very high degree of security and taking abnormal precautions at their normal meetings (about once in two weeks), since they are definitely not labelled with any political affiliation."[182] In other words, as Lunan clarified to the commission, the three wanted to hide their meetings with other Communists from their professional colleagues. Fauteux nudged Lunan to admit that these meetings were "Communist discussion groups."

Lunan demurred, calling any meeting "a social gathering,"[183] yet his report to Rogov had noted that "one or two have even opposed the introduction of new members to our group on the grounds that it would endanger their own security."[184] Lunan refused to acknowledge that "our group" referred to a Communist study cell that Mazerall had spoken of attending with Lunan, Halperin, and Smith.[185]

Fauteux's questions about recruitment were designed to get evidence of a conspiracy, so that he could turn Gouzenko's hearsay into evidence admissible in court. A direct confession of crimes under the Official Secrets Act would suffice, or, failing that, the government could still net even suspects who didn't confess as long as one suspect implicated the others in an illegal conspiracy.[186] Since *conspiring* to commit an indictable offence was illegal under the Criminal Code,[187] and since an offence against the Official Secrets Act was indictable, the suspect could be charged even without actually having done the offence that they conspired to do.[188] The Criminal Code in 1946 contained no definition of conspiracy, but the common law treated conspiracy as the agreement of two or more individuals to do "an unlawful act or to do a lawful act by unlawful means."[189] In other words, even if the goal was *lawful* – never mind altruistic and *un*lawful – a person couldn't use unlawful *means* to reach it. For example, until the Passage of the Trade Unions Act (1872), 'conspiring' with another person to leave an employer for higher wages elsewhere invited prosecution as a criminal conspiracy. And, vitally important, hearsay evidence was admissible in a conspiracy proceeding if "accompanied by independent proof of the conspiracy,"[190] so a conspiracy prosecution could open the door for Gouzenko's hearsay evidence. Lunan's testimony linking the suspects together was therefore what Fauteux and the government needed to tie Smith and Halperin to a Rogov-Lunan conspiracy. Mazerall's confession had already opened the door to his prosecution under the Official Secrets Act and under the Criminal Code's conspiracy provisions.[191] Nevertheless, even though the Mazerall case was mostly clear-cut, prosecutors would soon discover that they couldn't rely on the guilt-by-association clauses in the Official Secrets Act for prosecutions under the act and certainly not for conspiracy prosecutions under the act.[192]

Arrangements for the Rogov-Lunan meetings on street corners in Ottawa had been kept "as secret as possible." While Lunan from time to time came in his military uniform, Rogov always wore civilian attire. Both Lunan and Rogov usually arrived "on foot," though Rogov would have a car waiting in the wings.[193] Inviting Halperin, Smith, and Mazerall into the Rogov-Lunan conspiracy, Lunan proceeded cautiously. He told Rogov that he didn't want to give them "too great an assignment … at one time," and "for the time being" he didn't want "to characterize the work for what it is, but merely to let it be understood that it is work of a special conspiratorial nature, without mentioning my connection with you." For Smith, at least, the approach worked. After checking Lunan's "bona fides," Smith "promised to cooperate" and started a report on the NRC.[194] Even though Lunan tempered his commission testimony by saying that he might have overstated his success with the three group members, he did confirm that Smith had willingly joined the conspiracy.[195] By late March, Smith had begun giving information that the Soviets dearly wanted. "'Badeau' informs me," Lunan wrote in his report to Rogov, "that most secret work at present is on nuclear physics (bombardment of radio-active substances to produce energy). This is more hush-hush than radar." Smith had nothing to report on radar, but he revealed that the government had purchased a "radium producing plant" to facilitate the nuclear physics research at the University of Montreal and at McMaster.[196]

Trips, sickness, the demands of work stalled agents' cooperation, and there was a near misstep with Smith. Lunan said, "Badeau was very disturbed when I brought up the subject of money. I think he felt that it brought the subject of this work into a different (and more conspiratorial) focus."[197] Still, Smith reported in April about his work on "a battleship radar device for use in the Pacific. This is an extremely sensitive detecting devise which has been successfully tried out on the east coast."[198] Smith also met face to face with Rogov in Rogov's vehicle. While Lunan sat "in the front and smoked" beside Rogov's driver, Smith and Rogov talked in the back seat for forty-five minutes "in a low tone." Lunan found it "almost impossible to understand Jan under the circumstances" and could recall only a few phrases, mostly "about technical matters, electronic matters."[199] Later, in his own account, Rogov wrote that Badeau "brought valuable material" and that "we agreed upon further work.[200] By eliciting Lunan's confirmation of Rogov's documents and of secret information being given to the Soviets,[201] Fauteux put Smith squarely within an espionage conspiracy, and, bit by bit, transformed Gouzenko's hearsay evidence into evidence admissible in a criminal trial.

Halperin at first also went along willingly with Lunan's information requests, though, as Lunan told Rogov, "I don't think Bacon is sufficiently impressed with the conspiratorial nature of the work yet. But he is definitely keen and will be helpful."[202] Halperin agreed to describe the operations at Valcartier Explosives, about to become CARDE (Canadian Army Research Division, Explosives), a combined civilian and military organization. Since Halperin refused to hand over any actual documents or written reports, Lunan had to take notes during their conversations and then type out the results. In April, "Bacon's Report" detailed CARDE's planned development as an NRC-controlled "pilot explosives plant." It already had a ballistics lab, focusing on new explosives such as "DINA mixed with RDX [Research Developed Explosive] as a component in propellants," but its "Designs Branch" and "Field Trials Wings" would take over work currently done at Suffield and Valcartier. Halperin stressed the "importance of CARDE in controlling factory production."[203] Again, the assignment of this non-technical report seems to have been designed to draw Halperin into the GRU net.

At the Kellock-Taschereau Commission, eager to close the circle on conspiracy, Fauteux several times asked whether Halperin had provided the information requested by Rogov. Lunan said yes,[204] though sometimes he added, "By Jan, yes,"[205] as if he hadn't earlier identified Rogov as "Jan," forcing Fauteux to remind him of his earlier testimony. Nevertheless, while Lunan's testimony appeared to show that Halperin had joined the conspiracy, his commitment was limited. Early on, Halperin, the agent of choice to get at the grail of the atomic secret, was questioned about uranium and nuclear weapons, but Lunan hesitated to speak of "formulae and samples."[206] Halperin's reluctance became more pronounced sometime after mid-April. In an undated report to Rogov, Lunan explained that Halperin refused to provide a photograph or biography for the GRU and refused to write anything down. When Lunan asked for a uranium-235 sample, Halperin grew markedly colder: "It has become very difficult to work with him, especially after my request about Ur 235." Not only did Halperin emphasize that U-235 was "absolutely impossible to get," but he began to understand "the gist" of Lunan's requests "more fully" and, as Lunan remarked, "he does not like them very much."[207]

Early on, Halperin had ridiculed the government's tendency to label everything as "secret." Lunan said, "His attitude is that most of the so-called secret work is a joke and while it is officially on the secret list, those working on it can see no reason for secrecy."[208] This makes it difficult to assess whether Halperin was giving the Soviets only information that was publicly available, or giving them information that Halperin thought *should be* publicly available, or whether Halperin, afraid of incriminating himself, was simply vacillating about how far to go in his political involvement. The last seems the most likely. Halperin gave a broad technical account of "the general principles of the electron shell and the bomb detonator," but oral accounts were practically useless, since Lunan was not a scientist.[209] "Bomb detonator" probably referred to the proximity fuse or variable timed (VT) fuse, which could detonate an explosive based on proximity to its target. Prior to the invention of the VT fuse, detonation could only be triggered by a timer set at launch, by an altimeter, or by direct contact with a target. The fuse played a vital role as an anti-aircraft weapon in the war against Japan, and while the existence of the proximity fuse was not secret, its wiring and manufacturing process were top secret.[210]

At the Soviet embassy, Zabotin and Rogov faced growing pressure from Moscow to get more details on the atomic bomb, the information that they most wanted from Halperin.[211] However, on 5 July 1945, after several months of contact with Halperin, Lunan told Rogov that he had "spent a whole evening with 'Bacon' with most disappointing results." Halperin didn't want to take any risks in obtaining material that was obtainable by other means. On the question of atomic research and uranium production, he was "curious about the Chalk River plant and the manufacture of uranium," but he had no information to offer.[212] Even before the disappointing report, the GRU had tired of Halperin's stalling and shifted its hopes briefly to Durnford Smith. In May 1945,[213] Lunan excitedly told Rogov that Smith was willing to apply for a position at the University of Montreal's nuclear physics lab.[214]

But Moscow instead settled on Alan Nunn May as its best bet for nuclear intelligence in Canada. Nunn May's Communist credentials dated from his student days in Cambridge. He had contacted the Russians to warn them (mistakenly) that Nazi German might be developing a "dirty bomb" that could diffuse radioactive poison, and from that point on the GRU "booked" him as a potential source.[215] In 1942 at the behest of the British, Canada funded a research lab in Montreal to house a joint Anglo-Canadian nuclear research team. A secret British atomic weapons initiative (code-named "Tube Alloys") sent scientists – Nunn May among them – to the Montreal lab. Because MI5 was denied knowledge of the Tube Alloys project, no security checks were done on the scientists.[216] The British hoped for a close association with the Manhattan Project, but the Americans viewed the Montreal lab as a security threat and shared very little about the Manhattan Project. Montreal therefore focused on developing heavy water plutonium and constructing a nuclear reactor at Chalk River.[217]

Moscow's primary atomic source was, of course, British scientist Klaus Fuchs, who had joined Robert Oppenheimer's British-American team in 1943. A Soviet asset since 1941, Fuchs gave detailed information on the atomic bomb well into 1945.[218] Nevertheless, Gouzenko disclosed to MI5 that in early 1945 Moscow had directed Zabotin to contact "Alek" (Nunn May's second alias, in addition to "Primrose"), so GRU operative Lt. Pavel Angelov ("Baxter") showed up at Nunn

May's Montreal apartment, directing him to prepare a report on atomic energy research.[219] Nunn May also detailed the construction and operation of proximity shells that were "being adapted against the Japanese suicide-aviators by the American Navy,"[220] and he warned Moscow about the possible source Norman Veal, who in the presence of his wife had asked Nunn May if it "would be worth his (VEAL) [*sic*] while to hand over information about the atomic bomb."[221] In "This is a Disclosure of How I Became a Russian Spy," a document dictated from his deathbed, Nunn May admitted that he had borrowed from the National Research Council library (for Zabotin's team to copy) "the entire library of research documents on nuclear power (a great deal of which was provided by the USA)." He also told the Soviets about visits he made to a Manhattan Project laboratory in Chicago.[222]

Nunn May's reactivation not only solved the Halperin problem, but also ended any prospects of Smith moving to Montreal; Rogov told Lunan to cancel those plans.[223] Because Stalin was caught off-guard by the Hiroshima and Nagasaki detonations, he pushed harder for a Soviet atomic bomb, ordering Zabotin (and presumably other GRU station chiefs) to "take measures to organize the obtention [*sic*] of documentary materials of the atomic bomb: the technological, process, drawings, calculations."[224] Even before Hiroshima, Moscow had asked Nunn May to stay in Canada.[225] He couldn't. However, he still planned to bring information from the "Uranium Plant" (Chalk River) to Angelov. Zabotin told Moscow, "We (Angelov) handed over 500 dollars to him"[226] (the equivalent of $9,000 in 2026). On his deathbed, Nunn May would claim that he had been "tricked" into accepting such payments and had burned one of the payments afterwards.[227] Shortly after Hiroshima, he reported to Moscow on the central role of uranium-235 in the bomb.[228] He gave the Soviets "a slightly enriched sample" of U-235 in a glass tube[229] and "a very thin deposit" of U-233 "on a platinum foil" wrapped in paper, which Lt. Col. Petr Motinov, Nunn May's handler, immediately couriered to Moscow.[230] Motinov was greeted by none other than Stalin's security chief Lavrentiy Beriya.[231] Nunn May received US$200 and two bottles of whiskey;[232] Zabotin very soon received the Order of the Red Banner and the Order of the Red Star[233] (rather fleeting honours in Stalin's Russia); Motinov received radiation poisoning and had to have blood transfusions for the rest of his life.[234]

While Halperin initially cooperated with the Soviets and then pulled back, Ned Mazerall initially proved elusive to Lunan but eventually cooperated. The prospect of drawing Mazerall into the conspiracy appeared dim, and Lunan explained, "He has not been a very regular or enthusiastic supporter for several months but now he is showing more enthusiasm."[235] Lunan's testimony confirmed some of the things that Mazerall said. Smith had alerted Lunan about Mazerall's declining interest in the study group that Smith and Mazerall attended. Pressed by Fauteux, Lunan denied first-hand knowledge of the group but *supposed* that it was associated with the Communist Party.[236] Since Mazerall was "politically naive" and his wife "antagonistic" to his political participation, Lunan planned to "take things slow," to "develop his acquaintance as much as possible and gain his confidence by collaborating on some scientific articles."[237] Despite being difficult to contact,[238] Mazerall did promise to help, and through Lunan Rogov assigned him to get details on the "radio [radar] sets."[239] Mazerall eventually gave the Russians two documents about "electronic navigation devices."[240]

According to Lunan his own motives, like those of Smith, Halperin, and Mazerall, were purely "idealistic or political." Nobody wanted money "as a disbursement to cover expenses or otherwise,"[241] and he denied taking any money at any time from Rogov.[242] According to Rogov's records, however, money was "paid out" to Lunan and others on several occasions. During a meeting on 8 May 1945, for example, Rogov gave Lunan one hundred dollars as a "present for the wife."[243] It's true, nevertheless, that political motives were indeed central. At the same time, Lunan hedged about what exactly "political" meant – he seemed to use it as a euphemism for "Communist." He agreed with Fauteux that "political" referred to "Party sympathy," that the party in question was the Communist Party, and that his politics were tied to the Soviet Union,[244] yet, splitting hairs, he would not call supporters of the Labor-Progressive Party (LPP) Communists. One might lean towards the LPP or the Communist Party, Lunan argued, and not necessarily be a Communist. True, the LPP was the old Communist Party with a new name to gain a legal status, but not every supporter was a Communist: "The Labor-Progressive Party seeks its membership on the basis of a program which it has at any one time, and I do not think that it is a wholly Communist program or a revolutionary program. It is a program, as I see it, in order to advance the interests of Canada."[245] When Fauteux asked Lunan if he was a member "of the artists's [*sic*] branch of section 10 [*sic*] of the Communist party of Canada," Lunan equivocated. He acknowledged that he had been a member of "an artists' discussion group," but he added, "I was not aware that it was a branch of the Communist Party." Lunan testified that his affiliation with the group of six to twelve attendees dated from 1938, that they met every two weeks, and that they discussed "mostly politics; current events." Fauteux offered a translation: "You discussed the various theories of the Communist party; communism." Lunan agreed, but hedged again when asked if the meetings were "secret." His response, "not especially," soon graduated to an admission that potential new members of the Communist Party were invited to attend. Lunan acknowledged that he had attended social gatherings in Ottawa, but denied ever being a member of a Communist study group there.[246]

When Fauteux charged that Lunan was sheltered in "Section 10" of the Communist Party,[247] he meant "Section 13," a special membership category in which, as Merrily Weisbord explains, "middle-class teachers, scientists, and professionals were … grouped into closed clubs." Section 13 members "did not hand out leaflets, did not go to demonstrations, did not march on picket lines, did not, therefore, risk being photographed or arrested by the police … Few Party members knew and no one outside the Party was supposed to know that these one hundred or so 'darlings of the movement' were Party members."[248] In other words, Section 13 functioned as an underground membership category in order to protect professionals whose membership might cost them their jobs.[249] Although the *Final Report* of the Kellock-Taschereau Commission makes no reference to Section 13, the Communist sympathizers in this pool were potential recruits to do Soviet spying. Fred Rose would approach Section 13 members, Lunan among them, "who felt the Soviet Union was being denied help in a life-and-death struggle."[250] Because their colleagues didn't realize that they were Communists and because they knew how to work underground, they were the "perfect contacts."[251]

Lunan's reluctance to admit his membership in Section 13 was quite understandable, given that the Official Secrets Act's wartime jurisprudence allowed "known character" to be used as evidence of guilt. Fauteux dug into Lunan's personal connections with Hazen Size, Fred Poland, Matt Nightingale, Scot Benning, and Raymond Boyer – all associated with the Communist Party – and tried to link them to the spy conspiracy. Lunan acknowledged connections of one kind or another with them all. He had worked with Hazen Size to assist returnees from the Spanish Civil War.[252] Boyer he had met in Montreal through the Civil Liberties Union, an organization that, Lunan insisted, wasn't just "Communist" since, for example, the CCF's Eugene Forsey was a member. Fauteux tried to work in the conspiracy angle: "If I understand the situation, the Communists have their own secret organizations, their own groups, which carry on their secret operations, and they also join other groups which are operating in the open?"

LUNAN: "I think they feel free to join any group."

COMMISSIONER KELLOCK: "With the idea of controlling the other organization, if possible?"

LUNAN: "Well, with the idea of advancing their own opinions."[253]

If Kellock was prepared to invoke a common fear ever since the Winnipeg General Strike, Lunan was prepared to respond with public-relations language.

Eventually, Fauteux queried Lunan on the morality of his actions and the personal aspects of his political commitments, asking him why he agreed to act as Rogov's agent. Lunan said, "I reviewed what I had done in the light of my political ideas and my political principles, or if you like, my communist leanings."[254] Later he would speak of his wish for "a more humane society, a fairer distribution of wealth."[255] Certainly, because of Soviet sacrifices in the war against the Nazis, Communism in the West was never more popular than in the final years of World War II.[256] At the inquiry, Lunan cited his work helping International Brigade veterans who had fought in the Spanish Civil War, and his work for the Communist-linked Quebec Committee for Allied Victory, which advocated for the interests "of all people, in fighting against the axis."[257] Because of his work on the committee, he had been branded a Communist and had lost his job.

When he was recruited by Rogov, it was only after "a great struggle" that he could accept "this kind of work" (he avoided the word "spying"). He decided that his work would "advance the cause of international cooperation." Despite doubts, he said, "discussions of great numbers of scientist all over the world following the atom bomb raid tended to bear out my belief and balanced off to some extent my own misgivings." In the context of the UN, the Soviet Union would be an essential ally in a new cooperative international order. Thus, his spying wasn't "cheating Canada out of anything," just nudging it along the road to that cooperation.[258] Lunan conceded that he had not given "adequate conscious consideration to the question of loyalty." Still, the Soviet Union posed no threat to Canada, and he insisted, "In the front of my mind at all times was the thought that this was an ally." Without saying it in so many words, Lunan was justifying spying as legitimate as long as it was on the behalf of an ally. He did agree with Kellock that in his work for the GRU he put the interests of the Communist Party ahead of his sworn loyalty to Canada.[259] Kellock rephrased Lunan's words, "You thought the Communist party knew better what was in the interests of Canada than Canada herself?" Lunan agreed.[260] Decades later, in a more polemical attempt at self-justification, Lunan told Weisbord, "We accepted the illegal aspect. It's illegal but whose law is it: ... the law of the people who double-cross an ally."[261] In effect, Lunan was claiming that his spying obeyed a higher moral law, that blameworthy Canada must be defied in light of this higher imperative.

Lunan's testimony contained few revelations, but it did incriminate him, Smith, Halperin, and Mazerall, opening the door for Gouzenko's testimony and documents to be used against the four. Through his testimony about Fred Rose, Lunan verged on implicating the Canadian Communist Party in spying. In staccato notes, Malcolm MacDonald's deputy Stephen Holmes tallied up Lunan's score: "Only new details of any significance he has provided are of meeting when he took Smith personally to meet Rogov at clandestine rendezvous in latter's car at night ... He will not admit to being party member nor to attending study groups during clandestine period." Holmes complained that Lunan, impenitent, was still shielding the Communist Party, especially Fred Rose, who "it is clear ... recruited him."[262]

At the end of Lunan's testimony, Kellock advised him that he would be accused of giving the Russians "secret and confidential information" that could harm "the safety and interests of Canada." Lunan was invited to present evidence on his behalf or have counsel appear for him. After consulting with a lawyer, Lunan declined the invitation, and like Mazerall, he was convicted by a jury. On 18 November 1946, Ontario High Court Justice A.C. McRuer sentenced him to five years in the penitentiary. His appeal was dismissed.

6
Moscow Speaks

Following Mackenzie King's statement on 15 February 1946 divulging the Gouzenko affair, the Canadian government knew that subsequent press releases must be "partly governed by public feeling."[1] Moscow complicated this PR strategy on 20 February, before Lunan's testimony, when Soviet Deputy Commissar of Foreign Affairs Solomon Lozovsky (who would eventually be executed in 1952 during Stalin's purge of Jews[2]) invited the Canadian charge d'affaires in Moscow, Leon Mayrand, to a meeting. A day earlier, the Soviet press had published King's release without comment,[3] but when Mayrand arrived, Lozovsky read out a shortened version of a statement to be broadcast in the Soviet media the next day:[4] Moscow had "become aware" that "certain members" of the Soviet military attaché's staff in Ottawa had received information "of a secret nature" from Canadian nationals. However, because of the USSR's "more advanced technical attainment," the information "did not ... present great interest." Moreover, it was already available in published works, such as the "well known brochure of the American J.D. Smyth, "Atomic Energy."[5]

Then Moscow went on the offensive. It was "ridiculous to affirm that delivery of insignificant secret data of this kind could create any threat to the security of Canada." It was disappointing that the Canadian government had inappropriately chosen to sponsor an "unbridled anti-Soviet campaign" in the media, yet the Soviet Union would respond with diplomatic decorum: those "certain members" had been recalled. King must be responding to a UN speech, Moscow suggested, "where Soviet delegate spoke in favour of principle of democracy and independence of small countries" (*sic*).[6] Clearly, this powerful Soviet defence of democracy had caused "unpleasantness ... to Mr. King's friends" (presumably Britain and the US). The speech – about the continuing presence of British troops in Greece and those of the Soviet

Union in Eastern Europe[7] – had been given at a UN assembly in London on 4 February 1946 by Deputy Commissar for Foreign Relations Vyshinsky in response to an earlier speech by British Foreign Secretary Ernst Bevin.[8] Iran had lodged a complaint with the new UN Security Council against Soviet interference in its internal affairs. As soon as the British and Americans proposed an investigation, Moscow responded with a formal complaint to the Security Council that British troops in Greece threatened world peace. Bevin noticed that Moscow had ignored invitations from Britain to discuss Greece and only raised the issue after UN members complained about Russian intervention in Romania, Bulgaria, Poland, or Iran.[9] The Soviets now insinuated that King had become the lackey of his allies, an incorrect (though not impossible) claim. However, the notion that King and Bevin had been blind-sided by a Soviet defence of democracy seemed like the unwitting punchline to a joke – Moscow's tin ear arising out of the fact that at home, in Russia, intimidation could prop up the most inane propaganda.

Two days later, Canada's ambassador to the Soviet Union, Dana Wilgress, offered his take on the Soviet statement. Married to Russian-born Olga Buergin and speaking Russian himself, Wilgress had been a student of the Soviet Union since his appointment as Canadian trade commissioner in Russia at the end of World War I.[10] He found it somewhat absurd that the Soviets wanted to be notified before Canada investigated "grossly improper behaviour of some of its own citizens," behaviour that the Soviets had encouraged. He did, at the same time, understand why the Russians were highly sensitive to anti-Soviet media campaigns: "Conception of a free press is so foreign to the habit of mind of the Soviet people that however feeble this [defence] may sound abroad it doubtless sounds convincing inside Russia." Most importantly, although Moscow complained that an anti-Soviet campaign would discourage normal relations between Canada and the USSR, the acknowledgment of the military attaché's improper conduct" made it unlikely that the Soviets would break diplomatic relations.[11] MI5's Guy Liddell went further, calling Moscow's statement "very naive." By blaming their embassy staff, the Soviets were "sticking out their necks badly since when the Commission's report comes out it will be shown that all activities by their M.A. [military attaché] were directed in detail from Moscow."[12] Indeed, Gouzenko had identified Maj. Gen. Ivan Bolshakov, the GRU chief for the western hemisphere, as "the Director"[13] who in the GRU documents had sent detailed telegrams from Moscow and had told Zabotin how to handle the Canadian agents.[14] However, without the full report of the inquiry (still months away) to provide a context, the immediate release of the Zabotin-Bolshakov cables (replete with code names and GRU nomenclature) would have provoked wild speculations in the public square.

Wilgress suggested responding to the Moscow statement later on,[15] but Ottawa wanted to remain silent, to treat the matter "as essentially domestic house-keeping."[16] From the beginning of the inquiry, King had insisted that the investigation was *sub judice*: Ottawa couldn't speak even if it wanted to. This wishful thinking would last all of three days. In the meantime, the domestic and international press was in an uproar, and reports from Canadian embassies in London, Paris, and Washington on the reception of Moscow's statement funnelled that uproar directly to King, Norman Robertson, the Justice Department, the RCMP, and the inquiry commissioners.[17]

From Britain, High Commissioner Vincent Massey reported that Moscow's statement was received by the British press with "virtually no sympathy."[18] A.J. Cummings, political editor of the liberal *News Chronicle*[19] and author of the very popular "Spotlight on Politics" column,[20] had previously blamed the Allies' atomic secrecy, but now he dismissed the Soviet statement as "exceedingly clumsy and its accusations childish," little more than a "gratuitous attack upon the Canadian government."[21] In a similar vein, the mass circulation *Daily Telegraph* attributed the statement to "a state of mind which appears fantastic."[22] Both Labour's *Daily Herald* and the liberal *Manchester Guardian* considered spying as a routine activity of governments but condemned Moscow's excuses. The *Daily Herald*, somewhat parochially, saw "violent anti-British propaganda,"[23] while the *Guardian* spoke condescendingly about an "attack of spy fever" surging in Canada and the US, but added that the Soviet statement just perpetuated the viral contagion.[24] Only the Communist *Daily Worker* liked the Soviet statement: Moscow had "demolished Mr. King's effort to raise Goebbel's ghost. Mr. King's intention was to drag a reluctant United States into an anti-Soviet bloc which Britain was organizing."[25]

Despite the media attention, a two-day-long foreign policy debate in the British House of Commons apparently saw MPs making only "oblique" reference to Canadian developments,[26] leading Massey to wonder if Foreign Secretary Bevin and Anthony Eden, deputy leader of the opposition Conservatives, had actually read the Soviet statement and *Pravda*'s commentary. Massey attributed the "reticence" to the continuing influence of the 1924 "Zinoviev letter," in which a forged Comintern (Russian) directive urged the Communist Party of Great Britain into subversive activities as preparation for a revolution.[27] Could the Gouzenko affair be a similar Red Scare fraud? According to Massey, some Britons, failing to differentiate much between Canada and the

US, saw merely Canadian domestic politics at work. For example, *The Economist* "indirectly" associated the Gouzenko affair with "such activities as the Dies Committee" (a precursor to HUAC) in the US.[28] Given this complicated field, Massey believed that even the British press was following Bevin's example: "do nothing which might make the present breach with Russia irreparable."[29]

In France, the "right-wing" press was "wholly anti-Soviet," Ambassador Georges Vanier reported. *La Nation* regarded the Moscow statement as "an admission of guilt," while the "rabidly anti-Communist" *L'Ordre* printed a "cartoon of Truman and Stalin with latter hiding a bomb behind his back,"[30] reversing the actual state of affairs (though, of course, Stalin desperately wanted whatever was behind Truman's back). *L'Epoque*, meanwhile, published an unsubstantiated and inflammatory report that Québec premier Maurice Duplessis had "revealed" that during the war, under the guise of Resistance activities, Canadian- and American-based Soviet agents had received "directives from the French Communist Party."[31] On the other hand, an editorial in the Communist-affiliated *L'Humanité* treated Gouzenko's revelations as a Red Scare that, much like the Zinoviev letter, intended to undo the "good work done by the USSR at U.N.O." *L'Humanité* praised Moscow for resisting anti-Sovietism in Canada, "un des pays les plus réactionnaire de l'Empire Britannique où le Pétainisme règne à l'état larve" (one of the most reactionary countries of the British Empire where Pétainisme exists in larval form).[32] In more measured tones and with less teeth-gnashing than at the ends of the political spectrum, the socialist *Le Populaire* carried the headline "Moscou reconnait les faits et s'explique" (Moscow admits the facts and explains itself), and *Paris Matin* displayed "L'U.R.S.S. desavoue ses agents au Canada" (The USSR disavows its agents in Canada).[33]

Most interesting was Vanier's news from the French Resistance newspaper *Combat*, where Albert Camus was editor-in-chief.[34] Its New York correspondent P.F. Carus wrote that since September relations between Britain, the US, and the Soviet Union had been determined by "the Canadian affair," and that Gouzenko's revelations had convinced the US to keep the atomic bomb information secret, but that "Washington ne soutiendrait pas Ottawa" (Washington isn't supporting Ottawa): deciding that good relations with Moscow trumped Gouzenko, US Secretary of State James Byrnes had, without consulting London, initiated the December 1945 Moscow Conference.[35] *Combat* borrowed from Soviet propaganda, claiming that former ambassador Zarubin had shown Byrnes "information claiming provocation by Intelligence Service [i.e., the RCMP] was behind affair." Later, in response to the final report of the inquiry Moscow would continue to make the veiled charge that Gouzenko was a tool of the RCMP.[36]

Through *Pravda, Izvestia,* and the *New Times,* Moscow followed up its 20 February statement with a campaign to cast the Gouzenko revelations as a London-inspired anti-Soviet crusade. A 21 February editorial in *Pravda,* entitled "King as Bevin's Assistant," continued the Soviet attempt to dismiss King's 15 February statement as simply a "manoeuvre to assist British Foreign Minister [Bevin] who has put his government in very awkward position as a result of his attitude at London session of U.N.O."[37] *Izvestia* toed the same line, calling the Gouzenko revelations a failed "retaliation for reverses suffered" by Bevin and King "at hands of Soviet delegates to UNO."[38] If the issue arose in September, why, less than two weeks after the UNO meetings, had King suddenly acted? Either the Soviets had already dealt with the matter, *Pravda* said, or King wanted to negotiate with the Soviets. Clearly, faced with Bevin's scandalous failure and the great Soviet moral victory at the UN, King had been forced to change his tune.[39]

Moscow's *New Times,* meanwhile, asserted that the Gouzenko affair was paltry, but then leapt into massive hyperbole. Using a Russian expression that suggests a crude frame-up, the *New Times* said that King's "manoeuvre was so clearly stitched with *white thread* that the *Chicago Sun* has justly compared it to the Reichstag fire."[40] In a more effective commentary, entitled "Who is Mackenzie King," the *New Times* alleged that despite heading the Liberal Party, King had not "displayed ... liberalism in his post of Prime Minister." King-led governments had persecuted workers' organizations "and even passed a special decree declaring Communists outlaws." At the same time, "Fascist organizations ... flourished on Canadian soil under his protection": the "'Jeunesses Patriotes,' 'Parti National Social-Chretien' and 'Casques d'Acier' ... became notorious for their attacks on libraries and schools by burning, in public, progressive literature."[41] Of course, the *New Times* made no mention that many Canadian fascists, including PNSC founder Adrian Arcand, had been investigated and interned by the King government in 1940 under the Defence of Canada Regulations.[42] King, the *New Times* continued, had been "a fierce supporter of the [British] policy of appeasement which was planned to direct Hitler's aggression against the Soviet Union,"[43] so he was "an exactly suitable man for the next anti-Soviet campaign." Nevertheless, trying its best to relegate Gouzenko to the past, the *New Times* announced that the campaign had failed.[44]

In the US, the Canadian embassy reported that the "spy case was blown wide open again" by the Moscow statement. The *Times-Herald* headline "screamed … Russia Rebukes Canada for Atom." While the *New York Times* and *Washington Post* were more restrained, a *Philadelphia Inquirer* story carried a two-inch-tall headline, "Reds Admit Getting Canadian Secrets."[45] The anti-fascist and liberal *PM* continued its earlier line, complaining that Mackenzie King's "retreat into absolute silence" after 15 February encouraged … the wildest possible rumors" and "Red-baiting."[46] The Canadian embassy's analyst thought the Communist *Daily Worker's* headline "USSR Lashes 'Unfriendly' Act by Canada" captured the essence of even a United Press story,[47] since the UP story reported the Moscow statement without context or commentary except in the headline, "Reds Admit Securing Secret Data."[48] The *Daily Worker* also ran a cartoon depicting three perplexed Canadian mandarins sitting at a table, commiserating, "All right, they got our 'secrets,' but what makes me wild is their admitting it and telling us our 'secrets' are valueless!"[49] This belittling of the crimes occasionally appeared in the mainstream press too.

As one might expect, however, most American newspapers met Moscow's claims against King and the Canadian government with disbelief and ridicule. The *New York Times* "dismissed as fantastic" Moscow's claims that King was retaliating against the Soviet defence of democracy at the UNO. The *Times* correspondent in Ottawa, P.J. Philip, commended both King for his "unhurried wisdom" and Canada for "neither criticizing nor molesting the Soviet agents who had received information."[50] "Transparent nonsense," the *Washington Evening Star* called Moscow's claims. *The Star* asserted that Canada had no obligation to consult a foreign government suspected of spying on it, and that Canada had the right to detain any Canadian who was involved.[51] Punning ironically on Marxist economics, The *Cleveland Plain Dealer* said the Russians wanted "to confuse the issue and make capital out of it." The *Atlanta Journal* contrasted the Soviet "diatribe" with Canadian restraint, while other mass circulation dailies – *Chicago Daily News*, *Louisville Courier-Journal*, and *Baltimore Sun* – cast Moscow's attacks on Canada as "vitriolic," "preposterous," "immature," or "childish."[52] Even the militantly liberal *New Republic* rejected Moscow's assertion that the Gouzenko investigation was an anti-Soviet ruse. Behind the spy scare and all the posturing lay the real reason: "The Atomic-Arms Race is under way … Each day that it continues uncontrolled it gathers speed, bringing us closer to war."[53] The strongest denunciation of the Moscow statement came from the celebrated American journalist Dorothy Thompson, the first American journalist to be expelled from Germany for her anti-Nazi articles. The Kremlin's assaults on Canada and Mackenzie King, Thompson charged, constituted a form of "political blackmail." Moscow, like Hitler in the 1930s, was employing the "Big Lie" tactic. "By a miraculous abracadabra, which, as put forth in Soviet house organs, it is reprinted with a straight face in our own papers, Canada, not the Soviet Government, becomes the offender." The only defence against this was "the truth freely stated."[54]

Shortly after the release of the Moscow statement, Ambassador Wilgress had commented that Moscow's attempt to shape worldwide public opinion would have been more effective if it had avoided attacks on the Canadian government.[55] The newspaper evidence flowing from Canadian embassies in London, France, and the US to Ottawa suggests that he was right. Very soon, the Soviet overreach would contribute to Canada's decision to release an interim report on the Gouzenko inquiry, a report that would garner world-wide attention and leave the Moscow statement in tatters.

7
Accountability Crisis

20 February–3 March 1946

The storm of controversy generated by Mackenzie King's 15 February statement and the Soviets' 20 February response quickly became a PR headache. After King's statement, the blurry outlines of his Gouzenko policy came into clearer public focus, and some observers began to see the dark machinations of a Star Chamber. Because aspects of the policy challenged several basic norms of a democratic liberal order, many calls came, especially from the press and the suspects' families' lawyers, for the Liberal government to justify itself. What had been a security and intelligence crisis began to raise all sorts of questions about accountability. King's communications strategy therefore evolved from silence to piecemeal disclosure – but who should speak for the government? King shifted the responsibility for defending his Gouzenko policy to the commissioners and their lawyers, nudging them into the public sphere. A day after Moscow's media release and King's insistence that the government wouldn't respond, his foot soldiers along with the commission lawyers were drafting a statement to the press, but only, they said, about procedure.[1]

On 23 February, E.K. Williams and Gérald Fauteux issued a statement justifying the pre-inquiry methods – arrest, detain, interrogate. It was a bit of Mackenzie King sleight-of-hand to fend off the press. Since its "official" recipient was Justice Minister Louis St. Laurent, the statement amounted to the government handing its talking points to commission lawyers, who then mouthed them back to the government. Williams and Fauteux, technically legal counsel for what should have been a strictly independent royal commission, were transformed into publicists for an unpopular government policy. The statement defended the use of PC 6444 to detain and interrogate the suspects and called the move a success. The detention of "certain persons" had produced "a considerable amount of additional evidence, oral and documentary" confirming "the serious nature of [Gouzenko's] disclosures on which (orders for) interrogations were based." So far, thirteen people had been detained and interrogated "under PC 6444 dated the 6th of October 1945 and passed under the Provisions of the War Measures Act and continued under the Provisions of the TPA 1945."[2] However, Williams and Fauteux were not legal counsel to Mackenzie King or servants of the minister of justice: the Royal Commission that they served operated under PC 411, which did not rely in any way on either the War Measures Act or the TPA. It was not the commission but the detentions and the RCMP interrogations that, relying on PC 6444, occurred under those two acts.

Now, in the Canadian press, speculation gave way to questions, criticisms, and demands for government accountability, particularly about the condition of the suspects. Lawyers retained by family members raised the alarm that the state was trampling on fundamental rights. Ottawa lawyer H.P. Hill KC, retained "by the families of two civil servants in custody," protested the barring of legal advice to the suspects as "an extraordinary limitation of the principles of British justice."[3] For *habeas corpus*, the lawyer needed to consult with the client, but his clients had lost their rights: "No instructions can be given which would lead to their release." Hill complained that the Kellock-Taschereau Commission didn't seem to "trust the members of the local bar to keep silent about information given them by their client."[4] This and other affronts to the legal community were taken up by Ottawa lawyer Redmond Quain, who prepared a resolution to present to the Carlton County Bar Association.[5]

A.W. Beament appeared at a press conference, announcing that he represented David Shugar, detained at Rockcliffe, and that to detain people "incommunicado" was "not necessary for the legitimate use of police power."[6] Despite requests, neither Beament nor Shugar's wife had been allowed to see Shugar. Grace Shugar had written to the prime minister in protest, but he hadn't even acknowledged receiving her letter. At the same time, her husband had written her a letter, saying that the RCMP had interrogated him several times: "one is guilty here of whatever you're accused of," he wrote, "and if one doesn't agree to that, why, back to the guard room."[7]

On 25 February 1946, in an editorial salvo almost certainly written by editor-in-chief A.A. McIntosh, the *Globe and Mail* cast the Kellock-Taschereau Commission as a historic abuse of power by the state. Of the nameless suspects, McIntosh wrote, "Harsh as it may seem, the cold facts are that they have been detained under tactics suggestive of a totalitarian state." The state wouldn't say who was in detention or for how long. Without the right to *habeas corpus*, their detention could be endless. If not for the "gravity of it all, including Russia's admission of espionage on Canadian soil," McIntosh observed, "such methods could not be tolerated." PC 6444 was "a very vicious instrument," and though its use "must be suffered at this time," he wanted to hear "the fullest justification of its use."[8] Two days later, British diplomat Stephen Holmes reported that "lack of official information has caused Canadian press to turn its attention to question of rights and civil liberties of detainees," and he gave London a calibrated account of the lawyers' protests. He referred to lawyers (almost certainly Hill and Beament) "attacking Department of Justice for methods used," and he highlighted editorial comment about "'Gestapo' methods." Nevertheless, he hoped that an interim report and the release by Justice Minister St. Laurent of the "complete text of Order-in-Council (PC 6444)" might mitigate criticism of the government's actions.[9]

He was wrong. The *Ottawa Journal*, for example, found it extraordinary that during peace time PC 6444 could allow a minister to detain anybody and to decide the conditions and length of the incarceration: "13 individuals are held without charge, without hearing, denied visits from their families or consultation with such counsel as their families may engage. For them the Magna Charta does not exist; there is no such thing as *habeas corpus*." The *Journal* also touched on the search-and-seizure powers conferred under PC 6444. Even during the war, "if there had been uncovered a plot by Canadian citizens to supply information to Germany, Italy or Japan" the minister wouldn't have had greater powers. With the RCMP likely guiding the minister, did we really want "so much secret power ... in the hands of any police force or police official, or any cabinet minister"?[10] In his overview of editorial commentary, Stephen Holmes concluded that the release of the orders-in-council had done nothing to relieve "pressure of subject of civil liberties in Canadian press."[11]

Even though pragmatism and concerns about the state of his political capital often overrode his liberal ideals, King felt the weight of the criticisms. Reading the newspapers on 27 February, he was "much annoyed and distressed to find that no answer had gone to the woman [Grace Shugar] who had written to me about her husband being confined." King had handed the letter to Norman Robertson four days earlier with instructions that it be responded to "immediately." Worrying about the public's "general impression," King privately agreed that it was "wrong that those suspected should be detained indefinitely." Injecting himself into what was supposed to be an independent royal commission, King wanted Robertson to tell Williams and Fauteux and judges Kellock and Taschereau to shorten the inquiry and give the suspects back their legal rights. Sounding much like his critics, King lamented, "The whole proceedings are far too much like those of Russia itself."[12]

Of course, King's new guidance to the Kellock-Taschereau Commission posed an immediate threat to the commission's independence. Suddenly, his political agenda became the driving force for the inquiry's schedule and conduct. Late on 28 February, Williams and Fauteux met with King to develop a strategy to calm his anxieties. They offered King an "interim report" from the commissioners. It would be shown to cabinet on Saturday 2 March and released through the House of Commons on Monday. The report would send a volley at the Soviet statement of 20 February by detailing Soviet spying, listing the tasks given to GRU chief Zabotin by Moscow and the names of embassy personnel involved in the spying. It would also identify the areas of the Canadian government penetrated by Soviet espionage and announce that Woikin, Willsher, Mazerall, and Lunan had acted as Russian agents. By describing their espionage activities, the report would hopefully justify the King government's policy. Its release would coincide with the releases of Woikin, Willsher, Mazerall, and Lunan from detention under PC 6444 and their immediate arrest on criminal charges issued by the attorney general of Ontario. Moving four suspects to a regular court might also give the government some credit for heading back into normal court procedures and protections. The inclusion of Gordon Lunan in this theatre – on 28 February he was still a witness before the inquiry – depended on whether he sought legal counsel to address the inquiry's findings against him. He didn't.[13]

When cabinet examined the plan, Finance Minister J.L. Ilsley "asked a question as to whether publication of the report in advance of trial might not be in the nature of judgment in advance." King conceded that "there might be criticism on this score."[14] Earlier, on 15 February King had affirmed that until it was complete the Kellock-Taschereau Commission would remain "*sub judice*," which implied a silence running not only through the commission, but also through any subsequent proceedings in regular courts. As late as 19 February King, although he wanted to show that "the government has been fully justified in every step it has taken," said that publication of the evidence gathered by the inquiry couldn't happen with prosecutions "pending."[15] But in the *First Interim Report*, political imperatives and King's need for shelter from withering criticism would push aside the need to assure a fair trial for the suspects.

No royal commission's terms of reference prior to 1946 explicitly linked the commission's work to specific indictable offences. But since PC 411 referred directly to offences against the Official Secrets Act, the Kellock-Taschereau Commission took on a robust quasi-judicial character. As well, no Canadian statute required King to give Parliament a copy of the commission's report, yet the release of such reports had become common practice.[16] There was a legal reason for doing so. Canada had followed the British when, in 1840, The Parliamentary Papers Act was adopted to protect newspapers broadcasting commission reports. No criminal or civil proceeding could make news organizations liable for publishing papers printed by Parliament.[17] All legal responsibility lay on the Crown for the reports' contents. By releasing the report through Parliament, King would now invite the entire world to ignore the *sub judice* nature of the inquiry's findings, and even though technically he couldn't table the report in front of Parliament (since Parliament wasn't in session), he could maintain that fiction for a few days with little risk until Parliament resumed. For King, public discussion of the security threat trumped the obligation of the Liberal government to respect the courts and protect the defendants.

Of course, in his political calculations Mackenzie King needed to address international considerations too. For MI5 and British security officials, any release of a report filled with details about Soviet espionage in Canada would directly affect their handling of Alan Nunn May. A public report could be a red flag for him. The British had gone to lengths to collaborate with Canada on Nunn May, but in February Canada's appointment of the inquiry had forced MI5 to open an offensive against him. An initial interview went nowhere, and then, during a second interview on 20 February, he admitted giving the Russians samples of uranium and a report on atomic energy, and he signed a statement detailing his involvement with Soviet spying in Canada.[18] Remarkably, he was still left at liberty, because the question of whether he should be prosecuted in Britain or Canada remained unresolved. Since he had offended the official secrets acts of both countries, who should arrest him? At Canada's request, the British agreed to do the prosecuting.

May's liberty continued also because of another fact, embarrassing for Canada: his arrest would be the outcome of a normal British police investigation, while Canada, having pounded its suspects with the War Measures Act's draconian powers, hadn't delivered a single prosecution. Stephen Holmes relayed Canada's embarrassment to his superiors and supported Norman Robertson's proposal that action against Nunn May should only happen with the release of the *Interim Report* and the arrests of Woikin, Willsher, Mazerall, and Lunan.[19] Yet Nunn May's continued freedom – post-confession – posed a serious problem. How could British authorities let a self-confessed spy of such importance run at liberty? On 1 March, Undersecretary of State Orme Sargent told Holmes that "Primrose [Nunn May] cannot be left at liberty without risk of serious criticism in view of gravity of his admissions."[20] The plan was to arrest him "about 6 March" and to charge him under Britain's Official Secrets Act. In order to keep the Nunn May case under wraps until the Canadian inquiry could deliver Canadian prosecutions, the British director of public prosecutions would seek a remand, letting weeks pass before putting Nunn May on trial.[21]

Although the British had compromised, Canadian reciprocity – a central King policy since the beginning of the Gouzenko affair – now fell victim to the Liberals' PR woes. Canada's sudden decision to release a report on 4 March and announce the arrest of Canadians for spying unsettled the British plans, plans that had been made specifically to accommodate Canada. Canada's decision threatened to send Nunn May on a fast track to Moscow before he could be apprehended.

Would Canada shift the release date for the *First Interim Report*? No. Faced with fierce press criticism of his government's handling of the Gouzenko investigation, King dismissed the need for coordinated action with the British. Stephen Holmes told London that he saw no chance of persuading the Canadians to postpone the release of the *Interim Report*. He explained that King was fully aware of the difficulties he was creating but considered them secondary to the "urgent need … for corrective" to the "developing agitation" in Canada.[22] Again, MI5 had little choice but to change its plans, and on 4 March Nunn May was arrested.[23]

In addition to the *Interim Report*'s timing, the British struggled to get the Canadians to heed their concerns about its contents. Because Kathleen Willsher was a British national and an employee of the British government, London expected Ottawa to be open to consultation on her case. Again, Canadian domestic concerns trumped UK–Canadian collegiality. MI6's William Stephenson reluctantly told London, "Willsher was detained with UK authority. She is caught up in machinery of Commission and cannot now be SEGREGATED."[24] In fact, however, Wilshire's nationality counted *against* her. From King's perspective, it was important to keep Willsher in the line-up of spies in order to demonstrate that it wasn't just Canadians who could be lured by the Soviets. King confided to his diary that he hadn't complied with London's wish to "hold the announcement re Miss Willsher and Primrose until Wednesday." "It was important," King reflected, "that the public should see that British servants and scientists were involved and that the whole burden was not on the shoulders of the Canadian government in relation to its own civil servants." He was also pleased that the *Report* would disclose that "Russian espionage was not restricted to Canada or Britain but extended also to … the US."[25] King's determination to end his government's silence on Soviet espionage would also scotch British prime minister Attlee's strategy of avoiding questions about similar espionage in Britain. As late as 19 February, Attlee had parried Conservative Opposition MP Anthony Eden's questions about the Gouzenko affair by saying that the investigation was *sub judice* in Canada.[26]

In one matter, at least, the British were able to secure Canada's cooperation: William Stephenson persuaded the Canadians to scrub the Nunn May and atomic references from the *Interim Report*. Stephenson had explained to London that the interim report was "now being enlarged widely in scope in order that it may have strong impact." The Canadians wanted "to mention in their report leakage repeat leakage of atomic information."[27] For King, even though Nunn May hadn't yet been arrested, his inclusion in the report would, like Willsher's arrest, place Canadian treachery in a broader context. Although the British had reasonable grounds to exclude Nunn May from the *Interim Report,* they couldn't press the argument too vigorously. In late February Britain occupied a vulnerable position in post-war financial relations with Canada. Negotiators, including King and St. Laurent, had been discussing Canadian financial aid to lessen Britain's post-war debts. Britain hoped that Canada would forgive an outstanding British debt of $425 million incurred under the Commonwealth Air Training Plan and grant an interest-free loan of an additional $1.25 billion.[28] These negotiations reached a decisive point on the same weekend that King decided to issue the *Interim Report*. Holmes and Stephenson therefore cautioned London against a too-vigorous campaign to alter the Canadian report.[29] Nevertheless, in the end Stephenson was able to steer the Canadians away from Nunn May and the bomb: "I was able with assistance counsel to dissuade them" (*sic*).[30]

Even the US was forced to bend to Mackenzie King's will. US secretary of state James Byrnes, given a copy of the text before its release, immediately recognized its troubling import. He worried that Russia, confronted about its refusal to withdraw its troops from Iran, confronted about its troops in Manchuria, now potentially confronted by the *Interim Report,* would interpret this as "piling on," and he urged the Canadians to release only an abstract instead. But Canadian ambassador to the US Lester Pearson refused Byrnes's request to press such considerations on King.[31] Such tiptoeing around the Soviets wouldn't serve the prime minister's domestic or international political purposes.

Ultimately, it wasn't British or American priorities but a Canadian one – the domestic accountability crisis – that determined the release of the *First Interim Report*. If the King government's plan to shroud the Kellock-Taschereau Commission in secrecy had invited a wave of criticism, the *First Interim Report* gave King an opportunity to defend his government's dramatic action and to prove that Soviet spying wasn't just a Canadian problem.

8
The First Interim Report

4–8 March 1946

The *First Interim Report* was delivered to the public at noon on 4 March 1946.[1] At the same time, Emma Woikin, Kathleen Willsher, Ned Mazerall, and Gordon Lunan were released from detention under PC 6444, then immediately arrested on charges of offending against the Official Secrets Act and engaging in a conspiracy under the Criminal Code. They were taken to a special session of the Ottawa Police Court, where Magistrate Glenn Strike remanded them without bail until 11 March, and they walked down the steps in the central Ottawa police station to their temporary cells in the basement.[2]

Concerned that the prosecution of the four might touch on aspects of the investigation still before the inquiry, E.K. Williams pressed Justice Minister St. Laurent to ask the Ontario attorney general to hold the trials in camera. Malcolm MacDonald predicted that "such procedure will inevitably raise storm of protest from lawyers and also from press who will see themselves done out of some first-class copy particularly if Corby's [Gouzenko's] testimony were required."[3] However, St. Laurent, fed up with public criticism, categorically refused. Williams did get some satisfaction – the cases were remanded until the commissioners' work would be mostly complete.[4]

King, meanwhile, envisioned the release of the *First Interim Report* as a sacred public duty and as a sign of his centrality in world affairs: "It is a moment in the history of international relations, the importance and evidence of which cannot be overemphasized. I am only too conscious of the great gravity of the whole situation and of the tremendous responsibility that has come on my shoulders without wish or desire on my part but solely discharge [*sic*] of my public duties at a moment when I should have been happy to have been relieved of them altogether."[5]

King's grandiose pretentions weren't completely off the mark. The *First Interim Report*'s arrival in the public sphere was indeed a historical event. No longer could the "Big Three" of Britain, the US, and the Soviet Union pretend an image of unity. What Orwell, already in October 1945, had called the "Cold War" – "a peace with no peace" – the *Interim Report* exposed: a condition that would characterize relations between the Soviet Union and its former allies for decades.[6] A day after the report was released, Winston Churchill delivered his famous convocation address at Westminster College in Fulton, Missouri, metaphorically characterizing the Soviets' tighter and tighter control of Eastern Europe: "from Stettin in the Baltic to Trieste in the Adriatic, an iron curtain has descended across the Continent."[7] Through the summer and fall of 1945, Stalin, aware that Western governments had wedded themselves to post-war conciliation with Moscow, pushed ahead with his scheme to put Central and Eastern Europe under Soviet tutelage. Churchill, no longer prime minister of Great Britain but ever the realist in international affairs, announced publicly in March 1946 that the hope of a durable new order imagined by the West was a delusion. His dark overture announced the arrival of the Cold War.

The *Interim Report* repeated the statement released by King on 15 February 1946 that the Soviet Union had recruited and developed Canadian agents to obtain secret information from the Canadian government and the British high commissioner. The *Report* disclosed that "a former employee of the Russian Embassy at Ottawa, a cipher clerk of the Military Attaché," had produced authentic documents revealing the organizational structure of Soviet espionage.[8] Clearly showing that these clandestine networks operated under Moscow's control, the *Report* not only listed the Canadian targets of Soviet espionage given to Zabotin by the "Director," Maj. Gen. Ivan Bolshakov in Moscow, but also the names and titles of the embassy's Soviet spymaster Col. Zabotin and his main espionage associates, including Chief Assistant Military Attaché Lt. Col. Motinov, Assistant Military Attaché for Air Lt. Col. Rogov, subordinate of the Embassy Commercial Counsellor Maj. Sokolov, and Zabotin's Secretary Lt. Angelov. They carried out their activities in secret, their true identities obscured by "under-cover names." The *Report* explained that the Soviet Embassy kept "dossiers" on the "Canadian agents," listing the term of service for each as "length of time in net."

Soviet Military Intelligence Director for the Western Hemisphere Bolshakov's military and scientific expertise appeared throughout the list of GRU targets. The marching orders given to Canadian agents included demands for information on the materials, technological processes, and drawings required for the production of an atomic bomb; on the processing of uranium; on the electro-projector of the "V" bomb; on the production of other explosives and chemicals; on the transfer of the American troops (Infantry, Armoured, Tank) from Europe to the US and the Pacific; on telegrams going to and from the Department of External Affairs and the UK high commissioner; on NRC personnel and research programs; and more. The Soviets even wanted samples of uranium-235 and copies of all the documents held in the NRC library.[9] In climactic fashion, the *Interim Report* revealed who had leaked what information. Emma Woikin had given the Soviet embassy the contents of secret telegrams from the Department of External Affairs; Canadian army captain Gordon Lunan, working for the Soviet Lt. Col. Rogov, had gotten from Ned Mazerall, an engineer, two secret NRC reports on radar; Kathleen Willsher had disclosed secret documents from the UK high commissioner. "Many other agents were active," the *Report* concluded, so there was still much work to do.[10]

On the morning after the *Interim Report*'s release, Mackenzie King was "relieved to see from editorial comment ... that the public were now getting some real impression of the seriousness of the investigations and, with it, justification for the government's action."[11] The *Globe and Mail*, in an editorial titled "Russia Indicted," applauded the *Interim Report* for the clarity with which it showed a "network of undercover agents." Contrary to Soviet claims, "this nefarious scheme ... was organized under instructions from Moscow." Lunan came in for special attention: "Reports and instructions ... were relayed by this officer, for whom the possession of the King's commission was ... no bar to disloyalty." The *Globe* blamed "confused political beliefs and twisted values."[12]

Out west, under the heading "Our House Cleaning," the liberal *Winnipeg Free Press* was pleased that the *First Interim Report* would "put a stop to ... the absurd rumors that have been circulating and doing untold harm to many innocent reputations." And it would also "go a long way to justify the extraordinary measures taken by the Government in effecting arrests and holding the prisoners incommunicado." As King had hoped, the *Free Press* applauded the charges laid, "proof" that the government was returning "with all possible speed ... to the normal constitutional safeguards erected for the individual against the power of the state." At the same time, the suspects' actions constituted "vicious treason and moreover, treason committed in time of war," attacking "the safety of the state."[13]

In the US, the release of a report on Soviet espionage in Canada was an unlikely candidate to compete for coverage with Churchill's "iron curtain" speech, yet the *New York Times* gave similar and extended coverage to these linked events, promoting both to the front page,[14] printing the entire texts of both, and adding editorials praising both. The *Times* noted the "confidential information on the atom bomb, radar, and electronic shell fuses" leaked to the Soviets, and described the *Report* as "judicial and restrained." Contrary to Moscow's grievance that the Canadian investigation was an "unfriendly" act, "If unfriendly acts were committed, it was Soviet agents that committed them, not the Canadian government."[15]

The *First Interim Report* did garner some good will and, for at least a day, gave the King government relief from press criticism. The next day, however, after he had celebrated the indictment of the Soviet Union, the *Globe and Mail*'s A.A. McIntosh returned to his civil libertarian discourse to denounce the "totalitarian procedure" that the Liberal government had used. Why couldn't Canada have copied Britain's handling of Nunn May? There, authorities simply went to the University of London, arrested Nunn May, and charged him with violating the Official Secrets Act. No need to detain him incommunicado and deny him legal counsel as Canadian authorities did with their suspects. Unaware of the limits of hearsay evidence, McIntosh charged that even if the government needed War Measures Act powers, nothing in the *Interim Report* justified "the adoption of so vicious an instrument."

Likewise, McIntosh dismissed the *Interim Report*'s assertion that the suspects were offered legal counsel and an opportunity to present evidence: "Everything," he aptly observed, "depends upon when that opportunity was given ... It is not the custom of British justice to sweat a 'conviction' out of a suspected person before turning him over to his defender." Paraphrasing Locke, McIntosh granted that there were times when the security of the state required the subordination of individual rights, but this did not give licence to a government "to suspend all the judicial safeguards." He even invoked Churchill's Fulton Missouri speech, not for the descending iron curtain but for his reference to "the title deeds of freedom, which should lie in every cottage home." According to McIntosh, "there must be extremely grave reasons for denying to any cottager the fundamental right which independent justice should guarantee." Canadians should demand not only "the proof to convict the Soviet agents" but also "evidence to vindicate the King government."[16]

American reaction to the *Interim Report* stressed Moscow's direct role in the spying, the Canadian response, and the collateral damage to the US.[17] Except occasionally, as in the *Washington Post*, the headlines and articles focused on the results, not the process: "Canada Says Spies

Acted on Moscow Orders" (*New York Times*); "Canada Says Reds Spied on United States" (*Philadelphia Inquirer*); "Russia Spied on United States Army, Stole Secrets, Canada Reveals" (*Port Huron Michigan Times Herald*); and, under three-inch black-and-red headlines, "Canada Premier Charges: Moscow Sought United States Military Secrets" (*New York Journal-American*).[18] The *New York Herald Tribune*, at the time a newspaper equal to the *New York Times* in status,[19] pointed out (as Guy Liddell had expected) that evidence of Moscow's direction contradicted Soviet assertions that only low-level embassy personnel were involved.[20] Widely influential radio commentator Gabriel Heatter said the same.[21] H.V. Kaltenborn, in an ominous echo of the start of World War II, insisted, "We can't preserve peace by appeasing Stalin." The West had been generous to the Soviet Union but, Kaltenborn complained, "She bribes Canadians to get more."[22] Of course, there was very little evidence that bribery played a role, except perhaps in Lunan's case. Somewhat melodramatically, the *Washington Post* called the *First Interim Report* an "implicit confession that the Canadian Government is no longer sure of the loyalty of its most trusted servants," but the *Post* also, and more convincingly, found the "extra constitutional powers of search, seizure, also, imprisonment" disturbing. Do we dare "even for the sake of keeping our secrets, trust any government with such powers?"[23]

But the social imaginary was changing. *The Observer*'s Dorothy Thompson, who placed Gouzenko in dialogue with Churchill, gave a perceptive account of the evolution of American public opinion on East–West relations in early 1946. She asserted that "public opinion in America was not prepared" for Churchill's dramatic pronouncement on the state of the world. People "only vaguely apprehended" the "extent of the deterioration in the international situation." The reception of Churchill's speech was shaped by a mixture of "hope, disillusionment, doubt, inadequacy of information and partisan division," and the American press tended to play down alarming facts." In these ambivalent circumstances, the speech had been met with "fury from the Left." The Left, Thompson judged, linked the Gouzenko crisis with what the *Daily Worker* termed Churchill's proposal for "an Anglo-American war machine to rule the world," so the "grotesque spy scares created by the Canadian lie-factories" must be "part of the same preparation." "The Middle and the Right," on the other hand, listened to Churchill with cautious sympathy.[24] For Thompson and many others, the debate in the American media about Moscow's spying, set alongside the Kremlin's focus on American military capacity, was returning the West to an earlier ideological-battle mindset that had been dissipating, turning the Soviets from a wartime ally into a Cold War combatant. And if the war had given Americans confidence, these new developments couldn't help but undermine that.

In France, Georges Vanier reported that the "Right Wing and Centre press (*Le pays, L'Epoque, Le Figaro, Combat*)" was emphasizing "that agents acted on Moscow instructions and that Moscow now stands accused." The headline in *Le Figaro* was typical: "Le bureau d'espions recevait ses ordres de l'Ambassade Sovietique." *L'Ordre*'s headline announced, "Mackenzie King accuse Moscou." The *Paris Daily Mail* covered the *Report* in the most detail, under the headline "Moscow Gave Orders to A-Bomb Spies."[25] But, like the British *Daily Worker*,[26] the Communist papers in France – *L'Humanité* and *Franc-Tireur* – ignored the story.[27] Of the main Communist papers, only the American *Daily Worker* took on the *First Interim Report*, announcing, the "anti-Soviet scare is revived." It was "the anti-Soviet speeches of Secretary of State James F. Byrnes and Senator Arthur Vandenburg" that encouraged Ottawa in this nefarious campaign.[28] *The Daily Worker* managed to transform Moscow's institutional masterminding into the moral failing of a single individual, so that, according to *The Daily Worker*'s interpretation of the *Interim Report*, it was an "unnamed Soviet citizen" in Moscow who directed the "alleged" ring.[29]

In Britain, the *Manchester Guardian* provided another striking illustration of the transition in the social imaginary. The *Guardian* had downplayed King's 15 February announcement as a case of "spy fever." Now, with the *First Interim Report* exposing at least four spies, the Soviet embassy's role, and Moscow's masterminding, the traditionally left-leaning and very influential *Guardian* published what Vincent Massey described as a "bitter editorial" attacking the Soviet Union and inviting scrutiny of Western apologists for Soviet espionage. *Guardian* editor A.P. Wadsworth[30] pointed out that the *Interim Report* disclosed much more in the Canadian spy story than Moscow "would like us to believe." Moscow was animated by more than "scientific curiosity," since it asked about "the disposition of her Allies' troops." Because its "spirit of inquiry" appeared to have grown *after* the Allied victory, "Moscow had only itself to blame" for Allied suspicions. Wadsworth saved his most biting charge for those in the West who were excusing the British subjects implicated in the spying: "it will be interesting to see what the 'friend of the Soviet Union' here and elsewhere, have to say in extenuation [*sic*]. Or do spying and betrayal of trust become respectable when done at Russia's orders?"[31] *The Scotsman*,[32] likewise, was "less alarmed that the Soviets were spying than that British citizens were their instruments."[33] Similarly, the limited-circulation but influential *Time and Tide*[34] considered espionage an unseemly part of politics, but found it troubling that Russia could safely rely on "people whose services are assured to it on ideological grounds."[35]

When the Gouzenko affair erupted, Russian specialists in Canada's Department of External Affairs were debating the nature of the Soviet Union and Canadian policy vis-à-vis Moscow. Arnold Smith, recently returned from a three-year stint at the Canadian embassy in Moscow and now External Affairs' man at the Gouzenko inquiry, advocated a "get tough" policy.[36] In this, he shared the perspective of American diplomat and historian George Kennan, who sent his famous "Long Telegram" from Moscow to the US State Department in late February 1946, advocating a policy of containment against a Soviet Union ideologically committed to long-term conflict with the West.[37] Smith, too, believed that the mounting post-war tension between Russia and the West was primarily a product of the "character" of the Soviet government. He dismissed ideology or historical Russian security concerns as the basis for Soviet policy. In Smith's account, the Soviet Union was engaged in a policy of ruthless expansionism that grew out of "a nihilist pursuit of power."[38]

Others in the debate, including Ambassador Dana Wilgress, framed Soviet foreign policy in more moderate and conventional terms, arguing for a Canadian Soviet policy of tact and firmness, but one that remained open to conciliation and negotiation.[39] However, as Soviet intransigence in Eastern Europe, Iran, and elsewhere grew clearer, it pushed Ottawa's moderates to the right. "By the spring of 1946," David Bercuson has argued, "Wilgress's view of the Soviet regime had moved much closer to that of so-called 'hard-line' Americans such as George F. Kennan." The *First Interim Report* pushed Wilgress even further. In a mid-March 1946 memorandum to Ottawa, he responded to the *Report*. Understating earlier frictions, he observed that in the 1920s the principal friction between Canada and the Soviet Union concerned the "smuggling of books designed to spread Communism in Canada." Now, Soviet spying was siphoning information from Canadian Communists in order "to strengthen the Soviet Union as a military power."[40] In Wilgress's assessment, this change reflected a fundamental change in the Soviet Union from a Communist state to a nationalist one. While in the 1920s the Soviets had worked to secure "adherents to Communism from among the people in each country in which the Soviet Union was represented diplomatically," now Moscow focused less on the spread of Communist ideology and more on using Communist sympathizers in the West "for the good of the Soviet Union as a great power."[41]

In North America, Wilgress noted, many people still viewed the Soviet Union as it had been in the 1920s when it was "a country in which according to the doctrine of Marxism all men are treated as equals and where the aim of the government is to strive to have other countries follow this example." The Soviet Union was no longer that country, but "ideas sometimes take a long time to cross the Atlantic." The Soviet Union now had a privileged class, and the state served that class, both by deflecting a large proportion of the national income to it and by cementing its position, supposedly the same thing as "increasing the power of the Soviet Union."[42] For Wilgress, Canadian Communists who passed on secret information were "dupes of a foreign autocracy which exercises undisputed sway over millions of the fellow-men of these Canadians." He found it ironic that "these misguided individuals thought that they were furthering a cause, the ill-digested ideals of which had captured their imagination." He blamed "their own experiences in the economic depression of the thirties," whereas in fact, Woikin excepted, his claim overrated the influence of the suspects' personal financial circumstances. The more powerful cause lay in their youthful utopianism. He saw them as trading "the priceless boon of individual liberty" for "the mess of potage of economic security," but this was inaccurate, since they thought less about economic security than about an unjust economic system, and they had no real conception of Stalin's whole-hearted attack on individual rights and on lives. More astutely, Wilgress seems to have understood that many of the suspects were cobbling together an economic analysis of the thirties "with ideas prevalent in the Soviet Union in the twenties," resulting in "a plan of action entirely inappropriate to the conditions of the forties." What he wanted to fathom was why the suspects, who all had "so much in the way of opportunity," still betrayed their country on ideological grounds.[43] The question was reasonable, though Halperin, Shugar, and Gerson – all Jews – could have told him a thing or two about Canadian antisemitism in the 1930s and 1940s.[44]

Wilgress did not diminish the centrality of Stalin. Elsewhere, he observed that "to a dictator with the upbringing of Stalin the disunity of his western allies and the vagaries of their policies are circumstances that he just has to exploit." The former moderate on the Soviet Union now argued in favour of exposing "the true nature of Soviet aggression." By June 1946 Wilgress, the Canadian state's foremost authority on Soviet Russia, was convinced that the "Soviet Union is not interested in security through treaties[,] only in security through power."[45]

It was the *First Interim Report* that began the process of clarifying, not only for Wilgress but for the world, the challenge that the Soviet Union under Stalin posed to the construction of a stable world order after the war. Fifty years later, these findings would be confirmed and amplified through the disclosures of the Venona project and the opening of KGB (NKVD) and other archives.[46] However, in March 1946, while the *Interim Report* brought the King government some credit for its efforts to safeguard Canada and root out Soviet espionage, it offered only a weak antidote to libertarian claims that the government had embarked on a "totalitarian" policy.

9

Before the Royal Commission II

4–13 March 1946

In the wake of the publicity and debate generated by its *First Interim Report*, the Kellock-Taschereau Commission continued to work – still behind closed doors – interviewing the other suspects. Before the release of its *Second Interim Report* on 18 March, it would examine former RCAF Squadron leader Matt Nightingale, Dr. Raymond Boyer, Lt. Dr. David Shugar, and a records officer in the Department of Munitions and Supply, geological engineer Harold Gerson.

Matt Nightingale ("Leader"), 4 March

Like others taken into custody on 15 February, Matt Nightingale was held incommunicado and denied legal counsel. Although he didn't fully understand his legal position, he had no wish to incriminate himself. During Nightingale's first days at Rockcliffe, Malcolm MacDonald pegged him as "likely to sing." After his first RCMP interview Nightingale asked for pen and paper, but then produced the "most guarded document" with a few "half admissions."[1] When he arrived before the inquiry on 4 March 1946, he proved to be a study in equivocation, his testimony a cat-and-mouse game, as he tried to sell inquiry lawyers a story that his meetings with Soviet spies were job interviews. Although he played the game well enough, the holes in his alibis suggest that he did give information to the Soviets, and although none of it was high on the list of security concerns, it was secret.

Nightingale was born in 1906 to Quebeckers living in Mobile, Alabama. After his father died, Nightingale's mother brought him back to the family home in Lac Beauport. In 1928 he graduated from McGill University with an engineering degree. He joined the Bell Telephone

Squadron Leader Matt Nightingale, Royal Canadian Air Force (Library Archives Canada, Squadron Leader M.S. Nightingale – PA-129634)

Company, first as a "telephone engineer," then "transmission engineer," and eventually "district engineer." Halfway through the war, he volunteered for the Air Force. He would have joined earlier, he claimed, but Bell was engaged in war-related projects, so he stayed with the company until 1942.[2]

That December, Nightingale arrived at Air Force Headquarters, Directorate of Signals, in Ottawa and took charge of the technical side of RCAF phone communications until his discharge on 17 March 1945.[3] He designed the Eastern Air Command Fighter Control Network, which covered Newfoundland, the Labrador coast, and the Maritimes as far west as Mont Joli on the south shore of the St. Lawrence. According to Wing Commander G.M. Fawcett, lead administrative officer in the Directorate of Signals, this network included phone communications between radar posts, control rooms, and fighter stations. Nightingale was also the official liaison between RCAF headquarters and Defence Communications Ltd., a crown corporation created to install the "fighter network, Eastern Air Command."[4] He travelled to Washington in May 1943 to engage in "liaison on inter-communication (telephone)" and in March 1944 to Philadelphia to discuss work that the US Signal Corps had done for the RCAF on the Northwest Staging Route, a series of landing fields across the Canadian northwest from Grand Prairie to Fort Nelson to Whitehorse that connected Edmonton and Fairbanks, Alaska. Constructed jointly by Canada and the US from 1940 to 1944, the route proved "invaluable for the support of defence projects and for the delivery of aircraft to Alaska and the Soviet Union."[5] Fawcett testified that Nightingale had also helped design the Pacific coast program (equivalent to the Eastern Command) and a network of long telephone lines in Western Canada.[6] However, when Nightingale was asked about his duties at RCAF headquarters, he said that he was responsible for "Telephone lines" on Canada's east coast, and (misleadingly) that he had "Practically nothing" to do with work on the Pacific coast.[7]

The strongest evidence implicating Nightingale as a spy was a note in the handwriting of Lt. Col. Petr Motinov,[8] Zabotin's assistant military attaché, a note stolen by Gouzenko from Zabotin's safe. Motinov had recorded a brief history of Nightingale's association with the GRU and stated that he had "been taken away" from the "corporation" (code name for the Communist Party of Canada).[9] Since he was a commissioned officer working at the centre of RCAF telecommunications, it made sense for the GRU to hide his Communist associations, and someone higher up had evidently directed Zabotin to launder him. Nightingale could offer an insider's view of RCAF telecommunications from coast to coast and might also yield information on US defences. On 25 January 1945, Nightingale informed "Brent" (one of two code names for Lt. Col. Vassili Rogov) that he would be leaving the Air Force and returning to the Bell, and on 24 February 1945 the two met on the corner of Elgin and McLeod to update Nightingale's address and phone number. Zabotin asked for information about the "Network of Aerodromes in the country (both coasts)," and a "Map of the coast." On 24 March, in cryptic phrases, Zabotin wrote, "He will give the coast (BBC) and listening-in on the telephone,"[10] likely referring to "Bases Both Coasts" and wiretapping.

When Nightingale was taken into custody, he possessed several documents that he shouldn't have kept after leaving the Air Force. None of the documents was a security threat, Wing Commander Fawcett testified,[11] but although the *RCAF Manual Re Landings, Construction and Maintenance* wouldn't compromise Canadian security, it was "restricted" and Nightingale shouldn't have kept it.[12] A memorandum prepared by Nightingale on the Pacific Coast Program and one concerning test equipment turned over to the RCAF by Defence Communications Limited, Fawcett explained, "could not have been obtained in a proper way" and Nightingale shouldn't have possessed them at all. *Report of Survey Authorized by Northwest Air Command on Alaska Highway Telephone and Telegraph System* was published by Northwest Air Command after he left the Air Force. He had had access to the information that appeared in the document, but he shouldn't have kept a copy after he left the Air Force. With a couple of exceptions, Nightingale's documents should have been returned to the Air Force when he completed his "clearance" certificate in 1945.[13]

Confronted by Fauteux with the clearance certificate, Nightingale took no responsibility: "When I was discharged, as a matter of fact, I didn't take that around. That was taken around by the sergeant. That was the usual procedure; the sergeant took it around to the various officers for the officer and had it signed. It had to be signed before we could get cleared from our station." Did Nightingale sign the document? "I don't think so; no. No; that is right." But, looking at the actual document, which had a portion torn off, he admitted, "I might have signed it down here. I don't know." Fauteux pressed on: "Is it not a fact that the bottom part of the document that is missing is torn off and given to you when you have your clearance?"

NIGHTINGALE: "Probably. I think that may be true."
FAUTEUX: "So you have the stub missing from Exhibit 162, which was given to you?
NIGHTINGALE: "That seems to be correct. It is correct."

The point of the clearance certificate, Fauteux explained, was to ensure that all documents in an RCAF officer's possession, including any that he himself had authored, would be returned to the RCAF. Nightingale agreed.[14] So, why did he still have restricted RCAF material in his possession on 15 February 1946? Nightingale blamed "accident ... or possibly carelessness." He had thrown his engineering books into a pile, packed up his Ottawa possessions, and left for Montreal.[15]

Asked whether he had taken an "oath of secrecy," Nightingale fudged, "I imagine so." Pushed to give a less evasive answer, he added, "I couldn't remember, really." He thought that he might have signed something.[16] Asked about the document "Air Force Administration Orders – General Security," a document setting out detailed standards of conduct for Air Force personnel, Nightingale said that he had seen the document posted in various places. Fauteux drew his attention to the section declaring that it was "an offence to convey, or to attempt to convey by any method, to unauthorized persons information of documents, which are, or might be, harmful to security." Nightingale considered the security category "sort of vague." Perhaps it referred to anything that one thought "should not be disclosed ... It seemed to be left up to our discretion as to what was secret and what was not." Fauteux didn't think so: "There were plenty of documents marked secret?" Nightingale was forced to agree.[17]

Sam Carr, national organizer for the Labor Progressive Party, who constructed the initial GRU rings in Toronto and Ottawa (National Archives [Kew], KV 2/1633, Sam Carr)

With an eye towards conspiracy charges, Fauteux played the guilt-by-association card, getting Nightingale to admit that he knew many of the Communist Party members implicated by Gouzenko in Soviet espionage: Durnford Smith, Agatha Chapman, Fred Poland, Harold Gerson, Scot Benning, Gordon Lunan, Fred Rose, David Shugar. More problematic were Communist leader Sam Carr and the GRU's Lt. Col. Rogov, whom Nightingale claimed to have met as "Jean" on a train to Montreal.[18] If Nightingale wouldn't admit to being an actual or prospective GRU agent, why the relationship with Carr and Rogov, who stood at the centre of Soviet espionage? The story that Nightingale floated was impossible to credit, but he used it to admit the documented evidence while denying any illegal conduct.

A reference in Carr's GRU file implied that at some point Rogov gave responsibility for Nightingale to Carr.[19] Fauteux pursued this, particularly the puzzling reference in Zabotin's note that "Sam is known to him as WALTER."[20] If this esoteric information had come from Nightingale, the other statements in Zabotin's note would increase in credibility. Carr hadn't been among the 15 February arrests, yet, because he was named in Gouzenko's testimony and in GRU documents, the inquiry tried to subpoena him. Carr, however, had disappeared,[21] fleeing first to New York, then to France in May, and then, after a brief stay, on to Russia, carrying several documents about "atomic espionage activities."[22] Later, he would return to New York, where he and his wife Julia would live quietly until he was discovered in January 1949, arrested, and extradited to Canada to face a charge of conspiracy to offend the Official Secrets Act.[23]

Early in the war, as soon as Stalin announced (through the Communist International) that the Second World War was "an imperialist and unjust war," the leadership of the Canadian Communist Party immediately fell in line under the slogan "Withdraw Canada from the Imperialist War."[24] Canada responded by banning the Communist Party publications *The Clarion* and *Clarté* in the fall of 1939.[25] In the weeks leading up to the federal election of 26 March 1940, Communist Party candidates such as Leslie Morris dismissed the notion that Canada was fighting fascism and accused the nation of kowtowing to the British, who wanted "to impose the robber peace on Germany and destroy Russia."[26] Again Canada responded, and on 6 June 1940, through an amendment to the Defence of Canada Regulations, declared the Communist Party illegal, its members subject to detention. An order for Carr's arrest was issued, so he, like other leading Canadian Communists, went into hiding. Nevertheless, speakers such as Carr addressed underground meetings, and party militants mimeographed attacks on the war effort, charging that "for us in Canada the principal danger of fascism comes not from Nazi Germany but from the war policies of the King government."[27]

In hiding Carr remained, well past Hitler's invasion of the Soviet Union in June 1941. But then, abruptly, Operation Barbarossa transformed the Soviet Union into an ally, and Canadian Communist Party leader Tim Buck, toeing the Soviet line, reversed his stance on "the robber peace." He now called for "A Common Front for Victory."[28] Canada, having fought for a year alongside the Soviets, began freeing Communists held under the Regulations, and a deal was made with the Communist leaders still in hiding, including Carr, who surrendered to the RCMP on 25 September 1942. As promised, he was released eleven days later on a pledge "to support the Canadian war effort" and (more difficult) not to "belong to or support the Communist Party of Canada as long as it is an illegal organization."[29] The latter problem was solved in the summer of 1943 by the creation of the Labor-Progressive Party. Nevertheless, Carr had signed an "Undertaking" that he would "not participate in any propagandist or other activities of the Communist Party of Canada." He jettisoned that promise almost immediately. Upon his release from detention, Sergei Koudriavtsev invited him to collaborate with Sokolov on constructing a GRU network in Toronto and Ottawa. Carr kept an eye out for individuals who showed Communist sympathies and who were well placed to access information that the Soviets wanted.

Nightingale participated in Communist study groups in Lac Beauport and Montreal, and at one of those groups he met Carr: "I heard him in talks several times and we were introduced as Walter something-or-other."[30] After he moved to Ottawa, down to sometime in 1944, Nightingale participated in a few more groups at Scot Benning's residence and at Agatha Chapman's, attending "two or three times at most."[31] In Nightingale's telling, it wasn't until he saw a photo of Carr in the newspaper that he realized that "Walter" was Sam Carr.[32] Prodded by Fauteux, Nightingale admitted knowing that Carr was speaking on behalf of the Communist Party. He said that Carr talked about party opposition to the war "along usual Communist lines, of it being an imperialistic war, or something of the sort."[33]

Fauteux asked, did Nightingale have "Communistic sympathies"? Nightingale tried to make his responses simultaneously categorical and equivocal: "Absolutely, probably, yes."[34] He claimed that he was never a Communist Party member, though he had contributed small amounts to Communist election funds, including Fred Rose's.[35] He knew that the Montreal meetings were secret, illegal gatherings, composed of "full-fledged members of the Communist Party." In fall 1944 he had stopped attending. Had someone asked him to stop? "No, definitely no," he responded.[36] Despite this denial, his testimony dovetailed exactly with GRU records that sometime in 1944 the GRU had him "taken away" from the Communist Party.

Fauteux considered Nightingale's relationship with Lt. Col. Rogov central. Unlike Gordon Lunan's Rogov, a decisive man of action who got down to business and parcelled out detailed spying assignments, Nightingale's Rogov was a dawdler who, over the course of four meetings with Nightingale, chatted very generally about a possible employment opportunity for him in an unnamed foreign country. Rogov initiated the four meetings – one on a train trip to Montreal, one at Nightingale's Ottawa apartment, one on an Ottawa street corner, and one in a shady boarding house in Montreal. Each meeting, in Nightingale's telling, went nowhere. It is hard to imagine Rogov's boss, GRU chief Zabotin, sitting patiently for months while Rogov, his most important operative, drifted through inconclusive negotiations, framed as a job interview, to recruit a prospective GRU agent.

Nightingale described the meetings only in vague terms, with Rogov cast in the role of temporizing employment agent, Nightingale as the receptive but increasingly uninterested prospect. The first meeting took place by chance, Nightingale claimed, when he found himself beside Rogov for a two-hour train ride to Montreal "at the end of 1944 or the beginning of 1945" – "We just sat down together in the same seat." Rogov introduced himself as "Jean and some other name, some long name." Nightingale found him "hard to understand" and "gathered" that he was "in one of the legations or something at Ottawa," but didn't take Rogov's accent to be Russian and didn't ask which legation.[37] They discussed Nightingale's post–Air Force plans. When Rogov met Gordon Lunan, within minutes he had handed Lunan an envelope with a scheme to organize an espionage network. Nightingale's Rogov, a study in procrastination, could only bring himself to suggest that his unnamed country might need telephone engineers: "Very vaguely – the whole subject was vague – I gathered he wanted to know whether I would be interested in such a job."[38]

Was Rogov simply taking Nightingale's measure? Perhaps. Near the end of the ride, testified Nightingale, Rogov asked to see him again.[39] Rogov apparently offered no reason, but they agreed to meet in a week or so at Nightingale's Ottawa apartment. Nightingale expected a discussion about future employment, but Rogov didn't mention his country and Nightingale didn't ask. Fauteux feigned puzzlement: "He was inviting you to go and work in a country, and you never inquired what country it was?" Well, Nightingale was "curious," even though he wasn't very interested in a job outside Canada.[40]

Despite his avowed lack of interest, Nightingale welcomed Rogov to his apartment a week later. Nightingale called it "a very unsatisfactory discussion concerning my experience and what I was able to do as a telephone engineer." Once again, Nightingale described his experience as a telephone engineer to Rogov: "He went into more detail as to what my actual experience had been ... vaguely what I had done in the Air Force, not in detail." Did Rogov ask questions about tapping telephone lines? Possibly. Rogov did ask about "monitoring systems," which Nightingale took to mean "listening-in devices." He could not remember if they discussed "the question of the land-line connection system in Canada."[41] Although Rogov again kept silent about which country he represented, Nightingale somehow figured out that it was the Soviet Union and that Rogov "was a Russian from the Soviet Embassy."[42] Rogov's last name, however, still remained a mystery. Fauteux, with no little sarcasm, asked, "And were you still satisfied to use this fake name Jean?" "I was quite satisfied," Nightingale responded, "because I was not interested in his last name."[43] Again, Rogov failed to come up with a job offer, but he did want to meet Nightingale a third time.

They planned to meet on an Ottawa street corner, where, Nightingale explained, Rogov would "pick me up ... in a car with a friend." Nightingale, despite being "an innocent ass," as he put it, understood this unusual arrangement to mean that Rogov didn't want his friend to be seen entering Nightingale's place. A street-corner rendezvous between an RCAF officer and a Russian embassy official accompanied by an unidentified "friend" struck Fauteux as very unusual. Not so for Nightingale: "It did not raise very much question in my mind."[44] When Nightingale arrived at the designated street corner, he was surprised to encounter Rogov on foot, minus the "friend." As they walked, Rogov returned to his favorite subject – Nightingale either lacking the imagination to elaborate the "job interview" story or taking care to avoid possible contradictions: "We went over whether I was a telephone engineer or not, though not in those terms, and we did not get any further, as a matter of fact." At the meeting's conclusion Nightingale "definitely" told Rogov that he was leaving Ottawa and returning to work for Bell: "I was no longer interested in this proposition he seemed to have but had never put to me."[45]

Yet Nightingale's supposedly futile meetings with Rogov kept on going. A month into the Bell job in Montreal, Rogov called and invited Nightingale to his room for a drink. Nightingale declined but, ever cooperative, gave Rogov his address and phone number. He also agreed to give Rogov a summary of his experience and to meet again about the job he didn't want.[46] Gordon Lunan's recruitment of Smith, Halperin, and Mazerall had included a request to each for a biographical summary and photograph for inclusion in their GRU personnel file. Whatever really happened between Rogov and Nightingale, Rogov had evidently arrived at that stage in his recruitment of Nightingale: their final meeting took place in a Montreal boarding house. Nightingale gave Rogov the biographical summary. "I was only with him for about fifteen minutes at the most," Nightingale said, "because I had an appointment at eight o'clock to play bridge. He offered me a drink at his room which we had, and he asked me if I had the summary, that he would like to have it. He also asked me if I had a picture. It just so happened that in my billfold I had several old chauffeur's licenses and one of them had a picture on it which I tore off and gave to him."[47]

Nightingale's story of his relationship with the GRU operative Rogov did, in outline, echo Zabotin's note, but deceptively so. The note has Zabotin giving "Squadron Leader Mat Nantingale" (presumably Nightingale) several tasks from the GRU. There are no references to Russian job offers, only the references to "Network of Aerodromes in the country (both coasts)," "Map of the coast," and the expectation that Nightingale will "give the coast (BBC) and listening-in on the telephone," the latter implying that even Nightingale's tenure at Bell might be useful for any wire-tapping plans. The last section in Zabotin's note is headlined "Task," followed by "Recruiting," "Materials of the Company" and "DUBOK – GINI."[48] Zabotin's précis on Nightingale's fellow-suspect Raymond Boyer too had a reference to "GINI – (Jew) …

Owner of a chemistry story (pharmacy?) … He supplied a place for photography. Has a photolaboratory."[49] Boyer testified that "Gini" might be Reuben Ginsberg, a Communist who owned drugstores in Montreal.[50] Since *dubok* (camouflage) was used in spy terminology to indicate a "dead drop," it seems that Ginsberg's stores were used to pass material from Canadian agents to the Soviets while avoiding direct contact.[51]

The evidence suggests that Nightingale's job interview story was a tall tale. Because Zabotin wrote clipped diary-like entries meant for GRU eyes only, his note is far more credible than Nightingale's story. The prolonged bogus job interview could accommodate talk of coastal aerodromes, maps, and "listening in," allowing Nightingale to address the cryptic GRU documentary record while denying that he had entered a conspiracy to offend the Official Secrets Act. Why did Nightingale go to the fourth meeting with Rogov and why did he go to the trouble of preparing a summary of his skills and experience (accompanied by a photograph) when he wasn't even interested in the job? Curiosity. He had shown no curiosity about Rogov's legation, his last name, or the country that might offer Nightingale a job, but after repeated meetings that seemingly went nowhere, he expected the commissioners to believe that he went to the boarding-house meeting "sort of thinking that maybe [Jean/Rogov] will come to the point and give me some sort of an offer so I will find out after all this time what his proposition is."[52]

Nightingale's close colleague in the Air Force, Wing Commander Fawcett, testified that the network of aerodromes that Zabotin mentioned must refer to coastal networks in place to defend Canada and the US from attack, since "some of the aerodromes … were used only by the United States." Fawcett interpreted Zabotin's inquiry to be about the location of coastal aerodromes and "what communications there are between them and headquarters."[53] A "map of the coast" must mean the locations of coastal defence aerodromes, locations that, even after the end of the war, were secret. Some of this infrastructure had been dismantled, but the information sought by Zabotin could still be useful to a hostile foreign power if Canada needed to restore the air stations to operational capacity.[54] When Nightingale was detained, he had this information in his possession. As for Zabotin's reference to "listening in on the telephone," Fawcett observed that it extended beyond the technical question of tapping phone lines. Yes, Nightingale could tell Zabotin how to tap a phone, but of perhaps greater importance was Nightingale's ability, because of his service in the Air Force, to say "whose telephone lines should be tapped in order to obtain the most information."[55]

Fauteux probed Nightingale's narrative. How did Rogov know that Nightingale had information about RCAF aerodromes on both coasts? Nightingale's answer was ready: he had told Rogov that he was "partly responsible for providing the land-lines for the airports." Nightingale admitted having in his possession the coastal maps that Rogov sought, and that it would have been it possible to show them to Rogov, but insisted that he had told Rogov "Nothing specific ... I told him only that we were responsible for the design of those landlines connecting the airports."[56]

Fauteux tried a different tack by getting Nightingale to confirm that his address and phone number on the note were accurate and, more importantly, that he was the source of that information. Then Fauteux pointed to the words written after the address: "Sam is known to him as Walter." Kellock (referring to the source of the information rather than the actual note-writer, Zabotin) asked, "How would Rogov know to write it in his notebook ... unless you told him that information?" There was a lot at stake in Nightingale's response. If, as seemed unavoidable, he took credit for this information, it would imply that his portrayal of Rogov as employment agent was false, designed to mislead the inquiry, that he, knowing these code names, was involved in some sort of conspiracy with Rogov and Carr, that he had talked to Rogov about what he might do or *had done* for the GRU, and that he had an ulterior motive for retaining the secret RCAF documents. Nightingale refused to blink. "I do not know," he answered Kellock, "unless [Rogov] knew someone who knew me and knew I had known Sam Carr as Walter." Who could that be? Nightingale had no idea.[57]

Clearly, Nightingale's responses made no sense if he and Rogov had met by chance on a train. Fauteux pressed on. Had Nightingale ever *told* anyone that he knew Sam Carr as Walter? Nightingale could not remember "ever" telling anybody, but the other people at the study meetings four years earlier could have been aware of this.[58] Fauteux explicated the little dilemma to Nightingale: "How anybody four years later would remember that you knew Sam Carr as Walter in 1941 so as to have that piece of information written down in Rogov's or Motinov's notebook in 1945 – you will agree that that is a strange coincidence?" "It seems that way, yes," Nightingale responded.[59] Could Nightingale explain why his name should be associated with Sam Carr in a document held in the Russian embassy? His own name must be there because he had met Rogov, Nightingale countered, but he still could not explain its linkage to Sam Carr.[60] Simply put, some of the recorded facts just couldn't be assimilated to Nightingale's story of Rogov the employment agent.

Inquiry members dug at other vulnerabilities in Nightingale's story. Kellock pointed out that references to Nightingale's wife that Zabotin put in his note seemed to come directly from Nightingale. "She was going to England to her mother," the note read, "she does not like Canada." Nightingale explained that he had probably told Rogov about his first wife and their divorce.[61] Zabotin's record stated that Nightingale had been "detached from the Corporants" and was "reserved for the future." Did Nightingale know what "Corporants" referred to? No, but the previous week someone told him that it meant the Communist Party. Fauteux reminded Nightingale of his testimony that "at the end of 1944 you separated your connection with the study groups." Nightingale agreed, yet insisted that "it was not a question of stopping them" – he was merely returning to Montreal and thinking about getting married.[62] The interrogation continued, but Nightingale admitted nothing.

On 5 March, the second day of Nightingale's inquiry appearance, Malcolm MacDonald had told London that Nightingale "appears an accomplished liar but through tangle of evasions it is possible to see old pattern." MacDonald observed that "on his relations with Rogov" his lies were so "far fetched" that he was damaging his own case. While the documents found in Nightingale's possession were "not of high security rating," they would "probably be sufficient to make a legal case against him though he may possibly be able to evade more serious charges."[63] The next day, as the interrogation continued and Nightingale stuck tightly to his employment agent story, MacDonald conceded the match: the "greater part of entire day has been spent by Commission with Nightingale to no purpose." MacDonald thought that the inquiry would recommend charges against Nightingale, but a "good defence counsel might possibly get him acquitted."[64] He was right. In November 1946, when Nightingale was tried for offending the Official Secrets Act, a jury found him not guilty.[65]

Critics of the Kellock-Taschereau Commission, such as William Kardash, the Labor-Progressive Party's leader in Manitoba, pointed to the case of Matt Nightingale as an illustration of an abuse of state power triggered by overwrought and imaginary fears of Communist subversion. In the Manitoba legislature, during his response to the Stuart Garson government's Speech from the Throne, Kardash charged that the inquiry had been appointed on the "pretence … that the Soviet government has done something singularly sinister which friendly governments do not do." In actuality, "the secret investigation was merely the backdrop for a planned offensive against the growth of friendship and co-operation between Canada and the Soviet Union." Worse, "with the cheap staging of a Class "B' mystery thriller," Canada was "threatening to sabotage world peace." Echoing a line, he called the inquiry the equivalent of a "Reichstag fire now lit on Capitol Hill," and he charged the Liberals with trying to "drag the Labor-Progressive party into the spy case by hook or crook."[66] Even if Kardash believed what he said, the leadership of Communist parties of Canada, Britain, Australia, and the US directly abetted GRU and NKVD espionage networks against the West.[67]

Nightingale's case is a good example of the Liberal government's predicament. He had clearly been recruited by Sam Carr to spy for the Soviet Union, yet without a crystal ball it was impossible for Canadians (or the Soviets) to know if his information about the coastal defence system was important or worthless. Some information, notably secrets about the atomic bomb, radar, and other weaponry obtained from Nunn May, Smith, Boyer, and others had direct importance, but the value and threat of most of the spies' information wouldn't be known until the future arrived. Subsequent historical analyses, focused mainly on violations of individual rights, pay too little attention to the evidence generated by the Kellock-Taschereau Commission detailing the subversive activities of the Soviet GRU and its Canadian agents. The roles of the Canadian proxies, especially of the Labor-Progressive Party, are mostly ignored, while accounts of the anti-Communist preoccupations of the RCMP are privileged. And the actions of the Canadian state are subjected to close analysis, leading to a conclusion that state action was either unjustified or egregious or both.[68]

But in the spring of 1946, Matt Nightingale and others exposed by Gouzenko represented a prima facie threat to the security of Canada, the US, and Britain. The inquiry was by no means "a gauche proceeding ... the result of startled inexperience," as Canadian historian W.L. Morton asserted in 1947,[69] but a careful policy, the product of months of deliberation, during which various approaches were considered to address the novel challenges of Soviet espionage. While the denials of *habeas corpus* and of legal representation in 1946 were problematic, any failure of the Canadian liberal state to rein in the misguided Canadian proxies of the centrally managed Soviet threat would have been even more politically and morally untenable.

Raymond Boyer ("Professor"), 7 March

More forthcoming than Nightingale was Raymond Boyer. Boyer had gone through Montreal's Loyola College, Royal Military College, and McGill University, where he completed a PhD in 1933. After postgraduate work at Harvard and the University of Vienna, he spent six months in Paris before returning to Canada in 1937, at age thirty-one.[70] His journey towards Communism started in the late 1930s when the Quebec government brought in a sweeping assault on the Communist Party – the Padlock Law – which gave the attorney general power, without recourse to formal charges, to order the padlocking of any homes, apartments, or places of business deemed centres of Communist activity. Distribution of printed material "propagating … Communism or Bolshevism" became a crime[71] (though neither "Communist" nor "Bolshevik" was defined in the law).[72] Boyer joined the Civil Liberties Union (CLU) in 1938 to fight the Padlock Law, and by 1939 he was elected to the executive as secretary.[73] In those "united front" days, he also affiliated with the Friends of the Soviet Union, the League Against War and Fascism, and the Committee to Aid Spanish Democracy. Through a study group – "warm, intense, and inspiring" – led by Stanley Ryerson, he was introduced to the rigour of Marxist dialectics.[74] Without a leader, without fees, this "closed" group didn't participate in other study groups.[75] Books such as G.E.R. Gedye's *Fallen Bastions*, Ignazio Silone's *Bread and Wine*, John Reed's *Ten Days That Shook the World*, and Stefan Heym's *Hostages* rerouted Boyer's thinking: "These books showed me that the heroes of capitalism were not the people I admired." Now he found a new set of heroes to admire – and more, to imitate. "It was a tremendous change," he said.[76]

When war erupted Boyer sent a telegram to Mackenzie King offering his "services in any capacity."[77] His offer wasn't unusual. Communists initially embraced the Canadian declaration of war on Germany and fascism: as party secretary (leader) Tim Buck announced to a picnic crowd on 4 September 1939, Communists had always opposed Naziism and "Hitler's regime was doomed to fall before the democracies."[78] Yet Buck was forced to quickly swallow his anti-Nazi rhetoric two weeks later when, to legitimize the late-August 1939 Soviet non-aggression pact with Hitler, Stalin announced that the war was "imperialist and unjust" and that adherents of the Communist International must oppose it.[79] After a brief disorientation, Quebec Communists embraced Moscow's new party line and called for "a vast popular front of struggle against war, conscription and the imperialist regime."[80] Boyer may have received an acknowledgment of his offer to King, but nothing more.[81]

Because of the threat of vocational persecution and even prosecution, Boyer had remained a secret "Section 13" member of the Communist Party. As an anonymous member, he could serve the interests of Communism by appearing in the public sphere unburdened by

Dr. Raymond Boyer arraigned in a Montreal criminal court and charged with conspiring to offend the Official Secrets Act (Library Archives Canada, Dr Raymond Boyer – PA-129633)

people's ideological preconceptions. Yet his commitment to the party grew intense. Fred Rose had told him, "You've got to be able to hate because you can't love people unless you hate those who are doing things to them. That's what makes it possible for a communist to do things that a liberal can't do."[82] With religious zeal, Boyer embraced the notion that "you were a communist twenty-four hours a day,"[83] and he disparaged moderates as "scared of going further because of their careers." Even when the Soviet–Nazi non-aggression pact drove many from the party, Boyer stayed, because he had "faith in the leaders of the left-wing movement and their explanation of the world." He said, "I had gone beyond the liberal stage of questioning everything."[84]

Early on, liberals and non-Communist progressives dominated Boyer's Civil Liberties Union,[85] but it soon attracted the Communist left. Although pre-1939 Communist appeals for a common front against war and fascism now rang hollow, opposition to the recent Defence of Canada Regulations gave the CLU a new post-1939 agenda. Just as the "phoney war" ended and German troops swept across Holland, Belgium, Luxembourg, and into France, the CLU took the lead in organizing a national conference on civil liberties, planned for Montreal, 18–9 May 1940. At the same time, a wave of concern about fifth columns broke in the public square. The Canadian press reported on fifth columns supporting the German advance in the Low Countries,[86] while the *Globe and Mail* relayed concerns that Britain's Communist Party was "acting as a direct agent of a foreign power."[87] For similar reasons, France had banned the Communist Party since the beginning of the war. On 14 May 1940, days before the CLU-sponsored conference, an audience of three hundred at a Toronto Civil Liberties Association event was told that the "curtailment of liberties was essential to curb 'fifth column' elements in the Dominion,"[88] and across Canada there appeared calls for action against supposed local "fifth columns" undermining the war effort.[89]

In this climate, the organizing committee, on the final day of the conference, proposed a resolution indicting the Liberal government for attacking civil liberties via the Defence of Canada Regulations: "scores of prosecutions have been initiated; numerous persons have been arrested, fined or imprisoned; newspapers have been raided and suppressed; the right to strike has been endangered; freedom of speech has been curtailed [and] a political party [the Communist Party] has been declared illegal." Amendments to tone down the resolution's rhetoric were opposed by Communist spokesman A.E. Smith and by a large youth contingent[90] headed by Communist A.A. Macleod.[91] H. Larocque, representing the Pan-Canadian Union (a Quebec-based organization created in 1939 to foster national unity), objected to the preamble.[92] Without naming the Communist Party, he charged that there were two classes of people at the conference: "Those who came in good faith, and those who, under cover of the organization, would destroy democracy." When a chorus of boos arose from Macleod's youth contingent, Larocque replied, "Right here we have the fifth brigade. If this gathering adopts the resolution, it is working against democracy and against Canada."[93] The next day the *Montreal Daily Star* widened Larocque's charge: "the Canadian Civil Liberties Union is nothing more than a mask for the Communists, who are fully represented on its paid staff."

Responses to the CLU resolution landed quickly. Ten thousand people flocked to a 28 May public meeting organized by the Pan-Canadian Union and called on Ottawa to intern all alleged fifth columnists.[94] When the Montreal Youth Council's four-hundred-member "Parliament" refused to consider a "loyalty resolution" proposed by delegates from the Montreal YMCA, the *Daily Star* on 1 June warned of "the sinister influence of the Communist gang who occupy paid posts in the Canadian Union of Civil Liberties, whose activities we also commend to the very close and searching attention of the RCMP."[95] Some fifty representatives of Montreal's business and social organizations met on 6 June to create a "Canadian Column," committed to negating "fifth column activities in the city."[96] In effect, the National Conference on Civil Liberties transformed membership in the CLU into a badge of disloyalty. A 10 June RCMP security bulletin summed up the damage: the CLU, "which the Communist Party regard as the only remaining legal organization completely under its control," had shot itself in the foot "by arousing public reaction against it and causing many prominent citizens to withdraw their support."[97]

Boyer could not continue as secretary of the CLU without raising suspicions that he was part of a Soviet "fifth column." Quietly, he stepped aside but continued to participate in the underground campaign against the war. With *The Clarion* and *Clarté* banned, he let fellow-Communists print anti-war propaganda on a mimeograph machine in the basement of his Montreal home and on a printing press in his country house.[98]

Yet, in the middle of Boyer's career as an anti-war agitator, he received marching orders (probably from Stanley Ryerson, who directed Section 13 members) to join the Canadian weapons research effort. Boyer didn't "stop to wonder why."[99] Much of Boyer's story comes from his interviews with Merrily Weisbord three and a half decades after the Gouzenko affair, after time spent in Saint Vincent de Paul Penitentiary for a breach of the Official Secrets Act, after his break with international Communism, and after becoming a celebrated historian of penology in French Canada.[100] With Weisbord as a sympathetic audience, Raymond Boyer wove a romantic epic, a Raymond and Goliath story,[101] keeping mum about the fallout from his role in the CLU conference. At the end of his account, when asked about Fred Rose and passing information to the Soviet embassy, Boyer asserted that, yes, "sometimes a revolutionary has to do illegal things even if he doesn't want to."[102]

Three and a half decades earlier, called before the Kellock-Taschereau Commission, Boyer advanced a much more prosaic narrative about a man trying to do the right thing, always within conventional limits. He emphasized his conventional passage through higher education in the 1920s and early 1930s.[103] From 1937 until the outbreak of war – the time of his tumultuous personal and ideological upheaval that we have just recounted, when books, study groups, Communist friends, and CLU activism changed his whole outlook – Boyer told the inquiry, "I did not do anything."[104]

Having had no real response to his offer of war service from Mackenzie King, Boyer sent his offer in a different direction. Since the federal government – with professional associations such as the Institute of Chemistry, the Engineering Institute of Canada, and the Canadian Medical Association – was compiling lists of some twelve thousand Canadian professionals who had volunteered,[105] Boyer spoke to Foreign Affairs mandarin Dr. E.H. Coleman (still in the fall of 1939) about aiding the Canadian war effort. But this time, rather than again offering himself "in any capacity," Boyer now offered a very specific, very puzzling idea of how best to serve Canada. Since Russia was "a factor of tremendous importance in the war," and since it was vital for Canada to know what Russia thought, Boyer volunteered to go to Russia "without any diplomatic status or anything, in order to try and find out what Russia's real attitude to the war was."[106] Coleman might be excused if he wondered just what clarification a Canadian chemist could provide from the precincts of Moscow after General Secretary Stalin had announced that "the bourgeoisie of all the belligerent States bear equal responsibility" for the war.[107] Nevertheless, Coleman asked Boyer to put his thoughts in writing.

Soon, Foreign Minister Molotov would clarify the line that Stalin had decided on: that Russia "was extending our practical cooperation and rendering Germany political support in her efforts for peace."[108] But Boyer, in his undated letter to Coleman, explained, "I have no desire to continue working in chemistry, and I believe that the future of european [*sic*] civilization depends on the situation in Russia. Consequently I had intended to go to the Soviet Union in November and to study law there as a means of determining the factors which govern the policies of socialism. In preparation for this I have studied the Russian language for three years and it seems to me that I might prove useful as an observer in Moscow now that we are at war."[109] Since the unsigned copy available to the inquiry came from Boyer's safety deposit box, it's possible that Boyer never sent the letter to Coleman. If the letter was sent, Boyer's proposal went nowhere. Because it isn't clear whether Boyer chafed at the Soviet–Nazi non-aggression pact or found it easy to swallow, it's also unclear whom exactly Boyer meant to aid, Canada or Russia. Given the letter's language, it's even possible that the war was immaterial, that, still in the fervour of his ideological conversion, he wanted to experience Communism at the font, and that the war simply provided a pretext.

At the inquiry, of course, Boyer's strange plan for supporting the Canadian war effort immediately raised questions about his political affiliations. E.K. Williams asked him to confirm that he had been a member of the Communist Party for some time. "That is not correct," Boyer replied from his Section 13 perch with the usual Section 13 riposte: "I have worked very closely with Communists, but I have never held a party card nor paid dues."[110] He had made financial contributions to the party beginning sometime after 1939; some $130 dollars (the equivalent of about $2,800 in 2026 dollars) for election campaigns, and $150 (the equivalent of $3,275) to underwrite the publication of a book by Stanley Ryerson. Did he speak Russian? Rather than mention his three years of study, he said that he had taken some lessons. But he knew no Russian people and had no prospect of being received in Russia.[111]

In June 1940 Boyer mounted a new, rather different initiative to join the war effort. This time the chemist, who nine months earlier had had "no desire to continue working in chemistry," lobbied Dr. Otto Maass, head of chemistry at McGill, and offered his chemistry knowledge and skills. Why the change of heart? Because, Boyer told the inquiry, France had fallen and "the allied situation looked very desperate."[112] Given Boyer's devotion to the Communist Party and its position against the war (the Nazi invasion of the Soviet Union still a year away), the fall of France wasn't a credible explanation.[113] In later years, he told Weisbord that he returned to scientific research because he was directed to by the party and that he didn't understand why the party mandated him back into research supporting the war effort while other Communists were campaigning against the war. He must have had an inkling, but in any case his own motivations were quite consistent, from underground militant to prospective Russian lawyer to weapons researcher. If Section 13 membership was designed to obscure Boyer's affiliation with the Communist Party, it made sense to remove him from underground Communist activities now under government surveillance and to place him into a prestigious research establishment. Across Canada, the end of the "phoney war" in the spring of 1940 and the grim turn of events culminating in the fall of France in June triggered a "fifth column" crisis, with demands, especially in Montreal, that authorities ferret out anyone trying to undermine the war effort.[114] Dispatching Boyer into war research provided cover to use his Montreal residence as a safe house for party members gone underground and for organizational and anti-war activities. Later, when the Soviet Union was driven into an alliance with Canada, Boyer's access to highly secret weapons research would be exploited by the GRU.

War research at McGill was scheduled to begin in the fall of 1940, but it had already begun at the University of Toronto in the summer, so Boyer headed there to apply his knowledge to explosives associ-

Raymond Boyer (*left*) supervising RDX research at McGill in 1943 (McGill University Archives)

ated with "picric acid." His focus soon shifted to RDX, another explosive offering greater prospects of wartime use.[115] In September, Boyer returned to McGill to work with Dr. J.H. Ross under Maass, now the NRC's director of chemical warfare.[116] Robert Schiessler, a graduate student under Ross's supervision, had in 1939 discovered a new way of preparing RDX: the "McGill Process."[117] Boyer, in collaboration with British and American researchers, worked on refining RDX and producing it in volume.[118] While not on par with nuclear research, the RDX initiative was nevertheless vital for air-borne depth charges to attack German U-boats, for "Blockbuster" and "Tallboy" bombs to destroy domestic German war production, and for explosives used by special-ops forces behind enemy lines to destroy bridges, troop trains, ships, and aircraft.[119] Dr. Adrien Cambron, assistant director of the Chemistry Division of the NRC, told the inquiry that Canada had contributed to "practical methods of producing RDX on a large scale."[120] Despite collaboration with British and American scientists, it was the McGill process, the new reaction, that was crucial.[121]

From December 1942 on, RDX research in Canada was conducted under the direction of the NRC-created Associate Committee on Explosives (ACE). ACE included representatives from National Defence, the Department of Munitions and Supply, the Army Technical and Development Board, the NRC, and the Department of Mines and Resources. Boyer served as secretary of ACE's Research Subcommittee throughout the war, as well as on an international RDX committee comprising Canadian, American, and British scientists who met every two months until September 1944.[122] All of the research was carried on under protocols safeguarding it from unauthorized parties, with the Official Secrets Act as the bedrock.[123] Cambron, who as secretary for the ACE was responsible for classifying the research reports, told the inquiry that they were classified as "Top Secret, Secret or Confidential";[124] RDX reports only went to individuals on the "Circulation of Associate Committee Technical Reports" list[125] and to officials and scientists on equivalent bodies in Washington and London, such as the American Office of Scientific Research and Development (OSRD). All recipients would be required to treat the reports as secret.[126] In fact, "much of the new work was ... so hush-hush that it was never mentioned in the NRC Annual Reports."[127] Within this framework, Boyer, having sworn the standard NRC oath of confidentiality,[128] submitted reports to Maass, who forwarded them to the NRC in Ottawa.[129] Boyer composed a stream of research reports concerning RDX, all marked "secret," though he wasn't sure who classified them.[130] He knew that the British and Canadian governments in 1943 had publicly announced the new RDX manufacturing process,[131] but he also knew that the release of any information about RDX could come only from someone in "high authority."[132] Cambron testified that there were plans to release more information about RDX if all parties agreed, but the Americans had refused.[133]

The main stumbling block for the Americans was their distrust of the Soviets. Canada's relationship with the USSR was hardly better, despite the common purpose created by Hitler's obliteration of the Soviet–Nazi non-aggression pact. Trade disputes between Canada and the Soviet Union in the early 1930s, when the Bennett government imposed an embargo on trade with the Soviets, had added an antagonistic edge to the poor post-1917 relationship. Although the newly elected Mackenzie King government removed the embargo in 1936, that hardly spelled a thaw in relations.[134] The Soviet–Nazi non-aggression pact, alongside the Moscow-inspired campaign by the Canadian Communist Party against the war effort, quickly soured relations again. Yet when Germany shocked the world on 22 June 1941 by invading the Soviet Union, it looked as if fences might be mended. Early in 1942, the Soviet ambassador to Britain approached Vincent Massey, Canada's high commissioner in London, to ask if Canada would "receive one or two consular officers." By June, this overture had resulted in a formal agreement to exchange diplomatic representatives. Feodor Gusev, Soviet ambassador to Canada, arrived in October 1942, accompanied by a small delegation that included Sergei Koudriavtsev as first secretary.[135] Almost immediately, the Soviet embassy in Ottawa became the centre of an intelligence network under Koudriavtsev ("Leon"), who had served the GRU in Ankara and Berlin,[136] and Maj. Sokolov ("Davie"), nominally a commercial attaché.[137] Pavel Mikhailov ("Molier"), nominally a Soviet vice-consul in New York but really the GRU station chief, helped organize the Canadian network.[138]

Meanwhile, a newly created Canadian Aid to Russia Fund raised millions in support of the Soviet Union and its war effort.[139] In the summer of 1943, a second new organization, the National Council for Canadian-Soviet Friendship, held a mass "Salute to Russia" rally, featuring representatives from Canada's Armed Services and filling Toronto's Maple Leaf Gardens with a crowd that "spilled an overflow into the street."[140] Mackenzie King introduced keynote speakers and declared, "The importance of Russia's resistance has been so great that we hardly dare ask ourselves what might have happened if instead of standing firm, the Russians had yielded or had been beaten." He speculated that "Hitler and his Nazi legions, rich in oil and conquered territories, would then have been free to work their evil will in the West."[141]

Yet despite Canadian praise for the Soviet war effort, the nature of Canada's obligations under the initial 1941 alliance between Britain and the USSR and then under the Anglo-Soviet Technical Accord of September 1942 grew increasingly problematic. Under the Technical Accord, Britain and the USSR agreed to share information on all "weapons, devices, or processes ... deployed ... for the prosecution of the war against the common enemy." The American entry into the war complicated matters. Although it would channel over eleven billion dollars in military aid to the Soviet Union during the war,[142] the US, with no obligations under the 1942 accord, objected to the disclosure to the Soviets of new weapons or defensive capabilities developed in collaboration with Canada and Britain.[143] When Washington rejected requests from Moscow for information related to RDX,[144] Moscow sought the information in a clandestine way.

Montreal-based Labor-Progressive MP Fred Rose was the first Canadian active in Koudriavtsev's espionage network. Zabotin's notes indicate that Rose contacted "Davie" (Sokolov) in "May–June" 1942 to volunteer his services. Rose's Communist credentials were verified "through New York," and his work on behalf of Soviet intelligence began in September 1942.[145] According to Gouzenko, Koudriavtsev ("Leon") also contacted Sam Carr in October 1942 to invite him to collaborate. Carr was given charge of networks being developed in Toronto and Ottawa.[146] As the GRU and NKVD jostled for primacy, Vitali Pavlov, who arrived at the embassy in August 1942 nominally as first secretary but actually as the NKVD *rezident*, complained that "a number of people, who seemed to me to be the most promising sources of information, were already grabbed by my military 'neighbours' – workers in the GRU Residentura."[147] Neither Rose nor Carr was coerced into spying. Rose had previously been linked to the NKVD,[148] and Carr had been sent to Canada as a young man "for Comintern and intelligence work."[149] Both evidently thought that facilitating Soviet intelligence was integral to their leadership roles in the Communist Party of Canada. As organizers, party executives, and GRU recruiters, they could access Communist Party members (particularly those in Section 13) with whom they had long-standing personal relationships and who, through their party commitments, were susceptible to espionage requests.

Among those members was Raymond Boyer. Zabotin's notes contained material from "Before Reorganization" – in other words, the intelligence network in place before Zabotin's arrival in the fall of 1943. Under the heading "Fred's work" were the code names of three agents handled by Rose for the GRU: "1. Gray," "2. Green," and "3. Professor."[150] "Gray" was Harold Gerson; "Green" was never identified; "Professor" was specified as "Frenchman. Well known chemist, about 40 years. Works in the McGill University. Is one of the best specialists in BB [Russian abbreviation for explosives] on the American continent. Gives full information on BB and chemical plants. Very rich. He is afraid to work. (Gave the formula RDX up to the present there is no valuation (meaning by way of importance) from the Master.) Gave about OB" [Russian abbreviation for poison gas].[151] Clearly, as Gouzenko confirmed, "Professor" was Raymond Boyer.[152] Armed with Gouzenko's testimony and the GRU documentation, the RCMP took Boyer into custody, kept him without legal counsel, and brought him before the inquiry.

Under questioning, Boyer identified Sam Carr, Fred Rose, Fred Poland, Durnford Smith, Scot Benning, Gordon Lunan, and David Shugar as Communists or Labor-Progressive supporters.[153] Although he had met Col. Zabotin and Maj. Sokolov,[154] Boyer claimed that at the time of his arrest he "had no idea of the … extent of the intelligence network."[155] Later, he was surprised to learn that Gordon Lunan, someone he knew "intimately," was deeply involved in Soviet spying.[156] Boyer had even – perhaps unwittingly – placed a GRU spy in the Department of Munitions and Supply.[157] When Norman Lee, Harold Samuel Gerson's brother-in-law, asked Boyer to help "Sam" Gerson find employment. Boyer lobbied Dr. Ross in Munitions, and Gerson was hired.[158]

"Early in 1943," Fred Rose began conversations with Boyer about RDX. Rose invited Boyer to his apartment and, says Boyer, "He … asked me to reveal to him what we were doing in RDX."[159] In three or four meetings well into 1944,[160] while Rose took notes, Boyer told him about the new process to produce RDX, the materials involved, and the uses of RDX. Boyer explained that RDX was being developed as an explosive in several different compositions with beeswax, sometimes mixed with TNT and aluminum dust.[161] Because Rose lacked scientific expertise, and because he was probably trying to capture conversations after the event, his reports could be confusing. One telegram from Zabotin to Moscow began, "The Professor advised that the Director of the National Chemical Research Committee Stacey told him about the new plant under construction." Full of conflicting details about a "Pilot Plant at Grand Mere," Quebec, the telegram spoke of "experiments carried out with uranium" and of how "uranium may be used for filling bombs." It concluded with the assertion that the Americans had "invested 660 million dollars in this business."[162] Boyer thought that the telegram contained a "highly garbled account" of a conversation in which McGill colleagues had told him that the "Americans had spent a great deal of money on this atomic research," a conversation he may have mentioned to Rose. E.K. Williams therefore speculated, and Boyer agreed, that Rose had mixed up the RDX pilot plant with the uranium pilot plant.[163]

Boyer's testimony, Malcolm MacDonald told Orme Sargent, "has implicated Fred Rose deeply," making it necessary to take action against him. However, nobody came up with an immediate action plan and he disappeared. "Rose has gone underground," MacDonald reported, "and cannot be located at present by RCMP and it is not impossible that he has already left the country."[164] Boyer acknowledged that the RDX information he gave to Rose would be transmitted to Russia and that the "combinations and methods of use" would have been "new to the Russians."[165] Nevertheless, Boyer did not expect his information to be a game-changer.[166] The Russians might have "manufactured [RDX] in flasks in a laboratory, but … they could not build a plant around that information," he explained. Williams wasn't having it: "If the Russian chemists came to the Russian engineers with the information you gave," he said, "they could get to work and design a plant by which they could make RDX according to your formula." Boyer had to concede that possibility.[167]

At the inquiry, Boyer seemed quite willing to admit that he had contravened the Official Secrets Act,[168] and that he hadn't hesitated to give the Russians information that his oath of secrecy forbade. But his motives were ideological and altruistic, not pecuniary.[169] He explained that C.D. Howe, too, had wanted to offer the Russians the same information, but the Americans had prevented him from doing so. Howe indeed held the power to release the RDX information, yet that would have undercut Canada's national interest in maintaining the US as a bulwark of Canadian security. Boyer spoke as if he had a moral right to do what Howe didn't do: "It was unfortunate ... that there was not closer scientific liaison in connection with such information between the Russian war effort and ours ... I felt it was of great importance that the scientific war effort on the two fronts should be coordinated. That is all I have to say."[170]

Seeking *mens rea*, the guilty mind, behind this seemingly selfless motivation, Williams dug for an indication of Boyer's mental state, for any sense of wrongdoing. He nudged Boyer into admitting that he would never tell Dr. Ross or any of his scientific colleagues what he had done. "In other words," Williams explicated, "you did not want to let it be known to anybody that you had given that information to Rose?"[171] Boyer agreed, and he didn't protest when Kellock tied Boyer's motivations directly to his Communist leanings.[172] Kellock wondered if in cases such as Boyer's work with the Committee for Allied Victory, "there are times when the interests of the members of the Communist Party or its sympathizers do coincide with the interests of Canada?" Boyer responded much more categorically: "Every time so far as my work is concerned."[173] But not, Kellock tried to argue, in the case of RDX: "When it came to imparting information with regard to RDX to Rose, you could not say the same thing about that, could you?"[174] Boyer disagreed: "I still felt that it was of tremendous importance that there should be a full exchange of information between Russia and Canada and the United States and England."[175] Ultimately, it came down to a question of which moral obligation took precedence: "In that particular instance," Kellock concluded, "you were put in a position where you had to act contrary to the interests of Canada as laid down officially?" Boyer agreed.[176]

Boyer's two days of testimony ended on Friday morning, with Kellock concluding that Boyer had "communicated secret information to the agents of a foreign power." Only then, after saying "We are not a court ... We are just a Royal Commission," after disingenuously noting that Boyer hadn't asked for legal counsel, did Kellock offer him a lawyer and ask if he wanted to present any evidence. Boyer replied, "No, I have told you everything there is."[177] On the authority of PC 6444, he remained under detention at Rockcliffe until the commissioners were ready to release the *Second Interim Report* on 14 March.[178]

Assessing the motivations of scientists such Boyer in the Gouzenko affair, Donald Avery has argued that any explanation of Boyer's spying on behalf of the Soviet Union must consider "the Zeitgeist of the war years, when the Soviet Union was a valued ally."[179] Certainly, the wartime Canada–Soviet rapprochement marked an unprecedented, if brief, bonding between the two countries, a partial ground for Boyer's argument that the scientific war effort should be coordinated. However, in 1940 he stayed underground and campaigned against what Moscow had called Canada's imperialist war, until Moscow directed him to return to weapons research and to supply the secret information on new developments in explosives. During the inquiry, Boyer agreed that giving RDX information to the Soviets was rooted in his "Communist leaning or sympathy," and decades later, he summed up his spying in that resonant statement about a revolutionary needing to do illegal things "even if he doesn't want to."[180] Malcolm MacDonald put the matter more cynically: the GRU had hooked Boyer with "ideological and not a financial bait."[181] Contra Avery, dedication to the cause of international Communism trumped any "Zeitgeist" or "fairness to an ally" as Boyer's motivation. Individuals who joined the Communist Party became members of "a movement that demanded total commitment," Andrée Lévesque explains, "a community that considered itself above the confines of nations." They experienced what Stanley Ryerson termed a fundamental "change of mind."[182] Boyer, guided by Ryerson through an orthodox reading of Marx, Lenin, and Stalin, clearly experienced such a "change of mind" in 1938, a fundamental reordering of loyalties. Well before any matter of a coordinated war effort, Boyer had given his allegiance to the Soviet Union.

His political biography was not unique. Elsewhere too the Soviets found an unquestioning dedication to international Communism as defined by Moscow, and a willingness to consider the espionage propositions of local Communist leaders – "sometimes a revolutionary has to do illegal things even if he doesn't want to." The Venona decrypts, the records of Communist parties in the US, Britain, and Australia, and the brief opening of the Soviet intelligence archives all disclosed that Soviet spying flourished via national Communist Party officials.[183] In 1946, the Kellock-Taschereau Commission inquiry provided the world with its first detailed account of the relations between Soviet intelligence and a national Communist Party, a party that urged its adherents not just to theorize about utopia but to take action.[184]

David Shugar ("Prometheus"), 6 March

Even before the end of the war, as Kevin Riehle argues, the Soviet Union was preparing to fight against Britain and the US, and the "closer the end of the war approached, the more intense Soviet planning became."[185] Stalin saw little difference, Odd Arne Westad argues, between the British and the Americans on the one hand and Hitler and the Japanese on the other.[186] Although Stalin may not have actively sought a war against the West, he did consider it inevitable: "We are currently allied with the one faction [of capitalists] against the other," Bulgarian Communist Georgi Dimitrov heard him say in January 1945, "but in the future we will be against the first faction of capitalists, too."[187] He intended to be prepared, and Soviet agents in Canada were among those deployed to ensure this readiness. To focus, as some commentators have done,[188] on the relative importance or unimportance of various bits of intelligence gained by the Soviets from their Canadian agents misses the larger point: the GRU was building up a clandestine network. When Gouzenko defected, the program was in its early stages.

By July 1945, two months after the capitulation of Nazi Germany, Moscow's foreign policy concerns had shifted to the Soviet Union's post-war strategic position vis- à-vis the West and to ambitions in eastern and central Europe. In the wake of the momentous Potsdam conference, Soviet intelligence prioritized information about the atomic bomb and about American military resources in Europe. Where, the Soviets wanted to know, did their own military capacity stand in comparison to American might? What were the West's vulnerabilities? In Gouzenko's documentary cache were thirty-four GRU telegrams to and from Moscow in July: twenty-three sent by Zabotin), ("Grant") to Moscow, eleven sent to Zabotin from Moscow by his boss Ivan Bolshakov ("The Director"). While it is impossible to say whether these totals reflect typical monthly traffic, the telegrams do reveal Soviet concerns at the time.

The atomic bomb was, of course, front and centre. Even before the explosion of the first test bomb south of Los Alamos on 16 July, the GRU had been canvassing its Canadian prospects for atomic weapons information, and the urgency of this led Bolshakov to order Zabotin to "establish contact with Allan Nunn May."[189] On 28 July Bolshakov told Zabotin to ask "Alec" (Nunn May) for "detailed information on the progress of the work of uranium."

In early August, two days after the Americans dropped the bomb on Hiroshima, Zabotin reported to Bolshakov: "THE FACTS GIVEN BY ALEC: (1) The experiments with the atomic bomb were conducted in New Mexico, (with '49', '94-239'). The bomb thrown on Japan was made of uranium-235. It is known that the release of uranium-235 is produced to the amount of 400 grams daily at the magnetic separation plant in Clinton. The release of '49' is likely two times greater (some graphite units composed of 250 meda matts [*sic*] i.e. 250 grams a day)."[190] "49" was the Manhattan Project code for plutonium, based on its atomic number (94), with 94-239 referring to the plutonium isotope p-239. By "graphite units," Zabotin meant the 250-megawatt graphite reactor, known as Clinton Pile, at Oakridge, Tennessee. (Since the plant could produce 400 grams daily, the 250 grams a day seems to be his garbled version of 250 megawatts.) Zabotin concluded the telegram by telling Bolshakov that Nunn May had "handed over to us a platinum with 162 micrograms of Uranium 233 in the form of acid, contained in a thin lamina."[191]

The disposition of American troops in Europe was another major concern. On 11 August 1945, Bolshakov told Zabotin to get detailed information about "the transfer of the American troops from Europe to the USA and to the Pacific."[192] Citing divisional, corps, and group numbers, Bolshakov asked for specific information on over a dozen American military formations from armoured corps to armoured divisions to army groups. Were they still in Europe? What was their strength and composition? Were they going to be disbanded? "If so, give the dates and their destination after they are disbanded or moved." What were the Americans planning to do with the Brazilian Division and the First Air Force? Finally, had the US created a German headquarters for American troops? "If so, give the place where it is located and the name of Officers Commanding? … THIS IS URGENT."[193]

These geopolitical preoccupations led to growing demands on Soviet intelligence to recruit well-positioned agents in the Canadian armed forces. Matt Nightingale's case shows that this wasn't an entirely new initiative and that by early 1945 the recruitment assignment had fallen to Sam Carr. Gouzenko's documents reveal Carr as GRU talent spotter, recruiter, and agent intermediary. "Have we the possibilities," Vassili Rogov, Zabotin's intermediary, asked Carr, "of developing our work in the Ministry of National Defence, in the Ministry of Aviation, in the Ministry of Naval Fleet or even in their military staffs. [*sic*] At the present time these fields are very interesting to us, and we would like to have you expend your maximum efforts in that direction."[194] By July, Zabotin could pass along encouraging news to Bolshakov: "Sam promised

Lt. David Shugar, anti-submarine research officer in the Division of Warfare and Training (Library Archives Canada, Lieut. David Shugar – PA-129638)

to give us several officers from the central administration of the active forces."[195] Bolshakov was pleased: "We are definitely interested. Let Frank [Carr], after a final survey of the prospective persons, recommend one or two for our consideration."[196]

Carr had already served up a candidate: David Shugar. Since 1943 he had been on Carr's radar, and evidence suggests that in the spring of 1944, after Shugar joined the Royal Canadian Navy, Carr wanted to develop him as an agent. Carr told Rogov that Shugar was "a specialist in anti-submarine detection; Asdic." Although Moscow still had to vet him, Shugar was nevertheless assigned the code name "Prometheus" ("Prometey" in Russian).[197]

Carr's GRU file, compiled by Rogov and stolen by Gouzenko, contained "Assignment #1 Sam to Shugar." The assignment set out a series of requests for information about and "samples" of ASDIC technologies.[198] On 15 June 1945, six months after Shugar's first assignment, Carr had nothing from Shugar, but he reassured Rogov that Shugar would produce: "He has consented to work for us but with special caution. He has been under observation."[199] Why did Carr need to reassure Rogov? Was the initial assignment a test designed to confirm that Shugar was firmly in the GRU net?

Zabotin felt no qualms about Shugar's commitment and, perhaps wishing to be seen by Moscow as effective, told Bolshakov that he was bringing Shugar into direct contact with the GRU. Zabotin wrote, "I regard it expedient to give Brent [Rogov] the connection with Prometey [Shugar]."[200] Bolshakov vetoed the plan. From his perspective it seemed premature, even half-baked, with Shugar's recruitment stuck at a preliminary stage – he had produced nothing, and the Soviets knew very little about him. "Until the information re material are [*sic*] received from Prometheus and until his possibilities in the Navy Department are established, contact with him should be maintained through Frank," Bolshakov ordered. "Should it prove that Prometheus is a truly valuable man to us, direct contact may then be established." Not through "Brent" as Zabotin had suggested, but through "Chester" – Capt. Georgi Gourshkov, nominally Zabotin's chauffeur but likely an NKVD operative.[201] The dressing-down wasn't over. Bolshakov reminded Zabotin that he shouldn't use Carr's real name: "The pseudonym 'Sam' has long ago been changed to 'Frank.' In the future, use the latter."[202] Bolshakov also complained, "We have here almost no information on Prometheus except his family name and his place of employment." Since the construction of a file replete with picture, education, and work history was standard GRU protocol in the development of an agent, Carr's failure to extract this basic information cast doubt about Shugar's commitment.[203] Two days later, Carr received a new assignment: "Give the complete characteristics of Prometheus showing the duties of the department in which he works in the War Naval fleet and also write down biographical facts ascertained about his home and office work, his address and his telephone number." Carr should also suggest where "Pronet [typo for Prometey] would work in case of demobilization."[204]

Born in Opaeow, Poland, in 1915, Shugar had grown up in the working-class East End of Montreal, graduating from Baron Byng High School and McGill, where he completed a PhD in physics in 1940. Joining Research Enterprises, a Toronto Crown-owned company linked to the Department of Munitions and Supply,[205] Shugar did defence research first in the optical and then in the cathode ray division. By January 1943 he was elected secretary of the recently created Association of Technical Employees (ATE), and he quickly established himself as a militant.[206]

Research Enterprises fired Shugar "on the grounds of incompetence," but the real reason was clearly his union work, since the dismissal came in February 1943 during an ATE campaign to unionize the Research Enterprises technical and engineering staff. After a Labour Department hearing, he was reinstated,[207] and the controversy was publicized in the Labor-Progressive Party–run *Canadian Tribune*[208] (which had replaced the Communist Party's banned *Clarion*).[209] At the inquiry, Fauteux asked Shugar if he knew the editor or reporters at the *Tribune*. Did he give his friends there the story about union-busting at Research Enterprises? No, the ATE executive gave the *Tribune* the story, he responded, though he "undoubtedly" contributed to the press release.[210] Shugar was fired by Research Enterprises a second time in early 1944, this time supposedly because his qualifications were "too high." The federal Labour Department launched a second investigation, but Shugar decided to leave the company and join the Royal Canadian Navy,[211] working for the Directorate of Electrical Supply at Naval Services Headquarters in Ottawa.

Electrical Sub-Lt. Shugar began his naval career on 28 March 1944[212] and was soon assigned to take on research under Electrical Lt-Com. Norman M. Anderson, the anti-submarine research officer in the Division of Warfare and Training.[213] Transformed into a cutting-edge ASDIC specialist, Shugar gained privileged access to secure research establishments in Canada, Britain, and the US. Initially, his research dealt with oscillators and ASDIC recorder paper used in submarine detection.[214] Oscillators on naval vessels operated like radar, except that instead of emitting electromagnetic waves, the oscillator sent sound waves through the water. When the waves bounced back, operators could detect an object such as a submarine.[215] Existing oscillators, including those given to the Soviet Union by the British,[216] could detect only the distance and bearing of a submarine,[217] but Shugar was testing a new oscillator designed to ascertain the submarine's depth. The locational data was recorded on ASDIC "detector paper,"[218] and here, too, improvements were being made. Since Canadian work on "recorder paper" was more advanced than elsewhere, Canadians shared their findings with scientists in Britain and the US.[219]

When Fauteux turned from Shugar's job to questions about his Communist associations, two legal issues haunting the Kellock-Taschereau Commission came to the fore: guilt by association (including the naming of names) and the denial of legal representation. Fauteux named other suspects and showed photos of them, asking Shugar if he knew them. Because the Official Secrets Act placed importance on the "circumstances of the case," or the "conduct" and "known character" of an accused,[220] because the question of conspiracy was, by its very nature, tied to one's associations, and because the suspects and Canadian Communist officials had been identified in GRU documents as spying for the Soviets, Fauteux's questioning was not a McCarthyite way of identifying Communists. Rather, he was trying to unearth connections between conspirators. Fauteux's questions about Shugar's relations with the staff of the *Canadian Tribune* had been a testing-ground for questions that now dug into Shugar's Communist associations. What exactly was the relationship, Fauteux asked, between the banned Communist Party and the newly created (1943) Labor-Progressive Party? Shugar did not think there was much difference: the label changed, he said, but the party remained the same.[221] He admitted knowing Fred Poland and Raymond Boyer.[222] He didn't recognize Matt Nightingale, but had "met a man named Nightingale on the train once" among "a number of people going down to hear this fellow Paul Robeson."[223] Through the Canadian Association of Scientific Workers, Shugar, a member of the Ottawa branch, met Boyer, the national chair.[224] When Fauteux asked Shugar if Boyer was a Labor-Progressive Party member or had Communist leanings, an inconclusive sparring match erupted over the meaning of the word "Communist." Shugar finally declared that he himself wasn't a Communist.[225] Did Shugar then have "Communist leanings?" Shugar went silent.

When Fauteux shifted the focus of his questions to Shugar's participation in Labor-Progressive–inspired study groups, a procedural donnybrook erupted. At first Shugar affirmed that he had joined socialist study groups in Toronto and Montreal.[226] Asked to name others in these groups, he refused. "You are obliged to tell the names," Fauteux warned, "so please do not waste our time."

SHUGAR: "Can you explain to me why I am obliged to tell you the names?"

FAUTEUX: "Because that is the law; that you are obliged to answer any question that is put to you here."

SHUGAR: "I thought any questions pertaining to the subject under discussion."

FAUTEUX: "Well, we decide what questions relate to the subject under discussion.

SHUGAR: "Well, ... my legal counsel informed me that I need not answer, that I was at liberty to refuse to answer any questions."

Shugar stood firm that he had sworn only to answer "questions pertaining to the inquiry,"[227] so Kellock went on the attack: "Did you say you are refusing to answer? It is not a question of you rather not answering it; it is a question of either answering it or refusing to answer. Now what is it to be?" Again, silence from Shugar. Kellock told him that refusing to answer constituted contempt: "We have the power to punish you for contempt. So you can think it over, and we will adjourn until tomorrow morning at half-past ten."[228]

Alongside his objections to questions about his Communist affiliations, Shugar had several other legitimate objections to the inquiry. When the RCMP took him into custody on 15 February and told him that he was a suspected Soviet agent, Shugar had dismissed the investigation as "ridiculous."[229] Grace Shugar, lawyer A.W. Beament, and Shugar all challenged the inquiry's extraordinary procedures and, early in his detention, Shugar went on a hunger strike to protest the denial of legal counsel in particular. On 2 March, Taschereau told him that he was a material witness[230] and gave him the usual decoy promise: "If any findings are to be made against you, you will be given full opportunity to have counsel represent and to adduce evidence ... before the commission." When Shugar called his arrest and detention a "highly irregular" procedure, Taschereau responded, "The Commission is not concerned with that; we are just hearing the witnesses here."[231] This, of course, was an evasion. Not only were the extra-legal (though constitutional) detentions and interrogations intended to solve the legal problems inherent in the hearsay evidence of Gouzenko and his documents, but the term "suspects" had also been repeatedly used to describe the "witnesses" detained on 15 February.

More importantly, the form of Shugar's interrogation confirmed that he was a suspect. In his memoir, the RCMP's Cliff Harvison recalled that the detainees were told that "serious allegations" and evidence "tended to implicate them in the espionage activities of the USSR ... It was their right, if they so wished, to refuse to answer questions or provide information."[232] But RCMP interrogation protocols didn't mesh with the Inquiries Act. The commissioners, invoking a 1939 case, argued, "In view of this statutory obligation to speak, any idea that all persons whose conduct is being investigated before a Commission under the Statute should be cautioned before being required to give evidence, is based on a misconception." Ordinarily, under common law, criminal suspects wouldn't be obligated to speak, and they would be warned that their words could be used against them, since "confessions must be free from fear." A commission, however, possessed no power to punish crimes. Almost begging the question, the commissioners insisted that the right to remain silent "finds its application only when the person about to be interrogated is free to remain silent ... It does not and cannot be applied to a person who is under the compulsion of a statute to reveal to a Commission or other body the existence of facts of which he is aware."[233]

Shugar challenged the inquiry's premise, writing to the commissioners on 4 March (prior to his testimony) to protest his detention: "For eighteen days I have been detained by the RCMP in a manner contrary to all principles of justice under authorization bearing the signature of the Minister of Justice, and under charges which are not only false, but bear also evidence of fabrication." As a "British subject," he demanded either a lawyer or the dropping of all charges.[234] When he came to testify on 6 March, the commissioners challenged Shugar's letter. Taschereau gave a technically accurate but disingenuous rationalization, repeating the line about Shugar being "a material witness." Shugar, meanwhile, added other grievances. He wanted the letters he had written to his wife delivered. He wanted to see the document that authorized his "arrest." He wanted "to see the document or Order-in-Council or whatever it is setting up this commission." He wanted to protest the fact that he had been interrogated about his work in the navy by "a man in civilian clothes at the RCMP barracks." Shugar demanded that the commissioners, as members of the Supreme Court, remedy his situation at once. When he later repeated, "I would also like to complain about the gentleman who interrogated me and refused to show me his identification," Taschereau replied, "This Commission is not concerned with that."[235]

Acknowledging that Shugar et al. were suspects would have required the commissioners to let them use lawyers and present evidence. The suspects would still have been required to answer all questions, and it's unlikely that the inquiry would have been stalled by cross-examination of witnesses by the suspects' lawyers, because no such provision existed in the Inquiries Act. Confessions given freely before the inquiry would have been accepted without challenge in criminal proceedings, whereas any confession extracted by the inquiry from a *witness* detained incommunicado and denied counsel – hardly conditions for freely given confessions, as the criminal law required – could (and subsequently did) invite judicial scrutiny at criminal trials. Yet bringing the 15 February detainees before the inquiry via subpoena would have allowed them to coordinate their lies, obfuscations, and silences.

Shugar had every right to be confused by his status. The inclusion of police interrogation in E.K. Williams's revised Read/Varcoe scheme turned witnesses into suspects. The original Read/Varcoe included detention with interrogation by a commissioner. The commissioner's interrogation was dropped when the plan was formalized as PC 6444 to address the Nunn May situation, but E.K. Williams, by involving the

RCMP, wanted to create a theatre that would break the resolve of the suspects. The commissioners didn't "caution" the detainees because they were supposedly "witnesses," not suspects, but the style of the RCMP interrogations undermined the commissioners' rationale. No one told the RCMP interrogators that they shouldn't caution the detainees or suggest that there was evidence that might be used against them. The original Read-Varcoe plan was designed to preserve the identity of the detainees as *witnesses*, not suspects, yet Williams's use of Harvison and Anthony turned the detainees into suspects – psychologically effective, but legally questionable. Later, in their *Final Report*, the commissioners would invoke section 10 of the Official Secrets Act to justify the detentions, to say that an offender under the act "may be arrested without a warrant and detained by any constable or police officer."[236] However, the detainees were arrested under ministerial authority, not under the Official Secrets Act – and, again, an Official Secrets Act arrest would immediately turn them into *suspects*, invite *habeas corpus* proceedings, and prevent incommunicado detentions. This wouldn't have worked for spies. The best chance of securing incriminating evidence was their appearance before an inquiry as (nominally) "witnesses."

On 9 March, after Shugar's refusal to name names and Taschereau's threats of punishment for contempt, the debate resumed. Kellock lectured Shugar on the terms of the Inquiries Act, reading section 12 concerning access to counsel and the prohibition on commissioners reporting against anyone without giving an opportunity for the accused to answer any charges. Shugar began to reply, "The circumstances under which I have been detained; the manner in which I have been treated, and the method by which I am being interrogated – " but Kellock interrupted, "What have you to complain about?" Shugar explained his impression that he wasn't a witness but a guilty party. When Kellock insisted once again that Shugar was "just a witness here," Shugar pointed to his interrogation at Rockcliffe: "I was accused of passing on information to a foreign power. I was called upon to say that I had done so." Kellock dismissed Shugar's concerns.[237]

Shugar also disputed the terms of the oath he had sworn to answer questions. He had assumed that the questions would pertain only to the inquiry, and he couldn't agree that the commissioners should be the sole judges as to which questions were pertinent.[238] Kellock, on the contrary, could not imagine an inquiry in which witnesses decided "what questions were relevant and what questions were not."[239] When Shugar asked if his lawyer had been advised about the procedure, Kellock replied curtly, "You have no counsel here." Eventually, Shugar said that he understood the procedure but by no means agreed with it.[240]

Pressured by the commissioners, Shugar finally began to name names. In Ottawa, he had five or six times attended a study group that included Ned Mazerall, Durnford Smith, and perhaps Gordon Lunan. Shugar had met Smith at McGill in 1940 when both were PhD students, and when Shugar came to Ottawa they socialized frequently. Scotland Benning and Agatha Chapman he met while skiing in the spring of 1944,[241] and he grew to know her and "Sam" Gerson through social events at Benning's residence. The events were all "just talk and refreshments," Shugar claimed.[242] Like so many of the suspects, Shugar supposedly met Fred Rose on that great social mixer, the train, where one often met, just by chance, people who shared one's political philosophy: "I walked through the train looking for someone I knew. I bumped into [Rose] on the train and introduced myself." That was in October 1945.[243] With some prompting, Shugar recalled also meeting Rose in Montreal at a party for ex-service members at someone's residence, where Rose and Tim Buck made short speeches.[244]

Purely by chance, Shugar had also met several men from the Russian embassy. In May 1945, in search of a place to rent, he looked at an apartment being vacated by Hazen Size.[245] When the American Elizabeth Bentley, recruited by the NKVD in 1938, defected in the fall of 1945 she had listed Size among the NKVD's contacts.[246] A "secret Communist" and representative of Canada's National Film Board in Washington, Size gave the NKVD low-grade information drawn from conversations with Canadian and British embassy diplomats.[247] Shugar knew that Size had gone to Spain during the Spanish Civil War, but didn't know that he was a Communist.[248] Assessing the apartment, Shugar was surprised to find NKVD *rezident* Vitali Pavlov there with several other people. Shugar joined them for drinks and "chatted for an hour and a half" about architecture, engineering, town planning, and the reconstruction of Stalingrad.[249]

Shugar encountered Nicolai Zabotin and Sergei Koudriavtsev in yet another "accidental" meeting on a train between Toronto and Montreal, probably in the summer of 1944.[250] An old friend from McGill, "Morrison," who worked at the CBC, saw Shugar, mentioned that a couple of men from the Russian embassy were on the train, and said that he was going to talk with them. Would Shugar like to come along? The Russians turned out to be Koudriavtsev and Zabotin, whom Shugar recognized from an event in Maple Leaf Gardens where the "Colonel" had appeared on the platform. Shugar and Morrison chatted briefly with the Russians and then returned to their own car.[251]

Most importantly for the inquiry's purposes, Shugar had a relationship with Sam Carr, beginning in the fall of 1943. They met over lunch with Neil McDonald of the International Association of Machinists and at a social to raise funds for the *Canadian Tribune*.[252] Although Shugar may have disclosed at some point that he was engaged in "anti-submarine work," he insisted that he made it a policy not to talk about his work in any detail because it was "confidential."[253] Nevertheless, he added that under RCMP questioning he had lately come to a new understanding of his relationship with Carr. Perhaps Carr had been cultivating him for a purpose he didn't recognize at the time.[254] But Shugar placed his sudden "recognition" of Carr's real intent too late. A documentary trail stretching all the way to Moscow linked Shugar to Soviet intelligence. Was he or wasn't he a Soviet agent? While there was no specific record of him giving the GRU anything, Carr's GRU file did place Shugar in a conspiracy to offend the Official Secrets Act.

Failing to make headway with questions focused on Shugar's meetings with Carr, Fauteux brought out exhibit 19C, "Assignment No. 1. 16-12-44."[255] All the requests for information in "Assignment #1" were ASDIC-related. Commander Stanley Comach, Shugar's superior, had testified that the assignment was conveyed in imprecise, sometimes inaccurate, language. The opening request about "coastal hydro acoustic stations" probably referred to ASDIC harbour defence, a stationary form of ASDIC. Shugar never worked in harbour defence but "he certainly must have known of it," Comach said.[256] A reference to "working in the ultrasounds diapason" made no sense: the signal employed in an oscillator was "supersonic" just above the audible range.[257] But the request for "asdic which is used in a new submarine and other ships" seemed clearer, referring to devices available to the Canadian navy to detect submarines.[258] According to Comach, Shugar "was long enough in the Directorate to have picked up a knowledge of all of that."[259] Since "sonar" was the American usage for "ASDIC,"[260] questions about "sets of the Sonar's type" (also termed "hydro location finding sets") amounted to a request for information about American ASDIC devices. Comach thought that questions about "Situation of hydrophonic [underwater sound detection] sets in the ships of different classes"[261] concerned the location of oscillators on different ships. Best practice required that the proper function of an oscillator not be compromised by interference from the craft's propeller or the ship's pitch,[262] so the Russians might be asking for a confirmation of best practice.[263]

The last item in Assignment No.1 concerned information on "plants, workshops, scientific research institutions and laboratories in England and in the US which are making and planning the hydrophonic apparatus." The real purpose of the question, Comach thought, was the Soviets' interest in establishing "contact" with these organizations,[264] in other words, looking for spies. Neither the "Admiralty fellows" nor the Americans were going to volunteer information about where their military research was taking place, but Sugar could find out "if he made it his business."[265] On this matter, Shugar's travels could prove helpful. In 1944, he went to the US Bureau of Ships in Washington from September 3rd to the 29th, and across to Britain from October 23rd to December 3rd to discuss production of the location paper for submarine detention. He visited Fairlie, near Glasgow, where development and research on anti-submarine equipment took place;[266] Aberdeen, where a paper mill manufactured recorder paper; Slough, where experiments on compasses were conducted; Portsmouth and Braintree, where chemical labs were located; and finally, in January and February, Florida, where depth oscillators were being tested.[267] Asked about the requests in Assignment #1, Shugar confirmed that he would have been capable of providing such information, but that he hadn't been asked for it.[268]

However, these weren't the answers he had given during his Rockcliffe interrogation. Armed with the Rockcliffe transcripts, Fauteux and Williams attacked Shugar's inquiry testimony, thereby contradicting the commissioners' claims that the RCMP interrogations had nothing to do with the inquiry. Fauteux quoted the RCMP's lead interrogator Inspector Anthony's question – "I am asking you if Carr ever tried to obtain any of this information [Assignment #1] from you" – and Shugar's answer, "Yes, of course."[269] Shugar said, "I told [Carr] where I went to and the places I visited," including the Naval Research Laboratory in Washington and the US Naval Laboratory in Orlando.[270]

During the RCMP interrogation, Shugar had also admitted to a conversation with Carr about item no. 6 in exhibit 19C, "Assignment No. 1. 16-12-44." Rogov had directed Carr to seek Shugar's cooperation in the "passing of the planning and the test of examples of new types of the hydrophonic apparatus."[271] At the inquiry, however, Shugar suddenly couldn't remember that conversation. Commissioner Taschereau warned Shugar that it was not in his interest to answer a question with "yes" in one place and time and "no" in another.[272] Fauteux also asked, "Did you tell [Carr] how to use asdic?" Shugar responded "no." To the RCMP, Shugar had said, "I would not put it out of the bounds of possibility that I might have been asked how one used asdic."[273] To Fauteux at the inquiry, Shugar insisted that he hadn't answered even if Carr might have asked.[274] It was an almost too guarded way of dealing with interrogators: Were you asked the question? I don't know. Did you answer the question? No.

How did Shugar account for the GRU document that indicated he had consented to work for the GRU? He responded, "My impression …

would be that somebody was presuming that it was possible to get these facts from me."[275] When presented with other Russian embassy documents in which his name appeared, alongside a litany of references to ASDIC, he said, "I do not know what to make of it." More and more, Shugar parried Fauteux's questions in such ways. When invited to speculate on the origins of Assignment #1, he responded: "I don't know what I can say." When he was cornered: "Could you clarify that question?"[276] When Fauteux pointed out that someone had given Carr a series of questions to put to Shugar: "That would appear to be so."[277] When urged to recall conversations with Carr: "I have tried to think of that several times already."[278] His recollections always proved nebulous. Maybe Carr asked about "the use of radio location for detecting submarines," but Shugar said, "I recall vaguely … I am not quite sure of this."[279] Throughout his testimony Shugar acted deceptively and astutely: Anthony's interrogation could be challenged as coerced, but his testimony before the inquiry would be admissible in a future criminal proceeding.

Shugar had asserted that he was "a victim of fabricated evidence." He admitted knowing Carr and responding to some of Carr's questions about his work in the navy, but he testified that Carr must have been lying when he told the Russians that Shugar would work for the GRU. Why, Fauteux asked, would Carr make such a claim? Shugar had no answer.[280] Did he doubt the authenticity of the documents in which he was named? They did seem to him "a little fantastic."[281] Fauteux explained that the GRU also held documents incriminating people whom Shugar knew, including Gordon Lunan, Raymond Boyer, and Ned Mazerall. All had acknowledged that the documents in question were authentic and that they had worked for Soviet intelligence. What made Shugar's case any different? "I am not in a position to pass judgment on that," he said.[282] There the interrogation ended on 8 March and Shugar returned to Rockcliffe to await his destiny.

The following Wednesday, Shugar was again called before the inquiry, told that the commissioners would be reporting against him, and asked if he wished to confer with a lawyer. Several hours later, Shugar's lawyer A.W. Beament informed the commissioners that he would make no statement or present any evidence on behalf of Shugar.[283] Nothing that Shugar had said at the inquiry could support a criminal prosecution, Beament said. "It all boils down to one Carr having been directed by his Soviet friends to try and get some information from Shugar. Having failed to do so, he reports back that Shugar is being coy and is at his work in the Maritimes and he hopes for better results." Clearly, Beament concluded, "Dr. Shugar had not the same political views as the executive of the day, but that is not yet a crime, fortunately, in this country." This all took ten minutes.[284]

When the commissioners produced their *Second Interim Report* on 14 March 1946, they wrote that although Shugar denied giving secret information to the Soviet Union, he had offered no explanation for the documentary and testimonial evidence against him. The commissioners were not impressed by "the demeanour of Shugar, or by his denials." There was "no answer on the evidence before us, to a charge of conspiring to communicate secret information to an agent of the USSR."[285] However, the commissioners never actually laid out a specific charge, only hinted at hypothetical charges from time to time. Beament wanted a charge at the inquiry so that he could challenge the hearsay evidence. Was Shugar a "witness" or a "suspect," Beament wanted to know. If he was a suspect, what exactly was the crime?

Shugar was formally released by the Minister of Justice and immediately detained and charged by the RCMP with conspiracy to offend the Official Secrets Act. Following a preliminary hearing in late April, Police Magistrate Glenn Strike ruled that the Crown had failed to provide sufficient evidence to support the charge of conspiracy, and he ordered that Shugar be released.[286] Strike was pointing out the obvious. The evidence against Shugar was hearsay, drawn from the testimony of Gouzenko and from GRU documents referring to "Prometey." While inquiry testimony about Shugar's meetings with Carr might raise suspicions because of Carr's GRU involvement, that was not a sufficient basis for a conspiracy charge. Alternatively, the authorities could try to subpoena Carr to testify that Shugar had agreed to spy, but Carr had fled the country. Years later, when Carr stood trial for his own GRU work, he gave some indication of how he would have conducted himself in any trial against Shugar. Carr lied that "he knew no officials of the Russian Embassy here and was 'not anxious to know them.'"[287]

The dismissal of charges against Shugar heated the commissioners up again. On 3 May 1946, a week after Shugar walked out of Ottawa's Police Court, Gouzenko was recalled to answer questions about Shugar and the GRU. Did Gouzenko recall any communications about Shugar beyond those he brought with him from the embassy? In response, Gouzenko offered new hearsay evidence in a slightly different account of where the questions for Shugar came from. In one account, Gouzenko explained that Sam Carr had suggested developing Shugar as a spy and that Moscow had sent questions for him to answer.[288] In the other account, it was Vassili Rogov and Pantzenney (a naval officer well versed in ASDIC) who developed questions that Carr gave to Shugar. In both accounts, Shugar criticized the questions as too general – much had been written about hydrophonic technology and "he asked for more detailed and technical questions."[289] About two weeks later Moscow obliged and sent a big list, using the numbers of the specific ASDIC inventions. Carr was supposed to pass it on to Shugar, Gouzenko testified, but Shugar didn't have enough time to reply with all the information.[290] In Gouzenko's opinion, Shugar's request for more detailed questions proved that he had agreed to work for the GRU.[291]

The commissioners also renewed their investigation of Shugar's testimony about his scientific role at Naval Headquarters – which held access to all American and British confidential research. Shugar had claimed that *he* had "developed an entirely new paper" to record submarine movements. However, Stanley Comach, Shugar's superior, dismissed that notion completely: Shugar's role was one of liaison. The actual task of developing an improved paper, he explained, was taken on by Prof. F.E. Beamish,[292] the director of analytical chemistry research for Canada at the University of Toronto. Beamish confirmed Comach's account.[293] Shugar was the navy officer responsible for the recorder paper problem and he had brought the problem to Beamish. Beyond that, Beamish asserted, Shugar had "not the slightest to do with the development of it, nothing whatever." The recorder paper required the knowledge of analytical chemistry, but Shugar had practically no knowledge of chemistry.[294]

After Beamish's progress in resolving some of the recorder paper deficiencies, the decision was made to send Shugar to Britain to consult with specialists there. Because Shugar didn't understand the chemistry involved, Beamish's assistant Dr. J.E. Currah was chosen to accompany Shugar. However, a few days before the planned departure, Shugar abruptly informed Beamish that he intended to go alone. He couldn't take Currah but would contact Beamish from Britain when he was in discussion about the recorder paper. "It was almost ridiculous," Beamish told the inquiry, "that a man with so little knowledge, almost no knowledge of the detecting paper, should go to England and discuss the paper."[295] Beamish waited for Shugar's call from Britain. None came.[296]

When Shugar returned from Britain, he wanted Beamish to give him interim reports that Shugar would pass on to a British lab.[297] "He … specifically asked for certain formulae that we had never revealed because we felt they were not complete but … promising."[298] Later, at trial, Shugar insisted that he only wanted to avoid "further red tape" and to "hasten liaison between the two countries,"[299] though he didn't add that by "red tape" he meant the security protocols put in place by the NRC. Beamish objected and told Lt-Com. Anderson (the senior liaison officer in the project) that any information must go through regular chemical warfare channels. Nor would Beamish give Shugar "the latest impregnation formula," since it required further work and Beamish did "not wish to provide other laboratories with good ideas only half developed."[300] Perhaps because of Shugar's attitude generally or the way that Shugar kept Currah from joining the British mission, Beamish met with Anderson and demanded that Shugar be "removed from his liaison position, which meant that he could not visit the laboratory."[301] When Shugar regardless showed up there, he wasn't allowed to enter.[302]

Testimony from R.O. King, the director of scientific research and development at Naval Headquarters, raised more red flags. Shugar had told the inquiry that his "main interest since graduating from the university" was "the application of physics and mathematics to biology and medical work."[303] Before leaving the navy he began to search for a job, contacting medical institutions and then writing to Maj. Gen. Chisholm, federal deputy minister of health,[304] who eventually found him a research position at Health and Welfare.[305] At the inquiry Shugar had not mentioned wanting to stay in the navy.

According to King, however, Shugar had reached out to him twice, saying that he "wanted to stay in the navy" and work in the Directorate of Scientific Research.[306] Shugar was quite familiar with the directorate, where, in September 1945, King had established a library containing "secret documents, secret and confidential documents," including "all the reports in existence on anti-submarine work."[307] Shugar "spent a great deal of time in that secret library ... much more than any other officer,"[308] likely working to answer the "detailed and technical questions" that he had asked the Russians for. Nevertheless, King, having heard that Shugar had "made himself objectionable in Toronto," denied Shugar's job request.[309] Shugar's lobbying for a job at the directorate while hiding that fact from the inquiry fits plausibly with Carr's "promise" to Zabotin of "several officers from ... directorate of active force" for GRU work.[310]

When this new testimony was brought to the attention of Shugar's counsel, Beament commented that it added nothing other than evidence that "Dr. Shugar apparently was not popular with Beamish or King." Waving this distraction in front of the commissioners, Beament said that the inquiry was not conducting a "popularity competition," but then he added, more to the point, that he wanted the commissioners to specify their charge against Shugar. The commissioners' *Second Interim Report* had made a charge against him, but without the notice required by section 13 of the Inquiries Act.[311] Said Beament, "I have nothing to say until the Commission carries out what I submit is the statutory duty to give me the charge, not the evidence that prompts it."[312] The best Taschereau could offer was a question for Beament: wasn't "the reading of the evidence ... sufficient notice of what we have before us concerning Dr. Shugar, or do you want the charge put in writing?"[313] Kellock was only slightly less evasive, giving a hypothetical accusation rather than a specific charge: "the charge if it were being formulated to my mind would be a charge that he was one of the persons described in the Order-in-Council who had communicated, or who at least had agreed to communicate, or both."[314]

GRU documentary records and circumstantial evidence certainly raised suspicion of wrongdoing, but the fact remained that there was no *direct* evidence that Shugar had given the GRU anything, not even his phone number. Nevertheless, even without the deluge of suspicion unleashed by Gouzenko's revelations, Canadian military officers such as Shugar in security-sensitive positions needed to meet a high standard of conduct, since under the Official Secrets Act even the "circumstances of the case" or the "conduct" and "known character" of an accused could prove damaging.[315]

In the *Second Interim Report*, the commissioners asserted that Shugar had given "no answer on the evidence before us, to a charge of conspiring to communicate secret information to an agent of the USSR."[316] In their *Final Report*, tabled in the House of Commons on 16 July, the commissioners went further, charging that he had agreed to work for Soviet intelligence and that he "did in fact furnish information ... in furtherance of the objects of Zabotin's organization to the prejudice of the safety and interests of this country." Using section 3 (2) of the Official Secrets Act, they based their finding of guilt on "evidence including Shugar's conduct and character as revealed before us by him in the witness box" and "the evidence of other witnesses."[317] Yet, despite the Inquiries Act's requirement, Shugar hadn't been given notice of such charges and wasn't invited to address any charges at the inquiry.

In 1935, Supreme Court justice A.J. Davis had laid down a standard of conduct for executive inquiries. In *St. John and the Vancouver Stock and Bond Company Limited v. George L. Fraser*, Davis asserted that even an administrative tribunal (in this case an inquiry under British Columbia's Securities Fraud Prevention Act) "must act fairly and impartially."[318] Section 13 of the Inquiries Act – "no report shall be made against any person until reasonable notice shall have been given to him of the charge of misconduct alleged against him and he shall have been allowed full opportunity to be heard in person or by counsel"[319] – meant that Kellock and Taschereau had to name the "charge" they intended to report. However, in response to Beament's repeated demands for a specific charge, they offered only hypothetical statements and vague references to the evidence. Since they had no difficulty putting the charges into statutory language in their *Final Report*, but refused to do so earlier, their actions were neither fair nor impartial.

On 24 September 1946, Police Magistrate Glen Strike, who in April had dismissed a charge of conspiracy to offend the Official Secrets Act, now ordered Shugar to stand trial on that same charge.[320] Strike concluded that testimony had thrown "new light" on Shugar's possible involvement, making the suspicion of an offence "considerably stronger." Press reports described Dr. F.E.H. Beamish as the principal witness against Shugar in the preliminary hearing. In early December, Gouzenko testified at Shugar's trial, but Judge A.G. McDougall treated both his evidence and the Russian documents as hearsay, finding Shugar not guilty.[321]

Some authors have asserted that Shugar was innocent of any involvement with Soviet intelligence and was victimized by the Canadian state.[322] On the contrary, given Shugar's evasiveness and the general reliability of the GRU documents and of Gouzenko's testimony, it's likely that Shugar did agree to pass on sensitive information to the Soviets, though, for good evidentiary reasons, the hearsay evidence to support this conclusion wasn't admissible. Nevertheless, because Shugar was an officer in the Canadian armed forces, because he engaged in highly confidential work with access to research affecting Canadian, British, and American national security, the government clearly had no choice but to investigate the Soviet spy documents that implicated Shugar and to hold him accountable.

Harold Samuel Gerson ("Gray"), 11 March

"The gun being slightly elevated, some liquid RDX/TNT flowed back along the grooves into the chamber."[323] So ran the opening sentence of a two-page handwritten extract about the filling and firing of artillery shells that Gouzenko found in Col. Zabotin's safe in the Soviet embassy and handed over to the Canadian government. Before the inquiry, Gouzenko testified that the extract, possibly "in the handwriting of Gray or his wife" lay among material "given by Gray" to Maj. Sokolov.[324] Who was "Gray"? Harold Gerson, Gouzenko testified.[325]

The evidence against Gerson was more direct than that against Shugar. Dated 25 July 1945, the handwritten extract about a new explosive came from a report titled "Ordnance Board Investigation No.1, 206.[326] The Ordnance Board, a British agency responsible for designing armaments and munitions, published its reports in the "confidential" *Proceedings of the Ordnance Board*, reports that, in Canada, were stored in locked files at the

McGill engineering graduate and Munitions and Supply records manager Harold Gerson (RG 33/62, Royal Commission to Investigate the Communication of Secret and Confidential Information to Agents of a Foreign Power, vol. 5, "D971-80-19 SUPP C EX - Exhibit 115," photograph 125, microfilm T-3425/e011784684)

Ammunition Branch.[327] As a staff member there, Gerson had access to the *Proceedings*, and former director general of ammunition H.R. Malley thought the RDX extract written in Gerson's script would certainly be of interest to the Soviet Union: "RDX is a new type of filling and [the Russians] no doubt would wish to get all the information they could on it."[328]

Forty-year-old Gerson held an engineering degree from McGill. In July 1944, three years after beginning work for the Montreal-based crown corporation Allied War Supplies, he had moved to the Ammunition Branch of the Department of Munitions and Supply (DMS) in Ottawa as an assistant to Lt. Col. G. Ogilvie, director of filling. Even before his formal move there, he had "been lent" to the branch to coordinate the work of Allied War Supplies and the branch. As chief of records, Gerson coordinated munitions production, prepared and issued manufacturing and shipping schedules, and produced daily, weekly, and monthly production reports.[329] He also kept minutes of the Joint Gun Ammunition Production Committee, a planning and coordinating committee that connected the Ammunition Branch, the Inspection Board, and Allied War Supplies. He had wide access to "secret" records and reports. Although Malley testified that the word "secret" was used rather "promiscuously," and that there were no "top secret" files in the department, he also testified that it would be "inimical to the interests of Canada" for the files to be given to "unauthorized persons."[330] In November 1945, Gerson left DMS to join the War Assets Corporation.[331]

The handwriting in a letter from Gerson to Malley (Exhibit No. 214)[332] matched the writing in the extract taken from Zabotin's safe (Exhibit 28).[333] Malley, who saw Gerson's handwriting every day, considered the extract from the Soviet safe to be in Gerson's script,[334] and Gerson admitted that he had created the extract.[335] Still, in strictly legal terms, despite Gerson's handwriting matching "Gray's," despite material from Gerson arriving in the Soviet safe, and despite the material having been attributed to "Gray," Gouzenko's testimony that GRU agent "Gray" was Gerson[336] (based on conversations overheard in the Soviet embassy) was still considered hearsay.

Gerson acknowledged that he had seen copies of the *Proceedings of the Ordnance Board* and had borrowed them.[337] Yes, the *Proceedings* were confidential,[338] and neither Malley nor anyone in the DMS ever asked him to do research in the *Proceedings of the Ordnance Board*,[339] but his work as secretary of the Production Committee occasionally required him to make "extracts." At the same time, he claimed that he couldn't remember preparing any of the extracts ... only Exhibit 28, the one in his handwriting that the inquiry already possessed and that he couldn't deny. He also couldn't remember how many times he had made extracts or any of their specific subjects.[340]

Gerson was equally opaque about the use he made of the extracts. "I used them to assist me to carry out my duties," he told Williams. Did he copy the extracts to take them to committee meetings or use them when he was preparing the minutes? No. Mostly he needed them, he said, "for my own information." He couldn't remember where he stored them. "Probably in my office," he said; then, thinking the better of it, he removed the qualifier. Afterwards, he would "tear them up or throw them out."[341] He could not recall how long he kept them before destroying them, but he was quite definite about one thing: he had destroyed every single extract, including extracts that, earlier, he had claimed that he couldn't remember where they were.[342]

Aside from the fact that he was the one who had written extract Exhibit 28, the document seemingly remained a mystery to Gerson. He had copied it from the *Proceedings* document "O.B. Investigation No.1, 206," dated 25 July 1945, and graded "Confidential," but he couldn't remember when.[343] Why did he copy it? "I was probably interested in that information," was his non-answer. How did the document wing its way into the Russian embassy? He had no idea.[344] Gerson's lack of recall was a good strategic move. He must have known that an extract in his handwriting was the most compelling evidence against him, yet inconclusive, since (outside the GRU) Gouzenko was the only one who could claim that Gerson had given the GRU the extract, and Gouzenko's word was hearsay.

However, another document from the Gouzenko cache gave almost undeniable evidence, with no hearsay qualifications, that Gerson was "Gray." E.K. Williams dropped onto Gerson's lap what appeared to be a housekeeping question about his wife, Regina Schlein. Gerson said that she had been born in Radautz, Romania.[345] Did relatives of the family continue to reside there? Gerson thought so; he thought that the Schleins, Regina's parents, had received a letter from the Red Cross to that effect.[346] With his answer, Gerson unwittingly tied himself directly to evidence about "Gray" in a draft GRU telegram. Sometime in 1942, responding to inquiries, the Red Cross sent a letter to Regina, confirming that Schlein family members and relatives were alive and still in her native Romania. In 1944 "Gray" gave his Soviet handler, GRU Major Vsevolod Sokolov, a copy of the Red Cross letter and asked for GRU help in sending "money and other things" to his wife's family. "Gray's" relationship with Sokolov, it seems, had matured to the point that he felt comfortable asking for such assistance. What initially might have seemed like the GRU's Good Samaritan response was, in fact, an operational sleight-of-hand, whereby the GRU planned to use Gerson's Romanian relatives and friends as cover ("roofs," in GRU-speak) for illicit GRU mail. Zabotin approved an 8 April 1944 draft telegram to the "Director" Bolshakov in Moscow suggesting this use of "Gray's" wife's relatives and "many acquaintances among doctors and other specialists."[347] Lt. Col. Petr Motinov, who composed the telegram for Zabotin, concluded it with a terse summary that he knew Bolshakov would understand: "Roofs – the doctors and other specialists. Letters from Lesovia [Canada] – there are no suspicions against us."[348] Gouzenko testified that the GRU draft telegram was eventually sent to Moscow, but historian Kevin Riehle concludes that there is no evidence the illicit mail scheme ever came to fruition: "Gouzenko's compromise of Gerson likely prevented any follow-up."[349]

While the GRU scheme probably went nowhere, the telegram's simple contextual information linked Gerson closely to "Gray." "Gray's wife has relatives in Bukovina and Bucharest," Motinov explained. "Recently Gray handed over to Davie [Sokolov] a reply from the Canadian Red Cross of March 1942, wherein it was announced that the relatives of Gray's wife are in their own places, that is, in Roumania."[350] Presented with a translation of Motinov's draft telegram to Moscow, Gerson at first said that he couldn't remember any letter and that he had no idea why the Red Cross might send one. Then, reminded of his earlier testimony, he conceded that Regina might have written to the

Red Cross,[351] but he denied knowing Sokolov or handing him such a letter.[352] Maybe the GRU had another Canadian agent whose wife had been born in Romania, had received a letter from the Red Cross about her family members, and had (through her husband) solicited help from the GRU to send aid to Romania. This wasn't completely impossible, since Scotland Benning's wife (a sister of Regina Schlein) could, in theory, have done so, but Gouzenko had testified (and many details confirmed his testimony) that Benning's code name was "Foster,"[353] As well, Zabotin's notes indicated that Benning was handled by Nikolay Zheveinov ("Martin"), nominally a TASS (Telegraph Agency of the Soviet Union) agent at the embassy, not by Sokolov.[354] One of Gerson's explanations for contradicting his own testimony of the previous day about the letter to his wife was "It may have come to the family."[355] Did Gerson consider suggesting that Scot Benning's wife might have been the recipient of the Red Cross letter? If so, he quickly rejected that defence. How then could Red Cross correspondence about Gerson's relatives in Romania enter "the private and secret records of the Russian Embassy"? "You got me," Gerson responded. Kellock, perhaps hoping that a confession was in the offing, excitedly jumped in, "What is that?" But Gerson's phrase turned out merely to be slang for "I do not know, sir."[356]

The episode of the Red Cross letter gave clear support to the Gouzenko documents' portrayal of the relationship between Gerson and GRU's Maj. Sokolov. In Zabotin's notes about the spy network in place when he arrived in Canada in 1943, "Gray" was already part of the Sokolov-directed Montreal organization.[357] Yet the GRU's use of code names allowed Gerson still to falsely assert, against overwhelming circumstantial evidence, that he wasn't "Gray," that he didn't know Sokolov, and that he had no connection to Soviet intelligence.

Zabotin's notes also linked Gerson to Fred Rose.[358] Rose (later code-named "Debouz") was the first entry in Zabotin's account of the Montreal group "Directed by DAVIE [Sokolov]." Under the story of "FRED" and his acceptance in 1942 into GRU work, the title "FRED's Work" appeared, and, immediately below that, Zabotin had written "GRAY. Jew. The chief of the branch of the Directorate for procuring war materials for the allies. Taken to work on 1.9.42. Works well. Gives material on shells and cannon in film."[359] Zabotin's notes imply that Gerson was recruited and managed for the GRU by Rose, with Sokolov acting as their conduit to Zabotin. While Gerson denied any knowledge of Sokolov, he did admit knowing Rose socially: "Well, I would go to a party, and he would be there," Gerson explained. He had met Rose on a boat ride at a picnic in the mid-1930s.[360] Gerson might have spoken to Rose in similar social circumstances "a dozen times," but couldn't explain why Soviet documents credited him with giving the GRU information about munitions.[361]

Gerson's association with Rose was partly a product of his marriage to Regina Schlein. In Schlein family circles, Gerson acquired a sympathy for the Communist program, though he neither became a member of the party[362] nor attended Communist Party–inspired study groups – "I did my own reading," he said. He met Sam Carr a few times on "social occasions" at the Montreal home of Norman Lee, Gerson's brother-in-law, whom Gerson described as a "just another parlour pink."[363] This self-righteous dismissal of a person who doesn't act on his political beliefs makes a case for Gerson having taken a more active role on the Soviet behalf.

Despite his lack of attendance at Communist study groups, Gerson knew Fred Poland "socially," knew Matt Nightingale, who was "a very good friend" of Scotland Benning,[364] and had encountered Eric Adams at a party in Benning's home. Gerson recognized David Shugar, whom he had met "purely accidentally" – where else? – on a train going to Montreal.[365] Most importantly, Gerson knew Raymond Boyer. Gerson was hired at Allied War Supplies Corporation only after Lee asked Boyer to intervene. Initially, Gerson had applied unsuccessfully, but Lee contacted Boyer, who contacted an acquaintance, "Dr. Ross, over at the Department of Munitions and Supply," and presto, Gerson was hired.[366]

When Williams asked why his application had initially been rejected, Gerson said, "Because I was Jewish." Williams implied that this was only a subjective interpretation – how did Gerson know that was the reason? Gerson replied, "Here was a corporation with eighteen hundred people, and I was the only Jew working there."[367] Several of those implicated in the Gouzenko affair were Jewish, including Rose, Carr, Shugar, and Halperin. Did Canadian discrimination against Jews in that era[368] contribute to these men's willingness to assist Soviet intelligence? In Gerson's case, very likely. Later in the inquiry, invited to agree that "any Canadian" should give the inquiry his full cooperation, Gerson agreed and added "Even a second-class Canadian." Kellock asked, "What did you say?" Gerson answered, "I said, 'even a second-class Canadian' because I consider myself as a second-class Canadian, not as a first-class Canadian." Kellock must have laughed, thinking that Gerson was joking. Not so. Gerson immediately said, "That is not a laughing matter[,] Mr. Commissioner; it is very serious."[369]

Given the terms of PC 411, questions about Gerson's relationships with other suspects in the Gouzenko affair were more than just fishing expeditions. In particular, Gerson's relationship with his brother-in-law Benning drew scrutiny. Both had been employed in the DMS, both had been implicated by Gouzenko, and both were credited with specific intelligence information sent to Moscow, as noted on Zabotin's 5 January 1945 itemized list. Benning had been hired by Allied War Supplies in Montreal in June 1942 on Gerson's recommendation[370] and was transferred only a month later to the DMS in Ottawa.[371] Three items named "Corrections" and credited to "Gray" raised questions about the possibility of collaboration between Gerson and Benning in the service of the Soviets.[372] The "Gray"-credited items on Zabotin's list were dated 7 December 1944 (Secret), 27 November 1944, and 29 November 1944.[373] A long list of items, numbered 112–173, were credited to "Foster" [Benning], followed by the "Gray"-credited items. From the DMS, "Foster" had contributed supplements to contracts, correspondence with companies, reports, notes on reports, production of arms, and "Corrections."[374]

The "Corrections," Williams et al. concluded, referred to amendments made to monthly reports produced by the Economics and Statistics Branch of DMS titled *Forecast of War Production in Canada*. These reports – marked "SECRET," and "To be kept under lock and key"[375] – were cumulative, and corrections were made throughout a given month before the *Final Report* was issued. "Corrections" from the Ammunition Branch would be submitted by Gerson to the Statistics Branch, but in their final form these *Forecasts* were never made available again to the Ammunition Branch. Asked about his role in collecting data and preparing the *Forecast of War Production* reports, Gerson explained that he forwarded data for the Ammunition Branch to Benning in Statistics. There, Benning, who received similar data from several production branches of DMS, compiled monthly forecasts.[376] Malley speculated that, through Benning,[377] Gerson could secure "Corrections" from any other branch of DMS: Ship Building, Aircraft, Anti-Aircraft Equipment, Mechanical Transport, and Signals Instruments.[378] Although this was pure conjecture, somehow the "Corrections" credited to "Gray" had made it onto Zabotin's mail list of 5 January 1945.[379]

Other circumstantial evidence piled up against Gerson. On 2 August 1945, Zabotin telegraphed Moscow that the GRU had "received from Gray the whole correspondence on the question of the theory of the deformation ... of the shell in the channel of the barrel. Altogether about 150 pages."[380] According to Malley, this information was irrelevant to Ammunition Branch work, but in his opinion Gerson, even without a legitimate reason, could have accessed it through the

Ordnance Board Proceedings.[381] Gerson claimed that he knew nothing about the "deformation of the shell," so Kellock asked why he would copy out the subject matter of Exhibit No. 28 (filling shells with RDX/TNT, the material admittedly in Gerson's handwritting) and not also read Exhibit No 209 (the study of the deformation of a shell during firing). "I don't know," Gerson replied.[382]

In Exhibit 20C, dated 2 August 1945, Zabotin telegraphed Bolshakov that "Gray" had copied a May letter sent by the deputy minister of munitions and supplies, G.K. Shiels, to companies involved in ammunitions work: the Department of National Defence wanted an inventory of materiel to decide what portion of the war arsenal should be retained, with guns and mountings going to Lindsay Arsenal (Ontario); ammunition filling (i.e., putting explosives into shell casings) going to defence industries (Quebec); and radio and communications equipment going to the signals workshops (Eastview).[383] Such information about the arsenal, Malley testified, was confidential in May of 1945.[384] Gerson agreed[385] and acknowledged that he would have had access to Shiels's letter. Williams accused Gerson: "The Russian Embassy reports to Moscow that you have made it available to them,"[386] but Gerson repeated that he was not "Gray." Williams asked how Sheils's letter might have arrived in the hands of the GRU, but Gerson had no explanation.[387]

Williams moved on to Exhibit 23C,[388] a telegram from Bolshakov to "Grant" [Zabotin] dated 14 August 1945. Bolshakov complained that two 1944 reports from "Gray" on "technological questions" about "the production of war materials" failed to address questions about the production methods for "war materials, powder and chemical materials." Bolshakov wanted information about "1. The method and the technological processes of the production of munitions, explosives, (v.v) and explosive powders. 2. the formula for plastic explosives, the production of T.H and H.S, (their composition purpose and specific qualities). 3 the application of picrite and nitrate-gushchedina [the gun ammunition propellant nitroguanidine]. 4. the technic of producing the capsules of detonators and igniting capsules."[389] T.H. and H.S., which Malley testified should have been rendered "H.T. and H.S.," were the new plastic shell casings for bombs, replacing the older steel casings, a new development[390] that clearly interested the Russians. Commenting on Bolshakov's requests, Malley thought that Gerson could give the GRU information concerning the "filling" of ammunition and the production of empty shell casings and fuses. Although Gerson didn't have direct access to the "formula for plastic explosives" and the Ammunition Branch didn't have information on the "application of picrite and nitroguanidine," Gerson worked closely with the "Explosives Branch" and he could get the information there, along with information on producing "capsules of detonators and igniting capsules."[391] Questioned, Gerson claimed to have no idea what "reports" Bolshakov was referring to, though he did know about the production of igniting capsules,[392] and about picrite and nitroguanidine.[393]

More damningly, the telegraph traffic between the Soviet embassy and Moscow touched directly on details of Gerson's life. His superiors planned to move him to War Assets in November 1945, but Zabotin had urged "Gray" to take "all necessary measures for staying on his old job." On 28 August 1945 Zabotin told Bolshakov that since it might not be possible for "Gray" to continue in his current position, "Gray" would like Moscow to consider an alternative: opening "a geological-engineering consultative office." Zabotin said, "Gray is a geological engineer by profession and thereafter can head this office." Listing the expenses involved in establishing the operation and requested "$7,000 dollars a year," Zabotin learned from "Gray" "that Canada is entering a 'boom' period in the mining industry." "Gray" proposed creating his consulting office even before he left his current job. Zabotin concluded: "I beg to get your decision."[394] Gerson couldn't deny that in August 1945 great reductions in the staff of DMS were anticipated, that he was "a geologist by profession," or that in August 1945 he was considering opening an office as a geologist. He had discussed the idea with various people in Montreal and Ottawa and had sought financial backing. Even the amounts suggested in the Russian telegram for the creation of a consulting office were generally appropriate ... but he was not Gray.[395] Again, although Gouzenko's identification of Gerson as "Gray" was technically hearsay evidence, the ever-increasing weight of circumstantial evidence made it absurd to argue that Gouzenko was somehow mistaken.

Gerson's refusal to acknowledge the obvious truth threw a new importance onto conversations between Gerson and his RCMP interrogator, Detective Inspector Cliff Harvison. At Rockcliffe, Gerson had been "severely shaken" when confronted by the *Proceedings* extract.[396] He wanted to know what prison sentence he might face and admitted that "morally" he could not "bring himself to incriminate this person and that person."[397] At the inquiry, Harvison told the commissioners that Gerson had agreed that the handwriting in the extract looked "very much like his handwriting." He had indeed "made notes" like those in Exhibit 28 but didn't know "where his handwritten notes would be."[398] Harvison had appealed to Gerson to "assist his Government by supplying any information in his possession regarding Soviet espionage." Gerson had responded that "there were a number of personal problems connected with the decision" and that he found the whole business "extremely difficult." In the end, Harvison could only pull a half-baked confession out of Gerson: "He said that he realized that the picture ahead was very dark for him, that he had made mistakes; that he would have to face the music himself and that he would not be able to live with himself if he gave information that so-and-so had done such-and-such; and he used the expression, if I remember well, that he would not be able to live with himself if he 'put the finger on this man and that man.'"[399] Gerson admitted that Harvison's account of their conversation was "to a large extent correct'" and had no corrections or amendments to offer.[400]

E.K. Williams had hoped that RCMP interrogations would weaken the resolve of detainees, but in Gerson's case it seemed that the Rockcliffe experience could also firm up a suspect's resolution to deny all wrongdoing. In the face of compelling evidence, including Gerson's handwriting and GRU documentary records in which "Gray" exactly matched Gerson's biographical and professional data, Gerson still denied that he was "Gray."[401]

Gerson's testimony lasted for a day and a half. The evidence against him was mostly circumstantial, but overwhelming. No mention was made that the commissioners intended to report against him, though Taschereau's invitation to Gerson to make a statement or to have counsel appear on his behalf carried exactly that implication. Taschereau thus ignored section 13 of the Inquiries Act, which required that no report shall be made against any person "without reasonable notice" of the charge and the opportunity to be heard either in person or by a lawyer."[402] The commissioners wrote that Gerson had "communicated, over a considerable period, secret information to representatives of the Soviet Union in violation of the Official Secrets Act."[403] He was eventually sentenced to five years in prison.

10
In the House of Commons

14–21 March and 7 May 1946

In mid-March 1946 as Gerson was testifying, three months after the last sitting of Parliament, after the Drew Pearson disclosures, after the appointment of the Kellock-Taschereau Commission, after the detention of more than a dozen Canadians, after unfavourable press reports, Parliament was set to open. Mackenzie King's government, in power since 1935, had been re-elected in 1940 and again on 11 June 1945. In the latter election King had promised "full employment and … social security for the people of our country."[1] He staked out a middle ground between what he called the "extreme positions" of the Progressive Conservatives, "the party of private enterprise, of capitalism," and the CCF, "the party of public ownership, of socialism."[2] In December 1945, as the Soviet spying situation percolated, Parliament had approved the National Emergency Transitional Powers Act (TPA),[3] keeping limited emergency powers for cabinet until 31 March 1947.[4] The new law allowed orders-in-council approved under the War Measures Act (and not cancelled) to continue in force, so October's PC 6444 remained on the books.

Mackenzie King knew that when Parliament opened he would be under fire from the Opposition over the "Corby" case. In December, he had turned 71 and had become preoccupied with his legacy. Brooding over the soon-to-be-disclosed PC 6444, he complained to his diary in February, "A great cry will be raised having had a Commission sit in secret, and men and women arrested and detained under an Order-in-Council passed really under War Measures powers. I will be held up to the world as the very opposite of a democrat."[5] King's fears were justified. Leading newspapers, particularly the *Globe and Mail,* charged his government with "totalitarian" practices. Now the House would take up the cudgel.

Parliament reconvened on 14 March with a Speech from the Throne ... but not a word about the Corby case. Nevertheless, comments from CCF leader M.J. Coldwell to the *Ottawa Journal* two weeks earlier foreshadowed what King could expect: "When individuals are arrested and placed in custody and are not permitted for days to communicate with their relatives, friends or legal advisers, a serious abuse of civil liberties has occurred." After defeating totalitarianism in Germany and Italy, Coldwell intoned, "we must not permit totalitarian methods here."[6]

The *First Interim Report,* released to keep the attack dogs at bay, was generally well received and had given King some shelter. The *Second Interim Report* was delivered to the Justice Department the day Parliament reconvened so that King could use it, as he had the *First,* to defend his government. The *First Interim Report* had been followed by arrests and police court preliminary hearings. The *Second Interim Report* would again precipitate arrests, this time of the recent inquiry witnesses Matt Nightingale, Raymond Boyer, David Shugar, and Harold Gerson.

But throwing a wrench into King's plan was Fred Rose. Rose had emerged as a central figure in the spy case, and only days before the opening of Parliament, Raymond Boyer had directly implicated him. Lawyers told St. Laurent that any action against Boyer must include action against Rose, because a failure to arrest Rose would prejudice legal proceedings against Boyer. Could a sitting member of Parliament, St. Laurent asked, be arrested for offences under the Official Secrets Act?[7] Philippe Brais, KC, a former Montreal Crown prosecutor and well-connected Liberal retained by the Justice Department to prosecute Boyer, provided the most substantive justification. Citing Chapter 147, R.S.C., An Act Respecting the Senate and the House of Commons, Brais noted that a member of Parliament was subject to arrest if charged with "treason, felony, breach of peace or any indictable offence" – Rose could be charged under section 14 of the Official Secrets Act.[8] St. Laurent therefore had an information sworn and a warrant issued."[9] But the RCMP couldn't find Rose.[10] What if he tried to take his seat in the House of Commons when Parliament convened? Would he stand up and challenge the government's handling of the Gouzenko crisis?

When King arrived on Parliament Hill the afternoon of 14 March, St. Laurent, Robertson, and Hume Wrong caught him and told him that Rose had indeed surfaced in the House. They feared that he would avoid arrest by remaining there and that if the question of his arrest were raised in the House he would be given "undue prominence." Should the government still release the *Second Interim Report*? After hurried consultations, King decided to delay the release of the *Report* and also his speech about the spy investigation until after Rose was

MP Fred Rose (*left*) on his way to face conspiracy charges (Library Archives Canada, Fred Rose – PA-115249)

arrested.[11] Rose stayed in the Parliament buildings late that evening. When he tried to return to his Ottawa apartment, RCMP officers were waiting. They arrested him, transported him to Montreal,[12] and charged him with conspiring to offend the Official Secrets Act. He was released on high $10,000 bail, later raised to a stunning $25,000 (the equivalent of $450,000 in 2026) after a preliminary hearing.[13]

15 March 1946

Mackenzie King was not a fiery orator. The prime minister, said the *Ottawa Journal*'s Grattan O'Leary, was "not a Mr. Oppenheim, nor an Agatha Christie, much less an Edgar Wallace,"[14] the "King of Thrillers."[15] "Whether [King] is dealing with spies or the baby bonus," O'Leary wryly observed, "no shots disturb the stillness of his nights, nor weird wails come from dark forests to chill the hearts of his listeners."[16] So, when the prime minister stood in the House on 15 March to summarize the *Second Interim Report* and to announce that an MP had been arrested, his speech held many carefully shaped oversimplifications and omitted some crucial details.

He needed to defend the arrests of 15 February, because Parliament had been in recess that day. With several "witnesses" posing "a threat to the safety and interests of the state," the commissioners had "concurred" with the legal advice that St. Laurent should use PC 6444 to make arrests.[17] These suspects held strategic positions, and yet they had admitted, under oath, that they prioritized other loyalties over their loyalty to Canada. King had, he said, merely followed the advice of the commissioners, who feared that without the February arrests the detainees' communication with each other and with outsiders would defeat the inquiry.[18]

King answered press criticism about the purpose of the commissioners' interrogations. The detainees had been questioned to "see whether or not … a charge should be laid," King said (though St. Laurent would later deny that this was the reason behind the interrogations). Unintentionally, King implied that the inquiry was akin to a preliminary hearing, but without safeguards for the accused.[19] In his eyes, the interim reports consisted not of information and advice for the Crown to ponder, but of evidence to lead to criminal charges. Conveniently forgetting protections against self-incrimination in the Canada Evidence Act, he celebrated the utility of the Inquiries Act because witnesses were required to answer the questions put to them. He offered the Commons a disarming, even misleading, account of the commissioners' implementation of section 13 of the Inquiries Act: "When the commissioners come to the conclusion that *a charge* [our emphasis] should be laid against anyone who has been interrogated," he explained, "they bring before them the persons being interrogated and so inform them and ask them if they wish to retain counsel and if there is anything further they would like to say to the commission before the commission expresses the view that a warrant ought to be issued for their being taken into custody."[20] Everyone who had been charged, he said, had been offered this opportunity. Yet, counter to this, both commissioners had claimed that they were *not* required to disclose "the charge of misconduct alleged" against a witness that they intended to make to the Crown.[21]

While King spoke, judicial proceedings unleashed by the *Second Interim Report* were proceeding in Ottawa and Montreal. Like the *First Interim Report*, the *Second* was timed to match the release of four suspects detained under PC 6444 and their immediate rearrest by the RCMP. Raymond Boyer, who had implicated Fred Rose, appeared in court in Montreal on 15 March, was charged with offending the Official Secrets Act, and was released on an astronomical $10,000 bail.[22]

In Ottawa Harold Gerson, David Shugar, and Matt Nightingale were arraigned before Police Magistrate Glenn Strike. Shugar was released for lack of evidence, only to be later recharged and found not guilty. The others were charged under the Criminal Code for conspiracy and under the Official Secrets Act, then released on bail.[23]

In the House, the CCF's Coldwell immediately zeroed in on Rose. Even during times when the British Parliament had suspended the Habeas corpus Act, Coldwell observed, a special provision remained "that no member of Parliament shall be imprisoned during the sitting of Parliament until the matter in which he stands suspected shall be communicated to the house and the consent of the house obtained for his commitment." No matter whether Rose was detained under the Criminal Code or "special statutes," the Commons should be advised of any charges against him.[24] Of course, the idea of announcing in Parliament that the RCMP were looking for Rose was a non-starter, since it would have tipped Rose off. King replied matter-of-factly that charges had been laid against Raymond Boyer, Harold Gerson, Matt Nightingale, and David Shugar on the basis of the commissioners' recommendations.[25] Since the charges against Boyer involved a charge of conspiracy with "Debouz" and since evidence had identified "Debouz" as Fred Rose, "the honorable member for Cartier, Montreal," the Justice Department's legal opinions had recommended his arrest.[26]

More cautiously than Coldwell (given the patriotic minefield), Progressive Conservative leader John Bracken challenged King's methods. He sensed that the public supported the government "in searching out and in punishing crimes against the state," yet he, too, sang the praises of *habeas corpus* and "British justice." The only justifiable departure from regular procedures was "the safety of the state."[27] No problem for King. He was all for "the freedom of the individual," *habeas corpus*, and "human liberty." Platitudes, however, couldn't disguise that his government had denied the suspects *habeas corpus* and access to lawyers. He mounted himself onto Bracken's language and, returning to his 15 February strategy, emphasized that he would never curtail "the liberty of any individual" except when "the safety of the state" was the "main consideration."[28]

"Safety of the state" would remain King's bedrock defence, and it tapped a powerful symbolic root in British liberal-democratic discourse. If a political language is "a discursive field … something looser than a theory or ideology," as Mark Goldie argues,[29] its power nevertheless approximates the power of ideology. The Latin phrase *salus populi suprema lex esto* ("the safety of the people must be the supreme law") derived from Cicero's *De Legibus* (On the laws).[30] Locke placed *salus populi* at the heart of constitutional discourse, providing an ideological basis for unbridled emergency powers if something threatened the very existence of the state, of the public order.[31] In such a case, Crown prerogative meant the power to act "for the publick good, without the prescription of the law, and sometimes even against it."[32] Locke argued, in other words, that the social contract upon which the liberal state was based was not a "suicide pact" that privileged the rights of the individuals over the survival of the whole.[33]

While King might use safety-of-the-state language for rhetorical purposes, he wasn't prepared to acknowledge that his government had acted against the law. Through PC 6444, derived from the War Measures Act, Parliament had given cabinet almost unlimited authority to act with, in Locke's terms, "the prescription of the law."[34] Still, veteran politician that he was, King understood that his case for unprecedented actions against GRU spying had to be made in the Commons and to the public.[35] Canadian and international reaction to the *First Interim Report* had given him confidence that the inquiry would produce enough evidence to make that case. In preparation for his speech on the Gouzenko crisis (promised for Monday, 18 March[36]) he ordered twenty-five hundred English copies and one thousand French copies of *Documents Relating to the Proceedings of the Royal Commission*, including the *First* and *Second Interim* reports, to be printed.[37]

Papers in New York and Washington gave the *Second Interim Report* "fair prominence" on Saturday, according to the press analyst at Canada's Washington embassy, although the coverage was "scarcely as sensational" as a month ago. Rose's arrest got the most ink.[38] Since the release of the *First Interim Report*, said the analyst, "the spy scare in the United States has been mounting in intensity." The House Un-American Activities Committee (Dies Committee) was investigating possible leaks of atomic information from the Manhattan Project facility at Oak Ridge, and the US military had begun removing officers who might hold "subversive" opinions from positions of trust. Several members of Congress pressed for "a spy hunt in the State Department," and the National Catholic Welfare Council warned that the US government employed some 2,000 Communists, including at least 130 in "key positions." The *Washington Post* and *Indianapolis Star* detected "the recent Canadian scare" behind a Senate committee vote to let the military have jurisdiction over all phases of atomic energy development.[39] On the one hand, the press analyst said, the *Daily Worker* was complaining that the Canadian "spy scare" had been formulated precisely "to give the army militarists a club with which to crush all opposition to their conspiracy," while on the other, "reactionary sources" such as the *New*

York Journal American whipped up "enthusiasm for a witch hunt" and "pointed to Canada as showing the way to get rid of the Red menace."[40]

18 March 1946

Though the *First Interim Report* had gone some way to justify his government's Gouzenko policy, Mackenzie King had reason to be apprehensive about his speech to Parliament. Would Fred Rose, now on bail, return to Ottawa and try to take his seat in the House? Malcolm MacDonald registered the apprehension of official Ottawa: "Unless the House is prepared to take some action to suspend [Rose] pending trial, [Parliament] would certainly be best platform he could find for preparation of his defence."[41] As feared, Rose did, indeed, surface in the House for King's speech.[42]

First, John Bracken stood and, with only passing reference to Soviet spying, expressed his worries about the Liberals' assault on Canadian rights. The Conservative leader of the Opposition declared that he had no sympathy for "enemies of the state,"[43] but, verging on a liberal discourse descended from Locke, he quickly turned to individual rights rooted in a veneration of the common law. Speaking, he claimed, for "large numbers" of Canadians, he feared that the Liberal government was using "Star Chamber methods" and trampling on the "inalienable rights that British justice had secured for individuals." He wasn't quite ready to surrender the legal protections accorded under Canadian law. Even those "charged with crimes against the state" should be accorded those rights.[44]

Particularly fraught was the Liberal government's reliance on the War Measures Act. Section 3 limited its use to circumstances involving a "real or apprehended war, invasion or insurrection."[45] Could King convince Canadians that the15 February arrests belonged to an "apprehended war" when all the battles had ended the previous August?[46] In the only use of the War Measures Act to address a crisis other than war – the October Crisis of 1970 – Prime Minister Pierre Trudeau would point to "an apprehended insurrection."[47] If "a democratic society is to continue to exist," Trudeau announced over radio, "it must be able to root out the cancer of an armed, revolutionary movement that is bent on destroying the very basis of our freedom." Via the War Measures Act, "the full weight of government ... [could] be brought quickly to bear on all those persons advocating or practising violence as a means of achieving political ends."[48]

But King couldn't similarly point to a "real or apprehended war, invasion or insurrection." Nudging the House to think about a public that he said was concerned "above all" with "the deplorable question of espionage and disclosure of secret information to a foreign power,"[49] he resorted again to Locke's argument that in the difficult struggle for "the public good," governments must occasionally act "without the prescription of the Law and sometimes even against it."[50] With characteristic ambivalence, King gingerly embraced his role as defender of the liberal state: "I am prepared to take the whole responsibility *if necessary* for the steps that have been taken through the Minister of Justice" (our emphasis).[51] Describing Moscow's direct role in the spying, he fingered Zabotin, Motinov, Rogov, and Sokolov among others, and deplored their recruitment of Canadians.[52] The US and Britain had a "very great and grave concern" that their secrets were being lost through Canadian channels, King said. Quoting Gouzenko's claim that the Soviets were raising a fifth column in Canada,[53] King revealed the targets: explosives production, troop movements, atomic weapons technology, and stolen samples of weapon-grade uranium.[54]

Hoping that the credentials of his advisors would bolster the legitimacy of his government's action, King explained that the president of the Canadian Bar Association, E.K. Williams – "in whom members of the legal profession and the country would have every confidence"[55] – had been selected to advise the government. It was Williams who, to find out "how far-reaching this particular infiltration has been," suggested a commission of inquiry and who recommended that "certain persons should be kept incommunicado pending their interrogation and the taking of their evidence,"[56] Yes, these detentions were legally unprecedented. But against Bracken's condemnation of "police state" methods, King countered that his government had appointed Supreme Court justices precisely because "questions … of individual freedom were certain to arise." The Canadian public could trust Kellock and Taschereau. They, "above all, would be most anxious to protect the liberty of the subject, and to see that justice was done – and justice only."[57]

In response, the CCF's Coldwell returned to common law rights, to the long struggle for protections against an arbitrary state: "Through the ages our forefathers have fought vigorously to prevent secret trials and actions affecting the liberty of the subject without fair and proper trial." That struggle must continue. Yet in recent years, the War Measures Act and the Defence of Canada Regulations had been weaponized "not only against those who endeavoured to assist the enemy but against members of religious sects and, indeed, Canadians of Japanese origin." Certainly, punish "Quislings and traitors," but "act ... in accordance with established principles of justice." Coldwell speculated that the Liberals, not the Supreme Court justices, were pulling the inquiry's strings. He wanted answers about "stories" going around that he "could scarcely credit," stories that "savoured of the totalitarian system."[58]

Press reaction to King's speech was ambivalent. The liberal *Ottawa Evening Citizen* agreed that "there was a fairly extensive Soviet espionage organization in Canada." Because it had started three or four years ago, the spying couldn't have arisen only out of the secrecy around the atomic bomb. But why did the government deny legal counsel? Lawyers could be bound to secrecy, and their presence "would have gone far to reassure the public about what some suspected to be an arbitrary use of executive power."[59] Similarly, the *Halifax Chronicle* wondered why the more usual methods used to investigate Alan Nunn May in Britain were not applied in Canada. Why should the RCMP be "invested with the powers of a Gestapo"? And why should "a Minister of the Crown in a British nation … take unto himself the power of confining anybody he wishes to prison for an indefinite time without benefit of the advice of counsel"?[60] The (big L) Liberal *Winnipeg Free Press* reconsidered its earlier praise. Editor George Ferguson now thought that King had been foolish to take the advice of Williams and the commissioners that only unprecedented steps could keep the investigation from being foiled. Neither the *Second Interim Report* nor King's speech to the House gave any evidence that the "hateful procedure" recommended by the commissioners had "yielded the slightest result."[61] Given the suspects' revelations about providing the Soviets with atomic bomb secrets, troop movements, and technical specifications about explosives, the *Free Press* was arguing ideologically, against the evidence, but it echoed Bracken in deploring "Star Chamber methods." Perhaps uninformed about the legal precariousness of Gouzenko's hearsay testimony, Ferguson claimed there was no evidence that the inquiry would have been defeated had the detainees been allowed lawyers or communication with their families.

Conservative newspapers and politicians had the most difficult row to hoe, since King had co-opted their discourse of patriotism. The conservative *Ottawa Journal* shot off an anti-Communist polemic entitled "The Loyalty of Spies." It fixed on witnesses who had revealed "a loyalty which took priority over the loyalty owed by them to their own country, and for that reason they acted as they did, and would unquestionably have continued so to act had they not been detected."[62] The *Journal* mostly ignored King's speech, yet took issue with those who would minimize the threat of Soviet spying. Communism was "not an economic creed," but a "crusading faith." The unpleasant truth was that "throughout the world is a network of Communists, crusading and fanatical, whose loyalty is not to their own land or flag, but to the shrine of Moscow."[63] Such a network justified the use of a secret order-in-council "to deal with [a] … situation that was grave and delicate."[64]

At the same time, Conservative politicians still sought the weak links in King's handling of the situation. Arthur Smith KC, a celebrated defence lawyer and recent arrival in Ottawa as MP for Calgary West,[65] avoided any focus on the suspects' loyalties, or on the conspiracy to give classified information to the Soviets, but trained his beam on the problems of the government's procedures, particularly on PC 6444, which he called a "mistake."[66] Defence lawyer that he was, he appealed to the Magna Charta, which provided that "a man should have a fair and speedy trial." The evolution of the common law had thrown additional "safeguards around accused persons whose liberty might be at stake."[67] The state had euphemized its attack on these safeguards by speaking of the *detention* of individuals under PC 6444. In fact, several individuals had been "arrested without warrant" and not because they were "actively caught committing a crime." Not only were they kept incommunicado," but they were also "held for six days with glaring lights upon them." "Surely," Smith said, "it can never be said again in the Dominion of Canada that people were held for six days with glaring lights upon them."[68]

Smith questioned whether the witnesses had been given their rights under the Canada Evidence Act, which, in section 5(2), stated that if a witness objected to a question because the answer could criminate them, then although the witness was still compelled to answer, the answer couldn't be used against them in a criminal trial.[69] King had said that the witnesses had been offered counsel, but only after they had given testimony. "If that be so," Smith said, "Here you have people already in gaol, in solitary confinement … They are brought before this commission. There you have two Supreme Court judges whose names are well known, and who are no doubt known to them, eminent and able counsel, clerks, secretaries, stenographers and all that sort of thing which go with royal commissions … These people come in singly, and what happens? They are examined under oath … What in the world is the good of offering people counsel after they have been in solitary confinement, after they have been examined by this commission?" Unwittingly echoing E.K. Williams's 7 December report to the Department of Justice, Smith asserted that "there is nothing so aimed to break down will power and voluntary action as solitary confinement and being rushed in before a tribunal of that kind … Under these circumstances no one suggests that these would be voluntary statements … It is absolute nonsense." Smith dismissed King's assertions about "the safety of the state" and quoted Blackstone's ratio instead: "it is better that ten guilty men go free than one innocent man be convicted." "The people of this country," Smith thundered, "will always regret and will never live down the fact that we threw aside and abrogated the rights and liberties of our citizens. Indeed, sir, Canada now has seen black days."[70]

Given the job of answering was Minister of Justice St. Laurent, who seemed reluctant to assume that duty. He invoked Crown prerogative as a defence. References to "the safety of the state," the "security of the state," "the safety of the government," "the safety of our form of government in this country," and "the security of this state ... endangered by a conspiracy" all sailed close to Locke's "the safety of the people must be the supreme law," and St. Laurent bowed not to the Opposition, but only to the "tribunal of public opinion" as the final arbiter. Repeatedly, he warned of a subversive "fifth column." The purpose of the Kellock-Taschereau Commission was, he said, "to find out to what extent the security of this state has been endangered." How could one place the rights of the accused above dangers posed "by the infiltration of this fifth column into many ... public offices"?[71]

Then St. Laurent hedged. If there hadn't been a legal way to arrest the suspects, he said, he wouldn't have arrested them. But Parliament had granted cabinet authority to act through the War Measures Act. Even so, he had worried about the legitimacy of his actions, so that when E.K. Williams sought detentions under PC 6444, St. Laurent had protested, "I did not think in peace time it was proper that any member of the executive should have the kind of powers the order expressed." He recounted that he had demanded and received a letter from Taschereau and Kellock urging action under PC 6444. But even with the letter in hand, St. Laurent had acted only after searching his conscience, proceeding not just on the basis of well-defined constitutional authority (prerogative powers, Parliamentary imprimatur, or judicial sanction), but rather because, in a choice between "the safety of the state" and "some political discredit," he was prepared to suffer for Canada. Of course, he wasn't quite ready to take the fall alone: "I would choose to assume whatever political criticism might be directed against me *for following the advice* I got from counsel for the commission, *acting on instructions* from the commission" (our emphasis).[72]

No one caught in the inquiry's web was subject to a criminal prosecution, St. Laurent told the Commons. The Criminal Code dealt with "the prosecution or otherwise of individuals who have committed offences," he said, while investigations under the Inquiries Act "concerned the safety or good administration of the state." The inquiry had been appointed "to determine the extent to which [Russian spying] had vitiated the administrative life of this free country."[73] St. Laurent's account was, however, highly disingenuous. Justice Department lawyers understood that without proof of a conspiracy Gouzenko's documents and testimony would be inadmissible hearsay at a criminal trial. St. Laurent understood that the Inquiries Act's coercive powers – the power to require witnesses to answer even incriminating questions, the power to deny legal counsel who could explain the safeguards in the Canada Evidence Act – were being used precisely to solve this evidentiary deficit. Williams's December 1945 report showed that the Read/Varcoe plan was crafted precisely to fuse interrogations with "later prosecutions under Criminal Code."[74] As some "witnesses" soon realized, the inquiry had been structured to draw out evidence – preferably confessions or incriminating testimony – suitable for criminal trials.

St. Laurent was at pains to describe the inquiry as "fair, judicial, careful and prudent."[75] Almost immediately, Arthur Smith forced him to acknowledge that witnesses were only allowed lawyers *after* having been interrogated.[76] How could that be "fair"? St. Laurent responded with the patently false assurance that the witnesses' testimonies without benefit of counsel were "not to determine whether they had done anything personally, but to inform the commission what they know about the extent of this conspiracy."[77] The *Toronto Star* dismissed St. Laurent's explanation, since it didn't alter the fact that witnesses had been deprived of their legal rights. Even the Nuremberg defendants had lawyers.[78]

As King had done, St. Laurent misstated the practice of the commissioners around section 13 of the Inquiries Act. He told the Commons that before a negative report – a recommendation that a witness be criminally charged – was submitted to the government, "whenever the moment arises for them to have to answer the *charges* [our emphasis] against them, even before an adverse report is made about them by the commission, they are ... told what the facts are which indicate that they should be critically reported on by the commissioners" and invited to respond with the advice of legal counsel.[79] St. Laurent either hadn't read or was ignoring the transcript of the inquiry hearing of 16 May 1945 when Beament several times asked the commissioners to specify a charge against David Shugar.[80] St. Laurent also responded to the *habeas corpus* criticisms. The detainees could have "applied for and obtained a writ of *habeas corpus* but it would have done them no good," he said, because any judge would immediately have recognized that detentions under PC 6444 were legal. In "the leading case that decides the effect of the *War Measures Act*," the Supreme Court had confirmed that "things done under the *War Measures Act* had the effect of a statute to provide a legal cause for the detention of the man."[81]

Here, St. Laurent didn't specify the 1918 *Re George Edwin Gray* case, nor was he keen to. A closer look at the *habeas corpus* application by Ontario farmer George Gray would have revealed a decision more complicated than what St. Laurent needed.[82] *Re Gray* was, indeed, the precedent St. Laurent needed to nullify *habeas corpus*, but that was only part of the story. Justice Lyman Duff,[83] who had joined the majority decision, placed two important strictures on the use of the War Measures Act: an order-in-council approved under the act was "exercisable during war only" and must be "deemed advisable by reason of war."[84] Duff was simply underlining remarks made by E.L. Newcombe KC, deputy minister of justice, who had appeared before the court to defend the order. Newcombe had cited two limits to the governor-in-council's authority under the War Measures Act: that of time – it was limited to the period of the war – and that of purpose – it was limited to "the existence of apprehended war, invasion or insurrection."[85]

During the Second World War, judicial support for orders-in-council approved by the Liberal government typically invoked the war to justify the denial of civil liberties.[86] In 1941, explaining the reason for jailing the president of the Seamen's Union, Pat Sullivan, under the War Measures Act, Justice Hope quoted a 1918 case that appealed an order under the British Defence of the Realm Act.[87] There, Justice Thomas Scrutton argued that "a war could not be carried on according to the principles of Magna Charta." Since the "the success of totalitarian powers" relied on "subversive activities of agents within the gates," and since the struggle was "not only for the democratic way of life but for our very existence," the government must be free to "come near to suspending the very essence of our Constitution." Civil liberties could be "placed in pawn," and then be redeemed after victory.[88] In 1923, the Judicial Committee of the Privy Council had granted the federal government wide authority to address emergencies under the War Measures Act: the government must have "considerable freedom to judge" when an emergency existed. Only on "very clear evidence that the crisis has wholly passed away" could judges overrule the government.[89] In 1946 this ruling cut both ways. Clearly, Ottawa held carte blanche to act in relation to the war in Europe and the Far East, and even to decide when the war had ended, but did that authority extend to countering Soviet spying with a draconian order like PC 6444? Could St. Laurent realistically expect that when someone detained under PC 6444 applied for *habeas corpus*, Canadian judges would ignore the strictures that Lyman Duff, a chief justice of the Supreme Court, had placed on the War Measures Act?

Beyond the threat of a *habeas corpus* hearing, the Department of Justice likely denied legal counsel to the detainees to protect Kellock and Taschereau from an injunction that could hamstring their inquiry. The Kellock-Taschereau Commission had every right to investigate foreign spying, but the "witnesses" hadn't arrived at the inquiry voluntarily, or by subpoena, or by bench warrant[90] – no, the "witnesses" were detainees served up by St. Laurent. PC 6444 allowed him to detain and interrogate suspected spies, though not to place them before a commission of inquiry. Might an injunction against the inquiry be secured, against this highly irregular process? Anyone under a subpoena or a bench warrant could consult with a lawyer. Not so the detainees. A court might be persuaded that the detainees were suspects, not witnesses, since even King had implied as much. If suspects, why were they being interrogated by commissioners rather than by police? The Official Secrets Act's section 10 provided for the arrest of spies, and in their "Law and Procedure" section of the commission's *Final Report*, Kellock and Taschereau argued that the act placed no time limit on detentions.[91] But did the act allow for the detainees to be denied lawyers or to be placed in solitary confinement?[92] After a police interrogation, a suspect must be released or appear before a police magistrate in a preliminary hearing, as the British had done with Alan Nunn May. St. Laurent, in contrast, had put the detainees in a place where they had no choice but to answer all questions and incriminate themselves. Of course, that was the whole point of the commission: to secure incriminating testimony for use in criminal trials, and to bar lawyers who might put the searchlight of an injunction hearing on the use of PC 6444 and might thereby void the detainees' testimony.

Defending the government's Gouzenko policy, St. Laurent thanked Bracken for tolerating the lapse of memory back during the December 1945 debate on the TPA when St. Laurent had said that no *secret* orders-in-council existed. Apparently, he had simply forgotten about PC 6444 and PC 5991 after Alan Nunn May failed to meet his GRU contact in London.[93] Now St. Laurent regretted the use of PC 6444 to detain anyone. He gave a muddled account of the failure to construct an alternative process, suggesting that if he had thought the matter through, he would have come up with a clearer arrest order, an order that acknowledged the difficulties of investigating a conspiracy led by a foreign state.[94] He didn't mention on what authority he would have based the hypothetical order. Nor did he mention any consideration of the use of *Re Gray* to amend the Official Secrets Act.

In the event, the Opposition pursued the *habeas corpus* question, but nobody suggested an injunction against the inquiry. Since those detained at Rockcliffe were held incommunicado and denied lawyers, *habeas corpus* applications were unlikely. How exactly, Progressive Conservative Davie Fulton asked St. Laurent, can a person held incommunicado bring a writ of *habeas corpus*? St. Laurent responded shockingly: "It is no business of the custodian [i.e., St. Laurent] of a person who is held to provide opportunities for the issuing of such writs."[95] Even under the quite draconian Defence of Canada Regulations, St. Laurent was required to let detainees "make objections against the order either in person or by counsel, solicitor or agent." The minister must ensure that every detainee "is informed of his right to make objections under this Regulation."[96] Criticism of the Liberal government's Gouzenko policy even came from former Liberals. Once a powerful cabinet minister, Quebec MP Chubby Power broke with King in the fall of 1944 on the question of conscription, only to be re-elected in 1945 as an Independent Liberal.[97] In the House, he charged the Liberals with revoking the Magna Charta "after 731 years of existence" and of inviting a future totalitarianism into Canada. This precedent was dangerous.[98]

Inevitably, John Diefenbaker, the Progressive Conservatives' leading advocate for what his biographer termed "progressive causes," also took up the sword on behalf of the detainees.[99] Like all the Conservative critics, he claimed to have "no sympathy … for those who would undermine their country," but he wanted them subject to the law, not to "administrative lawlessness." In the past, the "safety of the state" had always been defined in relation to war or insurrection.[100] Neither PC 6444 nor PC 411 contained a reference to the "safety of the state," and St. Laurent hadn't shown anything that could seriously threaten the state.[101]

Diefenbaker thought that St. Laurent was lying about his faulty memory, that as "a former president of the Canadian Bar Association" he wasn't likely to forget "an order-in-council which did more to sweep aside the rights of individuals than any other order-in-council passed in the history of Canada?"[102] Parliament wouldn't have given St. Laurent his emergency transitional powers had it known of this secret order-in-council up his sleeve, allowing him to search, detain, and examine anyone without *habeas corpus*.[103] PC 6444 was more draconian than even section 21 of the Defence of Canada Regulations, because now the government could not only seize people but also interrogate them without allowing them a lawyer. Conveniently forgetting British colonization, Diefenbaker cried that during no other war or rebellion had any British government detained suspects and examined them without counsel.[104] The right of liberty – *habeas corpus* – had been the "great and abiding principle of British law all through the ages ... even in the darkest days." The Star Chamber was effective, of course, but it had denied "the Magna Charta – the principal bulwark of English liberty."[105] Meanwhile, in Britain, Alan Nunn May was being given all his rights. Why were Canadians treated differently? "Is it not passing strange that these people are detained until such time as they say something that implicates them? They are then granted the right to counsel."[106] In other words, the government jails people until they confess and then offers them lawyers. Diefenbaker's speech was celebrated in an editorial in the *Globe and Mail*, where A.A. McIntosh called it "a landmark in defence of civil liberties in Canada."[107]

Later that spring, during debates on the new Citizenship Act, Diefenbaker would push for including a "Bill of Rights," so that only parliament could suspend *habeas corpus* and so that nobody without a lawyer would be forced to incriminate themselves in front of a commission.[108] He thought Canadians were eager for such a bill: "The people of Canada have become liberty-conscious by reason of what has taken place in connection with the espionage investigation," he said.[109] He bristled at the fact that an "order in counsel independent of Parliament" could diminish the rights of Canadian citizens. As long as the War Measures Act remained in place, a government could "create emergencies real or apprehended" and then use those powers "to commit arbitrary acts."[110] Of course, as King's secretary of state, Paul Martin, reminded Diefenbaker, the inclusion of a bill of rights in the Citizenship Act wouldn't limit future parliaments. Only "an organic law" that Parliament couldn't change – i.e., a constitution – could do that. The "British system," with its precedents lying in common law, had never had that type of constitution.[111]

Diefenbaker wouldn't get his bill of rights until 1960 when he was prime minister,[112] but Dominique Clément, Ross Lambertson, and Frank K. Clarke among others have described how the Kellock-Taschereau Commission served as a catalyst for the growth of a civil rights movement in Canada,[113] and constitutional scholar B.L. Strayer argues that the excesses of the federal government and of the Kellock-Taschereau Commission during the Gouzenko affair ultimately helped lead to the section 15 non-discrimination clause of the Canadian Charter of Rights and Freedoms.[114]

11
Before the Royal Commission III

16–27 March

A.A. McIntosh's *Globe and Mail* encomium of Diefenbaker as the great defender of civil liberties must have irked Mackenzie King, namesake and grandson of 1837's "Great Rebel."[1] The day after Diefenbaker's triumph, King confided to his diary that he agreed with Diefenbaker: the government deserved to be criticized for "establishing the precedent of allowing persons to be detained, etc. without counsel." King wanted to free the suspects.[2]

Then, in a well-practised Mackenzie-King pivot, he blamed the commissioners for his government's actions. How "unfair" that "counsel and commissioners" should put the Liberal party into such an awkward position! While he wrote, "It is pretty difficult to make people see that to preserve the larger liberty of the nation itself the liberty of a few individuals has been thus thwarted,"[3] he appears to have had little appreciation of the work involved in investigating the Gouzenko disclosures. As of 15 March 1946, the day King released the *Second Interim Report,* the commissioners had been at the grindstone thirty-four days (including Saturdays) questioning witnesses morning, afternoon, and evening. Witnesses included Gouzenko, RCMP personnel, senior staff of the Department of Foreign Affairs and British High Commission, immediate supervisory staff of those suspects employed by the Canadian government or military, and civil and military administrators. The subject matter of the inquiry included the history, organization, and workings of Soviet espionage in Canada; Soviet tradecraft and the ways in which Canadians were recruited and handled within that network; travel schedules, work schedules, and office routines; security procedures; and the detainees' specific espionage-related activities. By 16 March 1946 the inquiry had accumulated 2,024 pages of testimony and over 250 exhibits (often many pages long). When the inquiry concluded on 27 June 1946, that had risen to 6,042 pages of testimony[4] and well over 600 exhibits, totalling over 9,000 pages.[5]

The Kellock-Taschereau Commission was a ground-breaking investigation. "The first major post-war insight into Soviet intelligence operations in the West,"[6] as Christopher Andrews called it, couldn't have happened without the painstaking work of the commissioners and their lawyers. In his diary, King had celebrated his sudden ascendance into a role in world history and he basked in the international (especially American) applause given to Canada for taking on Soviet intelligence. But now, with the work perhaps halfway done, the inquiry had become a political and public relations inconvenience.

Eric Adams ("Ernst"), 16 March

The difficulties can be seen in the case of Eric Adams, whom Gouzenko fingered as the GRU source "Ernst." Adams, thirty-nine years old, had graduated from McGill in 1929 with an engineering degree, and he followed this with a Harvard MBA in 1931. Through the early 1930s he lived in Montreal, working for Cockfield, Brown and Company, an advertising agency, before taking a position as an economist at CPR headquarters in 1935–36. For several years he worked for Coverdale and Colpitts, a firm of consulting engineers in New York.[7] Then, in 1939, he returned to Canada, first to Toronto where he started a private consulting firm, and soon to Ottawa in November 1940 to take a position with the Bank of Canada.

In Ottawa, Adams was immediately seconded to the Wartime Requirements Board where he remained until 24 May 1941. He moved to the Foreign Exchange Control Board as "Chief of Research and Statistics Section," reporting on international financial transactions affecting Canada. This work placed Adams at the centre of Canadian wartime finance via several high-level committees, including the Inter-Departmental Committee on Balance of Payments, the Advisory Committee on Foreign Exchange Conservation, the Executive Sub-committee on Export Control, the External Trade Advisory Committee (ETAC), and the Main Examining Committee of the Wartime Inventions Board. As a result, he had links to information from the Finance Department, External Affairs, Trade and Commerce, and the NRC. In September 1944 he began work unofficially with the Industrial Development Bank.[8]

Gouzenko's linking of "Ernst" to Adams illustrated the problem for Canadian authorities in dealing with Soviet spies. Although Gouzenko

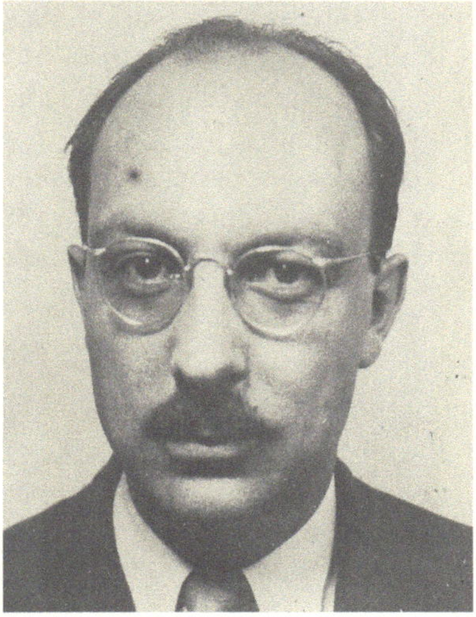

McGill- and Harvard-educated Bank of Canada bureaucrat Eric Adams (RG 33/62, Royal Commission to investigate the Communication of Secret and Confidential Information to Agents of a Foreign Power, vol. 5, "D971-80-19 SUPP C EX - Exhibit 115," photograph 129, microfilm T-3425/ e011784685)

had read Gousev's file on "Ernst," Gouzenko's account was sketchy, and he didn't even know where "Ernst" worked.[9] In any criminal trial the "Ernst"/Adams linkage would amount to hearsay, because it relied on information from a third party – Gousev – who couldn't be subpoenaed. Moreover, since Gouzenko would be considered a co-conspirator, anything he said in a courtroom would be tainted. The inquiry needed to prove that Adams, not just "Ernst," had violated the Official Secrets Act.

The day after King released the *Second Interim Report*, Adams was taken from detention at Rockcliffe to the conference room at the Justice Building. His first appearance before the inquiry did not go well. He was willing to swear that his testimony would be the truth, but he balked at the requirement that he answer every question.[10] Not until he got a lawyer would he answer every question.[11]A compromise was reached: he wouldn't have to answer every question. Round one, Adams.[12]

Fauteux began with questions about Adams's family origins, education, and work history, but Adams quickly halted him. This information was available "in a dozen different places," and, he said,[13] "not being a legal mind myself, I don't want to put myself in the position of answering even factually without legal counsel." Kellock responded that the commissioners would decide when it was time for Adams to get a lawyer, and that time hadn't yet arrived. Taschereau tried to explain that under sections 12 and 13 of the Inquiries Act Adams had no choice but to answer.[14] Adams remained adamant: "I refuse to answer without counsel."[15] Fauteux began again: Would Adams look at Exhibit No. 266?

Did Adams ever have any connection with the Russian embassy? Was Adams interested in spying for the Soviets? Did he ever meet Rogov? To these and other questions Adams responded, "No comment."[16] The inquiry adjourned. Adams was sent back to Rockcliffe.

Nine days later, the commissioners summoned Adams again and asked if he had changed his mind. He didn't know and needed a lawyer to decide. Finally, Kellock requested a name, and Adams responded, "Mr. Ahearn."

TASCHEREAU: So you want to see him?
ADAMS: Yes, I have asked to see a lawyer for thirty-eight days.[17]

The next morning, fifty-one-year-old John G. Ahearn QC, a veteran criminal defence lawyer, appeared.[18] After a one-hour consultation, the inquiry resumed with a request from Adams: "I ask for the protection of the court in this examination." Taschereau told Adams that he could have the protection of the commission, but noted that "whatever we may say will not give you more than the law affords you already by statute."[19] He did not tell Adams that the relevant law – section 5 of the Canada Evidence Act – required him to object to the future use of his testimony *every single time* that his answer might be incriminating. Later, Taschereau added that no protection existed for perjury.[20]

Even with legal representation and ground rules, Adams remained cagey. Did Exhibit No. 266, an application for national registration completed by "Eric George Adams," contain Adams's signature? "I am not sure of anything I have written if I cannot see the ink wet," Adams replied. Pressed as to whether he had made out the application, Adams said, "I do not deny or agree that I did."[21] He had sworn a multiplicity of oaths of secrecy and fidelity during his employment in the Canadian civil service, including one at the Bank of Canada[22] and another at the Foreign Exchange Control Board. Yet he was reluctant to acknowledge his signature on these documents: "It looks like my writing," he conceded. It took a while for Fauteux and the commissioners to bring him round to agreeing that there was "no doubt" that it was his signature on the documents.[23]

Kathleen Willsher had already testified in support of Gouzenko's claim that "Ernst" was Adams. From 1943 to September 1945, Adams had quizzed her on information tied to her work at the British High Commission. She had admitted giving him information, but never documents: he would ask questions and make notes on her replies. Gouzenko confirmed Willsher's account, testifying that "Ernst" had brought Willsher's information to the Russians.

Despite Gouzenko's testimony, Zabotin's mailing list of 5 January 1945 credited three documents directly to "Elli" (Willsher), including two memoranda concerning trade with Russia and marked "Secret," drafted by Canada's ambassador to the Soviet Union Dana Wilgress for Mackenzie King. The credit given to Willsher for the Wilgress correspondence seemed a mystery. Although she had testified that she had seen the substance of one of the letters at the British high commissioner's office, this was unlikely, Malcolm MacDonald said, because there was no "trace" of the correspondence being sent there.[24] MacDonald wrote, "ADAMS (who could have had access to Wilgress letters) may have shown her one and asked to obtain more information on the subject. She may therefore inadvertently have admitted to seeing it before recalling circumstances which she now wishes to hide in effort not to implicate ADAMS too deeply."[25] MacDonald was right: Adams did have access to the letters. So said Robert Bryce, the director of the Economic Division of the Department of Finance, who represented the deputy minister of finance on the External Trade Advisory Committee (ETAC), the committee that oversaw Canadian trade policy. And attending the ETAC meetings in 1944 was the Foreign Exchange Control Board's alternate rep, Eric Adams.[26]

The Wilgress correspondence would have been of particular interest to Moscow, Bryce testified, because of its insider information about British trade negotiations with the Soviets. Moscow had refused, the first letter said, an offer of credits from Britain to facilitate British exports. The Soviets also seemed to be changing their minds about buying communications technology from Britain. The second letter concerned supplies of Russian timber, required for the "reconstruction of bombed-out areas" in the UK, but Moscow was linking timber exports to more favourable trade credits. On both subjects, Wilgress disclosed political and economic problems should London not come to an agreement with the Soviets.[27] Bryce saw a copy of the letter about timber because it was referred to the Department of Finance and, as was customary, it was circulated to members of ETAC.[28] Although Adams's work had shifted to the Industrial Development Bank in the fall of 1944, he remained in Ottawa and was not formally replaced on the ETAC until 1945. As an alternate, he still could access ETAC's minutes and documentary record. He denied ever seeing the Wilgress letters,[29] yet since he admitted that he had continued to attend ETAC meetings in December 1944, he would have had access to the letters.[30] Most likely, he sought to obscure his connection to the Wilgress letters by submitting them to the Soviets under the name "Elli" rather than "Ernst."

Zabotin's notes on the GRU network (as of 1943) placed "Ernst" in the "Second Group (Ottawa Toronto)," organized by Sam Carr.[31] "Ernst" was employed "in the United Committee of Military Production of the war government (USA and Canada) (co-ordinator)."[32] He lived in Ottawa and provided the GRU with "detailed information about all kinds of industries, plans for the future." He was a "Good Worker" – he "gave materials daily"[33] – and Zabotin's 5 January 1945 mailing list credited him with twenty-five items.[34]

Among the items that "Ernst" had given to the Soviets was No.186, "Invention of Waterproofing."[35] Lesslie Reille Thompson, who had served on the Wartime Inventions Board and chaired its Main Examining Committee, testified that this likely meant Maj. A.F.P. Freeman's "waterproofing for maps, military maps, for use in tropical or extremely wet climates."[36] A related invention by Freeman was considered by the MEC on 7 December 1944, and "it was impossible to discuss" his new "battle board" invention ("a little device for looking at maps and having protection for your head and eyes in pouring rain") without discussing his earlier waterproofing invention.[37] Adams's term as the MEC's secretary ran from 14 Sept 1943 until early 1944, but he was asked to "continue in an unofficial and honorary capacity on account of the value of the work he had done for the Committee"[38] and he was present for the "battle board" discussion.[39] While the file on Freeman's waterproofing invention wasn't before the MEC at that time, Thompson explained, "it wouldn't have been seen as unusual if Adams asked to see the Freeman file."[40] This was significant because on 15 February 1946, during a search of Adams's Montreal office, the RCMP found a file titled "Minute Book of Main Examining Committee of NRC" containing over 200 pages of minutes and related documents, as well as a file titled "Inventions Board, M.E.C. Correspondence," containing some 175 pages of correspondence.[41] Adams could explain neither why the Main Examining minutes and related documents were in his possession[42] nor why the Russians would have credited him with the waterproofing document.[43]

"Ernst" also gave Zabotin over 100 pages of "Correspondence with Companies," though the GRU notes didn't detail the correspondence. Dean Marble, secretary of the Bank of Canada, assistant chair of the Foreign Exchange Control Board (FECB), and secretary of the Industrial Development Bank, doubted that the Russians would want to know about companies applying for funds from the Industrial Development Bank.[44] On the other hand, Adams's recent travel destinations and correspondence did raise questions because they were unrelated to his work in either the FECB or the Industrial Bank. Why did Adams visit the Aluminum Company of Canada[45] and the New York Shipbuilding Corporation in Camden, New Jersey?[46] Why would Adams write to the Civil Aeronautics Administration in Washington, DC, asking for a copy of the National Airport Plan prepared by the Civil Aeronautics Administration?[47] Why had Adams written to the US Senate Sub-committee on War Mobilization, asking for copies of its reports,[48] and to the Civil Aeronautics Board in Washington, DC, requesting a copy of "Overseas Air Service Patterns – Trans-Atlantic?[49] From Markle's point of view, Adams seemed to be using his formal position as chief of statistics and research at Canada's FECB to gather material far beyond his mandate, material that might indeed interest the Russians.[50] Questioned, Adams lamely countered that he didn't do this very often, and then he offered a non-explanation: "I may have written to some company some time asking for some piece of published information."[51]

Gouzenko and others had testified that GRU recruiters solicited people affiliated with the Communist movement. Given the evidence in the Russian documents, the investigation of Adams's political views and associations, as in the case of Shugar, wasn't a McCarthyite thought-police intrusion but an important investigation of motives. Adams acknowledged having read a few books written by Marx and Lenin.[52] The reading material seized on 15 February from Adams's extensive library included the *Manifesto of the Communist Party* and a number of works by Lenin – *Towards the Seizure of Power Book II, After the Seizure of Power, On the Road to Insurrection, From the Bourgeois to the Proletarian Revolution, The Communist International, What Is To Be Done, The Teachings of Karl Marx, The Struggle of the Bolshevik Party, The Tasks of the Proletariat in Our Revolution,* and *State and Revolution*[53] – classics all of Second Communist International theory and practice. Adams's copy of *State and Revolution* contained his underlining and marginal notes.[54]

However, when the commissioners and their lawyers asked Adams about his relationship to Communism, he tried to distance himself. He knew the name of a newspaper – *The Tribune* – reputed to be a Communist publication, and also the *Daily Worker*. "Occasionally" he read them.[55] He explained, "I think [Communism] is a political movement that has a lot of interest in it in these times, and that it is worth my while if I ever get the time to continue studying it as I started to."[56] Sam Carr he knew only by reputation, while Fred Rose he had met two or three years ago and he had been at Rose's residence to discuss politics a few times.[57] Was Adams a Communist? "No." What brought him to study Communism? "The interest of an inquiring mind, I guess, under modern conditions."[58]

Counter to his testimony, Adams's commitment to Stalinist Marxism ran far deeper than academic curiosity. In the summer of 1934, he and his wife Jo had travelled to the Soviet Union and, following the trip, he published five extensive articles in the *Financial Post* and a shorter article in the *Harvard Business School Alumni Bulletin*. Travellers to the Soviet Union in the 1930s usually received guided tours, and these arranged "visits to selected sites became the linchpin of presenting the Soviet system to outsiders."[59] Many of the pilgrims hoped to witness the unfolding of a socialist revolution and the dawning of a new social order. Leading British, American, and European intellectuals, labour activists, feminists, and travel writers, among others, visited the Soviet Union in the 1930s to touch the future. For example, the question in the title of Beatrice and Sidney Webb's *Soviet Communism: A New Civilization?* (1936)[60] answered itself, with the Webbs becoming, as one reviewed noted, "ardent apostles" of that new world.[61]

David Caute calls these Russian visitors "true sons and daughters of the Enlightenment, of the doctrine of Progress,"[62] while Lewis Feuer understands them as "heirs to the Platonic aspiration towards the status of philosopher-kings ... Whatever their philosophy, whether they were clergymen, existentialists, idealists, or scientific materialist, they responded warmly to the notion that their kind were ruling in the Soviet Union."[63] Some, Paul Hollander argues, were disaffected intellectuals, alienated from their home countries and casting about for a better organization of society. They found it in Stalin's Five-Year Plans and in the utopian accounts of Russia's socioeconomic transformation.[64]

The disaffected-intellectual characterization seems to fit Eric Adams. Social democrat John P. Humphrey knew Adams during their McGill days and debated politics with him in the 1930s. Humphreys, who went on to become the first director of the UN Human Rights Division and the primary author of the first draft of the UN Universal Declaration on Human Rights,[65] wrote in his diary that Adams's education as an engineer led him to expect "mathematically precise answers to problems, and so, when he switched his field to economics, he naturally gravitated towards Marxism – the one philosophy that claimed to offer precise answers." In the early 1930s, the Humphreys had socialized with the Adamses, but the men's political discussions frequently became so heated that Humphrey's wife suggested they see less of one another.[66]

In 1934, for almost two months, Eric and Jo Adams travelled Russia from north to south, visiting towns, cities, industrial sites, and collective farms.[67] Adams's five resulting articles in the *Financial Post* and for the *Harvard Business School Alumni Bulletin* reach the level of sales brochures.[68] Prior to his trip he had heard "about the impending famine in Russia" so, he reported, "I made a point of asking about the grain crop everywhere I went." Result: "all through the Ukraine … the crop is good."[69] He was particularly enchanted with "a little experimental station which the members of the collective had set up themselves. Here, they carried on tests on various kinds of soils … and the development of the best seeds, fertilizers, and methods of cultivation to use."[70] Almost invisible in Adams's "Russia To-day" are the turmoil and death that haunted Stalin's first Five-Year Plan. Stepping carefully, he notes that "a rapid change in the national economy, from predominantly agricultural to industrial" might cause what he euphemistically calls "complications and unforeseen strains in the system."[71] But, apart from a few dead animals, the upheavals were good: "So out went the kulaks (or a good many of them) and with them, in the winter of 1929–30 alone, one quarter of the cows, one third of the sheep, one half of the pigs and more than 10 per cent of the horses in the country."[72] Older people didn't always seem happy, but "the young people (under 35) whom I saw in all parts of the country looked both healthy and happy. Many of them had positively plump faces, and I must confess that I saw in them neither the dread of oppression nor the strain of the relentless drive of the Five Year Plans, as some observers in Russia profess to do. The little children are particularly fine. They are fat, happy, and bright." Via the Five-Year Plans, in fact, "the people have had their coöperative spirit greatly developed."[73] In the wake of collectivization, Adams only saw a transformed agriculture: "the land was well tilled and not covered with weeds." He counted dead livestock, but not the millions of starved humans.

Adams celebrated the Soviet Union's industrial advances. During the construction of the new tractor factory at Kharkov, "the people of the city contributed their free days in manual labor." The factory workers "consider that they are working for themselves and that the tractors that they make are their tractors." Adams said, "this feeling of working for themselves I found in every worker with whom I talked." The grounds surrounding the factory were "nicely parked and landscaped, a practice which is apparent in many places where a new plant has been built." The "workers' settlement" adjacent to the factory included "apartments, nursery, school, dispensary, stores, recreation grounds, etc. in fact everything to make the settlement completely self-contained."[74] Unlike Adams, contemporaneous sources who weren't pledged to sell an ideal provide a far less sanguine account of the 1932–34 famine: unbelievable suffering, mass deaths, and even cannibalism.[75] In addition to the state-inflicted starvation of five to ten million people,[76] Stalin's government engaged in mass political arrests and executions, and sent two to four million citizens to prisons or work camps.[77] Industrial workers suffered less than those in the countryside, but even they were not spared. At a "showplace" tractor plant in Kharkov, a "large colony of privileged foreign workers ... subsisted on a starvation diet"[78] ("privileged" because they *weren't* starving) while grappling with "despair at having to work alongside starving, stupefied and dazed Russian workers."[79] These conditions had been authoritatively reported (though without numerical estimates) in the Canadian press prior to the publication of Adam's articles.[80]

Historian of the Soviet Union Sheila Fitzpatrick calls accounts such as Adams's the "standard Western fellow traveller's tale of the visit to the Soviet Union." These tales emphasized "popular enthusiasm; support for science and education; high valuation of culture (high culture brought to the masses); welfare institutions, especially for workers, women, and children; economic growth under the Plan,"[81] and ignored "evidence of poverty, famine (in the early 1930s), begging, coercion, exclusion (of 'social aliens' with the wrong class background); GULAG, censorship, [and] internal surveillance." Ultimately, for Communists or Communist sympathizers visiting the Soviet Union, the pressure to make a glowing report of this new socialist world "was considered something close to a duty."[82] Yet Adams was supposedly not that kind of a visitor. *The Financial Post* (clearly on his say-so) introduced his articles with the assertion that he was "not a Communist" and that he sought to provide an "objective" account of conditions in the Soviet Union.[83]

Adams's unpublished work would have belied "not a Communist." In Adams's home, inside a grey looseleaf notebook, the RCMP found an eleven-page document entitled "Outline for a Research Project on a Comprehensive History of Canada" and a three-page handwritten document, "Special Questions for Research."[84] Before the untimely death in January 1945 of George Luxton, a graduate of McGill and Harvard who had joined the research branch of the Bank of Canada in 1940,[85] he and Adams had planned "an economic history of Canada, one that would reveal the economic sub-structure of the nation's development and divert students' attention from traditional constitutional lines of development."[86] The RCMP found Adams's outline and extensive bibliography for that book project. The outline treats Canadian economic development as the expression of a monopoly, with a "social program" of "enlightened paternalism" expressed through the "moulding of public philosophy (education)," and a political program that merges British, American, and Canadian capitalists in "a supra-national class interest" (with Canada as "a secondary imperialist power") that limits political participation via "tactics vs third parties." The result is "Parasitism of finance capital." As for culture, "low level and confused state reflects ruling class lack of clear objectives and environment of declining world class culture."[87]

The Soviet current of Third International Marxism of the Communist International embraced by Stanley Ryerson and other Canadian Communist leaders dominated Canadian Communism in the 1940s.[88] Ian McKay has argued that CCF leaders such as David Lewis and F.R. Scott, particularly in their widely read *Make This Your Canada* (1943), belonged very much to the same Marxist orthodoxy. However, although they credited Marx for showing the working class "a positive programme for political action ... for the purpose of supplanting capitalism by a new economic order,"[89] Lewis and Scott, contra McKay, moved far beyond Marx in intellectual and organizational debts to British trade unions, the international cooperative movement, the social gospel, and agrarian radicalism.[90] Their multivoiced language stood in contrast to the monological Marxism that in Ryerson, Tim Buck, and Adams took its cue from Stalin and his widely diffused primer *Dialectical and Historical Materialism*, first published in English in 1940.[91] Yet Marxist currents during the Communist International extended well beyond those that ran through Moscow, the most striking example being Antonio Gramsci's renovation of Second International Marxism. It is quite possible that Adams and Luxton, particularly in their emphasis on the role of finance capital in a colonial setting, might well have produced an innovative Marxist-inflected economic history of Canada.[92]

Fauteux tried to push Adams into acknowledging his Marxist ideals, but Adams, who had aspired to write Canadian history through Marx, now painted himself as a dabbler, someone who had only a nodding acquaintance with Communism. Fauteux mocked him, asking, "Is there anything secretive about being a Communist or being sympathetic to the Communist party, or its ideas?"[93] Of course, early in the Second World War, during the era of prosecutions under the Defence of Canada Regulations, membership in the Communist Party might land one in jail, as later on might Communist associations linked to a conspiracy under the Official Secrets Act. At the same time, by1946 the need for secrecy about Communist affiliations was also a product of Moscow's determination to draw sympathizers into GRU spying.

Kathleen Willsher had already testified about the Communist study groups that Adams led and about his role in Soviet spying. On street corners in Ottawa and Montreal, she had given him the British High Commission information that he wanted, and, for the Montreal trip he had paid her twenty-five dollars to cover travel expenses. At the inquiry, Adams tried to reframe her testimony. He would only admit that he had met her at "some party or other probably … [a] social gathering" in Ottawa,[94] but he didn't "remember" being the group's leader.[95] Was Willsher lying about the study groups she attended? "I do not know," he said.[96] First he claimed that he hadn't attended any study groups in Ottawa,[97] but later he tacitly conceded that Communist books were discussed, though he couldn't remember at whose house the meetings happened or who attended.[98] He refused to state, categorically, that Willsher's information was true or false – everything lay in a haze, somewhere on an individual relativist scale: "Her statement does not coincide with what I believe to be the truth." And again, "I do not want to be put in the position of saying somebody is a liar because somebody may be talking from their own opinion. I am giving my opinion." He couldn't "recall" asking Willsher for British High Commission information. Would he *deny* asking for information? Adams said, "I cannot go further than that."[99]

Adams tried to downgrade his handling of Willsher's spying into mere social visits. Yet Willsher had given precise details about where and when she met Adams, for example at the streetcar stop at the corner of Lisgar and Bank. Adams would pick her up in his car, ask her questions, and she would do her best to answer. Fauteux queried him, "Do you suppose, for one moment, that this is misconstruction, or invention, or the truth?" Adams called it a "misconstruction," suggesting that Willsher had turned a "casual conversation" into something else.[100] Willsher had testified that Adams came to Ottawa for meetings with her three or four times, and that Agatha Chapman made the arrangements. Did Willsher invent this testimony? Adams countered, "She has grossly misconstrued a few casual meetings." Adams denied that he came to Ottawa by car several times. "I may have come once in the car, that is all."[101] A few minutes later, he admitted that perhaps "once or twice … I had some occasion to let Miss Chapman know that I was going to be in Ottawa, and that I would like to see Miss Willsher … for social reasons."[102] Adams conceded that Willsher had come to his residence in Montreal once, but only for a "social" visit. He didn't know who had invited her – maybe his wife. Adams denied that he had given Willsher twenty-five dollars (which, adjusted for inflation, would be about $470 in 2026) to cover her travel expenses.[103] Had Willsher committed perjury by alleging that he gave her the twenty-five dollars? Adams replied, "I do not remember that." Would he deny that he had given Willsher the money? "I have no opinion on it," he said, "because I do not remember it."[104]

The commissioners subpoenaed Agatha Chapman,[105] who had participated in the study groups, hosting some at her own home."[106] Born in England in 1907, she arrived in Canada in 1918. By 1928, after two years at the University of Toronto, her progressive sympathies were already evident. Addressing the University College Women's Literary Society, she lamented that the "pitiful thing about [Walt] Whitman is that the masses for whom he wrote did not accept him, and the scholars for whom he had no thought, did."[107] She completed a bachelor of commerce (1930) and a master of arts in economics (1931) before moving to Montreal for work.[108] Not long afterwards, she connected with Irene Kon, and followed her to the advertising firm Young and Rubicam.[109] For Chapman, it was Kon and her father Louis who opened up a network of relationships with members of the Communist left.[110] During the Popular Front era, Louis served as the Montreal secretary of the supposedly apolitical Friends of the Soviet Union. Chapman joined the organization and served on the executive.[111]

Like so many others who became entangled in the Gouzenko affair, Chapman responded politically to the economic crises of the 1930s. Late in the decade, she joined a study group sponsored by the Fellowship for a Christian Social Order (FCSO),[112] which consisted of United Church ministers and university theologians rooted in the social gospel. Eventually, laymen such as Eugene Forsey were accepted too.[113] Forsey, in the FCSO-sponsored *Towards the Christian Revolution*,[114] declared, "Until Christians learn to understand and apply the lessons of Marxism they cannot enter into the Kingdom of Heaven."[115] Like many other progressives in Montreal, Chapman was galvanized by the Spanish Civil War and the Duplessis government's campaign against the left. In 1938 she joined the Montreal chapter of the Civil Liberties Union and within a year was elected to its executive[116] as the CLU fought first the Padlock Act and then the Defence of Canada Regulations.[117]

In 1938, Chapman left Young and Rubicam to join the Sun Life Insurance Company, but as treasurer on the CLU executive, she soon found herself at the centre of the CLU's May 1940 "fifth-column" storm. During the March federal election, when the Communist Party had dismissed Canada's struggle against Nazi Germany as an imperialist war, public outrage against Communists had flared across Canada. An anti-government resolution pushed by Communist-affiliated delegates at the CLU's national conference on civil liberties seemed to signal that the CLU was Moscow's stalking horse for a common front – not against fascism but against the Canadian war effort. With membership in the Montreal CLU now a symbol of disloyalty, Sun Life very quickly took steps to disassociate itself emphatically from the CLU. Chapman was given a choice: quit the CLU or be fired. She chose to be fired.[118] Shortly thereafter, in the US Communist journal *New Masses*, the CLU's executive secretary R.A.C. Ballantyne spoke about "paid staff ... being attacked in the Montreal press and about demands that he be jailed." "Weaker members of the Civil Liberties Union Executive Board," he said, "resigned under pressure,"[119] but two members of the executive (he and presumably Chapman) lost their jobs,[120] and he suspected that they would be blacklisted for the rest of the war.[121] Chapman's name does not appear in accounts of Montreal-based Communist study groups of the 1930s, yet her willingness to defy the pressure and to be labelled a Communist at a time when the Soviet Union was viewed as an ally of Nazi Germany expressed the strength of her commitment. According to Merrily Weisbord, at some point during the war Chapman became a Section 13 member of the Communist Party.[122]

Despite Ballantyne's well-founded blacklisting fears, Chapman surfaced in Ottawa at the beginning of September as an employee of the Bank of Canada, where she met Adams.[123] She testified that Adams and Willsher attended the study sessions at her Ottawa apartment, where Marxism was "sometimes" discussed and money was collected to buy periodicals such as *National Affairs Monthly* or *New Masses* and, on "special occasions," to support the Windsor strike, Aid to Russia, and the Canadian Soviet Friendship Council.[124] The "sometimes" was questionable: Fred Rose was a frequent visitor[125] and Ned Mazerall had accepted Fauteux's characterization of the Chapman gatherings as "a cell of the communist party."[126] However, Chapman denied being a go-between for Adams and Willsher. She hadn't communicated with him since he left Ottawa for Montreal at the beginning of 1945,[127] and she insisted that she couldn't recollect arranging for Willsher to meet Adams.[128]

Some historians see Chapman as an innocent victim.[129] Did she know that the study groups held at her apartment were used to cultivate and recruit agents for the GRU? It's possible that Chapman's involvement in Communism was purely ideological and her actions entirely above board, but Willsher's testimony about Chapman's role as go-between for Adams, alongside Chapman's evasiveness during the inquiry about that role, suggest that she probably knew. Still, none of her actions were criminal, as a subsequent trial would confirm. Dorise Neilsen, who visited Chapman with Rose and recalled her as "a friend," suggested that Chapman's suicide in 1963 could be explained in part by her loss of "faith in communism."[130] To this, one must add her arthritis and the fact that her post-war blacklisting made it impossible for her to get work commensurate with her talents.[131] As Judith Alexander says, while

Chapman's career held such promise, "one cannot escape the feeling that her life was blighted."[132]

At the conclusion of Adams's interrogation, the commissioners didn't indicate any charge that they intended to make. They invited him and his lawyer Ahearn to submit any information or testimony, but Adams only wanted to see the minutes of the Main Examining Committee of the Wartime Inventions Board included in the inquiry's record.[133] Afterwards, the commissioners recommended charges against Adams for conspiring to offend the Official Secrets Act.[134] Ultimately, Adams's non-answers paid off. Whereas Willsher – more or less Adams's dupe – received three years in the penitentiary, Adams, after a trial in October 1946 on one charge, was acquitted,[135] and the Crown eventually stayed the other charges.[136] In later years, among his notes, Adams had several partial drafts of what appear to be legal arguments exonerating Willsher and protesting her imprisonment. There's no evidence that he ever completed the work or sent it out.[137]

Scotland Benning ("Foster"), 22 March

The strategic nature of the targets chosen by the GRU for penetration by their Canadian agents grew increasingly apparent as the inquiry progressed. Clearly, Moscow viewed the Department of External Affairs, the British High Commission, the National Research Council, the Canadian Armed Forces,[138] the Bank of Canada, and the Department of Munitions and Supply (DMS) as strategic centres, and was playing a long game by recruiting well-placed agents such as "Foster," the GRU source who handed Moscow extensive records from the DMS.

It would be hard to exaggerate the importance of the DMS to the Canadian war effort. The energetic and ever-resourceful C.D. Howe, organizing the Canadian economy for war production,[139] made the DMS the administrative epicentre of the private and Crown corporations (some newly created[140]) that were producing staples and materiel for the Allied war effort. At its inception in April 1940, DMS employed 300 people, mostly in Ottawa. By April 1943 there were 5,000, including 3,000 in the "Temporary Buildings" in Ottawa, with the rest at "strategic purchasing or control points" in Canada, London (England), and Washington, DC.[141] Factoring in the private and crown corporations, some 900,000 people worked directly in war production.[142]

Every week (by June 1943) Canada produced six or more vessels (escort, cargo, or patrol), 80 planes, 4,000 motor vehicles and 450 fighting vehicles, 900 heavy guns, 525,000 rounds of "heavy ammunition," 25,000,000 rounds of small arms ammunition, 10,000 tons of explosive chemical, and four million dollars' worth of instruments and communications equipment.[143] To the Soviet Union, which Howe called Canada's "great and successful ally," Canada had sent 1,400 tanks, more than 2,000 Canadian Universal carriers, naval and Bren guns, anti-tank rifles, ammunition for heavy guns and small arms, machine tools, boots, gloves, textiles, clothing, and personal equipment.[144] In the last two years of the war, Canada donated $2 billion worth of Canadian-produced goods through the Canadian Mutual Aid Board, mostly to Britain and other Commonwealth countries, but the Soviet Union received $116 million dollars worth of aluminum and other base metals; wheat and flour; and electrical, radio, telephone, and automotive equipment.[145] As the war in Europe ended, Ottawa hoped that the Soviet Union would still want Canadian industrial equipment but would pay for it on credit. Extended negotiations went nowhere. Other allies accepted the credit terms; Moscow refused.[146]

In order to keep its complicated production structure running smoothly, DMS required some "one hundred formal reports" each month,[147] mainly from its Economics and Statistics Branch.[148] On Zabotin's list of items leaked to Moscow, many had come from DMS, and Gouzenko testified that Scotland Benning, code-named "Foster," had delivered seventy of those items.

Benning had joined the Ammunition Branch of DMS in 1942 and moved to Economics and Statistics in the early fall of 1943. Working in Production Statistics, he (alongside others) assembled statistics about gun and small arms ammunition, mechanical transport, and armoured fighting vehicles for a quarterly report entitled *Forecast of Canadian War Production*.[149] As the liaison officer for the Ammunition Branch he also connected with other production branches in the DMS, and, as joint secretary of the Canadian Munitions Assignment Committee[150] he helped to ensure timely and strategic assignment of Canadian-made munitions to other Allied forces.[151]

Gouzenko did not bring "Foster's" GRU file with him when he defected, but Zabotin's notes show that "Foster" had been serving Soviet intelligence since at least 1942, had been recruited by Sam Carr, and was "Assistant to the superintendent of the department of distribution of war production" at DMS. Through his handler Nikolay Zheveinov ("Martin"), "Foster" had given the Soviets information about "war material, guns and other kinds of supplies." According to Zabotin's notes, in the fall of 1943 "Foster" was "obtaining other work with promotion" and would soon "give better materials."[152] Indeed, in the fall of 1943 Benning was promoted from the Ammunition Branch to Economics and Statistics.[153]

Munitions and Supply statistics clerk Scotland Benning (Library Archives Canada, J. Scott Benning – PA-129637)

Benning had grown up in Anglo Montreal, downtown on Bishop Street. For six years he worked as a "cost clerk"[154] and, after a short time at the Allied War Supplies Corporation, where he was introduced to DMS record-keeping processes, he joined the DMS in June 1942. Maj. A.J. Lawrence, head of production control at Allied, testified that he had hired Benning on the recommendation of Harold Gerson, a GRU accomplice who also happened to be Benning's brother-in-law.[155] Gerson offered a slightly different account, saying that Ottawa-based Col. G. Ogilvie of DMS was looking for an administrative assistant, so Gerson suggested Benning.[156] In Benning's own account, he was reluctant to take the position, but Gerson convinced him that it was "a patriotic duty … a real step in assisting the general war effort."[157]

Hewing to the unforgiving clauses of the Official Secrets Act, the commissioners asked about Benning's associations, probing his "known character."[158] Later, "known character" would be dismissed by judges as a threat to civil liberties, but the close partnership between Soviet intelligence and leading Canadian Communists – party leaders recruiting spies for the GRU – made the associations relevant, especially for important players such as Lunan and Benning. Testimony had already shown the commissioners Benning's social and political connections to Raymond Boyer, Gordon Lunan, David Shugar,[159] and especially Matt Nightingale, who was Benning's "very good friend."[160] Kathleen Willsher recalled Benning's attendance at a study group led by Eric Adams at Agatha Chapman's place.[161] In fact, Ned Mazerall had testified that his encounter with Benning at a study group left him with the impression that Benning wasn't just an attendee, but a Communist Party functionary during the illegal period.[162]

Benning did his best to pretend that he barely knew many of his Labor-Progressive colleagues. The gathering at Agatha Chapman's, he suggested, wasn't a study group but "a social evening," even though everybody talked mostly economics and politics.[163] As for Boyer, Benning recalled meeting him only once, saying that Boyer was "slightly out of my class, speaking financially."[164] Boyer, however, had testified about knowing Benning for "a good many years," and about Benning's Labor-Progressive loyalties. Asked to explain the inconsistency, Benning responded lamely: "A man with his training might have a more retentive memory than mine."[165] Despite Ned Mazerall's testimony, Benning insisted that he hadn't come to a study-group secretaries' meeting at Agatha Chapman's to hear Fred Rose: Rose was "definitely not there."[166] Willsher, Shugar, and Adams he had met skiing.[167] Was the name "Adam" or "Adams"?[168] Benning wondered, despite Gerson's testimony that Adams had come to a party at Benning's home.[169]

Benning chronicled his odyssey of political awakening, arising out of a youthful conviction that the world could be a better place. Through their mutual involvement in the activities of the Spanish Medical Aid Committee, the China Relief Committee, and the League Against Fascism and War, he met Gordon Lunan in Montreal around 1938. "I was what you would call a parlour-pink, I believe," Benning explained, "or as some of the more orthodox would call an arm-chair Bolshevik."[170] His was in many respects a generational story: awakening into intellectual awareness during the Great Depression – watching its economic depredations and leaning more and more towards a radical political response.

Benning's political engagement began in 1930, during his final year of high school, when he became a pacifist and refused to participate in the school cadet program: "Shortly after that I did a fair amount of reading, mostly of a left-wing nature," he recalled.[171] Especially potent was Beverley Nicholls's *Cry Havoc*,[172] which one reviewer described as "not simply a bit of pacifist propaganda, but a thorough job of research into the activities of offensive preparations going on in the armament factories in England and on the Continent."[173] From there Benning moved on to *The Merchants of Death*,[174] a report on the international arms trade,[175] and to works by Harold Laski and John Strachey pronouncing capitalist democracy doomed and insisting that only a Marxist response could solve Depression woes.[176] Benning even dipped his toes into Marx but found him "a bit too cumbersome." Excepting R. Palme Dutt, Benning found "most of the more orthodox of the Communist writers" a similar struggle.[177]

His reading, Benning explained in his testimony, made him gravitate "to people holding rather liberal viewpoints," and he became "quite interested at one time in the [Montreal] Civil Liberties League or Union."[178] He joined the Spanish and Chinese Relief Committees and the League Against War and Fascism, "stuffing envelopes" and doing "things of that nature."[179] But he distanced himself from the committees' Communists: "I had my own suspicions," he explained, "and later they were pretty well founded, that they were composed equally of people who sincerely believed in it, with no particular axe to grind, and a fair sprinkling of people who I found out later were Communists." Had Benning ever been a member of the Communist or the Labor-Progressive Parties? "No. I never joined either of those parties," he said.[180]

Benning portrayed his relationship with Fred Rose and Sam Carr as similarly distant. With the Official Secrets Act's reverse onus clause, merely having the name or address of, or other information about, a suspected foreign agent could put one in jeopardy.[181] Benning had attended a 1938 Labour Day rally in Montreal where Carr spoke,[182] and had met both men at social events: "I bumped into [Rose] at these cocktail parties and musicales that the left-wing circles used to hold to raise funds for – what was the Communist paper called in those days? I think it was *The Clarion*, and then it became *The Tribune*." The contact was "purely social."[183] How then, Kellock asked, did Benning explain a telephone number and address for Rose in Benning's handwriting in a directory on his DMS desk? Benning replied, "I am afraid I cannot, sir. I may have put the numbers down as I was in the habit of putting down the numbers of everybody I had known or met at various times."[184]

Yet, despite Benning's supposedly incidental contact with leading Communists, no one contributed more to the 5 January 1945 consignment of intelligence to Moscow than "Foster," who brought seventy items.[185] "Foster" was Benning's code name, as evidenced by the exact description of his former role ("Assistant to the superintendent of the department of distribution of war production" at DMS)[186] and by Gouzenko's testimony that a Soviet embassy file prepared by Sergei Gousev named Benning as "Foster."[187] A related GRU document disclosed that "Foster ... Gave material about war material, guns, and other kinds of supplies."[188]

But Benning, waxing hyperbolic, was adamant that, even unconsciously, he hadn't passed any information to the Russians: "Consciously or unconsciously I have not given any information in writing, by word of mouth to anybody but authorized officials of the Canadian government."[189] Could Benning then explain why secret records in the

Russian embassy said that he had spied for the GRU? In fact, he could. Benning remembered *Out of the Night*,[190] a 1941 Book-of-the-Month-Club autobiography of "a Communist thug, saboteur, and spy." "Full of convincing and specific detail," one reviewer wrote, "it paints a frightening picture of the ruthless criminality of the international Communist movement."[191] "An awful lot of the book was a complete fabrication," Benning educated the commissioners, but one thing chimed with "other reading" he had done "in espionage": that spies could steal money from their superiors by pretending to pay informants. Perhaps, Benning suggested, a GRU operative had pretended to pay him! No spying took place, but the GRU operative may have cashed in by pretending that Benning was an informant. The defence was ludicrous, and it lacked one small detail. E.K. Williams immediately pounced: the Soviets kept a list of Canadians who had been paid for spying … and "Foster" wasn't on it.[192]

Because each item of Zabotin's 5 January list of materials from Canadian informants had been cryptically referenced, it proved difficult to identify the original documents. The commissioners turned to J.C. Dobie, a senior member of the Finance Statistics Division in Economics and Statistics, to identify the sources.[193] Of the seventy items credited to "Foster," twenty (totaling 120 pages and dating from November and December 1944) were particularly important. They concerned the production adjustments required as stage 1 of the war ended (with the soon-expected Victory in Europe Day) and stage 2 began (the push to defeat Japan).[194] Through this documentary record, Moscow could assess the military posture of Britain in Europe and in the Pacific.[195] For example, a 21 November 1944 telegram (item no. 116), designated "Top Secret" on Zabotin's list, set out London's revised production targets for Canadian factories.[196] Every production cable sent to H.J. Carmichael, coordinator of production at DMS, also crossed Benning's desk in Economics and Statistics, as Benning acknowledged.[197] He described that time of the war: "We were fluctuating rather madly, trying to keep these documents, similar ones, up to date," given the "very drastic reductions" expected at the end of stage 1.[198]

Dobie identified one of "Foster's" items as key, a telegram dated 29 November 1944 and coded as "Telva 2151."[199] With its statistical data about the production targets for ammunition, artillery shells, grenades, and fuses, the telegram's circulation was restricted,[200] but Benning had seen it because of his role in Economics and Statistics.[201] Why, Williams asked, would Zabotin's list have credited him with delivering Telva 2151? Even the Book of the Month Club failed Benning here: "I can offer no suggestions at all in that instance," he said.[202]

Connected to "Telva 2151" were a series of sixteen cables from the British Ministry of Supply to Canada's DMS between 16 and 23 November 1944. The British wanted Canada to make the production of selected artillery shells an "OVERRIDING PRIORITY," and urged that production facilities be "PUSHED TO THE VERY LIMIT."[203] The cables also requested vehicles, airplanes, weapons, small arms ammunition, installation kits (machine guns), signals production and instruments, Windsor and Universal Carriers (for anti-tank guns), and fuses (detonators).[204] On 1 August 1944, meeting with Canadian officials, John Maynard Keynes had explained Britain's financial position – the difficulties of getting through stage 2 (the Japanese phase of the war) with sufficient overseas reserves to weather stage 3 (the reconstruction of Britain's post-war economy).[205] To accomplish this, Britain asked Canada for debt forgiveness and loans,[206] culminating in the financial agreements of February 1946.[207] Since the Soviet Union wanted to know the military and political posture and capabilities of the West, intelligence gathered by Emma Woikin (External Affairs), Kathleen Willsher (British High Commission), Eric Adams (Bank of Canada), Harold Gerson (DMS), and Scott Benning (DMS) could give the Kremlin a hidden window into how well the West's financial and military capacity could resist Soviet post-war strategic ambitions, as well as whether London could mount a campaign in the Far East to regain its colonial possessions.

Benning recalled seeing some of this traffic.[208] He had access to the entire run of 30 November memoranda,[209] he said, but only took note of those related to his work.[210] Among the DMS items in GRU hands and credited to "Foster"[211] were No. 151 ("Supplement to Contracts," dated November 1944) and No. 193 ("Product'n of Arms for the Month of November," dated 12 December 1944), which appeared to be copies of the DMS November memoranda.[212] "Who, other than yourself," Williams asked Benning, "would be in a position to deliver this [No. 193] to the Russian Embassy?" Since Benning didn't know who else had worked on it, he said, many people *could* have handed the report to the Soviets.[213] He didn't contest any assertions that the items on Zabotin's list had come from the DMS memoranda, but he claimed that someone else must have done the spying. As for No.151, several people in Economics and Statistics worked on it. After being assembled, it was sent to a typing pool where a stencil was cut. Someone probably took the stencil elsewhere for reproductions, said Benning, because the Branch's printing shop was always busy. It was customary to have eighty to eighty-five copies of the document, sometimes more. Early on, copies were torn into shreds or given to a janitor to burn. Later, they were just "tossed around." In Benning's view, "hundreds of people ... could have had access to those documents."[214]

Other "Foster" items on Zabotin's list had come across Benning's desk at Economics and Statistics too.[215] A production report of aircraft by all of the companies – for example, Boeing (Vancouver) and Canadian Associated Aircraft (Montreal) – included numerical data and the types of aircraft produced: Hampton, Hurricane, Curtiss Hellcat.[216] A "Production of Ships" report[217] seemed to come from a multipage document, "Deliveries and Forecasts of Deliveries for 1944–45," containing cumulative data on ship construction and detailing the production of Corvettes, Frigates, Minesweepers, and Cargo ships.[218]

Given the provenance of some DMS items, Williams tried, unsuccessfully, to probe Benning's relationship with his brother-in-law Harold Gerson ("Gray"). Items No. 155[219] and No. 156[220] on Zabotin's list appeared to come from a 23 November 1944 sub-committee meeting of the Joint Gun Ammunition Production Committee,[221] for which Gerson took minutes. Gerson could have authored the material, Williams said, but Zabotin's list attributed the documents to Benning. Why else would his name be on the document?[222] Benning insisted that it was "very difficult to believe" that Gerson was giving information to the Russians,"[223] but most of all Benning objected to Williams using his name in relation to the GRU list: "I prefer if you use the name Foster, sir." Kellock replied, "Benning was used because the dossier on Benning in the Russian Embassy disclosed that James Scotland Benning's 'cover name' was 'Foster.'" Taschereau pointed to Gouzenko's testimony confirming the same.[224]

Benning lawyer H.P. Hill KC countered that, on the other hand, apparently nothing on Zabotin's list came from the Canadian Munitions Assignment Committee (Army), despite the fact that from 1943 Benning had served as the committee's joint secretary. It was perhaps the most important DMS committee for allocating munitions[225] and its discussions were top secret. The "sole criterion" for allocating munitions was "military expediency," so to jump the line, Britain or the US or even (through the Mutual Aid Board) Russia, China, Australia, New Zealand, and other allied nations might provide "in confidence ... details of critical military situations." Because of the sensitive military information, Benning explained, the chairman sometimes asked that no minutes be taken.[226] Yet despite all the critical military information, nothing in Gouzenko's stolen Soviet files had been linked to that committee.[227]

Ultimately, in the *Third Interim* and the *Final Report*, the commissioners used Gouzenko's hearsay evidence, a range of circumstantial evidence, Benning's relationship with Fred Rose and Harold Gerson, and Official Secrets Act, Sec. 3(2) about "known character" to accuse Benning of spying.[228] Since Rose and Gerson were agents of a foreign power,[229] the commissioners pointed at Benning's communication with the two.[230] Judging the secret Soviet documents to be accurate, the commissioners used the act's reverse onus clause to insist that it had been Benning's job to satisfy them that he hadn't given away Canadian secret information. "We are not so satisfied," they concluded.[231]

Benning was released from detention under PC 6444 and immediately rearrested on a charge of offending the Official Secrets Act. His jury trial took place in October 1946 before Chief Justice McRuer of the Ontario High Court,[232] with Gouzenko testifying that Benning was "Foster," one of Moscow's "most active agents."[233] In his charge to the jury, McRuer placed special emphasis on Benning's possession of Fred Rose's home and office phone numbers.[234] While cautioning the jury that Gouzenko's evidence "must be corroborated by other testimony since he was once a co-conspirator in the Russian espionage ring himself,"[235] McRuer implied that Benning's relationship with Rose met that evidentiary challenge. As one of the first judges to instruct a jury on the provisions of the Official Secrets Act, McRuer followed Parliament's lead. The Law Reform Commission later agreed that a broad reading of the act's evidentiary provisions "was fairly obviously Parliament's intention all along."[236] After a four-hour deliberation, the jury found Benning guilty, and McRuer sentenced him to five years in the penitentiary.

Benning appealed. Commissions of inquiry are rarely subject to judicial review, but because the Kellock-Taschereau proceedings were designed to produce criminal charges against the suspected spies, it was inevitable that a judicial gaze would fall on the findings of the inquiry. Benning argued that McRuer had misdirected the jury and had misinterpreted the meaning of the Official Secrets Act.[237] Concurring, the Ontario Court of Appeal issued a strong juridical critique of the Kellock-Taschereau finding against Benning and, by implication, against the wartime jurisprudence that informed the act.[238] Ontario Chief Justice R.S. Robertson dismissed Gouzenko's hearsay evidence. Yes, Gouzenko had revealed a conspiracy. However, in Benning's case, if there was no corroborating evidence "it is not evidence at all," Robertson said, and added that even the prosecution's arguments underscored this evidentiary rule. Since other members of Benning's DMS branch also had access to the documents credited to "Foster," there was no certainty that the documents came from Benning. No witness was called, Robertson noted, "who said the appellant had obtained, collected, recorded, published or communicated to another person or persons any document or information" contravening the Official Secrets Act.[239] Of course, in a conspiracy, such witnesses are rare. Robertson's most trenchant commentary was directed at the Crown's reliance on the Official Secrets Act to find "evidence" of Benning's guilt. Robertson agreed that Benning's association with "Gerson, and possibly in the case of Rose also" could be considered "communication with an agent of a foreign power." However, living in Ottawa, how could one *avoid* that?

The nature of the legal system is such that once a judge decides a case, their decision is voiced in a manner that discounts whatever doesn't fit the decision – in this case the disavowed connection of Benning and Rose, a connection that certainly wasn't a result of living in Ottawa. In addition, Robertson argued that "the circumstances in which Benning lived and worked made his frequent association with Gerson practically unavoidable," yet there was "not a particle of evidence from anyone that [Benning] ... knew anything of Gerson's connection with the conspiracy that Gouzenko describes.[240] This was hyperbole, not only because Gerson was Benning's brother-in-law, but also in regard to producing evidence: who exactly could be called upon to give "evidence" that Benning knew that Gerson was a spy? Perhaps for rhetorical effect, Robertson even gave credence to the fact that Benning had "denied the charge"![241]

More substantially, Robertson noted, simply *obtaining* information was not an offence under the statute, nor was it a feature of the formal charge against Benning. If half of Ottawa could in theory be charged with communicating with a foreign agent, then it seemed obvious to Robertson that a more limited interpretation of the act must have been intended. He rejected the idea that Parliament had intended that communication with an agent of a foreign power could supply "all the evidence needed for a conviction under s. 3(1)(c)."[242] He also rejected the reverse onus provisions of the act. Parliament couldn't have intended "to shift the whole burden of proving his innocence upon the accused simply because he had communicated with a foreign agent."[243] The three judges of the Ontario Court of Appeal all voted to quash Benning's conviction.[244]

Of course, counter to the Court of Appeal judges, who hewed closely to a civil liberties narrative, Parliament *had* intended much broader room for evidence. The 1867 Interpretation Act had called for a "fair, large and liberal construction and interpretation" of parliamentary statutes.[245] Given that the 1939 Official Secrets Act – supported by Arthur Meighen on behalf of the Conservatives and A.A. Heaps on behalf of the CCF – had been meant to attack any foreign conspiracies, and that like, for example, Canada's 2001 Anti-Terrorism Act, it attempted to address a danger whose extent wasn't yet known, the bolstering of Gouzenko's information and hearsay testimony was precisely the sort of situation that the Official Secrets Act envisioned, as we will argue. It was case specific; it wasn't encouraging system-wide denial of civil liberties via reverse onus and communication with foreigners.

The Appeal Court, however, took its own stance on Parliament's intention, and although its ruling in Benning's favour was understandable, it didn't reflect the truth of his involvement. Historian Amy Knight, in effect praising the gangland code of silence, says that Benning was among those who "wisely refused to confess," and she adds, inaccurately, that he was "acquitted at trial."[246] Yet even accounts sympathetic to him recognize his guilt. Drawing from conversations with his son and others who knew him, Merrily Weisbord has recounted how Benning's sister Paulette drew him to the Communist Party. Alongside Lunan and Boyer, he was a Section 13 Communist, and he remained loyal during the Soviet–Nazi non-aggression pact. After the banning of the Communist Party, he did underground work, and like other Section 13 members, that work prepared him for a role in GRU espionage.[247] The only disagreement between the Weisbord and the Gouzenko accounts is her assertion that Fred Rose, not Sam Carr, recruited Benning. In Weisbord's account, Benning's motive for spying arose out of a feeling that "the Soviet Union was being denied help in a life-and-death struggle."[248] The historical verdict on Benning must be the one that the Kellock-Taschereau Commission gave. His association with his brother-in-law Gerson doesn't implicate him, but the strong circumstantial evidence against him, combined with his evasiveness about that evidence and about his close association with Rose, argue that Gouzenko was right: Benning was "Foster." Here, as in the other cases, Gouzenko's hearsay evidence proved reliable, while Canada's necessary judicial protections allowed the guilty Benning to walk free.

Durnford Smith ("Badeau"), 19 March

If the Soviets didn't want the West to gain a strategic advantage after the war, neither did they want to concede a technological advantage. During the war, the development of receivers, antennas, and components designed for military purposes turned the resonant magnetron and microwave radar into a technology that gave the Allies a significant advantage in detecting German and Japanese fighter planes.[249] Although microwave radar research was centred on MIT's radiation

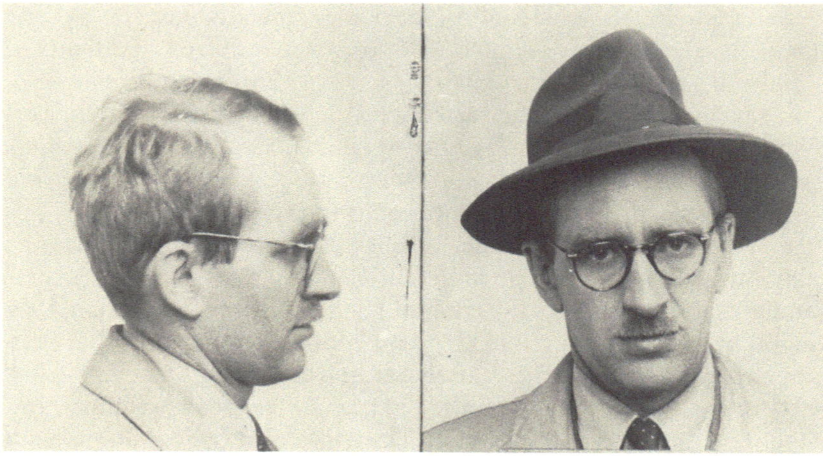

Durnford Smith, McGill PhD graduate and radar researcher at the National Research Council (RG 33/62, Royal Commission to Investigate the Communication of Secret and Confidential Information to Agents of a Foreign Power, vol. 5, "D971-80-19 SUPP C EX - Exhibit 115," photograph 119, microfilm T-3425/e011784683)

facility, Canadian scientists frequently visited the "Rad Lab,"[250] and Canada's NRC held the latest research in its Radio Branch documentary library.[251] Since Stalin predicted an inevitable confrontation with the capitalist West, work on radar, too, was important future-oriented work, and after the Cold War descended, radar intelligence (RADINT) technology would move on to guidance systems for intercontinental ballistic missiles.[252]

Lt. Col. Vassili Rogov identified a physicist, Durnford Smith – thirty-three years old, McGill trained, employed at the Radio Branch since 1942 – who might be persuaded to get the GRU some of that microwave radar intelligence. Later, Smith would reveal that his interest in Communism had begun at McGill in the 1930s, when he was a student.[253] Gordon Lunan testified that Rogov told him to recruit Smith. Initially, Smith was cautious, checking Lunan's "credentials." Nevertheless, Smith did reveal to Lunan that his work involved a "battleship radar device for use in the Pacific" and he "promised to cooperate."[254] In a clandestine meeting on an Ottawa street corner, Lunan introduced Smith to Rogov. Ned Mazerall, who worked with Smith and had likewise been recruited by Lunan, also testified that he and Smith had conspired together to get the secret information for Moscow.[255]

Called before the inquiry, Smith immediately asked to consult his lawyer, Aldous Aylen.[256] For "thirty-two days," during his detention, he had asked to see Aylen.[257] It was "unfair," he said, to insist that he swear oaths and testify without legal counsel. "Mr. Smith," Commissioner Kellock retorted, "there is not any question of fairness involved. You are here as a witness."[258] Quite aware of the trap, Smith objected that he had "a feeling" that he was "not really a witness."[259] Eventually the commissioners seemed to realize that interrogating Smith as a mere "witness" without legal counsel might unintentionally sabotage the use of his inquiry testimony in a subsequent criminal trial. For the moment, Kellock suggested that Smith take the oath to be truthful, and that they would discuss the question of legal counsel later.

As E.K. Williams began to ask questions about the handwriting on Smith's National Registration form, Smith figured out that Williams might be aiming to match the handwriting on GRU documents. Smith therefore said that he only "assumed" that some of the writing on the National Registration form was "probably" his.[260] Pressed to be more definitive, he kept qualifying every answer. "I think that is probably in my writing. That is years ago, and I have no direct memory."[261] But, like Eric Adams, his "inability" to remember ran up against intransigent facts, against for example the script in his job application letters.[262] "Yes," Smith conceded, "it must be mine." But even regarding the job applications, he claimed to have "no memory of writing these letters."[263]

Because testimony about relationships might open a door for later inquiries or characterize the witness, Williams pulled out a series of photographs. Smith said that he recognized Sam Carr and Fred Rose from pictures of them "in the newspaper."[264] He thought Fred Rose was a member of Parliament, but hadn't met him.[265] Adams, May, Gerson, Willsher, and Woikin were all strangers, as was Vassili Rogov, despite Lunan's testimony.[266] Smith did recognize Mazerall, Nightingale, Boyer, Shugar, Halperin, Benning, and Fred Poland.[267] Most importantly, Smith knew the man who had testified against him – Lunan – from occasional lunches and drinks at Montreal's Pointe-Claire Yacht Club.[268] There must be more, Williams thought: "Is that the full extent of your acquaintance with Captain Gordon Lunan?" "I believe so, yes, sir," Smith replied, qualifying and qualifying until Williams finally wrung a simple "Yes" out of him.[269] The last photo, taken from the "Badeau" dossier in the Soviet embassy, was a blurry head-and-shoulders photograph of Smith himself, clipped from a photograph of him standing in front of a house.[270] Smith had given Lunan the photograph along with some biographical notes that Rogov required for Smith's GRU dossier. Williams asked, "That is your own photograph, is it not?"[271]

Smith stopped answering. He again asked for legal counsel: "I am not endeavouring to obstruct you sir," he said to Kellock, "but I realize that, nevertheless, although I am a witness, I am in a serious position."[272] Kellock said, "There is no charge made against you as yet,"[273] but Smith rejected this obfuscation: "I have the feeling that what is actually happening is that I am being questioned by a prosecution, without the advantage of legal advice."[274] "Not so," Kellock dissembled, "Your conduct is being investigated, but there is no question of a prosecution."[275] Smith remained adamant: "Here we have lawyers who are questioning me. I do not know the intricacies of the law; I may be being led into a trap, for all I know, and that is why I am asking for counsel."[276] Following a brief recess, the commissioners said that they would reserve their decision on Smith's refusal to answer. It would soon become apparent that the commissioners – unlike the shrewd Williams – didn't realize that Smith was objecting because he knew that the photograph tied him to Soviet spying. Williams tried to show Smith another photograph from the Soviet embassy,[277] but Smith wouldn't answer, explaining, "I feel this is a question of principle. We have been without counsel, and this is a new type of procedure I believe."[278]

At that point, Kellock suddenly appeared to realize that the commissioners' refusal to grant Smith a lawyer, combined with the incriminating evidence and Williams's interrogation, might undermine a later criminal trial – undermine a central purpose of the inquiry. Kellock beat an awkward retreat: "Well, Mr. Smith, I did not realize when you objected to saying anything about Exhibit 119 [the photograph], just where Exhibit 119 had come from … You can appreciate that we have heard a great deal of evidence and all of it is not in the forefront of our minds at all times."[279] Shelving the fiction that there wasn't a plan to prosecute Smith, Kellock now claimed to "appreciate" why Smith wanted a lawyer. Under the circumstances, Smith could have a lawyer.[280]

H. Aldous Aylen KC arrived at the Justice Building, consulted with Smith, and announced that Smith was "quite ready and willing to answer any questions."[281] Of course, Smith had no intention of baring his soul to the inquiry, and he continued to hide behind a series of non-answers. Although the GRU's blurry head-and-shoulders shot of Smith appeared to prove his intimate connection with Soviet intelligence, he called the photo "unclear" and said, "It might bear a certain resemblance to me, but I could not be sure of it."[282] Williams urged Smith to examine the full photograph from which the headshot had been clipped, a photo of Smith standing in front of his home in Hull. Might that help Smith recognize himself? No. Smith speculated that the house could be one of any number of similar homes constructed during the war. Enlarged versions of the photograph were placed in front of Smith, he was given a magnifying glass, and Williams again asked him to identify his own image. He explained, "If I was not under oath, I would say that it looked like it." But since he was under oath, he could only say, "I am not sure." He wouldn't say that it wasn't him and he wouldn't say that it was.[283]

Rogov had told Lunan to ask Smith for "a full report on organization and personal, interlocking depts., etc of NDC [*sic*] plus any other information he considers useful"[284] – a simple and common task used to ease new recruits into the GRU net, testing them for more serious work. Smith "promised" to respond by 9 April 1945,[285] but didn't. Instead, he offered Lunan a copy of a dated *NRC Annual Report*. Lunan declined the offer.[286] Sometime in May, Smith added three pages of notes about his work in the Radio division, a sketchy account of NRC personnel copied from the 1941–42 *Annual Report*, a photograph of himself, and a biographical summary. "Badeau continues to be agreeable to our arrangement," Lunan told his handlers, "but is extremely cautious and takes a long time to commit himself to any course of action." Lunan tried to pass on some of Smith's scientific explanations too, but Lunan wasn't a scientist and he worried that the explanations lay beyond his limited knowledge.[287] Analysing Lunan's attempt to explain Smith's work, W.J. Henderson, Smith's superior in the Radio Branch, testified that some of the work described a "scanning antenna" linked to a radar device,[288] some a "T.R. cavity" (which allowed a microwave radar set to work with one antenna rather than two[289]), and some the "measuring [of] the Q of a resonant cavity"[290] (which determined how a receiver would respond to a radio frequency).[291] This last project, on which Smith had worked, could be shared with British scientists or Americans at MIT.'s Rad Lab,"[292] but was classified as "secret," and Smith had no right to offer it to the Soviets.[293]

Williams judged that some of the notes linked "Badeau" directly to Smith:[294] "I put it to you Mr. Smith that that is your handwriting." Again, Smith would neither affirm nor deny. Kellock found Smith's non-answer hard to credit: "You mean to say that you do not recognize your own handwriting when you see it." Smith shifted slightly: "I have no memory of writing these."[295] Shown the technical drawings and the writing on them, Smith agreed that the handwriting was "similar" to his, but he couldn't be sure.[296] Did the drawings and notes have anything to do with Smith's work at the NRC? Even here, he wouldn't give a categorical "yes." "I think that is so," he said. He identified a diagram in the notes as a "rotating coupling," but didn't know who made the drawing. "I suggest that you made it," Williams said, but Smith claimed that he couldn't remember.[297]

Smith identified another drawing in the notes as a "resonant cavity" and, after some prodding, conceded that the Radio Branch had worked on a resonant cavity in developing a "microwave zone position indicator" designed to detect "aeroplanes."[298] Was the reference to "40 element axial lines and one mixer to replace the old G.L. mark 3 treble sub mixer" relevant to Smith's work at the Research Council? "It could be, sir," Smith replied. Exasperated by Smith's non-stop hedging, Kellock burst out, "So, the proper answer to that question was not that it could be but that it was." Smith had to say "Yes."[299] But even to the question of whether his work at the Research Council was "secret," Smith stuck with his game plan, and would only reply that he "assumed" so.[300]

Taschereau tried a different tack. What was Smith's job in the Microwave division? He was there "to develop, invent, or produce useful equipment."[301] Who was involved with Smith in the work referenced in the documents that the GRU had obtained? "Henderson, Miller, myself, Cave, Retallack," he replied,[302] but he cautioned that the work in the Microwave division was also described in weekly and monthly reports circulating throughout the Radio Branch. Did Smith know of anybody who received the circular who had the same handwriting as he had? Smith didn't. Was it "not a fact," Taschereau continued, that Smith had authored the GRU documents? "I don't recall writing it, sir," Smith replied.[303] The author of the notes had written of one component that "we expect it to be operationally better." Who, Kellock wanted to know, other than a person directly involved in this work, could have written those words? "That is a little difficult for me to say, sir," Smith responded.[304] Taschereau offered his assistance: "It may very well have been written by you." "I suppose it is a possibility," Smith admitted.[305]

Taschereau invited Smith to explain his doubts about the handwriting. Who would have composed these notes other than Smith? Taking a page out of Scot Benning's defence, Smith speculated that perhaps someone had "forged" his handwriting to make it "appear" that he had created these documents.[306] Someone might be making money by implicating individuals in Soviet espionage: "I am wondering, if [Gouzenko] had any advantage in turning in people as implicated in this work and therefore took some means to get my handwriting forged."[307] Of course, Smith had no idea who might want to pay Gouzenko to forge documents.

Taschereau tried to force a conclusion: "If it is not written by you, it is a forgery. If it is not a forgery, it is written by you." "I suppose," Smith replied.[308] This irked Taschereau. Why couldn't Smith affirm or deny on oath that he had written these notes? Smith responded that the question was unfair, since it really meant, "Did you or did you not break the law?" After an extended discussion of what the question was, Smith steered the frustrated commissioners full circle back to his earlier non-answers: he wouldn't *deny* having created these documents, but that didn't mean that he was testifying that he "did write them."[309]

Alongside the handwritten notes from "Badeau," the commissioners also held a July 1945 summary that Rogov had prepared on Durnford Smith's progress as a GRU source. "Badeau" wanted "to work." He had given "written information on questions of research in the field of radio technique, of optics and separate apparatuses." In conversation, Smith had given Lunan an account of the "NRC from the top down," including the names of the "Committee of the Secret Council on Research Problems" and the composition of the "Research Council."[310] In the future, Smith wanted to "work on uranium," and Rogov therefore hoped that Smith might move beyond "Back's" [Lunan's] group, do "greater research," and make some useful "independent contacts."[311]

Williams confronted Smith with the "Scheme of the Research Group" given to Lunan by Rogov in March 1945, containing references to "Doruforth Smith" [*sic*], Smith's code name "Badeau," and an assignment for Smith. Lunan subsequently reported, "Badeau: ... He is preparing the report on his dept. as requested, also a full report on organization and personnel, inter-locking depts. etc, of NDC [*sic*] ... Badeau informs me that most secret work at present is on nuclear physics (bombardment of radio-active substances to produce energy). This is more hush-hush than radar and is being carried on at University of Montreal and at McMaster."[312] Smith was unmoved: yes, he knew about these developments from the newspapers. Did he know about the nuclear research when it was still secret? He didn't think so.[313]

Even more damningly, "Badeau's" GRU file was full of details. Under "Daruforth [*sic*] Smith," the file read "Pseudonym: 'Badeau,'" with his address, "145 Ste. Marie (Hull)," and his phone number, "3-3870." He worked as a "Scientific assistant engineer" in the "Radio Division" of the "Research Council," was thirty-three years old, and had two children – one six years old, the other six months: "He is member [*sic*] of the 'Labour Progressive Party.' He takes an active part in its work. Very sympathetic to us. Has a great desire to work for us."[314] Smith objected: his oldest child was *five,* not six years old; his job title did *not* include the word "Scientific;" and he had never held a Labor-Progressive membership. Was Smith aware of anyone else working for the NRC named Durnford Smith? "Not that I know of," he replied.[315] Asked about his sympathy for and desire to work for the Labor-Progressive Party, he said, "I know nothing about that."[316]

When Williams cited testimony from Ned Mazerall that Smith, along with Mazerall, Lunan, and David Shugar, had joined a Marxist and Communist study group, Smith repeated the same line: "I know nothing about that."[317] Kellock brought up Shugar's testimony that Smith was a member of an Ottawa-based study group. "All right; I will say yes," Smith conceded. He agreed that the group met every two weeks for two or three years, that money was collected to buy the "*Canadian Tribune, New Masses* ... papers like that,"[318] and that the members, including Smith, were sympathetic towards the Communist or Labor-Progressive Party.[319]

Because Gouzenko had pilfered so much of the incriminating evidence (Rogov's management notes, assignments, reports from Lunan on Smith, and the documents in Smith's handwriting) from Rogov's briefcase, stored in Zabotin's safe, Williams dug into Smith's relationship with Rogov. How could Smith's notes about radar make their way into Rogov's briefcase in the Russian embassy? Smith had no explanation. "I do not know that man," he reiterated when Williams again held up Rogov's photograph. But Lunan had testified that he had introduced Smith to "Jan" (Rogov]) and that together the three had driven the streets of Ottawa. No, Smith was "reasonably sure" that he had never ridden in a car with Rogov or Lunan. In a rare straightforward denial, Smith went so far as to say that Lunan "was mistaken."[320] According to Lunan, he invited Smith to meet him and Rogov at the corner of Carling and Harmer on the evening of 5 July 1945. Smith was supposed to bring details on NRC personnel and, if possible, an NRC telephone directory[321] – the non-sensitive "information ... obtainable from other sources"[322] and intended to ease Smith into the fold. Rogov subsequently added another, clearly more substantive assignment: bring "any kind of material on the American aeroplane radio locator of the type 'an/aps--10,'"[323] a recent innovation in airborne microwave radar achieved by American scientists at MIT.[324]

The NRC's Radio Documents library held a copy of Andrew Longacre's report, *AN/APS-10, Airborne Radar*, and on 25 June 1945 Smith had borrowed that report, returning it 12 July.[325] Smith admitted taking documents from the library home (though this was forbidden) about six times, insisting that he did so only for work on his PhD thesis.[326] Contrary to his excuse, the report had no connection to his thesis or to his work in the Radio division; yet since it dealt with "radio beams," he claimed that he "might be interested in it at any time."[327] Rogov's records, however, indicated that "Badeau" attended the 5 July meeting, that he brought "valuable materials,"[328] including "material on radio locators (radar) to be photographed,"[329] and that "Badeau" had "Completed" the assignment concerning "AN/APS-10" on "5 July 1945."[330] Lunan had testified that on 5 July Smith conferred with Rogov in his chauffeur-driven vehicle for "forty-five minutes."[331] Pressed to explicitly deny that he had attended the meeting and had given Rogov "valuable materials," Smith replied, "I don't admit it."[332] For him, it was merely a "strange coincidence" that Rogov had written approvingly that "Badeau's" AN/APS-10 assignment was completed at the very time that *AN/APS-10, Airborne Radar* happened to be in Smith's possession.[333] Although Smith had earlier been "disturbed" by Lunan's offer of money,[334] the "Badeau" notes for 5 July said that Rogov "Handed out 100 dollars; he [Smith] took the money readily. In the course of time he may become the head of a group."[335] Confronted with these notes from Rogov, Smith said he didn't know about that. Questioned again, he wouldn't directly deny attending a meeting with Lunan and Rogov or giving Rogov something at the meeting, but claimed, "I have no memory of it."[336]

During the 5 July meeting, "Badeau" "agreed to further work." Rogov, in a "special assignment"[337] given on "5-7-45," wanted intelligence about June 1945 tests of "a new photoflash bomb bursting, which had a 750 million candle power and special lenses for night photography." Rogov wanted to know the formula for the explosive material in the bomb, the "area of surface" illuminated by its flare, the duration of burning, and the "maximum height" from which photographs could be taken "with the aid of this bomb." He also wanted information about new photographic lenses and about the new work "in the field of aerial photography, color aerial photography and photography through clouds with the aid of infra-red rays."[338] This time, however, Rogov was asking the wrong person, since the questions lay outside of Smith's expertise and since he didn't have easy access to experimental results from the RCAF or from the Optics Section of the NRC's Physics Division.[339] With greater success, Rogov pushed for a more technical account of "an-aps-10." If possible, he would like to see samples of radio tubes and documentary material to photograph. He warned Smith to be surreptitious while gathering the information – Smith should display "no special activity." And one final order: "After reading this material burn it."[340]

Librarians at the Radio Branch documents library testified that Smith had twice deviated from his usual pattern of borrowing one or two items at a time. On 23 July 1945, he borrowed seven documents, all related to Rogov's 5 July assignment. Smith kept most of these documents until 31 August or 4 September 1945.[341] After a visit near the end of July to the MIT Rad Lab, Smith was allowed to take a "top-secret 4j34 magnetron" back to Ottawa, precisely the equipment that Rogov had requested.[342] Smith furnished Rogov with NRC library listings of items placed in the Radio Branch library. Soviet intelligence priorities in 1945 were broad, and these lists offered the GRU a menu of research and development reports, some of which might have been on topics unfamiliar to Moscow.[343] Using the NRC library lists, Rogov in early August assigned Smith to get three technical documents that Rogov wanted to photograph: "GL 14003" (*Application of Radar to Field Artillery*, which dealt with "gun-laying" or gun-positioning radar or anti-aircraft artillery); "Som. 14032" (*Intercept Work at Port Reyes, California*, which concerned the radar site where the US military tested coastal intercept radar directed at Japan); and "A.S.V. 14040" (*The Tactical Employment of S.C.R. 717C and AN/APQ5B in Blind Bombing of Land Installations*).[344] A.S.V. (Air to Surface Vessel) referred to airplane radars that scanned the sea for ships,[345] *S.C.R. 717C* to a type of navigational radar, and *AN/APQ5B* to an attachment that used radar to coordinate the release of bombs.[346]

Rogov must have been disappointed on August 18 when Smith arrived empty-handed, but Smith made up for that on 25 August, bringing the Soviets a motherlode of documents. One document on Rogov's wish list – *The Tactical Employment of S.C.R. 717C and AN/APQ5B in Blind Bombing of Land Installations* – wasn't available.[347] Nevertheless, Smith still had the undelivered documents borrowed on 23 July and he had gotten hold of both *Intercept Work at Port Reyes, California* and *Application of Radar to Field Artillery*.[348] He also brought several new documents, including work on magnetrons. Some of these documents carried warnings citing the British Official Secrets Act, while others warned of penalties under the American Espionage Act.[349]

From Rogov's point of view, the 25 August meeting was a success: Smith "Handed over a large quantity of radio literature and various reports, about ten books in all."[350] Zabotin, when he saw the cargo, was so pleased that he sent the "Director" a summary even before the documents could all be photographed and sent to Moscow. In a 27 August cable, Zabotin told Bolshakov that he had "received from 'Badeau' 17 top secret and secret documents (English, American and Canadian) on the question of magnet-, radio-locators for field artillery [and] three secret scientific-research journals of the year 1945." Because GRU tradecraft required their return to Smith within twenty-four hours, Zabotin was struggling to "photograph all the documents," totalling "about 700 pages." This espionage windfall inspired Zabotin with grandiose plans for the NRC that might have dumbfounded the cautious Smith: "I consider it necessary to examine the whole of the library of the scientific research council."[351]

Why, E.K. Williams asked, did Smith borrow a document titled *Application of Radar to Field Artillery – Preliminary Trials*? Smith couldn't remember.[352] Was he working on something related in the Radio Branch? He could not recall. Could he give the inquiry any explanation for borrowing this other than to fufil Rogov's wishes? Perhaps he borrowed it accidentally.[353] Was Smith seriously telling the commissioners that he had borrowed *Application of Radar to Field Artillery – Preliminary Trials* accidentally? He was just suggesting it as a possibility.[354] Williams judged that Zabotin's telegram to Moscow described the documents Smith had borrowed from the NRC documents library. "It might possibly be considered so," Smith conceded."[355] Williams asked, "Have you any explanation or idea about why Col. Zabotin should be telling the director in Moscow that he had, the Russian Embassy here, had got from Durnford Smith these secret documents?" Smith, of course, could give no explanation.[356]

Rogov hoped that Smith could complete the 5 July assignment: "Answer last letter regarding the new radio tubes, radio-locators (both for L=1, 2, 3 cm) and the other questions indicated in that letter." He also wanted "particulars about the 'Electron Shells'" and three books: "LG 13853; GL 14017 and P(RAD) 13920." The assignment ended with "P.S. – burn after reading."[357] When Smith met Rogov on 26 August at the corner of Osgood and Cumberland to return Smith's parcel of secret documents, Rogov again gave Smith $100 (the equivalent of $1,800 in 2026) and instructions for an "urgent meeting," which (one might guess) could have concerned the plan to promote Smith out of the Research Group. "Brent" (another Rogov code name) would trigger the meeting by phoning Smith and ending the conversation with the words "Mary sent her love for your children." The meeting would then take place in Hull at 9:00 p.m.: "Bado to walk down from Barr along Ste. Marie on the left side."[358] However, when Gouzenko defected, Moscow shut down its North American networks,[359] so we don't know if Smith ever got the call from "Brent."

Near the end of Smith's interrogation, Kellock summed up the case against him and then traced the arc of Smith's life to 1946. Born and raised in privileged Westmont, he had completed an MSc degree and was working on a PhD. He had worked at Bell Canada and the NRC, with "good prospects," and one of his "superiors" at the NRC "formed a pretty favorable idea" of his ability. "In light of those facts," Kellock asked, "what appealed to you in the Communist philosophy?" "Its logic, sir," Smith replied."[360] "Can you suggest to me any reason," Kellock wanted to know, "why any person in your position should have given any information, secret information, to the Russians or any other foreign power, apart from the fact that you were sympathetic to the Communist philosophy?" "No, sir," said Smith, "not at the moment."[361]

After the Kellock-Taschereau Commission ended, Smith would be charged with conspiracy to offend the Official Secrets Act.[362] At the end of 1946, on the basis of Ned Mazerall's testimony, Gouzenko's hearsay testimony, and the documentary cache, Carlton County Judge A.G. McDougall convicted Smith and sentenced him to five years in the penitentiary.[363] A subsequent appeal was dismissed.[364]

Fred Poland ("Polland"), 27 March

The evidence confirms that the commission lawyers were almost always right: eleven of the thirteen detainees, no matter whether they were convicted or acquitted in criminal courts, spied for the Soviets. The last two cases, shakier, would end inconclusively, though in one of them guilt is still the likely verdict, while in the other the suspect only dipped his toe into the world of espionage.

Col. Nikolai Zabotin's handwritten notes on the Soviet intelligence network that predated his arrival in Canada identified a "Second Group," based in Ottawa and Toronto, that had taken shape under Sam Carr. Among its members, he listed "Polland ... taken to work at the end of January." "Polland," in the "Ministry of Aviation" and working in the Toronto "Intelligence Branch," was "being transferred to Ottawa."[365] He had given the GRU "a map (plan) of the instructional schools"[366] – in other words, the Commonwealth Air Training bases. If Fauteux is correct, these events took place between October 1942 and the summer of 1943, just prior to Zabotin's arrival in Ottawa.[367] But Zabotin concluded his précis ambiguously: "Up to present is not working."[368]

Gouzenko's testimony gave only the most general account of "Poland's" association with Soviet intelligence: "Poland was described as a clever man and Colonel Zabotin proposed to Moscow in a telegram to hand him over to Neighbours ... the nickname for the N.K.V.D. Moscow replied that it was not worth while, to wait a while that he might develop into a good worker." Gouzenko concluded, "That was the only other time I saw the name of Poland and still I do not know whether it was his real name or his nickname."[369] Nevertheless, on the basis of one GRU document and Gouzenko's sketchy testimony, the RCMP arrested Fred Poland, an Air Force officer at RCAF headquarters in Ottawa.[370]

Poland, who played a central role in the RCAF Intelligence Directorate, had connections to other detainees. David Shugar had rented an apartment from him,[371] and he briefly shared one with Gordon Lunan.[372] He occasionally met Durnford Smith and Scot Benning for a drink,[373] and he knew Harold Gerson "socially."[374] Raymond Boyer met Poland in Montreal and found him to be "sympathetic to the old Communist Party and the present Labor-Progressive Party."[375]

Under Group Capt. H.R. Stewart, director of intelligence, Poland prepared broadcasts into occupied countries and oversaw the "re-education of German prisoners," eventually becoming the executive secretary of the Psychological Warfare Committee.[376] He supervised "security education throughout the RCAF," preparing, among other things, "security lectures" and "fortnightly Security Liaison letters." Because Poland was required to read all "security material" coming into the directorate, he also advised Stewart on "all matters of Security Policy," and, as secretary of the Security Sub-committee of the Canadian Joint Intelligence Committee (CJIC),[377] he helped coordinate intelligence with Britain and the US.[378] Members viewed the CJIC "as the natural body to organize and direct the future Canadian intelligence system." A CJIC memorandum, "Foreign Intelligence in Peacetime," recognized that "the atomic bomb was revolutionizing warfare and, for the purposes of intelligence, had placed a new premium on monitoring scientific and industrial developments and warding off surprise attack."[379] Poland also participated in the "Air Force Headquarters Committee on grading of classified documents." By the end of 1943, an effort was made to standardize security in Canada, Britain, and the US, so every Headquarters file had to be reviewed and classified. The classification "Top Secret" came into use because of this initiative.[380]

The Air Force Directorate of Intelligence had contact with the Soviet embassy through Zabotin and his deputy Rogov, but Capt. Stewart testified that communication with the Soviet embassy had always been exclusively Stewart's responsibility. He had no idea why several references to "Pavlov" – Vitali Pavlov, the NKVD's chief in Canada[381] – appeared in Poland's 1945 calendar pad.[382] Later, at trial, Poland would confirm that the "Pavlov" in his calendar pad was indeed Vitali.[383] Stewart told the commissioners that as the flight training schools associated with the British Commonwealth Air Training Plan spread across Canada, new updated maps of their locations were produced. These maps weren't confidential, but he considered it inappropriate for anyone under his command to give them to the Russians.

Malcolm MacDonald reported to London on 23 March 1946 that Fred Poland's legal counsel had secured a writ of *habeas corpus* (approved by Ontario High Court Chief Justice McRuer) questioning the legality of Poland's detention.[384] Authorities had to bring Poland to court by 30 March with documents showing why he was arrested.[385] MacDonald inferred that the "legality order in Counsel" (i.e., PC 6444) was at stake.[386] In other words, he and probably others on the Corby Committee had reason to fear that the entire foundation on which St. Laurent had detained the suspects without lawyers and without *habeas corpus* might be crumbling.

Under Canadian *habeas corpus* law, Ontario's McRuer issued an order of *certiorari* to review the government's actions, so the minister of justice or his representative must appear at Osgoode Hall to defend Poland's detention. While the Official Secrets Act placed no time limit on the detention, the Criminal Code required that detainees see a magistrate within a "reasonable time."[387] Earlier, St. Laurent had assured Parliament (without naming the *Re George Edwin Gray* case) that a 1918 precedent would convince courts to uphold the PC 6444 detentions. But he likely knew that any closer examination of *Re Gray* would reveal Justice Lyman Duff's strictures in that ruling – that the denial of *habeas corpus* was confined to wartime. No Wehrmacht threatened in 1946. Duff, former chief justice of the Supreme Court, had reiterated his strictures in the 1943 chemical manufacturers case. Relying on *Re Gray*, the Supreme Court unanimously agreed that, under the War Measures Act, St. Laurent could indeed regulate the production and sale of some chemicals. But, again, the decision held only for wartime.[388] Would the new struggle against Soviet spying provide the "essential conditions" required to hold someone without *habeas corpus* under a War Measures Act that had been proclaimed to fight Nazi Germany?

A minefield stretched out in front of Mackenzie King. If Poland – a suspected Soviet agent – were released by the court, St. Laurent would be duty-bound to arrest him immediately under the Official Secrets Act, again without charges, which would invite more *habeas corpus* challenges. An adverse ruling might also open the door to court action against the inquiry, possibly with demands that reports based on the testimony of *witnesses* placed before the inquiry through PC 6444 be destroyed and no reference to such testimony be allowed in the inquiry's *Final Report*. The political fallout would delight Moscow (and King's detractors), providing fodder for its complaints against Ottawa. Already weary of the inquiry, King would be forced to respond to the inevitable parliamentary and press outrage.

As it was, the political opposition didn't pose the strongest threat, but the courts did. After forty-one days in custody at Rockcliffe, Fred Poland finally appeared before the inquiry on the morning of 27 March

1946, but he refused to be sworn and he insisted on consulting his lawyer. When Eric Adams and David Shugar had refused to cooperate with the inquiry, both were sent back to Rockcliffe to stew and reconsider. But a *habeas corpus* hearing loomed in three days, so circumstances had changed. Only Poland and Israel Halperin were left to interrogate, and St. Laurent, at King's behest was pressing the commissioners to hurry up.[389] They relented, summoning Poland's lawyer Royden Hughes to the Justice Building.[390] Hughes announced that "writs of *habeas corpus* and *certiorari* have been issued and served," adding that "there might be a question of law as to whether this commission has under these circumstances any right ... to ask this witness to do anything."[391] Hughes urged commissioners not to question Poland until *habeas corpus* had been resolved.

Kellock pretended not to see Hughes's point: "What the proceedings in connection with *habeas corpus* have to do with [Poland's testimony] I am at a loss to understand."[392] Kellock might have been surprised to learn that Mackenzie King was losing sleep as he mulled over "cancelling the Order-in-Council giving power to detain persons brought before the Royal Commission." As soon as the *Third Interim Report* was ready, King planned to kill PC 6444. Ever the politician, he worried that "someone of the Opposition would anticipate our action and get credit for it by asking in the House for the immediate cancellation of the order."[393]

Hughes actually had to explain to Kellock – a Supreme Court justice – that *habeas corpus* would scuttle any testimony by Poland at the inquiry – there could be no other "court procedure other than to bring him up before the court on the writ [of *habeas corpus*], whether that was the Supreme Court of Canada or the Supreme Court of Ontario."[394] Kellock protested that the inquiry was "not a court at all," that (despite Hughes's argument) the *habeas corpus* writ wasn't an "interim injunction or something of that kind."[395] When Poland appeared before the inquiry on 28 March, a sparring session immediately broke out between Hughes and the commissioners. Hughes advised Poland that he had no obligation to answer questions, but Kellock and Taschereau maintained that even if *habeas corpus* freed Poland, he must still answer a subpoena and testify.[396] Hughes disagreed: "I say that this witness is under the protection of the court which issued *habeas corpus*. Part of that protection is that he has no right to be arrested by warrant of any other tribunal, nor is he liable to be summoned."[397] Kellock asked if Hughes was arguing that Poland hadn't been subpoenaed by the commission.[398] Hughes responded that he had no idea how Poland had "come before the Commission."[399] Of course, Kellock and Taschereau's complicity in the use of PC 6444 for Poland's detention and testimony would be laid bare during the *habeas corpus* proceeding only forty-eight hours away. To Hughes, Kellock said, "Your position and his seem to be perfectly clear that he refuses to be sworn and does not want to say anything or call any evidence."[400] Could Poland be a witness and an accused at the same time? By speaking of Hughes and Poland presenting evidence and calling witnesses, Kellock was effectively turning Poland into an accused (under sections 12 and 13 of the Inquiries Act) against whom they planned to make a charge. "Do you refuse to be sworn or what?" Kellock asked Poland. "I refuse to say a word to this Commission," Poland replied, "for fear of how it will be interpreted."[401]

It was all over. Though the commissioners had many questions for Poland, they had no appetite for sending him back to Rockcliffe if it meant taking a chance on serious political and professional repercussions should Chief Justice McRuer rule against the government. A subpoena could force Poland back before the inquiry, but that, too, would hand the inquiry's critics one more piece of artillery.

In the end, Poland gave no testimony. Nevertheless, citing the Official Secrets Act and evidence that he was sympathetic to the Labor-Progressive party, had been in contact with Vitali Pavlov (an "agent of a foreign power"), and had refused "to be sworn or to answer any questions" despite being "given fullest opportunity," the commissioners decided, with reason, that Poland had "completely failed to rebut the presumption of guilt" defined by the Official Secrets Act.[402] When Poland eventually stood trial under the act in January 1947, the Crown had only GRU documents, Gouzenko's sketchy testimony, and guilt-by-association evidence to offer. County Court judge Gordon A. MacDougald found him not guilty.[403]

Israel Halperin ("Bacon"), 22 and 27 March

Israel Halperin took a similar route to Poland's. When he initially appeared at the Justice Building on 22 March, he insisted that it was "the basic right of every Canadian citizen to have access to legal counsel." Just before his next appearance on 27 March, his wife successfully petitioned for *habeas corpus* in front of Supreme Court of Ontario justice Walter Schroeder.[404] This meant that, despite the War Measures Act, courts could review the legality of the PC 6444 detentions; that on 30 March two judges – Justice McRuer on Poland and Justice Schroeder on Halperin – would evaluate St. Laurent's claim that his actions were legal. If Poland or Halperin or both were granted freedom, King's government would be cast into a tyrannical light and the legal

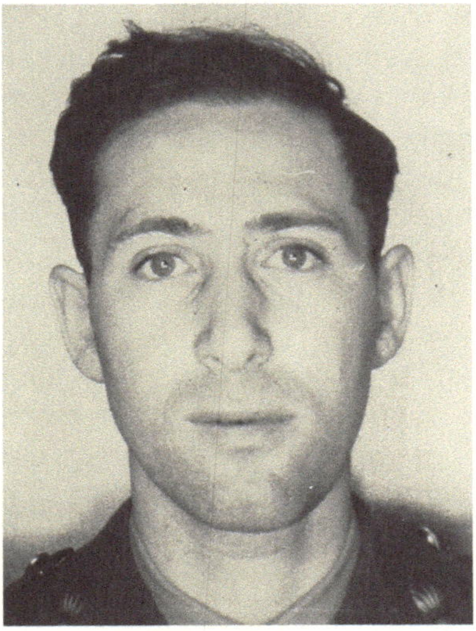

Princeton University–educated mathematician and Directorate of Artillery officer Maj. Israel Halpern (RG 33/62, Royal Commission to Investigate the Communication of Secret and Confidential Information to Agents of a Foreign Power, vol. 5, "D971-80-19 SUPP C EX - Exhibit 115," photograph 130, microfilm T-3425/ e011784686)

reputations of Supreme Court justices Kellock and Taschereau would take a beating. After King's crowing in Parliament about how Kellock and Taschereau had been carefully selected to protect the liberty of Canadians, King and the Liberals faced a political quagmire. Only the release of both Poland and Halperin before 30 March could ensure that the courts couldn't sink the inquiry.

When Halperin arrived at the inquiry on the morning of 27 March his lawyer, Senator Arthur Roebuck, stood beside him. Roebuck said that Halperin felt "duty bound" to assist the commission,[405] and that Halperin's testimony could be expedited if he received all the protections of the Canada Evidence Act. Kellock agreed.[406]

The son of Russian Jewish immigrants, Halperin was a thirty-five-year-old Torontonian with a PhD from Princeton. He did post-graduate work at Yale and Harvard and, since 1939, taught mathematics at Queen's.[407] After enlisting in the Canadian army in 1942, he worked on ballistics for the Directorate of Artillery.[408] He also served as the directorate's liaison officer with the Canadian Armament Research Division Establishment (CARDE),[409] a joint civilian/military organization at a military base in Valcartier, Quebec,[410] and by 1945 he was promoted to major.

Col. William van Steenburgh, who headed the Directorate of Artillery, had briefed officers on security and secrecy, giving each the manual on classified material,[411] but Halperin didn't remember reading anything about how to handle secret material. Instead, he said that he used his "common sense": "I would certainly not communicate to anybody who was not an authorized person any technical information."[412] But when Fauteux asked directly whether he had communicated to unauthorized people about the work he was doing, Halperin gave a syntactically convoluted non-answer: "Nothing that I would consider was either at that time or at this time as being misconduct."[413] Kellock wasn't satisfied. He wanted to hear Halperin's definition of "Top secret" and to know to whom Halperin would communicate such information. Halperin said that he understood "pretty well" what was "Top secret,"[414] yet he seemed to wink at official designations: "It was the custom for a long time to mark everything secret, even when it was obvious to everyone that it was not secret under any kind of system."[415] Had he given out information about the organization of his department?[416] "I have no recollection of that," he said.[417]

After a day of this sort of questioning – and two days shy of his *habeas corpus* hearing – Halperin astutely broke from his lawyer's advice. "I have come to the conviction," he said, "that this in effect is a prosecution with a charge not yet laid." He wanted the charge addressed in open court instead, where he would have better protections.[418] Roebuck withdrew, but Kellock decided to test Halperin's resolve anyway and directed Fauteux to question him. Halperin refused to answer.[419]

Angling for a way forward, Kellock, as he had done for Durnford Smith, told Halperin that no charge had been made against him. The inquiry was a "fact-finding body," and documents indicated that Halperin had given information to the Soviet embassy through Gordon Lunan.[420] He wanted Halperin to examine both an assignment Rogov had apparently given Halperin through Lunan and the resulting "Bacon's Report," Lunan's summary of an 18 April 1945 conversation with Halperin. Halperin appeared to reconsider his decision not to testify. He asked for a recess to confer with Roebuck again.[421]

"Bacon's Report" gave a detailed account of the personnel, organization, and activities at CARDE: the "Pilot explosives plant," the "Ballistics Laboratory," the "Designs Branch," and the "Field Trials Wing."[422] The Soviet "Scheme for the 'Research' Group" said that "Bacon," there identified as "Isidor Halperin"[423] and in another Soviet document as a professor of mathematics at Queen's,[424] had been asked to "give the organization and characters [*sic*] of Valcartier Explosives establishment's direction." This was the sort of non-classified assignment that the GRU used to draw recruits into the net – "What kind of the [*sic*] work is this organization engaged in?" – but Rogov also asked for real intelligence on "the prescription (formulas) of explosives and its samples" [*sic*].[425] He must have been pleased when Lunan reported that Halperin was "anxious to help."[426]

According to Col. Steenburgh, the notes gave "an exceptionally good description" of CARDE – only "someone on the inside" could have given it.[427] But even though the information was technically secret, it had zero security value.[428] On the other hand, "paragraph B," in which Halperin spoke about the tests of explosives DINA and albanite, was more problematic. Halperin had told Lunan, "They are using a new explosive 'DINA' mixed with RDX as a component in propellants," and he had described albanite, "a propellant containing DINA and picrite as an alternative to the standard British propellant containing Nitro-Glycerin and picrite."[429] "DINA" was a code name at the time, and Steenburgh confirmed that not only were the chemical compositions secret, but even the existence of these explosives was either "Top Secret," or "Secret." "Albanite" was on the US secret list, and "the Americans would have been very annoyed if that information had been released."[430] Yet Halperin, during his testimony, discussed DINA and albanite as if these propellants weren't classified "Top Secret" and "Secret."[431]

Rogov had directed Lunan (on 8 June 1945) to provide the "specifications" on the "electro-projector (the V-Bomb)" and details about new research on "explosive materials and artillery armaments." According to Rogov's marginal notes, Halperin had "promised to obtain" the information next time,[432] but ultimately he gave "no facts whatever" about new research on explosives. Lunan told Rogov that he had talked with Halperin for an entire evening in late June with only the "most disappointing results."[433] In fact, a series of undated notes in Rogov's handwriting said that Halperin had become very difficult to work with after Lunan broached the subject of uranium-235. Halperin did describe "the general principles of the electron shell and the bomb detonator," and told Lunan that "it would be possible to obtain instructions for it," but Lunan couldn't pry any more out of him, and Halperin refused to write anything down.[434]

By August 1945, Halperin had been a recruitment focus for several months. On 6 August 1945 Rogov asked Lunan, "Can Bacon after going to Queen's University maintain his connections with the artillery committees?" and "What possibilities will Bacon have for our work in Kingston?"[435] There is no record of Halperin's response, but clearly Rogov hadn't given up on him. When Lt. Henry J. Linney of the Canadian Military Intelligence (M.I.3A2) contacted Halperin, also in August, to do security clearances – "character investigations" – for CARDE personnel, Halperin didn't reveal that he himself was a recruitment target of Soviet military intelligence.[436] So why did Halperin, a man of formidable intelligence, continue to meet with Lunan and to entertain GRU requests? The evidence suggests that Halperin was struggling to decide exactly how far he was prepared to go for Moscow. He was a Communist and wanted to help, but he was also wise enough to recognize that his spy adventure might end badly.

Col. Steenburgh judged that references to the electro-projector or V-bomb concerned the "variable time fuse" (V-T) or proximity fuse, invented by scientists at the University of Toronto. This radar-controlled device detonated an explosive based on proximity to its target. Halperin was Steenburgh's liaison officer for this project.[437] And since Halperin had wanted to bring scientists working at Valcartier under the authority of the Artillery Directorate, Steenburgh had made him the liaison for that group as well.[438] Prior to the V-T fuse, detonation could only be triggered by direct contact with a target, a timer set at launch, or an altimeter, but by 1945 the fuse was amply proving its usefulness in Europe and especially in the Pacific, where shells triggered by V-T fuses provided a vital defence for American ships against Japanese airstrikes – the V-T fuse "knocked the Japanese air force out of the air." Although Halperin hadn't worked on the V-T fuse personally,[439] he agreed that his office held a copy of a document titled *Introduction to the Radio Proximity (VT) Fuse*,[440] published by Johns Hopkins University.[441] The V-T fuse's existence was no secret, and the Russians had watched a demonstration of it on Salisbury Plains in November 1944. However, no V-T fuses had ever been shipped to the Soviet Union, and the "wiring details" (which Halperin had) as well as "the details of manufacturing" were "still top secret and secret."[442] Only the Americans knew the details of the manufacturing process for the complete device.[443]

On Roebuck's advice, Halperin had been answering questions, but when Fauteux asked him to explain the purpose and operation of the fuse, Halperin again objected. He felt that Fauteux was asking for "things ... that can be used as evidence, presumably. In my opinion it is no longer a request for information; it is becoming a trial."[444] Still, Halperin did explain that the fuse was employed in artillery, that Canada and the US had jointly developed it, and that the work had been done at the University of Toronto.[445] The exchange finally hit a shoal when Fauteux asked if the shells guided by the V-T fuse were referred to as "electro-shells." Halperin had "never heard that term at all."[446] He had also never heard of an "electro-projector or a "V-Bomb,"[447] and he couldn't explain the role of electricity in the detonation of the V-Bomb.[448] He wanted to speak to Roebuck.[449]

When Halperin returned for his final appearance, he protested that the questions did not "seek information but were of a prosecutional type, which tried to get me by trickery to commit myself."[450] Once again, Roebuck was sent out. When Fauteux tried to talk about documents found in Lunan's GRU dossier that detailed Halperin's GRU contributions, Halperin announced, "I refuse to review any documents … I refuse to go on with this procedure."[451] Taschereau told Fauteux to present the documents to Halperin one by one and told the inquiry recorder to note every time that Halperin refused to answer Fauteux's questions. To Halperin, Kellock said, "Do you understand, witness, that by refusing to answer you commit an offence, which is contempt, for which you can be punished?"[452]

Fauteux read from the GRU's "Scheme of the Research Group": "Bacon – to give the organization and characters of Valcartier Explosives Establishment."[453] Taschereau asked, "What is your answer to what Mr. Fauteux read you?" Halperin replied, "That it is a lot of rubbish. I don't know this man Lunan, and I certainly didn't give him or anybody else any information to be communicated to a foreign power." Would he swear that he didn't know Lunan? "Yes," Halperin replied, "to the best of my remembrance I don't know Lunan."[454]

TASCHEREAU: Did you ever speak to him?
HALPERIN: I refuse to go on with this cross examination.
Fauteux introduced Halperin's telephone directory. Did Halperin recognize this book?[455]
HALPERIN: I must say that I now withdraw from the oath I gave.
TASCHEREAU: Oh no you cannot do that.
HALPERIN: I do it.
TASCHEREAU: You cannot do that.
HALPERIN: Am I here by compulsion?
TASCHEREAU: You are not here by compulsion.[456]
HALPERIN: Then I will walk out of the room.
TASCHEREAU: No you will stay.

Halperin rose, left the witness chair, and walked to the door.

TASCHEREAU: No you are not leaving this room.
HALPERIN: Then I have to tell you that I consider the oath invalid, and I will feel perfectly free to inform all of Canada exactly what happened here from now on; and I certainly will.

After a few more words, Taschereau asked whether Halperin had any explanation to give. He didn't, and declared, "I will not open my mouth here again."[457] This time he meant it.

Col. Steenburgh testified about Halperin's possible participation in GRU spying on the Directorate of Artillery, but near the end of his testimony he insisted on answering a question that he hadn't been asked: "No one has yet … asked me whether I consider the information of value or not of value to anyone on the receiving end. Based on the evidence that I have been shown [i.e., the GRU documents], the information as isolated bits of information is next to useless."[458] In other words, even if Halperin had passed on "Top Secret" or "Secret" information, he had given the GRU nothing of value. Lunan had said as much in his reports to Rogov. Halperin had refused to give the Russians a photograph or biographical information, to provide anything in writing, or to turn over serious intelligence.

Still, in the *Third Interim Report,* released 29 March 1946, the commissioners reported that Halperin's refusal to explain the "direct and circumstantial evidence against him," alongside his "general demeanour," convinced them that he had several times violated the Official Secrets Act.[459] In April, police magistrate Glenn Strike found sufficient evidence to warrant a trial.[460] But in the early spring of 1947 Gordon Lunan, the only person who could link Halperin directly to Soviet spying, refused to testify. Lunan received a one-year sentence for contempt of court,[461] while Halperin was acquitted. Judge Gordon MacDougall explained that Gouzenko's documents "were inadmissible, since the prosecution hadn't linked Halperin with other conspirators."[462] Years later, Lunan, in his memoir, no doubt feeling guilty for implicating Halperin, called him an unwitting victim.[463]

12
Loose Ends

On Friday, 29 March 1946, one day before the *habeas corpus* hearing and after forty-three days in custody, Israel Halperin, Fred Poland, Durnford Smith, Eric Adams, and Scotland Benning were released – then immediately rearrested by the RCMP.[1] They were formally charged at the Ottawa Police Court with offences against the Official Secrets Act.[2] On the same day, through a Canadian Press release, the inquiry released its *Third Interim Report* across the country.[3] The *Globe and Mail*'s front page highlighted the activities of the NKVD – the "Russian secret police … successor to the notorious OGPU." The NKVD, wrote Warren Baldwin, "infiltrated into Canada and are carrying on their activities in the country." He fingered Vitali Pavlov, second secretary and consul at the Soviet embassy, as the Canadian NKVD chief.[4]

It was King, itching to step away from the controversial order-in-council, who rose in the House of Commons on 1 April to read the letter from the commission lawyers indicating that they no longer needed PC 6444. He may have escaped the ignominy of having a judge overturn PC 6444, but the press congratulated itself for defending Canadian civil liberties and forcing King's move. Although the King government responded to popular will, A.A. McIntosh of the *Globe and Mail* still condemned it for employing "totalitarian methods" and for having "thrust aside … every principle of elementary British justice."[5]

Moscow added its voice. On 4 April, while Gouzenko testified at the preliminary hearings of Poland, Halperin, Smith, Adams, and Benning, the Russian embassy issued a release branding Gouzenko as "a criminal" who would be indicted if he returned to Russia. Canadian Communists hadn't quite coordinated their stories with this Soviet line, since a week earlier Malcolm MacDonald had noted that "in statement to Press last night Dorise Nielsen, former M.P. and leading Communist, maintained that CORBY is S.I.S. [MI6] plant."[6] The Moscow release charged that Canadian media reports intended "to cast a shadow and to discredit some of the diplomatic members of the Soviet Embassy in Canada, as for example on Messrs. V.G. Pavlov, I.T. Krotov and others." These reports were "completely fictitious and deserve no credit."[7]

Soviet internal documents said the opposite, and Moscow, with no mention of criminals or SIS plants, issued strict protocols to its agents to prevent a Gouzenko-like situation from happening again. On 7 April 1946 NKVD boss Vsevolod Merkulov (PETROV)[8] re-sent a directive to NKVD stations around the world. The cable "MOSCOW'S OBSERVATIONS ON GUZENKO'S [*sic*] DEFECTION AND INSTRUCTIONS TO RESIDENTS FOR TIGHTENING SECURITY" was to be "deciphered personally by the RESIDENT" (i.e., by the NKVD espionage head):

> As you know from the press, the former cipher clerk of the RESIDENCY of the Chief Intelligence Directorate of the Red Army in CANADA – GUZENKO [*sic*] has betrayed our country. Gouzenko stole and passed to the Canadian authorities several dozen incoming and outgoing cipher telegrams, personal dossiers on a valuable agent network. Operational work in the NEIGHBOURS' [i.e., the GRU's] RESIDENCY in CANADA was so organized that each operational worker had a detailed knowledge of the work of other members of the staff, the agent network, the times and places of meetings, the nature of the tasks of the CENTRE, and plans for operational measures. In the RESIDENCY personal dossiers on the agent network became common knowledge. In the work of the agent network extensive use was made of members of the FELLOW COUNTRYMEN'S organization who were known to authorities of the country for their progressive activity. Thus, GUZENKO'S work ... made it possible for the traitor to have at his disposal State secrets of great importance. G.'s testimony, and a number of documents introduced by the prosecution at the hearing, show that G. himself was prepared to betray his country long before the day on which he defected. In the RESIDENCY there was no study or training of people, the most elementary principles of security were ignored, complacency and self-satisfaction went unchecked. All this was the result of a decline in political vigilance and sense of responsibility for work entrusted by the Party and the Government. G.'s defection has caused great damage to our country and has, in particular, very greatly complicated our work in the American countries.

Merkulov promised new rules and ordered that they be followed scrupulously, but, even before the new rules arrived, the Resident should tighten security: "The work must be organized so that each member of the staff and agent can have no knowledge of our work beyond what directly relates to the task which he is carrying out."[9]

Merkulov's anger at the sudden winter for Soviet intelligence in North America was echoed in a curious way in the US by NKVD chief Grigory Dolbin, recently sent to Washington to replace Anatoly Gorsky as the new *rezident* after the defecting operative Elizabeth Bentley exposed Gorsky in November 1945.[10] Dolbin spoke no English when he arrived in the US, yet he was ordered to cultivate new contacts with Washington officials.[11] With his tenure dominated by the Gouzenko and Bentley defections, Dolbin, in a late March letter, complained, "The events in Canada and those that subsequently took place in the USA created in the country a situation of a drastic increase in counter-espionage activities in the country, not only by special [counterintelligence] organizations and agencies ... but also by various anti-espionage volunteer organizations, that have been founded." He was experiencing increased surveillance: "wiretapping in our employees' apartments and hotel rooms" and "miniature microphones in our senior workers' cars." Dolbin worried that more defections might be brewing. He singled out the behavior of Foreign Minister Molotov's close ally, Soviet chargé d'affaires Nickolai Novikov, who would eventually succeed Andrei Gromyko as Soviet ambassador to the US in June 1946.[12] Novikov was "rude to his subordinates" and people were "afraid of him," Dolbin complained. "Perhaps if circumstances were different, a situation like this wouldn't trouble us especially. However, the current situation in the USA is such that there is a possibility that the more unstable members of the colony could, having fallen out of their boss's favor and become frightened by his threats, make decisions that would not be desirable for us."[13]

Although he mouthed Marxist orthodoxies about communitarian values, his worries about capitalist propaganda and the effects of American life on Soviet nationals betrayed an implicit critique of the Soviet system and ideals: a "press campaign is trying to suggest to the average American that he lives in an environment where foreign gov'ts – even friendly ones, even those that Americans help out by giving a portion of their earnings in the form of taxes – are engaged in subversive anti-American work. This propaganda resonates with the average American, for whom a threat to his personal wealth and well-being is the greatest misfortune."[14] In Canada, Dolbin said, "the Canadian prime minister" had declared that Gouzenko, having seen the free Canadian elections, "became disenchanted with the Soviet Union, where everything was worse than it was in Canada." Because Americans and Canadians celebrated defections, it had become "easier for unstable people who have checkered pasts and are frightened at present to decide not to return to their Homeland."[15] Dolbin was recalled in early 1948, suffering from mental instability.[16]

"Berman," 2 April

Despite the release of the rest of the detainees and of the *Third Interim Report*, certain names that appeared in Gouzenko's cache raised question marks. Who was "Berman"? "Surensen"? "Hermine"? Why were GRU spies interested in them? To answer such questions, the inquiry began subpoenaing suspects who hadn't been arrested with the thirteen: S.S. Burman, Agatha Chapman, Dr. Henry Harris, Sam Carr, Ignacy Witczak, Fred Rose, and, with some difficulty, Hermina Rabinowitch.

A Montreal insurance agent with ties to the Communist Party appeared in GRU notes as "Berman." Gouzenko said that the notes in Lt. Col. Motinov's handwriting were draft telegrams, each addressed to "The Director" in Moscow. One concerned information that "Debouz" (Fred Rose) had secured from the Canadian minister of fisheries about a recent attempt on Hitler's life; a second concerned "Gray's" (Harold Gerson's) relatives in Bukovina and Bucharest; a third set out a plan for a meeting between "Berman" and a Soviet agent in London.[17] Because Moscow had responded that "Burman had been handed over to our people in London," Gouzenko judged that "Berman's" meeting with a Soviet agent did take place.[18] Zabotin also mentioned "Berman" in a telegram to Moscow confirming that "Debouz" had provided a "biography and photograph of Berman,"[19] which had been sent to Moscow with "Tunkin."[20]

The notes about "Berman's" London meeting described him as an "insurance agent" who had joined the Communist Party in 1938, with his wife following in 1939. "During the illegal period [beginning June 1940]," Motinov wrote, "he ['Berman'] worked in the central apparatus of the Party on organizational work."[21] Gouzenko believed that "Berman" wasn't a cover name, but a real name,[22] either "Berman" or "Burman," since Russian had no letter "u."[23] Based on Motinov's description and the Communist affiliation, the RCMP identified Samuel Saul Burman, a Montreal-based agent for North American Life.[24] He had been very active in the YMHA as a ski instructor, scout master, and event organizer, and he had volunteered in 1942 as a zone captain for the Combined Jewish Appeal,[25] but he drew RCMP attention because of his membership in the Friends of the Soviet Union.

Although an RCMP investigation concluded that Burman was "prominent in Communist subversive activities in Montreal,"[26] in his testimony he distanced himself from Communism. Nevertheless, he said that the Spanish Civil War moved him to raise money for the "Spanish Committee" that was "sending soldiers to Spain" and "looking after Spanish children,"[27] while opposition to the controversial padlock law seems to have drawn him to meetings of the Civil Liberties Union.[28] Were there Communists active in these organizations? "There may have been," he said," but they were not known to me."[29]

Because only one S.S. Burman appeared in Lovell's Montreal directory, it's very likely that the subpoenaed Burman was the one who wrote a letter to the *Montreal Gazette* (3 August 1942) protesting a 31 July editorial. The *Gazette* had argued that removing the ban against the Canadian Communist Party would damage the Liberal government politically among French Canadians and other Catholic ethnic minorities, who were deeply anti-Communist.[30] S.S. Burman castigated the *Gazette* for "driving a wedge" between Canadians and undermining the war effort. He argued that Ottawa could support the war effort by removing the ban on the Communist Party and freeing "interned Communists and antifascists."[31]

In 1943, at age thirty-five, Burman enlisted in the army as an officer cadet. He was soon promoted to lieutenant,[32] and he completed a "civil affairs staff course" supervised by the Department of External Affairs at the Royal Military College.[33] Those selected for civil affairs work studied history, government, and local administration directed at specific countries. As the Canadian First Army fought its way through northern Europe to Germany in the spring of 1945, Europe was a scene of destruction and disorder, and Civil Affairs officers dealt with the war's collateral damage. David Borys has described how Canadian Civil Affairs officers helped to liberate Europe by caring for "hungry, sick, dirty, and homeless civilians," and by assuming responsibility for the military government in occupied Germany.[34] Burman went overseas as a Civil Affairs officer in early September 1944[35] to Aldershot, England, and then, starting in March 1945, he worked as a Civil Affairs officer in Belgium, Holland, and Germany.[36] Neither he nor his fellow officers were young men fit for battle. Their work required individuals with life experience, professional knowledge (law, finance, politics, health), and knowledge of European languages. Officers specialized in areas such as public administration, relief, civil defence, and public safety.[37] Berman spent the summer and fall of 1945 doing such work in Germany.[38]

Questions arise. Why would Moscow let Motinov know that "Burman had been handed over to our people in London"?[39] Why had Fred Rose recruited "Berman"? Was his initial contact with the GRU in London intended to establish a way for him to share information about Allied resources, activities, and plans related to Germany's civilian administration? Certainly, intelligence about the post-war administration and reconstruction of Europe was highly sought, both by the Soviets and by Western powers. When a defeated Finland signed an armistice with the Allies in September 1944, it passed under the administration of an Allied Control Council headed by subsequent Comintern leader Andrei Zhdanov. Britain sent SIS "Political Representatives" or "Information Officers" – who were really undercover agents – to Finland and to other post-war Allied military administrations.[40] Via people like Berman, the Soviets were no doubt trying to achieve the same intelligence-gathering capacities. As the August 1945 telegrams from "the Director" (Bolshakov) to Zabotin made clear, Moscow was eager for insider information about American troops in Europe.[41] Civil Affairs officers were one potential intelligence source, and if the GRU could recruit agents in Canada, so much the better: those agents could then appear in Europe already in place and available to Soviet handlers.

That S.S. Burman had either worked for the GRU or planned to do so – that the RCMP's identification of Burman as "Berman" was correct – became clear at the inquiry. But Burman, subpoenaed to testify on 2 April 1946,[42] proved evasive, and Fauteux made little headway in his questioning. Motinov's draft telegram had set out arrangements for "Berman's" rendezvous with a Soviet agent in London.[43] They were supposed to meet on the third Sunday after "Berman's" departure "at 15 hours … in front of the office of the High Commissioner for Canada, London, S.W.1 (Canada House, Trafalgar Sq.)." This would have placed the meeting on 24 September 1944, but if it did not take place, it would "be transferred to the next Sunday at the same hours [*sic*] etc. until contact is established." Berman should "be in civilian clothes—brown suit (tweed) checkered, a raincoat but no hat, with a newspaper in his right hand."[44] The password would be "How's Elsie?" Berman" was to reply, "She's fine." Burman's wife's was named "Elsa," and he had taken to Britain "a pair of flannels," a brown tweed "sports jacket,"[45] and an army "trench coat," but no hat.[46] Around 26 September he had gone up to London for a couple of days' leave, but he "could not remember the exact dates."[47] He knew that Canada House lay "right at the corner of CHMQ [*sic*, CMHQ – Canadian Military Headquarters],"[48] but he denied that he had gone anywhere near Trafalgar Square in September.[49] He went to London again on the weekend of 28 October, but he insisted that he only visited CMHQ, not Canada House next door.[50] Fauteux wondered how Elsa's name and Burman's wardrobe for Britain would find its way into a GRU document without his complicity. Burman didn't know.[51]

The draft telegram to Moscow also contained a contingency plan: "If the meeting at the designated place should prove impossible, or inconvenient for us, Berman will send his address to his wife, the latter will give it to Debouz [Fred Rose], and the latter to us." In case the meeting had to be shifted to "Berman's living quarters," "Debouz" would alert Burman's wife, who would in turn "write Berman a letter with the following sentence: 'Ben has not been feeling too well.'"[52] Burman's brother "Barnett" was "known as Ben."[53] Burman claimed that he didn't know Rose, had "never met" him, and had no idea if his wife knew Rose or not. Yet Burman had attended meetings where Rose was present.[54] Burman did know Harold Gerson and Scotland Benning, because Ben Burman had married Harold Gerson's sister, while Gerson's wife and Benning's wife were sisters.[55]

Motinov had recorded that Berman "joined the Party in 1938," that "his wife had joined in 1939," and that "during the illegal period he worked in the central apparatus of the Party on organizational work." Burman called these statements "fantastic."[56] When Fauteux asked about Burman's participation in the "West End Club," an informal group of Labor-Progressive Party members, and his subscriptions to the *Canadian Tribune* and *National Affairs Monthly*, Burman gave vague and often contradictory responses. He was not a member of the club, though he might have attended a few meetings. Improbably, he claimed not to know if Elsa was a member of the Labor-Progressive Party. Or of the West End Club. He subscribed to the *Canadian Tribune*, which he considered "left-wing," but he wasn't prepared to call it Communist. He also subscribed to the CCF's *New Commonwealth* and may have bought a copy of *National Affairs Monthly* from a newsstand.[57]

Ultimately, as Fauteux's questioning stressed, it couldn't be chance that Burman's name, his wife's name, his brother's name, his wardrobe, the fact that he was in the insurance business, that he was from Montreal, and that he would be in London at a certain time all appeared in a GRU document. Could Burman explain this anomaly? No. Perhaps, Fauteux suggested, Burman might have been "an unconscious agent," unaware of the GRU's plans for him. Burman had no response.

> FAUTEUX: "You have no suggestion; you can give no explanation; you have nothing to say about that document?"
> BURMAN: "No, nothing at all."[58]

The circumstantial details, alongside Burman's political views and careful stonewalling, suggest that the commissioners were right to conclude that Burman was involved in GRU espionage: the "essential accuracy of the statements in the telegram with respect of Berman's family, occupation, political history, and civilian clothing" convinced them that the rest of the telegram was no less accurate – "The whole document was written in order to have Moscow arrange at that end for the meeting in London." However, the commissioners also concluded, again rightly, that they had no evidence to sustain a charge that Burman had given "secret and confidential information, the disclosure of which might be inimical to the safety and interests of Canada, to the agents of a foreign power."[59]

"Surensen," 4 April

On Thursday, 4 April 1946, someone who hadn't even been summoned showed up at the Kellock-Taschereau inquiry: Lt. Henning Sorensen, a Danish-born naval intelligence officer. The miscellaneous note that had implicated Fred Poland also referred to a GRU agent named "Surensen": "He works in "the Naval Ministry ... in Intelligence. Gave materials about construction of ships. Left for overseas." Like "Polland," he "worked up to April."[60] A separate note on Surensen read, "Did not work for us directly but for Sam's organization"[61] (which operated out of Toronto). Henning Sorensen explained that after the *Montreal Star* publicized the name "Surensen," "I had to take some steps to avoid suspicion being cast upon me ... I came here to ask for a statement to clear me of any suspicion because it is extremely annoying to me to have that name appear in the newspapers." He added, "I was not born in Canada, and always people are quite willing to believe the worst about you."[62]

But Sorensen's arrival at the inquiry as a result of personal feelings was something of a red herring. Reporting to London, Malcolm MacDonald revealed that Sorensen "came forward of his own accord after some prompting by the head of Naval Intelligence."[63] Until June 1944, Sorensen had worked at Ottawa's naval headquarters in the "Operational Intelligence Center," where he tracked "neutral shipping" to prevent "collaboration between supposedly neutral vessels and any of our enemies."[64] He was transferred to Military Intelligence in 1944 at Quebec's Farnham Internment Camp, administered by the Psychological Warfare Committee. Like "Surensen," Sorensen had "left for overseas." In September 1944 he was sent to England for a short course related to his work for the Psychological Warfare Committee. None of his work had anything to do with ship construction.[65] Lt. Commander George Tottenham, deputy director of naval intelligence, said that it would nevertheless have been easy for any naval officer to access the plans for ship construction;[66] Tottenham said that, since the Naval Construction library only recorded borrowing if the plans were removed from headquarters, as long as Sorensen looked at the plans in his office, no one would question him;[67] Sorensen wasn't so sure.[68] As for the Sam Carr connection, Sorensen had never lived in Toronto or been stationed there during his years in the navy.[69] He insisted that had never met Carr. Sorensen had only travelled to Toronto for family reasons, perhaps four times, most recently in late 1942 on his way "to visit his wife's people in Detroit."[70] He couldn't explain the references to "Surensen" in Zabotin's notes.[71]

A major thrust of Williams's questioning was to find out whether Sorensen was a Communist, especially since he had gone to Spain during the Spanish Civil War to support the Republicans.[72] Sorensen, in response, emphasized his associations with Frank Scott, Graham Spry, the CCF, and the Committee to Aid Spanish Democracy.[73] Indeed, the CCF's *New Commonwealth* contained a 17 October 1936 report from a "special correspondent," a Montreal native fluent in Spanish who had just crossed the frontier into Spain – Henning Sorensen. He represented the short-lived Spanish Medical Aid Committee[74] and was working with the Spanish government to address the Republic's medical needs.[75] "Being attracted to the C.C.F., would that mean that you would also be attracted to the Labor-Progressive party or the Communist party of Canada?" Williams asked. Sorensen disagreed: "I worked with a number of people in Spain which I found out were Communists after I had been working with them, and I will admit frankly that I got a certain respect for these people down there, the way they were fighting this civil war."[76]

When Kellock inquired whether Sorensen was a Communist, Sorensen denied it: "No ... My views are socialist. I have voted for the CCF at the last election."[77] Kellock wanted to hear Sorensen articulate the difference between socialists and communists. Sorensen explained that both groups were socialist, "that the aims of the Communists are also ultimate Socialism, but that the method is different." He favoured central planning and felt that "the capitalist system has a number of grave defects," but he said, "I am no fanatic in politics."[78]

His disavowals of Communism were false. Writing to the Central Committee of the Communist Party of Spain on 4 August 1937, Sorensen declared that he was a member of the Communist Party of Spain.[79] Following Sorensen's Spanish adventure, he worked for the Sun Life Company, but quit on 30 June 1940, and explained his resignation in a rather curious way: "I left the company in 1940, after – I don't know how to put it – an argument or disagreement with the chief of the Spanish Department."[80] However, it so happened that the tumultuous Montreal Civil Liberties Union conference had recently concluded, and Sun Life was purging employees who wouldn't disavow the now Communist-tainted CLU, of which Sorensen was a member. Agatha Chapman left the company on 5 July 1940, days after Sorensen did, because she refused to break with the CLU.[81] No doubt Sorensen was telling a partial truth about his departure: given his politics, he could have had "an argument or disagreement" with almost any member of the Sun Life administration. Roderick Stewart, who interviewed Sorensen for a biography of Norman Bethune and had access to Sorensen's unpublished autobiography, concluded that he was "likely … a member of the Communist Party of Canada."[82] Describing the recruitment of Alexander Foote and others by Soviet intelligence during their time in Spain, Hugh Thomas, though without any direct evidence, argues that Sorensen was recruited there by the GRU.[83] Certainly, Hazen Size, a co-worker with Sorensen in Bethune's Spanish project, was approached by Soviet agents.[84] Michael Cope, writing in 1962 from Havana about the new Castro regime, called Sorensen a "self-confessed Marxist and a voluntary member of Castro's Red-bossed militia." Sorensen told Cope that in May 1961 he had quit his job selling insurance in Vancouver and hurried to Havana: "At first I just came to have a look at the revolution here, but I found it so exciting I simply had to become part of it." Again, a curious coincidence: the new Soviet ambassador to Cuba (1960–62) was none other than Sergei Koudriavtsev, the GRU boss in Canada from 1942 to late 1944, prior to Zabotin's arrival and during "Surensen's" involvement. Sorensen became "senior translator in Cuba's propaganda department in the ministry of exterior relations."[85]

Because Sorensen had asked the commissioners to issue a statement clearing him of any involvement in Soviet espionage, and because they were obliged to examine the facts about Sorensen as part of their duty under the order-in-council, they, in their *Final Report*, included a six-page review of Sorensen's evidence.[86] Despite his request, they didn't state that he *wasn't* the GRU's "Surensen." Nevertheless, they did concede that they had no evidence that Henning Sorensen had offended the Official Secrets Act.[87] Sorensen must have been less than happy with such a lukewarm statement, but perhaps he was relieved that Williams's digging turned up nothing incriminating.

Ignacy Witczak, 5 April

Besides being fertile ground for recruiting GRU spies, the Spanish Civil War had been useful in other ways to the Soviet Union – witness the case of the real and the fake Ignacy Witczak. According to an MI5 file (that relied on Gouzenko), Moscow had given a fake

"Ignacy Witczak" "a Canadian passport which had belonged to a canadian [*sic*] citizen killed during the Spanish Civil War."[88] But the RCMP searched for and found the real Ignacy Witczak, who was very much alive. Should the Kellock-Taschereau inquiry investigate the case? It fell outside the inquiry's terms of reference, and it would "enlarge scope of Commission [*sic*] somewhat beyond purely Government employees as it would introduce Doctor SOBOLEV, Doctor Harris and Sam Carr." Yet the benefit of investigating "Witczak" was clear, as Malcolm MacDonald explained: "It would bring out with force the part played by C.P.[Communist Party]-Canada and this is of particular significance from point of view of public education."[89]

The real Witczak stood before the inquiry on 5 April 1946 and, through an interpreter, confirmed many of the details in the MI5 "Witczak" file. He was born in Poland in 1906, emigrated to Canada in 1930, worked on a farm in Leamington, Ontario, and became a naturalized Canadian in 1936. A Communist, he applied for a passport in 1937 in order to travel to Spain to serve in the Mackenzie-Papineau Battalion of the International Brigade.[90] At the military base in Albacete, Spain, he was told that passports were not taken to the front line because they might be destroyed.[91] Witczak turned his over. When he asked for it back upon leaving Spain, it turned out that the safe-keeping hadn't been so safe: he was told that a lorry had been hit during a bombardment and the passport had been ... destroyed.[92] Witczak knew others who, curiously, had had an identical "safe-keeping" experience, though he couldn't remember their names.[93] By 1939 he was repatriated to Canada. Did Witczak recognize the application for a new passport dated 1945? Had he signed these documents? No and no.[94] Clearly, Moscow had stolen the real Ignacy Witczak's passport, replaced his photo with one of a fake "Witczak," and dispatched that agent to the US as "a student in Los Angeles University."[95]

Meanwhile, as soon as Gouzenko made his espionage revelations, the fake "Witczak" suddenly vanished from his Los Angeles residence. The Gouzenko case in fact disrupted the entire GRU network in North America, and because the GRU sensed that the Americans and British were "enforcing a wholesale examination of people using Canadian passports ... Red Army Intelligence had given instructions for the recall of all agents carrying forged Canadian passports ... [T]here were a great many, especially in the Americas."[96] The FBI reported that "Witczak" had written his wife Bunia a coded letter from New York: "Doctors [FBI] in United States were informed, from Canada about HARRY'S ["Witczak's"] sickness." Apparently, "Witczak" had been "sleeping in railway stations and Turkish baths past few days." He had instructed Bunia "to close bank account slowly and dispose of furniture."

What had led to agent "Witczak's" exposure was the need to renew his false Canadian passport. For years, the Russians had exploited Canada as a source of documents for Soviet spies, especially for those who operated in the US. With false Canadian identity documents and passports, spies could cross from Canada to the US with little difficulty and remain there indefinitely. Fred Rose's NKVD work in the late 1930s primarily involved getting Canadian passports to the Ovakimian Soviet network in the US.[97] A "Top Secret" MI5 report linked Canadian passports, Tim Buck, and the "Tilton/Dozenberg" network circa 1928,[98] and cited individual cases, such as "HARRY I" using a Canadian passport to enter England in 1932,[99] and "ULANOVSKI" using one to enter the Low Countries and Denmark in 1935."[100]

But the process of renewing the fraudulent "Witczak" passport proved challenging. Col. Mikhail Milstein, inspecting Soviet espionage networks in Mexico, the US, and Canada,[101] had initiated the renewal process with Sam Carr in Ottawa in the summer of 1944. Later, he sent a Moscow telegram exulting in the "great possibilities of establishing this production of passports." (Gouzenko, because he coded the telegram, knew its contents.[102]) Rogov wanted to replicate those successful forgeries. Using the GRU code word for the forgers, he expressed the GRU's interest in determining if "possibly old shoemakers who disappeared several years ago" were available for the work.[103] They weren't. Carr, the Canadian point man, would have to recruit a new "shoemaker." Carr developed an agent – the "executor" – in the Passport Branch to do the work,[104] but delay after delay followed. First Carr found out that the passport would cost $5,000. Moscow objected that "$5,000 was a fantastic sum," and offered $3,000.[105] Then Carr became worried that the real Witczak was alive. No, Moscow responded, he had "died in 1937 in the Spanish war."[106] Even more problematic, the "executor" in the passport branch was all promise and no performance.[107] Rogov, who oversaw the project for the GRU, lamented, "It was some kind of drunken civil servant who was doing the work."[108]

The Witczak passport was part of a larger project for Rogov. He wanted Carr to summarize the "requirements which a person living as an 'illegal' must meet (nationality, citizenship, occupation, education, knowledge of languages, family and financial conditions etc.)." How could an "illegal" gain a legal grounding – through "a commercial undertaking, joining a business firm as a partner, what kind of firm, joining as a member any office, joining the army as a volunteer"? What documents must an "'illegal' ... possess (passport, different kinds of certificates, references, recommendation letters, etc.)" What were the most "expedient methods to slip into the country?"[109] Following up on a directive given to Zabotin by Bolshakov in Moscow, Rogov gave Carr assignments: "1. Write the report on documentation of passports and other documents pointing out by you (Frank) who concretely does such things. 2. What documents can be prepared and received through you."[110]

According to GRU records, Carr recruited others to assist him. Dr. Henry Harris, a Toronto optometrist and long-time associate of Carr, appeared to be a cut-out, an intermediary between Carr and Rogov. Meetings to deal with the passport project were arranged through Harris, he attended meetings, a few meetings were even held at his apartment,[111] and he was in attendance for discussions on how "evidence of naturalization and marriage" would be addressed for Ignacy and Bunia Witczak.[112] Appearing before the inquiry, Harris portrayed his relationship with Carr as purely personal. He acknowledged that he frequently travelled with Carr[113] – to Montreal, Ottawa, and New York – and shared hotel rooms with him. However, these trips were purely recreational. He just "loafed around."[114] They travelled to a ski resort in St. Agathe, Quebec, to "look at the skiing."[115] GRU documentation indicated that the "doctor" had been in Ottawa on specific dates and attended meetings to discuss passports. Harris agreed that he went to Ottawa on those dates, but he had not attended any meetings and didn't know Motinov or Rogov.[116] He had "no idea" why GRU documents would mention him. Perhaps someone else was using his name.[117]

In the inquiry's *Final Report*, the commissioners charged that Harris was one of several people "active in procuring a false Canadian passport for a Russian agent who was operating in the United States."[118] Eventually, Harris was charged with two counts of conspiracy to obtain and forge a false a passport in violation of the Official Secrets Act.[119] During his trial, Judge A.G. McDougall ruled that the "presumptions" set out in the Official Secrets Act – that the court could infer the guilt of an accused "from the circumstances of the case, or his conduct, or his known character"[120] – were relevant, "regardless of whether [the case] was one of conspiracy or of a direct violation" of the act.[121] For McDougall, it "was extremely difficult to believe that Harris continued to travel to Ottawa, Montreal, New York, and other cities merely to spend a short time with Carr when he saw him every day in Toronto."[122] He convicted Harris and sentenced him to five years' imprisonment.

The Ontario Court of Appeal quashed the conviction in June 1947, on the grounds that Harris had been charged under the conspiracy provisions of the Criminal Code, making the Official Secrets Act irrelevant, and that the Crown had failed to link Harris directly to a conspiracy. Chief Justice Robertson wrote, "Statements contained in documents purporting to be statements of acts done, or of things said by, or of arrangements made with a person charged with conspiracy, which documents are produced by a witness who did not write them [i.e., Gouzenko], does not know accused and who can give no evidence of any acts done by accused at any time or in any place, constitute hearsay evidence." Mere association with Carr was not enough, and no witness had established the truth of the statements in the documents – "the Court cannot proceed upon suspicion."[123]

Another Carr associate was also named. Since the real Witczak was unmarried, Bunia, the wife of the fake "Witczak," had to be referenced in the new passport. So, Carr recruited Dr. John Soboloff, his own doctor, to sign the new "Witczak" application. Questioned by the RCMP and later by the inquiry, Soboloff admitted that he had signed the "Witczak" application despite having no personal knowledge of any "Witczak."[124] Carr hadn't even shown Soboloff a photo of him.[125] Soboloff pled guilty to making a false statement to procure a passport, and he was fined five hundred dollars plus costs.[126]

Less conclusive was the investigation of the passport office. Adrienne Soulière held responsibility for the retrieval of stored files and possessed the only key to the file storage room,[127] though at least two other file clerks could retrieve files in Soulière's absence. Her records indicated that on 14 May 1945 and again on 27 August 1945, W.M. Pappin, a twenty-seven-year veteran of the passport service,[128] had requested the Witczak file.[129] Pappin denied this.[130] Nevertheless, the commissioners, relying on Soulière's testimony, concluded that "there would appear to have been only four male members of the Passport Office, who, as a practical matter, could have obtained the issue of the false passport," but the evidence singled out only one, W.M. Pappin.[131]

Pappin, on Soulière's evidence, was charged with conspiracy to secure a false passport. But the Crown's case suffered from irregularities in her testimony, because at times she claimed to remember Pappin asking for the Witczak file and at other times she seemed to rely purely on her records.[132] And then a new issue raised its head: her ongoing relationship with Emma Woikin, who had worked with Soulière in the passport office prior to her transfer to the cipher division of External Affairs. Soulière testified that Woikin had "visited the office about five times" in the summer of 1945 "principally to sell paintings she had made." "Woikin had never mentioned anything about the Witczak file," but she had once "'talked communism' to the girls in the file room and there had been an argument."[133]

The Crown's case collapsed. Both Witczak's birth date and the date of his arrival in Canada were wrong in the new application. Yet Pappin's colleagues in the passport office, Albert Cooper and C. Clancy, testified that Pappin was incapable of such an "incompetent job" of transferring simple data from the original to the fraudulent application form.[134] Soulière admitted that at the Royal Commission "she had been confused and worried by family troubles," and that "she had given an untrue statement to the commissioners."[135] As a result, Crown counsel J.J. Robinette and Judge A.G. McDougall agreed that "[a]nyone in the Passport office could have altered the 1937 file and attributed it to the accused." Pappin was acquitted of the charges.[136]

In mid-August 1945, the new "Witczak" passport still languishing in production, Bolshakov had wired Zabotin to demand an end to delays. Bolshakov ordered that the passport be sent to Moscow in "the next regular mail."[137] The fraudulent passport finally made its long-awaited Russian debut on 30 August 1945 … mere days before Gouzenko's defection. The fake "Witczak" in the US, therefore, never got to use it, because Philby's report to the Soviets about Gouzenko's defection almost immediately sent agent "Witczak" on the run.

The inquiry had also issued a subpoena for Carr to testify, but he had fled Canada for somewhere in Europe or the Soviet Union.[138] So the final chapter in the Witczak case had to wait until 1949, when Carr was arrested in New York.[139] Extradited and charged with conspiracy to forge a Canadian passport,[140] Carr was convicted in April 1949 and sentenced to six years in penitentiary. Half a year later, his appeal was dismissed.[141]

"Skelton," 16 April

One of the GRU notes stolen by Gouzenko said that if "Eric" wanted to speak to "Frank" (Sam Carr) in Toronto, he would phone Dr. Henry Harris's optical clinic through "Skelton."[142] The use of a cut-out such as "Skelton" signalled GRU tradecraft. Generally, cut-outs were nearly anonymous with a low public profile. Freda Linton ("Frieda"), an employee at the International Labour Office (ILO) in Montreal in the early 1940s and then at the National Film Board in Ottawa, served as a cut-out between Maj. Sokolov and his Montreal agents,[143] and later between Fred Rose and Raymond Boyer.[144] Grace Marsh ("Galya"), a Montreal high school teacher, was the cut-out between Fred Rose and his agents Raymond Boyer and Harold Gerson.[145] Hermina Rabinowitch, another Montreal ILO employee, provided cover (as we will show) for communication between the GRU resident in New York and a watchmaker who funnelled financial support to the GRU in Switzerland.[146]

While cut-outs were only small cogs, their existence meant that the GRU wanted to shield something from official Canadian eyes, so E.K. Williams attempted to uncover the identity of "Skelton." Initially, "Skelton" seemed to be a code name for a buffer between the GRU and a Canadian agent code-named "Eric," but it didn't take Canadian officials long to figure out that neither "Skelton" nor "Eric" were code names. Rogov, inheriting Sergei Koudriavtsev's network and perhaps making a hasty note, had made unguarded references to a person actually named "Skelton" and to Eric Adams, recruited for the GRU by Sam Carr in 1942.[147] When Mackenzie King read the transcript of Gouzenko's testimony, King immediately connected "Skelton" to Alexander Skelton, the son of his long-time advisor, undersecretary of state for external affairs O.D. Skelton.[148] "Sandy Skelton's name comes in in reference to being an intermediary," King noted in his diary on 20 February 1946, and he added, "I have never felt sure of him and his sympathies."[149] King even had reservations about Skelton senior: "There was a strong feeling I know among many that Dr. Skelton was much too sympathetic with the Communist outlook."[150] Alexander (Sandy) Skelton was invited to the inquiry.[151]

The forty-year-old Skelton was both a leading figure in the Canadian civil service and a man who burned life's candle at both ends. A 1927 economics graduate of Queens University, he became a Rhodes Scholar and a middleweight boxing champion. He studied at Oxford but abandoned his program during the final year in favour of yachting in the Mediterranean and failed to get his degree.[152] Nevertheless, he was recruited in 1935 to head the Research Division of the new Bank of Canada. There he built a career on brilliance and a capacity for work. At the same time, he acquired a bear cub as a pet and earned a reputation as a hard-drinking socializer, his "frenzied bursts of intense output punctuated by liquid lunches."[153] Already at age thirty-two, as secretary for the Rowell-Sirois Commission, Skelton played a central role in formulating the institutional structure of post-war Canada and advancing the welfare state.[154]

In his testimony, Skelton revealed that he knew Adams "very well" and had met Sam Carr "once several years ago," but hadn't had contact with the Russian embassy, with Col. Rogov, or with Lt. Col. Motinov. No, Adams didn't ask him to communicate with anybody. Less believably, Skelton, who hired Adams and Agatha Chapman to work at the Bank of Canada,[155] professed to have had not a clue about Adams's Communist sympathies: "No, this whole development has been a great surprise because I know Adams quite well from the work and also outside the work and there was no indication, even of sympathies in that direction, much less of active work."[156] Untrue. According to Stanley Ryerson, who stood "at the centre of Canadian [Communist] party life,"[157] Skelton "got involved in progressive circles in the thirties" and not only "knew Eric Adams, a Party member, very well" but also "showed a friendly interest in Communist Party leaders." Nevertheless, Ryerson, recognizing the limits of Skelton's sympathies, called him a "reform Liberal."[158]

Skelton's domestic circumstances also suggested much closer ties to Communism than he admitted. His ten-year marriage to American Kathleen Green[159] ended in 1939 when he took up with a Scottish woman, Janet Turner Jackson,[160] part of "the small communist movement in interwar Montreal."[161] Turner Jackson's mother, in particular, emerged as a Communist activist, and Kathleen Willsher testified that her own commitment to Communism was rekindled by study sessions at "Mrs. Turner's" in Ottawa as early as 1936.[162]

Skelton met Turner Jackson when she was acting as a courier for Fred Rose, "carrying papers" to Skelton from Rose.[163] Although she didn't disclose the subject matter,[164] it seems likely that the documents related to the Communist Party of Canada's 123-page submission in 1938 to the Rowell-Sirois Commission of which Skelton was secretary.[165] Skelton had contributed to the Communist submission, and Turner Jackson was his conduit to Fred Rose and the Communist Party officials preparing the report.[166] Skelton and Turner Jackson moved into a riverboat on the Ottawa River,[167] and in 1941 her husband Stanley Jackson secured a divorce based on his wife's adultery.[168] Living with Skelton didn't change the politics of Turner Jackson (who now called herself Turner Skelton). Florence Adamson (a secretary in the prime minister's office), who arranged a meeting in the early 1940s between Turner Skelton and Harry Ferns (a self-described Communist, also in the PMO), described her as a "red hot socialist."[169]

Skelton knew that the inquiry into Soviet espionage was interested in his common-law partner's mother, Mrs. Turner, but under questioning he behaved as if he didn't know why. Did he know anything about study groups held at the Turner residence? Was he aware that the GRU used such study groups as a recruitment field for espionage agents? Gingerly, Skelton danced around his Communism connections: no, he wasn't aware of any study groups at the Turner residence or of encountering Eric Adams there. At the same time, confronted by the cryptic GRU reference to "Skelton" in Gouzenko's testimony, he said, "I assume it refers to me,"[170] and he expressed no surprise or indignation that an inquiry into Soviet espionage had set its sights on his extended family.

E.K. Williams appears to have deliberately avoided asking Skelton whether Janet Turner Skelton had assisted the GRU. Instead, he invited Skelton to brainstorm, in a kind of pin-the-tail-on-the-donkey exercise: "Could you think of any other person named Skelton that this note might refer to?"[171] Skelton proved immediately helpful. He theorized that "Skelton" wasn't a person at all, but a mechanism employed by Eric Adams to make unauthorized use of the Bank of Canada private telephone exchange whereby "officers of the Bank" communicated between Ottawa and Toronto or Montreal via "direct wires."[172] To call Toronto, Skelton would just say "This is Skelton speaking,"[173] and the switchboard operator would connect him directly to the number he wanted. According to Skelton, the code name enigma had a simple solution: "It might very well be that someone was using the wire in my name."[174]

The GRU using the Bank of Canada's privileged network, available to only a handful of executives, as a cut-out to protect its agent Eric Adams from exposure? Highly improbable. Cut-outs were intended to hide GRU purposes behind the ordinary, not call attention to themselves by grasping at executive privilege. Calls via the Bank of Canada from Eric Adams to Dr. Henry Harris, a known associate of Communist organizer Sam Carr, would offer not cover but exposure. Telephone operators familiar with the voices of the few executives authorized to use the special privilege would likely become suspicious at hearing a strange-voiced "Skelton" on the line. Sergei Koudriavtsev, the senior Soviet operative in charge of building the GRU network prior to Zabotin's arrival, would have immediately red-flagged this high-wire act had Adams suggested it.

A more likely explanation than the Bank of Canada executive-phone theory was that Skelton was protecting his common-law partner, Turner Skelton. Her liminal position within Ottawa society made her an ideal cut-out for the GRU. Adams (via an anonymous telephone) could call "Skelton," asking for a meeting with Sam Carr. "Skelton" (via an anonymous telephone) could then call Harris's clinic to arrange the meeting. All standard GRU tradecraft – no executive lines, no puzzled switchboard operators, no involvement of non-GRU third parties. And Turner Skelton, having been a courier for Fred Rose, had experience in this kind of work.

Alexander Skelton's story proposed a direct, partly public, connection between the agent Adams and his GRU handlers. The commissioners, remembering Adams's other GRU involvements, were too ready to accept Skelton's fiction, and concluded erroneously in their *Final Report* that Adams, "using Mr. Skelton's name," had secretly used his position at the Bank of Canada to make espionage-related calls to Sam Carr in Toronto.[175] A better explanation is that "Skelton" was not a password but, like "Eric," an actual person, most likely Janet Turner Skelton. Alexander Skelton's deceptive and imaginative answers to the inquiry on a range of subjects suggest that he was quite aware of this. According to Merrily Weisbord, "The commission did not publicly investigate members of the political and military establishments, such as Alex Skelton, who, given the same treatment as the Communists, might have suffered their fate."[176] In fact, however, Skelton did appear before the inquiry, despite the paucity of evidence against him, and an account of his testimony was made public in the *Final Report*. It may be that the commissioners, like Weisbord, didn't have enough evidence to see just where the "Skelton" trail led.

"Dear Hermina," 20 May

One loose end in the Gouzenko documents seemed too important to ignore, but initially the Kellock-Taschereau Commission decided to ignore it anyway. In December 1943, a member of a Swiss-based Soviet spy network had contacted Hermina (Germina) Rabinowitch, an employee of the ILO office in Montreal, asking her to serve as a financial conduit – another kind of cut-out – between the GRU in Canada, the GRU in New York, a New York–based watch company, and spies in Geneva. As with the case of "Ignacy Witczak," the ramifications were international.

There were problems with pursuing the case. During World War II, a Russian-inspired transnational spy network – the "Rote Kapelle" (red orchestra) – spread across Europe to fight the Nazis. After the freeing of Europe, the network still followed Moscow's dictates,[177] but now against the Western capitalist liberators. The Rabinowitch case suggested that part of the Rote Kapelle's Swiss chapter was being financed via Canadian channels, but Rabinowitch, protected by diplomatic immunity, was beyond the reach of an inquiry subpoena. Also, strategic considerations hovered: Britain's MI6 worried that any probe of her might stray into sensitive intelligence matters in Paris and Egypt.

It seemed doubtful that the Kellock-Taschereau Commission would call her to testify. She hadn't violated the Official Secrets Act,[178] and it could be argued that by serving as a financial cut-out for the Rote Kapelle she had been *aiding* the Allies' anti-Nazi fight. Nevertheless, there were ideological and pragmatic reasons for the inquiry to follow up on her. Ideologically, both the West and Russia fully understood their alliance as a marriage of convenience. It wasn't just strident anti-Communists such as E.K. Williams who predicted that once Hitler was defeated it would be difficult to find common ground with an ally who insisted that the governmental and economic systems of Western democracies must be overthrown. The Soviets, very guarded about their secrets, understood the marriage's limits even better. On the more pragmatic side, the commissioners wanted to know exactly how Soviet intelligence operations worked, who was involved, and whether it could be weaponized against Western interests in the post-war setting. In early March, as the inquiry widened its scope to include "Witczak" and his passport, Britain's Malcolm MacDonald began lobbying for an investigation of Rabinowitch and the Swiss network. He thought that she might "be able to give information of some considerable value to us in Europe and also bring out USA link." London agreed, as long as the "scope" of the probe were limited to prevent a "plunge into what might be an interminable investigation."[179] Still, the ILO had to be persuaded to remove Rabinowitch's diplomatic immunity, and the commission had to be pushed to invite her.[180]

On 24 April 1946, the RCMP advised Roger Hollis in London that it had been "definitely decided" that Rabinowitch would not be called before the inquiry.[181] But less than a month later, the resident director of the ILO office in Montreal suspended her and removed her diplomatic immunity.[182] Judging by the signature on a letter from External Affairs, it must have been Arnold Smith, perhaps External Affairs' most vigorous critic of the Soviet Union, who pushed for an investigation. The next day, the RCMP delivered a subpoena to Rabinowitch.[183]

Rabinowitch, who spoke Russian, French, German, and English, was born in Lithuania to Jewish parents. She attended school in St. Petersburg in pre-revolutionary Russia, and in Königsberg, Germany, graduating from Heidelberg University with a PhD in economics and social science. After serving with the Soviet Trade Delegation in Berlin she worked for the ILO in Geneva and eventually in Montreal from 1941 to 1945.[184] While she wouldn't face charges under the Criminal Code or the Official Secrets Act, she could lose her job and worse. Because she held only a Lithuanian passport, invalid since the summer of 1940 when Lithuania was transformed into a Soviet republic, Rabinowitch was technically stateless. Her appearance before the inquiry would ultimately put her under surveillance, close employment doors, and restrict her travel to Britain, France, and the US.[185]

A request for Soviet money came to Rabinowitch from Geneva in December 1943 through her cousin Alexander Abramson, a senior employee of the ILO there. The telegram, arriving in an ILO diplomatic pouch, urged Rabinowitch to contact the Soviet embassy in Ottawa and request financial assistance for Rachel Dübendorfer, a German from Warsaw who, like Abramson, worked for one of the Rote Kapelle chapters – the "Rote Drei" (red three)[186] – operating in Switzerland since 1936–37. Dübendorfer had joined a discussion group in Rabinowitch's Geneva home, and participants joked that Dübendorfer checked with Moscow before she took a position on any subject.[187] The Rote Kapelle consisted of over one hundred agents – "Belgium (17 agents), France (35), Switzerland (17), and Germany (48)" – who gave Moscow "critical military, political, and economic information on the Nazi war machine."[188] Although the Nazis broke up the Rote Kapelle in 1942–43,[189] the Rote Drei lasted slightly longer, until 1943–44.[190] In the fall of 1943, the Germans demanded that the Swiss adhere to their obligations as a neutral country, so Swiss authorities began arresting Rote Drei members,[191] including Dübendorfer. She was jailed for a short time and felt abandoned by the Soviets. Rabinowitch, complying with Abramson's request, travelled to Ottawa and asked to meet with Gregori Tounkin, counsellor at the Soviet embassy,[192] but the Russians didn't know who she was talking about and offered nothing. Rabinowitch went away "rather furious."[193]

Why would the Russians be interested in Dübendorfer? "Because she was probably working for them," Rabinowitch testified.[194] She insisted that she had been "very annoyed with Abramson" for his request[195] and hadn't known "what kind of work Dübendorfer was engaged in."[196] Alexander Foote, who served in the Rote Drei after being recruited in Spain while with the International Brigade, inferred that "Hermina knew nothing about the Swiss network" (i.e., about Rachel Dübendorfer's intelligence work) at the outset. Otherwise, Rabinowitch would have gone straight to the military attaché.[197] Motinov ("Lamont") at the Soviet embassy made a similar assessment: "She did not know anything about SISI's [Dübendorfer's] work previously."[198]

The evidence, however, including a second letter to Rabinowitch in open code,[199] is more complex, suggesting that she may not have comprehended what she was getting into, but that she slowly grew wiser, and that she knew more than she admitted in her testimony. GRU records disclosed that early in 1944 Rabinowitch received a second letter from Abramson, which included Dübendorfer's synopsis of her sad tale:

> We live in the former apartment and work with the old firm. Two weeks ago SISI sent you a telegram. Tell us how did your journey to GISEL's

> parents turn out. My health is excellent. ALBERT is sick and will probably leave his profession for a long time, he is in bed. Relations with LUCY are good, she is a very good woman. GISEL's family for some reason is no longer interested, although up to the present she was a support … SISI's position is sad. Please inform GISEL's parents that they must hand over 6,700 dollars. This sum must be handed over by you. There are no other possibilities. GISEL must bear these expenses.[200]

In his memoir *A Handbook for Spies,* Alexander Foote provided a mostly accurate guide to this text.[201] "Sisi" or "Cissie" was Dübendorfer. The "old firm" was Soviet military intelligence in Moscow, while "Gisel" was, more specifically, the "Red Army Intelligence Service" or GRU. In other words, Dübendorfer wanted to know how Rabinowitch's contact with the Soviets had turned out. Rote Drei leader Sandor Radó ("Albert") had gone underground, while Dübendorfer and her main intelligence source, "Lucy" (Rudolf Roessler), remained active, but for some reason Soviet intelligence had abandoned Dübendorfer. She wanted support again. At the inquiry – no doubt to keep up the fiction that she hadn't involved herself in a spy network – Rabinowitch pretended not to grasp the code: "I did not quite understand what this note was about.[202]

But she understood well enough to act appropriately to the message. She lobbied the Soviets again on Dübendorfer's behalf. GRU records indicated that Rabinowitch wrote to the Soviet embassy on 9 March 1944 and enclosed Dübendorfer's new appeal. This time, Tounkin passed the message to NKVD chief Vitali Pavlov, who consulted Moscow, only to be told that "Rachel" was the Red Army's person and that (since the NKVD wanted the GRU to cough up the money) he should "do nothing."[203] It took a third appeal from Dübendorfer in April – this time for $10,000 – to finally spur the GRU into action. Dübendorfer asked, "Please advise ZNAMENSKY 19 [the address of GRU headquarters in Moscow] that SISI lives and works as of old with LUCY … but finances came to an end." For Dübendorfer to continue her work, "GISEL's family must transfer 10,000 dollars. HERMINA must make the transfer personally through N.Y. in connection with the wishes of Mister HELMARS."[204]

Sergei Koudriavtsev ("Leon")[205] was sent to Montreal with a letter from "Gisel," commending "Dear Hermina" for her contribution to the GRU's work and deputizing her to deliver the money to the Helbein Watch Company in New York: "We ask you to forward ten thousand dollars to that watch company according to Sisi's instructions."[206] By the end of July, she reported to Koudriavtsev that she had delivered the

$10,000[207] and, by early August 1944, that the funds had been received in Geneva.[208] At that time, with Rabinowitch's commitment to the GRU evidently growing, Koudriavtsev asked her to prepare a report on the ILO, on the "the characteristics of the institution."[209] She not only delivered the report but also declared, "I am, of course, at your disposal for any supplementary information as well as for the translation into Russian,"[210] and she agreed to a September meeting.[211]

When Rabinowitch appeared before the inquiry on 20 May 1946, she had no idea that it had seen these documentary records, so she deflected the questions via misdirection, contrived answers, and falsehoods. She said that Abramson told her that Dübendorfer was "in extremely difficult financial position; more than that, in misery."[212] Abramson asked for Rabinowitch's help because she was his cousin, but she couldn't explain why the request had to be directed to the Soviet embassy in Canada. "Does every Russian citizen stranded about the world write to any Russian embassy any place, and ask for $10,000, and expect to get it?" Kellock asked. Rabinowitch didn't think so.[213] What made Dübendorfer's financial problems relevant to the Soviet embassy in Canada? Rabinowitch answered falsely that Dübendorfer – a German national – wasn't German, but "of Russian origin."[214] She offered a similar misdirection when she explained that Abramson worried about Dübendorfer's financial circumstances because he was "a friend of hers." Later, Abramson, evidently having failed to coordinate his story with Rabinowitch, would pretend that the money was needed to aid "Russian prisoners of war."[215]

As Fauteux disclosed new characters and events from the GRU documentary trail, Rabinowitch's yarn grew ever more strained. She admitted arranging for money to be sent to Geneva, but suddenly there were two separate charity cases – Dübendorfer and Abramson. Abramson, she said, was "always in difficulty."[216] Rabinowitch had asked "somebody … who had business between Switzerland and the United States to give Abramson if possible some money,"[217] "somebody" running "a big firm," a watch company … but she could not recall the name.[218] With some help from Fauteux, she managed to recall that the company – the Helbros Watch Company – and the "somebody": company president William Helbein.[219] "Abramson asked me to go and tell them his name," she said.[220] She did, and luckless Abramson got his relief money. Not only that: Helbein was kind enough to carry it personally to Switzerland.[221]

But the Helbein money for Abramson, she tried to explain, had nothing to do with the Soviet money for Dübendorfer – the two separate charity cases involved "two different transactions."[222] At this point, Fauteux presented a "Dear Hermina" letter from "Gisel" (the GRU), thanking Rabinowitch for her help and asking her to deliver a letter to "Sisi" and ten thousand dollars to "that watch company." All expenses would be paid.[223] Rabinowitch denied ever seeing the letter, and when Fauteux began pursuing the letter's details, she grew silent. He offered her an opportunity to confer with legal counsel.[224]

When the inquiry resumed, Rabinowitch was more forthcoming, though still guarded. She revealed that Koudriavtsev had arranged for her to travel to New York where, at a hotel on 45th Street, a man gave her ten thousand dollars to deliver to the Helbros Watch Company for transfer to Dübendorfer via Abramson.[225] Rabinowitch likely didn't know that the money was supplied by Pavel Mikhailov ("Molier"), who (under the cover of the Soviet consulate) headed the GRU *rezidentura* in New York and who had been deeply involved in the construction of the Canadian GRU network prior to the arrival of Zabotin.[226]

Asked why the Russians in New York couldn't just run the money across town themselves but needed her, a Canadian, to travel all the way to the US to deliver it to Helbein, Rabinowitch displayed either an intuitive or more likely a schooled grasp of her role as a cut-out: "Because I was the cousin of Abramson," she answered, "and there was nothing so particular about that."[227] She agreed that the Russians wanted to avoid suspicion that they were involved. The $10,000 (the equivalent of $182,000 in 2026) for "Sisi" seemed "strange" to Rabinowitch "because the amount of money was so high and because of this whole secrecy,"[228] but she assumed that "Gisel" was someone connected with Moscow and that "Sisi" must be working for the Russians."[229]

Rabinowitch defended her decision to participate in this scheme as "humanitarian": "Even when I understood that ['Sisi'] probably worked for the Russians, I did not find it as harmful as I would have found it, for instance, today. The whole atmosphere of the war, and the whole war effort, and so on, and Switzerland being cut off, and I knowing that it was anti-fascist work, I didn't have the feeling that that is something immoral."[230] Even more importantly, she wanted to ensure the welfare of her aged parents in Lithuania as the Soviet army advanced: "I had perhaps the foolish idea that with rendering a service to Abramson and to Rachel I might have some kind of possibilities in helping my parents, who were in very great danger there in Lithuania."[231] After the war, she would learn that both her parents had died in a German concentration camp.[232] By May 1946, at the inquiry, she was full of regret, admitting: "In this whole business, I was used just like a tool, and was foolish enough to let myself into this business."[233]

Although the inquiry had no access to Abramson and William Helbein, the FBI later interrogated them. Helbein denied that Rabinowitch had given him ten thousand dollars to transfer to Switzerland.[234] Rather (he and his office manager Jack Wolff agreed), eight weeks before Rabinowitch's appearance a mysterious woman had dropped off ten thousand dollars in an envelope at the Helbros Watch Company, saying that the money belonged to Bertha Helbein, William's sister-in-law in Geneva. Bertha Helbein agreed. She had lent thousands of Swiss francs to Dübendorfer during World War II, but only for "some Soviet Relief Organization."[235] It didn't take much for the FBI to conclude that William Helbein was indeed a financial conduit between the GRU and Dübendorfer.[236]

Abramson, during a five-hour MI6 interrogation in 1947, denied that he had "ever done any work for any espionage organization of any power." He was friends with Dübendorfer and had sent "telegrams to Rabinowitch in Montreal in the belief that the money was for Soviet Prisoners of War." He didn't actually receive money from Canada and only grasped the true nature of Dübendorfer's work after her release from prison, at which time she divulged "the reasons for her arrest."[237] Clearly, Abramson was lying, as his MI6 interrogator saw.[238] The author of the MI6 report concluded that Rabinowitch had, at least temporarily, stopped working for Soviet intelligence after GRU officer Maria Poliakova's departure from Switzerland, but that Rabinowitch "retained her sympathies and loyalties to the Soviet [*sic*] and was a willing collaborator in Canada."[239] This may have been partially accurate, since she did give Koudriavtsev the report he wanted on ILO operations.[240] But she claimed that she didn't go to the planned September 1944 meeting with Koudriavtsev,[241] which may also have been true. Despite having placed herself at Koudriavtsev's disposal in August, she said that she was "fed up."[242]

On 30 August, the US announced that she was banned from ever entering the country, and a day later the ILO in Washington announced that Rabinowitch had already, more than a month earlier, complied with a request that she resign from her ILO position.[243] She left Canada six months later and found work at the Immigration Branch of France's Ministry of Labour, but in 1951 she was "expelled from that country through ministerial decree." She ended up in Israel.[244]

13
The Final Report

When the inquiry ended on 27 June the commissioners began to put together their findings, and on Friday, 12 July, Mackenzie King received the first bound copy – 733 pages – of the *Final Report*. He confided that he was "sorry for this." He feared that Russia would accuse Canada of trying to destroy Communism and that the Gouzenko affair would strain Canada's international relations.[1] Because the *Final Report* named several members of the Soviet legation, King decided to play the diplomat and let the Soviets slip the identified spies quietly out of Canada prior to any public request. He invited the Soviet charge d'affaires, Nikolai Belokhvostikov, to appear at his office at 5:30 p.m. on the 12th.[2] Several members of the Soviet legation had already left. Ambassador Zaroubin,[3] Nikolai Zabotin,[4] and Vassili Rogov all sailed for Russia in the wake of Gouzenko's revelations, while GRU Maj. Vsevolod Sokolov and his wife vanished from Ottawa without any official notification.[5] Gregory Popov replaced Zabotin in December, but by March he was gone too. In early February he had been arrested in Toronto's red-light district, jailed for being drunk and disorderly in a public place, and charged with having a concealed weapon. He had $600 in his possession and a receipt for $150 signed "Chester." A note on the receipt ("Basis: telegram from Center Jan 17, 1946"), with its code word for GRU headquarters ("Center"), hinted at Popov's status as a GRU operative.[6] External Affairs intervened, and Popov was released from jail.[7] Since his route back to Russia took him through the US, the FBI, at William Stephenson's suggestion, tried to lean on him to defect in Gouzenko's footsteps. Stephenson forecast "a reasonable chance of success since … he must be aware of what awaits him if he returns."[8]

When Belokhvostikov arrived for the meeting on Friday evening, King gave him seventeen names – all Soviet embassy employees who had directed spying in Canada. Six were still in Ottawa: Vitali

Pavlov, Ivan Krotov, A.M. Farafontov, J.G. Levin (or Levine), and (so King thought) Maj. Sokolov and his wife. King knew that Moscow couldn't very well pull all the spies out of Canada before the publication of the Kellock-Taschereau *Final Report* – coming on Monday – but he hoped that Moscow would expedite their removal.[9] Norman Robertson suggested giving Belokhvostikov a copy of the *Final Report*, but King quickly nixed that. Privately, he was "amazed" at Robertson: this near misstep showed "how tired [Robertson] is, or he could never have thought of letting a document of the kind get into the hands of the enemy before it was even presented to Parliament. One could be assured that between now and Monday next, the whole business would have been gone over by Russian lawyers and others, and probably given in part to the public before our own press and parliament and people had any knowledge of it."[10]

On Monday, Belokhvostikov sent a half-hearted volley back at King. Reiterating Moscow's 20 February statement after the first arrests, Belokhvostikov criticized "the provocative character of the campaign started against some members of the Soviet Embassy in Ottawa based on the false evidence of criminal Gouzenko who is under the investigation of the Canadian police." Nevertheless, Pavlov, Krotov, Farafontov, and Levin were packing to leave.[11] No mention of the Sokolovs.

Governments are recipients of royal commission reports, not their authors, but King and leading figures in External Affairs had as much influence on the *Final Report* as did the commissioners. Already in February, King had laid down strictures. By no means should the authors limit themselves "entirely to the guilt of our own people." On the contrary, the Russians were responsible, for they had drawn the Canadians "into a net" and had organized a "complete system of espionage throughout Canada."[12] No worries if the *Report* offended Moscow. On the other hand, Hume Wrong had lobbied for a soft report, "a surgical operation," and he defended his position by saying, "we must make an effort to re-establish working relations with the Soviet Government." Although the strongest anti-Communist in External Affairs – Arnold Smith – was chosen to write the Soviet pages of the report,[13] Wrong told him that the text shouldn't "draw general conclusions about Soviet activities in foreign countries but should confine itself to describing the detailed sample of the way they carried on in Canada and the way in which these activities were directed by Soviet agencies in Moscow."[14] Smith, for his own part, wanted to "debunk the nihilistic totalitarianism and separate it clearly from left-wing ideology and socialism." He had less interest in the Russian response than in the Canadian audience: "the Report was designed to influence and wake up public opinion about [Communist] conspiracy [but] not against the Russians."[15]

When the moment in the House of Commons arrived, King – so impatient since February to step away from an inquiry that was eroding his political capital – now lavished praise on the commissioners, the lawyers, and the inquiry staff: "Their task has been long and arduous. They have worked at it unremittingly and with a high sense of public duty."[16] What he found most "outstanding" was that the report confirmed that his government had been right all along and that it revealed "the seriousness of the situation which the government asked the commission to investigate."[17] The report, King said, showed Russian espionage in Canada dating from the creation of the Canadian Communist Party in 1924 and portrayed Moscow as the central antagonist in an assault on Western national security. He was pleased to confirm that the commissioners had absolved Soviet ambassador Zaroubin, who had no knowledge of the spying, but he emphasized the commissioners' findings that "membership in Communist organizations or a sympathy towards Communist ideologies was the primary force" that led Canadians astray. Soviet agents and their Canadian associates were also illegally procuring Canadian passports and citizenship documents, and the GRU here was "helping to supervise and finance ... agents operating in certain European countries."[18]

Prosecutions had started, and more would follow, King told the Commons. In February, he had initially kept the spies' names confidential, with the investigation *sub judice*. However, facing relentless pressure in Canada and elsewhere, King's *sub judice* position quickly dissolved, and the names of the implicated had been released in the interim reports, long before trials and even charges. King read the list of the shamed into the parliamentary record: Eric Adams, Scotland Benning, Raymond Boyer, Harold Gerson, Israel Halperin, Gordon Lunan, Allan Nunn May, Ned Mazerall, Matt Nightingale, Fred Poland, David Shugar, Durnford Smith, Kathleen Willsher, and Emma Woikin. Some names in the *Final Report* – Sam Carr and Fred Rose – didn't fall into the category of public officials or individuals in positions of trust (and were therefore outside the official terms of reference of the inquiry), but they "were members of Zabotin's organization and took an active part in recruiting agents." (Though Rose was a member of Parliament, his *position* in the state stood outside and above those occupied by "public officials and individuals in positions of trust" designated in PC 6444 and PC 411. The detention and interrogation of Rose could be achieved only if he was charged with "treason, felony, breach of peace or any indictable offence," i.e., under the Official Secrets Act.[19]) Rose had already been tried and convicted in June. Carr would eventually be convicted of conspiracy to commit an indictable offence, uttering forged documents, and counselling Soboloff to make false statements. As in the case of Halperin, King, relying on the commissioners, accused the innocent alongside the guilty: W.M. Pappin (uttering forged documents – acquitted) and John Soboloff (making a false statement for the purpose of procuring a passport – guilty).[20] King named others who, the commissioners charged, had either organized cells to help recruit spies or had acted as cut-outs between GRU agents: Agatha Chapman, Freda Linton,[21] Henry Harris, and S.S. Burman.[22] He didn't mention that the commissioners had found no basis for charges against Burman.

Punish the guilty, yes, but King believed that "publicity, education and full understanding are better preventatives."[23] He therefore saw the report as an antidote to Canadians being tempted by future Soviet spy recruitment schemes. The commissioners had arrived at a similar perspective, wanting, on the one hand, "as complete an account as possible of the illegal activities" and, on the other, a more popular document "for all to read."[24] Such, indeed, Wilfrid Eggleston of *Saturday Night* found it to be, calling it an "omnibus thriller."[25]

King wanted the *Final Report* spread far and wide. It would be the press doing the spreading, because the *Report* itself turned out to cost more than what most people would pay and there were few copies to be had. Edmund Cloutier, who held the hammer on the print run, initially offered 4,500 copies at $1.50 each (the equivalent of $27 in 2026). About 1,765 copies were sent to government departments, police, and the military, but since the RCMP received only 200, they had to be rationed.[26] In the Privy Council Office, press officer Mark McClung lobbied for a lower price – $1.00 – to ensure that more people, not just "foreign Embassies, Communists, lawyers," and others who had a legal interest, would buy it.[27] McClung failed but, perhaps in compromise, the press received 125 copies free of charge.[28]

Douglas How's Canadian Press stories were the first accounts of the *Final Report* in English Canada. He stressed the "fifth column" threat,[29] particularly via the Labor-Progressive Party and Canadian Communists, and gave a cumulative account in the December 1946 *MacLean's* of the *Final Report* as "a massive, unprecedented indictment" in which "the implications of international Communism were laid bare for all to see."[30] The *Montreal Gazette*,[31] Toronto's *Globe and Mail*,[32] and Regina's *Leader-Post*[33] all stressed the role of the LPP, with headlines such as "Communist Party Main Source of Recruits for Spy Network Here."[34] Quebec's French language papers likewise emphasized the threat to national security and the subversive role of the Communist Party:

La Press, Quebec's largest daily, announced, "Énorme travail clandestine de Moscou" (Moscow's big clandestine operation); *La Patrie* and *Le Soleil* followed suit.[35] The vehemently anti-Communist *L'Action catholique* stressed that "Le Comintern existe encore et continue son oeuvre nefaste" (the Comintern still exists and continues its nefarious work),[36] and the lead story in *L'Action catholique* said that the Canadian "fifth column" took orders from Moscow, "selon la politique du comintern dont la prétendue dissolution fut la plus grande des farces des communistes en ces dernières années" [(according to the policy of the Comintern whose alleged dissolution was the greatest Communist fabrication in recent years).[37]

Editorial opinion in both languages ran in the same direction, treating Canadian Communists, including Tim Buck, Sam Carr, and Fred Rose, as agents of Moscow.[38] Pulling back from his earlier attacks on the Liberal government's totalitarian tactics, A.A. McIntosh of the *Globe and Mail* theorized that the "rank and file" might not have known that the LPP was "so absolutely a servant of the Communist 'Centre' in Moscow," but now they had no excuse for not recognizing that every task the LPP undertook, no matter how small, served Moscow's "master plan," that Communism "is a religion, whose fanatics recognize but one god," and that their god resided in Moscow.[39] The *Winnipeg Tribune*'s Gerald Allison agreed with the indictment of the LPP, but he didn't want it banned. A ban "would merely make martyrs of Canadian Communists and drive them underground where their activities would not come under as close public scrutiny." A ban was also unnecessary since the LPP had been "discredited in the eyes of the public."[40] *Winnipeg Free Press* editorialist Grant Dexter, on the other hand, worried more about the government's threat to Canadian freedoms. Ottawa, not Moscow, had launched an "Attack on Freedom." He wasn't worried about Communists, but about the state's "hateful" methods – by, in other words, PC 6444.[41] Still, the headlines on the front page of the *Free Press* followed conventional lines – "Soviet 'Fifth Column' in Canada, Report Reveals" and "Say Spies Obtained Many Secrets."[42]

The LPP's counterblast came in the August edition of *National Affairs Monthly*.[43] Veteran Communist and Stalin loyalist Leslie Morris[44] pointed to the historical narrative of anti-Communism, a bourgeois vilification of Communism that stretched back to the Cologne Communist trial, where convictions relied on forgeries that supposedly linked the 1848 Revolution to Marx and the London-based International Workingmen's Association.[45] Morris also cited the forgeries (supported by conservative monarchists) that treated the 1871 Paris Commune as the masterwork of Marx in London,[46] the claims that Lenin was a

German "spy,"[47] and the lame-footed denouement of the 1928 British ARCOS Affair, when British police raided the offices of the All-Russian Co-operative Society and the Soviet Trade delegation in London, but failed to produce "usable evidence of Soviet espionage."[48] Morris could point at historical vilifications, but in the Gouzenko affair there were no forged documents or conspiracies, so he was reduced to the hyperbolic and vague claim that the "slimy charge of 'betrayal' and 'espionage'" only revealed "the fear of the bourgeoisie for the fate of their own system." The "bourgeois ideologists" (Kellock and Taschereau) had based their report on the "twisted and distorted views of exposed informers, ambitious police and miserable traitors like Gouzenko." While the world was searching for peace, the Canadian government was "poison[ing] the waters."[49]

In the US papers – which had also received free copies of the *Final Report* – Associated Press (AP) and United Press (UP) stories appeared under provocative headlines: "Red Spies in Canada Sought United States Post-war Defence Plans" (*Washington Post*), "Canada Says Red Spies Got Top Secrets" (*Philadelphia Inquirer*), "Top Soviet Agent in United States Now" (*Indianapolis Star*), and "Red Spy Rings Still Active Canada Hints" (*Chicago Tribune*). There followed details about the Soviet theft of radar research and of Western post-war defence plans, about the transporting of uranium-235 to Moscow, and about the presence of a supposed "super-spy" in the US. The *New York Times* discussed the role of the Communist Party as a base for spy recruitment,[50] while the *Los Angeles Examiner* reported that the US and Canada were consulting on how to protect their military and political secrets.[51]

Alarmed editorial commentary showed just how chilly this new Cold War was growing. "[The *Final Report*] is not a happy or reassuring report," a *Sacramento Bee* editorial observed. "It bristles with disclosures which the average American would prefer to believe are untrue." The *Bee* quoted Gouzenko on preparations in Moscow for a Third World War, a nightmarish prospect, especially from a "supposedly friendly" ally. A pessimistic assessment followed: "the Commissioners' report throws a drab light upon the world outlook and indicates the way to lasting peace will be a hard road, with or without another war."[52] More troubling than the specific information that GRU spying had acquired, according to the *New York Times*, was "the revelation of their operating methods ... [designed] to develop in Canada a fifth column." Either blissfully, or perhaps only rhetorically ignorant, the *Times* breathed relief that such things couldn't happen in America: "Attorney General Tom Clark informs us that the United States is 'entirely on top of the espionage situation.'"[53] Of course, atomic spy Klaus Fuchs, for one, wouldn't be exposed until 1950.[54] Less confident than Clark, the *Washington Times Herald* believed that the report from "our Canadian friends" should be a warning for the US that "the Russian network in Canada had and has branches in this country ... and this country has a lot more things to be ferreted out than has Canada." The *Times Herald* declared its support for an American spy system, presumably for the relatively untested CIA, and urged a seemingly extra-constitutional procedure that might have given E.K. Williams, Kellock, and Taschereau pause: "We think that the United States should call back some of Wild Bill's [Bill Donovan][55] boys and let them start rooting around under the no-holds-barred OSS [Office of Strategic Services] procedure to see what they can turn up."[56]

In Britain, those who sought the detailed accounts of the actual *Report* got only crumbs from Ottawa, while, again, the press's second-hand summations shaped the national discussion. MI5 Chief Percy Sillitoe requested forty-two copies of the *Final Report* for the Home Office, Bow Street Magistrates, New Zealand, Australia, and elsewhere. The RCMP sent him two.[57] Two weeks later, Sillitoe asked again: "This report … appears to us to be a document of such importance that we should like in due course to circulate copies to our representatives in this country and in other parts of the world."[58] He would be happy to pay for the copies. The RCMP sent him two more.[59] In London, borrowed copies were passed around. MI5's Roger Hollis lent his copy to Home Office undersecretary Sir Alexander Maxwell for the home secretary to study, but Hollis wanted it back as soon as possible.[60] At the end of August, MI5 finally got its forty copies. By early fall, London had sent copies to intelligence offices in Egypt, Rhodesia, Eritrea, Palestine, Lebanon, Cyprus, Trinidad, Kenya, Gibraltar, Malta, Singapore, Burma, Hong Kong, and Malaya. Nevertheless, in January 1947 Sillitoe was still fielding unfulfillable requests for copies, and he apologized to H.F. Cartmel-Robinson, acting governor of Northern Rhodesia, saying, "The Canadians greatly underestimated the demand."[61] British MPs wanted copies too. In October 1946, MP Sir Ernest Graham-Little asked the undersecretary of state for Dominion affairs to supply copies for MPs. At a minimum, could he "place a copy in the Library of the House of Commons?"[62] A month later, he was indeed "able to borrow the single copy placed in the House of Commons library." Apparently, however, copies were "readily obtainable in Australia," where the *Report* "caused profound anxiety."[63] The British shortfall was soon remedied: by April 1947 Canada had printed over 10,000 English copies and 1,750 French copies of the *Report*,[64] and, by April 1948 the British government Stationary Office had imported and sold more than 4,000 copies at 7s ($1.40).[65]

British newspapers, relying on what the Reuters correspondent in Ottawa absorbed from the Canadian press, pointed at the fifth-column threat: "the NKVD – Russian Security Police – have a powerful organization in Canada," and "there was intended to be a large-scale post-war expansion of the network."[66] Editorial comment was more limited in Britain than in Canada, because the interim reports had already received much attention and because by mid-July 1946 other, more dramatic Soviet actions – the push for control in Central and Eastern Europe – were taking centre stage.[67] Still, the *Birmingham Gazette* prioritized the *Final Report*'s old news about Alan Nunn May, born in Birmingham, and about his delivery of uranium-233 samples to the Russian Lt. Angelov.[68] The *London Times* condemned the GRU for its secret cells. To use a "conspiratorial technique developed in less fortunate countries to promote an underground struggle against tyranny" was "singularly inappropriate" in a democratic society.[69]

Pravda denounced the *Final Report* on 3 August 1946. In "A Sorry Finale to a Shameful Comedy – Canadian Spy Investigation Engineered to Harm USSR," Moscow showed little interest in calming its recent allies or in mending relationships. David Zaslavsky's five-page article spoke in the internecine Soviet political discourse of falsehood and character assassination. Pretending that the *Report*'s charges were based only on Gouzenko's word rather than on the stolen Soviet documents, Zaslavsky called the *Report* "an exposition of idle talk, scandalous fabrication and shameless lies of a certain Igor Gouzenko, a traitor to the Soviet Motherland, a perfidious deserter."[70] The Canadian government's campaign was meant to damage the Soviet Union politically.[71] "With studied procrastination," the commission had revived "all the worn out, long-compromised machinery of anti-Soviet lies" that not only harmed the Soviet embassy and the LPP, but also created "an atmosphere of savage anti-democratic terror ... in Canada."[72] It was the Reichstag fire all over again. As Hitler had done, Canada was using this new hoax as a pretext to round up Communists.[73]

Not quite sure whether he was recounting a grave injustice or an inconsequential bit of satire, Zaslavsky swung between the two. From "savage anti-democratic terror" and the warning that "a dastardly provocateur" [Gouzenko? RCMP Communist specialist John Leopold?] was leading Canada "by the nose," reducing the country to "a weapon in an international intrigue,"[74] Zaslavsky suddenly pivoted to mockery, insinuating that the whole affair was utterly trivial. Kellock and Taschereau had sorted the testimony out "as assiduously as the cock sorted out the dung-heap" – they failed "to discover a single grain of truth."[75] Like the warlord "Toptygin" in Nikolai Schedrin's "The Bear in the Voivodeship" (1884), the Canadian government "promised great bloodshed and ended by eating a sparrow."[76]

Lastly, innuendo: there was "indeed a secret organization in Canada, but ... not where the Commission looked for it." Zaslavsky wouldn't name it but offered clues: "This organization, which has great power, takes into its service an employee of a foreign Mission, dissipates him, bribes him, and trains him to act against his country. With his aid it steals secret documents from the Soviet Embassy."[77] Evidently, Zaslavsky meant the RCMP.[78] His polemic was broadcast to the world via Radio Moscow and issued in English as a bulletin by *Soviet Monitor* in London,[79] with a toned-down version appearing in the Labor-Progressive Party's *Canadian Tribune*.[80]

After the *Final Report* came out, British high commissioner Alexander Clutterbuck sent London a twelve-page summary as part of a twenty-eight-page report, saying that the Gouzenko affair was "no isolated phenomenon."[81] As unaware of Kim Philby and the Cambridge Five as the Americans were of Klaus Fuchs and others, Clutterbuck could only say that Russian subversion extended to many countries, including, "apparently," the UK and the US. Analysing the inquiry's domestic impact, he said that during the war Canadian authorities had been "at pains to emphasize, indeed to over-emphasize, the role of 'heroic' Russia," but the new revelations had caused a "sharp reaction against Communism," reviving "a deep-rooted prejudice of Communism and all its works."[82] Nevertheless, because other, more important events – presumably those in Eastern Europe and the Middle East – were damaging relations "between Russia and the Anglo-Saxon powers," the Canadian events had turned into "minor pieces" in a larger game.[83] Clutterbuck didn't fail to note the widespread criticism of the inquiry's methods: "many of these practices were distasteful to liberal Canadian opinion;" Minister of Justice St. Laurent hadn't been happy about defending them.[84] And Clutterbuck reproached the *Report*'s authors for sometimes wading into rhetoric: "the attempt to give dramatic effect has led at times to unjustifiably extravagant language; the search for brilliance has not always led to an impartial conclusion." Too often, the report presented inferences as self-evident facts,[85] with the result that it did occasionally look like an anti-Soviet polemic.

Clutterbuck's measured tone hardly confirmed Zaslavsky's claim that the West had launched an ideological campaign against Moscow, but some British officials wanted to launch precisely such a campaign. Irritated by Moscow's anti-British rhetoric, Christopher Warner, an assistant under-secretary in the British Foreign Office, called in April 1946 for a "retaliatory publicity drive against Communism."[86]

As relations with the Soviet Union worsened,[87] the idea gained traction with Ernst Bevin and Clement Attlee,[88] and early in 1948 the secret Information Research Department (IRD) was born[89] – essentially a propaganda department that deliberately popularized terms such as "the Kremlin" so as to cast the Soviet Union as a malevolent other.[90]

With the *Final Report* in the public sphere, it seemed by August 1946 that the King government had achieved some success and closure in the Gouzenko crisis. But an important hurdle remained. The Civil Liberties Committee (CLC) of the Canadian Bar Association (CBA) had written a report critical of the Kellock-Taschereau Commission. Come late August, at the CBA's annual meeting – this year in E.K. Williams's hometown of Winnipeg – the CBA would vote on whether to approve that CLC report. Approval could hand Moscow a propaganda rod with which to beat the West. Mackenzie King had pointed at the president of the CBA, E.K. Williams, and Supreme Court justices Kellock and Taschereau as proof against any charges that the commission was imperilling Canadian liberties. The Bar Association's approval of the CLC report would explode King's defence of his government's actions and taint the legal reputations of everyone associated with the inquiry. The commissioners, by curtailing their interrogations of Poland and Halperin, had avoided the risk and ignominy of a judge ordering the suspects to be released via *habeas corpus*. But there was no way to shut down the CLC vote.

The commissioners anticipated CLC arguments and tried to pre-empt them via the *Final Report*'s section 11, "Law and Procedure," perhaps the only section authored by the commissioners themselves.[91] In it, they contended that their critics had failed to grasp the special provisions of the Official Secrets Act (OSA), intended to defend the "safety and interests of the State." These provisions, the commissioners believed, meant that Parliament considered the disclosure of secret or confidential information to a foreign power to be more serious than ordinary criminal offences.[92]

That may have been true, but the OSA, consolidating the British Official Secrets Act of 1911 and that of 1920, had been approved in the late spring of 1939 in a patriotic rush.[93] In Britain, the threat of war in 1911 and the push after World War I to integrate orders approved under the Defence of the Realm Act into the existing British Official Secrets Act had resulted in expedited legislation and little scrutiny.[94] In Canada, too, both Parliament and the Senate approved the OSA with virtually no debate. As Europe descended into World War II, the CCF's A.A. Heaps, representing labour-dominated Winnipeg North, declared that "in times such as the present, every nation has the right to protect itself," and he thought that "Hon. Members cannot be anything but wholeheartedly in favor of such a measure."[95] No one objected. Imagining the most likely offenders to be recent unnaturalized or naturalized immigrants, a few MPs wanted a clause on deportation for offenders (Heaps hoping to send fascists back to Germany, others hoping to send Communists back to the Soviet Union).[96] In the Senate, Conservative Arthur Meighen was also "whole-heartedly infavour." He mocked the Liberals for proposing legislation that outdid Meighen's harsh section 98 of the Criminal Code (that had banned unlawful associations in the aftermath of the Winnipeg General Strike), and he congratulated "the Government on their conversion."[97] Senate approved the bill without amendment.[98]

The commissioners didn't mention that the OSA's special provisions had never been tested in Canadian courts, but they themselves, having made use of the OSA, understood its questionable features quite well and, with studied innocence, suggested that perhaps it might be advisable to amend the OSA "to provide additional safeguards."[99] Later commentators on the legislation were not as circumspect. The 1969 Royal Commission of Security described the OSA as "an unwieldy statute, couched in very broad and ambiguous language" and called for it to be revised.[100] Similarly, the 1979 MacDonald Commission recommended that it be replaced, and that espionage be grouped in the Criminal Code "with all other national security offences."[101]

Despite their doubts about the OSA, the commissioners didn't hesitate to use its most draconian features. Responding to the fierce criticisms of the 15 February detentions under PC 6444, the commissioners argued that the search-and-detention features of PC 6444 simply replicated the prudent, if unusual, powers of the OSA.[102] Police could, under the OSA, make a warrantless arrest and detain anyone without a charge, merely on suspicion "of having committed" or "being about to commit" an offence.[103] Although sections 652 and 664 of the Criminal Code required that detainees be brought before a judge within a "reasonable time," the OSA set no time limits on detentions.[104] Releasing a security threat would defeat the law's very purpose.

Generally, of course, section 668 of the Criminal Code ensured that a magistrate would examine any charge against a person. The commissioners, however, argued that since the OSA and PC 6444 allowed a person to be arrested *without* charge, merely on suspicion of being about to commit an offence,[105] there existed no charge for a magistrate to examine.[106] Thus, under PC 6444, as under the OSA, magistrates simply had no role in deciding on the validity of the detention. As Martin Friedland argues, offences against the OSA were indictable offences and subject to section 27(2) of the Interpretation Act, which meant they were subject to the Criminal Code (s. 652 and s. 668): any detainee must be brought before a judge "within a reasonable time and in any event within 24 hours." In the absence of evidence to bring a charge under the OSA, the accused must be released. This interpretation, Friedland notes, had also been placed on the comparable British section of the OSA.[107] PC 6444, however, was no parliamentary statute and therefore not subject to the Interpretation Act or the Criminal Code. Nevertheless, the constitutionality of the order could have been drawn into question through a *habeas corpus* hearing. This vulnerability was never mentioned or defended by the commissioners, though they must have been aware of it, given that their fear of such hearings for Poland and Halperin had rushed the conclusion of those interrogations.

Naturally, the commissioners focused, rightly so, on "the secret records of the Russian Embassy" that implicated the detainees, records that "indicated strongly" that the GRU network was "still functioning."[108] In order to stop secret information from being given to a foreign power, PC 6444 allowed the prime minister or minister of justice to order suspects to be detained and interrogated, with the detention conditions entirely at the prime minister's or minister of justice's discretion. These powers were "purely preventive ... and not punitive";[109] in other words, PC 6444 was intended to prevent further breaches of Canadian security, to gain insight into "the organization of the Fifth Column and the various spy rings," to find out who was "being drawn into the net" to spy for the Soviets, and to "[exonerate] those who had been placed under suspicion but who in fact were innocent."[110]

The commissioners also argued that the inquiry's interrogations and accusations made against the detainees reflected section 3(2) of the OSA. Even without proving that an accused "was guilty of any particular act," a conviction could be based on evidence of a "purpose" prejudicial to the state drawn from "the circumstances of the case," or the accused's "conduct," or their "known character."[111] Purpose, conduct, known character: they all justified an accusation and trial even without any illegal act – the *actus reus* (guilty act) so basic to criminal law. War or no war, the OSA's section 3(3) went even further. Under 3(3), a charge could be laid purely on evidence that an individual had communicated with, or tried to communicate with, an agent of a foreign power.[112] Under 3(4)(a), the *accused*, not the Crown, was responsible for proving their innocence, despite the fundamental common law principle of the presumption of innocence.[113] And section 9 prohibited even acts "preparatory" to the illegal act.[114]

Although the inquiry was shaped by the Justice Department's need to solve the hearsay evidence problem by producing confessions, the commissioners rejected criticisms that the inquiry was *aimed* towards criminal prosecutions. No actual or prospective legal proceeding, they claimed, gave the detainees immunity from testifying.[115] The commissioners treated the detainees as criminal suspects, yet rejected any obligation to explain section 5 of the Canada Evidence Act to "witnesses" detained under PC 6444. Ordinarily, a criminal *suspect* must be explicitly informed of the right to remain silent, the commissioners conceded, but this didn't apply to a *witness*, "to a person who is under the compulsion of a statute [the Inquiries Act] to reveal to a Commission ... facts of which he is aware." It was, they argued, a "misconception" to believe that "all persons whose conduct is being investigated before a Commission ... should be cautioned before being required to give evidence."[116] They cited Sir Robert Collier in a Judicial Committee of the Privy Council judgment that the obligation to caution applies "to accused persons only, and has no application whatever to Witnesses."[117] For example, in 1946 a person charged with manslaughter has no right of legal counsel when ordered to appear at a coroner's inquest into matters related to the manslaughter charge. The commissioners claimed that they, like coroners, had the *discretion* to allow anyone whose "conduct is being investigated" to have access to a lawyer, but that such access became a *requirement* only if a charge were made during the investigation.[118] Until then, the detainees remained merely *witnesses*.

In this argument, the commissioners carefully side-stepped the way in which the suspects had been taken into custody and PC 6444's conditions of detention. A witness before a corner's inquiry – or before a royal commission – was summoned through subpoena (or, in extreme cases, a bench warrant)[119] and could get legal advice if they wanted it. However, when the commissioners decided to follow E.K. Williams's advice and bring in the Gouzenko suspects for interrogation, they did so via PC 6444. No subpoena was served on any of those detained on 15 February 1946.[120] Moreover, unlike witnesses subpoenaed by a coroner, all the suspects were held incommunicado with no access to lawyers during the RCMP interrogations. Claims that similar conditions of detention had been contemplated in the provisions of the OSA simply do not hold water. Ultimately, contrary to the commissioners' defence, these features of PC 6444 didn't replicate the prudential features of the OSA.

In 1945, Canada's existing security and intelligence infrastructure was unimpressive and was geared towards discrete acts of espionage. Meanwhile, the carefully constructed Soviet spy network on the scale disclosed by Gouzenko amounted to a threat for which Canada was mostly unprepared, forcing King and his advisors to cobble together an emergency framework. Decades later, in the wake of 9/11, Canada was still trying to construct a viable intelligence and security framework. At a conference urgently convened in the fall of 2001 to debate new security and intelligence policies under consideration by the Canadian government, Wesley Wark, Canada's leading intelligence and security historian, ruminated on the difficulties of countering security threats from actors who operated in a clandestine manner, used compartmentalization, cut-outs, "deep cover," and "sleeper" agents.[121] "We are at war," said Wark, "or at least in a war. Our problem is that we don't yet understand the nature of this war on terrorism, or its future."[122] Wark might have been describing, *mutatis mutandis*, the 1945 challenges that the Canadian state faced when Gouzenko's disclosures revealed a danger that Ottawa couldn't address with the tools at hand.

Was it because they were judges of the Supreme Court of Canada that the commissioners were unwilling, in the "Law and Procedure" section of the *Final Report*, to acknowledge that they abetted the state's imperfect adaptation of emergency legislative tools? They refused to acknowledge the illiberal aspects of state investigative methods required to come to grips with what, after all, the commissioners correctly called "a malignant growth, the full penetration of which we did not know, but which was alive and expanding, working in secret below ground, directed against the safety and interests of Canada," a growth "made up of Canadian citizens" who were devoted to a foreign power, "believing it to be the supreme exponent of ideas to which they had given themselves as much as if they were its citizens."[123]

The commissioners concluded their "Law and Procedure" section by insisting that whenever a charge was made against any witness before the inquiry, they had adhered to section 13 of the Inquiries Act and had ensured that those individuals were "allowed full opportunity to be heard in person or by counsel."[124] Not quite. Even when the commissioners intended to charge a witness, they refused to state the charge, and yet they still wanted to hear responses from the witnesses and their legal counsel. A.W. Beament rightly protested that the commissioners ignored the intent of section 13 of the Inquiries Act by refusing to specify charges.

The Civil Liberties Committee of the Canadian Bar Association, in any case, conceded the technical "legality" of the Gouzenko proceedings, but it was deeply concerned with the state's use of emergency powers "in time of peace," and feared that these powers might create precedents for future inquiries. As early as August 1944, long before

Gouzenko's defection, the CBA had warned the Liberal government that it should not try to extend the War Measures Act beyond the end of the war. Of particular concern was the word "apprehended": the state could invoke emergency powers during a "war, invasion, or insurrection, real or apprehended." In terms of the act, the state merely had to *say* that a war, invasion, or insurrection existed for a war, invasion, or insurrection to *exist*.[125] For the CBA, the state could thus abuse its authority and extend its powers beyond any real threat of war.[126] At its August 1945 annual meeting, the CBA repeated the warning,[127] and then, a few months later, almost as if prophesied, PC 6444 materialized – exactly the kind of misuse of state power that the country's lawyers had feared. The CLC report condemned this misuse.

Consideration of the CLC report at the Royal Alexandra Hotel in Winnipeg was scheduled for 30 August 1946, the final day of the meeting. It would be voted on by the CBA membership. Out-of-town registration had surpassed that of any previous annual meeting, probably because of the civil liberties question that "haunted the proceedings" from the beginning.[128] Before the meeting, the *Winnipeg Free Press* threw its weight behind the CLC, challenging the CBA to "condemn the Government for the procedure it followed" in the Gouzenko inquiry procedure. The *Free Press* understood, and explicitly stated, that the CBA would thereby "also be condemning some of the most distinguished members of the bench and bar in Canada."[129]

As E.K. Williams presided over the President's Dinner on Thursday evening, he knew that he led the list of distinguished CBA members facing possible censure the next day. Others at the dinner who had reason to fear the CLC report included commission counsel Gerald Fauteux, Hon. F.P. Brais (past president of the association who had successfully prosecuted Fred Rose in June), Chief Justice J.C. McRuer (dominion vice-president of the association whose ruling in May 1946 had allowed Ned Mazerall's inquiry testimony to be used against him in his trial[130]), the Hon. Mr. Justice J.E. Read (formerly legal advisor to the Department of Foreign Affairs, now Canada's member of the International Court of Justice, who had co-authored the rationale for the creation and use of PC 6444), and W.P. Fillmore (president of the Manitoba Law Society and member of the CLC who, in his remarks to the gathering, had celebrated Williams and Blais as "spy-swatters").[131]

The CLC report, read verbatim to the assembly,[132] set out the alleged abuses perpetrated by the Liberal government and the Kellock-Taschereau Commission. Detained suspects should have had the right to remain silent, but the commissioners had used the Inquiries Act to compel testimony. The suspects should have been charged with a crime and been given *habeas corpus* – otherwise, they could claim false imprisonment or malicious prosecution – but, through PC 6444, the state had taken away these rights.[133] The suspects should have been warned that their answers could be used against them in a criminal trial, but they hadn't been allowed to communicate with lawyers before being questioned and hadn't been warned about self-incrimination during the inquiry. Although the suspects weren't charged after their 15 February "detention," they were nevertheless interrogated by two Supreme Court judges and subsequently sent to criminal trials, with, in at least one case, the suspect's inquiry testimony admitted as evidence. That individual "was convicted and sentenced to imprisonment."[134] Finally, the commissioners had assigned guilt or innocence, even though the suspects had had no lawyers and hadn't been tried.[135] The CLC rejected the government's appeal to "the safety of the State."[136] Wartime might justify procedural departures, but if a government removes the normal constitutional safeguards in peacetime, "we are, indeed in grave danger of having substituted for the rule of law ... the alien principles of the Totalitarian State."[137]

The CLC report included several recommendations. Paramount was the recommendation that section 5 of the Canada Evidence Act be amended to ensure that all witnesses be informed of the right to remain silent, and that their testimony in a criminal trial be admitted only when they consciously waive that right.[138] As well, it was "detrimental to the proper administration of justice" for governments to appoint inquiries "into the conduct of persons suspected of having committed criminal offences." That practice must stop. Finally, commissions should also stop publishing reports that charged individuals with criminal offences, or that placed suspicion upon them. How could such individuals get fair trials?[139] Much of the CLC report had been composed by R.M. Wiles Chitty, who, throughout the war, had used his *Fortnightly Review* to reject Ottawa's justification of emergency procedures and to assail the government as totalitarian, primarily because of what Chitty took to be its interference with property rights.[140] He argued that "even if the State be in direct peril we are still a democracy, and we must adhere to democratic principles."[141] Winnipeg lawyer John MacLean KC agreed: *Salus populi suprema lex esto* (the safety of the people must be the supreme law) was no legal principle. Rather, it amounted to the "negation of all law," he argued, "a reversion to the primordial instinct of self-preservation." And he, too, wasn't convinced that the Gouzenko affair amounted to a "state of emergency."[142]

The opposition to the CLC report was more nuanced. F.P. Fillmore didn't reject the statutory recommendations proposed by the committee, yet the same time he couldn't agree that Canada was "in a state of normal peace." In fact, the Soviet Union's increasing provocations were creating "as great an emergency as created at any time during the war."[143] Likewise, W.B. Scott KC, brother of civil liberties advocate Frank Scott, was tempted to nail his colours to civil liberties, but the Soviet espionage system, so "skillfully and secretly organized, and so far-reaching in its ramifications ... could not be reached or investigated by ordinary judicial process."[144] The state of emergency justified setting up the commission. In terms of the vote, he feared that "not two per cent of the people in this room ... have read the Report or know the score."[145] Adopting the CLC report "would amount to a vote of censure on the Commissioners," and "the only people who would benefit and chuckle over that" would be the Soviets.[146] Likewise, Senator J.T. Haig, a Conservative, agreed with the CLC recommendations but not with the commentary.[147] He proposed an amendment that the CBA approve only the recommendations in the CLC report. The amendment carried.[148]

Mackenzie King, St. Laurent, Kellock, Taschereau, Read, Varcoe, McRuer, Williams, Fauteux, and Munsell were safe. The *Globe and Mail* and *Saturday Night*'s B.K. Sandwell slammed the CBA for failing to take a strong stand against the commission's "departures from judicial methods" and "betrayal of rights." Still, Sandwell thought that the CBA's support of the recommendations had brought to bear "an immense moral force … in support of the ancient principles concerning the administration of justice."[149]

Epilogue

By July 1946, confessions in hand, the state had put Emma Woikin, Kathleen Willsher, and Ned Mazerall behind bars. Fred Rose was also in jail on the testimony of Raymond Boyer and Gouzenko. More trials were scheduled for the fall, but unlike the cases already processed, the prosecutions weren't supported by confessions or other direct evidence and the Crown balanced unsteadily on the more questionable guilt-by-association provisions of the Official Secrets Act. Given the hearsay evidence, perhaps it was not surprising that the trials did not go well for the Crown. On 18 October W.M. Pappin was appropriately acquitted on charges related to securing a false passport,[1] and in the following weeks Eric Adams,[2] Matt Nightingale,[3] and Agatha Chapman also walked free despite their activities on behalf of the Soviets. In Chapman's case, Judge A.G. MacDougall stopped the trial without even inviting the defence to present a case, saying that no jury would convict Chapman on the Crown's evidence.[4]

Still, British high commissioner Alexander Clutterbuck was surprised. He reported to London: "The three acquittals have come as a surprise and somewhat of a jolt to many who had accepted, without question, the conclusions of the Royal Commission."[5] The "jolt" in the Nightingale case occurred when "the judge ... warned against accepting the evidence of an accomplice (Gouzenko)."[6] For Clutterbuck this was all the more "striking," since Adams and Nightingale were "two persons who were flatly reported by the Royal Commission to be important agents of the Soviet espionage organization." Clearly, these acquittals implied a criticism of the royal commission.[7] While the reputation of the government and the royal commission suffered, Clutterbuck thought that, at the same time, the acquittals" also pleased many Canadians worrying about the future of civil liberties, and showed "that justice in the Canadian courts continues to be meted out without fear or favour."[8]

Sensing which way the wind was blowing, David Shugar's defence counsel A.W. Beament asked the new minister of justice, J.L. Ilsley, that copies of the *Final Report* add a note stating that "certain people branded as guilty have been exonerated in the courts."[9] Ilsley took up the suggestion but gave Beament rather more than he asked for. At the end of January 1947, an addendum listed those charged with crimes and their standing: acquitted, convicted, or awaiting trial. But the scorecard was qualified immediately by a declaration: "It should not be assumed that in any case the evidence before the Royal Commission and that adduced in the criminal proceedings was the same." Seeing this addendum, John Diefenbaker leapt up in the House of Commons and demanded to know who was engaging in "a gratuitous attack on the courts ... Who authorized the addition of these words which cast doubts on the judgment of our courts?"[10] Ilsley refused to respond, saying that Diefenbaker's allegations did not constitute a proper question.

High Commissioner Clutterbuck judged that Diefenbaker wasn't alone in his objection and that the government's action of indirectly commenting on the outcome of trials hadn't been well received: "Many Canadians feel that this ambiguous statement casts an unjust shadow of suspicion on persons who have been acquitted ... and it has served to increase the public uneasiness as to the methods adopted by the Royal Commission."[11] In a debate a few months later on Canada's human rights obligations under the new United Nations Charter, Ilsley and Diefenbaker revisited the controversy, Diefenbaker telling the Commons that the addendum disclosed "a spirit of resentment because the courts of the country saw fit not to allow the declaration of a royal commission." He wanted to ensure that Canadians weren't "deprived of reputations by an executive that is exasperated by the results in the courts."[12] Ilsley responded that if fairness required the first part of the addendum – to highlight the acquittals – the second part was also required because the government didn't want to appear to be "criticizing or repudiating the work of the commission." And it was true that the acquittals came, at least in part, because the evidence from the stolen Soviet documents and from Gouzenko wasn't allowed in criminal court.[13]

Likely it was Commissioner Kellock – as some have argued – who insisted on the addendum's final sentence.[14] It would have been extraordinary for the Department of Justice to add or delete anything from a royal commission report without consulting the putative authors. Secondly, in the "Law and Procedure" section, the commissioners had asserted that their inquiry carried "a formal equality with the other institutions of the State such as the Courts, Houses of Parliament and Privy Council,"[15] and that this "formal equality" extended to their findings: no matter what a court might do with charges arising from the inquiry, the "findings of the Commission, arrived at under its own procedure, and on the evidence before it, are not affected and remain valid."[16] The commissioners' wished-for parity between the inquiry and the courts was one feature of a novel account of the institutional status of Canadian inquiries. The commissioners also asserted that this "formal equality" meant that the inquiry, while "sitting, and until its existence terminates, is not subordinate to any body."[17] Writing in 1934, D.M. Gordon, a "pioneer of Canadian administrative law scholarship,"[18] had laid the groundwork for part of Kellock's account. Gordon had argued that commissioners have an absolute procedural discretion within the terms of their mandate.[19] The Ontario Appeal Court cited Gordon in *Re Ashby* (1934), affirming that "an administrative tribunal ... possesses a complete, absolute and unfettered discretion and, having no fixed standards to follow, it is guided by its own ideas of policy and expediency."[20] Kellock took this procedural discretion a step further: an inquiry, he said, "is independent in every sense ... not subject to or under the control of the Courts."[21] This was simply not true. Commissions of inquiry functioned under the authority of a statute – the Inquiries Act – so their activities were and had been subject to judicial review.[22] Though in historical terms Kellock's account provides an important benchmark of Canadian state formation, several grounds for judicial review of inquiry proceedings and findings were open both to the courts and to those who felt wronged by an inquiry.[23] In other words, Kellock's account was hyperbolic, well outside the terms of reference contained in PC 411.

The perceived excesses of the Kellock-Taschereau Commission gave impetus to a post-war civil liberties campaign that insisted upon the legal defences for those called to testify at inquiries. Combined, the repressive Defence of Canada Regulations, the treatment of Japanese Canadians during World War II, and the Kellock-Taschereau Commission's methods catapulted Canadians into a new post-war era of rights advocacy, culminating in 1982 with the Charter of Rights and Freedoms.[24] Under the 1982 Charter, executive inquiries retain the power to subpoena witnesses and require testimony but, under section 7, compelled testimony cannot be used in any subsequent trials against the witness.[25] Section 13 also gives explicit protection against self-incrimination. Subsequent Supreme Court judgments have affirmed and extended these protections. In *Phillips v. Nova Scotia (Commission of Inquiry into the Westray*

Mine Tragedy of 1995), the Supreme Court affirmed that "a witness who is compelled to testify before a Commission of Inquiry will receive the protection of section 13 of the Charter against the self-incriminatory use of his or her testimony and, as well, protection under section 7 of the Charter against the use of evidence which had been derived from that testimony."[26]

As might be expected, the Soviet penetration of vital branches of the Canadian wartime state necessitated a new intelligence regime. Even before Gouzenko, the military's Canadian Joint Intelligence Committee (CJIC), created in 1942, had been deliberating about post-war security arrangements and, completely unaware of the revelations that Gouzenko was in the process of making, the CJIC in September 1945 proposed a Joint Coordinating Bureau of Intelligence.[27] As the Gouzenko affair continued to simmer, Lt. General Charles Foulkes, chief of the Canadian general staff, reworked the CJIC proposal into a recommendation for a new civilian intelligence bureau.[28] However, by February 1946 the Gouzenko crisis actually disrupted this process,[29] as macro security concerns gave way to micro concerns. In their July *Final Report*, Kellock and Taschereau recommended that Canada establish coordinated safeguards to prevent the kinds of infiltration they had seen,[30] recommendations that Norman Robertson had anticipated when he created a "Security Panel" for government departments.[31] In any case, the actual work of investigation of "personal lives and political associations" fell again to the RCMP.[32]

The Gouzenko crisis haunted security and intelligence services in Canada for decades. RCMP Inspector Terry Guernsey, convinced that Gouzenko's leads might reveal deeper NKVD roots in Canada, initiated an unofficial probe.[33] After the defections of Donald Maclean and Guy Burgess in 1951, the spy investigations in the US, and the suicide of Herbert Norman,[34] Special Branch leadership in 1958 officially authorized the "Operation Feather Bed" probe. It generated files on over three hundred and fifty individuals during a decades-long failed search for more moles in Canada and elsewhere.[35]

Only in 2012 was a heavily redacted "Feather Bed file"[36] released by CSIS in response to a freedom-of-information request.[37] Who were the agents of subversion? Feather Bed justified its attentions on certain people by recalling the experience of the 1930s and 1940s – the Gouzenko era of ideological spies: "Experience has shown that the motivation of almost all high calibre agents has been ideological and that these persons use their influential positions to further the careers of others of similar ilk."[38] This logic pointed investigators back to the generation of mandarins who had come of age during the militant

Communism and fascism of the 1930s. A Feather Bed commentary, "From Communism to Soviet Spy: A Study in the Motivation of Some Soviet Agents,"[39] explained that the spies exposed by Gouzenko were overwhelmingly idealists and intellectuals, and that "idealistic intellectuals saw the USSR as the strongest bulwark against the new barbarism."[40] According to Gouzenko's roadmap, there could be other still-hidden spy networks predating him. Feather Bed cited evidence from "a recent [unnamed] defector and other delicate information pointing to current high level government penetration."[41]

Interpreting affiliation with Communism as a potential mark of disloyalty to Canada, Feather Bed investigators generated a long list of "Suspected Underground Members" of the Communist Party of Canada holding influential positions within the federal government in Ottawa, and warned that "[t]he majority of them are in very senior, indeed some of the most senior, Canadian Government positions."[42] This overreaction turned the celebrated Canadian mandarin Robert Bryce into a central target.[43] Bryce had studied economics at Cambridge in 1932–34, at the same time that the Soviets were recruiting fellow students Donald Maclean and Kim Philby there. In 1936, Bryce and Herbert Norman were leaders among Cambridge's Communist students,[44] and later, at Harvard, the two led a Marxist study group.[45] Working for a while at Sun Life, Bryce knew Agatha Chapman,[46] and in Ottawa he rose to become deputy minister of finance, clerk of the Privy Council, the prime minister's economic advisor on the constitution, and Canadian director of the International Monetary Fund.[47] Feather Bed heard allegations that Bryce "sponsored Agatha Chapman for government service during the war,"[48] so he and others were placed under surveillance. However, as Jim Bronskill observes, there is "no evidence the highly confidential investigation ever identified a Soviet agent."[49] It seems that, unlike the Cambridge Five and the spies outed by Gouzenko, the other Canadian officials who had tried out Communism during their university days had abandoned the more radical aspects of their thinking as they matured.

In Britain, the Gouzenko crisis "led to a rapid tightening of lackadaisical, almost non-existent security procedures."[50] A report, "The Spread of Communism Throughout the World and the Extent of Its Direction from Moscow," which included an extensive summary of the Kellock-Taschereau findings,[51] led Britain's Joint Intelligence Committee (JIC) to conclude in 1946 that if war broke out with the Soviet Union, Britain's Communist Party posed "an acute source of danger,"[52] and that counter-actions should be taken.[53] Prime Minister Clement Attlee established and chaired a secret committee – the Cabinet Committee on

Subversive Activities.[54] At its first meeting on 16 June 1947, the committee accepted a report, again relying on the Kellock-Taschereau *Final Report*'s "mass of concrete evidence" about Soviet recruitment.[55] Bottom line: "the Communist party which has foreign support, and is subservient to a foreign power, at present constitutes the principal danger."[56] Less than a year later, Attlee announced a new "purge procedure" to exclude Communists and fascists from some posts in the British civil service.[57]

In the US, coincident with the release of the Kellock-Taschereau *Final Report* in July 1946, the House Civil Service Committee called for a review of security in the American civil service. President Truman created the Commission on Employee Loyalty four months later. Some American historians have called the threat of Communist subversion directed by Moscow simply a chimera and berated the Truman administration for exaggerating the Communist threat, but the release of Comintern, KGB, and Venona records in the 1990s has undercut that criticism.[58]

Moscow certainly understood the damage that Gouzenko's defection posed to Soviet espionage in the West. A 1950 KGB assessment pointed out that following "the treachery of the traitor to the Homeland, Gouzenko, in Canada, American counter-intelligence agencies increased their work against us and were able to strike heavy blows against our agent network in the USA."[59] Then, in November 1945, "Myrna" (Elizabeth Bentley) struck the "most appreciable blow against our operations" and "betrayed over 40 of our most valuable agents to American authorities."[60] Stalin demanded a detailed report and a strategy to counter the Gouzenko damage. Probably in May 1946 after firing Vsevolod Merkulov as NKVD chief, Stalin ordered the Politburo to create the Malenkov inquiry into the security failures around Gouzenko, Bentley, and perhaps Konstantin Volkov.[61] Both the GRU and the NKVD came under scrutiny.

Restructuring his governing apparatus since late 1945, Stalin was reminding everyone that despite his age and increasing frailty, the *Vozhd* was still in charge.[62] Nominally, the purpose of the commission was to "explore mistakes committed under Merkulov's leadership" of the NKVD, but its real purpose was to send a cautionary message to Leventiy Beria ("Merkulov's patron and protector") that everyone in the Kremlin served at Stalin's pleasure.[63] On 17 June 1941, Merkulov had warned Stalin that well-placed Soviet agents in Berlin had revealed that within days Hitler would unleash a blitzkrieg directed at Russia. Stalin responded, "You can tell your 'source' from Ger. air force headquarters to go f — his mother. This is not a 'source' – it's someone spreading disinformation. J. St."[64] In August 1946, Stalin berated Merkulov for the opposite response – for having been less quick to listen to his sources during the Gouzenko affair. In announcing the findings of the inquiry, Stalin released a Politburo resolution that he himself had drafted: "Comrade Merkulov, occupying a responsible position, has not conducted himself with full honesty, has not informed the Central Committee of the serious situation at the security services, and he has concealed from the Central Committee, until the very last moment, the failure of its work abroad."[65]

As in the US, so in Canada, the Gouzenko affair left Soviet spying in limbo. Vladimir Burdin (sometimes Bourdine) arrived in Ottawa from Washington in 1948, nominally as the Soviet embassy's first secretary and then cultural attaché, but actually as Vitali Pavlov's replacement as NKVD *rezident*.[66] Almost immediately, Burdin complained to the Centre in Moscow about post-Gouzenko conditions: "The residency not merely lost all its previous contacts in Canadian circles but did not even try to acquire new ones … The Soviet colony closed in on itself and shut itself off from the outside world, becoming wholly preoccupied with its own internal affairs."[67] This was hardly news. Moscow responded that the Ottawa residency was "stuck in a rut,"[68] and that his job was to get it moving again. Eventually, with help from the Canadian Communist Party, Burdin developed a new network of Canadian agents and demonstrated, despite Feather Bed's failure, that the availability of the ideologically committed spy in Canada was not limited to those adherents of Moscow who came of age in the 1930s.[69]

Stalin ultimately decided against exacting revenge on Gouzenko, so he would live until 1982, when he died of a heart attack at age sixty three; but almost a decade after Stalin's death Soviet security decided that KGB defectors should pay the price. The 1961 defection of Maj. Anatoliy Golitsyn,[70] who exposed scores of Soviet spies, including Kim Philby, revived Moscow's determination to mete out punishment beyond the Soviet Union to "enemies of the people." In November 1962 KGB Chairman Vladimir Semichastny approved an aspirational plan for "special actions" against "particularly dangerous traitors,"[71] with the executions to be carried out by specially trained assassins from the "Thirteenth Department."[72] Former GRU Lt. Igor Gouzenko hadn't been KGB. No matter; his defection still rankled. His name was first on the list.[73]

Gouzenko's troubling voice – threatened, surviving – would have had little effect in 1945–6 without an institutional setting to amplify it. At that time, three important voices had begun to express, powerfully, the new realities of the post-war geopolitical order: George

Kennan, in his "Long Telegram," had called for the containment of Soviet expansionism;[74] Winston Churchill had identified the descent of an "Iron Curtain;" and Stalin proxy Andrei Zhdanov, in his "New Aspects of World Conflict" speech at the founding meeting of the Cominform in September 1947,[75] would name the West as the Kremlin's principal adversary.[76] But it was through the Kellock-Taschereau Commission's 1946 *Agents of a Foreign Power Final Report,* despite its flaws, despite its restrictions on civil liberties, that the details and full weight of the intelligence and security challenges facing the West emerged publicly in a nascent Cold War.

Note on Sources

The emergence of security and intelligence history and our contribution to that historiography is to be found in the release of vital British (MI5, MI6), American (Venona), and Soviet (NKVD / KGB) archival sources and their wide availability through digitization. On its own, the release of Soviet archival records constitutes a foundational chapter in security and intelligence history. The opening of British and American intelligence records, while historically unprecedented, followed a mostly prosaic institutional process. In a similar way, the passage to the public sphere of the records of the Kellock-Taschereau inquiry involved mostly the churning of institutional machinery; even so, their release marked an important transition in Canadian archival practice.

The availability of Gouzenko-related records held at the British National Archives at Kew (TNA) proved of vital importance to our account of the Canadian espionage crisis of 1945–46. Beginning in 2003, a large body of MI5 and Foreign Office records on the Gouzenko crisis were released to the British Public Records Office and are now held at TNA. The COVID crisis proved an unlikely boon to our research. Because researchers were denied access to TNA, beginning 24 April 2020 that institution opted to provide existing digitized records available for download free of charge. Through this generous policy we were able to use a wide range of files that extended our understanding of key players in this story and opened new avenues to understanding the Canadian, British, and American perspective on this Soviet-driven intelligence and security crisis.

The British files concerning the Gouzenko affair held within the British Security Service (MI5) personal files are organized as the KV 2 series, listed as TNA, KV 2/ 1419-28, Igor Gouzenko, Corby Case. The file identified as KV 2/1427 contains digital copies of the GRU documents delivered by Gouzenko to the RCMP and the translated versions prepared (some 297 pages) by RCMP translator Mervyn Black. During the inquiry, each translation was presented to Gouzenko for his assessment of their accuracy. KV 2/1428 contains a copy of the report titled "Soviet Espionage in Canada," completed in November 1945. While these records are available on Canadiana Héritage, the digital copies held at the British National Archives are superior reproductions. However, because it was possible to link notes directly to the versions available on Canadiana Héritage, we have done so. The contents of KV 2/1419-KV 2/1428 address the Gouzenko crisis from Gouzenko's defection and extend beyond fall 1946 when the final report of the Kellock-Taschereau inquiry was released. Our endnotes provide a guide to most vital records held in this archive.

Additional British National Archives sources examined for our study include: Ivan Alekseevich Bolshakov, KV 2/3105; Rachel Dübendorfer/Paul Boettcher, KV 2/1619-20; Sam Carr, KV 2/1632-33; Alexander Allan Foote, KV 2/1613; Emil Julius Klaus Fuchs, KV 2/1245; Sergei and Vera Koudriavtsev, KV 2/1650; Freda Linton, KV 2/1896; KV 2/Grace Marsh, 1571; Alan Nunn May, KV 2/2212-13; Hermina Rabinowitz (Rabinowitch), KV 2/1634; Alexander and Helene Rado, KV 2/1648; Frederick Rosenberg (Fred Rose), KV 2/1015; Ignacy Samuel and Buna Genah Witczak, KV 2/1635; KV 3/ 350, The Case of the Rote Kapelle (Red Orchestra); KV 2/ 4728 and KV 2/4737, Harold Adrian Russell Philby; KV 2/4674 through KV 2/4676, Constantin Volkov; and KV 4/ 466-67, Liddell (Guy Liddell) Diaries. A copy of the British Joint Intelligence Sub-committee September 1946 report titled "The Spread of Communism Throughout the World and the Extent of Its Direction from Moscow" is available in TNA, Records of the Cabinet Office (CAB) 79-52-6.

Records made available by Canadian archival institutions were also vital to this study. When the Kellock-Taschereau inquiry came to an end in June 1946, the records of the inquiry – transcripts of testimony, thousands of pages of exhibits including the documents Gouzenko took from the Soviet embassy, inquiry correspondence, and a miscellany of other documents including press reports related to the inquiry – were transferred to the Office of the Privy Council. There they remained until 1948, when they were transferred to the Public Archives of Canada. Policy related to the release of government records remained at that time in a very formative state, though because of their security-related importance there was no question of releasing these records. In 1966 an order-in-council, the Public Records Order (PC 1966-1749), transferred authority from the Dominion Archivist to the federal cabinet to determine the access status for records created after 1939. Under a thirty-year rule adopted by the Trudeau government in 1969, the Kellock-Taschereau records were due for release in 1978. However, in 1977 the government reviewed the records and ordered that they be withheld from the public for an additional ten years.

Security concerns in Britain that echoed across the Atlantic prompted this withholding and, in the House of Commons, created a theatre of the absurd as the Opposition accused Trudeau of somehow being in league with Soviet espionage. Following a second review of the documents completed in the early fall of 1981, on 8 October 1981 through order-in-council P.C. 1981-2766, the records were released without fanfare or even public disclosure. The 110 pages of documents taken from the Soviet embassy by Gouzenko and several thousand pages of additional inquiry exhibits remained sequestered until 7 January 1985, when they were released to the public. Until 2014, researchers interested in these documents were required to travel to Library Archives Canada in Ottawa. The time and expense associated with researching some 9,000 pages of testimony and related documentation posed serious challenges for interested researchers. These challenges were removed in 2014 through an arrangement involving Library Archives Canada and CKRN (Canadian Research Knowledge Network) to place the entire body of Kellock-Taschereau inquiry records on the Canadiana Héritage site.

A detailed finding aid for the inquiry testimony and exhibits is available for downloading at Library Archives Canada. At the Canadiana site Reels T-1368-1370 contain the testimony given before the inquiry, while reels 3423-3434 contain a range of documentary evidence – including exhibits – associated with the inquiry. These include copies of the documentary records (translated) turned over to Canadian authorities by Igor Gouzenko (reels 3423–24), additional exhibits placed before the inquiry (reels 3425–33), and correspondence including subpoenas issued by the inquiry, press clippings related to the origins and progress of the inquiry, and reports concerning international press coverage of the inquiry provided by the Department of External Affairs (reel 3434).

The work of Timothy Sayle and others associated with the Bill Graham Center for Contemporary International History (University of Toronto) and the creation of *Canada Declassified*, a digital repository for records released under the Canadian Access to Information Act, have also contributed to the archival foundation of our research into the Gouzenko security and intelligence crisis. References to two bodies of records held in *Canada Declassified* appear in this book. The first is a body of records released by CSIS as one PDF file with no indication of original order or provenance. However, it is self-evident that these records were generated by the RCMP investigation triggered by Gouzenko's defection and his disclosures concerning Soviet spying in Canada. They include vital correspondence from the commissioner of the RCMP to J. Edgar Hoover, Louis St. Laurent, and Commissioner Wood's subordinates, and documents related to the investigation and detention of those implicated by Gouzenko. This body of records also includes detailed reports produced for the Justice Department and the Kellock-Taschereau inquiry based on police interviews with Gouzenko and field investigations of those implicated by him in Soviet espionage.

The second body of records consulted at *Canada Declassified*, titled "The Feather Bed File," was the product of an investigation of federal civil servants initiated in the 1950s on the premise that at the highest levels Canada's federal civil service was riddled with Soviet agents not exposed by the Gouzenko investigation. Feather Bed was the Canadian counterpart to the post-Gouzenko search for moles in London and Washington that blighted careers and ruined reputations in the search for Soviet agents.

We have also relied on Soviet and American records made available through the Woodrow Wilson Center for International Scholars. The indefatigable work of John Earl Haynes in the production of his "Index and Concordance to Alexander Vassiliev's Notebooks and Soviet Cables Deciphered by the National Security Agency's Venona Project" facilitated our search for Soviet records related to the Gouzenko crisis. The Haynes Index and Concordance provides researchers with a key to nine notebooks composed by former KGB operative Alexander Vassiliev based on his research in KGB operational files. The Index and Concordance also provides a guide to twelve compilations of NKVD/KGB cables deciphered by the US National Security Agency's Venona project. The Vassiliev and Venona records provide a documentary record of Kim Philby's reports to Moscow about Gouzenko's defection, Soviet reaction to the Gouzenko-triggered intelligence debacle, and Moscow's operational response to the crisis.

Notes

Introduction

1 Released on 6 August 1945, the statements appeared in the *New York Times* a day later. "New Age Ushered; Day of Atomic Energy Hailed by President, Revealing Weapon," *New York Times*, 7 August 1945, 1.
2 Stimson's Statement, *New York Times*, 7 August 1945, 4.
3 On Milstein, see "A Model Soviet General," *New York Times*, 20 November 1992, 30; Mikhail Abramovich Milstein, *Сквозь годы войн и нищеты* (Through the years of wars and poverty) (Moscow: Itar-Tass, 2000), 92 (hereafter cited as "Through the years"). On Fyodor Kuznetsov, see Viktor Suvorov, *Inside Soviet Military Intelligence* (New York: Macmillan, 1984), 179.
4 Milstein, Through the years, 90–1.
5 Library and Archives Canada, RG33-62, *Royal Commission to Investigate the Facts Relating to and the Circumstances Surrounding the Communication, by Public Officials and Other Persons in Positions of Trust of Secret and Confidential Information to Agents of a Foreign Power* fonds, Reel T-3423, Exhibit 23HH, Incoming telegram in the handwriting of Lieut. Koulatov, to Grant, no. 11931, 22.8.45. https://heritage.canadiana.ca/view/oocihm.lac_reel_t3423/712. Hereafter cited as LAC RG33-62 Agents of a Foreign Power fonds.
6 The most detailed account of the events of Gouzenko's defection appears in testimony before the Kellock-Taschereau Commission. LAC, RG33-62, Agents of a Foreign Power fonds, Reel T-1368, Igor Gouzenko testimony, 372–86. https://heritage.canadiana.ca/view/oocihm.lac_reel_t1368/423.
7 Ben Macintyre, *A Spy Among Friends: Kim Philby and the Great Betrayal* (New York: Crown, 2014) 102. For the MI5 record on the Volkov affair and the subsequent investigation of Kim Philby's role in thwarting Volkov's defection see TNA, KV 2/4674,4675, and 4676, Constantin Volkov.

8 Christopher Andrew, *Defend the Realm: The Authorized History of MI5* (New York: Alfred Knopf, 2009), 342.

9 Later, the Kellock-Taschereau inquiry served as an inspiration and model for the Australian Royal Commission on Espionage in 1954. For this, see Robert Manne, *The Petrov Affair: Politics and Espionage* (Sydney: Pergamon, 1987), 70.

10 Allen Weinstein and Alexander Vassiliev, *The Haunted Wood: Soviet Espionage in America: The Stalin Era* (New York: Random House, 1999), 104.

11 See John Gaddis, *We Know Now: Rethinking Cold War History* (Oxford: Clarendon, 1997); Odd Arne Westad, *The Cold War: A World History* (New York: Basic Books, 2017), esp. 60–2; Norman M. Naimark, *Stalin and the Fate of Europe* (London: Harvard University Press, 2019).

12 See, for example, Dominique Clément, "Spies, Lies, and a Commission: A Case Study in the Mobilization of the Canadian Civil Liberties Movement," *Left History* 7, no. 2 (2000): 53–79; Frank K. Clarke, "Debilitating Divisions: The Civil Liberties Movement in Early Cold War Canada, 1946–48," in *Whose National Security?: Canadian State Surveillance and the Creation of Enemies*, ed. Gary Kinsman, Mercedes Steedman, and D.K. Buse (Toronto: Between the Lines, 2000), 171–87; Christopher MacLennan, *Toward the Charter: Canadians and the Demand for a National Bill of Rights* (Montreal & Kingston: McGill-Queen's University Press, 2003), 33–60; Ross Lambertson, *Repression and Resistance: Canadian Human Rights Activists* (Toronto: University of Toronto Press, 2005), 143–95; B.L. Strayer, "In the Beginning ...: The Origins of Section 15 of the Charter," *Journal of Law & Equality* 5, no. 1 (2006): 15.

13 On Canadian anti-Communism, see Reg Whitaker, "Official Repression of Communism During World War II," *Labour/Le Travail* 17 (1986): 135–66; Reg Whitaker, Gregory S. Kealey, and Andrew Parnaby, *Secret Service: Political Policing in Canada from the Fenians to Fortress America* (Toronto: University of Toronto Press, 2012), 179–85.

14 Some of the principal works that have inspired us in writing "*P.S. Burn After Reading*" include J.L. Granatstein and David Stafford, *Spy Wars: Espionage and Canada from Gouzenko to Glasnost* (Toronto: McClelland & Stewart, 1990); John Earl Haynes, Harvey Klehr, and Fridrikh Igorevich Firsov, *The Secret World of American Communism* (New Haven: Yale University Press, 1995); Weinstein and Vassiliev, *The Haunted Wood*; Philip Deery, "'The Secret Battalion': Communism in Britain During the Cold War," *Contemporary British History* 13, no. 4 (1999): 1–28; Christopher Andrew and Mitrokhin, *The Mitrokhin Archive: The KGB in Europe and the West* (London: Penguin, 2000); Herbert Romerstein and Eric Breindel, *The Venona Secrets: Exposing Soviet Espionage and American Traitors* (Washington, DC: Regnery, 2000); Philip Deery, "Decoding the Cold

War: Venona, Espionage and 'The Communist Threat,'" in *Arguing the Cold War*, ed. Peter Love and Paul Strangio (n.p.: Red Rag, 2001), 107–15; Christopher Andrew, *Defend the Realm: The Authorized History of MI5* (New York: Alfred Knopf, 2009); Harvey Klehr, John Earl Haynes, and Alexander Vassiliev, *Spies: The Rise and Fall of the KGB in America* (New Haven: Yale University Press, 2009); Keith Jeffery, *The Secret History of MI6: 1909–1949* (New York: Penguin, 2010); K.A. Cuordileone, "The Torment of Secrecy: Reckoning with American Communism and Anticommunism after Venona," *Diplomatic History* 35, no. 4 (2011): 615–42; Daniel W.B. Lomas, "Labour Ministers, Intelligence and Domestic Anti-Communism, 1945–1951," *Journal of Intelligence History* 12, no. 2 (2013): 113–33; Daniel W.B. Lomas, *Intelligence, Security and the Attlee Governments, 1945–51: An Uneasy Relationship* (Manchester: Manchester University Press, 2017); and Jonathan Haslem, *Near and Distant Neighbours: A New History of Soviet Intelligence* (Oxford: Oxford University Press, 2015).

15 James McCook, London, "Espionage Report Widely Circulated," *Regina Leader Post*, 29 April 1948, 6.

16 On King's career, see H. Blair Neatby, "William Lyon Mackenzie King," *Dictionary of Canadian Biography*, http://www.biographi.ca/en/bio/king_william_lyon_mackenzie_17E.html. For the diary, see Library Archives Canada, William Lyon Mackenzie King, Secret and Confidential Diary Relating to Russian Espionage Activities, 6 September–31 October 1945.

17 Amy Knight, *How the Cold War Began: The Igor Gouzenko Affair and the Hunt for Soviet Spies* (New York: Carroll & Graf, 2005), 11.

18 For a summary of inquiries prior to 1949, see K.B. Callard, "Commissions of Inquiry in Canada 1867–1949," unpublished report for the Privy Council Office, 1950. A copy of this document is held in the library at the University of Waterloo, Waterloo, Ontario.

19 John Locke, *Two Treatises of Government*, ed. Peter Laslett (Cambridge: Cambridge University Press, 1967), §158, 391. On coercive inquiries circa 1946, see Callard, "Commissions of Inquiry in Canada," 33.

Chapter 1: The Gouzenko Question

1 On Robertson, see J.L. Granatstein, *A Man of Influence: Norman A. Robertson and Canadian Statecraft 1929–68* (Ottawa: Deneau, 1981), 168–82.

2 On Gouzenko's military rank, see LAC, Agents of a Foreign Power fonds, Reel T-1368, Gouzenko testimony, 23, https://heritage.canadiana.ca/view/oocihm.lac_reel_t1368/85.

3 Vadim J. Birstein, "Soviet Military Counterintelligence from 1918–1939," *International Journal of Intelligence and Counterintelligence* 25, no. 1 (2012): 87.

4 The National Archives, KV 2/1428, "Soviet Espionage in Canada," 2.

5 TNA, KV 2/1428, "Soviet Espionage in Canada," 4. Mark Kristmanson has pondered the possibility that Gouzenko's defection was "the product of a Britsh intelligence operation." *Plateaus of Freedom: Nationality, Culture, and State Security in Canada 1940–1960* (Toronto: University of Toronto Press, 2003), 149–50. Gregory Johnson has pointed out that, coincident with Gouzenko's defection, NKVD officer Konstantin Volkov's planned defection in Ankara was undone by Kim Philby, head of Soviet Counterintelligence in MI6. For any similar defection, if Philby knew early enough, he would have informed Moscow, and Gouzenko would have suffered the same fate as Volkov. Gregory A. Johnson, "Plateaus of Freedom: Nationality, Culture, and State Security in Canada, 1940–1960 (Review)," *Canadian Historical Review* 85, no. 4 (2004): 873.

6 On the importance of the subject matter for this conference and its failure to build anything other than distrust, see Alan Bullock, *Ernest Bevin: Foreign Secretary 1945–1951* (New York: W.W. Norton, 1983), 129–37.

7 On Rivett-Carnac's recollections of the Gouzenko affair, see Charles Rivett-Carnac, *Pursuit in the Wilderness* (London: Jarrolds, 1967), 303–21. On the evolution of the security service in the RCMP, see Canada, *Commission of Inquiry Concerning Certain Activities of the Royal Canadian Mounted Police*, 2nd report, vol. 1, *Freedom and Security under the Law* (Ottawa: Privy Council Office, 1981), 54–71; and Lawrence Aronsen, "'Peace, Order and Good Government' During the Cold War: The Origins and Organization of Canada's Internal Security Program," *Intelligence and National Security* 1, no. 3 (1986): 357–380.

8 On Malcolm MacDonald and the Gouzenko Affair, see Malcolm MacDonald, *People and Places: Random Reminiscences of the Rt. Hon. Malcolm MacDonald* (London: Collins, 1969), 182–201; and Clyde Sanger, *Malcolm MacDonald: Bringing an End to Empire* (Montreal & Kingston: McGill-Queen's University Press, 1995), 246–7. The extended record of correspondence by MacDonald and Holmes constitutes a unique and vital record of the British and Canadian response to the Gouzenko affair. MacDonald and Holmes were in almost constant communications with Mackenzie King, Robertson, and Wrong on the Canadian side and with the permanent undersecretary of state for foreign affairs in Britain, first Sir Alexander Cadogan, then Sir Harold Orme Sargent. Unfortunately, this Foreign Office communication was routed through the MI6 British Security Coordination operation in New York to MI6 in London to the desk of Kim Philby, Soviet Counter-Intelligence, prior to delivery to the Foreign Office and MI5.

9 Malcolm MacDonald notes the inclusion of Holmes on the Corby Committee. MacDonald, *People and Places*, 184.

10 Granatstein, *A Man of Influence*, 175.

11 TNA, KV 2/1425, Sir Alexander Cadogan from Malcolm MacDonald, no. 259/260, 10.9.45, serial 2a.

12 On St. Laurent's career in politics, see Robert Bothwell, "Louis-Stephen St. Laurent," *Dictionary of Canadian Biography*, http://www.biographi.ca/en/bio/st_laurent_louis_stephen_20E.html.

13 On Cadogan, see Gore-Booth, revised by G.R. Berridge, "Sir Alexander George Montagu Cadogan," *Oxford Dictionary of National Biography*, https://doi.org/10.1093/ref:odnb/32234.

14 TNA, KV 2/1425, N.A. Robertson to Cadogan, no. 251, 9.9.45, s. 1a.

15 Christopher Andrew, *Defend the Realm: The Authorized History of MI5* (New York: Alfred Knopf, 2009), 341.

16 TNA, KV 2/1425, MacDonald to Cadogan, no. 251, 10.9.45, s. 12a.

17 Andrew, *Defend the Realm*, 348. In 1981, the McDonald inquiry concluded that the Gouzenko crisis alerted the West "to the urgent need to strengthen [its] ... defences against Soviet espionage and clandestine Communist involvement in political life." Canada, *Commission of Inquiry Concerning Certain Activities of the Royal Canadian Mounted Police*, 2nd report, vol. 1, *Freedom and Security under the Law* (Ottawa: Privy Council Office, 1981), 61.

18 TNA, KV 2/1425, MacDonald to Cadogan, no. 251, 10.9.45, s. 2a.

19 LAC, WLMK, Secret and Confidential Diary, 10 September 1945, 8. The Regulations for the Defence of Canada had been approved under the War Measures Act in 1939. Defence of Canada Regulations (Ottawa: King's Printer, 1939), https://archive.org/details/defenceofcanadar1939cana/page/32/mode/2up. Twelve of the regulations affecting civil liberties were revoked on 16 August 1945. See Lester H. Phillips, "Canada's Internal Security," *Canadian Journal of Economics and Political Science* 12, no. 1 (1946): 18.

20 For the order and related directives, see LAC, RG13-A-2, Espionage Appointment of Royal Commission to Investigate Prosecution of Persons Under Official Secrets Act (1946), vol. 2121, file 150262, PC 1945-5991, 10 September 1945.

21 LAC, WLMK, Secret and Confidential Diary, 10 September 1945, 8. These developments are described in J.W. Pickersgill and D.F. Forster, *The Mackenzie King Record*, vol. 3, *1945–1946* (Toronto: University of Toronto Press, 1970), 14.

22 The British Security Coordination was an umbrella organization for the work of British security organizations throughout North and South America during World War II. On the BSC, see William S. Stephenson, ed. *British Security Coordination: The Secret History of British Intelligence in the Americas 1940–1945* (New York: Fromm, 1988). On the use of the BSC communications establishment during the Gouzenko affair, see TNA, KV 2/1425, Malcolm MacDonald to Sir Alexander Cadogan, no. 252,

9.9.45, s. 3A. For an account of the technological innovation required for the creation of this secure communications network, see John Ferris, *Intelligence and Strategy: Selected Essays* (London: Routledge, 2005), 171–4. The operations centre for HYDRA was located at the BSC training camp near Oshawa, Ontario. For an account of HYDRA as a feature of Camp X, see David Stafford, *Camp X – 1941–45* (Toronto: Lester & Orpen Dennys, 1986), 171–5.

23 For an account from a British perspective of Philby's subversive role in the Gouzenko affair, see Christopher Andrew, *Defend the Realm*, 342–9, and Keith Jeffery, *The Secret History of MI6, 1909–1949* (New York: Penguin, 2010), 656–60.

24 "Guy Liddell," in Nigel West, *Historical Dictionary of British Intelligence*, 2nd ed. (New York: Rowman & Littlefield, 2014), 346.

25 TNA, KV4/466, Liddell Diaries, 11 September 1945, 198–9.

26 Kreshin, whose real name was Boris Krötenschild., was the 3rd secretary and consul general of the London embassy. He was also known as Boris Krotov. On Krötenschild, see Boris Volodarsky, *Stalin's Agent: The Life and Death of Alexander Orlov* (Oxford: Oxford University Press, 2015), 397, 488, 669.

27 Jeffery, *The Secret History of MI6*, 657.

28 See "Fitin, Pavel Mikhailovich: Chief of KGB Foreign Intelligence from 1939 until 1946," in John Earl Haynes, *Index and Concordance to Alexander Vassiliev's Notebooks and Soviet Cables Deciphered by the National Security Agency's Venona Project*, rev. 11/1/2014, 137, https://www.wilsoncenter.org/article/venona-project-and-vassiliev-notebooks-index-and-concordance.

29 Wilson Center Digital Archive, London KGB – Moscow Center Cables Decrypted by the National Security Administration's Venona Project, Transcribed by Students of the Mercyhurst College, Institute for Intelligence Studies, Arranged by John Earl Haynes, Library of Congress, "Comment on the Accuracy of Stanley's Information (1945), Moscow to London, 17 September 1945," in Wilson Center, 2011, 17, https://www.wilsoncenter.org/sites/default/files/media/documents/article/Venona-London-KGB.pdf.

30 Wilson Center Digital Archive, Alexander Vassiliev Papers, Manuscript Division, Library of Congress, Vassiliev Notebooks, White Notebook no. 2, 27, https://digitalarchive.wilsoncenter.org/document/vassiliev-white-notebook-2.

31 Wilson Center, Venona Project – London – KGB, Moscow to London, no.47, 18 September 1945, To BOB from VICTOR, "SAFEGUARDING OF THE AGENT NETWORK IN VIEW OF THE NEWS FROM CANADA," 20.

32 Wilson Center, Venona Project – London – KGB, Moscow to London, no. 34, 21 September 1945, To BOB from VICTOR, "Reorganization of

contact with 'Khiks' [likely 'HICKS,' code name of Guy Burgess], 'ADAM' [unidentified], 'DZhONSON' [unidentified], AND 'STENLI' ['STANLEY,' code name for Kim Philby]," 8–9.

33 Wilson Center, Venona Project – London – KGB, Moscow to London, no. 64(a), 21 September 1945, To BOB from VICTOR, "'BOB' ORDERED TO EXERCISE SPECIAL CARE IN MEETINGS," 23. The National Security Agency noted that "[t]his message carries, externally, the top priority used on this lane."

34 Wilson Center, Venona Project – London – KGB, Moscow to London, no. 34, 21 September 1945, To BOB from VICTOR, "Reorganization of contact with 'Khiks' [likely 'HICKS,' code name of Guy Burgess], 'ADAM' [unidentified], 'DZhONSON' [unidentified], AND 'STENLI' ['STANLEY,' code name for Kim Philby]," 8–9.

35 On Gromov, see Wilson Center, Haynes, *Index and Concordance*, 154, 158, 228, 323, 442–3, 461, 463; Wilson Center, Vassiliev Notebooks, Black Notebook, "Cipher telegram to Vadim [Anatoly Borisovich Gromov], KGB cable no. 7673, 21 October 1945, 57; https://digitalarchive.wilsoncenter.org/document/vassiliev-black–notebook.

36 TNA, KV 2/1421, MacDonald to Cadogan, no. 161, 18.2.46, s. 60A.

37 TNA, KV 2/1425, 48000 (Sir William Stephenson, British Security Coordination chief New York) to CSS (MI6 director general Sir Stewart Menzies), no. CXG. 326, 17.9.45. s. 11A. Through their Ottawa liaison officer Glen Bethel, the FBI had almost immediate access to Gouzenko. John F. Fox, "The Impact of the Gouzenko Affair on FBI Counter-Espionage and Security Relations with Canada," in *The Gouzenko Affair: Canada and the Beginnings of Cold War Counter-Espionage*, ed. J.L. Black and Martin Rudner (Ottawa: Centre for Research on Canadian-Russian Relations, 2006), 63–4.

38 LAC, WLMK, Secret and Confidential Diary, 23 October 1945, 14.

39 Stuart Wood, "Tools for Treachery," *Canadian Spokesman* 1, no. 2 (1941): 1–6, quoted in W.E. Mann & John Allan Lee, *RCMP vs. the People: Inside Canada's Security Service* (Don Mills: General Publishing, 1979), 118.

40 *Canada Declassified*, Canadian Security Intelligence Service, "RCMP Special Branch Lectures," https://declassified.library.utoronto.ca/exhibits/show/rcmp-special-branch-lectures/rcmp-special-branch-lectures.

41 *Canada Declassified*, CSIS, Corby Case, vol. 1, S.T. Wood, Commissioner Royal Canadian Mounted Police to The Hon. Louis St. Laurent, Minister of Justice and Attorney General of Canada, 27 September 1945, 00093-00094, https://declassified.library.utoronto.ca/files/original/85eb4cd89d0ecd7882908fdd194c8751.pdf.

42 *Canada Declassified*, CSIS, Corby Case, vol. 1, S.T. Wood, Commissioner Royal Canadian Mounted Police to The Hon. Louis St. Laurent, Minister of

Justice, and Attorney-General for Canada, 12 October 1945, 000134-000135, https://declassified.library.utoronto.ca/files/original/85eb4cd89d0ecd7882908fdd194c8751.pdf.

43 On St. Laurent's anti-Communism, see Philip Girard, "St-Laurent, Judging, Justice, and the Death Penalty in the Shadow of the Cold War," in *The Unexpected Louis St-Laurent: Politics and Policies for a Modern Canada*, ed. Patrice Dutil (Vancouver: UBC Press, 2020), 338–9.

44 Reg Whitaker, "Official Repression of Communism During World War II," *Labour/Le Travail* 17 (1986): 150.

45 *Canada Declassified*, CSIS, Corby Case, Wood to St. Laurent, 12 October 1945, 000134-000135, https://declassified.library.utoronto.ca/files/original/85eb4cd89d0ecd7882908fdd194c8751.pdf.

46 Luigi Bruti Liberati, "The Internment of Italian Canadians," in *Enemies Within: Italians and Others, Internees in Canada and Abroad*, ed. Franca Iacovetta, Roberto Perin, and Angelo Principe (Toronto: University of Toronto Press, 2000), 86–7.

47 M.L. Friedland, *Cases and Materials on Criminal Law*, 5th ed. (Toronto: University of Toronto Press, 1978), 163.

48 Wes Wilson, "The Political Use of Criminal Conspiracy," *University of Toronto Faculty Law Review* 20, no. 2 (1984): 60–78.

49 Reinhold Kramer and Tom Mitchell, *When the State Trembled: How A.J. Andrews and the Citizens Broke the Winnipeg General Strike* (Toronto: University of Toronto Press, 2010), 239–42.

50 *Canada Declassified*, CSIS, Corby Case, Wood to St. Laurent, 12 October 1945, 000134-000135, https://declassified.library.utoronto.ca/files/original/85eb4cd89d0ecd7882908fdd194c8751.pdf.

51 *Canada Declassified*, CSIS, Corby Case, Wood to St. Laurent, 27 September 1945, 00093-00094, https://declassified.library.utoronto.ca/files/original/85eb4cd89d0ecd7882908fdd194c8751.pdf.

52 Amy Knight, *How the Cold War Began: The Igor Gouzenko Affair and the Hunt for Soviet Spies* (New York: Carroll & Graf, 2005), 76.

53 Canadian authorities had previously demonstrated limited competence in handling an international espionage case. See Erik D. Jens, "The 'Great Gouzenko': Political, Intelligence, and Psychological Factors in the Defection That Triggered the Cold War," *American Intelligence Journal* 32 (2015): 188.

54 On Nunn May, see Brian Cathcart, "Britain's First Convicted Atom Spy," *The Independent* (London), 29 January 2003, 18; and Nigel Fountain and Richard Norton-Taylor, "Scientist Spy Exposed by Gouzenko," *Globe & Mail*, 1 February 2003, 11.

55 See TNA, KV 2/1425, MI5 "Memorandum," 24.9.45. The memorandum accompanied correspondence from G.M. Liddell to the commissioner of

the RCMP. TNA, KV 2/1425, Liddell to the Commissioner, 24.9.46, s. 20A. For Nunn May's confession, see TNA, KV 2 – 2212, Alan Nunn May to New York, no. 451, 20.2.46, "Top Secret," no serial number. See also Kevin Riehle, "Soviet Intent at the Dawn of the Cold War: Igor Gouzenko's Revelations about GRU Intelligence Tasking," *Journal of Intelligence History* (2021), 14n87, https://doi.org/10.1080/16161262.2021.1892997.

56 TNA, KV 2/1425, Liddell to RCMP (for Hollis), 19.9.45, s. 15A.

57 Dominique Clément has suggested that British security authorities exercised a kind of hegemony in the handling of the Gouzenko affair. He points to MI6 agent Peter Dwyer's role coordinating the Canadian, American, and British response. According to Clément, the "British encouraged the Canadian government to use an Order-in-Council to detain and interrogate the suspects." Clément, "Canada's Integration into Global Intelligence-Sharing Networks," *Intelligence and National Security* 33, no. 7 (2018): 1055–6, https://doi.org/10.1080/02684527.2018.1518290.

58 John Erskine Read, since 1929, had served as legal counsel for the Department of Foreign Affairs. He left the Canadian government in February 1946 when he was elected to the newly created United Nations Court of International Justice. "John Erskine Read," *Globe & Mail*, 7 February 1946, 7; "Canada Member of World Court Lauds UNO," *Globe & Mail*, 20 February 1946, 8.

59 Frederick Percy Varcoe, who almost certainly had announced that Justice harboured "grave doubts" about prosecutions based solely on Gouzenko's documentary record and testimony, had been deputy minister of justice since 1941. On Varcoe, see Richard W. Pound, *Chief Justice W.R. Jackett: By the Law of the Land* (Montreal & Kingston: McGill-Queen's University Press, 1999), 60–5.

60 TNA, KV 2/1425, Hume Wrong to Robertson (copy to Cadogan), no. 478, 6.10.45, s. 57a. Wrong's attribution of the plan to Read and Varcoe appears here, and for this reason we call it the "Read/Varcoe" plan.

61 On the Official Secrets Act see *Crimes Against the State, Working Paper 49* (Ottawa: Law Reform Commission of Canada, 1986), 8–10.

62 *Canada Declassified*, CSIS, Corby Case, vol. 1, Commissioner S.T. Wood to J. Edgar Hoover, Director, Federal Bureau of Investigation, 3 October 1945, 00099-00101, https://declassified.library.utoronto.ca/files/original/85eb4cd89d0ecd7882908fdd194c8751.pdf.

63 Robertson was in England with Mackenzie King. TNA, KV 2/1425, Wrong to Robertson (copy to Cadogan), no. 478, 6.10.45, s. 57a.

64 Charles W. Fricke. *5000 Criminal Definitions, Terms and Phrases* (Los Angeles: Legal Book Store), 17.

65 See *R. v. Christie* in E.G. Ewaschuk, "Hearsay Evidence," *Osgoode Hall Law Journal* 16, no. 2 (1978): 437.

66 TNA, KV 2 /1423, P.A. Clutterbuck, Office of the Commissioner from Great Britain, Ottawa, to Viscount Addison, Secretary of State for Dominion Affairs, London, no. 454, 25.11.46, 4, s. 247A.

67 (1946) 88 C.C.C 114 at 125 (Que. C.A.); Matthew R. Goode, *Criminal Conspiracy in Canada* (Toronto: Carswell, 1975), 245.

68 TNA, KV 2/1425, Wrong to Robertson (copy to Cadogan), no. 478, 6.10.45, s. 57a.

69 Reginald Whitaker and Gary Marcuse, *Cold War Canada: The Making of a National Security State, 1945–1957* (Toronto: University of Toronto Press, 1994), 51.

70 Tom Mitchell, "1846, Canada's First Inquiries Act," *Journal of Canadian Studies* 55, no. 3 (2021): 574–82.

71 TNA, KV 2/1425, Wrong to Robertson (copy to Cadogan), no. 478, 6.10.45, s. 57a.

72 On trials arising from the Kellock-Taschereau inquiry, see Barbara J. Falk and Tyler Wentzell, "The Enemy Within: A Review and Comparison of Early Cold War Canadian and American Spy Trials," in *Canadian State Trials*, vol. 5: *World War, Cold War, and Challenges to Sovereignty, 1939–1990*, ed. Barry Wright, Susan Binnie, and Eric Tucker (Toronto: University of Toronto Press, 2022), 177–227.

73 TNA, KV 2/1425, Wrong to Robertson (copy to Cadogan), no. 478, 6.10.45, s. 57a.

74 See Regulation 24.2. b and c, *Defence of Canada Regulations* (Ottawa: King's Printer, 1939), 30–2, https://archive.org/details/defenceofcanadar1939cana/page/32/mode/2up. For an account of the early operations of the Regulations, see F.A. Brewin, "Civil Liberties in Canada During Wartime," *Bill of Rights Review* 1, no. 2 (1941): 112–21.

75 TNA, KV 2/1425, Wrong to Robertson (copy to Cadogan), No. 478, 6.10.45, s. 57a.

76 *Revised Statutes of Canada* (R.S.C.) 1927, c. 59, Canada Evidence Act (Ottawa: King's Printer, 1927), 1524.

77 *Defence of Canada Regulations* (Ottawa: King's Printer, 1939), 30, https://archive.org/details/defenceofcanadar1939cana/page/32/mode/2up.

78 Section 685 of the *Criminal Code* states that "[n]othing herein contained shall prevent any prosecutor from giving in evidence any admission or confession, or other statement, made at any time by the person accused or charged, which by law would be admissible as evidence against him." R.S.C. c. 146, *Criminal Code* (Ottawa: King's Printer, 1927), 224.

79 LAC, WLMK, Secret and Confidential Diary, 7 October 1945, 2.

80 Pickersgill and Forster, *The Mackenzie King Record*, vol. 3, 34.

81 In his memoir Arnold Heeney, in 1945 secretary to the Privy Council, stated that he drafted PC 6444 and took it around for signature "by four ministers, a quorum of Council for such purposes." Heeney secured the signatures of Minister of Justice St. Laurent, on whose "instructions" he had drafted the order, Ilsley, and two other ministers he does not name. Arnold Heeney, *The Things That Are Caesar's: Memoirs of a Canadian Public Servant* (Toronto: University of Toronto Press, 1972), 85.

82 *Defence of Canada Regulations* (Ottawa: King's Printer, 1939), 30, https://archive.org/details/defenceofcanadar1939cana/page/32/mode/2up.

83 A copy of PC 6444 was released to Parliament and the public on 14 March 1946 in a document titled *Documents Relating to the Proceedings of the Royal Commission established by Order-in-Council PC 411 of February 5, 1946, including the First and Second Interim Reports of the Royal Commission* (Ottawa: King's Printer, 1946), 9–10. For this publication, see TNA, KV 2/1423, Documents Relating to the Proceedings of the Royal Commission, s. 170A.

84 TNA, KV 2/1423, Documents Relating to the Proceedings of the Royal Commission, s. 170A, 9–10. Whitaker and Marcuse state incorrectly that King and three other ministers approved PC 6444. On 6 October King was on the Queen Mary, docked in Great Britain. Whitaker and Marcuse, *Cold War Canada*, 42.

85 This new openness may well have been prompted by parliamentary criticism of "secret" order PC 6444. See J.R. Mallory, "Delegated Legislation in Canada: Recent Changes in Machinery," *Canadian Journal of Economics and Political Science* 19, no. 4 (1953): 463.

86 Both had joined the RCMP as teenagers and both worked their way to senior positions in the Criminal Investigations branch. Anthony began his career as an RCMP member of the Canadian Expeditionary Force in Siberia and ended his life in policing as chief of the Edmonton police force. "Death Ends Long Career of Edmonton Police Chief," *Lethbridge Herald*, 26 March 1966, 2. Harvison, who ended his career as commissioner, left an account of his role in the Gouzenko affair in a published autobiography: C.W. Harvison, *The Horsemen* (Toronto: McClelland & Stewart, 1967), 127–47.

87 TNA, KV4/466, Guy Liddell Diaries, 6 October 1945, 257–8.

88 For a sample of these reports, see TNA, KV/2-2213, Alan Nunn May, H. Hunter to Mr. Marriott, "Alan Nunn May" (Top Secret), 18 and 28 December 1945, ss. 254A and 254B.

89 TNA, KV 2/ 4728, Philby, Harold Adrian Russell, Letter from H.A.R. Philby to MI5, undated [January 1952?], s. 239ca.

90 TNA, KV 2 /4728, Evelyn McBarnet [MI5], 15 January 1952, s. 239cb.

91 Harvison, *The Horsemen*, 151.
92 "Orders-in-Council Upheld by Supreme Court Judges," *Globe & Mail*, 20 July 1918, 1.
93 "Orders-in-Council Upheld by Supreme Court Judges," *Globe & Mail*, 20 July 1918, 1. Gray was subsequently sentenced by court martial to ten years in jail for "disobeying a lawful command." On the sentence, see Library Archives Canada, RG73-C-6, vol. 561, 434927. On *Re Gray*, see Patricia I. McMahon, "Conscription and the Courts: The Case of George Edwin Gray, 1918," in *Canadian State Trials*, vol. 4: *Security, Dissent, and the Limits of Toleration in War and Peace, 1914–1939*, ed. Barry Wright, Eric Tucker, and Susan Binnie (Toronto: University of Toronto Press, 2015), 132–72.
94 In the Matter of a Reference as to the Validity of the Regulations in relation to Chemicals Enacted by the Governor General in Council of Canada on the 10th Day of July, 1941, P.C. 4996, and of an Order of the Controller of Chemicals, dated the 16th Day of January, 1942, made pursuant thereto, 3, 13, https://decisions.scc-csc.ca/scc-csc/scc-csc/en/item/2784/index.do.
95 The Fort Frances Pulp and Paper Company Limited (Appeal No. 69 of 1923) v The Manitoba Free Press Company Limited and others (Ontario) [1923] UKPC 64 (25 July 1923), 7, https://www.bailii.org/uk/cases/UKPC/1923/1923_64.html.
96 TNA, KV 2/1425, Liddell to RCMP, 23.9.45, s. 17A.
97 TNA, KV 2/1425, Note, 9.10.45, signed Roger Hollis, s. 62B.
98 TNA, KV 2/1425, For Hollis from MI5, no. 24, 27.10.45, s. 68Y.
99 TNA, KV 2/1425, For Hollis from MI5, no. 24, 27.10.45, s. 68Y.
100 TNA/KV 2/1425, Ernest Bevin to the Prime Minister, TOP SECRET, The Corby Case, 27 October 1945, s. 68a.
101 TNA, KV 2/1425, MacDonald to Cadogan, no. 622, 31.10.45, s. 71a.
102 Wood concluded the letter with a request that St. Laurent return the report when "it has served its purpose." *Canada Declassified*, CSIS, Corby Case, vol. 1, S.T. Wood, Commissioner Royal Canadian Mounted Police to The Hon. Louis St. Laurent, Minister of Justice, and Attorney-General for Canada, 9 November 1945,000347, 2021, https://declassified.library.utoronto.ca/files/original/85eb4cd89d0ecd7882908fdd194c8751.pdf.
103 TNA, KV 2/1428, "Soviet Espionage in Canada."
104 The report was dated 5 January 1944, but it was made clear during Gouzenko's testimony that the date recorded should have been 5 January 1945, because the items on the list were received by GRU personnel from their Canadian agents from October to December 1944. LAC, RG33-62, Agents of a Foreign Power fonds, Reel T-3423, Exhibit 16A, Record of the Materials Sent to the Address of the Director (Record of the Materials

Sent), 5 January 1945, 254–61, https://heritage.canadiana.ca/view/oocihm.lac_reel_t3423/254.

105 TNA, KV 2/1425, 48,000 (Stephenson) to C.S.S (Menzies), no. 554, 19.10.45, s. 68a.

106 TNA, KV 2/1425, 48,000 (Stephenson) to C.S.S. (Menzies), no. 554, 19.10.45, ss. 65B, 65C.

107 TNA, KV 2.1425, Neville Butler to "Dear Tom" (T.E. Bromley), with Draft Agreement on procedure for dealing with the "Corby" case (attached), and the annex dealing with Nunn May, 14.11.45, s. 87d.

108 TNA, KV 2/1425, For MI5 from Hollis, no. 764, 19.11.45, s. 87c.

109 Wilson Center, Vassiliev Notebooks, White Notebook #2, "Message 'Bob' from London sent 'S's data in a cipher cable dated 20 November 1945," KGB cable, file 70545, 27–28, https://digitalarchive.wilsoncenter.org/document/vassiliev-white-notebook-2. In 1963 Philby would admit that he had given the Russians "all the British information on the Guzenko [*sic*] case." TNA, KV 2/ 4237, Philby, Harold Adrian Russell, "Meeting with PEACH at 1600 hours on Friday 11 January 1963," Document 2 at 16.

110 Wilson Center, Vassiliev Notebooks, White Notebook #2, KGB cable, File 70545 "Myrna," "Message 'Bob' from London sent 'S's data in a cipher cable dated 20 November 1945," 28, https://digitalarchive.wilsoncenter.org/document/vassiliev-white-notebook-2.

111 Kim Philby, quoting telegrams from J. Edgar Hoover to security officials in Great Britain and Canada, told Moscow that Hoover had asked that joint measures be postponed until the FBI completed its investigation of what appeared to be a Soviet spy network in the United States. Allen Weinstein and Alexander Vassiliev, *The Haunted Wood: Soviet Espionage in America: The Stalin Era* (New York: Random House, 1999), 104.

112 Wilson Center, Vassiliev Notebooks, Black Notebook, "Plan of measures for the 1st Department, 1st Directorate of the KI to improve intelligence work in the USA. Approved by S. Savchenko 16.03.50," 81, https://digitalarchive.wilsoncenter.org/document/vassiliev-black-notebook.

113 For an account of this development from a British perspective, see TNA, KV4/467, Guy Liddell Diaries, 20 November 1945, 2–3. From the American side, see Weinstein and Vassiliev, *The Haunted Wood,* 104–5.

114 On the Byrnes-initiated Moscow conference of December 1945, see Bullock, *Ernest Bevin,* 199–200, 206–12.

115 Daniel W.B. Lomas, I*ntelligence, Security and the Attlee Governments, 1945–51: An Uneasy Relationship* (Manchester: Manchester University Press, 2017), 156.

116 TNA, KV 2/1425, Lord Halifax to Cadogan (copy to MacDonald), no. 820, 28.11.45, s. 94a.

117 Wilson Center, Vassiliev Notebooks, White Notebook #2, File 70545 "Myrna" [code name Elizabeth Bentley, a.k.a. "Clever Girl"], V. Merkulov to Comrades I.V. Stalin, V.M. Molotov, and L.P. Beria, 24 November 1945, 28–9, https://digitalarchive.wilsoncenter.org/document/vassiliev-white-notebook-2.

118 Wilson Center, Vassiliev Notebooks, White Notebook #2, File 70545, "Bob" from London "S's" information, 26.11.45, 32, https://digitalarchive.wilsoncenter.org/document/vassiliev-white-notebook-2.

119 Wilson Center, Vassiliev Notebooks, White Notebook #2, File 70545," Bob" from London "S's" information, 27.11.45, 33, https://digitalarchive.wilsoncenter.org/document/vassiliev-white-notebook-2.

120 For this account of the plan, see TNA, KV 2/1425, MacDonald to Cadogan (copy to Halifax), nos. 855–6, 2.12.45, s. 95.

121 On Wood's anti-Communist initiatives prior to the Gouzenko affair, see John Stanton, "Government Internment Policy, 1939–45," *Labour/Le Travail* 31 (1993): 203–41.

122 Canada *Declassified*, CSIS, Corby Case, vol. 3, S.T. Wood, Commissioner Royal Canadian Mounted Police to The Hon. Louis St. Laurent, Minister of Justice and Attorney General of Canada, 3 December 1945, 00403-00406, https://declassified.library.utoronto.ca/files/original/5aabe4992d1c863bbe950bb24df1506f.pdf.

123 TNA, KV 2/1425, MacDonald to Cadogan (copy to Halifax), nos. 860–2, 4.12.45, ss. 98a and 98b.

Chapter 2: Read/Varcoe Redux

1 TNA, KV 2/1425, MacDonald to Cadogan (copy to Halifax), no. 856, 2.12.45, s. 95.

2 On the challenges (and opportunities) of mounting criminal conspiracy prosecutions, see Wes Wilson, "The Political Use of Criminal Conspiracy," *University of Toronto Faculty Law Review* 20, no. 2 (1984): 60–78.

3 TNA, KV 2/1425, MacDonald to Cadogan (copy to Halifax), no. 856, 2.12.45, s. 95.

4 He served as a commissioner on Uniformity of Laws for Manitoba (1922–24); convener of the Canadian Bar Association committee on Comparative Provincial Legislation and Law Reform (1923–32); honorary treasurer, Canadian Bar Association (1932–44); Dominion vice-president, 1944–45; honorary member, American Bar Association; and vice-president, International Association of Insurance Counsel.

5 Archives of Manitoba, Esten Kenneth Williams Papers, MG 14, B 39, as quoted in Dale Brawn, *The Court of Queen's Bench of Manitoba 1870–1950: A Biographical Approach* (Toronto: University of Toronto Press, 2006), 335.

6 For this language, see Mark Goldie, "Retrospect – The Ancient Constitution and the Languages of Political Thought," *Historical Journal* 62, no. 1 (2019): 4.
7 "Williams Doubts Empire Falling," *Winnipeg Tribune*, 22 April 1947, 7.
8 "Williams Against Mayor and Vicar Debating Issue," *Winnipeg Free Press*, 14 February 1934, 2.
9 Dale Gibson, *Substantial Justice Law, and Lawyers in Manitoba 1670–1970* (Winnipeg: Peguis, 1972), 233.
10 "Canada's Quislings," *Winnipeg Tribune*, 16 January 1942, 13. Williams was joining a chorus of attacks on the Communist left during the early years of the war. See Reg Whitaker, "Official Repression of Communism During World War II," *Labour/Le Travail* 17 (1986): 135–66.
11 Locke, *Two Treaties of Government*, § 16, 296–297.
12 Eric M. Adams, "The Idea of Constitutional Rights and the Transformation of Canadian Constitutional Law, 1930–1960," unpublished PhD diss., University of Toronto, 2009, 88.
13 There are at least two versions of the report extant. Dominique Clément references a redacted version held in the records of the Department of Justice. See his reference to Library Archives Canada, Records of the Department of Justice, RG 13, vol. 2119, 2121, E.K. Williams, "The Corby Case" [Top Secret memorandum to William Lyon Mackenzie King], 5 [*sic*] December 1945, in Clément, "Spies, Lies and a Commission: A Case Study in the Mobilization of the Canadian Civil Liberties Movement," *Left History* 7, no. 2 (2000): 74nn19, 20. A longer version held in RCMP / CSIS records saw light of day in 2018 and is the version relied on for this book. See *Canada Declassified*, CSIS, Corby Case, vol. 3, RCMP Registry, "The Corby Case, The Documents," 000416-000422, https: / / declassified.library.utoronto.ca / files / original / 5aabe4992d1c863bbe950bb24df1506f.pdf.
14 On the Mathers inquiry see Tom Mitchell, "'Ultra Vires and Void': An Executive Inquiry Takes on Manitoba's Legislative Building Crisis (And Wins)," *Manitoba Law Review* 44, no. 3 (2021), https: / / journals.library.ualberta.ca / themanitobalawjournal / index.php / mlj / article / view / 1277. For Perdue's inquiry, see Manitoba, Legislative Assembly, "Royal Commission Appointed to Investigate the Charges in the Statement of C.P. Fullerton, KC," *Sessional Papers*, no. 18 (1916).
15 See, for example, North West Dealers Ass'n v. Hyndman; United Grain Growers, Ltd. v. Hyndman, [1921] DLR 61 at 548; Braaten v. Sargent and Attorney-General for British Columbia, British Columbia Supreme Court, Seaton, J. [1967] DLR 61 S.L.R (2d) 678; Reference Re A Commission of Inquiry into the Police Department of the City of Charlottetown, Prince Edward Island Supreme Court, in Banco, Nicholson, C.J.P.E.I., Darby and McQuaid, [1977], DL Reports 74 (3d) 422; A.G. of Que. and Keable v. A.G.

of Can. et al [1979] 1 S.C.R. at 218; Terrance Patrick O'Hara and John Earl Kirkbride v. Her Majesty the Queen in Right of the Province of British Columbia, the Attorney General of the Province of British Columbia, Malcolm A. Matheson, Mary Saunders and Richard M. MacIntosh and the Attorney General for Ontario et al. [1987] CSC Reports, 591.

16 TNA, KV 2/1428, "Soviet Espionage in Canada," 5.

17 *Canada Declassified*, CSIS, "The Corby Case, The Documents," 000416, https://declassified.library.utoronto.ca/files/original/5aabe4992d1c863bbe950bb24df1506f.pdf.

18 A cut-out in an espionage network is an individual who undertakes activities that allow others more senior or in more sensitive positions to remain anonymous. Bob Burton, *Top Secret: The Dictionary of Espionage and Intelligence* (New York: Kensington, 2005), 49.

19 *Canada Declassified*, CSIS, "The Corby Case, The Documents," 000417, https://declassified.library.utoronto.ca/files/original/5aabe4992d1c863bbe950bb24df1506f.pdf.

20 *Canada Declassified*, CSIS, "The Corby Case, The Documents," 000417, https://declassified.library.utoronto.ca/files/original/5aabe4992d1c863bbe950bb24df1506f.pdf.

21 Harrison W. Moore, "Executive Commissions of Inquiry," *Columbia Law Review* 13, no. 6 (1913): 518.

22 Norman McCord and A.W. Purdue, *The Short Oxford History of the Modern World: British History 1815–1914*, 2nd ed. (Oxford: Oxford University Press, 2007), 212.

23 Frédéric Moret, *The End of the Urban Ancient Regime in England* (Newcastle upon Tyne: Cambridge Scholars, 2015), 35.

24 The Right Honorable the Viscount Caldecote, "The King's Prerogative," *Cambridge Law Journal* 7, no. 3 (1941): 815.

25 *First Report of the Commissioners Appointed to Inquire into the Municipal Corporations of England and Wales* (London: Charles Knight, 1835), 4, https://babel.hathitrust.org/cgi/pt?id=nyp.33433014090470&view=1up&seq=8.

26 Hugh McDowall Clokie and J. William Robinson. *Royal Commissions of Inquiry: The Significance of Investigations in British Politics* (Stanford: Stanford University Press, 1937), 85–6; "The Corporation Commission," *The Law Magazine* 11, no. 1 (1834): 68–82.

27 *Report of Her Majesty's commissioners appointed to inquire into the state, discipline, studies, and revenues of the University and Colleges of Oxford: together with evidence and an appendix.* (London: William Lowes and Sons, 1852), 32.

28 Provincial Statutes of Canada 1846, c. 39, An Act to empower Commissions for inquiring into matters connected with the public business, to take evidence on oath. The Australian colony of Victoria (1854) and, later, New

Zealand (Commissioners' Power Act 1867) approved similar legislation. In 1902, the new Commonwealth of Australia (established 1901) adopted a Royal Commissions Act. Stephen Goudge and Heather MacIvor, *Commissions of Inquiry* (Toronto: LexisNexis Canada, 2019), 41.

29 *The Report of the Royal Commission To Investigate the Facts Relating to and the Circumstances Surrounding the Communication, by Public Officials and Other Persons in Positions of Trust of Secret and Confidential Information to Agents of a Foreign Power* (Ottawa: King's Printer, 1946), 8, https://publications.gc.ca/site/eng/9.699909/publication.html. Hereafter cited as *The Report of the Royal Commission (Final Report).*

30 Tom Mitchell, "1846, Canada's First Inquiries Act," *Journal of Canadian Studies* 55, no. 3 (2021): 574–82.

31 *Report of the Departmental Committee on the Procedure of Royal Commissions* (London: King's Printer, 1910), 12.

32 Peter G. Richards, "The Tribunal Act 1921," *Public Administration* 28, no. 2 (1949): 123–128; Jason Beer, ed., *Public Inquiries* (Oxford: Oxford University Press, 2011), 6.

33 T.K. Ramsay, *Government Commissions of Inquiry* (Montreal: John Lovell, St Nicholas Street, 1863), 3–6.

34 D. Girouard, "The Bill of Oaths, the Prorogation, and the Royal Commission," *Revue Critique de Legislation et de Jurisprudence du Canada* 3, no. 2 (1873–75): 195–6.

35 *Montreal Herald and Commercial Gazette*, 19 August 1863, 2.

36 *Montreal Herald and Commercial Gazette*, 31 August 1863, 2. His decision prompted a dissenting critical commentary by Montreal lawyer T.K. Ramsay, who dismissed Monk's judgment as an assault on the common law principal that only the courts could adjudicate criminal charges levelled by the state against a citizen. Ramsay, *Government Commissions of Inquiry*, 3–6.

37 Provincial Statutes of Canada 1846, c. 39, An Act to empower Commissions.

38 "Quebec Boodle Investigation," *The Globe*, 11 December 1888, 1.

39 Statutes of Canada 1889, c. 33, An Act to make further provision respecting inquiries concerning Public Matters.

40 For Thompson's explanation of the need for the legislation, see House of Commons, *Debates*, 7 March 1889, 504. See also *Debates of the Senate*, 20 February 1889, 40. Thompson contributed to an ongoing Benthamite-inspired campaign to make all witnesses competent and compellable. See Desmond H. Brown, "Be Sworn and Give Evidence: The Evolution of the Competent Witness in the Context of the Canadian Evidence Act," *Manitoba Law Journal* 22 (1994): 349–93.

41 Thompson in House of Commons, *Debates*, 3 March 1893, 1675, as quoted in Brown, "Be Sworn and Give Evidence," 390.

42 For a summary of the debate in Commons and Senate, see Ronald D. Noble, "The Struggle to Make the Accused Competent in England and Canada," *Osgoode Hall Law Journal* 8, no. 2 (1970): 270–2.
43 R.S.C 1893, c. 31, An Act Respecting Witnesses and Evidence.
44 Statutes of Canada 1898, c. 53, An Act to Amend the Canada Evidence Act 1893.
45 Godson v. Toronto (City), (1890) 18 S.C.R. 36, 53.
46 Godson v. Toronto (City), (1890) 18 S.C.R. 36, 44.
47 As quoted in Robert D. Howe, "The Applicability of the Rules of Natural Justice to Investigatory and Recommendatory Functions," *Osgoode Hall Law Journal* 12, no. 1 (1974): 180.
48 T.R. O'Donnel, "O'Connor v. Waldron – Defamation – Privilege – Judicial and Administrative Tribunals," *Alberta Law Quarterly* 2, no. 4 (1936): 118.
49 Roach, "The Administrative Law Scholarship of D.M. Gordon," *McGill Law Journal* 34, no. 1 (1989): 2.
50 D.M. Gordon, "Administrative Tribunals and the Courts," *Law Quarterly Review* 49, 1 (1933): 94.
51 Re Ashby et al. [1934] O.R. 42 Ontario Court of Appeal, 18 May 1934.
52 Howe, "Applicability of the Rules of Natural Justice," 181.
53 Howe, "Applicability of the Rules of Natural Justice," 179.
54 See also Goudge and MacIvor, *Commissions of Inquiry*, 76–8.
55 *Canada Declassified*, CSIS, "The Corby Case, The Documents," 000419, https://declassified.library.utoronto.ca/files/original/5aabe4992d1c863bbe950bb24df1506f.pdf.
56 *Canada Declassified*, CSIS, "The Corby Case, The Documents," 000420, https://declassified.library.utoronto.ca/files/original/5aabe4992d1c863bbe950bb24df1506f.pdf.
57 In British political discourse the phrase "enemies of the state" first appeared as an anti-Catholic reference. See for example the pamphlet by Anonymous, *A remonstrance presented to His Maiestie by the Parliament in June, ann. dom. 1628, 3° Caroli Regis vvherein is discovered the great danger that England and Ireland lay under, and the Parliaments care to have secured them : as also the names of some of the enemies of the state, as Dr. Laud, &c.* London: n.p., 1642.
58 Locke's account appears in his discussion titled "Dissolution of Government." Locke, *Two Treatises of Government*, ed. Peter Laslett (Cambridge: Cambridge University Press, 1967), §231, 436.
59 J.L. Granatstein, *The Ottawa Men: The Civil Service Mandarins 1935–1957* (Toronto: University of Toronto Press, 1982), 247.
60 *Canada Declassified, CSIS*, "The Corby Case, The Documents," 000419, https://declassified.library.utoronto.ca/files/original/5aabe4992d1c863bbe950bb24df1506f.pdf.

61 *Canada Declassified*, CSIS, "The Corby Case, The Documents," 000421, https://declassified.library.utoronto.ca/files/original/5aabe4992d1c863bbe950bb24df1506f.pdf.
62 On Departmental Inquiries, see R.S.C 1906, c. 104, An Act Respecting Public and Departmental Inquiries, Part II, Departmental Inquiries (King's Printer, 1906), 1779–81.
63 *Canada Declassified*, CSIS, "The Corby Case, The Documents," 000422, https://declassified.library.utoronto.ca/files/original/5aabe4992d1c863bbe950bb24df1506f.pdf.
64 *Canada Declassified*, CSIS, "The Corby Case, The Documents," 000418, https://declassified.library.utoronto.ca/files/original/5aabe4992d1c863bbe950bb24df1506f.pdf.
65 Later, when the US Senate Sub-committee investigating Soviet intelligence activities sought Gouzenko as a star witness, the Canadian government declined. The *New York Times* suggested that one reason for this was the red-baiting nature of the American hearings. *New York Times*, "The Gouzenko Case," 3 December 1953, 2D.
66 Whitaker, "Official Repression of Communism," 148.
67 "Robert Taschereau – Served as Chief Justice of the Supreme Court," *Globe & Mail*, 28 July 1970, 3.
68 Whitaker, "Official Repression of Communism," 148.
69 Hon. Mr. Justice R.L. Kellock, *Report on the Halifax Disorders May 7th–8th 1945* (Ottawa: King's Printer, 1945.)
70 "Roy Lindsay Kellock – Headed Inquiry into Soviet espionage," *Globe & Mail*, 13 December 1975, 5.

Chapter 3: PC 411

1 Daniel W.B. Lomas, *Intelligence, Security and the Attlee Governments, 1945–51: An Uneasy Relationship* (Manchester: Manchester University Press, 2017), 157. For the date of the meeting, see TNA, KV 2/1426, memorandum, JHM [John Marriott] no. F.c2, 25.1.46, s. 113a.
2 TNA, KV 2/1426, MacDonald to Cadogan, no. 79, 1.2.46, s. 114a.
3 For the substance of Pearson's account, see TNA, KV 2/1426, MacDonald to Cadogan, nos. 90 and 91, 4.2.46, s. 116a.
4 John F. Fox, "The Impact of the Gouzenko Affair on FBI Counter-Espionage and Security Relations with Canada," in *The Gouzenko Affair: Canada and the Beginnings of Cold War Counter-Espionage*, ed. J.L. Black and Martin Rudner (Ottawa: Centre for Research on Canadian-Russian Relations, 2006), 67. C (MI6 chief Sir Stewart Menzies) appointed William Stephenson as MI6's man in America under the cover of a British passport control officer in New York. Menzies directed Stephenson "to investigate

enemy activities, to institute adequate security measures against the sabotage of British property and to organize American public opinion in favour of aid to Britain." Keith Jeffery, *The Secret History of MI6: 1909–1949* (New York: Penguin, 2010), 440.

5 Amy Knight, "The Allies and the Gouzenko Affair," in *The Gouzenko Affair: Canada and the Beginnings of Cold War Counter-Espionage*, ed. J.L. Black and Martin Rudner (Ottawa: Centre for Research on Canadian-Russian Relations, 2006), 105.

6 Dennis Molinaro, "How the Cold War Began ... with British Help: The Gouzenko Affair Revisited," *Labour/Le Travail* 79 (2017): 151–3.

7 Library Archives Canada, Diaries of William Lyon Mackenzie King 1893–1950, 4 February 1946, 2.

8 For a certified copy of PC 411, see LAC, RG33-62, Agents of a Foreign Power fonds, T-3423, Exhibit 1, PC 411, 2-5, https://heritage.canadiana.ca/view/oocihm.lac_reel_t3423/104. Neither judge received any extra compensation for his work on the inquiry. House of Commons, *Debates*, 10 February 1947, 241. On Kellock, see "Headed Inquiry into Espionage in Canada," *Globe & Mail*, 13 December 1975, 5; on Taschereau, see "Robert Taschereau," *Globe & Mail*, 28 July 1970, 6, and "Served as Chief Justice of the Supreme Court," *Globe & Mail*, 28 July 1970, 3.

9 Statutes of Canada 1945, c. 25, The National Emergency Transitional Powers Act (Transitional Powers Act), 177–180.

10 Transitional Powers Act, s. 5, 179.

11 Transitional Powers Act s. 4, 179.

12 Louis St. Laurent in House of Commons, *Debates*, 19 March 1946, 92–3.

13 *Canada Declassified*, CSIS, "The Corby Case, The Documents," 000417, https://declassified.library.utoronto.ca/files/original/5aabe4992d1c863bbe950bb24df1506f.pdf.

14 For the phrase "in legal custody," see LAC, RG33-62, Agents of a Foreign Power fonds, T-3423, PC 6444, https://heritage.canadiana.ca/view/oocihm.lac_reel_t3423/103.

15 LAC, Diaries of WLMK, 4 February 1946, 2. Malcolm MacDonald reported to Cadogan that "Mackenzie King has given all clear to proceed by Royal Commission immediately. This is subject to approval by Cabinet tomorrow, but approval forgone conclusion." TNA, KV 2/1426, MacDonald to Cadogan, no. 93, 4.2.46, s. 117a.

16 LAC, RG33-62, Agents of a Foreign Power fonds, T-3423, Exhibit 1, PC 411, 2–5, https://heritage.canadiana.ca/view/oocihm.lac_reel_t1368/65.

17 Statutes of Canada, 1939, c. 49, Official Secrets Act (Ottawa: King's Printer, 1939), 450–1.

18 TNA, KV 2/1423, Documents Relating to the Proceedings of the Royal Commission, s. 170A. Prosecutions under the Official Secrets Act required

the imprimatur of the federal minister of justice. Official Secrets Act, s. 12, 456.

19 Official Secrets Act, s. 3, 450–1.

20 "Halperin Is Acquitted on Espionage Charges," *Globe & Mail*, 5 March 1947, 8.

21 LAC, RG33-62, Agents of a Foreign Power fonds, T-3423, Exhibit 1, PC 411, 2–5, https://heritage.canadiana.ca/view/oocihm.lac_reel_t3423/101.

22 Eric M. Adams states erroneously that PC 411 was authorized under The Transitional Powers Act. There is a reference to the War Measures Act in PC 6444, but there is no reference to the National Emergency and Transitional Powers Act in PC 411. See Adams, "The Idea of Constitutional Rights and the Transformation of Canadian Constitutional Law, 1930–1960," unpublished PhD diss., University of Toronto, 2009, 153.

23 TNA, KV 2/1426, MacDonald to Cadogan, no. 107, 7.2.46, s. 125a.

24 TNA, KV 2/1426, MacDonald to Cadogan, no. 102, 5.2.46, s. 118a.

25 *Canada Declassified*, CSIS, prepared for the Commission, Corby Case vol. 1, https://declassified.library.utoronto.ca/files/original/06e0c7c3e1fbdccff470275834eb1d7c.pdf.

26 LAC, RG33-62, Agents of a Foreign Power fonds, Reel T-3423, Exhibit 25AA, Page out of notebook in Col. Zabotin's handwriting, 763, https://heritage.canadiana.ca/view/oocihm.lac_reel_t3423/763.

27 LAC, RG33-62, Agents of a Foreign Power fonds, Reel T-3423, Exhibit 25 BB, Page out of notebook in Col. Zabotin's handwriting, Before reorganization, 765.

28 TNA, KV 2/1426, MacDonald to Cadogan, no. 106/107, 7.2.46, s. 125a.

29 LAC, RG33-62, Agents of a Foreign Power fonds, T-1368, 2, https://heritage.canadiana.ca/view/oocihm.lac_reel_t1368/64.

30 LAC, RG33-62, Agents of a Foreign Power fonds, T-1368, David Shugar testimony, 1905, https://heritage.canadiana.ca/view/oocihm.lac_reel_t1368/1978.

31 On Mundell, see Richard W. Pound, *Chief Justice W.R. Jackett – By the Law of the Land* (Montreal & Kingston: McGill-Queen's University Press, 1999), 56.

32 "Magistrate to Commit Lunan, 'Spy Cell Head,'" *Globe & Mail*, 3 April 1946, 13.

33 LAC, RG33-62, Agents of a Foreign Power fonds, T-1368, 8, https://heritage.canadiana.ca/view/oocihm.lac_reel_t1368/70. In his autobiography, former RCMP acting head of the Criminal Investigation Branch Rivett-Carnac observed that "Inspector Leopold assisted the Royal Commissioners, and two other officers had been specially selected to deal with the initial questioning of the suspects." Charles Rivett-Carnac, *Pursuit in the Wilderness* (London: Jarrolds, 1967), 316.

34 LAC, RG33-62, Agents of a Foreign Power fonds, Reel T-1368, 9, https://heritage.canadiana.ca/view/oocihm.lac_reel_t1368/71.

35 In August 1943 Moliere (Pavel Mikhailov, Soviet vice-consul, New York) advised Moscow that "Fred [Rose], our man in LESOVIA, has been elected to the LESOVIAN parliament. His personal opportunities undoubtedly are improving, but warn LION [*sic*] [Sergei M. Koudriavtsev, LEON) about increasing caution to the maximum." Wilson Center, Venona Project, USA-GRU, New York to Moscow, no. 1328, 12 August 1943, to the DIRECTOR from MOLIERE [Zabotin], 172.

36 *The Report of the Royal Commission* (*Final Report*), 15, https://publications.gc.ca/site/eng/9.699909/publication.html. In January 1944 Zabotin cabled Moscow that "I consider that DAVIE [Sokolov] and LEON [Koudriavtsev] have done a great deal for the country and the Red Army and that therefore the first two ought to be recommended for a government award." Wilson Center, Venona Project, Ottawa–GRU, Ottawa to Moscow, no. 52, 25 January 1944, To the DIRECTOR from GRANT [Zabotin], "DAVIE, LEON AND MARTIN FOR AWARDS (1944), 5. "Leon's" name is sometimes spelled "Kudryavtzev."

37 TNA, KV 2/1428, "Soviet Espionage in Canada," 22.

38 TNA, KV 2/1428, "Soviet Espionage in Canada," 22–3; Kevin Riehle, "Soviet Intent at the Dawn of the Cold War," 8, https://doi.org/10.1080/16161262.2021.1892997.

39 LAC, RG33-62, Agents of a Foreign Power fonds, Reel T-1368, Gouzenko testimony, 23–44, https://heritage.canadiana.ca/view/oocihm.lac_reel_t1368/85.

40 LAC, RG33-62, Agents of a Foreign Power fonds, Reel T-1368, Gouzenko testimony, 118, https://heritage.canadiana.ca/view/oocihm.lac_reel_t1368/179.

41 For copies of these documents, see LAC, RG33-62, Agents of a Foreign Power fonds, Reel T-3423, Exhibits 20A–20VV, Outgoing telegrams, 431–612, https://heritage.canadiana.ca/view/oocihm.lac_reel_t3423/431, and Exhibits 23A to 23JJ, From Director to Grant, 649–738, https://heritage.canadiana.ca/view/oocihm.lac_reel_t3423/649. For the MI5 files, see TNA, KV 2/1427, Corby Case (vol. I), part 1. Telegrams from Ottawa to Moscow, s. 70–95, part 2. Telegrams from Moscow to Ottawa, ss. 96–107.

42 LAC, RG33-62, Agents of a Foreign Power fonds, Reel T-1368, Gouzenko testimony, 140–1, https://heritage.canadiana.ca/view/oocihm.lac_reel_t1368/201.

43 LAC, RG33-62, Agents of a Foreign Power fonds, Reel T-1368, Gouzenko testimony, 132, https://heritage.canadiana.ca/view/oocihm.lac_reel_t1368/193.

44 LAC, RG33-62, Agents of a Foreign Power fonds, Reel T-1368, Gouzenko testimony, 123, https://heritage.canadiana.ca/view/oocihm.lac_reel_t1368/184.

45 For a detailed account of the nomenclature and evolution of Soviet security and espionage organizations, see "Appendix No. 3 – Espionage Organizations of the USSR between 1918 and March 1954, in Commonwealth of Australia," *Report of the Royal Commission on Espionage* (Sydney: Government Printer for New South Wales, 1955), 430–3.

46 LAC, RG33-62, Agents of a Foreign Power fonds, Reel T-1368, Gouzenko testimony, 125, https://heritage.canadiana.ca/view/oocihm.lac_reel_t1368/186.

47 LAC, RG33-62, Agents of a Foreign Power fonds, Reel T-1368, Gouzenko testimony, 126, https://heritage.canadiana.ca/view/oocihm.lac_reel_t1368/187.

48 For a speculative account of why Stalin directed the dissolution of the Third International, see Robert H. McNeal, "The Legacy of the Comintern," *International Journal* 21, no. 2 (1966): 199–204. See also TNA, CAB 79-52-6, Meeting with Directors of Intelligence, "The Spread of Communism Throughout the World and the Extent of Its Direction from Moscow," Report by the Joint Intelligence Sub-Committee, JIC (46)70(O) (Final), 23 September 1946 (Limited Circulation), 61–2. On the fate of the records of the Comintern, see Kerry Taylor, "The Comintern Archives, Moscow," *Labour History* 64 (1993): 139.

49 LAC, RG33-62, Agents of a Foreign Power fonds, Reel T-1368, Gouzenko testimony, 80, https://heritage.canadiana.ca/view/oocihm.lac_reel_t1368/142. Captain Georgi Gourshkov (Chester) was nominally Zabotin's chauffeur. TNA, KV 2/1428, "Soviet Espionage in Canada," 23.

50 LAC, RG33-62, Agents of a Foreign Power fonds, Reel T-1368, Gouzenko testimony, 59, https://heritage.canadiana.ca/view/oocihm.lac_reel_t1368/121. For the "mail list," see LAC, RG33-62, Agents of a Foreign Power fonds, Reel T-3423, Exhibit 16A, Record of the Materials Sent, 254–61, https://heritage.canadiana.ca/view/oocihm.lac_reel_t3423/254.

51 LAC, RG33-62, Agents of a Foreign Power fonds, Reel T-1368, Gouzenko testimony, 59, https://heritage.canadiana.ca/view/oocihm.lac_reel_t1368/121.

52 LAC, RG33-62, Agents of a Foreign Power fonds, Reel T-1368, Gouzenko testimony, 60–2, https://heritage.canadiana.ca/view/oocihm.lac_reel_t1368/122

53 LAC, RG33-62, Agents of a Foreign Power fonds, Reel T-3423, Exhibit 16A, Record of the Materials Sent, nos. 109 and 110, 254, https://heritage.canadiana.ca/view/oocihm.lac_reel_t3423/254.

54 LAC, RG33-62, Agents of a Foreign Power fonds, Reel T-1368, Igor Gouzenko testimony, 63, https://heritage.canadiana.ca/view/oocihm.lac_reel_t1368/125.

55 LAC, RG33-62, Agents of a Foreign Power fonds, Reel T-1368, Gouzenko testimony, 65, https://heritage.canadiana.ca/view/oocihm.lac_reel_t1368/127.
56 LAC, RG33-62, Agents of a Foreign Power fonds, Reel T-1368, Gouzenko testimony, 66–7, https://heritage.canadiana.ca/view/oocihm.lac_reel_t1368/129.
57 LAC, RG33-62, Agents of a Foreign Power fonds, Reel T-3423, Exhibit 16A, Record of the Materials Sent, no. 175, 258, https://heritage.canadiana.ca/view/oocihm.lac_reel_t3423/258.
58 LAC, RG33-62, Agents of a Foreign Power fonds, Reel T-1368, Gouzenko testimony, 68–9, https://heritage.canadiana.ca/view/oocihm.lac_reel_t1368/130.
59 LAC, RG33-62, Agents of a Foreign Power fonds, Reel T-1368, Gouzenko testimony, 71, https://heritage.canadiana.ca/view/oocihm.lac_reel_t1368/133.
60 LAC, RG33-62, Agents of a Foreign Power fonds, Reel T-1368, Gouzenko testimony, 70, https://heritage.canadiana.ca/view/oocihm.lac_reel_t1368/132.
61 LAC, RG33-62, Agents of a Foreign Power fonds, Reel T-3423, Exhibit 16A, Record of the Materials Sent, no. 180, 259, https://heritage.canadiana.ca/view/oocihm.lac_reel_t3423/259.
62 LAC, RG33-62, Agents of a Foreign Power fonds, Reel T-3423, Exhibit 19B, File marked Frank, "Translation of text covered by note," 407, https://heritage.canadiana.ca/view/oocihm.lac_reel_t3423/407. For Gouzenko's commentary on Nightingale, see LAC, RG33-62, Agents of a Foreign Power fonds, Reel T-1368, Gouzenko testimony, 110–11, https://heritage.canadiana.ca/view/oocihm.lac_reel_t1368/171.
63 LAC, RG33-62, Agents of a Foreign Power fonds, Reel T-3423, Exhibit 19C, File marked Frank, To Sam for Shugar, Assignment no. 1, 16.12.45, 419, https://heritage.canadiana.ca/view/oocihm.lac_reel_t3423/419. For Gouzenko's testimony on this document, see LAC, RG33-62, Agents of a Foreign Power fonds, Reel T-1368, Gouzenko testimony, 99, 101, https://heritage.canadiana.ca/view/oocihm.lac_reel_t1368/161.
64 On Rogov, see TNA, KV 2/1428, "Soviet Espionage in Canada," 22.
65 LAC, RG33-62, Agents of a Foreign Power fonds, Reel T-3423, Exhibit 17H, File marked "Back," Course of Meetings, 327, https://heritage.canadiana.ca/view/oocihm.lac_reel_t3423/327. For Gouzenko's testimony on "Back" and this document, see LAC, RG33-62, Agents of a Foreign Power fonds, Reel T-1368, Gouzenko testimony, 86–7, https://heritage.canadiana.ca/view/oocihm.lac_reel_t1368/148.
66 LAC, RG33-62, Agents of a Foreign Power fonds, Reel T-3423, Exhibit 17B, File marked "Back," Scheme of the Group "Research," 318,

https://heritage.canadiana.ca/view/oocihm.lac_reel_t3423/318. For Gouzenko's testimony on "Back" and this document, see LAC, RG33-62, Agents of a Foreign Power fonds, Reel T-1368, Gouzenko testimony, 84–6, https://heritage.canadiana.ca/view/oocihm.lac_reel_t1368/1170.

67 LAC, RG33-62, Agents of a Foreign Power fonds, Reel T-1368, Gordon Lunan (Lunan) testimony, 1099–1102, https://heritage.canadiana.ca/view/oocihm.lac_reel_t1368/1159.

68 LAC, RG33-62, Agents of a Foreign Power fonds, Reel T-3423, Exhibit 18D, File marked "Back," Assignment for Badeau, no. 3, Given through Back 6.8.45, 339, https://heritage.canadiana.ca/view/oocihm.lac_reel_t3423/339.

69 LAC, RG33-62, Agents of a Foreign Power fonds, Reel T-3423, Exhibit 17H, File marked "Back," Course of Meetings, 327, https://heritage.canadiana.ca/view/oocihm.lac_reel_t3423/327. For Gouzenko's testimony about these payments, see LAC, RG33-62, Agents of a Foreign Power fonds, Reel T-1368, Gouzenko testimony, 93–4, https://heritage.canadiana.ca/view/oocihm.lac_reel_t1368/155.

70 LAC, RG33-62, Agents of a Foreign Power fonds, Reel T-1368, Gouzenko testimony, 73–4, https://heritage.canadiana.ca/view/oocihm.lac_reel_t1368/135.

71 TNA, KV 2/1428, "Soviet Espionage in Canada," 2. Repeated in LAC, RG 33 62, T-1368, Gouzenko testimony, 360, https://heritage.canadiana.ca/view/oocihm.lac_reel_t1368/410.

72 Mikhail Abramovich Milstein, *Сквозь годы войн и нищеты* (Through the years of wars and poverty) (Moscow: Itar-Tass, 2000), 84–5.

Chapter 4: PC 6444

1 On this subject see Peter Desbarats, "The Independence of Public Inquiries: Dixon V. Canada," *Alberta Law Review* 36, no. 1 (1997): 252–7.

2 LAC, Diaries of WLMK, 16 February 1946, 2.

3 LAC, Diaries of WLMK, 20 February 1946, 1.

4 TNA, KV 2/1426, RCMP to Hollis, no. 103, 7.2.46, s. 124a.; TNA, KV 2/1426, no. 401, Hollis to RCMP, 6.2.46, s. 123a.

5 TNA, KV 2/1426, MacDonald to Cadogan, no. 119, 11.2.46, s. 129a.

6 TNA, KV 2/1426, Holmes to Cadogan, no. 122, 13.2.46, s. 131a.

7 TNA, KV 2/1426, MacDonald to Cadogan, no. 126, 13.2.46, s. 131a.

8 TNA, KV 2/1426, MacDonald to Cadogan, no. 133, 13.2.46, s. 131a.

9 Louis St. Laurent in House of Commons, *Debates*, 19 March 1946, 89.

10 LAC, RG 33-62, T-3433, Agents of a Foreign Power fonds, R.C. 11, Correspondence – Commission Counsel to Commissioners and Minister of Justice, E.K. Williams and Gerald Fauteux to The Rt. Hon. Louis

St. Laurent, Re: Royal Commission – P.C. 411, 14 February 1946, 1, 940, https://heritage.canadiana.ca/view/oocihm.lac_reel_t3433/940.

11 LAC, RG33-62, Agents of a Foreign Power fonds, Reel T-3433, To Louis St. Laurent, Minister of Justice, 14 February 1946, 940, https://heritage.canadiana.ca/view/oocihm.lac_reel_t3433/940.

12 LAC, RG 33-62, T-1368, Agents of a Foreign Power fonds, Commissioner Taschereau, 147–8, https://heritage.canadiana.ca/view/oocihm.lac_reel_t1368/208.

13 LAC, RG 33-62, T-1368, Agents of a Foreign Power fonds, Commissioner Kellock, 149, https://heritage.canadiana.ca/view/oocihm.lac_reel_t1368/210.

14 LAC, RG 33-62, T-3433, Agents of a Foreign Power fonds, R.C. 11, Correspondence – Commission Counsel to Commissioners and Minister of Justice, E.K. Williams and Gerald Fauteux to The Rt. Hon. Louis St. Laurent, Re: Royal Commission – P.C. 411, 14 February 1946, 1, 940, https://heritage.canadiana.ca/view/oocihm.lac_reel_t3433/940. Although arrangements for Kathleen Willsher's arrest had been made in October, her name did not appear on that list because Malcolm MacDonald was seeking approval from London for Willsher's detention under PC 6444. TNA, KV 2/1426, MacDonald to Cadogan, no. 134, 13.2.46, s. 134a.

15 *The Report of the Royal Commission* (*Final Report*), 671, https://publications.gc.ca/site/eng/9.699909/publication.html.

16 TNA, KV 2/1425, Wrong to Robertson, no. CXG. 491, 8.9.45, s. 60A.

17 LAC, Diaries of WLMK,15 February 1946, 1.

18 LAC, Diaries of WLMK, 15 February 1946, 1.

19 Darling J. in *Shipton's Case* (1915) 3 K.B. 676 at 684 as cited in *The Report of the Royal Commission* (*Final Report*), 678, https://publications.gc.ca/site/eng/9.699909/publication.html.

20 Library Archives Canada, J. King Gordon Papers, MG 30, C241, vol. 70/15, "Report of a Fact-Finding Committee," Civil Liberties Association of Ottawa, 1.

21 See P.C. 6444, https://heritage.canadiana.ca/view/oocihm.lac_reel_t3423/103.

22 For the change to 7 a.m., see Diaries of WLMK, 15 February 1946, 1, and TNA, KV 2, 1426, Holmes to Cadogan, no. 142, 14.2.46, s. 137a. For the arrests at 3 a.m., see TNA, KV 2, 1426, Holmes to Cadogan, no. 138, 14.2.46, s. 135A.

23 LAC, Gordon Papers, Report, 1.

24 TNA, KV 2/1421, MacDonald to Cadogan, no. 150, 16.2.46, s. 59 A.

25 TNA, KV 2 1422, MacDonald to Cadogan, no. 198, 22.2.46, s. 71a.

26 TNA, KV 2 1422, Holmes to Cadogan, no. 240, 28.2.46, s. 83a.

27 TNA, KV 2/1426, Wrong to Robertson, no. 400, 6.2.46, s. 120a and unnumbered, 4.2.46, s. 115a.
28 LAC, RG33-62, Agents of a Foreign Power fonds, Reel T-3433, Exhibit 5, Malcolm MacDonald, Office of the High Commissioner for the United Kingdon to The Right Hon. L.S. St. Laurent, Minister of Justice, 14 February 1946, http://heritage.canadiana.ca/view/M.P., oocihm.lac_reel_t3433/672.
29 *The Report of the Royal Commission* (*Final Report*), 227, https://publications.gc.ca/site/eng/9.699909/publication.html.
30 TNA, KV 2/1426, MacDonald to Cadogan, no. 148, 15.2.46, s. 142a. On Willsher's arrest, see Clyde Sanger, *Malcolm Macdonald: Bringing an End to Empire* (Montreal & Kingston: McGill-Queen's University Press, 1995), 249, and Malcolm MacDonald to the Minister of Justice, 14 February 1946, LAC, RG33-62, Agents of a Foreign Power fonds, Reel T-3433, 672, https://heritage.canadiana.ca/view/oocihm.lac_reel_t3433/672.
31 TNA, KV 2/1426, MacDonald to Cadogan, TOP SECRET, no. 133, 13.2.46, s. 133a.
32 TNA, KV 2/1426, Robertson to Wrong, no. 109, 8.2.46, s. 126a.
33 In late January 1946, Lunan had approached Paul Martin with an offer to arrange a meeting with Soviet diplomat Andrey Vyshinsky. TNA, KV 2/1426, Wrong to Robertson, script, undated, s. 130a.
34 Merrily Weisbord, *The Strangest Dream: Canadian Communists, the Spy Trials, and the Cold War* (Toronto: Lester & Orpen Dennys, 1983), 146.
35 On Vitali Pavlov's activities as NKVD chief in Canada under cover of his nominal designation as second secretary in the Soviet embassy, see "Vitali Pavlov" in *The Report of the Royal Commission* (*Final Report*), passim, 20–6, https://publications.gc.ca/site/eng/9.699909/publication.html.
36 LAC, WLMK, Diaries of WLMK, 15 February 1946, 1.
37 TNA, KV 2/1426, MacDonald to Cadogan, no. 144, 15.2.46, s. 140a.
38 TNA, KV 2/1421, MacDonald to Cadogan, no. 150, 16.2.46, s. 59A.
39 "Prime Minister Issues Statement on Espionage," *Globe & Mail*, 16 February 1946, 1. For a copy of the original draft, see TNA, KV 2/1426, Cadogan from MacDonald, Top Secret, nos. 144, 145,146, 15.2.46, s. 140a.
40 *Winnipeg Tribune*, 18 February 1946, 1. MacDonald reported this to London the same day. TNA, KV 2/1421, MacDonald to Cadogan, no. 160,18.2.46, s. 61A. Lester Pearson also reported that American newspapers had taken notice of the Ottawa disclosure. LAC, RG33-62, Agents of a Foreign Power fonds, Reel T-3434, Canadian Ambassador to the United States to Secretary of State for External Affairs, Canada, 19 February 1946, WA-828, 397, https://heritage.canadiana.ca/view/oocihm.lac_reel_t3434/397.
41 LAC, Diaries of WLMK, 20 February 1946, 1.
42 TNA, KV 2/1421, MacDonald to Cadogan, no. 165, 19.2.46, s. 63A.

43 Sonia Orwell and Ian Angus, *The Collected Essays, Journalism and Letters of George Orwell*, vol. 4: *In Front of your Nose* (London: Secker & Warburg, 1968), 6. In the US Walter Winchell popularized the term "Cold War." Jacqueline Foertsch, *American Culture in the 1940s* (Edinburgh: Edinburgh University Press, 2008), 55–6.
44 LAC, RG33-62, Agents of a Foreign Power fonds, Reel T-3434, The Canadian Ambassador, Paris to the Secretary of State for External Affairs, no. 68 (Confidential), 16 February 1946, 375, https://heritage.canadiana.ca/view/oocihm.lac_reel_t3434/375.
45 LAC, RG33-62, Agents of a Foreign Power fonds, Reel T-3434, "The High Commissioner for Canada in Great Britain to the Secretary of State for External Affairs," Canada (signed Massey), no. 473, 16 February 1946, 379, https://heritage.canadiana.ca/view/oocihm.lac_reel_t3434/379.
46 See the espionage fiction of Edward Phillips Oppenheim, including *The Kingdom of the Blind* (1917) and *The Great Impersonation* (1920). William A.S. Sarjeant, "Edward Phillip Oppenheim," *Oxford Dictionary of National Biography* (Oxford: Oxford University Press, 2022), https://doi.org/10.1093/ref:odnb/35319.
47 LAC, RG33-62, Agents of a Foreign Power fonds, Reel T-3434, "The High Commissioner for Canada in Great Britain to the Secretary of State for External Affairs, Canada, no. 481, 18 February 1946, 376–7, https://heritage.canadiana.ca/view/oocihm.lac_reel_t3434/376.
48 *Reynolds News* was "an organ of the Left" published by the Co-operative Press Co., a subsidiary of the Co-operative Society. Dennis Griffiths, ed., *The Encyclopedia of the British Press 1422–1992* (New York: St. Martin's Press, 1992), 485.
49 The *Daily Herald* was owned in part by the British Trades Union Congress. Griffiths, *Encyclopedia of the British Press*, 179–80.
50 Massey almost certainly meant the mass-circulation *Daily Express*, owned by Lord Beaverbrook. On this publication, see Griffiths, *Encyclopedia of the British Press*, 183.
51 LAC, RG33-62, Agents of a Foreign Power fonds, Reel T-3434, "The High Commissioner for Canada in Great Britain to the Secretary of State for External affairs," Canada, no. 481, 18 February 1946, 376–7, https://heritage.canadiana.ca/view/oocihm.lac_reel_t3434/376.
52 LAC, RG33-62, Agents of a Foreign Power fonds, Reel T-3434, "The High Commissioner for Canada in Great Britain to the Secretary of State for External Affairs, Canada SECRET," no. 505, 20 February 1946, 402, https://heritage.canadiana.ca/view/oocihm.lac_reel_t3434/402.
53 On Martin's complicated relationship with Stalin's Soviet Union, see Adrian Smith, "Kingsley (Basil) Martin," *Oxford Dictionary of National Biography*, https://doi.org/10.1093/ref:odnb/34902.

54 LAC, RG33-62, Agents of a Foreign Power fonds, Reel T-3434, "The High Commissioner for Canada in Great Britain to the Secretary of State for External Affairs, Canada, SECRET," no. 526, 22 February 1946, 421, https://heritage.canadiana.ca/view/oocihm.lac_reel_t3434/421.
55 Christopher Andrew, *Defend the Realm: The Authorized History of MI5* (New York: Alfred Knopf, 2009), 344.
56 British security services considered intelligence matters in Commonwealth counties to be "domestic" and therefore the responsibility of MI5. Andrew, *Defend the Realm*, 349. Because of Hollis's alleged mishandling of the Gouzenko file, British journalist Chapman Pincher later falsely accused Hollis (who subsequently became director-general of MI5) of being a Soviet agent. See Haden B. Peake, "The Intelligence Officer's Bookshelf," *Studies in Intelligence*, March 2008, 81; and David Levy, "The Roger Hollis Case Revisited," *International Journal of Intelligence and CounterIntelligence* 32, no. 1 (2019): 146–58.
57 Pearson served as ambassador from 1 January 1945 to the summer of 1946. On his tenure in Washington, see John English, *Shadow of Heaven: The Life of Lester Pearson*, vol. 1: *1897–1948* (Toronto: Lester & Orpen Dennys, 1989), 253–98.
58 LAC, RG33-62, Agents of a Foreign Power fonds, Reel T-3434, Canadian Ambassador to the United States to Secretary of State for External Affairs, Canada, CONFIDENTIAL, 18 February 1946, WA-826, 382–385, https://heritage.canadiana.ca/view/oocihm.lac_reel_t3434/382.
59 This almost certainly referred to Andrei Shevchenko, a Soviet-educated engineer, described by David Dallin as "perhaps the most inept and grotesque spy in the history of espionage." Dallin, *Soviet Espionage* (New Haven: Yale University Press, 1955), 450–3. On 17 February 1946, Pearson turned his sights on the US State Department and a claim that "a Russian agent named Shimishenko had been employed for some time in USA, was known to FBI who had been forced to allow him to leave the country in spite of information against him." Malcolm MacDonald made inquiries and reported that the FBI "presume Pearson was referring to Andrei Nanovich Schavchenko, for some time official of Soviet Purchasing Commission ... in USA." TNA, KV 2/1422, MacDonald to Sargent, no. 314, 7.3.46, s. 115A. On Shevchenko, see also John Earl Haynes, *Index and Concordance to Alexander Vassiliev's Notebooks and Soviet Cables Deciphered by the National Security Agency's Venona Project*, revised 11/1/2014, "Raina, Andrey Ivanovich: Soviet intelligence officer. Used the pseudonym Andrey Shevchenko when in the United States in WWII," 26, https://www.wilsoncenter.org/article/venona-project-and-vassiliev-notebooks-index-and-concordance.
60 On the fictional creation of "Alfred Adamson," see Ann Hegedorn, *Sleeper Agent: The Atomic Spy in America Who Got Away* (New York: Simon and Shuster, 2022).

61 LAC, RG33-62, Agents of a Foreign Power fonds, Reel T-3434, Canadian Ambassador to the United States to Secretary of State for External Affairs, Canada, CONFIDENTIAL, 18 February 1946, WA-826, 384, https://heritage.canadiana.ca/view/oocihm.lac_reel_t3434/384.

62 LAC, RG33-62, Agents of a Foreign Power fonds, Reel T-3434, Canadian Ambassador to the United States to Secretary of State for External Affairs, Canada, CONFIDENTIAL, 18 February 1946, WA-826, 384, https://heritage.canadiana.ca/view/oocihm.lac_reel_t3434/384. Pearson shared the same information in Canada through a contribution to the *Globe & Mail*. Drew Pearson, "Soviet Agent in Custody Says Writer," *Globe & Mail*, 16 February 1946, 1.

63 LAC, RG33-62, Agents of a Foreign Power fonds, Reel T-3434, Canadian Ambassador to the United States to Secretary of State for External Affairs, Canada, CONFIDENTIAL, 18 February 1946, WA-826, 385, https://heritage.canadiana.ca/view/oocihm.lac_reel_t3434/385.

64 LAC, RG33-62, Agents of a Foreign Power fonds, Reel T-3434, Canadian Ambassador to the United States to Secretary of State for External Affairs, Canada, Confidential, 20 February 1946, WA-866, 411, https://heritage.canadiana.ca/view/oocihm.lac_reel_t3434/41.

65 On Bridges, see Spencer C. Tucker, ed., *The Encyclopedia of the Korean War: A Political, Social, and Military History*, 2nd ed, vol. 1 (Santa Barbara: ABC-CLIO, 2010), 101.

66 LAC, RG33-62, Agents of a Foreign Power fonds, Reel T-3434, Canadian Ambassador to the United States to Secretary of State for External Affairs, Canada, CONFIDENTIAL, 18 February 1946, WA-826, 385, https://heritage.canadiana.ca/view/oocihm.lac_reel_t3434/385.

67 Cedric W. Foster (1900–75), American Heritage Center, University of Wyoming, https://archiveswest.orbiscascade.org/ark:80444/xv577862.

68 LAC, RG33-62, Agents of a Foreign Power fonds, Reel T-3434, Canadian Ambassador to the United States to Secretary of State for External Affairs, Canada, CONFIDENTIAL, 18 February 1946, WA-824, 387, https://heritage.canadiana.ca/view/oocihm.lac_reel_t3434/387.

69 On his journalistic career, see "Bill Cunningham of Boston Herald," *New York Times*, 18 April 1960, 29.

70 LAC, RG33-62, Agents of a Foreign Power fonds, Reel T-3434, Canadian Ambassador to the United States to Secretary of State for External Affairs, Canada, CONFIDENTIAL, 18 February 1946, WA-824, 388, https://heritage.canadiana.ca/view/oocihm.lac_reel_t3434/388.

71 On Childs, see Wolfgang Saxon, "Marquis W. Childs Is Dead at 87; Won a Pulitzer for Commentary," *New York Times*, 2 July 1990, 52.

72 LAC, RG33-62, Agents of a Foreign Power fonds, Reel T-3434, Canadian Ambassador to the United States to Secretary of State for External Affairs,

Canada, 20 February 1946, WA-859, 407, https://heritage.canadiana.ca/view/oocihm.lac_reel_t3434/407.

73 Paul Milkman, *PM: A New Deal for Journalism, 1940–1948* (New Brunswick, NJ: Rutgers University Press, 1997).

74 LAC, RG33-62, Agents of a Foreign Power fonds, Reel T-3434, Canadian Ambassador to the United States to Secretary of State for External Affairs, Canada, 20 February 1946, WA-859, 407, https://heritage.canadiana.ca/view/oocihm.lac_reel_t3434/407.

75 On Eid, see "Lief Eid, 67, Correspondent for NBC News until 1966," *New York Times*, 30 March 1976, 28.

76 LAC, RG33-62, Agents of a Foreign Power fonds, Reel T-3434, Canadian Ambassador to the United States to Secretary of State for External Affairs, Canada, CONFIDENTIAL, 18 February 1946, WA-824, 387, https://heritage.canadiana.ca/view/oocihm.lac_reel_t3434/387.

77 LAC, RG33-62, Agents of a Foreign Power fonds, Reel T-3434, Canadian Ambassador to the United States to Secretary of State for External Affairs, Canada, CONFIDENTIAL, 18 February 1946, WA-824, 387, https://heritage.canadiana.ca/view/oocihm.lac_reel_t3434/387.

78 Stoddard was described by his biographer as a writer who "dramatically set forth the dire perils of the coloured races, biological degeneration, and revolutionary movements which supposedly organized the immense residue of inferior humans into a grand assault against civilization." James Robert Backman, "Thomas Lothrop Stoddard: The Bio-sociological Battle for Civilization," PhD diss., University of Rochester, 1967, 10, https://www.proquest.com/dissertations-theses/theodore-lothrop-stoddard-bio-sociological-battle/docview/288139825/se-2.

79 LAC, RG33-62, Agents of a Foreign Power fonds, Reel T-3434, Canadian Ambassador to the United States to Secretary of State for External Affairs, Canada, CONFIDENTIAL, 18 February 1946, WA-824, 388, https://heritage.canadiana.ca/view/oocihm.lac_reel_t3434/388.

80 See Dwayne Ryan Menezes and Heather N. Nicol, eds., *The North American Arctic: Themes in Regional Security* (London: University College London Press, 2019), 26. For a detailed account, see Dr. J.T. Wilson, "Exercise Musk-Ox, 1946," *Polar Record* 5, nos. 33–34 (1947): 14–26.

81 Pearson may have been referring to the case of Seattle-based Soviet naval lieutenant Nikolai Gregorevitch Redin. See Daniel J. Leab, "The Red Menace and Justice in the Pacific Northwest: The Trial of the Soviet Naval Lt. Nikolai Gregorevitch Redin," *Pacific Northwest Quarterly* 87, no. 2 (1996): 82–93.

82 LAC, RG33-62, Agents of a Foreign Power fonds, Reel T-3434, Canadian Ambassador to the United States to Secretary of State for External Affairs, Canada, CONFIDENTIAL, 18 February 1946, WA-824, 388, https://heritage.canadiana.ca/view/oocihm.lac_reel_t3434/388.

83 LAC, RG33-62, Agents of a Foreign Power fonds, Reel T-3434, Canadian Ambassador to the United States to Secretary of State for External Affairs, Canada, 18 February 1946, WA-815, 392, https://heritage.canadiana.ca/view/oocihm.lac_reel_t3434/392.

84 LAC, RG33-62, Agents of a Foreign Power fonds, Reel T-3434, Canadian Ambassador to the United States to Secretary of State for External Affairs, Canada, Confidential, 20 February 1946, WA-866, 409, https://heritage.canadiana.ca/view/oocihm.lac_reel_t3434/409.

85 LAC, RG33-62, Agents of a Foreign Power fonds, Reel T-3434, Canadian Ambassador to the United States to Secretary of State for External Affairs, Canada, 19 February 1946, WA-839, 399, https://heritage.canadiana.ca/view/oocihm.lac_reel_t3434/399.

86 LAC, RG33-62, Agents of a Foreign Power fonds, Reel T-3434, Canadian Ambassador to the United States to Secretary of State for External Affairs, Canada, 20 February 1946, WA-859, 404, https://heritage.canadiana.ca/view/oocihm.lac_reel_t3434/404.

87 On Davies, see "Joseph E. Davies, Diplomat, Is Dead," *New York Times*, 10 May 1958, 21.

88 LAC, RG33-62, Agents of a Foreign Power fonds, Reel T-3434, Canadian Ambassador to the United States to Secretary of State for External Affairs, Canada, 20 February 1946, WA-859, 405, https://heritage.canadiana.ca/view/oocihm.lac_reel_t3434/405.

89 LAC, RG33-62, Agents of a Foreign Power fonds, Reel T-3434, Canadian Ambassador to the United States to Secretary of State for External Affairs, Canada, Confidential, 20 February 1946, WA-866, 411, https://heritage.canadiana.ca/view/oocihm.lac_reel_t3434/411.

90 LAC, RG33-62, Agents of a Foreign Power fonds, Reel T-3434, Canadian Ambassador to the United States to Secretary of State for External Affairs, Canada, Confidential, 20 February 1946, WA-866, 412, https://heritage.canadiana.ca/view/oocihm.lac_reel_t3434/412.

91 LAC, RG33-62, Agents of a Foreign Power fonds, Reel T-3434, Canadian Ambassador to the United States to Secretary of State for External Affairs, Canada, Confidential, 20 February 1946, WA-866, 411, https://heritage.canadiana.ca/view/oocihm.lac_reel_t3434/411.

92 David Lawrence was a conservative political columnist who wrote a column syndicated at one time in over three hundred newspapers. Beginning in 1946, he was the founding editor of *US News and World Report*. "David Lawrence, the Columnist, Is Dead," *New York Times*, 12 February 1973, 30.

93 LAC, RG33-62, Agents of a Foreign Power fonds, Reel T-3434, Canadian Ambassador to the United States to Secretary of State for External Affairs, Canada, Confidential, 20 February 1946, WA-866, 410, https://heritage.canadiana.ca/view/oocihm.lac_reel_t3434/410.

94 LAC, RG33-62, Agents of a Foreign Power fonds, Reel T-3434, Canadian Ambassador to the United States to Secretary of State for External Affairs, Canada, Confidential, 20 February 1946, WA-866, 409, https://heritage.canadiana.ca/view/oocihm.lac_reel_t3434/409.
95 Mikhail Abramovich Milstein, *Сквозь годы войн и нищеты* (Through the years of wars and poverty) (Moscow: Itar-Tass, 2000), 92 (hereafter cited as "Through the years").
96 Milstein, Through the years, 92.
97 See Odd Arne Westad, *The Cold War: A World History* (New York: Basic Books, 2017), 41, 48–9.
98 See, for example, Raymond L. Garthoff, *Soviet Leaders and Intelligence: Assessing the American Adversary During the Cold War* (Washington, DC: Georgetown University Press, 2015), 96–7.

Chapter 5: Before the Royal Commission I

1 Kellock observed that the "governing principle is stated by Lord Sumner in *Ibrahim v. The King*, [1914] A.C. 599, 609–10." M.L. Friedland, *Cases and Materials on Criminal Law*, 5th ed. (Toronto: University of Toronto Press, 1978), 88.
2 Later, during the interrogation of David Shugar, Gérald Fauteux quoted Shugar's response to a question concerning a conversation Shugar had with Sam Carr. LAC, RG33-62, Agents of a Foreign Power fonds, Reel T-1369, Commission counsel Fauteux, 2058, https://heritage.canadiana.ca/view/oocihm.lac_reel_t1369/67.
3 C.W. Harvison, *The Horsemen* (Toronto: McClelland & Stewart, 1967), 157.
4 TNA, KV 2/1421, MacDonald to Cadogan, no. 161, 18.2.46, s. 60A.
5 TNA, KV 2/1421, MacDonald to Cadogan, no. 162, 18.2.46, s. 60A.
6 TNA, KV 2/1422, MacDonald to Cadogan, no. 186, 21.2.46, s. 70a.
7 TNA, KV 2/1421, MacDonald to Cadogan, no. 179, 20.2.46, s. 67A.
8 TNA, KV 2/1421, MacDonald to Cadogan, no. 164, 18.2.46, s. 60a.
9 TNA, KV 2/1421, MacDonald to Cadogan, no. 167, 19.2.46, s. 62A.
10 TNA, KV 2/1422, MacDonald to Cadogan, no. 187, 21.2.46, s. 71a.
11 TNA, KV 2/1421, MacDonald to Cadogan, no. 163, 18.2.46, s. 60a.
12 TNA, KV 2/1422, MacDonald to Cadogan, no. 186, 21.2.46, s. 70a.
13 TNA, KV 2/1422, MacDonald to Cadogan, no. 186, 21.2.46, s. 70a.
14 TNA, KV 2/1422, MacDonald to Cadogan, no. 197, 22.2.46, s. 71a.
15 TNA, KV 2/1421, MacDonald to Cadogan, no. 161, 18.2.46, s. 60a.
16 TNA, KV 2/1421, MacDonald to Cadogan, no. 178, 20.2.46, s. 67A.
17 TNA, KV 2/1421, MacDonald to Cadogan, no. 150, 16.2.46, s. 59A
18 TNA, KV 2/1421, MacDonald to Cadogan, no. 169, 18.2.46, s. 62A.

19 TNA, KV 2/1421, MacDonald to Cadogan, no. 181, 20.2.46, s. 67A.
20 TNA, KV 2/1421, MacDonald to Cadogan, no. 163, 18.2.46, s. 60a.
21 TNA, KV 2/1421, MacDonald to Cadogan, no. 178, 20.2.46, s. 67A.
22 TNA, KV 2/1421, MacDonald to Cadogan, no. 167, 19.2.46, s. 62A.
23 TNA, KV 2/1422, MacDonald to Cadogan, no. 198, 22.2.46, s. 71a.
24 TNA, KV 2/1421, MacDonald to Cadogan, no. 164, 18.2.46, s. 60a.
25 TNA, KV 2/1422, Holmes to Cadogan, no. 229, 27.2.46, s. 82a.
26 TNA, KV 2/1422, Holmes to Cadogan, no. 240, 28.2.46, s. 83a.
27 TNA, KV 2/1422, Holmes to Sargent, no. 283, 3.3.46, s. 99a. At the end of February 1946 Sir Orme Sargent, a career diplomat (and growing Russophobe), replaced Sir Alexander Cadogan as British undersecretary of state for foreign relations. In February 1946 Cadogan was appointed Britain's permanent representative to the UN. On Sargent, see Ritchie Ovendale, "Sir (Harold) Orme Garton Sargent," *Oxford Dictionary of National Biography*, https://doi.org/10.1093/ref:odnb/35948.
28 TNA, KV 2/1422, MacDonald to Cadogan, no. 203, 23.2.46, s. 74a.
29 The portion is marked "group mut." (short for "group mutilated"), meaning that words are missing because the code was mutilated at that spot.
30 TNA, KV 2/1422, Holmes to Sargent, no. 253, 1.3.46, s. 87a.
31 TNA, KV 2/1421, MacDonald to Cadogan, no. 168, 19.2.46, s. 62A.
32 TNA, KV 2/1422, MacDonald to Cadogan, Nos. 196–7, 22.2.46, s. 71a.
33 TNA, KV 2/1422, Holmes to Sargent, no. 282, 3.3.46, s. 99a.
34 LAC, RG33-62, Agents of a Foreign Power fonds, Reel T-1368, Emma Woikin testimony, 588, https://heritage.canadiana.ca/view/oocihm.lac_reel_t1368/641.
35 June Callwood, *Emma* (Toronto: Stoddart, 1984), 48.
36 LAC, RG33-62, Agents of a Foreign Power fonds, Reel T-3424, Exhibit 81, "Emma Woikin, Application for Employment, Department of Foreign Affairs," 457, https://heritage.canadiana.ca/view/oocihm.lac_reel_t3424/457; Callwood, *Emma*, 73.
37 Callwood, *Emma*, 77–8.
38 LAC, RG33-62, Agents of a Foreign Power fonds, Reel T-1368, Gouzenko testimony, 68–9, https://heritage.canadiana.ca/view/oocihm.lac_reel_t1368/130.
39 LAC, RG33-62, Agents of a Foreign Power fonds, Reel T-1370, Gouzenko testimony, 5041, https://heritage.canadiana.ca/view/oocihm.lac_reel_t1370/1213.
40 LAC, RG33-62, Agents of a Foreign Power fonds, Reel T-1370, Gouzenko testimony, 5041, https://heritage.canadiana.ca/view/oocihm.lac_reel_t1370/1213.
41 Callwood, *Emma*, 109.

42 LAC, RG33-62, Agents of a Foreign Power fonds, T-1370, Gouzenko testimony, 5041, https://heritage.canadiana.ca/view/oocihm.lac_reel_t1370/1213.

43 The 1934 Named Doukhobor "Declaration of the Union of Spiritual Communities of Christ in Canada" declares, in only slightly veiled terms, a resistance to state demands. Because the communities are submitted only to God, "We … by this have liberated ourselves from the guardianship and power established by men." *Iskra: Voice of the Doukhobors*, September 2016, 5.

44 LAC, RG33-62, Agents of a Foreign Power fonds, Reel T-1368, Woikin testimony, 681–82, https://heritage.canadiana.ca/view/oocihm.lac_reel_t1368/735.

45 Callwood, *Emma*, 57–8, 63–6.

46 LAC, RG33-62, Agents of a Foreign Power fonds, T-1370, Gouzenko testimony, 5041, https://heritage.canadiana.ca/view/oocihm.lac_reel_t1370/1213.

47 LAC, RG33-62, Agents of a Foreign Power fonds, Reel T-1368, Woikin testimony, 596, https://heritage.canadiana.ca/view/oocihm.lac_reel_t1368/649.

48 LAC, RG33-62, Agents of a Foreign Power fonds, Reel T-1368, Woikin testimony, 594, https://heritage.canadiana.ca/view/oocihm.lac_reel_t1368/647.

49 LAC, RG33-62, Agents of a Foreign Power fonds, Reel T-1368, Gouzenko testimony, 234–5, https://heritage.canadiana.ca/view/oocihm.lac_reel_t1368/295.

50 LAC, RG33-62, Agents of a Foreign Power fonds, Reel T-1368, Stanislas Daley (Daley) testimony, 569–76, 585, https://heritage.canadiana.ca/view/oocihm.lac_reel_t1368/569.

51 LAC, RG33-62, Agents of a Foreign Power fonds, Reel T-1368, Woikin testimony, 608–11, 615, 622, https://heritage.canadiana.ca/view/oocihm.lac_reel_t1368/669.

52 LAC, RG33-62, Agents of a Foreign Power fonds, Reel T-1368, Woikin testimony, 645, https://heritage.canadiana.ca/view/oocihm.lac_reel_t1368/699.

53 LAC, RG33-62, Agents of a Foreign Power fonds, Reel T-1368, Woikin testimony, 620, https://heritage.canadiana.ca/view/oocihm.lac_reel_t1368/674.

54 LAC, RG33-62, Agents of a Foreign Power fonds, Reel T-3423, Exhibit 16A, Record of the Materials Sent, no. 175, copies of telegrams (10), forms (3), and photos (110), 258, https://heritage.canadiana.ca/view/oocihm.lac_reel_t3423/258.

55 LAC, RG33-62, Agents of a Foreign Power fonds, Reel T-1368, Daley testimony, 574, https://heritage.canadiana.ca/view/oocihm.lac_reel_t1368/627.

56 Kenneth O. Morgan, "Christopher Addison, first Viscount Addison (1869–1951), politician." *Oxford Dictionary of National Biography*, https://www.oxforddnb.com/view/10.1093/ref:odnb/9780198614128.001.0001/odnb-9780198614128-e-30342.

57 "Communists in Balkans Reported Seizing Power," *Globe & Mail*, 23 May 1945, 1.

58 "Mr. Churchill's Address Calling for United Effort for World Peace," *New York Times*, 6 March 1946, 4.

59 "Communists in Balkans Reported Seizing Power," *Globe & Mail*, 23 May 1945, 1.

60 Cyril E. Black, "The Start of the Cold War in Bulgaria: A Personal View," *Review of Politics* 41, no. 2 (1979): 170. See also Geoffrey Roberts, "Ideology, Calculation, and Improvisation: Spheres of Influence and Soviet Foreign Policy 1939–45," *Review of International Studies* 25 (1999): 655–73.

61 Black, "Start of the Cold War,"163–202.

62 Peter Weiler, "British Labour and the Cold War: The Foreign Policy of the Labour Governments, 1945–1951," *Journal of British Studies* 26, no. 1 (1987): 62–3.

63 "Plan Elections in Bulgaria," *Globe & Mail*, 18 June 1945, 7.

64 See, for example, "Regard Bulgaria as Test Ground of New Charter," *Globe & Mail*, 21 August 1945, 3.

65 LAC, RG33-62, Agents of a Foreign Power fonds, Reel T-3423, Exhibit 24B, From the Secretary of State for Dominion Affairs to the Secretary of State External Affairs Ottawa, 24 August 1945, 746–7, https://heritage.canadiana.ca/view/oocihm.lac_reel_t3423/746.

66 Sir Alvary Gascoigne was a member of the British foreign service for thirty-four years. In 1945 he was a British political representative in Hungary with the rank of minister. He was British ambassador to the Soviet Union at the time of Stalin's death in 1953. "Alvary Gascoigne, British Envoy, 76," *New York Times*, 21 April 1970, 43.

67 On Miklós and these developments, see Laszlo Borhi, *Hungary in the Cold War 1945–1956: Between the United States and the Soviet Union* (Budapest: Central European University Press, 2004), 33–6.

68 LAC, RG33-62, Agents of a Foreign Power fonds, Reel T-3423, Exhibit 24D, From The Secretary of State for Dominion Affairs to the Secretary of State External Affairs Ottawa, 31 August 1945, 754, https://heritage.canadiana.ca/view/oocihm.lac_reel_t3423/754.

69 The *Tito–Šubašić* agreements were the product of negotiations between Josip Tito, head of the Yugoslav partisans, and Ivan Šubašić, prime minister of the Yugoslav government in exile, concerning the creation of a coalition government in post–World War II Yugoslavia. See Hugh de Santis, "In Search of Yugoslavia: Anglo-American Policy and Policy-Making 1943–45," *Journal of Contemporary History* 16, no. 3 (1981): 541–63.

70 LAC, RG33-62, Agents of a Foreign Power fonds, Reel T-3423, Exhibit 24B, From the Secretary of State for Dominion Affairs to the Secretary of State External Affairs Ottawa, 24 August 1945, 746, https://heritage.canadiana.ca/view/oocihm.lac_reel_t3423/746.
71 Barbara Jelavich, *History of the Balkans: Twentieth Century* (Cambridge: Cambridge University Press, 1983), 269–70.
72 LAC, RG33-62, Agents of a Foreign Power fonds, Reel T-3423, Exhibit 24A, From the Secretary of State for Dominion Affairs to the Secretary of State External Affairs Ottawa, 24 August 1945, 743, https://heritage.canadiana.ca/view/oocihm.lac_reel_t3423/743. Addison referred to General Mikailovic, but meant Dragoljub "Draža" Mihailović, who had been made a general and appointed minister of war by the Yugoslav government-in-exile in 1942. L.S. Stavrianos, *The Balkans since 1453* (New York: Rinehart, 1959), 778.
73 "Chetniks" was "a Serbian term with revered historical associations. A Chetnik was literally a member of a Cheta or military detachment that had fought against the Turks in the nineteenth century." Stavrianos, *The Balkans since 1453*, 773.
74 de Santis, "In Search of Yugoslavia," 558–60.
75 LAC, RG33-62, Agents of a Foreign Power fonds, Reel T-3423, Exhibit 24B, From the Secretary of State for Dominion Affairs to the Secretary of State External Affairs Ottawa, 24 August 1945, 746, https://heritage.canadiana.ca/view/oocihm.lac_reel_t3423/746.
76 de Santis, "In Search of Yugoslavia," 541–63.
77 On this theme, see Barbara Jelavich, *History of the Balkans*, 322–5.
78 Geoffrey Roberts, "Stalin at the Tehran, Yalta, and Potsdam Conferences," *Journal of Cold War Studies* 9, no. 4 (2007): 35–6, https://www.jstor.org/stable/26926079.
79 LAC, RG33-62, Agents of a Foreign Power fonds, Reel T-3423, Exhibit 24C, From the Secretary of State for Dominion Affairs to the Secretary of State External Affairs Ottawa, 28 August 1945, 750–1, https://heritage.canadiana.ca/view/oocihm.lac_reel_t3423/750. On Britain's position on Spain at Potsdam, see David Wingeate Pike, "Franco and the Axis Stigma," *Journal of Contemporary History* 17, no. 3 (1982): 390–1.
80 LAC, RG33-62, Agents of a Foreign Power fonds, Reel T-1368, Stanislas Daley testimony, 572–4, https://heritage.canadiana.ca/view/oocihm.lac_reel_t1368/625.
81 Obert Louis Benson and Michael Warner, eds., *Venona: Soviet Espionage and the American Response, 1939–1957* (Washington, DC: National Security Agency and Central Intelligence Agency, 1996), xix n. 36. For an account of how Soviet cipher codes were broken, see p. xv.
82 TNA, KV 2/1428, Soviet Espionage in Canada, 55.

83 Amy Knight, *How the Cold War Began: The Igor Gouzenko Affair and the Hunt for Soviet Spies* (New York: Carroll & Graf, 2005), 121. Callwood claims that Woikin gave Sokolov only "the most innocuous material that crossed her desk." Callwood, *Emma*, 109.

84 LAC, RG33-62, Agents of a Foreign Power fonds, Reel T-1368, Woikin testimony, 689, https://heritage.canadiana.ca/view/oocihm.lac_reel_t1368/743.

85 LAC, RG33-62, Agents of a Foreign Power fonds, Reel T-1368, Woikin testimony, 668, https://heritage.canadiana.ca/view/oocihm.lac_reel_t1368/722; Callwood, *Emma*, 131.

86 LAC, RG33-62, Agents of a Foreign Power fonds, Reel T-1368, Emma Woikin testimony, 1148, 1150, https://heritage.canadiana.ca/view/oocihm.lac_reel_t1368/1209.

87 "Woikin Pleads Guilty on 2 Remaining Counts," *Globe & Mail*, 11 April 1946, 1.

88 Mayrand got his information from Canadian diplomat Arnold Smith and American diplomat George Kennan. *Canada Declassified*, CSIS, RCMP Central Registry, vol. I, Leon Mayrand, Charge de Affairs, Canadian Embassy, Moscow to The Right Honourable Secretary of State for External Affairs 3 August 1945, 000046, https://declassified.library.utoronto.ca/files/original/85eb4cd89d0ecd7882908fdd194c8751.pdf.

89 Leonard Schapiro, relying on Alfred Burmeister and Igor Gouzenko, argues that after the Comintern was "dissolved" the Central Committee of the Communist Party of the Soviet Union (CPSU) suddenly acquired a Foreign Affairs Department. This, for all practical purposes, became Comintern's new incarnation. Shapiro, "The International Department of the CPSU: Key to Soviet Policy," *International Journal* 32, no. 1 (1976–77): 42. On the dissolution of the existing Comintern organization beginning in the purges of 1937, see Alfred Burmeister, *Dissolution and Aftermath of the Comintern: Experiences and Observations, 1937–1947* (New York: Research Program on the USSR–East European Fund, 1955).

90 Alexander Trapeznik, "'Agents of Moscow' at the Dawn of the Cold War: The Comintern and the Communist Party of New Zealand," *Journal of Cold War Studies* 11, no. 1, (2009): 149.

91 Andrew Thorpe, "Comintern 'Control' of the Communist Party of Great Britain, 1920–43," *English Historical Review* 113, no. 452 (1998): 662.

92 See for example Philip Deery, "Decoding the Cold War: Venona, Espionage and 'The Communist Threat,'" in *Arguing the Cold War*, ed. Peter Love and Paul Strangio (n.p.: Red Rag, 2001), 107–15; and H. Klehr, J.E. Haynes, and F.I. Firsov, *The Secret World of American Communism* (New Haven: Yale University Press, 1995).

93 Official Secrets Act, s. 3.2, 451.

94 LAC, RG33-62, Agents of a Foreign Power fonds, Reel T-1368, Kathleen Willsher testimony, 850, https://heritage.canadiana.ca/view/oocihm.lac_reel_t1368/911.

95 On Moscow and the dynamics of the popular front strategy in Canada, see John Manley, "Communists Love Canada!": The Communist Party of Canada, the "People" and the Popular Front, 1933–1939," *Journal of Canadian Studies* 36, no. 4 (2002): 59–86.

96 David Caute, *The Fellow-Travellers: Intellectual Friends of Communism*, rev. and updated (New Haven: Yale University Press, 1988), 168–9.

97 LAC, RG33-62, Agents of a Foreign Power fonds, Reel T-1368, Willsher testimony, 765, https://heritage.canadiana.ca/view/oocihm.lac_reel_t1368/825.

98 LAC, RG33-62, Agents of a Foreign Power fonds, Reel T-1368, Willsher testimony, 762, https://heritage.canadiana.ca/view/oocihm.lac_reel_t1368/822.

99 LAC, RG33-62, Agents of a Foreign Power fonds, Reel T-1368, Willsher testimony, 759, https://heritage.canadiana.ca/view/oocihm.lac_reel_t1368/819.

100 See for example David McKnight, "The Comintern's Seventh Congress and the Australian Labor Party," *Journal of Contemporary History* 32, no. 3 (1997): 395; Philip Deery, "'The Secret Battalion': Communism in Britain During the Cold War," *Contemporary British History* 13, no. 4 (1999): 1–28; Klehr, Haynes, and Firsov, *Secret World of American Communism*; Allen Weinstein and Alexander Vassiliev, *The Haunted Wood: Soviet Espionage in America: The Stalin Era* (New York: Random House, 1999); Herbert Romerstein and Eric Breindel, *The Venona Secrets: Exposing Soviet Espionage and America's Traitors* (Washington, DC: Regnert, 2000); David McKnight, "Rethinking Cold War History," *Labour History* 95 (2008): 185–96; Alexander Trapeznik, "'Agents of Moscow' at the Dawn of the Cold War: The Comintern and the Communist Party of New Zealand," *Journal of Cold War Studies* 11, no. 1 (2009): 124–49; and K.A. Cuordileone, "The Torment of Secrecy: Reckoning with American Communism and Anticommunism after Venona," *Diplomatic History* 35, no. 4 (2011): 615–42.

101 Robert Comeau and Bernard Dionne, *Communists in Québec 1936–1956 – The Communist Party of Canada/Labor – Progressive Party* (Montreal: Presses de l'Unité, 1982), 53–4.

102 Deery, "Decoding the Cold War," 107.

103 LAC, RG33-62, Agents of a Foreign Power fonds, Reel T-1368, Willsher testimony, 778, https://heritage.canadiana.ca/view/oocihm.lac_reel_t1368/838.

104 LAC, RG33-62, Agents of a Foreign Power fonds, Reel T-1368, Willsher testimony, 780, https://heritage.canadiana.ca/view/oocihm.lac_reel_t1368/840.
105 LAC, RG33-62, Agents of a Foreign Power fonds, Reel T-1368, Willsher testimony,782, https://heritage.canadiana.ca/view/oocihm.lac_reel_t1368/842.
106 LAC, RG33-62, Agents of a Foreign Power fonds, Reel T-1368, Willsher testimony, 788, https://heritage.canadiana.ca/view/oocihm.lac_reel_t1368/848.
107 LAC, RG33-62, Agents of a Foreign Power fonds, Reel T-1368, Willsher testimony, 788, https://heritage.canadiana.ca/view/oocihm.lac_reel_t1368/848.
108 LAC, RG33-62, Agents of a Foreign Power fonds, Reel T-1368, Willsher testimony, 811–12, https://heritage.canadiana.ca/view/oocihm.lac_reel_t1368/871.
109 LAC, RG33-62, Agents of a Foreign Power fonds, Reel T-1368, Willsher testimony, 757, https://heritage.canadiana.ca/view/oocihm.lac_reel_t1368/817.
110 LAC, RG33-62, Agents of a Foreign Power fonds, Reel T-1368, Willsher testimony, 792, https://heritage.canadiana.ca/view/oocihm.lac_reel_t1368/852.
111 LAC, RG33-62, Agents of a Foreign Power fonds, Reel T-1368, Willsher testimony, 793, https://heritage.canadiana.ca/view/oocihm.lac_reel_t1368/853.
112 On this general subject, see Robert B. Bryce and Matthew J. Bellamy, *Canada and the Cost of World War II: The International Operations of Canada's Department of Finance, 1939–1947* (Montreal & Kingston: McGill-Queen's University Press, 2005), 203–11.
113 LAC, RG33-62, Agents of a Foreign Power fonds, Reel T-1368, Robert Bryce testimony, 2619, https://heritage.canadiana.ca/view/oocihm.lac_reel_t1369/639.
114 LAC, RG33-62, Agents of a Foreign Power fonds, Reel T-1368, Willsher testimony, 804, https://heritage.canadiana.ca/view/oocihm.lac_reel_t1368/864.
115 The document described as a "Manuscript" and "Notes on the Conference" dated 20-12-44 was listed as number 186 in the materials forwarded by Zabotin on 5 January 1945 to the director in Moscow. LAC, RG33-62, Agents of a Foreign Power fonds, Reel T-3423, Exhibit 16A, Record of the Materials Sent, no. 186, Ernst, Manuscript, Notes from the Conference, 20.12.44, 259, https://heritage.canadiana.ca/view/oocihm.lac_reel_t3423/259.
116 LAC, RG33-62, Agents of a Foreign Power fonds, Reel T-1368, Willsher testimony, 805, https://heritage.canadiana.ca/view/oocihm.lac_reel_t1368/865.

117 LAC, RG33-62, Agents of a Foreign Power fonds, Reel T-1368, Willsher testimony, 829, https://heritage.canadiana.ca/view/oocihm.lac_reel_t1368/890.
118 LAC, RG33-62, Agents of a Foreign Power fonds, Reel T-1368, Willsher testimony, 834, https://heritage.canadiana.ca/view/oocihm.lac_reel_t1368/895.
119 LAC, RG33-62, Agents of a Foreign Power fonds, Reel T-1368, Willsher testimony, 841, https://heritage.canadiana.ca/view/oocihm.lac_reel_t1368/902.
120 LAC, RG33-62, Agents of a Foreign Power fonds, Reel T-1368, Willsher testimony, 852, https://heritage.canadiana.ca/view/oocihm.lac_reel_t1368/913.
121 LAC, RG33-62, Agents of a Foreign Power fonds, Reel T-1368, Willsher testimony, 852–3, https://heritage.canadiana.ca/view/oocihm.lac_reel_t1368/913.
122 LAC, RG33-62, Agents of a Foreign Power fonds, Reel T-1368, Willsher testimony, 856, https://heritage.canadiana.ca/view/oocihm.lac_reel_t1368/917.
123 LAC, RG33-62, Agents of a Foreign Power fonds, Reel T-1368, Commissioner Kellock, 1195, https://heritage.canadiana.ca/view/oocihm.lac_reel_t1368/1256.
124 LAC, RG33-62, Agents of a Foreign Power fonds, Reel T-1368, Willsher testimony, 1195, https://heritage.canadiana.ca/view/oocihm.lac_reel_t1368/1256.
125 LAC, RG33-62, Agents of a Foreign Power fonds, Reel T-1368, Willsher testimony, 1198, https://heritage.canadiana.ca/view/oocihm.lac_reel_t1368/1259.
126 LAC, RG33-62, Agents of a Foreign Power fonds, Reel T-1368, Willsher testimony, 1199, https://heritage.canadiana.ca/view/oocihm.lac_reel_t1368/1260.
127 "Mary [*sic*] Willsher Given Three Years in Prison on Espionage Charges," *Globe & Mail*, 4 May 1946, 17.
128 LAC, RG33-62, Agents of a Foreign Power fonds, Reel T-1368, Ned Mazerall testimony, 955, https://heritage.canadiana.ca/view/oocihm.lac_reel_t1368/1016.
129 LAC, RG33-62, Agents of a Foreign Power fonds, Reel T-1368, Mazerall testimony, 959, https://heritage.canadiana.ca/view/oocihm.lac_reel_t1368/1020.
130 LAC, RG33-62, Agents of a Foreign Power fonds, Reel T-1368, Mazerall testimony, 966–7, https://heritage.canadiana.ca/view/oocihm.lac_reel_t1368/1027. Robert Edmonds was a native of Toronto. In the late 1930s he was employed as a reporter for CBC Radio prior to joining the new National Film Board in 1942. Edmonds left Canada in 1949 and settled

in Chicago, where he joined the faculty of Columbia College as the first director of its Film Department. "An Interview with Robert Edmonds," Columbia College *Alumni Newsletter*, Fall 1985, 2, http://digitalcommons.colum.edu/alumnae_news.

131 LAC, RG33-62, Agents of a Foreign Power fonds, Reel T-1368, Gouzenko testimony, 197, https://heritage.canadiana.ca/view/oocihm.lac_reel_t1368/258.

132 LAC, RG33-62, Agents of a Foreign Power fonds, Reel T-1368, Gouzenko testimony, 92, https://heritage.canadiana.ca/view/oocihm.lac_reel_t1368/154.

133 TNA, KV 2/1421, MacDonald to Cadogan, no. 161, 18.2.46, s. 60A.

134 LAC, RG33-62, Agents of a Foreign Power fonds, Reel T-1368, Mazerall testimony, 966, https://heritage.canadiana.ca/view/oocihm.lac_reel_t1368/1027.

135 LAC, RG33-62, Agents of a Foreign Power fonds, Reel T-1368, Mazerall testimony, 968, https://heritage.canadiana.ca/view/oocihm.lac_reel_t1368/1029.

136 LAC, RG33-62, Agents of a Foreign Power fonds, Reel T-1368, Mazerall testimony, 975, https://heritage.canadiana.ca/view/oocihm.lac_reel_t1368/1036.

137 LAC, RG33-62, Agents of a Foreign Power fonds, Reel T-1368, Mazerall testimony, 973, https://heritage.canadiana.ca/view/oocihm.lac_reel_t1368/1034.

138 LAC, RG33-62, Agents of a Foreign Power fonds, Reel T-1368, Mazerall testimony, 986, https://heritage.canadiana.ca/view/oocihm.lac_reel_t1368/1046.

139 The first was a "Long-Term Proposal" prepared by Dr. McKinley of the NRC that concerned civil aids to air navigation; the second was a report titled "Airborne Distance Indicator" prepared by Mazerall and edited by McKinley. LAC, RG33-62, Agents of a Foreign Power fonds, Reel T-1368, Mazerall testimony, 988–9, https://heritage.canadiana.ca/view/oocihm.lac_reel_t1368/1048.

140 LAC, RG33-62, Agents of a Foreign Power fonds, Reel T-1368, Mazerall testimony, 992, https://heritage.canadiana.ca/view/oocihm.lac_reel_t1368/1052.

141 LAC, RG33-62, Agents of a Foreign Power fonds, Reel T-1368, Commission counsel Fauteux, 997–9, https://heritage.canadiana.ca/view/oocihm.lac_reel_t1368/1057.

142 LAC, RG33-62, Agents of a Foreign Power fonds, Reel T-1368, Mazerall testimony, 994–5, https://heritage.canadiana.ca/view/oocihm.lac_reel_t1368/1054.

143 See for example Lunan's commentary on "Bagley" in LAC, RG33-62, Agents of a Foreign Power fonds, Reel T-3423, Exhibit 17F, File marked

"Back," Organizational Letter About the Group "Research," 5.7.45, 303, https://heritage.canadiana.ca/view/oocihm.lac_reel_t3423/303.

144 LAC, RG33-62, Agents of a Foreign Power fonds, Reel T-1368, Mazerall testimony, 1018, https://heritage.canadiana.ca/view/oocihm.lac_reel_t136/1079.

145 LAC, RG33-62, Agents of a Foreign Power fonds, Reel T-1368, Mazerall testimony, 1025, https://heritage.canadiana.ca/view/oocihm.lac_reel_t136/1086.

146 LAC, RG33-62, Agents of a Foreign Power fonds, Reel T-1368, Mazerall testimony, 1030–1, https://heritage.canadiana.ca/view/oocihm.lac_reel_t1368/1091.

147 LAC, RG33-62, Agents of a Foreign Power fonds, Reel T-1368, Mazerall testimony, 1035, https://heritage.canadiana.ca/view/oocihm.lac_reel_t1368/1096.

148 LAC, RG33-62, Agents of a Foreign Power fonds, Reel T-1368, Mazerall testimony, 1032–3, https://heritage.canadiana.ca/view/oocihm.lac_reel_t1368/1093.

149 Col. George A. Drew, "Workers in Russia Starving," *Globe & Mail*, 18 August 1937, 1.

150 Timothy Snyder, *Bloodlands: Europe Between Hitler and Stalin* (New York: Basic Books, 2010), 107.

151 LAC, RG33-62, Agents of a Foreign Power fonds, Reel T-1368, Mazerall testimony, 1032–1103, https://heritage.canadiana.ca/view/oocihm.lac_reel_t1368/1093.

152 LAC, RG33-62, Agents of a Foreign Power fonds, Reel T-1368, Mazerall testimony, 1034–5, https://heritage.canadiana.ca/view/oocihm.lac_reel_t1368/1095.

153 TNA, KV 2/1422, MacDonald to Cadogan, no. 238, 28.2.46, s. 83a.

154 TNA, KV 2/1422, MacDonald to Cadogan, no. 239, 28.2.46, s. 83a.

155 LAC, RG33-62, Agents of a Foreign Power fonds, Reel T-1368, Mazerall testimony, 1201–2, https://heritage.canadiana.ca/view/oocihm.lac_reel_t1368/1262.

156 "Magistrate to Commit Lunan, 'Spy Cell Head,'" *Globe & Mail*, 3 April 1946, 13.

157 TNA, KV 2/1423, Documents Relating to the Proceedings of the Royal Commission, s. 170A, First Interim Report, 14.

158 1946_R v Mazerall_*Ontario Reports*, 1946, 511–21, https://archive.org/details/ontarioreports1946.

159 TNA, KV 2/1422, MacDonald to Cadogan, no. 240, 28.2.46, s. 83A.

160 TNA, KV 2/1422, MacDonald to Sargent, no. 252, 1.3.46, 252, s. 87a.

161 In his autobiography Lunan applauded those who refused to answer questions put to them by the inquiry, but he offers no explanation for his decision to provide extensive testimony to the same body. See Gordon

Lunan, *Redhanded: Inside the Spy Ring That Changed the World* (Montreal: Optimum, 2005).

162 *Rex v. Harris*, 4 June 1947, O.R. 461–468.

163 LAC, RG33-62, Agents of a Foreign Power fonds, Reel T-1368, Lunan testimony, 1087–8, https://heritage.canadiana.ca/view/oocihm.lac_reel_t1368/1147.

164 LAC, RG33-62, Agents of a Foreign Power fonds, Reel T-1368, Lunan testimony, 1092, 1094, 1096, https://heritage.canadiana.ca/view/oocihm.lac_reel_t1368/1152.

165 Rogov's records of the meeting indicate that it took place on at the corner of Edward Avenue and Daly at 9 p.m. No date is given, but on the basis of Lunan's testimony it would seem that the meeting took place in early March 1945. LAC, RG33-62, Agents of a Foreign Power fonds, Reel T-3423, Exhibit 17H, File marked "Back," The Course of Meetings, Contents of Meeting, 5.7.45 (Course and Contents 5.7.45), 327, https://heritage.canadiana.ca/view/oocihm.lac_reel_t3423/327.

166 LAC, RG33-62, Agents of a Foreign Power fonds, Reel T-1368, Lunan testimony, 1097–8, https://heritage.canadiana.ca/view/oocihm.lac_reel_t1368/1157.

167 LAC, RG33-62, Agents of a Foreign Power fonds, Reel T-3423, Exhibit 17B, File marked "Back," Scheme of the Group "Research" (Scheme), 318, https://heritage.canadiana.ca/view/oocihm.lac_reel_t3423/318.

168 On Foote's unusual career in espionage, see "Allen Alexander Foote" in Nigel West, *Historical Dictionary of British Intelligence*, 2nd ed. (New York: Rowman & Littlefield, 2014), 218–19.

169 Alexander Foote, *Handbook for Spies* (Garden City, NY: Doubleday, 1949). For the Australian system, see chap. 6, "The GRU Apparatus in Australia," 70–2, in Hon. Mr. Justice W.F.L. Owen, Hon. Mr. Justice R.F.P. Philp, and Hon. Mr. Justice G.C. Ligertwood, *Report of the Royal Commission on Espionage* (Canberra: Government of Australia, 1955), https://nla.gov.au/nla.obj-2587286978/view?partId=nla.obj-2588970516#page/n3/mode/1up.

170 TNA, KV 2/1424, Igor Gouzenko, Copy of Note on Foote's comments on the Royal Commission Report, 14.11.47, 1, s. 258a.

171 Yuri Modin, Jean-Charles Deniau, and Aguieszka Ziarek, *My Five Cambridge Friends* (London: Headline, 1994). Former MI6 officer David Cornwell, under his nom de plume John Le Carré, creates a good deal of the drama in his classic *Tinker, Tailor, Soldier, Spy* through its focus on the activities of Soviet intelligence operatives associated officially with the Soviet embassy in London.

172 LAC, RG33-62, Agents of a Foreign Power fonds, Reel T-3423, Exhibit 17H, File marked "Back," Course and Contents, 327–8, https://heritage.canadiana.ca/view/oocihm.lac_reel_t3423/327.

173 LAC, RG33-62, Agents of a Foreign Power fonds, Reel T-3423, Exhibit 17B, File marked "Back," Scheme, 318, https://heritage.canadiana.ca/view/oocihm.lac_reel_t3423/318.
174 LAC, RG33-62, Agents of a Foreign Power fonds, Reel T-1368, Lunan testimony, 1102, https://heritage.canadiana.ca/view/oocihm.lac_reel_t1368/1152.
175 LAC, RG33-62, Agents of a Foreign Power fonds, Reel T-3423, Exhibit 17D, File marked "Back," Organizational Letter about the "Research" Group from "Back," Ottawa, March 28 (Organizational Letter Ottawa, 28 March), 320, https://heritage.canadiana.ca/view/oocihm.lac_reel_t3423/320.
176 LAC, RG33-62, Agents of a Foreign Power fonds, Reel T-1368, Lunan testimony, 1111, https://heritage.canadiana.ca/view/oocihm.lac_reel_t1368/1171.
177 LAC, RG33-62, Agents of a Foreign Power fonds, Reel T-1368, Lunan testimony, 1113, https://heritage.canadiana.ca/view/oocihm.lac_reel_t1368/1173.
178 On Lunan and the Quebec Committee for Allied Victory, see Lunan, *Redhanded*, 136.
179 LAC, RG33-62, Agents of a Foreign Power fonds, Reel T-1368, Lunan testimony, 1108, https://heritage.canadiana.ca/view/oocihm.lac_reel_t1368/1168.
180 LAC, RG33-62, Agents of a Foreign Power fonds, Reel T-3423, Exhibit 17D, File marked "Back," Organizational Letter Ottawa, 28 March, 320, https://heritage.canadiana.ca/view/oocihm.lac_reel_t3423/320.
181 LAC, RG33-62, Agents of a Foreign Power fonds, Reel T-1368, 1114, https://heritage.canadiana.ca/view/oocihm.lac_reel_t1368/1174.
182 LAC, RG33-62, Agents of a Foreign Power fonds, Reel T-3423, Exhibit 17D, File marked "Back," Organizational Letter Ottawa, 28 March, 320, https://heritage.canadiana.ca/view/oocihm.lac_reel_t3423/320.
183 LAC, RG33-62, Agents of a Foreign Power fonds, Reel T-1368, Lunan testimony, 1117–18, https://heritage.canadiana.ca/view/oocihm.lac_reel_t1368/1177.
184 LAC, RG33-62, Agents of a Foreign Power fonds, Reel T-3423, Exhibit 17D, File marked "Back," Organizational Letter Ottawa, 28 March, 320, https://heritage.canadiana.ca/view/oocihm.lac_reel_t3423/320.
185 LAC, RG33-62, Agents of a Foreign Power fonds, Reel T-1368, Lunan testimony, 1117–20, https://heritage.canadiana.ca/view/oocihm.lac_reel_t1368/1177.
186 On the challenges attending a successful conspiracy prosecution for conspiracy, see Matthew R. Goode, *Criminal Conspiracy in Canada* (Toronto: Carswell, 1975), 231–55.

187 R.S.C. 1927, Criminal Code, c. 146, s. 573 (Ottawa: King's Printer, 1927), 849.
188 Official Secrets Act, c. 49, s. 14, 456.
189 Peter MacKinnon, "Developments in the Law of Criminal Conspiracy," *Canadian Bar Review* 96 (1981): 301. In 1954 a variant of this definition was placed in the Criminal Code only to be repealed in 1984. The section read: "Everyone who conspires with anyone (b) to effect a lawful purpose by unlawful means, is guilty of an indictable offence and is liable to imprisonment for two years." R.S.C., Criminal Code, 1970, c. 34, s. 423 (2).
190 Goode, *Criminal Conspiracy in Canada,* 245.
191 Mazerall was charged with conspiracy under the Criminal Code and two counts of offending the Official Secrets Act. "Mazerall Trial Waits Ruling on Probe Evidence," *Globe & Mail,* 18 May 1946, 3.
192 On this, see Martin Friedland, *National Security: The Legal Dimensions* (Ottawa: Commission of Inquiry Concerning Certain Activities of the Royal Canadian Mounted Police, 1980), 31–41.
193 LAC, RG33-62, Agents of a Foreign Power fonds, Reel T-1368, Lunan testimony, 1183–4, https://heritage.canadiana.ca/view/oocihm.lac_reel_t1368/1244.
194 LAC, RG33-62, Agents of a Foreign Power fonds, Reel T-3423, Exhibit 17D, File marked "Back," Organizational Letter Ottawa, 28 March, 320, https://heritage.canadiana.ca/view/oocihm.lac_reel_t3423/320.
195 LAC, RG33-62, Agents of a Foreign Power fonds, Reel T-1368, Lunan testimony, 1122–3, https://heritage.canadiana.ca/view/oocihm.lac_reel_t1368/1182.
196 LAC, RG33-62, Agents of a Foreign Power fonds, Reel T-3423, Exhibit 17D, File marked "Back," Organizational Letter Ottawa, 28 March, 321, https://heritage.canadiana.ca/view/oocihm.lac_reel_t3423/321.
197 LAC, RG33-62, Agents of a Foreign Power fonds, Reel T-3423, Exhibit 17E, File marked "Back," Organizational Letter of 18.4.45, 323, https://heritage.canadiana.ca/view/oocihm.lac_reel_t3423/323.
198 LAC, RG33-62, Agents of a Foreign Power fonds, Reel T-3423, Exhibit 17E, File marked "Back," Organizational Letter of 18.4.45, 323, https://heritage.canadiana.ca/view/oocihm.lac_reel_t3423/323.
199 LAC, RG33-62, Agents of a Foreign Power fonds, Reel T-1368, Lunan testimony, 1185–9, https://heritage.canadiana.ca/view/oocihm.lac_reel_t1368/1246.
200 LAC, RG33-62, Agents of a Foreign Power fonds, Reel T-3423, Exhibit 17H, File marked "Back," Course and Contents 5.7.45, 328, https://heritage.canadiana.ca/view/oocihm.lac_reel_t3423/328.
201 LAC, RG33-62, Agents of a Foreign Power fonds, Reel T-1368, Lunan testimony, 1160–1, https://heritage.canadiana.ca/view/oocihm.lac_reel_t1368/1221.

202 LAC, RG33-62, Agents of a Foreign Power fonds, Reel T-3423, Exhibit 17D, File marked "Back," Organizational Letter Ottawa, 28 March, 321, https://heritage.canadiana.ca/view/oocihm.lac_reel_t3423/321.

203 LAC, RG33-62, Agents of a Foreign Power fonds, Reel T-3423, Exhibit 17E, File marked "Back," Bacon's Report, 18.4.45, 324, https://heritage.canadiana.ca/view/oocihm.lac_reel_t3423/324.

204 LAC, RG33-62, Agents of a Foreign Power fonds, Reel T-1368, Lunan testimony, 1125–6, https://heritage.canadiana.ca/view/oocihm.lac_reel_t1368/1185.

205 LAC, RG33-62, Agents of a Foreign Power fonds, Reel T-1368, Lunan testimony, 1159, https://heritage.canadiana.ca/view/oocihm.lac_reel_t1368/1220.

206 LAC, RG33-62, Agents of a Foreign Power fonds, Reel T-3423, Exhibit 17D, File marked "Back," Organizational Letter Ottawa, 28 March, 321, https://heritage.canadiana.ca/view/oocihm.lac_reel_t3423/321.

207 LAC, RG33-62, Agents of a Foreign Power fonds, Reel T-3424, Exhibit 32, Page from Lt. Col. Rogov's briefcase. Handwriting of Lt. Col. Rogov in red. Remainder all in handwriting of Levine or Gousev, Back's Group, Material no. 1, 16, https://heritage.canadiana.ca/view/oocihm.lac_reel_t3424/16. This is Rogov's note based on a note from Lunan. The typed version of Rogov's note drops the first paragraph in Lunan's handwritten note held in MI5 records. TNA KV 2/1427, Miscellaneous Notes taken from Grant's Safe, untitled handwritten document, 13. The isotope uranium-235 (U-235) can sustain a nuclear chain reaction required for a nuclear explosion.

208 LAC, RG33-62, Agents of a Foreign Power fonds, Reel T-3423, Exhibit 17D, File marked "Back," Organizational Letter Ottawa, 28 March, 321, https://heritage.canadiana.ca/view/oocihm.lac_reel_t3423/321.

209 RG33-62, Agents of a Foreign Power fonds, Reel T-3424, Exhibit 32, Page from Lt. Col. Rogov's briefcase, Back's Group, Material no. 1, 16–17, https://heritage.canadiana.ca/view/oocihm.lac_reel_t3424/17. For Lunan's testimony on this document, see LAC, RG33-62, Agents of a Foreign Power fonds, Reel T-1368, Lunan testimony, 1176, https://heritage.canadiana.ca/view/oocihm.lac_reel_t1368/1237. On the nuclear physics associated with the concept of the "electron shell," see Richard Rhodes, *The Making of the Atomic Bomb* (New York: Simon & Shuster, 1986), 115–16.

210 Fredrik Nebeker, *Dawn of the Electronic Age: Electrical Technologies in the Shaping of the Modern World* (Hoboken, NJ: John Wiley and Sons, 2009), 438–42.

211 On the background to nuclear research in Canada during World War II, see Donald Avery, "Atomic Scientific Co-operation and Rivalry among

Allies: The Anglo-Canadian Montreal Laboratory and the Manhattan Project, 1943–1946," *War in History* 2, no. 3 (1995): 274–305.

212 LAC, RG33-62, Agents of a Foreign Power fonds, Reel T-3423, Exhibit 17F, Organizational Letter of 5.7.45., 325, https://heritage.canadiana.ca/view/oocihm.lac_reel_t3423/325.

213 It must have been May because written reports from Lunan exist for March, April, and June.

214 For the note, see LAC, RG33-62, Agents of a Foreign Power fonds, Reel T-3423, Exhibit 27, Photostat one Sheet taken from Lt. Col. Rogov's briefcase, 801, https://heritage.canadiana.ca/view/oocihm.lac_reel_t3423/801. For a legible copy of this document, see TNA, KV 2/1427, Corby Case (vol. 5), Miscellaneous Notes taken from Grant's safe, s. 13. The note came from Rogov's briefcase stored in Grant's safe. On this point, see LAC, RG33-62, Agents of a Foreign Power fonds, Reel T-1368, Gouzenko's testimony, 121, https://heritage.canadiana.ca/view/oocihm.lac_reel_t1368/182.

215 Brian Cathcart, "Nunn May – Safety of Mankind," *The Independent* (London), 29 January 2003, 18; Jeevan Vasagar, "Spy's Deathbed Confession: Atom Physicist Tells How Secrets Given to Soviet Union," *The Guardian*, 27 January 2003, https://www.theguardian.com/uk/2003/jan/27/science.internationaleducationnews.

216 TNA, KV4/466, Guy Liddell Diaries, 17 September 1945, 206.

217 On these developments, see James Eayrs, *In Defence of Canada: Peacemaking and Deterrence* (Toronto: University of Toronto Press, 1972) 266–9, and Donald Avery, "Atomic Scientific Co-operation and Rivalry," 274–305.

218 In a late-1946 MI5 minute, Michael Serpell noted that when the Gouzenko case "first broke an attempt was made to recollect a number of cases of communists or communist suspects employed on the Tube-Alloy project." Serpell recalled that "[t]he case of Fuchs escaped our attention at that time but I suggest that it is one of considerable importance." TNA, KV 2/1245, Emil Julius Fuchs, memorandum, M.F. Serpell, Minute 49, B.1.c, 13.11.46.

219 For the "Statement by Igor Gouzenko taken on 14th March 1946," given to MI5 concerning Moscow's directions concerning Nunn May, see TNA, KV 2/ 2213, Alan Nunn May, E.J.P. Cussen, Minute Sheet 13, s. 371. See also LAC, RG33-62, Agents of a Foreign Power fonds, Reel T-1368, Gouzenko testimony, 137–8, https://heritage.canadiana.ca/view/oocihm.lac_reel_t1368/198. On Angelov, see TNA, KV 2/1428, "Soviet Espionage in Canada," 23.

220 LAC, RG33-62, Agents of a Foreign Power fonds, Reel T-3423, Exhibit 20EE, Telegram from Col. Zabotin, To the Director, no. 242, 9.7.1945, 475, https://heritage.canadiana.ca/view/oocihm.lac_reel_t3423/475.

221 LAC, RG33-62, Agents of a Foreign Power fonds, Reel T-3423, Exhibit 20 FF, Telegram from Col. Zabotin, To the Director, no. 243, 9.8.1945, 488, https://heritage.canadiana.ca/view/oocihm.lac_reel_t3423/488.

222 Cathcart, "Nunn May – Safety of Mankind,"18.

223 LAC, RG33-62, Agents of a Foreign Power fonds, Reel T-1368, Lunan testimony, 1179, https://heritage.canadiana.ca/view/oocihm.lac_reel_t1368/1240. For Rogov's decision, see LAC, RG33-62, Agents of a Foreign Power fonds, Reel T-3423, Exhibit 21A, Notes of Lt. Col. Rogov, Results of last meeting of Back's group (research), 5, 629, https://heritage.canadiana.ca/view/oocihm.lac_reel_t3423/629.

224 David Holloway, *Stalin and the Bomb: The Soviet Union and Atomic Energy 1939–1956* (New Haven: Yale University Press, 1994), 129. For the directive from Moscow, see LAC, RG33-62, Agents of a Foreign Power fonds, Reel T-3423, Exhibit 23HH, Incoming telegram in the handwriting of Lieut. Koulakov, "To Grant," N 11931, 22.8.45, 712, https://heritage.canadiana.ca/view/oocihm.lac_reel_t3423/712.

225 LAC, RG33-62, Agents of a Foreign Power fonds, Reel T-3423, Exhibit 23AA, Incoming telegram in the handwriting of Lieut. Koulakov, "To Grant," N 10458, 30.7.45, 654, https://heritage.canadiana.ca/view/oocihm.lac_reel_t3423/654.

226 LAC, RG33-62, Agents of a Foreign Power fonds, Reel T-3423, Exhibit 20GG, "To the Director," no. 244, no date, 497, https://heritage.canadiana.ca/view/oocihm.lac_reel_t3423/497.

227 Cathcart, "Nunn May – Safety of Mankind," 18.

228 LAC, RG33-62, Agents of a Foreign Power fonds, Reel T-3423, Exhibit 20DD, "To the Director," no. 241, 9.7.45, 468, https://heritage.canadiana.ca/view/oocihm.lac_reel_t3423/468.

229 See Gouzenko's account, LAC, RG33-62, Agents of a Foreign Power fonds, Reel T-1370, Gouzenko testimony, 5254–6, https://heritage.canadiana.ca/view/oocihm.lac_reel_t1370/1428.

230 TNA, KV 2/1428, "Soviet Espionage in Canada," 22.

231 Kevin Riehle, "Soviet Intent at the Dawn of the Cold War," 14, relying on Mikhail Tolochko, *Military Intelligence Officers of the 20th Century* (Minsk: Literatura, 1997), https://doi.org/10.1080/16161262.2021.1892997.

232 LAC, RG33-62, Agents of a Foreign Power fonds, Reel T-3423, Exhibit 30A, Page torn from notebook of Lt. Col. Motinov in handwriting of Motinov, Alek, 834, https://heritage.canadiana.ca/view/oocihm.lac_reel_t3423/834. For Nunn May's account of these transactions, see TNA, KV 2-2212, Alan Nunn May, Telegram to New York, no. 451, "Top Secret," 20 February 1946, "Signed Statement from Alan Nunn May without caution."

233 Christopher Andrew, *The Defence of the Realm: The Authorized History of MI5* (Toronto: Penguin, 2009), 341.
234 Knight, *How the Cold War Began*, 30. Kevin Reihle cites Motinov's autobiography on this subject. Riehle, "Soviet Intent at the Dawn of the Cold War," 14n87, https://doi.org/10.1080/16161262.2021.1892997.
235 LAC, RG33-62, Agents of a Foreign Power fonds, Reel T-3423, Exhibit 17D, "Organizational Letter Ottawa, March 28," 321, https://heritage.canadiana.ca/view/oocihm.lac_reel_t3423/321.
236 LAC, RG33-62, Agents of a Foreign Power fonds, Reel T-1368, Lunan testimony, 1129, https://heritage.canadiana.ca/view/oocihm.lac_reel_t1368/1189.
237 LAC, RG33-62, Agents of a Foreign Power fonds, Reel T-3423, Exhibit 17D, "Organizational Letter Ottawa, March 28," 321, https://heritage.canadiana.ca/view/oocihm.lac_reel_t3423/321.
238 LAC, RG33-62, Agents of a Foreign Power fonds, Reel T-1368, Lunan testimony, 1165, https://heritage.canadiana.ca/view/oocihm.lac_reel_t1368/1226.
239 LAC, RG33-62, Agents of a Foreign Power fonds, Reel T-1368, Lunan testimony, 1166, https://heritage.canadiana.ca/view/oocihm.lac_reel_t1368/1227.
240 LAC, RG33-62, Agents of a Foreign Power fonds, Reel T-1368, Lunan testimony, 1166–7, https://heritage.canadiana.ca/view/oocihm.lac_reel_t1368/1227; Lunan testimony, 1142, https://heritage.canadiana.ca/view/oocihm.lac_reel_t1368/1203.
241 LAC, RG33-62, Agents of a Foreign Power fonds, Reel T-1368, Lunan testimony, 1212, https://heritage.canadiana.ca/view/oocihm.lac_reel_t1368/1273.
242 LAC, RG33-62, Agents of a Foreign Power fonds, Reel T-1368, Lunan testimony, 1212, https://heritage.canadiana.ca/view/oocihm.lac_reel_t1368/1273.
243 LAC, RG33-62, Agents of a Foreign Power fonds, Reel T-3423, Exhibit 17H, File marked "Back," Course and Contents of Meetings, 327, https://heritage.canadiana.ca/view/oocihm.lac_reel_t3423/327.
244 LAC, RG33-62, Agents of a Foreign Power fonds, Reel T-1368, Lunan testimony, 1211–12, https://heritage.canadiana.ca/view/oocihm.lac_reel_t1368/1272.
245 LAC, RG33-62, Agents of a Foreign Power fonds, Reel T-1368, Lunan testimony, 1234, https://heritage.canadiana.ca/view/oocihm.lac_reel_t1368/1295.
246 LAC, RG33-62, Agents of a Foreign Power fonds, Reel T-1368, Lunan testimony, 1234–5, https://heritage.canadiana.ca/view/oocihm.lac_reel_t1368/1295.

247 LAC, RG33-62, Agents of a Foreign Power fonds, Reel T-1368, Lunan testimony, 1234–5, https://heritage.canadiana.ca/view/oocihm.lac_reel_t1368/1295.

248 Merrily Weisbord, *The Strangest Dream: Canadian Communists, the Spy Trials, and the Cold War* (Toronto: Lester & Orpen Dennys, 1983), 91.

249 Andrée Lévesque, "The Transnational Experience of Some Canadian Communists," in *Left Transnationalism: The Communist International and the National, Colonial, and Racial Questions*, ed. Olesksa Drachewych and Ian McKay (Montreal & Kingston: McGill-Queen's University Press, 2019), 198n12.

250 Weisbord, *The Strangest Dream*, 130. Weisbord recounts Lunan's entry into the Communist Party in the late 1930s, his introduction to the disciplined "underground" work during the illegal period in the early years of World War II, and his recruitment into Soviet espionage, pp. 93–4.

251 Weisbord, *The Strangest Dream*, 130.

252 Montreal-born architect Hazen Size worked with Norman Bethune's Hispano-Canadian Blood Transfusion Institute during the Spanish Civil War. On his return to Montreal in November 1937, he became active in the Committee to Aid Spanish Democracy and the Friends of the Mackenzie-Papineau Battalion. Library and Archives of Canada, Hazen Size Finding Aid, http://data2.archives.ca/pdf/pdf001/p000001562.pdf.

253 LAC, RG33-62, Agents of a Foreign Power fonds, Reel T-1368, Lunan testimony, 1243–4, https://heritage.canadiana.ca/view/oocihm.lac_reel_t1368/1304.

254 LAC, RG33-62, Agents of a Foreign Power fonds, Reel T-1368, Lunan testimony, 1250, https://heritage.canadiana.ca/view/oocihm.lac_reel_t1368/1310.

255 Gordon Lunan, quoted in Knight, *How the Cold War Began*, 19.

256 Odd Arne Westad, *The Cold War: A World History* (New York: Basic Books, 2017), 55.

257 LAC, RG33-62, Agents of a Foreign Power fonds, Reel T-1368, Lunan testimony, 1251, https://heritage.canadiana.ca/view/oocihm.lac_reel_t1368/1311.

258 LAC, RG33-62, Agents of a Foreign Power fonds, Reel T-1368, Lunan testimony, 1252–3, https://heritage.canadiana.ca/view/oocihm.lac_reel_t1368/1312.

259 LAC, RG33-62, Agents of a Foreign Power fonds, Reel T-1368, Lunan testimony, 1258–60, https://heritage.canadiana.ca/view/oocihm.lac_reel_t1368/1318.

260 LAC, RG33-62, Agents of a Foreign Power fonds, Reel T-1368, Lunan testimony, 1260, https://heritage.canadiana.ca/view/oocihm.lac_reel_t1368/1320.

261 Weisbord, *The Strangest Dream*, 130–1. The person whom Weisbord gives the pseudonym "Norman" is clearly Gordon Lunan, since all of the details match Lunan's life. Lunan doesn't specify the "double-cross," but it could refer to the Allies' unwillingness to share the atomic bomb with the Soviets, or to the painfully slow opening of a second front while the Soviet Union was suffering great losses during World War II.

262 TNA, KV 2/1422, Holmes to Sargent, no. 252, 1.3.46, s. 87a.

Chapter 6: Moscow Speaks

1 TNA, KV 2/1426, MacDonald to Cadogan, no. 122, 13.2.46, s. 131a.

2 On Lozovsky, see Joshua Rubenstein and Valdimir Pavolich Naumov, eds., *Stalin's Secret Pogrom: The Postwar Inquisition of the Jewish Anti-Fascist Committee* (New Haven: Yale University Press, 2001), 218–85.

3 LAC, RG33-62, Agents of a Foreign Power fonds, Reel T-3434, Canadian Ambassador to the United States to Secretary of State for External Affairs, Canada, Confidential, 20 February 1946, WA-866, 408, https://heritage.canadiana.ca/view/oocihm.lac_reel_t3434/408.

4 LAC, RG33-62, Agents of a Foreign Power fonds, Reel T-3434, "The Charge D'Affaires, Canadian Embassy, Moscow, USSR, to the Secretary of State for External affairs, Ottawa," TOP SECRET, no. 24, 20 February 1946, 555, https://heritage.canadiana.ca/view/oocihm.lac_reel_t3434/555.

5 LAC, RG33-62, Agents of a Foreign Power fonds, Reel T-3434, "The Charge D' Affairs, Canadian Embassy, Moscow, USSR to The Secretary of State for External Affairs, Ottawa, no. 25, 21 February 1946, 418, https://heritage.canadiana.ca/view/oocihm.lac_reel_t3434/418.

6 LAC, RG33-62, Agents of a Foreign Power fonds, Reel T-3334, "The Charge D' Affairs, Canadian Embassy, Moscow, USSR to The Secretary of State for External Affairs, Ottawa, no. 25, 21 February 1946, 418–20, https://heritage.canadiana.ca/view/oocihm.lac_reel_t3434/418.

7 Andrey Vyshinsky, described as a leading "henchman" of Joseph Stalin, served as the state prosecutor during the Moscow show trials of 1936–38. In 1945 he was deputy minister of foreign affairs under Vyacheslav Molotov. On Vyshinsky, see Martin McCauley, *Who's Who in Russia since 1900* (London: Routledge, 1997), 225.

8 See "Excerpts from Vishinsky's and Bevin's Talks to UNO Security Council," *New York Times*, 5 February 1946, 2.

9 Alan Bullock, *Ernest Bevin: Foreign Secretary 1945–1951* (New York: W.W. Norton, 1983), 219–22.

10 For his Russian experience, see Dana Wilgress, "From Siberia to Kuibyshev: Reflections on Russia, 1919–1943," *International Journal* 22 (1967): 364–75.

11 LAC, RG33-62, Agents of a Foreign Power fonds, Reel T-3434, Memorandum, 23 February 1946, SECRET, L. Dana Wilgress (see initials p. 4), Canadian Ambassador to the Soviet Union, 460–4, https://heritage.canadiana.ca/view/oocihm.lac_reel_t3434/460.
12 TNA, KV4/467, Guy Liddell Diaries, 21 February 1946, 116.
13 LAC, RG33-62, Agents of a Foreign Power fonds, Reel T-1368, Gouzenko testimony, 202–3, https://heritage.canadiana.ca/view/oocihm.lac_reel_t1368/263.
14 TNA, KV 2/3105, Bolshakov Ivan Alekseevich, "Soviet Intelligence Album," 014. These telegrams wouldn't be made public for decades. Robert Sheppard and James Rusk, "Cabinet Frees Spy Ring Testimony, Doesn't Tell Anyone," *Globe & Mail*, 15 October 1981, 10. Later, when Bolshakov was appointed Soviet military attaché to the US in 1948, Gouzenko identified him as the man who in 1945 had headed Soviet Military Intelligence for Canada and the US. TNA, KV 2/3105, no. 2704, Bolshakov Ivan Alekseevich, "J.A. Cimperman, American Embassy, London, to Dear Mr. Marriott, Leconfield House, London," 17 May 1949, s. 20a. He was also identified by Ismail Akhmedov, former GRU operative. TNA, KV 2/3105, no. 2739, Bolshakov Ivan Alekseevich, "J.A. Cimperman, American Embassy, London, to Dear Mr. Marriott, Leconfield House, London," 7 July 1949, s. 23a. On Akhmedov, see Ismail Akhmedov, *In and Out of Stain's GRU: A Tartar's Escape from Red Army Intelligence* (Frederick, MD: University Publications of America, 1984). For Akhmedov's account of Bolshakov, see TNA, KV 2/3105, Bolshakov Ivan Alekseevich, R. Thistlethwaite to Director General of the Security Service, London, SECRET, Subject: Major-General Ivan Alekseevich Bolshakov, 23 December 1948, s. 13a.
15 LAC, RG33-62, Agents of a Foreign Power fonds, Reel T-3434, Memorandum, 23 February 1946, SECRET, initials, L. Dana Wilgress, Canadian Ambassador to the Soviet Union, 460, https://heritage.canadiana.ca/view/oocihm.lac_reel_t3434/460.
16 TNA, KV 2/1422, Secretary of State for External Affairs to High Commissioner for Canada, London, no. 491, 23.2.46, s. 76a.
17 See for example LAC, RG33-62, Agents of a Foreign Power fonds, Reel T-3434, "From the High Commissioner for Canada in the United Kingdom, London referred by direction of The Secretary of State for External Affairs to the Royal Commission of Inquiry, Justice and the Royal Canadian Mounted Police for Information and Necessary Action," 378, https://heritage.canadiana.ca/view/oocihm.lac_reel_t3434/378.
18 LAC, RG33-62, Agents of a Foreign Power fonds, Reel T-3434, "The High Commissioner Great Britain to the Secretary of State for External Affairs, Canada, SECRET," no. 526, 22 February 1946, 422, https://heritage.canadiana.ca/view/oocihm.lac_reel_t3434/422.

19 Linton Andrews and Marc Brodie, "Cummings, Arthur John (1882–1957), journalist and author." *Oxford Dictionary of National Biography*, https://doi-org.berlioz.brandonu.ca/10.1093/ref:odnb/32662.
20 Dennis Griffiths, ed., *The Encyclopedia of the British Press 1422–1992* (New York: St. Martin's Press, 1992), 179–80.
21 LAC, RG33-62, Agents of a Foreign Power fonds, Reel T-3434, "The High Commissioner Great Britain to the Secretary of State for External Affairs, Canada, SECRET," no. 526, 22 February 1946, 422, https://heritage.canadiana.ca/view/oocihm.lac_reel_t3434/422.
22 LAC, RG33-62, Agents of a Foreign Power fonds, Reel T-3434, "The High Commissioner Great Britain to the Secretary of State for External Affairs, Canada, SECRET," no. 526, 22 February 1946, 422-3, https://heritage.canadiana.ca/view/oocihm.lac_reel_t3434/422.
23 LAC, RG33-62, Agents of a Foreign Power fonds, Reel T-3434, "The High Commissioner Great Britain to the Secretary of State for External Affairs, Canada, SECRET," no. 526, 22 February 1946, 422–3, https://heritage.canadiana.ca/view/oocihm.lac_reel_t3434/422.
24 LAC, RG33-62, Agents of a Foreign Power fonds, Reel T-3434, "The High Commissioner Great Britain to the Secretary of State for External Affairs, Canada, SECRET," no. 526, 22 February 1946, 422, https://heritage.canadiana.ca/view/oocihm.lac_reel_t3434/422.
25 LAC, RG33-62, Agents of a Foreign Power fonds, Reel T-3434, "The High Commissioner Great Britain to the Secretary of State for External Affairs, Canada, SECRET," no. 526, 22 February 1946, 423, https://heritage.canadiana.ca/view/oocihm.lac_reel_t3434/423. While William "Bill" Rust was nominally editor of the *Daily Worker* in 1946, Rajani Palme Dutt set the editorial line. On Dutt and the Moscow line, see John Callaghan, "Dutt, (Rajani) Palme (1896–1974), political leader." *Oxford Dictionary of National Biography*, https://doi-org.berlioz.brandonu.ca/10.1093/ref:odnb/31055.
26 LAC, RG33-62, Agents of a Foreign Power fonds, Reel T-3434, "The High Commissioner Great Britain to the Secretary of State for External Affairs, Canada, SECRET," no. 526, 22 February 1946, 421, https://heritage.canadiana.ca/view/oocihm.lac_reel_t3434/421.
27 On this still controversial subject, see Gill Bennett, *The Zinoviev Letter: The Conspiracy That Never Dies* (Oxford: Oxford University Press, 2018).
28 LAC, RG33-62, Agents of a Foreign Power fonds, Reel T-3434, "The High Commissioner Great Britain to the Secretary of State for External Affairs, Canada, TOP SECRET," no. 573, 26 February 1946, 471, https://heritage.canadiana.ca/view/oocihm.lac_reel_t3434/471. The reference is to Martin Dies Jr., the first chair of the House Committee on Un-American Activities in the United States Congress, created in 1938. On the committee, see Nancy Lopez, "'Allowing Fears to Overwhelm Us': A Re-Examination of

the House Special Committee on Un-American Activities, 1938–1944," Unpublished PhD diss., Rice University, 2002, https://www.proquest.com/docview/276382292?pq-origsite=primo.

29 LAC, RG33-62, Agents of a Foreign Power fonds, Reel T-3434, "The High Commissioner Great Britain to the Secretary of State for External Affairs, Canada, SECRET," no. 526, 22 February 1946, 421, https://heritage.canadiana.ca/view/oocihm.lac_reel_t3434/421.

30 LAC, RG33-62, Agents of a Foreign Power fonds, Reel T-3434, "The Canadian Ambassador, Paris, to the Secretary of State for External Affairs," no. 78, Confidential, 21 February 1946, 437–8, https://heritage.canadiana.ca/view/oocihm.lac_reel_t3434/437.

31 LAC, RG33-62, Agents of a Foreign Power fonds, Reel T-3434, "The Canadian Ambassador, Paris, to the Secretary of State for External Affairs," no. 79, Confidential, 22 February 1946, 449, https://heritage.canadiana.ca/view/oocihm.lac_reel_t3434/449.

32 Accents have been added to all non-accented French telegraph quotations. LAC, RG33-62, Agents of a Foreign Power fonds, Reel T-3434, "The Canadian Ambassador, Paris, to the Secretary of State for External Affairs," no. 78, Confidential, 21 February 1946, 437, https://heritage.canadiana.ca/view/oocihm.lac_reel_t3434/437.

33 LAC, RG33-62, Agents of a Foreign Power fonds, Reel T-3434, "The Canadian Ambassador, Paris, to the Secretary of State for External Affairs," no. 78, Confidential, 21 February 1946, 437, https://heritage.canadiana.ca/view/oocihm.lac_reel_t3434/437.

34 *Combat* was established in 1941 as a clandestine publication of the non-Communist left. Katherine Knorr, "Albert Camus: Being Right about the Left," *New York Times*, https://www.nytimes.com/1996/02/23/style/IHT-albert-camusbeing-right-about-the-left.html.

35 LAC, RG33-62, Agents of a Foreign Power fonds, Reel T-3434, "The Canadian Ambassador, Paris, to the Secretary of State for External Affairs," no. 82, Confidential, 27 February 1946, 478–9, https://heritage.canadiana.ca/view/oocihm.lac_reel_t3434/478. On the Moscow conference, see Bullock, *Ernest Bevin: Foreign Secretary*, 199–200, 206–12.

36 TNA/KV 2/1423, Extract from Daily Digest of World Broadcasts, during period 2.8.46–3.8.46, "Pravda," Article by Zaslavsky, "A Sorry Finale to a Shameful Comedy," 5, s. 240a.

37 LAC, RG33-62, Agents of a Foreign Power fonds, Reel T-3434, "The Charge D' Affairs, Canadian Embassy, Moscow, USSR to the Secretary of State for External Affairs, Ottawa," 21 February 1946, no. 26, TOP SECRET, 447, https://heritage.canadiana.ca/view/oocihm.lac_reel_t3434/447.

38 LAC, RG33-62, Agents of a Foreign Power fonds, Reel T-3434, "The Charge D' Affairs, Canadian Embassy, Moscow, USSR to the Secretary of State for

External Affairs, Ottawa, TOP SECRET," 22 February 1946, no. 27, 551, https://heritage.canadiana.ca/view/oocihm.lac_reel_t3434/551.

39 LAC, RG33-62, Agents of a Foreign Power fonds, Reel T-3434, "The Charge D' Affairs, Canadian Embassy, Moscow, USSR to the Secretary of State for External Affairs, Ottawa, SECRET," 24 February 1946, no. 32, 464, https://heritage.canadiana.ca/view/oocihm.lac_reel_t3434/464.

40 LAC, RG33-62, Agents of a Foreign Power fonds, Reel T-3434, "The Charge D' Affairs, Canadian Embassy, Moscow, USSR to the Secretary of State for External Affairs, Ottawa, TOP SECRET," 3 March, 1946, no. 37, 493, https://heritage.canadiana.ca/view/oocihm.lac_reel_t3434/493. For "white thread," see Elinor Lipper, *Eleven Years in Soviet Prison Camps* (San Francisco: Hauraki, 2015), 181.

41 LAC, RG33-62, Agents of a Foreign Power fonds, Reel T-3434, "The Charge D' Affairs, Canadian Embassy, Moscow, USSR to the Secretary of State for External Affairs, Ottawa, SECRET," 3 March 1946, no. 38, 490–1, https://heritage.canadiana.ca/view/oocihm.lac_reel_t3434/490

42 On the investigation and internment of Canadian fascists under the Mackenzie King government, see Reg Whitaker, Gregory S. Kealey, and Andrew Parnaby, *Secret Service: Political Policing in Canada from the Fenians to Fortress America* (Toronto: University of Toronto Press, 2012), 159–60; Gregory Kealey, *Spying on Canadians: The Royal Canadian Mounted Police and the Origins of the Long Cold War* (Toronto: University of Toronto Press, 2017), 199. On the internment of Adrian Arcand, see "Arcand Action Believed Plot against the State," *Globe & Mail*, 20 June 1940, 5.

43 On King's complicated relationship with European fascism, see Roy MacLaren, *Mackenzie King in The Age of the Dictators: Canada's Imperial and Foreign Policies* (Montreal & Kingston: McGill-Queen's University Press, 2019), 252–62.

44 LAC, RG33-62, Agents of a Foreign Power fonds, Reel T-3434, "The Charge D' Affairs, Canadian Embassy, Moscow, USSR to the Secretary of State for External Affairs, Ottawa, SECRET," 3 March 1946, no. 38, 491–2, https://heritage.canadiana.ca/view/oocihm.lac_reel_t3434/491.

45 LAC, RG33-62, Agents of a Foreign Power fonds, Reel T-3434, "The Canadian Ambassador to the United States, to the Secretary of State for External Affairs, Canada," WA-893 Confidential, 22 February 1946, 424, https://heritage.canadiana.ca/view/oocihm.lac_reel_t3434/424.

46 Special Correspondent, "Canadians Want to Know the Facts," *PM*, 21 February 1946, 7.

47 LAC, RG33-62, Agents of a Foreign Power fonds, Reel T-3434, "The Canadian Ambassador to the United States, to the Secretary of State for External Affairs, Canada," WA-893 Confidential, 22 February 1946, 424, https://heritage.canadiana.ca/view/oocihm.lac_reel_t3434/424.

48 "Reds Admit Securing Secret Data," *Lodi News Sentinel*, Lodi, CA, 21 February 1946, https://shorturl.at/zt81Z.
49 TNA, KV 2/1422, "Gabriels," *Daily Worker*, 23 February 1946, s. 73a.
50 LAC, RG33-62, Agents of a Foreign Power fonds, Reel T-3434, "The Canadian Ambassador to the United States to the Secretary of State for External Affairs, Canada," WA-893 Confidential, 22 February 1946, 425, https://heritage.canadiana.ca/view/oocihm.lac_reel_t3434/425.
51 LAC, RG33-62, Agents of a Foreign Power fonds, Reel T-3434, "The Canadian Ambassador to the United States to the Secretary of State for External Affairs, Canada," WA-899 Confidential, 23 February 1946, 454–5, https://heritage.canadiana.ca/view/oocihm.lac_reel_t3434/454.
52 LAC, RG33-62, Agents of a Foreign Power fonds, Reel T-3434, "The Canadian Ambassador to the United States to the Secretary of State for External Affairs, Canada," WA-930 Confidential, 26 February 1946, 468, https://heritage.canadiana.ca/view/oocihm.lac_reel_t3434/468.
53 "A World Made for War," *The New Republic*, 14, no. 9, 4 May 1946, 1.
54 LAC, RG33-62, Agents of a Foreign Power fonds, Reel T-3434, "The Canadian Ambassador to the United States to the Secretary of State for External Affairs, Canada," WA-978 Confidential, 1 March 1946, 486, https://heritage.canadiana.ca/view/oocihm.lac_reel_t3434/486.
55 Wilgress thought that Moscow's rhetorical assault of Canada was directed mostly at "the Soviet people themselves and communist parties in other countries." LAC, RG33-62, Agents of a Foreign Power fonds, Reel T-3434, Memorandum, 23 February 1946, SECRET, initials, L. Dana Wilgress, Canadian Ambassador to the Soviet Union, 460, https://heritage.canadiana.ca/view/oocihm.lac_reel_t3434/460.

Chapter 7: Accountability Crisis

1 TNA, KV 2.1422, MacDonald to Cadogan, no. 184, 21.2.46, s. 69a.
2 "Hint Others Will Be held in Spy Probe," *Globe & Mail*," 25 February 1945, 1.
3 "No Further Arrests in Spy-Hunt," *Winnipeg Tribune*, 26 February 1946, 1.
4 LAC, Gordon Papers, Report, 1.
5 "Security of Friendly Powers Involved in Ottawa Spy Probe," *Winnipeg Tribune*, 27 February 1946, 1.
6 "No Further Arrests in Spy-Hunt," *Winnipeg Tribune*, 26 February 1946, 1, 5.
7 "Security of Friendly Powers Involved in Ottawa Spy Probe," *Winnipeg Tribune*, 27 February 1946, 1.
8 "Action Extraordinary," *Globe & Mail*, 15 February 1946, 6.
9 TNA, KV 2/1422, MacDonald to Cadogan, no. 224, 27.2.46, s. 79a.
10 *Ottawa Journal*, 28 February 1946, as quoted in LAC, Gordon Papers Report, 7–8.

11 TNA, KV 2/1422, MacDonald to Cadogan, No. 242, 28.2.46, s. 84a.
12 LAC, Diaries of WLMK, 27 February 1946, 1.
13 TNA, KV 2/1422, Holmes to Sargent, no. 253, 1.3.46, s. 87a.
14 LAC, Diaries of WLMK, 2 March 1946, 2.
15 LAC, Diaries of WLMK, 19 February 1946, 1.
16 Watson Sellar, "A Century of Royal Commissions," *Canadian Bar Review* 25, no. 1 (1949): 27.
17 Parliamentary Papers Act 1840 as quoted in Sellar, "A Century of Royal Commissions," 27.
18 Christopher Andrew, *Defend the Realm: The Authorized History of MI5* (New York: Alfred Knopf, 2009), 347–8.
19 TNA, KV 2/1422, Holmes to Cadogan, no. 216, 26.2.46, s. 77a.
20 TNA, KV 2, 2212, For Holmes from Sargent, no. 493, 1.3.46, s. 302.b.
21 TNA, KV 2/2212, Sargent to Holmes, no. 493, 1.3.46, s. 302b.
22 TNA, KV 2/1422, following for Sargent from Holmes repeated Halifax, CXG 266 of 2.3.46, s. 91a.
23 TNA, KV/2 -2213, Inspector Whitehead, Special Report, Subject, Alan Nunn May, Metropolitan Police, Special Branch, 5 March 1946, Further to the Case of Dr. Alan Nunn May.
24 TNA, KV 2/1422, 48,000 for C.S.S, CXG.264, 2.3.46, s. 90A.
25 LAC, Diaries of WLMK, 3 March 1946, 4.
26 LAC, RG33-62, Agents of a Foreign Power fonds, Reel T-3434, To N.A. Robertson, Under-Secretary of State for External Relations, Ottawa from Stephen L. Holmes, Office of the High Commission for the United Kingdom, Ottawa 27 February 1946, 483, https://heritage.canadiana.ca/view/oocihm.lac_reel_t3434/483.
27 TNA, KV 2/1422, C.S.S. only from 48,000, CXG.265, 2.3.46, s. 90A.
28 On this subject, see Robert B. Bryce and Matthew J. Bellamy, *Canada and the Cost of World War II: The International Operations of Canada's Department of Finance, 1939–1947* (Montreal & Kingston: McGill-Queen's University Press, 2005), 296–309. On what was agreed to, see Warren Baldwin, "Canada's Loan, Debt Cancellation to Aid Britain in Trade Recovery," *Globe & Mail*, 8 March 1946, 1.
29 TNA, KV 2/1422, following for C.S.S only, CXG 265, 2.3.46., s. 90A.
30 TNA, KV 2/1422, C.S.S. only from 48,000, CXG.265, 2.3.46, s. 90A.
31 LAC, Diaries of Mackenzie King, 3 March 1946, 4.

Chapter 8: The First Interim Report

1 On the release of the report, see "Reveal Four Names in Spy Case," *Winnipeg Free Press*, 4 March 1946, 1. The complete text of the *Interim Report* appeared almost immediately in the press. See "Ottawa Issues Interim Spy Report," *Globe & Mail*, 4 March 1946, 19.

2 Kenneth C. Cragg, "4 Remanded in Custody Til March 11," *Globe & Mail*, 5 March 1946, 1. The story drew international attention. The *New York Times* published photographs of Ned Mazerall and Gordon Lunan being "booked" at Ottawa Police headquarters. See *New York Times*, 5 March 1946, 2.
3 TNA, KV 2 1422, MacDonald to Sargent, no. 321, 8.3.46., 321, s. 121A.
4 TNA, KV 2 1422, MacDonald to Sargent, no. 330, 8.3.46., s. 119A.
5 LAC, Diaries of Mackenzie King, 4 March 1946, 2.
6 Historian Amy Knight believes that the Gouzenko affair and the publicity given it through the Kellock-Taschereau inquiry and its findings marked the beginning of the Cold War. See the title and introduction of Knight, Knight, *How the Cold War Began: The Igor Gouzenko Affair and the Hunt for Soviet Spies* (New York: Carroll & Graf, 2005). Most historians of the Cold War have ignored the Gouzenko affair in their accounts of its origins. See John Gaddis, *We Know Now: Rethinking Cold War History*; (Oxford: Clarendon, 1997); Odd Arne Westad, *The Cold War: A World History* (New York: Basic Books, 2017); Norman M. Naimark, *Stalin and the Fate of Europe* (London: Harvard University Press, 2019).
7 "Mr. Churchill's Address Calling for United Effort for World Peace," *New York Times*, 6 March 1946, 4.
8 TNA, KV 2/1423, Documents Relating to the Proceedings of the Royal Commission, s. 170A, *First Interim Report*, 11.
9 TNA, KV 2/1423, Documents Relating to the Proceedings of the Royal Commission, s. 170A, *First Interim Report*, 11–13.
10 TNA, KV 2/1423, 170A, Documents Relating to the Proceedings of the Royal Commission, s. 170A, *First Interim Report*, 14.
11 LAC, Diaries of WLMK, 5 March 1946, 1.
12 "Russia Indicted," *Globe & Mail*, 5 March 1946, 6.
13 "Our House Cleaning," *Winnipeg Free Press*, 5 March 1946, 11.
14 "Four Named in Ottawa," *New York Times*, 5 March 1946, 1, 3; "Briton Speaks Out," *New York Times*, 6 March 1946, 1, 5. In a separate article the *Times* announced that the speech had been well received in London. "Churchill Speech Hailed in London," *New York Times*, 6 March 1946, 6.
15 "Canada's Spy Case," *New York Times*, 5 March 1946, 24.
16 "Totalitarian Procedure," *Globe & Mail*, 6 March 1946. A.A. McIntosh edited the *Globe & Mail* from 1936 to 1948. W.H. Kesterton, *A History of Journalism in Canada* (Toronto: McClelland & Stewart, 1967), 85.
17 LAC, RG33-62, Agents of a Foreign Power fonds, Reel T-3434, Canadian Ambassador to the United States to Secretary of State for External Affairs, Canada, CONFIDENTIAL, 7 March 1946, WA-1091, 508, https://heritage.canadiana.ca/view/oocihm.lac_reel_t3434/508.
18 LAC, RG33-62, Agents of a Foreign Power fonds, Reel T-3434, Canadian Ambassador to the United States to Secretary of State for External Affairs,

Canada, CONFIDENTIAL, 5 March 1946, WA-1047, 504–5, https://heritage.canadiana.ca/view/oocihm.lac_reel_t3434/504.

19 Jacqueline Foertsch, *American Culture in the 1940s* (Edinburgh: Edinburgh University Press, 2008), 46.

20 LAC, RG33-62, Agents of a Foreign Power fonds, Reel T-3434, Canadian Ambassador to the United States to Secretary of State for External Affairs, Canada, CONFIDENTIAL, 7 March 1946, WA-1091, 508–9, https://heritage.canadiana.ca/view/oocihm.lac_reel_t3434/508.

21 LAC, RG33-62, Agents of a Foreign Power fonds, Reel T-3434, Canadian Ambassador to the United States to Secretary of State for External Affairs, Canada, CONFIDENTIAL, 5 March 1946, WA-1046, 503, https://heritage.canadiana.ca/view/oocihm.lac_reel_t3434/503.

22 LAC, RG33-62, Agents of a Foreign Power fonds, Reel T-3434, Canadian Ambassador to the United States to Secretary of State for External Affairs, Canada, CONFIDENTIAL, 5 March 1946, WA-1046, 503, https://heritage.canadiana.ca/view/oocihm.lac_reel_t3434/503.

23 LAC, RG33-62, Agents of a Foreign Power fonds, Reel T-3434, Canadian Ambassador to the United States to Secretary of State for External Affairs, Canada, CONFIDENTIAL, 5 March 1946, WA-1039, 501, https://heritage.canadiana.ca/view/oocihm.lac_reel_t3434/501.

24 Dorothy Thompson, "US Not Ready for Churchill Speech," *The Observer*, 10 March 1946, 5.

25 LAC, RG33-62, Agents of a Foreign Power fonds, Reel T-3434, The Canadian Ambassador, Paris to the Secretary of State for External Affairs, no. 98 (CONFIDENTIAL), 5 March 1946, 497, https://heritage.canadiana.ca/view/oocihm.lac_reel_t3434/497.

26 LAC, RG33-62, Agents of a Foreign Power fonds, Reel T-3434, "The High Commissioner Great Britain to the Secretary of State for External Affairs, Canada, SECRET," no. 633, London, 6 March 1946, 512, https://heritage.canadiana.ca/view/oocihm.lac_reel_t3434/512.

27 LAC, RG33-62, Agents of a Foreign Power fonds, Reel T-3434, The Canadian Ambassador, Paris to the Secretary of State for External Affairs, no. 98 (CONFIDENTIAL), 5 March 1946, 497, https://heritage.canadiana.ca/view/oocihm.lac_reel_t3434/497.

28 On Vandenburg and the Cold War, see Laurence S. Kaplan, *The Conversion of Senator Arthur H. Vandenburg: From Isolation to International Engagement* (Lexington: University Press of Kentucky, 2015).

29 LAC, RG33-62, Agents of a Foreign Power fonds, Reel T-3434, Canadian Ambassador to the United States to Secretary of State for External Affairs, Canada, CONFIDENTIAL, 5 March 1946, WA-1047, 506, https://heritage.canadiana.ca/view/oocihm.lac_reel_t3434/506.

30 On A.P. Wadsworth and the political character of the *Guardian*, see "A.P. Wadsworth, Newsman, Is Dead," *New York Times*, 5 November 1956, 31.

31 "Russia's Spies," *The Manchester Guardian*, 5 March 1946, 4, as quoted in LAC, RG33-62, Agents of a Foreign Power fonds, Reel T-3434, "The High Commissioner Great Britain to the Secretary of State for External Affairs, Canada, SECRET," no. 627, London, 4 March 1946, 489, https://heritage.canadiana.ca/view/oocihm.lac_reel_t3434/489.

32 *The Scotsman* has been described as "widely influential in Scotland and "a leading exemplar of responsible journalism." "*The Scotsman*," *Encyclopedia Britannica*, https://www.britannica.com/topic/The-Scotsman.

33 LAC, RG33-62, Agents of a Foreign Power fonds, Reel T-3434, "The High Commissioner Great Britain to the Secretary of State for External Affairs, Canada, SECRET," no. 661, London, 8 March 1946, 514, https://heritage.canadiana.ca/view/oocihm.lac_reel_t3434/514.

34 For the history of this influential review of politics and culture, see *Time and Tide*, https://www.timeandtidemagazine.org/.

35 LAC, RG33-62, Agents of a Foreign Power fonds, Reel T-3434, "The High Commissioner Great Britain to the Secretary of State for External Affairs, Canada, SECRET," no. 661, London, 8 March 1946, 514, https://heritage.canadiana.ca/view/oocihm.lac_reel_t3434/514.

36 Lawrence Aronsen and Martin Kitchen, *The Origins of the Cold War in Comparative Perspective* (New York: St. Martin's Press, 1988), 176.

37 Kennan's analysis appeared a year later in an article authored by Kennan but attributed to X in *Foreign Affairs*. See X, "The Sources of Soviet Conduct," *Foreign Affairs* 25 (1947): 566–82. For an informed discussion of this theme, see Raymond L. Garthoff, *Soviet Leaders and Intelligence: Assessing the American Adversary During the Cold War* (Washington, DC: Georgetown University Press, 2015), 1–16.

38 Don Page and Don Munton, "Canadian Images of the Cold War 1946–7," *International Journal* 32, no. 3 (1977): 589.

39 On this debate, see Page and Munton, "Canadian Images of the Cold War," 583–9, and David Bercuson, "'A People So Ruthless as the Soviets': Canadian Images of the Cold War and the Soviet Union, 1946–1950," in *Canada and the Soviet Experiment: Essays on Canadian Encounters with Russia and the Soviet Union, 1900–1991*, ed. David Davies (Toronto: Canadian Scholars, 1994), 91.

40 LAC, RG33-62, Agents of a Foreign Power fonds, Reel T-3434, To the Honorable Secretary of State for External affairs, Canada from L.D. Wilgress (from L.D. Wilgress), Moscow, 27 March 1946 SECRET, no. 118, 546, https://heritage.canadiana.ca/view/oocihm.lac_reel_t3434/546.

41 LAC, RG33-62, Agents of a Foreign Power fonds, Reel T-3434, L.D. Wilgress, Moscow, 27 March 1946, SECRET, no. 118, 546, https://heritage.canadiana.ca/view/oocihm.lac_reel_t3434/546.

42 LAC, RG33-62, Agents of a Foreign Power fonds, Reel T-3434, L.D. Wilgress, Moscow, 27 March 1946, SECRET, no. 118, 546, https://heritage.canadiana.ca/view/oocihm.lac_reel_t343/546.

43 LAC, RG33-62, Agents of a Foreign Power fonds, Reel T-3434, L.D. Wilgress, Moscow, 27 March 1946, SECRET, no. 118, 546–7, https://heritage.canadiana.ca/view/oocihm.lac_reel_t3434/546.
44 Blair Fraser, who knew some of the suspects, argues that alongside ideological and personal motives, antisemitism, which Harold Gerson said turned them into "second-class Canadians," may also have played a role. See Fraser, "Backstage at Ottawa: Why Did They Spy," *MacLean's*, 1 September 1946, 69.
45 Bercuson, "A People So Ruthless," 91.
46 On the Venona Project, see John Earl Haynes and Harvey Klehr, *Venona: Decoding Soviet Espionage in America* (New Haven: Yale University Press, 1999). On Soviet archives, see Allen Weinstein and Alexander Vassiliev, *The Haunted Wood: Soviet Espionage in America: The Stalin Era* (New York: Random House, 1999).

Chapter 9: Before the Royal Commission II

1 TNA, KV 2/1421, MacDonald to Cadogan, no. 167, 19.2.46, s. 62A.
2 LAC, RG33-62, Agents of a Foreign Power fonds, Reel T-1368, Squadron Leader M.S. Nightingale (Nightingale) testimony, 1333–6, https://heritage.canadiana.ca/view/oocihm.lac_reel_t1368/1408.
3 For a complete record of Nightingale's postings, see LAC, RG33-62, Agents of a Foreign Power fonds, Reel T-1368, Wing Commander M.A. McNeil (McNeil) testimony, 1317, https://heritage.canadiana.ca/view/oocihm.lac_reel_t1368/1388.
4 LAC, RG33-62, Agents of a Foreign Power fonds, Reel T-1368, Wing Commander G.M. Fawcett (Fawcett) testimony, 1333–6, https://heritage.canadiana.ca/view/oocihm.lac_reel_t1368/1408.
5 Coates, Kenneth S., "Northwest Staging Route." *The Canadian Encyclopedia*. Historica Canada, https://www.thecanadianencyclopedia.ca/en/article/northwest-staging-route.
6 LAC, RG33-62, Agents of a Foreign Power fonds, Reel T-1368, Fawcett testimony, 1337–8, https://heritage.canadiana.ca/view/oocihm.lac_reel_t1368/1408.
7 LAC, RG33-62, Agents of a Foreign Power fonds, Reel T-1368, Nightingale testimony, 1377, https://heritage.canadiana.ca/view/oocihm.lac_reel_t1368/1408.
8 On Motinov, see TNA, KV 2/1420, The Intelligence Department of the Red Army in Moscow and Ottawa, Canadian Network, Lieut-Col. Petr Motinov, 5b.
9 LAC, RG33-62, Agents of a Foreign Power fonds, Reel T-3423, Exhibit 29A, Page torn from notebook of Lt. Col. Motinov titled Squadron Leader, 1337–8, https://heritage.canadiana.ca/view/oocihm.lac_reel_t3423/826.

10 LAC, RG33-62, Agents of a Foreign Power fonds, Reel T-3423, Exhibit 29A, Page torn from notebook of Lt. Col. Motinov titled Squadron Leader, 1337–8, https://heritage.canadiana.ca/view/oocihm.lac_reel_t3423/826.

11 LAC, RG33-62, Agents of a Foreign Power fonds, Reel T-1368, Fawcett testimony, 1345, https://heritage.canadiana.ca/view/oocihm.lac_reel_t1368/1416.

12 LAC, RG33-62, Agents of a Foreign Power fonds, Reel T-1368, Fawcett testimony, 1341–3, https://heritage.canadiana.ca/view/oocihm.lac_reel_t1368/1412.

13 LAC, RG33-62, Agents of a Foreign Power fonds, Reel T-1368, Fawcett testimony, 1346–51, https://heritage.canadiana.ca/view/oocihm.lac_reel_t1368/1417.

14 LAC, RG33-62, Agents of a Foreign Power fonds, Reel T-1368, 1385–6, https://heritage.canadiana.ca/view/oocihm.lac_reel_t1368/1456.

15 LAC, RG33-62, Agents of a Foreign Power fonds, Reel T-1368, Nightingale testimony, 1392, https://heritage.canadiana.ca/view/oocihm.lac_reel_t1368/1464.

16 LAC, RG33-62, Agents of a Foreign Power fonds, Reel T-1368, Nightingale testimony, 1380, https://heritage.canadiana.ca/view/oocihm.lac_reel_t1368/1451.

17 LAC, RG33-62, Agents of a Foreign Power fonds, Reel T-1368, Nightingale testimony, 1387–90, https://heritage.canadiana.ca/view/oocihm.lac_reel_t1368/1459.

18 LAC, RG33-62, Agents of a Foreign Power fonds, Reel T-1368, Nightingale testimony, 1394–5, 1402, https://heritage.canadiana.ca/view/oocihm.lac_reel_t1368/1466.

19 LAC, RG33-62, Agents of a Foreign Power fonds, Reel T-3423, Exhibit 19B, "Translation of the text covered by the note," 407, https://heritage.canadiana.ca/view/oocihm.lac_reel_t3423/407.

20 LAC, RG33-62, Agents of a Foreign Power fonds, Reel T-3423, Exhibit 29A, Page torn from notebook of Lt. Col. Motinov titled Squadron Leader, 826, https://heritage.canadiana.ca/view/oocihm.lac_reel_t3423/826.

21 The doctrine of diplomatic immunity placed embassy personnel beyond the reach of Canadian law: no subpoena would bring Nikolai Zabotin or any of his subordinates before the inquiry to answer questions about Nightingale and the GRU. On this, see R. St. J. MacDonald, "Public International Law Problems Arising in Canadian Courts," *University of Toronto Law Journal* 11, no. 2 (1956): 237.

22 TNA, KV 2, 1633, V2, Sam Carr, France/Canada, Sam Carr in France, no. 5762, 29 September 194 [*sic*], no serial.

23 TNA, KV 2, 1633, V2, Sam Carr, "Russian Agent Arrested in US," *Daily Telegraph*, 28 January 1949, s. 109a.

24 Norman Penner, *Canadian Communism: The Stalin Years and Beyond* (Toronto: Methuen, 1988), 161–5.
25 Ivan Avakumovic, *The Communist Party of Canada: A History* (Toronto: McClelland & Stewart, 1975), 142.
26 "Morris Launches Campaign," *Winnipeg Free Press*, 11 March 1940, 19.
27 Avakumovic, *The Communist Party of Canada*, 140
28 Penner, *Canadian Communism*, 182.
29 Penner, *Canadian Communism*, 186–7.
30 LAC, RG33-62, Agents of a Foreign Power fonds, Reel T-1368, Nightingale testimony, 1403, https://heritage.canadiana.ca/view/oocihm.lac_reel_t1368/1475.
31 LAC, RG33-62, Agents of a Foreign Power fonds, Reel T-1368, Nightingale testimony, 1410, https://heritage.canadiana.ca/view/oocihm.lac_reel_t1368/1482.
32 LAC, RG33-62, Agents of a Foreign Power fonds, Reel T-1368, Nightingale testimony, 1403, https://heritage.canadiana.ca/view/oocihm.lac_reel_t1368/1475.
33 LAC, RG33-62, Agents of a Foreign Power fonds, Reel T-1368, Nightingale testimony, 1433, https://heritage.canadiana.ca/view/oocihm.lac_reel_t1368/1505.
34 LAC, RG33-62, Agents of a Foreign Power fonds, Reel T-1368, Nightingale testimony, 1428, https://heritage.canadiana.ca/view/oocihm.lac_reel_t1368/1500.
35 LAC, RG33-62, Agents of a Foreign Power fonds, Reel T-1368, Nightingale testimony, 1416, https://heritage.canadiana.ca/view/oocihm.lac_reel_t1368/1488.
36 LAC, RG33-62, Agents of a Foreign Power fonds, Reel T-1368, Nightingale testimony, 1430, https://heritage.canadiana.ca/view/oocihm.lac_reel_t1368/1502.
37 LAC, RG33-62, Agents of a Foreign Power fonds, Reel T-1368, Nightingale testimony, 1437–9, https://heritage.canadiana.ca/view/oocihm.lac_reel_t1368/1509.
38 LAC, RG33-62, Agents of a Foreign Power fonds, Reel T-1368, Nightingale testimony, 1441, https://heritage.canadiana.ca/view/oocihm.lac_reel_t1368/1513.
39 LAC, RG33-62, Agents of a Foreign Power fonds, Reel T-1368, Nightingale testimony, 1441, https://heritage.canadiana.ca/view/oocihm.lac_reel_t1368/1513.
40 LAC, RG33-62, Agents of a Foreign Power fonds, Reel T-1368, Nightingale testimony, 1444, https://heritage.canadiana.ca/view/oocihm.lac_reel_t1368/1516.

41 LAC, RG33-62, Agents of a Foreign Power fonds, Reel T-1368, Nightingale testimony, 1447, https://heritage.canadiana.ca/view/oocihm.lac_reel_t1368/1519.
42 LAC, RG33-62, Agents of a Foreign Power fonds, Reel T-1368, Nightingale testimony, 1451, https://heritage.canadiana.ca/view/oocihm.lac_reel_t1368/1523.
43 LAC, RG33-62, Agents of a Foreign Power fonds, Reel T-1368, Nightingale testimony, 1453, https://heritage.canadiana.ca/view/oocihm.lac_reel_t1368/1525.
44 LAC, RG33-62, Agents of a Foreign Power fonds, Reel T-1368, Nightingale testimony, 1456, https://heritage.canadiana.ca/view/oocihm.lac_reel_t1368/1528.
45 LAC, RG33-62, Agents of a Foreign Power fonds, Reel T-1368, Nightingale testimony, 1463, https://heritage.canadiana.ca/view/oocihm.lac_reel_t1368/1535.
46 LAC, RG33-62, Agents of a Foreign Power fonds, Reel T-1368, Nightingale testimony, 1465, https://heritage.canadiana.ca/view/oocihm.lac_reel_t1368/1537.
47 LAC, RG33-62, Agents of a Foreign Power fonds, Reel T-1368, Nightingale testimony, 1469, https://heritage.canadiana.ca/view/oocihm.lac_reel_t1368/1541.
48 LAC, RG33-62, Agents of a Foreign Power fonds, Reel T-3423, Exhibit 29A, translation of page torn from notebook of Lt. Col. Motinov titled Squadron Leader, 826, https://heritage.canadiana.ca/view/oocihm.lac_reel_t3423/826.
49 LAC, RG33-62, Agents of a Foreign Power fonds, Reel T-3423, Exhibit 25 BB, Page out of notebook in Col. Zabotin's handwriting, Before Reorganization, 3. Professor, 765, https://heritage.canadiana.ca/view/oocihm.lac_reel_t3423/765.
50 LAC, RG33-62, Agents of a Foreign Power fonds, Reel T-1368, Boyer testimony, 1797, https://heritage.canadiana.ca/view/oocihm.lac_reel_t1368/1870.
51 LAC, RG33-62, Agents of a Foreign Power fonds, Reel T-1368, Gouzenko testimony, 277, https://heritage.canadiana.ca/view/oocihm.lac_reel_t1368/327.
52 LAC, RG33-62, Agents of a Foreign Power fonds, Reel T-1368, Nightingale testimony, 1469, https://heritage.canadiana.ca/view/oocihm.lac_reel_t1368/1541.
53 LAC, RG33-62, Agents of a Foreign Power fonds, Reel T-1368, Fawcett testimony, 1360, https://heritage.canadiana.ca/view/oocihm.lac_reel_t1368/1431.

54 LAC, RG33-62, Agents of a Foreign Power fonds, Reel T-1368, Fawcett testimony, 1361–3, https://heritage.canadiana.ca/view/oocihm.lac_reel_t1368/1431.
55 LAC, RG33-62, Agents of a Foreign Power fonds, Reel T-1368, Fawcett testimony, 1363–4, https://heritage.canadiana.ca/view/oocihm.lac_reel_t1368/1434.
56 LAC, RG33-62, Agents of a Foreign Power fonds, Reel T-1368, Nightingale testimony, 1480, https://heritage.canadiana.ca/view/oocihm.lac_reel_t1368/1552.
57 LAC, RG33-62, Agents of a Foreign Power fonds, Reel T-1368, Nightingale testimony, 1473, https://heritage.canadiana.ca/view/oocihm.lac_reel_t1368/1545.
58 LAC, RG33-62, Agents of a Foreign Power fonds, Reel T-1368, Nightingale testimony, 1474, https://heritage.canadiana.ca/view/oocihm.lac_reel_t1368/1546.
59 LAC, RG33-62, Agents of a Foreign Power fonds, Reel T-1368, Nightingale testimony, 1475, https://heritage.canadiana.ca/view/oocihm.lac_reel_t1368/1547.
60 LAC, RG33-62, Agents of a Foreign Power fonds, Reel T-1368, Nightingale testimony, 1478, https://heritage.canadiana.ca/view/oocihm.lac_reel_t1368/1550.
61 LAC, RG33-62, Agents of a Foreign Power fonds, Reel T-1368, Nightingale testimony, 1484, https://heritage.canadiana.ca/view/oocihm.lac_reel_t1368/1556.
62 LAC, RG33-62, Agents of a Foreign Power fonds, Reel T-1368, Nightingale testimony, 1481–2, https://heritage.canadiana.ca/view/oocihm.lac_reel_t1368/1553.
63 TNA, KV 2/1422, MacDonald to Sargent, no. 306, 5.3.46, s. 110A.
64 TNA, KV 2/1422, MacDonald to Sargant, no. 315, 7.3.46, s. 114A.
65 "Nightingale Acquitted of Russian Spy Charge," *Globe & Mail*, 8 November 1946, 17.
66 "Report Shows Canadian Espionage – Kardash," *Winnipeg Free Press*, 9 March 1946, 1.
67 For an account of these developments, see Philip Deery, "'The Secret Battalion': Communism in Britain During the Cold War," *Contemporary British History* 13, no. 4 (1999): 1–28; David McKnight, "Rethinking Cold War History," *Labour History* 95 (2008): 185–96; and K.A. Cuordileone, "The Torment of Secrecy: Reckoning with American Communism and Anticommunism after Venona," *Diplomatic History* 35, no. 4 (2011): 615–42.
68 See for example W.L. Morton, "Canada and Foreign Affairs," *Canadian Historical Review* 28, no. 2 (1947), 183–93; Reginald Whitaker and Gary Marcuse, *Cold War Canada: the Making of a National Security State,*

1945–1957 (Toronto: University of Toronto Press, 1994), 37–8, 43–8; Dominique Clément, "Spies, Lies, and a Commission: A Case Study in the Mobilization of the Canadian Civil Liberties Movement," *Left History* 7, no. 2 (2000): 53–79; Reg Whitaker, Gregory S. Kealey, and Andrew Parnaby, *Secret Service: Political Policing in Canada from the Fenians to Fortress America* (Toronto: University of Toronto Press, 2012), 179–85; Ian Leigh, "Secret Proceedings in Canada," *Osgoode Hall Law Journal* 34, no. 1 (1996): 113–74.

69 Morton, "Canada and Foreign Affairs," 187.

70 LAC, RG33-62, Agents of a Foreign Power fonds, Reel T-1368, Boyer testimony, 1701, https://heritage.canadiana.ca/view/oocihm.lac_reel_t1368/1773.

71 Ross Lambertson, *Repression and Resistance: Canadian Human Rights Activists* (Toronto: University of Toronto Press, 2005), 45.

72 Michiel Horn, *The League for Social Reconstruction: Intellectual Origins of the Democratic Left in Canada, 1930–1942* (Toronto: University of Toronto Press, 1980), 113.

73 "Civil Liberties Union," *The Labor World*, 13 May 1939, 7.

74 LAC, RG33-62, Agents of a Foreign Power fonds, Reel T-1368, 1763–5, https://heritage.canadiana.ca/view/oocihm.lac_reel_t1368/1836. Merrily Weisbord, *The Strangest Dream: Canadian Communists, the Spy Trials, and the Cold War* (Toronto: Lester & Orpen Dennys, 1983), 55, 74. For Stanley Ryerson's account of a similar study group he led in this era, see his "Comrade Bethune," in Wendell MacLeod, Stanley B. Ryerson, and Libbie Park, *Bethune: The Montreal Years* (Toronto: J. Lorimer, 1978) 151–6.

75 Fred Taylor told Merrily Weisbord that he and Gordon Lunan also belonged to this group. Weisbord, *The Strangest Dream*, 73.

76 Weisbord, *The Strangest Dream*, 74–5.

77 LAC, RG33-62, Agents of a Foreign Power fonds, Reel T-1368, Boyer testimony, 1702, https://heritage.canadiana.ca/view/oocihm.lac_reel_t1368/1774.

78 "Fights Naziism," *Winnipeg Free Press*, 4 September 1939, 18.

79 Penner, *Canadian Communism*, 161.

80 Robert Comeau and Bernard Dionne, *Communists in Québec 1936–1956 – The Communist Party of Canada/Labor – Progressive Party* (Montreal: Presses de l'Unité, 1982), 8.

81 LAC, RG33-62, Agents of a Foreign Power fonds, Reel T-1368, Boyer testimony, 1702, https://heritage.canadiana.ca/view/oocihm.lac_reel_t1368/1774.

82 Weisbord, *The Strangest Dream*, 94.

83 Weisbord, *The Strangest Dream*,76.

84 Weisbord, *The Strangest Dream*, 100.

85 For its leading members in 1938, see Lambertson, *Repression and Resistance*, 48.

86 See "The Dutch accelerated their campaign against 'fifth column' elements in their cities" in "Dutch Troops Withdraw to Water Defense Lines," *Winnipeg Tribune*, 13 May 1940, 2.
87 "Reds in Britain May Be Banned," *Globe & Mail*, 25 April 1940, 1.
88 "Fifth Column Operates Here, Speakers Warn," *Globe & Mail*, 14 May 1940, 4.
89 "Citizens Seek Police Probe of 5th Column," *Globe & Mail*, 15 May 1940, 4.
90 On this group, see B.K. Sandwell, "Saviors of Liberty," *Saturday Night*, 25 May 1940, 3.
91 James Naylor described MacLeod, who was national chair of the LAWF, as "a Communist for sure." Naylor, *The Fate of Labour Socialism: The Co-operative Commonwealth and the Dream of a Working-Class Future* (Toronto: University of Toronto Press, 2016), 213.
92 In 1939 the Pan-Canadian Union was created by Jean-Charles Harvey, editor of Quebec's *Le Jour*, to build Canadian national unity. "Pan-Canadian Union," *Winnipeg Free Press*, 6 November 1939, 11.
93 "3 Who Oppose Communism Booed at Rally," *Montreal Daily Star*, 20 May 1940, 3. See also "Civil Liberties Guard Is Urged," *Globe & Mail*, 20 May 1940, 10.
94 "10,000 Ask Ottawa to Intern All Fifth Columnists in Canada," *Montreal Daily Star*, 28 May 1940, 3.
95 "Fit Subjects For Internment," *Montreal Daily Star*, 3 June 1940, 10.
96 "Canadian Column to Be Formed Here," *Montreal Gazette*, 6 June 1940, 11.
97 "Secret Bulletin, No. 33, June 10, 1940," in *R.C.M.P. Security Bulletins – The War Series, 1939–41*, ed. Gregory S. Kealey and Reg Whitaker (Athabasca: Athabasca University Press, 1989), https://journals.lib.unb.ca/index.php/RCMP/article/view/9641.
98 Weisbord, *The Strangest Dream*, 87.
99 Weisbord, *The Strangest Dream*, 110.
100 See, for example, Raymond Boyer, *Les crimes et les châtiments au Canada français du XVIIe au XXe siècle* (Montreal: Cercle du Livre de France, 1966).
101 Thelma Oliver observes that Merrily Weisbord conveyed her story of the Communist Party c. 1946 in the Bardic tradition so as to celebrate the "spirit of the wonderful, committed, principled and selfless people she had known growing up in Montreal." While Weisbord's Bardic manner may have a distorting effect, the raw material she worked with, drawn from interviews, can be taken at face value. In 2002, the Society for Socialist Studies held a conference on the book, and several of those interviewed for *The Strangest Dream* were in attendance. For Thelma Oliver's review, see her "A Chronicle of Defeat," *Winnipeg Free Press*, 3 March 1984, 49. For the conference, see Irwin Block, "Ex-Communists to Hold Walkabout; Graying Reds Recall Radical Era," *Montreal Gazette*, 31 May 1995, A1.

102 Weisbord, *The Strangest Dream*, 130.
103 LAC, RG33-62, Agents of a Foreign Power fonds, Reel T-1368, Boyer testimony, 1701, https://heritage.canadiana.ca/view/oocihm.lac_reel_t1368/1773.
104 LAC, RG33-62, Agents of a Foreign Power fonds, Reel T-1368, Boyer testimony, 1702, https://heritage.canadiana.ca/view/oocihm.lac_reel_t1368/1774.
105 R.A. Farquharson, "Register Made of Manpower on Four Fronts," *Globe & Mail*, 17 February 1940, 13.
106 LAC, RG33-62, Agents of a Foreign Power fonds, Reel T-1368, Boyer testimony, 1702–3, https://heritage.canadiana.ca/view/oocihm.lac_reel_t1368/1774.
107 Penner, *Canadian Communism*, 161.
108 "Red 'Neutrality,'" *Globe & Mail*, 7 November 1939, 6.
109 LAC, RG33-62, Agents of a Foreign Power fonds, Reel T-3425, Exhibit 189, "Dr. E.H. Coleman, Under Secretary of State, Ottawa [undated]," 494, https://heritage.canadiana.ca/view/oocihm.lac_reel_t3425/494.
110 LAC, RG33-62, Agents of a Foreign Power fonds, Reel T-1368, Boyer testimony, 1703, https://heritage.canadiana.ca/view/oocihm.lac_reel_t1368/1775. For variations on the usual riposte, see Scotland Benning and Agatha Chapman on the question of their Communist Party membership. LAC, RG33-62, Agents of a Foreign Power fonds, Reel T-1369, 3273–74, 3849, https://heritage.canadiana.ca/view/oocihm.lac_reel_t1369/1315.
111 LAC, RG33-62, Agents of a Foreign Power fonds, Reel T-1368, Boyer testimony, 1704, https://heritage.canadiana.ca/view/oocihm.lac_reel_t1368/1776.
112 LAC, RG33-62, Agents of a Foreign Power fonds, Reel T-1368, Boyer testimony, 1704, https://heritage.canadiana.ca/view/oocihm.lac_reel_t1368/1776.
113 On 4 June 1940 the Communist Party was declared illegal under s. 39C (newly added) of the Defence of Canada Regulations. The order banned the Communist Party, the Young Communist League, the Canadian Labor Defence League, and the League for Peace and Democracy, along with a variety of Canadian fascist organizations. For the order, see Order-in-Council 2363, 4 June 1940, published in *The Canada Gazette*, 6 June 1940, https://recherche-collection-search.bac-lac.gc.ca/eng/home/record?app=cangaz&IdNumber=6792.
114 "Fifth Column Operates Here, Speakers Warn," *Globe & Mail*, 14 May 1940, 4; "Demands Grow to Curb 5th Column and Spur War Efforts in Canada," *Montreal Gazette*, 22 May 1940, 10; "Rally to Fight 5th Column," *Montreal Daily Star*, 22 May 1940, 3.

115 LAC, RG33-62, Agents of a Foreign Power fonds, Reel T-1368, Boyer testimony, 1705, 1707–8, https://heritage.canadiana.ca/view/oocihm.lac_reel_t1368/1777.
116 On J.H. Ross and RDX at McGill, see Wilfrid Eggleston, *National Research in Canada: The NRC 1916–1966* (Toronto: Clarke Urwin, 1978), 199–201. On Canada and RDX, see Colin F. Baxter, *The Secret History of RDX: The Super Explosive that Help Win World War II* (Lexington: University Press of Kentucky, 2018), 63–74.
117 John T. Edward, "The Preparation of RDX by the McGill Process," unpublished PhD diss., McGill University, April 1942, 1, https://escholarship.mcgill.ca/concern/theses/8623j214t.
118 Edward, "The Preparation of RDX," 1.
119 Baxter, *The Secret History of RDX*, 4–5.
120 LAC, RG33-62, Agents of a Foreign Power fonds, Reel T-1368, Dr. Adrien Cambron (Cambron) testimony, 1639, https://heritage.canadiana.ca/view/oocihm.lac_reel_t1368/1711.
121 LAC, RG33-62, Agents of a Foreign Power fonds, Reel T-1368, Cambron testimony, 1640, https://heritage.canadiana.ca/view/oocihm.lac_reel_t1368/1712.
122 LAC, RG33-62, Agents of a Foreign Power fonds, Reel T-1368, Boyer testimony, 1718–9, https://heritage.canadiana.ca/view/oocihm.lac_reel_t1368/1791.
123 Wilfrid Eggleston, *National Research in Canada: The NRC 1916–1966* (Toronto: Clarke Urwin, 1978), 123.
124 LAC, RG33-62, Agents of a Foreign Power fonds, Reel T-1368, Cambron testimony, 1664, https://heritage.canadiana.ca/view/oocihm.lac_reel_t1368/1736.
125 LAC, RG33-62, Agents of a Foreign Power fonds, Reel T-1368, Cambron testimony, 1643, https://heritage.canadiana.ca/view/oocihm.lac_reel_t1368/1715.
126 LAC, RG33-62, Agents of a Foreign Power fonds, Reel T-1368, Cambron testimony, 1646–7, https://heritage.canadiana.ca/view/oocihm.lac_reel_t1368/1718.
127 Eggleston, *National Research in Canada*, 123.
128 LAC, RG33-62, Agents of a Foreign Power fonds, Reel T-1368, Boyer testimony, 1715, https://heritage.canadiana.ca/view/oocihm.lac_reel_t1368/1788.
129 LAC, RG33-62, Agents of a Foreign Power fonds, Reel T-1368, Boyer testimony, 1713, https://heritage.canadiana.ca/view/oocihm.lac_reel_t1368/1786.
130 LAC, RG33-62, Agents of a Foreign Power fonds, Reel T-1368, Boyer testimony, 1729, https://heritage.canadiana.ca/view/oocihm.lac_reel_t1368/1802.

131 LAC, RG33-62, Agents of a Foreign Power fonds, Reel T-1368, Boyer testimony, 1731, https://heritage.canadiana.ca/view/oocihm.lac_reel_t1368/1804.
132 LAC, RG33-62, Agents of a Foreign Power fonds, Reel T-1368, Boyer testimony, 1733, https://heritage.canadiana.ca/view/oocihm.lac_reel_t1368/1806.
133 LAC, RG33-62, Agents of a Foreign Power fonds, Reel T-1368, Cambron testimony, 1648, https://heritage.canadiana.ca/view/oocihm.lac_reel_t1368/1720.
134 For a detailed overview of Canada–Soviet relations in the 1930s, see Norman Hillmer, "Canada and the 'Godless Country,' 1930–1939," in *Canada and the Soviet Experiment: Essays on Canadian Encounters with Russia and the Soviet Union, 1900–1991*, ed. David Davies (Toronto: Canadian Scholars, 1994), 57–74.
135 LAC, RG33-62, Agents of a Foreign Power fonds, Reel T-3433, Exhibit 543, Précis Showing the History of the Establishment of the USSR, Diplomatic Mission in Canada, 83–9, https://heritage.canadiana.ca/view/oocihm.lac_reel_t3433/83.
136 For Koudriavtsev's MI5 dossier, see TNA, KV 2/1650, Sergei Koudriavtsev/Vera Koudriavtsev.
137 LAC, RG33-62, Agents of a Foreign Power fonds, Reel T-3423, Exhibit 25BB, Page out of notebook in Col. Zabotin's handwriting, Before Reorganization, 771, https://heritage.canadiana.ca/view/oocihm.lac_reel_t3423/771.
138 TNA, MI5, KV 2/ 1427, Corby Case (vol. 5), Miscellaneous Notes taken from Grant's Safe, "Before Reorganization." For Gouzenko's account of this document and of Pavel Mikhailov ("Molier"), see LAC, RG33-62, Agents of a Foreign Power fonds, Reel T-1368, Gouzenko testimony, 247–50, https://heritage.canadiana.ca/view/oocihm.lac_reel_t3423/771.
139 J.L. Granatstein, "Changing Alliances: Canada and the Soviet Union, 1939–1945," in *Canada and the Soviet Experiment: Essays on Canadian Encounters with Russia and the Soviet Union, 1900–1991*, ed. David Davies (Toronto: Canadian Scholars, 1994), 81.
140 "Russia Is Imperative to Stable Peace Hope," *Globe & Mail*, 23 June 1943, 1.
141 Quoted in "Russia Is Imperative to Stable Peace Hope," *Globe & Mail*, 23 June 1943, 1.
142 Robert J. McMahon, *The Cold War: A Very Short Introduction*, 2nd ed. (Oxford: Oxford University Press, 2021), 18.
143 Donald Avery, *The Science of War: Canadian Scientists and Allied Military Technology During the Second World War* (Toronto: University of Toronto Press, 1998),, 214.
144 Avery, *The Science of War*, 217–18.

145 LAC, RG33-62, Agents of a Foreign Power fonds, Reel T-3423, Exhibit 25BB, Page out of notebook in Col. Zabotin's handwriting, Before Reorganization, 771, https://heritage.canadiana.ca/view/oocihm.lac_reel_t3423/771.

146 TNA, KV 2/1428, "Soviet Espionage in Canada," 27. See also TNA, KV 2 / 1650. Koudriavtsev, Sergei and Koudriavtsev, Vera.

147 Vitaliy Pavlov, *Operatziya "Sneg"* (Operation "Snow") (Geya: Moscow, 1996), 69, as quoted in Herbert Romerstein and Eric Breindel, *The Venona Secrets: Exposing Soviet Espionage and American Traitors* (Washington, DC: Regnery, 2000), 194.

148 In his account of the state of Soviet espionage before his arrival, Zabotin noted that Rose had been employed by the "Neighbours" (the NKVD and the GRU referred to one another as "neighbours"). LAC, RG33-62, Agents of a Foreign Power fonds, Reel T-3423, Exhibit 25BB, Page out of notebook in Col. Zabotin's handwriting, Before Reorganization, Director Davie, 1. Fred, 763, 771, https://heritage.canadiana.ca/view/oocihm.lac_reel_t3423/771.

149 Romerstein and Breindel, *The Venona Secrets*, 196.

150 LAC, RG33-62, Agents of a Foreign Power fonds, Reel T-3423, Exhibit 25BB, Page out of notebook in Col. Zabotin's handwriting, Before Reorganization, 3. Professor, 771, 763, https://heritage.canadiana.ca/view/oocihm.lac_reel_t3423/771.

151 LAC, RG33-62, Agents of a Foreign Power fonds, Reel T-3423, Exhibit 25AA, Page out of notebook in Col. Zabotin's handwriting, 3. Professor, 763, https://heritage.canadiana.ca/view/oocihm.lac_reel_t3423/763.

152 LAC, RG33-62, Agents of a Foreign Power fonds, Reel T-1368, Gouzenko testimony, 61, https://heritage.canadiana.ca/view/oocihm.lac_reel_t1368/123.

153 LAC, RG33-62, Agents of a Foreign Power fonds, Reel T-1368, Boyer testimony, 1751, 1752, 1760–5, 1767–8, https://heritage.canadiana.ca/view/oocihm.lac_reel_t1368/1824.

154 LAC, RG33-62, Agents of a Foreign Power fonds, Reel T-1368, Boyer testimony, 1750, 1754–5, https://heritage.canadiana.ca/view/oocihm.lac_reel_t1368/1823.

155 Weisbord, *The Strangest Dream*, 173.

156 Weisbord, *The Strangest Dream*, 131.

157 LAC, RG33-62, Agents of a Foreign Power fonds, Reel T-1368, Boyer testimony, 1766, https://heritage.canadiana.ca/view/oocihm.lac_reel_t1368/1839.

158 LAC, RG33-62, Agents of a Foreign Power fonds, Reel T-1368, Boyer testimony, 1766–7, https://heritage.canadiana.ca/view/oocihm.lac_reel_t1368/1839. Boyer was referring to F.M. Ross, director general of Naval Armament and Equipment Branch, Department of Munitions and Supply. See LAC, RG33-62, Agents of a Foreign Power fonds, Reel T-3427, Exhibit

210J, Department of Munitions and Supply, 694, https://heritage.canadiana.ca/view/oocihm.lac_reel_t3427/694.

159 LAC, RG33-62, Agents of a Foreign Power fonds, Reel T-1368, Boyer testimony, 1777, https://heritage.canadiana.ca/view/oocihm.lac_reel_t1368/1850.

160 LAC, RG33-62, Agents of a Foreign Power fonds, Reel T-1368, Boyer testimony, 1790, https://heritage.canadiana.ca/view/oocihm.lac_reel_t1368/1863.

161 LAC, RG33-62, Agents of a Foreign Power fonds, Reel T-1368, Boyer testimony, 1785, https://heritage.canadiana.ca/view/oocihm.lac_reel_t1368/1858.

162 LAC, RG33-62, Agents of a Foreign Power fonds, Reel T-3434, Exhibit 35A, "To the Director," no date, 53, https://heritage.canadiana.ca/view/oocihm.lac_reel_t3434/53.

163 LAC, RG33-62, Agents of a Foreign Power fonds, Reel T-1368, Boyer testimony, 1803–6, https://heritage.canadiana.ca/view/oocihm.lac_reel_t1368/1876.

164 TNA, KV 2/1422, MacDonald to Sargent, no. 338, 11.3.46, s. 126A.

165 LAC, RG33-62, Agents of a Foreign Power fonds, Reel T-1368, Boyer testimony, 1777–8, 1786, https://heritage.canadiana.ca/view/oocihm.lac_reel_t1368/1851.

166 LAC, RG33-62, Agents of a Foreign Power fonds, Reel T-1368, Boyer testimony, 1778, https://heritage.canadiana.ca/view/oocihm.lac_reel_t1368/1851.

167 LAC, RG33-62, Agents of a Foreign Power fonds, Reel T-1368, Boyer testimony, 1781, https://heritage.canadiana.ca/view/oocihm.lac_reel_t1368/1854.

168 LAC, RG33-62, Agents of a Foreign Power fonds, Reel T-1368, Boyer testimony, 1778, https://heritage.canadiana.ca/view/oocihm.lac_reel_t1368/1851.

169 LAC, RG33-62, Agents of a Foreign Power fonds, Reel T-1368, Boyer testimony, 1791, https://heritage.canadiana.ca/view/oocihm.lac_reel_t1368/1864.

170 LAC, RG33-62, Agents of a Foreign Power fonds, Reel T-1368, Boyer testimony, 1791, https://heritage.canadiana.ca/view/oocihm.lac_reel_t1368/1864.

171 LAC, RG33-62, Agents of a Foreign Power fonds, Reel T-1368, Commission counsel E.K. Williams, 1798. https://heritage.canadiana.ca/view/oocihm.lac_reel_t1368/1871.

172 LAC, RG33-62, Agents of a Foreign Power fonds, Reel T-1368, Boyer testimony, 1844, https://heritage.canadiana.ca/view/oocihm.lac_reel_t1368/1917.

173 LAC, RG33-62, Agents of a Foreign Power fonds, Reel T-1368, Boyer testimony, 1844, https://heritage.canadiana.ca/view/oocihm.lac_reel_t1368/1917.
174 LAC, RG33-62, Agents of a Foreign Power fonds, Reel T-1368, Commissioner Kellock, 1844, https://heritage.canadiana.ca/view/oocihm.lac_reel_t1368/1917.
175 LAC, RG33-62, Agents of a Foreign Power fonds, Reel T-1368, Boyer testimony, 1844, https://heritage.canadiana.ca/view/oocihm.lac_reel_t1368/1917.
176 LAC, RG33-62, Agents of a Foreign Power fonds, Reel T-1368, Commissioner Kellock, 1845, https://heritage.canadiana.ca/view/oocihm.lac_reel_t1368/1918..
177 LAC, RG33-62, Agents of a Foreign Power fonds, Reel T-1368, Boyer testimony, 1847–8, https://heritage.canadiana.ca/view/oocihm.lac_reel_t1368/1920.
178 Boyer was allowed visits with his wife. Prior to his final appearance before the inquiry, she brought him news that his father had retained a lawyer on his behalf. LAC, RG33-62, Agents of a Foreign Power fonds, Reel T-1368, Boyer testimony, 1848, https://heritage.canadiana.ca/view/oocihm.lac_reel_t1368/1921.
179 Avery, *The Science of War*, 220.
180 Weisbord, *The Strangest Dream*, 130.
181 TNA, KV 2 1422, MacDonald to Cadogan, no. 197 and no. 197, 22.2.46, s. 71a.
182 Andrée Lévesque, "The Transnational Experience of Some Canadian Communists," in *Left Transnationalism: The Communist International and the National, Colonial, and Racial Questions*, ed. Olesksa Drachewych and Ian McKay (Montreal & Kingston: McGill-Queen's University Press, 2019), 184.
183 John Earl Haynes, Harvey Klehr, and Fridrikh Igorevich Firsov, *The Secret World of American Communism* (New Haven: Yale University Press, 1995); Allen Weinstein and Alexander Vassiliev, *The Haunted Wood: Soviet Espionage in America: The Stalin Era* (New York: Random House, 1999); Romerstein and Breindel, *The Venona Secrets*; Haynes and Klehr, *Venona: Decoding Soviet Espionage in America*. See also Philip Deery, "Decoding the Cold War: "Venona, Espionage and 'The Communist Threat,'" in *Arguing the Cold War*, ed. Peter Love and Paul Strangio (n.p.: Red Rag, 2001), 107–15; David McKnight, "Rethinking Cold War History," 185–96; Cuordileone, "The Torment of Secrecy," 615–42.
184 *The Report of the Royal Commission* (*Final Report*), 11–89, https://publications.gc.ca/site/eng/9.699909/publication.html.
185 Kevin Riehle, "Soviet Intent at the Dawn of the Cold War: Igor Gouzenko's Revelations about GRU Intelligence Tasking," *Journal of Intelligence History* (2021), 5, https://doi.org/10.1080/16161262.2021.1892997.

186 Odd Arne Westad, *The Cold War: A World History* (New York: Basic Books, 2017), 48.
187 Ivo Banac, ed., *The Diary of Georgi Dimitrov, 1933–1949* (New Haven: Yale University Press, 2003), 358.
188 Avery, *The Science of War*, 245–8.
189 LAC, RG33-62, Agents of a Foreign Power fonds, Reel T-1368, Gouzenko testimony, 137–8, https://heritage.canadiana.ca/view/oocihm.lac_reel_t1368/198.
190 LAC, RG33-62, Agents of a Foreign Power fonds, Reel T-3423, Exhibit 20DD, N 241, To the Director, 9.8.45, 464, 466, https://heritage.canadiana.ca/view/oocihm.lac_reel_t3423/466. Thanks to Dr. John Rice, professor emeritus, Brandon University Physics Department, for clarifying these details. The "9.7.45" date placed on telegram 241 is erroneous, since the contents make it evident that the date should read "9.8.45," as noted in the English translation two pages later; https://heritage.canadiana.ca/view/oocihm.lac_reel_t3423/464.
191 LAC, RG33-62, Agents of a Foreign Power fonds, Reel T-3423, Exhibit 20DD, N 241, To the Director, 9.8.45, 468, https://heritage.canadiana.ca/view/oocihm.lac_reel_t3423/466. In other telegrams Nunn May is sometimes referred to as Alek. See for example LAC, RG33-62, Agents of a Foreign Power fonds, Reel T-3423, Exhibit 20EE, N 243, Grant to the Director, 9.7.45, 478, https://heritage.canadiana.ca/view/oocihm.lac_reel_t3423/478. On this subject, see also Nunn May's confession to MI5 on 20.2.46. TNA, KV 2/2212, to New York, no. 451, Top Secret, 20.2.46, no serial number.
192 LAC, RG33-62, Agents of a Foreign Power fonds, Reel T-3423, Exhibit 23B, Incoming telegram in the handwriting of Lieut. Koulakov, Director to Grant, no. 11273, 11.8.45, 660, https://heritage.canadiana.ca/view/oocihm.lac_reel_t3423/660.
193 LAC, RG33-62, Agents of a Foreign Power fonds, Reel T-3423, Exhibit 23B, Incoming telegram in the handwriting of Lieut. Koulakov, Director to Grant, 11.8.45, no. 11273, 660, https://heritage.canadiana.ca/view/oocihm.lac_reel_t3423/660.
194 LAC, RG33-62, Agents of a Foreign Power fonds, Reel T-3423, Exhibit 19D, File marked "Frank," Task #2 of 15.6.45, 408–12, https://heritage.canadiana.ca/view/oocihm.lac_reel_t3423/412.
195 LAC, RG33-62, Agents of a Foreign Power fonds, Reel T-3423, Exhibit 20A, N 232, To the Director, 2.8.45, 434, https://heritage.canadiana.ca/view/oocihm.lac_reel_t3423/434.
196 LAC, RG33-62, Agents of a Foreign Power fonds, Reel T-3423, Exhibit 23EE, Incoming telegram in the handwriting of Lieut. Koulakov, N 11437, To Grant, Your Telegram 232, N 11437, 14.8.45, 688, https://heritage.canadiana.ca/view/oocihm.lac_reel_t3423/688.

197 LAC, RG33-62, Agents of a Foreign Power fonds, Reel T-1368, Gouzenko testimony, 101, https://heritage.canadiana.ca/view/oocihm.lac_reel_t1368/162.
198 LAC, RG33-62, Agents of a Foreign Power fonds, Reel T-3423, Exhibit 19C, File marked "Frank," Assignment #1 Sam to Shugar, 16.12.45, 401, https://heritage.canadiana.ca/view/oocihm.lac_reel_t3423/401. The date should read "16.12.44." Since the original document was removed from the Soviet embassy on 5 September 1945, a document correctly dated 16.12.45 couldn't have existed at that time.
199 LAC, RG33-62, Agents of a Foreign Power fonds, Reel T-3423, Exhibit 19D, File marked "Frank," Task #2 of 15.6.45, 410, https://heritage.canadiana.ca/view/oocihm.lac_reel_t3423/410.
200 LAC, RG33-62, Agents of a Foreign Power fonds, Reel T-3423, Exhibit 20A, N 232, To the Director, 2.8.45, 434, https://heritage.canadiana.ca/view/oocihm.lac_reel_t3423/434.
201 LAC, RG33-62, Agents of a Foreign Power fonds, Reel T-3423, Exhibit 23EE, Incoming telegram in the handwriting of Lieut. Koulakov, N 11437, To Grant, Your Telegram 232, 14.8.45, 688, https://heritage.canadiana.ca/view/oocihm.lac_reel_t3423/688. The RCMP thought that Gourshkov was also a NKVD operative. TNA, KV 2/1428, "Soviet Espionage in Canada," 23.
202 LAC, RG33-62, Agents of a Foreign Power fonds, Reel T-3423, Exhibit 23DD, Incoming telegram in the handwriting of Lieut. Koulakov, N 11436, To Grant, Re no. 227, 14.8.45, 682, https://heritage.canadiana.ca/view/oocihm.lac_reel_t3423/682.
203 LAC, RG33-62, Agents of a Foreign Power fonds, Reel T-3423, Exhibit 23EE, Incoming telegram in the handwriting of Lieut. Koulakov, N 11437, To Grant, Your Telegram 232, 14.8.45, 688, https://heritage.canadiana.ca/view/oocihm.lac_reel_t3423/688.
204 LAC, RG33-62, Agents of a Foreign Power fonds, Reel T-3423, Exhibit 19H, File marked "Frank," Assignment given 16.8.45, 416, https://heritage.canadiana.ca/view/oocihm.lac_reel_t3423/416.
205 LAC, RG33-62, Agents of a Foreign Power fonds, Reel T-1368, Shugar testimony, 1920, https://heritage.canadiana.ca/view/oocihm.lac_reel_t1368/1993.
206 "Oust Mitchell, Alter Policies, Demand Voiced," *Globe & Mail*, 18 January 1943, 4.
207 LAC, RG33-62, Agents of a Foreign Power fonds, Reel T-1368, Shugar testimony, 1911, https://heritage.canadiana.ca/view/oocihm.lac_reel_t1368/1984.
208 LAC, RG33-62, Agents of a Foreign Power fonds, Reel T-3425, Exhibit 200, "Order Investigation of Unionist's Discharge," *Canadian Tribune*, 6

March 1943, 5, 605, https://heritage.canadiana.ca/view/oocihm.lac_reel_t3425/605; LAC, RG33-62, Agents of a Foreign Power fonds, Reel T-3425, Exhibit 201, "Trades Council Fights Firing," *Canadian Tribune*, 13 March 1943, 3, 634, https://heritage.canadiana.ca/view/oocihm.lac_reel_t3425/634.

209 LAC, RG33-62, Agents of a Foreign Power fonds, Reel T-1368, Shugar testimony, 1914, https://heritage.canadiana.ca/view/oocihm.lac_reel_t1368/1987.

210 LAC, RG33-62, Agents of a Foreign Power fonds, Reel T-1369, Shugar testimony, 2120, https://heritage.canadiana.ca/view/oocihm.lac_reel_t1369/139.

211 LAC, RG33-62, Agents of a Foreign Power fonds, Reel T-3425, Exhibit 199, "New Excuse for Firing: 'The Man Is Too Good,'" *Canadian Tribune*, 5 February 1944, 3, 621, https://heritage.canadiana.ca/view/oocihm.lac_reel_t3425/621.

212 *The Canadian Navy List for September 1944* (Ottawa: King's Printer, 1944), 552, http://www.forposterityssake.ca/RCN-DOCS/NAVY%20LISTS/1944-09-SEP-VOL2.pdf.

213 *The Canadian Navy List for September 1944* (Ottawa: King's Printer, 1944), 535, http://www.forposterityssake.ca/RCN-DOCS/NAVY%20LISTS/1944-09-SEP-VOL2.pdf.

214 LAC, RG33-62, Agents of a Foreign Power fonds, Reel T-1368, Shugar testimony, 1925–7, https://heritage.canadiana.ca/view/oocihm.lac_reel_t1368/1998.

215 LAC, RG33-62, Agents of a Foreign Power fonds, Reel T-1368, Shugar testimony, 1928, https://heritage.canadiana.ca/view/oocihm.lac_reel_t1368/2001.

216 LAC, RG33-62, Agents of a Foreign Power fonds, Reel T-1368, Comack testimony, 1884, https://heritage.canadiana.ca/view/oocihm.lac_reel_t1368/1957.

217 LAC, RG33-62, Agents of a Foreign Power fonds, Reel T-1368, Comack testimony, 1886, https://heritage.canadiana.ca/view/oocihm.lac_reel_t1368/1959.

218 LAC, RG33-62, Agents of a Foreign Power fonds, Reel T-1368, Shugar testimony, 1928, https://heritage.canadiana.ca/view/oocihm.lac_reel_t1368/2001.

219 LAC, RG33-62, Agents of a Foreign Power fonds, Reel T-1368, Shugar testimony, 1929, https://heritage.canadiana.ca/view/oocihm.lac_reel_t1368/2002.

220 Official Secrets Act, s. 3.2.3, 450–1.

221 LAC, RG33-62, Agents of a Foreign Power fonds, Reel T-1368, Shugar testimony, 1915–16, https://heritage.canadiana.ca/view/oocihm.lac_reel_t1368/1988.

222 LAC, RG33-62, Agents of a Foreign Power fonds, Reel T-1368, Shugar testimony, 1952, https://heritage.canadiana.ca/view/oocihm.lac_reel_t1368/2025.
223 LAC, RG33-62, Agents of a Foreign Power fonds, Reel T-1368, Shugar testimony, 1953, https://heritage.canadiana.ca/view/oocihm.lac_reel_t1368/2026. On Paul Robson's appearances in Canada in 1945 – one in Toronto at a Labor-Progressive Party rally and one in Windsor in support of Ford Motor workers – see Laurel Sefton-MacDowell, "Paul Robeson in Canada: A Border Story," *Labour/Le Travail* 51 (2003): 180–1.
224 LAC, RG33-62, Agents of a Foreign Power fonds, Reel T-1368, Shugar testimony, 1953, https://heritage.canadiana.ca/view/oocihm.lac_reel_t1368/2026. On the Canadian Association of Scientific Workers, see Avery, *The Science of War*, 222.
225 LAC, RG33-62, Agents of a Foreign Power fonds, Reel T-1368, Shugar testimony, 1954–7, https://heritage.canadiana.ca/view/oocihm.lac_reel_t1368/2027.
226 LAC, RG33-62, Agents of a Foreign Power fonds, Reel T-1368, Shugar testimony, 1962, https://heritage.canadiana.ca/view/oocihm.lac_reel_t1368/2035.
227 LAC, RG33-62, Agents of a Foreign Power fonds, Reel T-1368, Shugar testimony, 1964, https://heritage.canadiana.ca/view/oocihm.lac_reel_t1368/2037.
228 LAC, RG33-62, Agents of a Foreign Power fonds, Reel T-1368, Shugar testimony, 1967, https://heritage.canadiana.ca/view/oocihm.lac_reel_t1368/2040.
229 TNA, KV 2/1421, MacDonald to Cadogan, no. 164, 18.2.46, s. 60A.
230 LAC, RG33-62, Agents of a Foreign Power fonds, Reel T-1368, Commissioner Taschereau, 1306, https://heritage.canadiana.ca/view/oocihm.lac_reel_t1368/1377.
231 LAC, RG33-62, Agents of a Foreign Power fonds, Reel T-1368, Commissioner Taschereau testimony, 1307, https://heritage.canadiana.ca/view/oocihm.lac_reel_t1368/1378.
232 C.W. Harvison, *The Horsemen* (Toronto: McClelland & Stewart, 1967), 157.
233 *The Report of the Royal Commission* (*Final Report*), 672–4, https://publications.gc.ca/site/eng/9.699909/publication.html. The commissioners cited *The King v. Walker*, 1939 S.C.R. 214; Reg. v. Coote, L.R4 Privy Council 599; *Gach v. The King*, 1943, S.C.R. 250; and Rex v. Barnes, 49 O.L.R. 374.
234 LAC, RG33-62, Agents of a Foreign Power fonds, Reel T-3434, Exhibit R.C. 16, David Shugar to the Royal Commission, 4 March 1946, 79, https://heritage.canadiana.ca/view/oocihm.lac_reel_t3434/79.

235 LAC, RG33-62, Agents of a Foreign Power fonds, Reel T-1368, Shugar testimony, 1602–8, https://heritage.canadiana.ca/view/oocihm.lac_reel_t1368/1674. Shugar was interrogated by Inspector M.F.E. Anthony. Early on, Harvison and Anthony agreed that Harvison would interrogate detainees from Montreal while Anthony would question those in Toronto. Harvison, *The Horsemen*, 157.

236 Official Secrets Act, S.10, 455.

237 LAC, RG33-62, Agents of a Foreign Power fonds, Reel T-1368, Shugar testimony, 1982–4, https://heritage.canadiana.ca/view/oocihm.lac_reel_t1368/2056.

238 LAC, RG33-62, Agents of a Foreign Power fonds, Reel T-1368, Shugar testimony, 1984, https://heritage.canadiana.ca/view/oocihm.lac_reel_t1368/2057..

239 LAC, RG33-62, Agents of a Foreign Power fonds, Reel T-1368, Shugar testimony, 1985, https://heritage.canadiana.ca/view/oocihm.lac_reel_t1368/2058.

240 LAC, RG33-62, Agents of a Foreign Power fonds, Reel T-1368, Shugar testimony, 1985, https://heritage.canadiana.ca/view/oocihm.lac_reel_t1368/2058.

241 LAC, RG33-62, Agents of a Foreign Power fonds, Reel T-1368, Shugar testimony, 1987–8, 1993, https://heritage.canadiana.ca/view/oocihm.lac_reel_t1368/2066.

242 LAC, RG33-62, Agents of a Foreign Power fonds, Reel T-1368, Shugar testimony, 2000–1, https://heritage.canadiana.ca/view/oocihm.lac_reel_t1369/10.

243 LAC, RG33-62, Agents of a Foreign Power fonds, Reel T-1368, Shugar testimony, 1995, https://heritage.canadiana.ca/view/oocihm.lac_reel_t1368/2068.

244 LAC, RG33-62, Agents of a Foreign Power fonds, Reel T-1369, Shugar testimony, 1998, 1996, https://heritage.canadiana.ca/view/oocihm.lac_reel_t1369/05.

245 LAC, RG33-62, Agents of a Foreign Power fonds, Reel T-1369, Shugar testimony, 2015, https://heritage.canadiana.ca/view/oocihm.lac_reel_t1369/24.

246 "Montrealer Cited as Spy at US Probe," *Globe & Mail*, 6 June 1949, 1.

247 Haynes and Klehr, *Venona: Decoding Soviet Espionage*, 384. For an account of Bentley's connection with Size and the Canadian embassy, including Bentley's gratuitous 1951 references to Lester Pearson, see John English, *Shadow of Heaven: The Life of Lester Pearson*, 1897–1948 (Toronto: Lester & Orpen Dennys, 1989), 301–9.

248 LAC, RG33-62, Agents of a Foreign Power fonds, Reel T-1369, Shugar testimony, 2019, https://heritage.canadiana.ca/view/oocihm.lac_reel_t1369/28.
249 LAC, RG33-62, Agents of a Foreign Power fonds, Reel T-1369, Shugar testimony, 2016, https://heritage.canadiana.ca/view/oocihm.lac_reel_t1369/25.
250 LAC, RG33-62, Agents of a Foreign Power fonds, Reel T-1369, Shugar testimony, 2020, https://heritage.canadiana.ca/view/oocihm.lac_reel_t1369/29.
251 LAC, RG33-62, Agents of a Foreign Power fonds, Reel T-1369, Shugar testimony, 2025, https://heritage.canadiana.ca/view/oocihm.lac_reel_t1369/34. Shugar thought the encounter took place in the summer of 1944 or 1945. Because Koudriavtsev was posted to London at the end of 1944, the train meeting must have taken place in the summer of 1944, months into Shugar's career in Asdic. TNA, KV 2/1428, "Soviet Espionage in Canada," 23.
252 LAC, RG33-62, Agents of a Foreign Power fonds, Reel T-1368, Shugar testimony, 1990–2, https://heritage.canadiana.ca/view/oocihm.lac_reel_t136/2064.
253 LAC, RG33-62, Agents of a Foreign Power fonds, Reel T-1369, Shugar testimony, 2033–5, https://heritage.canadiana.ca/view/oocihm.lac_reel_t1369/42.
254 LAC, RG33-62, Agents of a Foreign Power fonds, Reel T-1369, David Shugar testimony, 2090–1, https://heritage.canadiana.ca/view/oocihm.lac_reel_t1369/99.
255 LAC, RG33-62, Agents of a Foreign Power fonds, Reel T-3423, Exhibit 19C, Assignment #1 Sam to Shugar, 16-12-44 [? The document's date – 16.12.45 – should read "16.12.44."], https://heritage.canadiana.ca/view/oocihm.lac_reel_t3423/419.
256 LAC, RG33-62, Agents of a Foreign Power fonds, Reel T-1368, Comack testimony, 1877, https://heritage.canadiana.ca/view/oocihm.lac_reel_t1368/1950.
257 Item two in Assignment #1 referred to "Common review of the Caproni's stability of the USA and Great Britain." Comach did not know what this referred to. The only Caproni he was familiar with was an aircraft. LAC, RG33-62, Agents of a Foreign Power fonds, Reel T-1369, Comack testimony, 1878. https://heritage.canadiana.ca/view/oocihm.lac_reel_t1368/1951.
258 LAC, RG33-62, Agents of a Foreign Power fonds, Reel T-1368, Comack Testimony, 1879, https://heritage.canadiana.ca/view/oocihm.lac_reel_t1368/1952.
259 LAC, RG33-62, Agents of a Foreign Power fonds, Reel T-1368, Comack testimony, 1880, https://heritage.canadiana.ca/view/oocihm.lac_reel_t1368/1953.

260 LAC, RG33-62, Agents of a Foreign Power fonds, Reel T-1368, Comack testimony, 1880, https://heritage.canadiana.ca/view/oocihm.lac_reel_t1368/1953.
261 LAC, RG33-62, Agents of a Foreign Power fonds, Reel T-1368, Comack testimony, 1881, https://heritage.canadiana.ca/view/oocihm.lac_reel_t1368/1954.
262 LAC, RG33-62, Agents of a Foreign Power fonds, Reel T-1368, Comack testimony, 1882, https://heritage.canadiana.ca/view/oocihm.lac_reel_t1368/1955.
263 LAC, RG33-62, Agents of a Foreign Power fonds, Reel T-1368, Comack testimony, 1884, https://heritage.canadiana.ca/view/oocihm.lac_reel_t1368/1957.
264 LAC, RG33-62, Agents of a Foreign Power fonds, Reel T-1368, Comack testimony, 1885, https://heritage.canadiana.ca/view/oocihm.lac_reel_t1368/1958.
265 LAC, RG33-62, Agents of a Foreign Power fonds, Reel T-1368, Comack testimony, 1889, https://heritage.canadiana.ca/view/oocihm.lac_reel_t1368/1962.
266 LAC, RG33-62, Agents of a Foreign Power fonds, Reel T-1368, Comack testimony, 1870, https://heritage.canadiana.ca/view/oocihm.lac_reel_t1368/1943.
267 LAC, RG33-62, Agents of a Foreign Power fonds, Reel T-1368, Shugar testimony, 1947–8, https://heritage.canadiana.ca/view/oocihm.lac_reel_t1368/2020.
268 LAC, RG33-62, Agents of a Foreign Power fonds, Reel T-1369, Shugar testimony, passim, 2035–58, https://heritage.canadiana.ca/view/oocihm.lac_reel_t1369/44.
269 LAC, RG33-62, Agents of a Foreign Power fonds, Reel T-1369, Shugar testimony, 2058, https://heritage.canadiana.ca/view/oocihm.lac_reel_t1369/67.
270 LAC, RG33-62, Agents of a Foreign Power fonds, Reel T-1369, Shugar testimony, 2059–62, https://heritage.canadiana.ca/view/oocihm.lac_reel_t1369/68.
271 LAC, RG33-62, Agents of a Foreign Power fonds, Reel T-1369, Shugar testimony, 2064, https://heritage.canadiana.ca/view/oocihm.lac_reel_t1369/73.
272 LAC, RG33-62, Agents of a Foreign Power fonds, Reel T-1369, Commissioner Taschereau, 2066, https://heritage.canadiana.ca/view/oocihm.lac_reel_t1369/75.
273 LAC, RG33-62, Agents of a Foreign Power fonds, Reel T-1369, Shugar testimony, 2086, https://heritage.canadiana.ca/view/oocihm.lac_reel_t1369/95.

274 LAC, RG33-62, Agents of a Foreign Power fonds, Reel T-1369, Shugar testimony, 2087, https://heritage.canadiana.ca/view/oocihm.lac_reel_t1369/96.
275 LAC, RG33-62, Agents of a Foreign Power fonds, Reel T-1369, Shugar testimony, 2091, https://heritage.canadiana.ca/view/oocihm.lac_reel_t1369/100.
276 LAC, RG33-62, Agents of a Foreign Power fonds, Reel T-1369, Shugar testimony, 2092, https://heritage.canadiana.ca/view/oocihm.lac_reel_t1369/101.
277 LAC, RG33-62, Agents of a Foreign Power fonds, Reel T-1369, Shugar testimony, 2093, https://heritage.canadiana.ca/view/oocihm.lac_reel_t1369/102.
278 LAC, RG33-62, Agents of a Foreign Power fonds, Reel T-1369, Shugar testimony, 2094, https://heritage.canadiana.ca/view/oocihm.lac_reel_t1369/104.
279 LAC, RG33-62, Agents of a Foreign Power fonds, Reel T-1369, Shugar testimony, 2095, https://heritage.canadiana.ca/view/oocihm.lac_reel_t1369/105.
280 LAC, RG33-62, Agents of a Foreign Power fonds, Reel T-1369, Shugar testimony, 2106, https://heritage.canadiana.ca/view/oocihm.lac_reel_t1369/116.
281 LAC, RG33-62, Agents of a Foreign Power fonds, Reel T-1369, Shugar testimony, 2099, https://heritage.canadiana.ca/view/oocihm.lac_reel_t1369/109.
282 LAC, RG33-62, Agents of a Foreign Power fonds, Reel T-1369, Shugar testimony, 2136, https://heritage.canadiana.ca/view/oocihm.lac_reel_t1369/155.
283 LAC, RG33-62, Agents of a Foreign Power fonds, Reel T-1369, A.W. Beament (Beament) testimony, 2513, https://heritage.canadiana.ca/view/oocihm.lac_reel_t1369/533.
284 LAC, RG33-62, Agents of a Foreign Power fonds, Reel T-1369, Beament testimony, 2513, https://heritage.canadiana.ca/view/oocihm.lac_reel_t1369/533.
285 TNA, KV 2/1423, s. 170A, *Documents Relating to the Proceedings of the Royal Commission, Second Interim Report,* 20.
286 "Orders Halperin To Stand Trial, Releases Shugar," *Globe & Mail,* 25 April 1946.
287 Douglas How, "His Red Link Minus Deceit, Carr Claims," *Globe & Mail,* 8 April 1949, 1.
288 LAC, RG33-62, Agents of a Foreign Power fonds, Reel T-1370, Gouzenko testimony, 5069–70, https://heritage.canadiana.ca/view/oocihm.lac_reel_t1370/1241.

289 LAC, RG33-62, Agents of a Foreign Power fonds, Reel T-1370, Gouzenko testimony, 5069–70, https://heritage.canadiana.ca/view/oocihm.lac_reel_t1370/1241, 5283, https://heritage.canadiana.ca/view/oocihm.lac_reel_t1370/1458.

290 LAC, RG33-62, Agents of a Foreign Power fonds, Reel T-1370, Gouzenko testimony, 5284, https://heritage.canadiana.ca/view/oocihm.lac_reel_t1370/1459.

291 LAC, RG33-62, Agents of a Foreign Power fonds, Reel T-1370, Gouzenko testimony, 5069–70, https://heritage.canadiana.ca/view/oocihm.lac_reel_t1370/1241.

292 Dr. Frederick Earl Beamish graduated from McMaster University, taught analytical chemistry at the University of Toronto from 1928 to 1974, and earned an international reputation as a specialist in gold and platinum. https://discoverarchives.library.utoronto.ca/index.php/frederick-earl-beamish-fonds.

293 For Comach's account of the distribution of responsibilities, see LAC, RG33-62, Agents of a Foreign Power fonds, Reel T-1368, Comach testimony, 1860–1, https://heritage.canadiana.ca/view/oocihm.lac_reel_t1368/1933.

294 LAC, RG33-62, Agents of a Foreign Power fonds, Reel T-1370, Beamish testimony, 4925, https://heritage.canadiana.ca/view/oocihm.lac_reel_t1370/1098.

295 LAC, RG33-62, Agents of a Foreign Power fonds, Reel T-1370, Beamish testimony, 4932, https://heritage.canadiana.ca/view/oocihm.lac_reel_t1370/1105.

296 LAC, RG33-62, Agents of a Foreign Power fonds, Reel T-1370, Beamish testimony, 4918, https://heritage.canadiana.ca/view/oocihm.lac_reel_t1370/1091.

297 LAC, RG33-62, Agents of a Foreign Power fonds, Reel T-1370, Beamish testimony, 4919, https://heritage.canadiana.ca/view/oocihm.lac_reel_t1370/1092.

298 LAC, RG33-62, Agents of a Foreign Power fonds, Reel T-1370, Beamish testimony, 4922–3, https://heritage.canadiana.ca/view/oocihm.lac_reel_t1370/1095.

299 Later at trial Shugar didn't disagree on this point. "Gave Russia No Data, Shugar Says in Defense," *Globe & Mail*, 30 November 1946, 7.

300 Dr. F.E. Beamish to Lieut. Commander N.W. Anderson, 9 January 1945, Exhibit #508. LAC, RG33-62, Agents of a Foreign Power fonds, Reel T-3432, 826. Beamish copied his letter to Dr. R. McIntosh, Maass's assistant at McGill. https://heritage.canadiana.ca/view/oocihm.lac_reel_t3432/826; LAC, RG33-62, Agents of a Foreign Power fonds, Reel T-3432, Exhibit 509, Professor F.E. Beamish to Dr. R. McIntosh, McGill

University 11 January 1945, 831, https://heritage.canadiana.ca/view/oocihm.lac_reel_t3432/831.

301 LAC, RG33-62, Agents of a Foreign Power fonds, Reel T-1370, Beamish testimony, 4921, https://heritage.canadiana.ca/view/oocihm.lac_reel_t1370/1094.

302 LAC, RG33-62, Agents of a Foreign Power fonds, Reel T-1370, Beamish testimony, 4924, https://heritage.canadiana.ca/view/oocihm.lac_reel_t1370/1097.

303 LAC, RG33-62, Agents of a Foreign Power fonds, Reel T-1369, Shugar testimony, 2026, https://heritage.canadiana.ca/view/oocihm.lac_reel_t1369/35.

304 LAC, RG33-62, Agents of a Foreign Power fonds, Reel T-1369, Shugar testimony, 2027, https://heritage.canadiana.ca/view/oocihm.lac_reel_t1369/36. On Chisholm, see Griffin, J., and Nathan Baker. "Brock Chisholm," *The Canadian Encyclopedia*, Historica Canada, https://www.thecanadianencyclopedia.ca/en/article/brock-chisholm.

305 LAC, RG33-62, Agents of a Foreign Power fonds, Reel T-1369, Shugar testimony, 2027, https://heritage.canadiana.ca/view/oocihm.lac_reel_t1369/36.

306 LAC, RG33-62, Agents of a Foreign Power fonds, Reel T-1370, King testimony, 5032–3, https://heritage.canadiana.ca/view/oocihm.lac_reel_t1370/1204.

307 LAC, RG33-62, Agents of a Foreign Power fonds, Reel T-1370, King testimony, 5037, https://heritage.canadiana.ca/view/oocihm.lac_reel_t1370/1209.

308 LAC, RG33-62, Agents of a Foreign Power fonds, Reel T-1370, King testimony, 5037, https://heritage.canadiana.ca/view/oocihm.lac_reel_t1370/1209.

309 LAC, RG33-62, Agents of a Foreign Power fonds, Reel T-1370, King testimony, 5032–3, https://heritage.canadiana.ca/view/oocihm.lac_reel_t1370/1204.

310 LAC, RG33-62, Agents of a Foreign Power fonds, Reel T-3423, Exhibit 20A, N 232, To the Director, 2.8.45, 434, https://heritage.canadiana.ca/view/oocihm.lac_reel_t3423/434.

311 LAC, RG33-62, Agents of a Foreign Power fonds, Reel T-1370, Beament testimony, 5231, https://heritage.canadiana.ca/view/oocihm.lac_reel_t1370/1405.

312 LAC, RG33-62, Agents of a Foreign Power fonds, Reel T-1370, Beament testimony, 5035, https://heritage.canadiana.ca/view/oocihm.lac_reel_t1370/1409.

313 LAC, RG33-62, Agents of a Foreign Power fonds, Reel T-1370, Commissioner Taschereau, 5234, https://heritage.canadiana.ca/view/oocihm.lac_reel_t1370/1408.

314 LAC, RG33-62, Agents of a Foreign Power fonds, Reel T-1370, Commissioner Kellock, 5230–1, https://heritage.canadiana.ca/view/oocihm.lac_reel_t137/1404.

315 On "wartime jurisprudence" in Canada, see Eric M. Adams, "The Idea of Constitutional Rights and the Transformation of Canadian Constitutional Law, 1930–1960," unpublished PhD diss., University of Toronto, 2009, 88.

316 TNA, KV 2/1423, 170A, *Documents Relating to the Proceedings of the Royal Commission, Second Interim Report,* 20.

317 *The Report of the Royal Commission* (*Final Report*), 313, https://publications.gc.ca/site/eng/9.699909/publication.html.

318 St. John v. Fraser, 1935 SCR 441 (SCC), https://canlii.ca/t/21v2z.

319 Inquiries Act, s. 13, 258.

320 "New Disclosures Mean that Dr. Shugar Must Stand Trial," *Globe & Mail,* 25 September 1946, 15.

321 Ottawa (CP), "Dr. D. Shugar Is Acquitted," *Medicine Hat Daily News,*" 7 December 1946, 1.

322 Lambertson, *Repression and Resistance,* 143–95; Amy Knight, *How the Cold War Began: The Igor Gouzenko Affair and the Hunt for Soviet Spies* (New York: Carroll & Graf, 2005), 145; Reg Whitaker, "The Gouzenko Affair," in *Canadian State Trials,* vol. 5: *World War, Cold War, and Challenges to Sovereignty, 1939–1990,* ed. Barry Wright, Susan Binnie, and Eric Tucker (Toronto: University of Toronto Press, 2022), 150–1.

323 LAC, RG33-62, Agents of a Foreign Power fonds, Reel T-3423, Exhibit 28, Document in handwriting of Gray (Gerson), 817, https://heritage.canadiana.ca/view/oocihm.lac_reel_t3423/817.

324 LAC, RG33-62, Agents of a Foreign Power fonds, Reel T-1368, Gouzenko testimony, 272–4, https://heritage.canadiana.ca/view/oocihm.lac_reel_t1368/322.

325 LAC, RG33-62, Agents of a Foreign Power fonds, Reel T-1368, Gouzenko testimony, 135, 273, https://heritage.canadiana.ca/view/oocihm.lac_reel_t1368/323.

326 LAC, RG33-62, Agents of a Foreign Power fonds, Reel T-3426, Exhibit 209, O-B Investigation no. 1, 206, 201, https://heritage.canadiana.ca/view/oocihm.lac_reel_t3426/201.

327 LAC, RG33-62, Agents of a Foreign Power fonds, Reel T-1369, H.R. Malley, Director General Ammunitions Branch, Department of Munitions and Supply, (Malley) testimony, 11 March 1946, 2201, https://heritage.canadiana.ca/view/oocihm.lac_reel_t1369/220.

328 LAC, RG33-62, Agents of a Foreign Power fonds, Reel T-1369, Malley testimony, 2205, https://heritage.canadiana.ca/view/oocihm.lac_reel_t1369/224.

329 LAC, RG33-62, Agents of a Foreign Power fonds, Reel T-1369, Malley testimony, 2195–6, https://heritage.canadiana.ca/view/oocihm.lac_reel_t1369/214.

330 LAC, RG33-62, Agents of a Foreign Power fonds, Reel T-1369, Malley testimony, 2198, https://heritage.canadiana.ca/view/oocihm.lac_reel_t1369/217.

331 LAC, RG33-62, Agents of a Foreign Power fonds, Reel T-1369, Harold Samuel Gerson testimony, 2269–74, https://heritage.canadiana.ca/view/oocihm.lac_reel_t1369/288.

332 LAC, RG33-62, Agents of a Foreign Power fonds, Reel T-3427, Exhibit 214, "H.R. Malley to L.L. Price," 30 November 1945, 744–5, https://heritage.canadiana.ca/view/oocihm.lac_reel_t3427/745.

333 LAC, RG33-62, Agents of a Foreign Power fonds, Reel T-3427, Exhibit 28, Document in handwriting of Gray (Gerson), 817, https://heritage.canadiana.ca/view/oocihm.lac_reel_t3423/817.

334 LAC, RG33-62, Agents of a Foreign Power fonds, Reel T-1369, Malley testimony, 2192, https://heritage.canadiana.ca/view/oocihm.lac_reel_t1369/211.

335 LAC, RG33-62, Agents of a Foreign Power fonds, Reel T-1368, Gerson testimony, 2385, https://heritage.canadiana.ca/view/oocihm.lac_reel_t1369/404.

336 LAC, RG33-62, Agents of a Foreign Power fonds, Reel T-1368, Gouzenko testimony, 272–3, https://heritage.canadiana.ca/view/oocihm.lac_reel_t1368/323.

337 LAC, RG33-62, Agents of a Foreign Power fonds, Reel T-1369, Gerson testimony, 2353, https://heritage.canadiana.ca/view/oocihm.lac_reel_t1369/372.

338 LAC, RG33-62, Agents of a Foreign Power fonds, Reel T-1369, Gerson testimony, 2354, https://heritage.canadiana.ca/view/oocihm.lac_reel_t1369/273.

339 LAC, RG33-62, Agents of a Foreign Power fonds, Reel T-1369, Gerson testimony, 2367, https://heritage.canadiana.ca/view/oocihm.lac_reel_t1369/386.

340 LAC, RG33-62, Agents of a Foreign Power fonds, Reel T-1369, Gerson testimony, 2354–5, https://heritage.canadiana.ca/view/oocihm.lac_reel_t1369/373.

341 LAC, RG33-62, Agents of a Foreign Power fonds, Reel T-1369, Gerson testimony, 2358–60, https://heritage.canadiana.ca/view/oocihm.lac_reel_t1369/379.

342 LAC, RG33-62, Agents of a Foreign Power fonds, Reel T-1369, Gerson testimony, 2361, https://heritage.canadiana.ca/view/oocihm.lac_reel_t1369/380.

343 LAC, RG33-62, Agents of a Foreign Power fonds, Reel T-1369, Gerson testimony, 2385, https://heritage.canadiana.ca/view/oocihm.lac_reel_t1369/404.
344 LAC, RG33-62, Agents of a Foreign Power fonds, Reel T-1369, Malley testimony, 2205, https://heritage.canadiana.ca/view/oocihm.lac_reel_t1369/224.
345 LAC, RG33-62, Agents of a Foreign Power fonds, Reel T-1369, Gerson testimony, 2305, https://heritage.canadiana.ca/view/oocihm.lac_reel_t1369/324.
346 LAC, RG33-62, Agents of a Foreign Power fonds, Reel T-1369, Gerson testimony, 2306, https://heritage.canadiana.ca/view/oocihm.lac_reel_t136/325.
347 On the meaning of "Roofs" and "Lesovia," see LAC, RG33-62, Agents of a Foreign Power fonds, Reel T-1368, Gouzenko testimony, 301–2, https://heritage.canadiana.ca/view/oocihm.lac_reel_t1369/350.
348 LAC, RG33-62, Agents of a Foreign Power fonds, Reel T-3424, Exhibit 34A, To the Director from Grant, 28.4.44, 46, https://heritage.canadiana.ca/view/oocihm.lac_reel_t3424/46.
349 Kevin Riehle, *Soviet Defectors: Revelations of Renegade Intelligence Officers, 1924–1954* (Edinburgh: Edinburgh University Press, 2020), 156.
350 LAC, RG33-62, Agents of a Foreign Power fonds, Reel T-3424, Exhibit 34A, To the Director from Grant, 28.4.44, 43, https://heritage.canadiana.ca/view/oocihm.lac_reel_t3424/43.
351 LAC, RG33-62, Agents of a Foreign Power fonds, Reel T-1369, Gerson testimony, 2459–1, https://heritage.canadiana.ca/view/oocihm.lac_reel_t1369/479.
352 LAC, RG33-62, Agents of a Foreign Power fonds, Reel T-1369, Gerson testimony, 2460–1, https://heritage.canadiana.ca/view/oocihm.lac_reel_t1369/480.
353 LAC, RG33-62, Agents of a Foreign Power fonds, Reel T-1368, Gouzenko testimony, 107, https://heritage.canadiana.ca/view/oocihm.lac_reel_t1369/168.
354 LAC, RG33-62, Agents of a Foreign Power fonds, Reel T-3423, Exhibit 22A, Page out of notebook in Col. Zabotin's handwriting, Second Group, Foster, 642, https://heritage.canadiana.ca/view/oocihm.lac_reel_t3423/642.
355 LAC, RG33-62, Agents of a Foreign Power fonds, Reel T-1369, Gerson testimony, 2460, https://heritage.canadiana.ca/view/oocihm.lac_reel_t1369/480.
356 LAC, RG33-62, Agents of a Foreign Power fonds, Reel T-1369, Gerson testimony, 2460–1, https://heritage.canadiana.ca/view/oocihm.lac_reel_t1369/480.

357 LAC, RG33-62, Agents of a Foreign Power fonds, Reel T-3423, Exhibit 25BB, Page out of notebook in Col. Zabotin's handwriting, Before Re-organization, Fred's work, 1 Gray, 772, https://heritage.canadiana.ca/view/oocihm.lac_reel_t3423/771. Gouzenko pointed out that the translation rendered as "Director" in the exhibit should read "Directed by." LAC, RG33-62, Agents of a Foreign Power fonds, Reel T-1368, 247, https://heritage.canadiana.ca/view/oocihm.lac_reel_t1368/308.

358 LAC, RG33-62, Agents of a Foreign Power fonds, Reel T-1368, Gouzenko testimony, 247, https://heritage.canadiana.ca/view/oocihm.lac_reel_t1368/308.

359 LAC, RG33-62, Agents of a Foreign Power fonds, Reel T-34223, Exhibit 25BB, Page out of notebook in Col. Zabotin's handwriting, Before re-organization, Second Group, Director Davie, Fred's Work 1. Gray, 771, https://heritage.canadiana.ca/view/oocihm.lac_reel_t3423/771.

360 LAC, RG33-62, Agents of a Foreign Power fonds, Reel T-1369, Gerson testimony, 2284–6, https://heritage.canadiana.ca/view/oocihm.lac_reel_t1369/504.

361 LAC, RG33-62, Agents of a Foreign Power fonds, Reel T-1369, Gerson testimony, 2457, https://heritage.canadiana.ca/view/oocihm.lac_reel_t1369/477.

362 LAC, RG33-62, Agents of a Foreign Power fonds, Reel T-1369, Gerson testimony, 2482–3, https://heritage.canadiana.ca/view/oocihm.lac_reel_t1369/502

363 LAC, RG33-62, Agents of a Foreign Power fonds, Reel T-1369, Gerson testimony, 2483, 2485, https://heritage.canadiana.ca/view/oocihm.lac_reel_t1369/505.

364 LAC, RG33-62, Agents of a Foreign Power fonds, Reel T-1369, Gerson testimony, 2290, https://heritage.canadiana.ca/view/oocihm.lac_reel_t1369/510.

365 LAC, RG33-62, Agents of a Foreign Power fonds, Reel T-1369, Gerson testimony, 2298, https://heritage.canadiana.ca/view/oocihm.lac_reel_t1369/317.

366 LAC, RG33-62, Agents of a Foreign Power fonds, Reel T-1368, Boyer testimony, 1767, https://heritage.canadiana.ca/view/oocihm.lac_reel_t1368/1840.

367 LAC, RG33-62, Agents of a Foreign Power fonds, Reel T-1369, Gerson testimony, 2293, https://heritage.canadiana.ca/view/oocihm.lac_reel_t1369/312.

368 The Gouzenko affair added to the general animus against Jews in Canada. Gerald Tulchinsky, *Canada's Jews: A People's Journey* (Toronto: University of Toronto Press, 2008), 284–327.

369 LAC, RG33-62, Agents of a Foreign Power fonds, Reel T-1369, Gerson testimony, 2496, https://heritage.canadiana.ca/view/oocihm.lac_reel_t1369/516.
370 LAC, RG33-62, Agents of a Foreign Power fonds, Reel T-1369, Gerson testimony, 2476–7, https://heritage.canadiana.ca/view/oocihm.lac_reel_t1369/496.
371 LAC, RG33-62, Agents of a Foreign Power fonds, Reel T-1369, R.W. MacLean (Maclean) testimony, 3171, http://heritage.canadiana.ca/view/oocihm.lac_reel_t1369/1213. Maclean, as secretary of the Department of Reconstruction and Supply, had possession of the records of Munitions and Supply.
372 LAC, RG33-62, Agents of a Foreign Power fonds, Reel T-3423, Exhibit 16A, Record of the Materials, nos. 196, 197, 198, 260, https://heritage.canadiana.ca/view/oocihm.lac_reel_t3423/260.
373 LAC, RG33-62, Agents of a Foreign Power fonds, Reel T-3423, Exhibit 16A, Record of the Materials Sent, nos. 196, 197, 198, 260, https://heritage.canadiana.ca/view/oocihm.lac_reel_t3423/260.
374 LAC, RG33-62, Agents of a Foreign Power fonds, Reel T-3423, Exhibit 16A, Record of the Materials Sent, Foster, 255, https://heritage.canadiana.ca/view/oocihm.lac_reel_t3423/260.
375 See for example LAC, RG33-62, Agents of a Foreign Power fonds, Reel T-3427, Exhibit 218, *Forecast of War Production in Canada for 1944 and 1ST and 2ND QTRS. of 1945*, Ottawa, 1 July 1944, Department of Munitions and Supply, Economics and Statistics Branch, 782, https://heritage.canadiana.ca/view/oocihm.lac_reel_t3427/782.
376 LAC, RG33-62, Agents of a Foreign Power fonds, Reel T-1369, Gerson testimony, 2379–80, https://heritage.canadiana.ca/view/oocihm.lac_reel_t1369/398.
377 LAC, RG33-62, Agents of a Foreign Power fonds, Reel T-1369, Malley testimony, 2222, https://heritage.canadiana.ca/view/oocihm.lac_reel_t1369/241.
378 For the categories, see LAC, RG33-62, Agents of a Foreign Power fonds, Reel T-3427, Exhibit 218a, *Monthly Supplement to Quarterly Forecast of War production for October 1st, 1944*, Department of Munitions and Supply, Economics and Statistics Branch, 774, https://heritage.canadiana.ca/view/oocihm.lac_reel_t3427/774.
379 LAC, RG33-62, Agents of a Foreign Power fonds, Reel T-3423, Exhibit 16A, Record of the Materials Sent, items 196–8, 260, https://heritage.canadiana.ca/view/oocihm.lac_reel_t3423/254.
380 LAC, RG33-62, Agents of a Foreign Power fonds, Reel T-3423, Exhibit 20A, Telegram no. 232, To the Director from Grant, 2.8.45, 435, https://heritage.canadiana.ca/view/oocihm.lac_reel_t3423/435.

381 LAC, RG33-62, Agents of a Foreign Power fonds, Reel T-1369, Malley testimony, 2223–5, https://heritage.canadiana.ca/view/oocihm.lac_reel_t1369/242.
382 LAC, RG33-62, Agents of a Foreign Power fonds, Reel T-1369, Gerson testimony, 2402, https://heritage.canadiana.ca/view/oocihm.lac_reel_t1369/421.
383 LAC, RG33-62, Agents of a Foreign Power fonds, Reel T-3427, Exhibit 215, "G.K. Sheils to All Crown Plants under Private Management, Crown-Owned Companies, Directors General of Production Branches," 5 May 1945, 750–4, https://heritage.canadiana.ca/view/oocihm.lac_reel_t3427/750.
384 LAC, RG33-62, Agents of a Foreign Power fonds, Reel T-1369, Malley testimony, 2211, https://heritage.canadiana.ca/view/oocihm.lac_reel_t136/230.
385 LAC, RG33-62, Agents of a Foreign Power fonds, Reel T-1369, Gerson testimony, 2376, https://heritage.canadiana.ca/view/oocihm.lac_reel_t1369/395.
386 LAC, RG33-62, Agents of a Foreign Power fonds, Reel T-1369, Commission counsel Williams, 2410, https://heritage.canadiana.ca/view/oocihm.lac_reel_t1369/430.
387 LAC, RG33-62, Agents of a Foreign Power fonds, Reel T-1369, Gerson testimony, 2413, https://heritage.canadiana.ca/view/oocihm.lac_reel_t1369/433.
388 For Gouzenko's interpretation of this telegram, see LAC, RG33-62, Agents of a Foreign Power fonds, Reel T-1368, Gouzenko testimony, 206–8, https://heritage.canadiana.ca/view/oocihm.lac_reel_t1368/267.
389 LAC, RG33-62, Agents of a Foreign Power fonds, Reel T-3423, Exhibit 23CC, Incoming telegram in the handwriting of Lieut. Koulakov, no. 11295, To Grant from the Director, 14.8.45, 669, https://heritage.canadiana.ca/view/oocihm.lac_reel_t3423/669.
390 LAC, RG33-62, Agents of a Foreign Power fonds, Reel T-1369, Malley testimony, 2235, https://heritage.canadiana.ca/view/oocihm.lac_reel_t1369/254.
391 LAC, RG33-62, Agents of a Foreign Power fonds, Reel T-1369, Malley testimony, 2236, https://heritage.canadiana.ca/view/oocihm.lac_reel_t1369/255.
392 LAC, RG33-62, Agents of a Foreign Power fonds, Reel T-1369, Gerson testimony, 2415–17, https://heritage.canadiana.ca/view/oocihm.lac_reel_t1369/435.
393 LAC, RG33-62, Agents of a Foreign Power fonds, Reel T-1369, Gerson testimony, 2418, https://heritage.canadiana.ca/view/oocihm.lac_reel_t1369/438. Nitrocellulose served as a replacement for gunpowder in

firearms. J. Naas, "Nitrocellulose," *Encyclopedia of Toxicology*, 2nd ed., https: / / www.sciencedirect.com / topics / chemical-engineering / nitrocellulose.

394 LAC, RG33-62, Agents of a Foreign Power fonds, Reel T-3423, Exhibit 20MM, no. 263, To the Director, 25.8.45, 541–2, https: / / heritage .canadiana.ca / view / oocihm.lac_reel_t3423 / 541.

395 LAC, RG33-62, Agents of a Foreign Power fonds, Reel T-1369, Gerson testimony, 2423, https: / / heritage.canadiana.ca / view / oocihm.lac_reel _t1369 / 443.

396 TNA, MI5, KV 2 / 1422, Holmes to Cadogan, no. 229, 27.2.46, s. 82a.

397 TNA, MI5, KV 2 / 1422, Holmes to Sargent, no. 283, 3.3.46, s. 99a.

398 LAC, RG33-62, Agents of a Foreign Power fonds, Reel T-1369, RCMP Inspector C.W. Harvison testimony, 2427, https: / / heritage.canadiana.ca / view / oocihm.lac_reel_t1369 / 447.

399 LAC, RG33-62, Agents of a Foreign Power fonds, Reel T-1369, Harvison testimony, 2428, https: / / heritage.canadiana.ca / view / oocihm.lac_reel _t1369 / 448.

400 LAC, RG33-62, Agents of a Foreign Power fonds, Reel T-1369, Gerson testimony, 2427–8, https: / / heritage.canadiana.ca / view / oocihm.lac_reel _t1369 / 447.

401 Later, on this evidence, two juries would convict Gerson of conspiracy to violate the Official Secrets Act. "Gerson Guilty a Second Time," *Globe & Mail*, 10 October 1947, 1.

402 Statues of Canada, 1912, An Act to Amend the Inquiries Act, c. 28, s. 13, 258.

403 TNA, KV 2 / 1423, s. 170A, *Documents Relating to the Proceedings of the Royal Commission, Second Interim Report, 17.*

Chapter 10: In the House of Commons

1 William Lyon Mackenzie King, *Canada and the War: Victory, Reconstruction and Peace: Mackenzie King to the People*, 1945 (Ottawa?: s.n., 1945), 15.

2 King, *Canada and the War*, 121.

3 The National Emergency Transitional Powers Act, S.C. 1945, c. 25.

4 The National Emergency Transitional Powers Act remained in force until 31 March 1947, only to be replaced by the Continuation of Transitional Measures Act, which stayed in place until 30 April 1951. For the act, see The Continuation of Transitional Measures Act, S.C. 1947, c. 16; Peter Niemczak and Philip Rosen, "Emergency Powers Act," https: / / publications.gc.ca / Collection-R / LoPBdP / BP / prb0114-e.htm.

5 LAC, Diaries of WLMK, 13 February 1946, 2.

6 *Ottawa Journal*, 28 February 1946, as quoted in LAC, Gordon Papers, Report, 9.

7 "To The Honourable L.S. St. Laurent, KC, Minister of Justice, Ottawa, 14 March 1946 from E. K. Williams, Gérald Fauteux and D.W. Mundell, Counsel for the Commission," in Hon. W.L.M. King in House of Commons, *Debates*, 15 March 1946, 4.

8 "Brais & Campbell, Royal Bank Building, 360 St. James St. West, Montreal, March 12, 1946, to E.K. Williams, G.H Fauteux, Justice Building, Ottawa (Secret and Confidential)" in Hon. W.L.M. King in House of Commons, *Debates*, 15 March 1946, 6–7.

9 TNA, KV 2/1422, MacDonald to Sargent, No.368, 14.3.46, s. 136A.

10 TNA, KV 2/1422, MacDonald to Sargent, no. 338, 11.3.46, s. 126A.

11 LAC, Diaries of WLMK, 14 March 1946, 2.

12 See Fred Rose, Montreal Jail, Bordeaux, Que., to Louis St. Laurent, Minister of Justice, 9 July 1946, in Unpublished Sessional Papers, 2nd Session of the 20th Parliament, 1946, no. 132g, RG 14, D2, vol. 502, 1.

13 "Rose Released on $10,000 Bail," *Winnipeg Free Press*, 15 March 1946, 1.

14 "Mr King's Spy Story," *Ottawa Journal*, 20 March 1946.

15 David Glover, "Edgar Richard Horatio Wallace," *Oxford Dictionary of National Biography*, https://www.oxforddnb.com/view/10.1093/ref:odnb/9780198614128.001.0001/odnb-9780198614128-e-36703.

16 "Mr King's Spy Story," *Ottawa Journal*, 20 March 1946.

17 W.L.M. King in House of Commons, *Debates*, 15 March 1946, 7.

18 W.L.M. King in House of Commons, *Debates*, 15 March 1946, 7.

19 W.L.M. King in House of Commons, *Debates*, 15 March 1946, 7.

20 W.L.M. King in House of Commons, *Debates*, 15 March 1946, 7. Section 13 of the Inquiries Act required that "no report shall be made against any person until reasonable notice shall have been given to him of the charge of misconduct alleged against him and he shall have been allowed full opportunity to be heard in person or by counsel." Statutes of Canada, 1912, An Act to Amend the Inquiries Act, c. 28, s. 13, 258.

21 LAC, RG33-62, Agents of a Foreign Power fonds, Reel T-1370, Commissioner Kellock, 5230–1, 5234, https://heritage.canadiana.ca/view/oocihm.lac_reel_t1370/1404.

22 "Claim McGill Professor Gave Secret of RDX Explosive to Russians," *Globe & Mail*, 16 March 1946, 1.

23 Kenneth C. Cragg, "Charges Laid against Three More," *Globe & Mail*, 16 March, 1946, 1, 4.

24 M.J. Coldwell in House of Commons, *Debates*, 15 March 1946, 4.

25 W.L.M. King in House of Commons, *Debates*, 15 March 1946, 4.

26 King tabled the correspondence from Williams, Fauteux, Mundell, and Philippe Brais upon which St. Laurent had based his decision to have Rose charged and arrested. W.L.M. King in House of Commons, *Debates*, 15 March 1946, 5.

27 John Bracken in House of Commons, *Debates*, 15 March 1946, 8.
28 W.L.M. King in House of Commons, *Debates*, 15 March 1946, 8.
29 Mark Goldie, "Retrospect: The Ancient Constitution and the Languages of Political Thought," *Historical Journal* 62, no. 1 (2019): 4.
30 "Salus populi suprema lex esto, n." *OED Online*, September 2022, https://www.oed.com/dictionary/salus-populi-suprema-lex-esto_n?tab=factsheet#24430585.
31 Locke described *salus populi suprema lex esto* as "certainly so just and fundamental a Rule, that he, who sincerely follows it cannot dangerously err." John Locke, *Two Treatises of Government*, ed. Peter Laslett (Cambridge: Cambridge University Press, 1967), §158, 391.
32 Locke, *Two Treatises of Government*, §160, 393.
33 For a prominent use of this phrase, see Justice Robert H. Jackson's dissenting opinion in Terminiello v. City of Chicago, 337 U.S. 1 (1949), https://supreme.justia.com/cases/federal/us/337/1/.
34 Locke, *Two Treatises of Government*, §160, 393.
35 Locke's account of prerogative power in a liberal state contained a caution: "If there comes to be a question between the executive power and the people about a thing claimed as a prerogative," he observed, "the tendency of the exercise of such prerogative, to the good or hurt of the people, will easily decide that question." Locke, *Two Treatises of Government*, §160, 393.
36 The *Report* was published in the *Globe & Mail*. "Commission Recommends New Spy Charges Against Four Additional Canadians," *Globe & Mail*, 16 March 1946, 7.
37 For this document see TNA, KV 2/1423, s. 170A, Documents Relating to the Proceedings of the Royal Commission of the Royal Commission.
38 LAC, RG33-62, Agents of a Foreign Power fonds, Reel T-3434, Canadian Ambassador to the United States to Secretary of State for External Affairs, Canada, CONFIDENTIAL, 16 March 1946, WA-1224, 517, https://heritage.canadiana.ca/view/oocihm.lac_reel_t3434/517
39 See for example "How the Army's Hush Hush Can Ruin Us," *PM*, 8 March 1946, 2.
40 LAC, RG33-62, Agents of a Foreign Power fonds, Reel T-3434, Canadian Ambassador to the United States to Secretary of State for External Affairs, Canada, CONFIDENTIAL, 16 March 1946, WA-1224, 518–19, https://heritage.canadiana.ca/view/oocihm.lac_reel_t3434/518
41 TNA, KV 2/1422, MacDonald to Sargent, no. 380, 15.3.46, s. 141A.
42 TNA, KV4/467, Guy Liddell Diaries, 18 March 1946, 135.
43 John Bracken in House of Commons, *Debates*, 18 March 1946, 37.
44 John Bracken in House of Commons, *Debates*, 18 March 1946, 37.
45 See "State of Apprehended War Exists Proclamation Says," *Lethbridge Herald*, 2 September 1939, 16. The existence of a state of war was

proclaimed 10 September 1939. PC 2626, Proclamations and Orders-in-Council Passed Under the Authority of the War Measures Act R.S.C. (1927) C. 206 (Ottawa: King's Printer, 1940), 52.

46 The National Emergency Transitional Powers Act approved in December 1945 came into force 1 January 1946. Section 5 of that statute declared that "on and after that day [1 January 1946], the war against Germany and Japan shall be deemed, for purposes of the War Measures Act, no longer to exist." The National Emergency Transitional Powers Act, 1945, C. 25, Statutes of Canada, 9–10 George VI, 20th Parliament, 1st Session (1945), 177–80.

47 Library Archives Canada, Canada Gazette, Part II, vol. 104, Ottawa, 16 October 1970, 1, https://recherche-collection-search.bac-lac.gc.ca/eng/home/record?app=cangaz&IdNumber=13861.

48 *Canadian News Facts*, 1970, 527.

49 W.L.M. King in House of Commons, *Debates*, 18 March 1946, 44.

50 Locke, *Two Treatises of Government*, §160, 393. On Locke and prerogative, see Thomas Poole, "Constitutional Exceptionalism and the Common Law," *International Journal of Constitutional Law* 7, no. 2 (2009): 247–74, https://doi.org/10.1093/icon/mop006.

51 W.L.M. King in House of Commons, *Debates*, 18 March 1946, 47.

52 W.L.M. King in House of Commons, *Debates*, 18 March 1946, 45.

53 W.L.M. King in House of Commons, *Debates*, 18 March 1946, 47.

54 W.L.M. King in House of Commons, *Debates*, 18 March 1946, 49.

55 W.L.M. King in House of Commons, *Debates*, 18 March 1946, 48.

56 W.L.M. King in House of Commons, *Debates*, 18 March 1946, 48.

57 W.L.M. King in House of Commons, *Debates*, 18 March 1946, 50.

58 J.R. Coldwell in House of Commons, *Debates*, 18 March 1946, 56.

59 "The Prime Minister's Case," *Ottawa Evening Citizen*, 20 March 1946.

60 *Halifax Chronicle*, 18 March 1946, as quoted in LAC, Gordon Papers, Report, 13.

61 "The Spy Catcher's Defence," *Winnipeg Free Press*, 21 March 1946.

62 "The 'Loyalty' of Spies," *Ottawa Journal*, 16 March 1946.

63 "The 'Loyalty' of Spies," *Ottawa Journal*, 16 March 1946.

64 "Mr. King's Spy Story," *Ottawa Journal*, 20 March 1946.

65 On Smith, see "Former Member for Calgary Riding Art Smith Dies," 21 December 1951, *Medicine Hat News*, 1.

66 Arthur Smith in House of Commons, *Debates*, 19 March 1946, 83.

67 Arthur Smith in House of Commons, *Debates*, 19 March 1946, 83. This was an overly simple account of Canadian developments. As an expert criminal defence lawyer, Smith had to be aware of the strong Benthamite current in Canadian legal reform circles that had pushed law reform in the direction of facilitating criminal prosecutions. See for example Neil Brooks,

"The Law Reform Commission of Canada's Evidence Code," *Osgoode Hall Law Journal* 16, no. 2 (1978): 241–320; Alanah Josey, "Jeremy Bentham and Canadian Evidence Law: The Utilitarian Perspective on Canadian Mistrial Applications," *Manitoba Law Review* 42, no. 4 (2019): 291–313.

68 Arthur Smith in House of Commons, *Debates*, 19 March 1946, 85.

69 R.S.C 1927, Canada Evidence Act, C. 59, Part 1, s. 5(2), 2. The approval of section 13 of the Charter of Rights and Freedoms in 1982 provided absolute protection against self-incrimination: "A witness who testifies in any proceedings has the right not to have any incriminating evidence so given used to incriminate that witness in any other proceedings, except in a prosecution for perjury or for the giving of contradictory evidence." "Charter protection for incrimination cited in retrial order," *Globe & Mail*, 22 November 1985, A5. The Canada Evidence Act was amended in 1993 to reflect the protection provided in the Charter. See R.S.C 1993, Canada Evidence Act, C.5, Part 1, s. 5(2), 2.

70 Arthur Smith in House of Commons, *Debates*, 19 March 1946, 85–8.

71 Louis St. Laurent in House of Commons, *Debates*, 19 March 1946, 88–91.

72 Louis St. Laurent in House of Commons, *Debates*, 19 March 1946, 89.

73 Louis St. Laurent in House of Commons, *Debates*, 19 March 1946, 89.

74 TNA, KV 2/1425, Hume Wrong to Norman Robertson (copy to Sir A. Cadogan) no. 478, 6.10.45, s. 57a.

75 Louis St. Laurent in House of Commons, *Debates*, 19 March 1946, 89.

76 Louis St. Laurent in House of Commons, *Debates*, 19 March 1946, 91.

77 Louis St. Laurent in House of Commons, *Debates*, 19 March 1946, 91.

78 *Toronto Star*, 23 March 1946, as quoted in LAC, Gordon Papers, Report, 5–6.

79 Louis St. Laurent in House of Commons, *Debates*, 19 March 1946, 91.

80 LAC, RG33-62, Agents of a Foreign Power fonds, Reel T-1370, 5229–40, https://heritage.canadiana.ca/view/oocihm.lac_reel_t1370/1403.

81 Louis St. Laurent in House of Commons, *Debates*, 19 March 1946, 92.

82 For the case, see In Re George Edwin Gray, (1918) 57 S.C.R. 150. https://www.canlii.org/en/ca/scc/doc/1918/1918canlii533/1918canlii533.html.

83 On the remarkable career of The Right Honourable Sir Lyman Poore Duff, PC, GCMG, see https://www.scc-csc.ca/judges-juges/bio-eng.aspx?id=lyman-poore-duff.

84 In Re George Edwin Gray, (1918) 57 S.C.R. 150,https://www.canlii.org/en/ca/scc/doc/1918/1918canlii533/1918canlii533.html. For additional commentary on this case, see Patricia Peppin, "Emergency Legislation and Rights in Canada: The War Measures Act and Civil Liberties," *Queen's Law Journal* 18, no. 1 (1993): 148–9.

85 "Diverse Views in Supreme Court on habeas corpus," *Globe & Mail*, 19 July 1918, 4. On Newcombe's role in drafting the War Measures Act, see F. Murray Greenwood, "The Drafting and Passage of the War Measures Act in 1914 and 1927: Object Lessons in the Need for Vigilance," in *Canadian Perspectives on Law and Society: Issues in Legal History*, ed. W. Wesley Pue and Barry Wright (Ottawa: Carleton University Press, 1988), 302–3.
86 On this subject, see James Francis, "The War Measures Act: A Summary of the Cases Reported," *Canadian Bar Review* 19, no. 6 (1941): 453.
87 Ronnfeldt v. Phillips (1918), 35 T.L.R (1918), 47. On Scrutton and the case against Ronnfeldt, see David Foxton, *The Life of Thomas E. Scrutton* (Cambridge: Cambridge University Press, 2013), 210.
88 Ex parte Sullivan, [1941] 1 D.L.R. 676, [1941] O.W.N. 49, as quoted in Francis, "The War Measures Act," 453.
89 The Fort Frances Pulp and Paper Company Limited (Appeal no. 69 of 1923) v The Manitoba Free Press Company Limited and others (Ontario) [1923] UKPC 64 (25 July 1923), 7, https://www.bailii.org/uk/cases/UKPC/1923/1923_64.html.
90 Commissioners of inquiry have no direct authority to enforce a subpoena. John D. Richard, "Judicial Review in Canada," *Duquesne Law Review* 45, no. 3 (2007): 501.
91 The Report of the Royal Commission (Final Report), 654, https://publications.gc.ca/site/eng/9.699909/publication.html.
92 Official Secrets Act, 1939, c. 49, s. 10, Statutes of Canada, 1939, 455.
93 Louis St. Laurent in House of Commons, *Debates*, 19 March 1946, 92–3.
94 Louis St. Laurent in House of Commons, *Debates*, 19 March 1946, 92–3.
95 Louis St. Laurent in House of Commons, *Debates*, 19 March 1946, 92.
96 Defence of Canada Regulations (Ottawa: King's Printer, 1939) 30, https://archive.org/details/defenceofcanadar1939cana/page/32/mode/2up.
97 On "Chubby" Power, see Norman Ward, ed., *C.G. Power, A Party Politician: The Memoirs of Chubby Power* (Toronto: Macmillan, 1966).
98 C.G. Power in House of Commons, *Debates*, 21 March 1946, 170–2.
99 Denis Smith, *Rogue Tory: The Life and Legend of John G. Diefenbaker* (Toronto: Macfarlane Walter & Ross, 1995), 157; Asa Mckercher, "Sound and Fury: Diefenbaker, Human Rights, and Canadian Foreign Policy," *The Canadian Historical Review* 97, no. 2 (2016): 165–94.
100 J.G. Diefenbaker in House of Commons, *Debates*, 21 March 1946, 137.
101 J.G. Diefenbaker in House of Commons, *Debates*, 21 March 1946, 136.
102 J.G. Diefenbaker in House of Commons, *Debates*, 21 March 1946, 138.
103 J.G. Diefenbaker in House of Commons, *Debates*, 21 March 1946, 138.
104 J.G. Diefenbaker in House of Commons, *Debates*, 21 March 1946, 138. Michael Lobban has noticed that "[a]s the British empire expanded in

Africa, many political leaders found themselves detained and deported from their homelands, deprived of their liberty without that due process of law which Britons had long regarded as the hallmark of their constitutional culture." Lobban, *Imperial Incarceration: Detention without Trial in the Making of British Colonial Africa* (Cambridge: Cambridge University Press, 2021), 419.

105 J.G. Diefenbaker in House of Commons, *Debates*, 21 March 1946. 140. Here he referenced a source: William Sharp M'Kechnie, *Magna Carta: A Commentary on the Great Charter of King John*, 2nd ed. (Glasgow: James MacLehose & Sons, 1914).

106 J.G. Diefenbaker in House of Commons, *Debates*, 21 March 1946, 139.

107 A.A. McIntosh, "Price of Liberty," *Globe & Mail*, 23 March 1946, 6.

108 J.G. Diefenbaker in House of Commons, *Debates*, 7 May 1946, 1300.

109 J.G Diefenbaker in House of Commons, *Debates*, 7 May 1946, 1300.

110 J.G. Diefenbaker in House of Commons, *Debates*, 7 May 1946, 1301.

111 Paul Martin in House of Commons, *Debates*, 7 May 1946, 1310–1.

112 Christopher MacLennan, *Toward the Charter: Canadians and the Demand for a National Bill of Rights* (Montreal & Kingston: McGill-Queen's University Press, 2003), 126–51.

113 Dominique Clément, "Spies, Lies, and a Commission: A Case Study in the Mobilization of the Canadian Civil Liberties Movement," *Left History* 7, no. 2 (2000): 53–79; Ross Lambertson, *Repression and Resistance: Canadian Human Rights Activists* (Toronto: University of Toronto Press, 2005), 143–95; Frank K. Clarke, "Debilitating Divisions: The Civil Liberties Movement in Early Cold War Canada, 1946–48," in *Whose National Security?: Canadian State Surveillance and the Creation of Enemies*, ed. Gary Kinsman, Steedman, and D.K. Buse (Toronto: Between the Lines, 2000).

114 B.L. Strayer, "In the Beginning ...: The Origins of Section 15 of the Charter," *Journal of Law & Equality* 5, no. 1 (2006): 15.

Chapter 11: Before the Royal Commission III

1 A.A. McIntosh, "Price of Liberty," *Globe & Mail*, 23 March 1946, 6. For a reference to William Lyon Mackenzie as the "Great Rebel," see "Sale of Historic Farm Recalls Great Rebel's Escape," *Globe & Mail*, 27 March, 1943, 2. For King's pride in his grandfather the "rebel," see LAC, Diaries of WLMK, 28 February 1946, 4.

2 LAC, Diaries of WLMK, 22 March 1946, 2–3.

3 LAC, Diaries of WLMK, 22 March 1946, 2–3.

4 LAC, RG33-62, Agents of a Foreign Power fonds, Reel T-1370, 6042, https://heritage.canadiana.ca/view/oocihm.lac_reel_t1370/2018.

5 For a record of the exhibits accumulated by the inquiry, see LAC, RG33-62, Agents of a Foreign Power fonds, "List of Exhibits," Reel T-3423, 12–82, https://heritage.canadiana.ca/view/oocihm.lac_reel_t3423/12.
6 Christopher Andrew, *Defend the Realm: The Authorized History of MI5* (New York: Alfred Knopf, 2009), 341.
7 LAC, RG33-62, Agents of a Foreign Power fonds, Reel T-1369, Eric Adams testimony, 3465–6, https://heritage.canadiana.ca/view/oocihm.lac_reel_t1369/1517.
8 His position was made official on 1 January. Duncan McDowall, *The Sum of the Satisfactions: Canada in the Age of National Accounting* (Montreal & Kingston: McGill-Queen's University Press, 2008), 87–104.
9 LAC, RG33-62, Agents of a Foreign Power fonds, Reel T-1368, Gouzenko testimony, 70, https://heritage.canadiana.ca/view/oocihm.lac_reel_t1368/132.
10 LAC, RG33-62, Agents of a Foreign Power fonds, Reel T-1369, Adams testimony 2638, https://heritage.canadiana.ca/view/oocihm.lac_reel_t1369/660.
11 LAC, RG33-62, Agents of a Foreign Power fonds, Reel T-1369, Adams testimony, 2641. 9/663, https://heritage.canadiana.ca/view/oocihm.lac_reel_t1369/662.
12 LAC, RG33-62, Agents of a Foreign Power fonds, Reel T-1369, Adams testimony, 2642, https://heritage.canadiana.ca/view/oocihm.lac_reel_t1369/663.
13 LAC, RG33-62, Agents of a Foreign Power fonds, Reel T-1369, Adams testimony, 2647, https://heritage.canadiana.ca/view/oocihm.lac_reel_t1369/668.
14 LAC, RG33-62, Agents of a Foreign Power fonds, Reel T-1369, Adams testimony, 2648, https://heritage.canadiana.ca/view/oocihm.lac_reel_t1369/669.
15 LAC, RG33-62, Agents of a Foreign Power fonds, Reel T-1369, Adams testimony, 2648, https://heritage.canadiana.ca/view/oocihm.lac_reel_t1369/669.
16 LAC, RG33-62, Agents of a Foreign Power fonds, Reel T-1369, Adams testimony, 2649, https://heritage.canadiana.ca/view/oocihm.lac_reel_t1369/670.
17 LAC, RG33-62, Agents of a Foreign Power fonds, Reel T-1369, Adams testimony, 3417, https://heritage.canadiana.ca/view/oocihm.lac_reel_t1369/1467.
18 On Ahearn, see *Winnipeg Free Press*, 18 July 1978, 5.
19 LAC, RG33-62, Agents of a Foreign Power fonds, Reel T-1369, Commissioner Taschereau, 3461, https://heritage.canadiana.ca/view/oocihm.lac_reel_t1369/1512.

20 LAC, RG33-62, Agents of a Foreign Power fonds, Reel T-1369, Commissioner Taschereau, 3464, https://heritage.canadiana.ca/view/oocihm.lac_reel_t1369/1515.
21 LAC, RG33-62, Agents of a Foreign Power fonds, Reel T-1369, Adams testimony, 3462, https://heritage.canadiana.ca/view/oocihm.lac_reel_t1369/1513.
22 For these documents, see LAC, RG33-62, Agents of a Foreign Power fonds, Reel T-3430, Exhibit 272, Personal file of Eric Adams with Foreign Exchange Control Board, Oaths of Fidelity and Secrecy A, B, C, 648–51, https://heritage.canadiana.ca/view/oocihm.lac_reel_t3430/648.
23 LAC, RG33-62, Agents of a Foreign Power fonds, Reel T-1369, Adams testimony, 3474, https://heritage.canadiana.ca/view/oocihm.lac_reel_t1369/1525.
24 See the testimony of Stephen Holmes, deputy high commissioner, on this at LAC, RG33-62, Agents of a Foreign Power fonds, Reel T-1368, Stephen Holmes (Holmes) testimony, 729, https://heritage.canadiana.ca/view/oocihm.lac_reel_t1368/789.
25 TNA, KV 2/1422, Holmes to Sargent, no. 228, 27.2.46, s. 82A.
26 LAC, RG33-62, Agents of a Foreign Power fonds, Reel T-1369, Robert Bryce (Bryce) testimony, 2614, https://heritage.canadiana.ca/view/oocihm.lac_reel_t1369/634. The committee also included representatives from Finance, External Affairs, Munitions and Supply, Wartime Prices and Trade, and National Revenue. For an account of Bryce's early career in the Canadian state, see Robert Bryce, *Maturing in Hard Times: Canada's Department of Finance through the Great Depression* (Montreal & Kingston: McGill-Queen's University Press, 1986) and Robert B. Bryce and Matthew J. Bellamy, *Canada and the Cost of World War II: The International Operations of Canada's Department of Finance, 1939–1947* (Montreal & Kingston: McGill-Queen's University Press, 2005).
27 For the letters, see LAC, RG33-62, Agents of a Foreign Power fonds, Reel T-3424, Exhibit 95, Wilgress to King 11 October 1944, 710–5; and Exhibit 96, Wilgress to King 3 November 1944, 719–24, https://heritage.canadiana.ca/view/oocihm.lac_reel_t3424/710.
28 LAC, RG33-62, Agents of a Foreign Power fonds, Reel T-1369, Bryce testimony, 2616, https://heritage.canadiana.ca/view/oocihm.lac_reel_t1369/636.
29 LAC, RG33-62, Agents of a Foreign Power fonds, Reel T-1369, Adams testimony, 3497–3500, https://heritage.canadiana.ca/view/oocihm.lac_reel_t1369/1548.
30 LAC, RG33-62, Agents of a Foreign Power fonds, Reel T-1369, Adams testimony, 3507, https://heritage.canadiana.ca/view/oocihm.lac_reel_t1369/1558.

31 LAC, RG33-62, Agents of a Foreign Power fonds, Reel T-3423, Exhibit 22A, Page out of notebook in Col. Zabotin's handwriting, Second Group, 2. ERNST, 642–3, https://heritage.canadiana.ca/view/oocihm.lac_reel_t3423/642.

32 Part of the committee title was missing; Gouzenko filled it in. LAC, RG33-62, Agents of a Foreign Power fonds, Reel T-1368, Gouzenko testimony, 143, https://heritage.canadiana.ca/view/oocihm.lac_reel_t1368/204.

33 LAC, RG33-62, Agents of a Foreign Power fonds, Reel T-3423, Exhibit 22A, Page out of notebook in Col. Zabotin's handwriting, Second Group, 2. ERNST, 642–3, https://heritage.canadiana.ca/view/oocihm.lac_reel_t3423/642.

34 LAC, RG33-62, Agents of a Foreign Power fonds, Reel T-3423, Exhibit 16A, Record of the Materials Sent, nos. 180–90, 195, 199–213, https://heritage.canadiana.ca/view/oocihm.lac_reel_t3423/259.

35 LAC, RG33-62, Agents of a Foreign Power fonds, Reel T-3423, Exhibit 16A, Record of the Materials Sent, no. 186, Ernst, Copy, Invention of Waterproofing, 20.12.44, 4 pages, 46, https://heritage.canadiana.ca/view/oocihm.lac_reel_t3423/259.

36 LAC, RG33-62, Agents of a Foreign Power fonds, Reel T-1369, Lesslie Reille Thompson (Thompson) testimony, 2629–30, https://heritage.canadiana.ca/view/oocihm.lac_reel_t1369/649.

37 LAC, RG33-62, Agents of a Foreign Power fonds, Reel T-1369, Thompson testimony, 2630–1, 2635, https://heritage.canadiana.ca/view/oocihm.lac_reel_t1369/650.

38 LAC, RG33-62, Agents of a Foreign Power fonds, Reel T-1369, Thompson testimony, 2628, https://heritage.canadiana.ca/view/oocihm.lac_reel_t1369/648.

39 For the minutes of the 7 December meeting of the MEC, see LAC, RG33-62, Agents of a Foreign Power fonds, Reel T-3430, Exhibit 282A, Minutes of the 7 December meeting of the MEC, 770. The reference to Freeman appears on page 2. https://heritage.canadiana.ca/view/oocihm.lac_reel_t3430/770; https://heritage.canadiana.ca/view/oocihm.lac_reel_t1369/651.

40 LAC, RG33-62, Agents of a Foreign Power fonds, Reel T-1369, Thompson testimony, 2631, https://heritage.canadiana.ca/view/oocihm.lac_reel_t1369/651. For the file, see LAC, RG33-62, Agents of a Foreign Power fonds, Reel T-3430, Exhibit 281A, Department of National Defence Invention file of Major Freeman, Report on a waterproof map surfaced for operational working in any weather, 751, https://heritage.canadiana.ca/view/oocihm.lac_reel_t3430/751.

41 LAC, RG33-62, Agents of a Foreign Power fonds, Reel T-1369, testimony of RCMP Staff Sargent J.H. Pepper (Pepper) testimony, 2524,

https://heritage.canadiana.ca/view/oocihm.lac_reel_t1369/544. For these documents, see LAC, RG33-62, Agents of a Foreign Power fonds, Reel T-3430, Exhibit 239, Minute Book of Main Examining Committee of National Research Council, found in Montreal office of Eric Adams, 15, https://heritage.canadiana.ca/view/oocihm.lac_reel_t3430/15; and Exhibit 240 Inventions Board, M.E.C, Correspondence, found in Montreal Office of Eric Adams, 299, https://heritage.canadiana.ca/view/oocihm.lac_reel_t3430/299.

42 LAC, RG33-62, Agents of a Foreign Power fonds, Reel T-1369, Adams testimony, 3510–11, https://heritage.canadiana.ca/view/oocihm.lac_reel_t1369/1561.

43 LAC, RG33-62, Agents of a Foreign Power fonds, Reel T-1369, Adams testimony, 3653, https://heritage.canadiana.ca/view/oocihm.lac_reel_t1369/1703.

44 LAC, RG33-62, Agents of a Foreign Power fonds, Reel T-1369, Dean G. Marble (Markle) testimony, 2568, https://heritage.canadiana.ca/view/oocihm.lac_reel_t1369/588.

45 LAC, RG33-62, Agents of a Foreign Power fonds, Reel T-1369, Markle testimony, 2569, https://heritage.canadiana.ca/view/oocihm.lac_reel_t1369/589.

46 LAC, RG33-62, Agents of a Foreign Power fonds, Reel T-1369, Markle testimony, 2597, https://heritage.canadiana.ca/view/oocihm.lac_reel_t1369/617.

47 LAC, RG33-62, Agents of a Foreign Power fonds, Reel T-3430, Exhibit 27A, Letters Found in Office Desk of Eric Adams, 703, https://heritage.canadiana.ca/view/oocihm.lac_reel_t3430/703.

48 The main committee was the Committee on Military Affairs, dealing with cartels and national security. LAC, RG33-62, Agents of a Foreign Power fonds, Reel T-1369, Markle testimony, 2598–9, https://heritage.canadiana.ca/view/oocihm.lac_reel_t1369/618. For the letter, see LAC, RG33-62, Agents of a Foreign Power fonds, Reel T-3430, Exhibit 275A, Letters Found in Office Desk of Eric Adams, 704, https://heritage.canadiana.ca/view/oocihm.lac_reel_t3430/704.

49 LAC, RG33-62, Agents of a Foreign Power fonds, Reel T-1369, Markle testimony, 2599, https://heritage.canadiana.ca/view/oocihm.lac_reel_t1369/619. For the letter, see LAC, RG33-62, Agents of a Foreign Power fonds, Reel T-3430, Exhibit 275A, Civil Aeronautics Administration, 4 December 1944, Washington DC,706, https://heritage.canadiana.ca/view/oocihm.lac_reel_t3430/706.

50 LAC, RG33-62, Agents of a Foreign Power fonds, Reel T-1369, Markle testimony, 2598–9. https://heritage.canadiana.ca/view/oocihm.lac_reel_t1369/618.

51 LAC, RG33-62, Agents of a Foreign Power fonds, Reel T-1369, Adams testimony, 3649–50, https://heritage.canadiana.ca/view/oocihm.lac_reel_t1369/1699.
52 LAC, RG33-62, Agents of a Foreign Power fonds, Reel T-1369, Adams testimony, 3538, https://heritage.canadiana.ca/view/oocihm.lac_reel_t1369/1589.
53 For the complete list, see LAC, RG33-62, Agents of a Foreign Power fonds, Reel T-3429, Exhibit 228, RCMP prepared list of books found at the residence of Eric Adams, 642, https://heritage.canadiana.ca/view/oocihm.lac_reel_t3429/642.
54 LAC, RG33-62, Agents of a Foreign Power fonds, Reel T-1369, Adams testimony, 3641–2, https://heritage.canadiana.ca/view/oocihm.lac_reel_t1369/1691.
55 LAC, RG33-62, Agents of a Foreign Power fonds, Reel T-1369, Adams testimony, 3532, https://heritage.canadiana.ca/view/oocihm.lac_reel_t1369/1583.
56 LAC, RG33-62, Agents of a Foreign Power fonds, Reel T-1369, Adams testimony, 3536, https://heritage.canadiana.ca/view/oocihm.lac_reel_t1369/1587.
57 LAC, RG33-62, Agents of a Foreign Power fonds, Reel T-1369, Adams testimony, 3562, https://heritage.canadiana.ca/view/oocihm.lac_reel_t1369/1612.
58 LAC, RG33-62, Agents of a Foreign Power fonds, Reel T-1369, Adams testimony, 3536, 3538, https://heritage.canadiana.ca/view/oocihm.lac_reel_t1369/1587.
59 Michael David Fox, *Showcasing the Great Experiment: Cultural Diplomacy and Western Visitors to the Soviet Union, 1921–1941* (Oxford: Oxford University Press, 2121), 98.
60 Beatrice & Sidney Webb, *Soviet Communism: A New Civilization?* (London: Longmans & Green, 1936).
61 J.M. O'Sullivan, "Soviet Communism: A New Civilization," *Studies: An Irish Quarterly Review* 25, no. 97 (1936): 156.
62 David Caute, *The Fellow-Travellers: Intellectual Friends of Communism*, rev. and updated (New Haven: Yale University Press, 1988), 3.
63 Lewis S. Feuer, "The Fellow Travellers," *Survey* 20, nos. 2/3 (1974): 206–7.
64 Paul Hollander, *Political Pilgrims: Travels of Western Intellectuals to the Soviet Union, China, and Cuba, 1928–1978* (New York: University Press of America, 1981), 77–80.
65 On his role in the international development of human rights, see John P. Humphrey, *Human Rights and the United Nations: A Great Adventure* (New York: Transnational, 1984).

66 A.J. Hobbins, "Humphrey and the Old Revolution: Human Rights in the Age of Mistrust," *Fontanus* 8 (1995), 124, https://doi.org/10.26443/fo.v8i.124.
67 LAC, RG33-62, Agents of a Foreign Power fonds, Reel T-1369, Adams testimony, 3465, https://heritage.canadiana.ca/view/oocihm.lac_reel_t1369/1516.
68 The articles were Eric Adams, "Russia Today – Living Conditions Show Improvement – Equality of Wages Has Been Abandoned as Policy," *Financial Post*, 17 November 1935, 8; Eric Adams, "Russia Today – Special Rewards Given to Best Among Workers – Prices High or Low According to Rouble Rate," *Financial Post*, 1 December 1935, 8; Eric Adams, "Russia Today – Industrial Development Proceeds on Big Scale – Special Attention Paid to Scientific Research," *Financial Post*, 8 December 1935, 11; Eric Adams, "Russia Today – Transportation Programme is Large Factor in Second Five-Year Plan – Air Services Stressed," *Financial Post*, 15 December 1935, 8; Eric Adams, "Russia Today – The Collectivization of Farms Is Speeded Up, Possibly More Rapidly Than Peasants Like It," *Financial Post*, 29 December 1935, 8.
69 Adams, "Russia Today – The Collectivization of Farms Is Speeded Up," *Financial Post*, 29 December 1935, 8.
70 Adams, "Russia Today – The Collectivization of Farms Is Speeded Up," *Financial Post*, 29 December 1935, 8.
71 Adams, "Russia Today – The Collectivization of Farms Is Speeded Up," 8.
72 Adams, "Russia Today – The Collectivization of Farms Is Speeded Up," 8.
73 Eric G. Adams, "A Short View of Russia Today," *Harvard Business School Alumni Bulletin* 11, no. 2 (February 1935), 101–6.
74 Adams, "Russia Today – Industrial Development Proceeds on Big Scale,"11.
75 Dana G. Dalrymple, "The Soviet Famine of 1932–1934," *Soviet Studies* 15, no. 3 (1964): 258.
76 "Famine over Russia," *Winnipeg Free Press*, 2 September 1933, 19.
77 Robert Conquest, *The Great Terror: A Reassessment* (Oxford: Oxford University Press, 1990), 311. See as well Robert Conquest, *The Harvest of Sorrow: Soviet Collectivization and the Terror-Famine* (New York: Oxford University Press, 1986); Lubomyr Luciuk, ed., *Holodomor: Reflections on the Great Famine of 1932–1933 in Soviet Ukraine* (Kingston: Kashtan, 2008); Norman Naimark, *Stalin's Genocides* (Princeton: Princeton University Press, 2010). For an authoritative historical account of this era in Soviet history, see Anne Applebaum, *Red Famine: Stalin's War on Ukraine* (New York: Doubleday, 2017).
78 Fred Beal, *Word from Nowhere* (London: R. Hale, 1937), 236, as quoted in Dalrymple, "The Soviet Famine of 1932–1934," 274.

79 Beal, *Word from Nowhere*, 239, as quoted in Dalrymple, "The Soviet Famine of 1932–1934," 274.
80 "Do Famine Conditions Now Obtain in Russia," *Winnipeg Free Press*, 27 May 1933, 26; "Cardinal Asks Aid to Russia," *Winnipeg Free Press*, 26 August 1933, 24; "Russia's Heavy Death Toll From Famine," *Lethbridge Herald*, 21 September 1933, 44; "Ukrainians Protest Atrocities in Ukraine," *Dauphin Herald and Press*, 2 November 1933, 1,5; "Millions of Russians Face Starvation, Says Geneva Investigator," *Winnipeg Evening Tribune*, 20 July 1934, 1; William Henry Chamberlain, "Farewell to Russia," *Atlantic Monthly*, as quoted in *Lethbridge Herald*, 15 December 1934, 4. Chamberlain's article appeared in the *Atlantic Monthly*, no. 154, November 1934.
81 Sheila Fitzpatrick, "Australian Visitors to the Soviet Union: The View from the Soviet Side," in *Political Tourists: Travellers from Australia to the Soviet Union in the 1920s–1940s*, ed. Sheila Fitzpatrick and Carolyn Rasmussen (Melbourne: Melbourne University Press, 2008), 15.
82 Fitzpatrick, "Australian Visitors," 15.
83 See for example Adams, "Russia Today – Living Conditions Show Improvement," 8.
84 LAC, RG33-62, Agents of a Foreign Power fonds, Reel T-3430, Exhibit 245, Outline for a Research Project on a Comprehensive History of Canada, 510, https://heritage.canadiana.ca/view/oocihm.lac_reel_t3430/510. This exhibit was returned to Adams and not included with the Kellock-Taschereau fonds. For the document see LAC, George Eric Adams fonds R8274, Box 2, File 1: "Research Project – E.G. Adams – Comprehensive History of Canada" (13 pp.).
85 Alex Skelton, "Edward Arthur George Luxton, 1914–1945," *Canadian Journal of Economics and Political Science* 11, no. 3 (1945): 478–9.
86 Duncan McDowall, *The Sum of the Satisfactions: Canada in the Age of National Accounting* (Montreal & Kingston: McGill-Queen's University Press, 2008), 92.
87 LAC, George Eric Adams fonds R8274, Box 2, File 1: Research Project – E.G. Adams – Comprehensive History of Canada, "Outline for a Research Project on a Comprehensive History of Canada," 4–5.
88 For an introduction to the development of Marxist-inspired Canadian historical writing in Canada, see Gregory S. Kealey's account of the life and work of Stanley Bréhaut *Workers and Canadian History* (Montreal & Kingston: McGill-Queen's University Press, 1995), 48–54; Brian McDougall, "Stanley Ryerson and the Materialist Conception of History: A Study in the Stalinist Distortion of Marxism," master's thesis, Carleton University, 1981, 1–20; and Bryan Palmer, "Historical Materialism and the Writing of Canadian History: A Dialectical View," *Journal of the Canadian Historical Association* 17, no. 2 (2006): 33–40.

89 Ian McKay, "For a New Kind of History: A Reconnaissance of 100 Years of Canadian Socialism," *Labour/Le Travail* 46 (2000): 96, 99–100.
90 David Lewis and Frank Scott, *Make This Your Canada: A Review of CCF History and Policy* (Toronto: Central Canada Publishing, 1943), 75–88.
91 Palmer, "Historical Materialism," 48. See also McDougall, "Stanley Ryerson," 1–20.
92 We thank Bryan Palmer for making this point during his insightful comments on the Adams / Luxton "Outline for a Research Project on a Comprehensive History of Canada." E-mail message to Tom Mitchell, 1 August 2024.
93 LAC, RG33-62, Agents of a Foreign Power fonds, Reel T-1369, Adams testimony, 3602, https://heritage.canadiana.ca/view/oocihm.lac_reel_t1369/1652.
94 LAC, RG33-62, Agents of a Foreign Power fonds, Reel T-1369, Adams testimony, 3547, https://heritage.canadiana.ca/view/oocihm.lac_reel_t1369/1598.
95 LAC, RG33-62, Agents of a Foreign Power fonds, Reel T-1369, Adams testimony, 3551, https://heritage.canadiana.ca/view/oocihm.lac_reel_t1369/1602.
96 LAC, RG33-62, Agents of a Foreign Power fonds, Reel T-1369, Adams testimony, 3551, https://heritage.canadiana.ca/view/oocihm.lac_reel_t1369/1602.
97 LAC, RG33-62, Agents of a Foreign Power fonds, Reel T-1369, Adams testimony, 3546, https://heritage.canadiana.ca/view/oocihm.lac_reel_t1369/1597.
98 LAC, RG33-62, Agents of a Foreign Power fonds, Reel T-1369, Adams testimony, 3553, https://heritage.canadiana.ca/view/oocihm.lac_reel_t1369/1604.
99 LAC, RG33-62, Agents of a Foreign Power fonds, Reel T-1369, Adams testimony, 3608, https://heritage.canadiana.ca/view/oocihm.lac_reel_t1369/1658.
100 LAC, RG33-62, Agents of a Foreign Power fonds, Reel T-1369, Adams testimony, 3618, https://heritage.canadiana.ca/view/oocihm.lac_reel_t1369/1668.
101 LAC, RG33-62, Agents of a Foreign Power fonds, Reel T-1369, Adams testimony, 3617, https://heritage.canadiana.ca/view/oocihm.lac_reel_t1369/1667.
102 LAC, RG33-62, Agents of a Foreign Power fonds, Reel T-1369, Adams testimony, 3619, https://heritage.canadiana.ca/view/oocihm.lac_reel_t1369/1669.
103 LAC, RG33-62, Agents of a Foreign Power fonds, Reel T-1369, Adams testimony, 3548, https://heritage.canadiana.ca/view/oocihm.lac_reel_t1369/1599.

104 LAC, RG33-62, Agents of a Foreign Power fonds, Reel T-1369, Adams testimony, 3549–50, https://heritage.canadiana.ca/view/oocihm.lac_reel_t1369/1600.
105 LAC, RG33-62, Agents of a Foreign Power fonds, Reel T-3434, RG19, Subpoena, Agatha Chapman, 29 March 1946, 104, https://heritage.canadiana.ca/view/oocihm.lac_reel_t3434/104.
106 LAC, RG33-62, Agents of a Foreign Power fonds, Reel T-1369, Chapman testimony, 3822, https://heritage.canadiana.ca/view/oocihm.lac_reel_t1369/1878.
107 "Whitman's Poetry Subject of Paper by Miss Chapman," *The Varsity* (University of Toronto undergraduate newspaper), 28 November 1928, 1.
108 LAC, RG33-62, Agents of a Foreign Power fonds, Reel T-3430, Exhibit 274A, "Agatha Chapman, Application for position Bank of Canada," 677, https://heritage.canadiana.ca/view/oocihm.lac_reel_t3430/677.
109 LAC, RG33-62, Agents of a Foreign Power fonds, Reel T-1369, Agatha Chapman (Chapman) testimony, 3801, https://heritage.canadiana.ca/view/oocihm.lac_reel_t1369/1857; "Une agence de publictié s'établit à Montréal," *La Patrie*, 19 August 1934; Josephine Mackay, "Irene the Lionhearted" (video, 52 minutes), 2002, https://vucavu.com/en/groupe-intervention-video/2006/irene-the-lionhearted.
110 On Kon's work of networking in the Montreal Communist left, see John Virtue, *Fred Taylor: Brother in the Shadows* (Montreal & Kingston: McGill-Queen's University Press, 2008), 80–1, and Merrily Weisbord, *The Strangest Dream: Canadian Communists, the Spy Trials, and the Cold War* (Toronto: Lester & Orpen Dennys, 1983), 70–6.
111 LAC, RG33-62, Agents of a Foreign Power fonds, Reel T-1369, Chapman testimony, 3836, https://heritage.canadiana.ca/view/oocihm.lac_reel_t1369/1892.
112 LAC, RG33-62, Agents of a Foreign Power fonds, Reel T-1369, Chapman testimony, 3836, https://heritage.canadiana.ca/view/oocihm.lac_reel_t1369/1892.
113 Eugene Forsey, *A Life on the Fringe* (Toronto: Oxford University Press, 1990), 58–9.
114 R.B.Y Scott and Gregory Vlastos, eds., *Towards the Christian Revolution* (Chicago: Willett, Clarke, 1936).
115 Eugene Forsey, "A New Economic Order," in *Towards the Christian Revolution*, ed. R.B.Y Scott and Gregory Vlastos (Chicago: Willett, Clarke, 1936), 139.
116 "Civil Liberties Union," *The Labor World*, 13 May 1939, 7.
117 Ross Lambertson, *Repression and Resistance: Canadian Human Rights Activists* (Toronto: University of Toronto Press, 2005), 53.

118 Chapman's dismissal has been confirmed in two sources: Faith Johnston, *Great Restlessness: The Life and Politics of Dorise* Nielsen (Winnipeg: University of Manitoba Press, 2006), 162; and in his autobiography Gordon Lunan reports that Chapman was fired from Sun Life Company for belonging to the Civil Liberties Union. Gordon Lunan, *The Making of a Spy* (Montreal: R. Davies, 1995), 95.

119 See "Form Vigilance Committee CLU Montreal," *Montreal Gazette*, 28 May 1937; "Hepburn's Attacks on Dons Denounced," *Montreal Gazette*, 20 April 1939, 5; "Civil Liberties Union," *The Labor World*, 13 May 1 939, 7.

120 Gordon Lunan reports that Chapman, Norman Lee, and M.J. Brierley were dismissed by Sun Life. Lunan, *Redhanded: Inside the Spy Ring That Changed the World* (Montreal: Optimum, 2005), 82.

121 Joseph Starobin, "Canada's Civil Liberties," *New Masses*, 34, no. 4 (16 July 1940), 8.

122 Weisbord, *Strangest Dream*, 152.

123 LAC, RG33-62, Agents of a Foreign Power fonds, Reel T-1369, Agatha Chapman (Chapman) testimony, 3820, https://heritage.canadiana.ca/view/oocihm.lac_reel_t1369/1876.

124 LAC, RG33-62, Agents of a Foreign Power fonds, Reel T-1369, Chapman testimony, 3831, 3838–9, https://heritage.canadiana.ca/view/oocihm.lac_reel_t1369/1887.

125 Faith Johnston, *Great Restlessness*, 200, 265.

126 LAC, RG33-62, Agents of a Foreign Power fonds, Reel T-1368, Mazerall testimony, 966, https://heritage.canadiana.ca/view/oocihm.lac_reel_t1368/1029.

127 LAC, RG33-62, Agents of a Foreign Power fonds, Reel T-1369, Chapman testimony, 3839, https://heritage.canadiana.ca/view/oocihm.lac_reel_t1369/1895.

128 LAC, RG33-62, Agents of a Foreign Power fonds, Reel T-1369, Chapman testimony, 3841, https://heritage.canadiana.ca/view/oocihm.lac_reel_t1369/1897.

129 See for example Judith Alexander and Duncan McDowall, "The Trial and Tribulations of Miss Agatha Chapman: Statistics in a Cold War Climate," *Queen's Quarterly* 22 (September 2007), https://www.thefreelibrary.com/The+trial+and+tribulations+of+Miss+Agatha+Chapman%3A+statistics+in+a...-a0172383120.

130 Faith Johnston, *Great Restlessness*, 200, 265.

131 Amy Knight, *How the Cold War Began: The Igor Gouzenko Affair and the Hunt for Soviet Spies* (New York: Carroll & Graf, 2005), 184; Alexander and McDowall, "Trial and Tribulations of Miss Agatha Chapman."

132 Judith Alexander, "Agatha Louisa Chapman," in *A Biographical Dictionary of Women Economists*, ed. Robert W. Dimand, Mary Ann Dimand, and Evelyn L. Forget, (Cheltenham, UK: Edward Elgar, 2000), 106.

133 LAC, RG33-62, Agents of a Foreign Power fonds, Reel T-1369, Adams testimony, 3668, https://heritage.canadiana.ca/view/oocihm.lac_reel_t1369/1718.

134 On this legal strategy, see "Ottawa Watches Next Move in Adams Spy Case," *Winnipeg Tribune*, 4 November 1946, 8.

135 On the trial, see "Talks with Woman 'Office-Gossipy' Alleged Spy Says in His Defense," *Globe & Mail*, 22 October 1946, 8; "Miss Willsher Says Adams Got 2nd Front Data," *Winnipeg Tribune*, 18 October 1946, 3.

136 "Surplus Charges Ditched in Spy Cases," *Winnipeg Tribune*, 5 February 1947, 3.

137 LAC, R8274, Eric George Adams fonds, Vol. 17, File 14, Kathleen Mary Willsher notes, 1947, Draft – Confidential, Memorandum for the Minister of Justice Re: Espionage Cases, 29 July 1947.

138 Rogov, in his words, wanted Carr to develop agents "in the Ministry of National Defence, in the Ministry of Aviation, in the Ministry of Naval Fleet or even in their military staffs [*sic*]." LAC, RG33-62, Agents of a Foreign Power fonds, Reel T-3423, Exhibit 19D, File marked "Frank," Task #2 of 15.6.45, 412, https://heritage.canadiana.ca/view/oocihm.lac_reel_t3423/412.

139 Robert Bothwell, "Clarence Decatur Howe," in *Dictionary of Canadian Biography*, vol. 18, University of Toronto/Université Laval, 2003–, http://www.biographi.ca/en/bio/howe_clarence_decatur_18E.html.

140 The latter included Research Enterprises in Toronto where David Shugar worked prior to joining the Canadian navy. Howe created Research Enterprises to address the Canadian military requirements for radar systems and optical instruments. W.E. Knowles Middleton, *Radar Development in Canada: The Radar Branch of the National Research Council of Canada 1939–1946* (Waterloo: Wilfred Laurier University Press, 1981), 40–4.

141 J. de N. Kennedy, *History of the Department of Munitions and Supply: Canada in the Second World War*, vol. 1 (Ottawa: King's Printer, 1950), viii, https://babel.hathitrust.org/cgi/pt?id=mdp.39015081266820&view=1up&seq=12.

142 Kenneth C. Cragg, "World Leader in Base Metals, Canada 4th as War Producer – Howe Details Arms Output of $4 Billion," *Globe & Mail*, 12 June 1943, 1.

143 Cragg, "World Leader in Base Metals, Canada 4th," *Globe & Mail*, 12 June 1943, 1. For the full record (with tables) of Howe's speech in Parliament, see Hon. C.D. Howe, Minister of Munitions and Supply in House of Commons, *Debates*, 11 June 1943, 3543–57.

144 "Canadian War Goods Help Allies Everywhere," *Globe & Mail*, 12 June 1943, 3.
145 Bryce and Bellamy, *Canada and the Cost of World War II*, 157.
146 Bryce and Bellamy, *Canada, and the Cost of World War II*, 157.
147 Kennedy, *History of the Department of Munitions and Supply*, vol. 1, ix, https://babel.hathitrust.org/cgi/pt?id=mdp.39015081266820&view=1up&seq=12.
148 Economics and Statistics also coordinated the work of DMS with the British Ministry of Supply (London) and the Combined Production and Resources Board (Washington). Kennedy, *History of the Department of Munitions and Supply*, vol. 2, 321, https://babel.hathitrust.org/cgi/pt?id=mdp.39015081266812&view=1up&seq=6.
149 LAC, RG33-62, Agents of a Foreign Power fonds, Reel T-1369, Jean Maurice Rochon testimony, 3184, https://heritage.canadiana.ca/view/oocihm.lac_reel_t1369/1226. For Benning's assignment of responsibilities in Munitions and Supply, see LAC, RG33-62, Agents of a Foreign Power fonds, Reel T-3431, Exhibit 399, "Proposed List of Duties for Mr. Benning," 9 September 1943, 861–8, https://heritage.canadiana.ca/view/oocihm.lac_reel_t3431/861.
150 On the origins and work of this high-level committee, see C.P. Stacey, *Arms, Men, and Governments: The War Policies of Canada 1939–1945* (Ottawa: Queen's Printer, 1970), 172, https://www.canada.ca/content/dam/themes/defence/caf/militaryhistory/dhh/official/book-1970-policies-ww2-en.pdf.
151 LAC, RG33-62, Agents of a Foreign Power fonds, Reel T-1369, Rochon testimony, 3181–4, https://heritage.canadiana.ca/view/oocihm.lac_reel_t1369/1223. "War Supplies Limited was a Crown company incorporated on 13 May 1941 to negotiate and receive orders from departments of the United States government for war supplies manufactured in Canada." Stacey, *Arms, Men, and Governments*, 172. https://www.canada.ca/content/dam/themes/defence/caf/militaryhistory/dhh/official/book-1970-policies-ww2-en.pdf.
152 LAC, RG33-62, Agents of a Foreign Power fonds, Reel T-3423, Exhibit 22A, page out of notebook in Col. Zabotin's handwriting, Second Group, Foster, 642, https://heritage.canadiana.ca/view/oocihm.lac_reel_t3423/642.
153 LAC, RG33-62, Agents of a Foreign Power fonds, Reel T-1369, Maclean testimony, 3171–2, https://heritage.canadiana.ca/view/oocihm.lac_reel_t1369/1214.
154 On his attendance at McGill 1929–31, see TNA, KV 2/1428, Soviet Espionage in Canada, James Scotland Benning, 57.
155 LAC, RG33-62, Agents of a Foreign Power fonds, Reel T-1369, Major A.J. Lawrence (Lawrence) testimony, 2171, https://heritage.canadiana.ca/view/oocihm.lac_reel_t1369/190.

156 For Gerson's account of his role in Benning's hiring, see LAC, RG33-62, Agents of a Foreign Power fonds, Reel T-1369, Gerson testimony, 2476–7, https://heritage.canadiana.ca/view/oocihm.lac_reel_t1369/496.

157 For Benning's account, see LAC, RG33-62, Agents of a Foreign Power fonds, Reel T-1369, Benning testimony, 3335–6, https://heritage.canadiana.ca/view/oocihm.lac_reel_t1369/1377.

158 Official Secrets Act, 1939, c. 49, s. 3(2), 451.

159 LAC, RG33-62, Agents of a Foreign Power fonds, Reel T-1368, Shugar testimony, 1993, https://heritage.canadiana.ca/view/oocihm.lac_reel_t1368/2066.

160 LAC, RG33-62, Agents of a Foreign Power fonds, Reel T-1369, Gerson testimony, 2290, https://heritage.canadiana.ca/view/oocihm.lac_reel_t1369/309.

161 LAC, RG33-62, Agents of a Foreign Power fonds, Reel T-1368, Willsher testimony, 760, https://heritage.canadiana.ca/view/oocihm.lac_reel_t1368/820.

162 LAC, RG33-62, Agents of a Foreign Power fonds, Reel T-1368, Mazerall testimony, 1023–5, https://heritage.canadiana.ca/view/oocihm.lac_reel_t1368/1084.

163 LAC, RG33-62, Agents of a Foreign Power fonds, Reel T-1369, Benning testimony, 3410, https://heritage.canadiana.ca/view/oocihm.lac_reel_t1369/1460.

164 LAC, RG33-62, Agents of a Foreign Power fonds, Reel T-1369, Benning testimony, 3268, https://heritage.canadiana.ca/view/oocihm.lac_reel_t1369/1310.

165 LAC, RG33-62, Agents of a Foreign Power fonds, Reel T-1369, Benning testimony, 3413, https://heritage.canadiana.ca/view/oocihm.lac_reel_t1369/1463.

166 LAC, RG33-62, Agents of a Foreign Power fonds, Reel T-1369, Benning testimony, 3408–9, https://heritage.canadiana.ca/view/oocihm.lac_reel_t1369/1458.

167 LAC, RG33-62, Agents of a Foreign Power fonds, Reel T-1369, Benning testimony, 3278, 3401, 3410, https://heritage.canadiana.ca/view/oocihm.lac_reel_t1369/1520.

168 LAC, RG33-62, Agents of a Foreign Power fonds, Reel T-1369, Benning testimony, 3278–9, https://heritage.canadiana.ca/view/oocihm.lac_reel_t1369/1320.

169 LAC, RG33-62, Agents of a Foreign Power fonds, Reel T-1369, Gerson testimony, 2299, https://heritage.canadiana.ca/view/oocihm.lac_reel_t1369/318.

170 LAC, RG33-62, Agents of a Foreign Power fonds, Reel T-1369, Benning testimony, 3269, https://heritage.canadiana.ca/view/oocihm.lac_reel_t1369/1311.

171 LAC, RG33-62, Agents of a Foreign Power fonds, Reel T-1369, Benning testimony, 3272, https://heritage.canadiana.ca/view/oocihm.lac_reel_t1369/1314.
172 Beverley Nichols, *Cry Havoc* (London: Jonathan Cape, 1933).
173 "Beverley Nicholls' *Cry Havoc*" (Review), *Kirkus Review*, 1 September 1933, https://www.kirkusreviews.com/book-reviews/a/beverley-nichols-3/cry-havoc-5/.
174 H.C. Engelbrecht and F.C. Hanighen, *Merchants of Death: A Study of the International Armament Industry* (New York: Dodd, Mead, 1934); LAC, RG33-62, Agents of a Foreign Power fonds, Reel T-1369, Benning testimony, 3272, https://heritage.canadiana.ca/view/oocihm.lac_reel_t1369/1314.
175 Freda White, "Merchants of Death: A Study of the International Armament Industry" (Review), *International Affairs* 13, no. 6 (1934): 861–2.
176 LAC, RG33-62, Agents of a Foreign Power fonds, Reel T-1369, Benning testimony, 3272, https://heritage.canadiana.ca/view/oocihm.lac_reel_t1369/1314; Florence Finch Kelly, "Harold Laski Considers the Present State of Democracy," *New York Times*, 11 June 1933, 42.
177 LAC, RG33-62, Agents of a Foreign Power fonds, Reel T-1369, Benning testimony, 3272, https://heritage.canadiana.ca/view/oocihm.lac_reel_t1369/1314.
178 LAC, RG33-62, Agents of a Foreign Power fonds, Reel T-1369, Benning testimony, 3272–3, https://heritage.canadiana.ca/view/oocihm.lac_reel_t1369/1314.
179 LAC, RG33-62, Agents of a Foreign Power fonds, Reel T-1369, Benning testimony, 3273, https://heritage.canadiana.ca/view/oocihm.lac_reel_t1369/1315.
180 LAC, RG33-62, Agents of a Foreign Power fonds, Reel T-1369, Benning testimony, 3274, https://heritage.canadiana.ca/view/oocihm.lac_reel_t1369/1316.
181 Official Secrets Act, 1939, c. 49, ss. 3(3), 3(4), and 4(a), 451. On the "reverse onus" provisions of the Official Secrets Act, see Eric M. Adams, "The Idea of Constitutional Rights and the Transformation of Canadian Constitutional Law, 1930–1960," unpublished PhD diss., University of Toronto, 2009, 157n77.
182 LAC, RG33-62, Agents of a Foreign Power fonds, Reel T-1369, Benning testimony, 3268, 3274, https://heritage.canadiana.ca/view/oocihm.lac_reel_t1369/1316.
183 LAC, RG33-62, Agents of a Foreign Power fonds, Reel T-1369, Benning testimony, 3275–6, https://heritage.canadiana.ca/view/oocihm.lac_reel_t1369/1317.
184 LAC, RG33-62, Agents of a Foreign Power fonds, Reel T-1369, Benning testimony, 3402, https://heritage.canadiana.ca/view/oocihm.lac_reel_t1369/1452.

185 "Ernst" came second with thirty-four items. For the complete list, see LAC, RG33-62, Agents of a Foreign Power fonds, Reel T-3423, Exhibit 16A, Record of the Materials Sent, 254–61, https://heritage.canadiana.ca/view/oocihm.lac_reel_t3423/254.
186 LAC, RG33-62, Agents of a Foreign Power fonds, Reel T-1369, Commission Counsel Williams, 3287, https://heritage.canadiana.ca/view/oocihm.lac_reel_t1369/1329. For the document, see LAC, RG33-62, Agents of a Foreign Power fonds, Reel T-3423, Exhibit 22A, Page out of notebook in Col. Zabotin's handwriting, Second Group, Foster, 642, https://heritage.canadiana.ca/view/oocihm.lac_reel_t3423/642.
187 LAC, RG33-62, Agents of a Foreign Power fonds, Reel T-1368, Gouzenko testimony, 145, https://heritage.canadiana.ca/view/oocihm.lac_reel_t1368/206.
188 LAC, RG33-62, Agents of a Foreign Power fonds, Reel T-3423, Exhibit 22A, Page out of notebook in Col. Zabotin's handwriting, Second Group, Foster, 642, https://heritage.canadiana.ca/view/oocihm.lac_reel_t3423/642.
189 LAC, RG33-62, Agents of a Foreign Power fonds, Reel T-1369, Benning testimony, 3288, https://heritage.canadiana.ca/view/oocihm.lac_reel_t1369/1330.
190 Jan Valtin, *Out of the Night: The Memoir of Richard Julius Krebs Alias Jan Valtin* (New York: Alliance, 1941).
191 John V. Fleming, "The 'Truth' About Jan Valtin," *Princeton University Library Chronicle* 67, no. 1 (2005): 70.
192 LAC, RG33-62, Agents of a Foreign Power fonds, Reel T-1369, Commission counsel Williams, 3288–9, https://heritage.canadiana.ca/view/oocihm.lac_reel_t1369/1331.
193 "Alumni News," *The Queen's Review* 19, no. 1 (1945): 29.
194 For this data, see LAC, RG33-62, Agents of a Foreign Power fonds, Reel T-3423, Exhibit 16A, Record of Materials Sent, items titled Telegrams, Corrections, Contracts, Notes to Contr., Corrections to Contracts, Supplements to Contracts, and Document, 254–61, https://heritage.canadiana.ca/view/oocihm.lac_reel_t3423/254.
195 LAC, RG33-62, Agents of a Foreign Power fonds, Reel T-1369, J.C. Dobie (Dobie) testimony, 3208, https://heritage.canadiana.ca/view/oocihm.lac_reel_t1369/1250.
196 LAC, RG33-62, Agents of a Foreign Power fonds, Reel T-1369, Dobie testimony, 3209–10, https://heritage.canadiana.ca/view/oocihm.lac_reel_t1369/1251.
197 LAC, RG33-62, Agents of a Foreign Power fonds, Reel T-1369, Benning testimony, 3302, https://heritage.canadiana.ca/view/oocihm.lac_reel_t1369/1344.

198 LAC, RG33-62, Agents of a Foreign Power fonds, Reel T-1369, Benning testimony, 3302–3, https://heritage.canadiana.ca/view/oocihm.lac_reel_t1369/1344.

199 LAC, RG33-62, Agents of a Foreign Power fonds, Reel T-3423, Exhibit 16A, Record of Materials Sent, no. 114, Telegram no. 2151, 29 November 1944, 5 pages, 255. "Telva" was a designation used to identify cables from the British Ministry of Supply to DMS in Ottawa, https://heritage.canadiana.ca/view/oocihm.lac_reel_t3423/255. For this explanation, see LAC, RG33-62, Agents of a Foreign Power fonds, Reel T-1369, Dobie testimony, 3202, https://heritage.canadiana.ca/view/oocihm.lac_reel_t1369/3423.

200 LAC, RG33-62, Agents of a Foreign Power fonds, Reel T-1369, Dobie testimony, 3203–4, https://heritage.canadiana.ca/view/oocihm.lac_reel_t1369/1246.

201 LAC, RG33-62, Agents of a Foreign Power fonds, Reel T-1369, Benning testimony, 3329, https://heritage.canadiana.ca/view/oocihm.lac_reel_t1369/1371.

202 LAC, RG33-62, Agents of a Foreign Power fonds, Reel T-1369, Benning testimony, 3330, https://heritage.canadiana.ca/view/oocihm.lac_reel_t1369/1372.

203 LAC, RG33-62, Agents of a Foreign Power fonds, Reel T-3432, Exhibit 405B Carmichael from Banks, 26.10.44, Top Secret, 101, https://heritage.canadiana.ca/view/oocihm.lac_reel_t3432/101. The cables were Exhibits 405C through 405R.

204 For these cables, see LAC, RG33-62, Agents of a Foreign Power fonds, Reel T-3432, Exhibits 405C 16 November 1944, Carmichael from Berry; 405D 16 November 1944, Carmichael from Berry; 405E 18 November 44, Carmichael from Berry ; 405F 18 November 44, Carmichael from Berry; 405G 18 November 44, Carmichael from Berry; 405H 18 November 44, Carmichael from Berry; 405I 18 November 44 Carmichael from Berry; 405J 17 November 44 Carmichael from Berry; 405K 17 November 44 Carmichael from Berry; 405L 18 November 44 Carmichael from Berry; 405M 22 November 44 Carmichael from Berry; 405N 22 November 44 Carmichael from Berry; 405O 22 November 44 Carmichael from Berry; 405P 22 November 44 (all "TOP SECRET"); Carmichael from Berry (RESTRICTED); 405Q 22 November 44 Carmichael from Berry (RESTRICTED); 405R 23 November 44 Carmichael from Berry (RESTRICTED), 102–21; https://heritage.canadiana.ca/view/oocihm.lac_reel_t3432/102.

205 "Notes on Meeting in Office of Minister of Finance to Discuss United Kingdom Financing August 1, 1944," in *Documents on Canadian External Relations*, ed. John F. Hilliker, vol. 10, pt. I, 1944–45 (Ottawa: Department of External Affairs and International Trade, 1990), 543.

206 On these developments, see Chris Madsen, "Dollars, Diplomacy and Fleets: John Maynard Keynes and Stage II Naval Requirements for War Against Japan," *International Journal of Maritime History* 19, no. 1 (2007): 107–44.

207 For the documentary trail of these negotiations on "War Supplies and Finance," see Hilliker, ed., *Documents on Canadian External Relations*, 539–715.

208 LAC, RG33-62, Agents of a Foreign Power fonds, Reel T-1369, Benning testimony, 3329, https://heritage.canadiana.ca/view/oocihm.lac_reel_t1369/1371.

209 For this cable traffic, see https://heritage.canadiana.ca/view/oocihm.lac_reel_t3432/126.

210 LAC, RG33-62, Agents of a Foreign Power fonds, Reel T-1369, Benning testimony, 3329, https://heritage.canadiana.ca/view/oocihm.lac_reel_t1369/1371.

211 LAC, RG33-62, Agents of a Foreign Power fonds, Reel T-3423, Exhibit 16A, Record of Materials Sent, no. 120, "Correct. of Contracts," November 1944, 13 pages, 255, https://heritage.canadiana.ca/view/oocihm.lac_reel_t3423/255; LAC, RG33-62, Agents of a Foreign Power fonds, Reel T-1369, Dobie testimony, 3218, https://heritage.canadiana.ca/view/oocihm.lac_reel_t1369/1260.

212 LAC, RG33-62, Agents of a Foreign Power fonds, Reel T-3423, Exhibit 16A, Record of Materials Sent, no. 151, "Supplement to Contracts," November 1944, 13 pages, 256, https://heritage.canadiana.ca/view/oocihm.lac_reel_t3423/257; no. 192, "Product'n of Arms for the Month of November," 12 December 1944, 11 pages, 260, https://heritage.canadiana.ca/view/oocihm.lac_reel_t3423/260; LAC, RG33-62, Agents of a Foreign Power fonds, Reel T-1369, Benning testimony, 3298, https://heritage.canadiana.ca/view/oocihm.lac_reel_t1369/1340. A copy of the 1 October 1944 Monthly Supplement was archived in the commission's records. LAC, RG33-62, Agents of a Foreign Power fonds, Reel T-3427, Exhibit 218a, Monthly Supplement to Quarterly Forecast of War Production for October 1st, 1944, Department of Munitions and Supply, Economics and Statistics Branch, 773–81, https://heritage.canadiana.ca/view/oocihm.lac_reel_t3427/773; LAC, RG33-62, Agents of a Foreign Power fonds, Reel T-1369, Dobie testimony, 3219, https://heritage.canadiana.ca/view/oocihm.lac_reel_t1369/1261.

213 LAC, RG33-62, Agents of a Foreign Power fonds, Reel T-1369, Benning testimony, 3298–9, https://heritage.canadiana.ca/view/oocihm.lac_reel_t1369/1341.

214 LAC, RG33-62, Agents of a Foreign Power fonds, Reel T-1369, Benning testimony, 3319–20, https://heritage.canadiana.ca/view/oocihm.lac_reel_t1369/1361.

215 LAC, RG33-62, Agents of a Foreign Power fonds, Reel T-1369, Commission counsel E.K. Williams, 3332, https://heritage.canadiana.ca/view/oocihm.lac_reel_t1369/1374; LAC, RG33-62, Agents of a Foreign Power fonds, Reel T-3423, Exhibit 16A, Record of the Materials Sent, no. 112, "Production Sam," October 1944," 2 pages, 254, https://heritage.canadiana.ca/view/oocihm.lac_reel_t3423/254.

216 LAC, RG33-62, Agents of a Foreign Power fonds, Reel T-1369, Dobie testimony, 3194, https://heritage.canadiana.ca/view/oocihm.lac_reel_t1369/1236. For the document cited by Dobie, see LAC, RG33-62, Agents of a Foreign Power fonds, Reel T-3432, Exhibit 402A, "Semimonthly Aircraft Production Report," 15–31 October 1944, 59, https://heritage.canadiana.ca/view/oocihm.lac_reel_t3432/59; LAC, RG33-62, Agents of a Foreign Power fonds, Reel T-1369, Dobie testimony, 3197, https://heritage.canadiana.ca/view/oocihm.lac_reel_t1369/1239.

217 LAC, RG33-62, Agents of a Foreign Power fonds, Reel T-3423, Exhibit 16A, Record of the Materials Sent, no. 113, "Production of Ships," October 1944, 5 pages, 254, https://heritage.canadiana.ca/view/oocihm.lac_reel_t3423/254.

218 LAC, RG33-62, Agents of a Foreign Power fonds, Reel T-3432, Exhibit 403 "Deliveries and Forecasts of Deliveries for 1944–45," 71–4, https://heritage.canadiana.ca/view/oocihm.lac_reel_t3432/71.

219 LAC, RG33-62, Agents of a Foreign Power fonds, Reel T-3423, Exhibit 16A, "Record of the Materials Sent, no. 155, Report 23.11.44, 14 pages, annotated: "See who was secretary of the meeting," 257, https://heritage.canadiana.ca/view/oocihm.lac_reel_t3423/257.

220 LAC, RG33-62, Agents of a Foreign Power fonds, Reel T-3423, Exhibit 16A, "Record of the Materials Sent, No.156, Report 23.11.44, 14 pages, annotated: "See who was secretary of the meeting," 257, https://heritage.canadiana.ca/view/oocihm.lac_reel_t3423/257.

221 LAC, RG33-62, Agents of a Foreign Power fonds, Reel T-3432, Exhibit 411, "Report of the Minutes of the Sub-Committee Meeting of the Joint Gun Ammunition Production Committee," 24 November 1944, 226–34, https://heritage.canadiana.ca/view/oocihm.lac_reel_t3432/226.

222 LAC, RG33-62, Agents of a Foreign Power fonds, Reel T-1369, Commission counsel Williams, 3310, https://heritage.canadiana.ca/view/oocihm.lac_reel_t1369/1352.

223 LAC, RG33-62, Agents of a Foreign Power fonds, Reel T-1369, Benning testimony, 3304, https://heritage.canadiana.ca/view/oocihm.lac_reel_t1369/1346.

224 LAC, RG33-62, Agents of a Foreign Power fonds, Reel T-1369, Commissioner Taschereau, 3312–13, https://heritage.canadiana.ca/view/oocihm.lac_reel_t1369/1355.

225 Stacey, *Arms, Men, and Governments*, 172, https://www.canada.ca/content/dam/themes/defence/caf/militaryhistory/dhh/official/book-1970-policies-ww2-en.pdf.
226 LAC, RG33-62, Agents of a Foreign Power fonds, Reel T-1369, Benning testimony, 3677–8, https://heritage.canadiana.ca/view/oocihm.lac_reel_t1369/1727.
227 LAC, RG33-62, Agents of a Foreign Power fonds, Reel T-1369, Benning testimony, 3680, https://heritage.canadiana.ca/view/oocihm.lac_reel_t1369/1729.
228 Official Secrets Act, 1939, c. 49, 451.
229 *The Report of the Royal Commission (Final Report)*, 443, https://publications.gc.ca/site/eng/9.699909/publication.html.
230 Official Secrets Act, 1939, c. 49, 451.
231 Official Secrets Act, 1939, c. 49, 451; *The Report of the Royal Commission (Final Report)*, 444–5, https://publications.gc.ca/site/eng/9.699909/publication.html.
232 J. Patrick Boyer, *A Passion for Justice: How "Vinegar Jim" McRuer Became Canada's Greatest Law Reformer* (Blue Butterfly Books, 1988).
233 "Benning Trial Shows Deeper Spy Inroads," *Winnipeg Free Press*, 25 October 1946, 4. In 1946, a trial judge could admit evidence of the acts and declarations of alleged co-conspirators before the conspiracy itself had been proved on condition that by the conclusion of the trial evidence was provided that the accused had participated in the conspiracy. Peter McKinon, "Conspiracy and Sedition as Canadian Political Crimes," *McGill Law Journal*, 23 (1977): 629.
234 "Convicted as a Spy, Benning Given Five Year Term," *Globe & Mail*, 30 October 1946, 1.
235 "Warns Evidence of Cipher Clerk Requires Support," *Globe & Mail*, 23 October 1946, 17.
236 "Crimes Against the State," Working Paper 49 (Ottawa: Law Reform Commission of Canada, 1986), 40
237 "Benning Still Held, Awaiting Bail of $6,000," *Globe & Mail*, 2 November 1946, 9.
238 Adams, "The Idea of Constitutional Rights," 88.
239 Rex v Benning [1947] O.R., 370–1, https://archive.org/details/ontarioreports1947/page/370/mode/2up?q=benning.
240 Rex v Benning [1947] O.R., 374, https://archive.org/details/ontarioreports1947/page/374/mode/2up?q=benning.
241 Rex v Benning [1947] O.R., 371, https://archive.org/details/ontarioreports1947/page/371/mode/2up?q=benning.
242 Rex v Benning [1947] O.R., 373, https://archive.org/details/ontarioreports1947/page/373/mode/2up?q=benning. Section 3(1)(c) of

the Official Secrets Act stated that anyone who "obtains, collects, records, or publishes, or communicates to any other person any secret official code word, or pass word, or any sketch, plan, model, article, or note, or other document or information which is calculated to be or might be or is intended to be directly or indirectly useful to a foreign power; he shall be guilty of an offence under this Act."

243 Rex v Benning [1947] O.R., 376, https://archive.org/details/ontarioreports1947/page/376/mode/2up?q=benning.

244 Rex v Benning [1947] O.R., 378, https://archive.org/details/ontarioreports1947/page/378/mode/2up?q=benning. See also "Lack of Evidence Cited, Spy Conviction Quashed," *Globe & Mail*, 25 April 1947, 8.

245 Interpretation Act, s. 12. as quoted in Lorne Neudorf, "Canada's First Act: The History and Role of the Interpretation Act," in *Legislating Statutory Interpretation: Perspectives from the Common Law World*, ed. Christopher Hunt, Lorne Neudorf, and Micah Rankin, (Toronto: Thomson Reuters, 2018), 10.

246 Knight, *How the Cold War Began*, 173.

247 LAC, Rick Stow fonds, Accession 2019-0030, Interview with Paulette Benning Buchanan, 1990-11-11. The scope and content note states that, according to Paulette, in 1938 she and "her brother Scott joined the [Communist] Party together, becoming members of closed club 'Section 13.' Hers was a safe house in the illegal period. It was often the site of meetings of the leadership. Paulette discusses various instances where her brother shared information with the Soviets and the various repercussions."

248 Weisbord, *The Strangest Dream*, 107–8, 130.

249 Robert Burdini, *The Invention That Won the War* (New York: Simon & Schuster, 1996), 42.

250 Robert Burdini, *The Invention That Won the War*, 13.

251 See W.E. Knowles, *Radar Development in Canada: The Radio Branch of the National Research Council of Canada 1939–46* (Waterloo: Wilfrid Laurier University Press, 1981).

252 Shlomo Shapiro, "Cold War Radar Intelligence: Operation 'Cerberus,'" *Journal of Intelligence History* 6, no. 2 (2006): 61, https://doi.org/10.1080/16161262.2006.10555132.

253 LAC, RG33-62, Agents of a Foreign Power fonds, Reel T-1369, Smith testimony, 3034, https://heritage.canadiana.ca/view/oocihm.lac_reel_t1369/1076.

254 LAC, RG33-6, Agents of a Foreign Power fonds, Reel T-3423, Exhibit 17E, File marked "Back," Course of Meeting," 17.4.45, 299, https://heritage.canadiana.ca/view/oocihm.lac_reel_t3423/299.

255 LAC, RG33-62, Agents of a Foreign Power fonds, Reel T-1368, Durnford Smith testimony (Smith testimony), 1018, https://heritage.canadiana.ca/view/oocihm.lac_reel_t1369/1079.
256 Ottawa-based lawyer H. Aldous Aylen KC studied law at McGill University and Osgoode Hall. In 1950, age fifty-two, he was appointed to the Ontario Supreme Court. "Jurist Served as RFC [Royal Flying Corp] Pilot in 1914–18 War," *Globe & Mail*, 4 October 1963, 52.
257 LAC, RG33-62, Agents of a Foreign Power fonds, Reel T-1369, Smith testimony, 2795, https://heritage.canadiana.ca/view/oocihm.lac_reel_t1369/836.
258 LAC, RG33-62, Agents of a Foreign Power fonds, Reel T-1369, Commissioner Kellock, 2795, https://heritage.canadiana.ca/view/oocihm.lac_reel_t1369/836.
259 LAC, RG33-62, Agents of a Foreign Power fonds, Reel T-1369, Smith testimony, 2796, https://heritage.canadiana.ca/view/oocihm.lac_reel_t136/837.
260 LAC, RG33-62, Agents of a Foreign Power fonds, Reel T-1369, Smith testimony, 2801, https://heritage.canadiana.ca/view/oocihm.lac_reel_t1369/842.
261 LAC, RG33-62, Agents of a Foreign Power fonds, Reel T-1369, Smith testimony, 2801, https://heritage.canadiana.ca/view/oocihm.lac_reel_t1369/842.
262 LAC, RG33-62, Agents of a Foreign Power fonds, Reel T-3430, Exhibit 284 Q-R, Correspondence, 795–6, https://heritage.canadiana.ca/view/oocihm.lac_reel_t3430/795.
263 LAC, RG33-62, Agents of a Foreign Power fonds, Reel T-1369, Smith testimony, 2804–5, https://heritage.canadiana.ca/view/oocihm.lac_reel_t1369/845.
264 LAC, RG33-62, Agents of a Foreign Power fonds, Reel T-1369, Smith testimony, 2815, https://heritage.canadiana.ca/view/oocihm.lac_reel_t1369/856.
265 LAC, RG33-62, Agents of a Foreign Power fonds, Reel T-1369, Smith testimony, 2816, https://heritage.canadiana.ca/view/oocihm.lac_reel_t1369/857.
266 LAC, RG33-62, Agents of a Foreign Power fonds, Reel T-1368, Lunan testimony, 1188, https://heritage.canadiana.ca/view/oocihm.lac_reel_t1368/1249.
267 LAC, RG33-62, Agents of a Foreign Power fonds, Reel T-1369, 2816–19, https://heritage.canadiana.ca/view/oocihm.lac_reel_t1369/857.
268 LAC, RG33-62, Agents of a Foreign Power fonds, Reel T-1369, 2832–3, https://heritage.canadiana.ca/view/oocihm.lac_reel_t1369/873.

269 LAC, RG33-62, Agents of a Foreign Power fonds, Reel T-1369, Smith testimony, 2831–3, https://heritage.canadiana.ca/view/oocihm.lac_reel_t1369/872.
270 LAC, RG33-62, Agents of a Foreign Power fonds, Reel T-3423, Exhibit 18B, File marked "Badeau," 320, https://heritage.canadiana.ca/view/oocihm.lac_reel_t3423/336.
271 LAC, RG33-62, Agents of a Foreign Power fonds, Reel T-1369, Commission counsel Williams, 2821, https://heritage.canadiana.ca/view/oocihm.lac_reel_t1369/862.
272 LAC, RG33-62, Agents of a Foreign Power fonds, Reel T-1369, Smith testimony, 2821, https://heritage.canadiana.ca/view/oocihm.lac_reel_t1369/862.
273 LAC, RG33-62, Agents of a Foreign Power fonds, Reel T-1369, Commissioner Kellock, 2821, https://heritage.canadiana.ca/view/oocihm.lac_reel_t1369/862.
274 LAC, RG33-62, Agents of a Foreign Power fonds, Reel T-1369, Smith testimony, 2822, https://heritage.canadiana.ca/view/oocihm.lac_reel_t1369/863.
275 LAC, RG33-62, Agents of a Foreign Power fonds, Reel T-1369, Commissioner Kellock, 2822, https://heritage.canadiana.ca/view/oocihm.lac_reel_t1369/863.
276 LAC, RG33-62, Agents of a Foreign Power fonds, Reel T-1369, Smith testimony, 2823, https://heritage.canadiana.ca/view/oocihm.lac_reel_t1369/864.
277 LAC, RG33-62, Agents of a Foreign Power fonds, Reel T-1369, Commission counsel Williams, 2823, https://heritage.canadiana.ca/view/oocihm.lac_reel_t1369/864.
278 LAC, RG33-62, Agents of a Foreign Power fonds, Reel T-1369, Smith testimony, 2823–4, https://heritage.canadiana.ca/view/oocihm.lac_reel_t1369/864.
279 LAC, RG33-62, Agents of a Foreign Power fonds, Reel T-1369, Commissioner Kellock, 2824, https://heritage.canadiana.ca/view/oocihm.lac_reel_t1369/865.
280 LAC, RG33-62, Agents of a Foreign Power fonds, Reel T-1369, Commissioner Kellock, 2823–4, https://heritage.canadiana.ca/view/oocihm.lac_reel_t1369/864.
281 LAC, RG33-62, Agents of a Foreign Power fonds, Reel T-1369, Aldous Aylen K.C (Aylen) testimony, 2826, https://heritage.canadiana.ca/view/oocihm.lac_reel_t1369/867.
282 LAC, RG33-62, Agents of a Foreign Power fonds, Reel T-1369, Smith testimony, 2827, https://heritage.canadiana.ca/view/oocihm.lac_reel_t1369/868.

283 LAC, RG33-62, Agents of a Foreign Power fonds, Reel T-1369, Smith testimony, 2831, https://heritage.canadiana.ca/view/oocihm.lac_reel_t1369/872.

284 LAC, RG33-62, Agents of a Foreign Power fonds, Reel T-3423, Exhibit 17D, File marked "Back," Organizational Letter Ottawa, 28 March, 320, https://heritage.canadiana.ca/view/oocihm.lac_reel_t3423/320.

285 LAC, RG33-62, Agents of a Foreign Power fonds, Reel T-3423, Exhibit 17D, File marked "Back," Organizational Letter Ottawa, 28 March, 320, https://heritage.canadiana.ca/view/oocihm.lac_reel_t3423/320.

286 LAC, RG33-62, Agents of a Foreign Power fonds, Reel T-3423, Exhibit 17E, File marked "Back," Organizational Letter, 18.4.45, 322, https://heritage.canadiana.ca/view/oocihm.lac_reel_t3423/322.

287 For the note, see LAC, RG33-62, Agents of a Foreign Power fonds, Reel T-3423, Exhibit 27, Photostats taken from Lt. Col. Rogov's briefcase, 801, https://heritage.canadiana.ca/view/oocihm.lac_reel_t3423/801. For a legible copy of this document, see TNA, KV 2/1427, Corby Case (vol. 5) Miscellaneous Notes taken from Grant's safe, s. 13. The note came from Rogov's briefcase stored in Grant's safe. On this point, see LAC, RG33-62, Agents of a Foreign Power fonds, Reel T-1368, Gouzenko's testimony, 121, https://heritage.canadiana.ca/view/oocihm.lac_reel_t1368/182.

288 LAC, RG33-62, Agents of a Foreign Power fonds, Reel T-1369, W.J. Henderson (Henderson) testimony, 2682, https://heritage.canadiana.ca/view/oocihm.lac_reel_t1369/722.

289 LAC, RG33-62, Agents of a Foreign Power fonds, Reel T-1369, Henderson testimony, 2683, https://heritage.canadiana.ca/view/oocihm.lac_reel_t1369/723.

290 LAC, RG33-62, Agents of a Foreign Power fonds, Reel T-1369, Henderson testimony, 2686, https://heritage.canadiana.ca/view/oocihm.lac_reel_t1369/726.

291 LAC, RG33-62, Agents of a Foreign Power fonds, Reel T-1369, Henderson testimony, 2687, https://heritage.canadiana.ca/view/oocihm.lac_reel_t1369/727.

292 LAC, RG33-62, Agents of a Foreign Power fonds, Reel T-1369, Henderson testimony, 2680, https://heritage.canadiana.ca/view/oocihm.lac_reel_t1369/720.

293 LAC, RG33-62, Agents of a Foreign Power fonds, Reel T-1369, Henderson testimony, 2685, https://heritage.canadiana.ca/view/oocihm.lac_reel_t1369/725.

294 For the notes, see LAC, RG33-62, Agents of a Foreign Power fonds, Reel T-3423, Exhibit 17K-M, File marked "Back," Photostatic copy of notes by Durnford Smith, 280–3, https://heritage.canadiana.ca/view/oocihm.lac_reel_t3423/280.

295 LAC, RG33-62, Agents of a Foreign Power fonds, Reel T-1369, Smith testimony, 2837–8, https://heritage.canadiana.ca/view/oocihm.lac_reel_t1369/879.
296 LAC, RG33-62, Agents of a Foreign Power fonds, Reel T-1369, Smith testimony, 2840, https://heritage.canadiana.ca/view/oocihm.lac_reel_t1369/881.
297 LAC, RG33-62, Agents of a Foreign Power fonds, Reel T-1369, Smith testimony, 2841, https://heritage.canadiana.ca/view/oocihm.lac_reel_t1369/882.
298 LAC, RG33-62, Agents of a Foreign Power fonds, Reel T-1369, Smith testimony, 2845–7, https://heritage.canadiana.ca/view/oocihm.lac_reel_t1369/886.
299 LAC, RG33-62, Agents of a Foreign Power fonds, Reel T-1369, Smith testimony, 2848, https://heritage.canadiana.ca/view/oocihm.lac_reel_t1369/889.
300 LAC, RG33-62, Agents of a Foreign Power fonds, Reel T-1369, Smith testimony, 2846–7, https://heritage.canadiana.ca/view/oocihm.lac_reel_t1369/887.
301 LAC, RG33-62, Agents of a Foreign Power fonds, Reel T-1369, Smith testimony, 2851, https://heritage.canadiana.ca/view/oocihm.lac_reel_t1369/892.
302 LAC, RG33-62, Agents of a Foreign Power fonds, Reel T-1369, Smith testimony, 2851–2, https://heritage.canadiana.ca/view/oocihm.lac_reel_t1369/892.
303 LAC, RG33-62, Agents of a Foreign Power fonds, Reel T-1369, Smith testimony, 2851–2, https://heritage.canadiana.ca/view/oocihm.lac_reel_t1369/892.
304 LAC, RG33-62, Agents of a Foreign Power fonds, Reel T-1369, Smith testimony, 2854, https://heritage.canadiana.ca/view/oocihm.lac_reel_t1369/895.
305 LAC, RG33-62, Agents of a Foreign Power fonds, Reel T-1369, Smith testimony, 2855, https://heritage.canadiana.ca/view/oocihm.lac_reel_t1369/896.
306 LAC, RG33-62, Agents of a Foreign Power fonds, Reel T-1369, Smith testimony, 2856, https://heritage.canadiana.ca/view/oocihm.lac_reel_t1369/897.
307 LAC, RG33-62, Agents of a Foreign Power fonds, Reel T-1369, Smith testimony, 2857, https://heritage.canadiana.ca/view/oocihm.lac_reel_t1369/898.
308 LAC, RG33-62, Agents of a Foreign Power fonds, Reel T-1369, Smith testimony, 2859, https://heritage.canadiana.ca/view/oocihm.lac_reel_t1369/900.

309 LAC, RG33-62, Agents of a Foreign Power fonds, Reel T-1369, Smith testimony, 2864–5, https://heritage.canadiana.ca/view/oocihm.lac_reel_t1369/905.
310 Lunan did not receive anything in writing from Smith about the NRC. Notes in Lunan's handwriting that Lunan said were based on conversations with Smith were filed in Lunan's GRU dossier. For Rogov on this point, see LAC, RG33-62, Agents of a Foreign Power fonds, Reel T-3423, Exhibit 21A, Notes of Lt. Col. Rogov, Results of last meeting of Back's group (research), 2, 626, https://heritage.canadiana.ca/view/oocihm.lac_reel_t3423/626.
311 LAC, RG33-62, Agents of a Foreign Power fonds, Reel T-3423, Exhibit 21A, Notes of Lt. Col. Rogov, Results of last meeting of Back's group (research), 5, 629, https://heritage.canadiana.ca/view/oocihm.lac_reel_t3423/629.
312 LAC, RG33-62, Agents of a Foreign Power fonds, Reel T-3423, Exhibit 17D, Organizational Letter Ottawa, 28 March, 320, https://heritage.canadiana.ca/view/oocihm.lac_reel_t3423/320.
313 LAC, RG33-62, Agents of a Foreign Power fonds, Reel T-1369, Smith testimony, 2883, https://heritage.canadiana.ca/view/oocihm.lac_reel_t1369/924.
314 LAC, RG33-62, Agents of a Foreign Power fonds, Reel T-3423, Exhibit 18B, Durnford Smith GRU Registration card, 337, https://heritage.canadiana.ca/view/oocihm.lac_reel_t3423/337.
315 LAC, RG33-62, Agents of a Foreign Power fonds, Reel T-1369, Smith testimony, 2963, https://heritage.canadiana.ca/view/oocihm.lac_reel_t1369/1004.
316 LAC, RG33-62, Agents of a Foreign Power fonds, Reel T-1369, Smith testimony, 2890, https://heritage.canadiana.ca/view/oocihm.lac_reel_t1369/931.
317 LAC, RG33-62, Agents of a Foreign Power fonds, Reel T-1369, Smith testimony, 2898, https://heritage.canadiana.ca/view/oocihm.lac_reel_t1369/939.
318 LAC, RG33-62, Agents of a Foreign Power fonds, Reel T-1369, Smith testimony, 2903, https://heritage.canadiana.ca/view/oocihm.lac_reel_t1369/944.
319 LAC, RG33-62, Agents of a Foreign Power fonds, Reel T-1369, Smith testimony, 2906, https://heritage.canadiana.ca/view/oocihm.lac_reel_t1369/947.
320 LAC, RG33-62, Agents of a Foreign Power fonds, Reel T-1369, Smith testimony, 2876–7, https://heritage.canadiana.ca/view/oocihm.lac_reel_t1369/918.
321 LAC, RG33-62, Agents of a Foreign Power fonds, Reel T-3423, Exhibit 17G, Assignment Number 1, Given to Back's Group (Research)given

8.6.45, 307, https://heritage.canadiana.ca/view/oocihm.lac_reel_t3423/307.

322 Kevin Riehle, "Soviet Intent at the Dawn of the Cold War: Igor Gouzenko's Revelations about GRU Intelligence Tasking," *Journal of Intelligence History* (2021), 37, https://doi.org/10.1080/16161262.2021.1892997.

323 LAC, RG33-62, Agents of a Foreign Power fonds, Reel T-3423, Exhibit 17G, Assignment Number 1, Assigned to Group Back (Research) assigned on 8.6.45, 324, https://heritage.canadiana.ca/view/oocihm.lac_reel_t3423/326.

324 R.C. Borde, and E.C. Williams, *Radar Mapping of the Chicago-New York Airway* (Indianapolis: Civil Aeronautics Administration and Technical Development and Evaluation Centre, 1950), 2, https://www.google.ca/books/edition/Technical_Development_Report/DHksLT04oZsC?hl=en&gbpv=1&dq=an/aps-10+war&pg=PA1&printsec=frontcover. Each document in the Radio documents library had a unique identifier: s. number and title. LAC, RG33-62, Agents of a Foreign Power fonds, Reel T-1369, 2694–, 5, https://heritage.canadiana.ca/view/oocihm.lac_reel_t1369/734. A seven-page report had been written in 1944 by Andrew Longacre, a scientist at the Radiation Laboratory. Longacre, AS/APS-10, Airborne Radar, Cambridge, MA: Radiation Laboratory, Massachusetts Institute of Technology, 1944 (7 pages). See also "Andrew Longacre," *Physics Today* 32, no. 2 (1979): 70, https://doi.org/10.1063/1.2995424.

325 Williams misstated the return date. Radio Branch librarian Claire Pigeon gave the correct date in her testimony before the inquiry. LAC, RG33-62, Agents of a Foreign Power fonds, Reel T-1369, Pigeon testimony, 2695–7, https://heritage.canadiana.ca/view/oocihm.lac_reel_t1369/735.

326 LAC, RG33-62, Agents of a Foreign Power fonds, Reel T-1369, Smith testimony, 2911, 9, https://heritage.canadiana.ca/view/oocihm.lac_reel_t1369/952.

327 LAC, RG33-62, Agents of a Foreign Power fonds, Reel T-1369, Smith testimony, 2913, https://heritage.canadiana.ca/view/oocihm.lac_reel_t1369/954.

328 LAC, RG33-62, Agents of a Foreign Power fonds, Reel T-3423, Exhibit 17H, File marked "Back," The Course of Meetings, 5.7.45, 328, https://heritage.canadiana.ca/view/oocihm.lac_reel_t3423/328.

329 LAC, RG33-62, Agents of a Foreign Power fonds, Reel T-3423, Exhibit 18, Badeau file, The Course of Meetings, 5.7.45, 328, https://heritage.canadiana.ca/view/oocihm.lac_reel_t3423/346.

330 LAC, RG33-62, Agents of a Foreign Power fonds, Reel T-3423, Exhibit 17G, File marked "Back," Assignment Number I, Given to Back's Group (Research) 8-6-45, Badeau, 326, https://heritage.canadiana.ca/view/oocihm.lac_reel_t3423/326.

331 LAC, RG33-62, Agents of a Foreign Power fonds, Reel T-1368, Lunan testimony, 1189, https://heritage.canadiana.ca/view/oocihm.lac_reel_t1368/1250.

332 LAC, RG33-62, Agents of a Foreign Power fonds, Reel T-1369, Smith testimony, 2908, https://heritage.canadiana.ca/view/oocihm.lac_reel_t1369/949.

333 LAC, RG33-62, Agents of a Foreign Power fonds, Reel T-1369, Smith testimony, 2916, https://heritage.canadiana.ca/view/oocihm.lac_reel_t1369/957.

334 LAC, RG33-62, Agents of a Foreign Power fonds, Reel T-3423, Exhibit 17E, File marked "Back," Organizational Letter of 18.4.45, 322, https://heritage.canadiana.ca/view/oocihm.lac_reel_t3423/322.

335 LAC, RG33-62, Agents of a Foreign Power fonds, Reel T-3423, Exhibit 18, File marked "Badeau," The Course of Meetings, 5.7.45, 346, https://heritage.canadiana.ca/view/oocihm.lac_reel_t3423/346.

336 LAC, RG33-62, Agents of a Foreign Power fonds, Reel T-1369, Smith testimony, 2919, https://heritage.canadiana.ca/view/oocihm.lac_reel_t1369/960.

337 LAC, RG33-62, Agents of a Foreign Power fonds, Reel T-3423, Exhibit 18, File marked "Badeau," The Course of Meetings, 5.7.45, 346, https://heritage.canadiana.ca/view/oocihm.lac_reel_t3423/346.

338 LAC, RG33-62, Agents of a Foreign Power fonds, Reel T-3423, Exhibit 18C, File marked "Badeau," Assignment Number 1, 5.7.45, 366, https://heritage.canadiana.ca/view/oocihm.lac_reel_t3423/366.

339 LAC, RG33-62, Agents of a Foreign Power fonds, Reel T-1369, Smith testimony, 2972, https://heritage.canadiana.ca/view/oocihm.lac_reel_t1369/1013.

340 Rogov wanted a "basic description of the features of the contrivance transmitting and receiving radio tubes for L=3 and L=1 cm. and their technical manufacture," details on the "tube '4j-33,'" and information about "New York work … [on] radio locators [radar] for anti-aircraft artillery and aeroplanes with L=3 and L=1 cm." Also helpful would be recent work on the "T-R Switch," "types of radio antennae for L=3 and L=1 cm," and the work going on at the "Boyd Station." LAC, RG33-62, Agents of a Foreign Power fonds, Reel T-3423, Exhibit 18C-1, File marked "Badeau," Assignment Number 2, Given 6.7.45, 370, https://heritage.canadiana.ca/view/oocihm.lac_reel_t3423/370.

341 The documents were "Mixers, TRS, and Crystals"; "The Gas Discharge T-R Switch VII: Pulsed Operation of the Ignitor Electrode"; "Gas Discharge T-R Switch VIII: A Method of Analyzing Leakage Power"; "Wide-Band T-R Switch for LW/AW. Mk. V"; "Magnetrons; Review of the Present Knowledge of Factors Influencing Crystal Protection and a

Summary of Tests made ... on Ten S-Band Systems Using 721A TR Tubes"; and "Testing of 'S' and 'X' Band Magnetrons." LAC, RG33-62, Agents of a Foreign Power fonds, Reel T-1369, 2744, 2748, 2752, 2756–7, 2764, https://heritage.canadiana.ca/view/oocihm.lac_reel_t1369/784.

342 Donald Avery, *The Science of War*, 92.

343 Kevin Riehle, email message to Tom Mitchell, 27 February 2023.

344 LAC, RG33-62, Agents of a Foreign Power fonds, Reel T-3423, Exhibit 18D, File marked "Badeau," Assignment for Badeau, Number 3, Given Through Back, 6.8.45, 339, https://heritage.canadiana.ca/view/oocihm.lac_reel_t3423/339.

345 See for example Simon Watts, *Airborne Maritime Surveillance Radar*, vol. 1: *British ASV Radars in WWII 1939–1945* (San Francisco: Morgan & Claypool, 2018.)

346 Office of the Chief of Naval Operations, Radar Bulletin no. 2A (Radtwo A): The Tactical Use of Radar in Aircraft, Part Two, 91, https://www.ibiblio.org/hyperwar/USN/ref/RADTWOA/RADTWOA-2.html#an/apq5b.

347 LAC, RG33-62, Agents of a Foreign Power fonds, Reel T-1369, Pigeon testimony, 2702–3, https://heritage.canadiana.ca/view/oocihm.lac_reel_t1369/742.

348 LAC, RG33-62, Agents of a Foreign Power fonds, Reel T-1369, Pigeon testimony 2699, 2701, https://heritage.canadiana.ca/view/oocihm.lac_reel_t1369/739.

349 Smith's documents included "A Resonant Cavity Method of Measuring Relative Permittivity and Loss Tangent"; "Tuning and Setting up of the TIM X-Band Mixer Used in ARI, 5578"; "Treatment of Echo Box Problems by Lagrangian Procedures, Part 2, March 1945"; "Broad-Band Wattmeter for Use at X-Band"; "An Electronic Modulator for CW Magnetrons"; "Magnetrons for Wavelengths below 2 cms"; and three publications of the Telecommunications Research Establishment (TRE), Britain's principal telecommunications research and development organization: T.R.E. Journal; Secret T.R.E. Report no. T 1784; and Confidential, T.R.E. Report no. T 1816. For Smith's borrowing record and more detail on each of these items, see LAC, RG33-62, Agents of a Foreign Power fonds, Reel T-1369, 2711–22, https://heritage.canadiana.ca/view/oocihm.lac_reel_t1369/751.

350 LAC, RG33-62, Agents of a Foreign Power fonds, Reel T-3423, Exhibit 18D, File marked "Badeau," Course of Meetings, 25.8.45, 347, https://heritage.canadiana.ca/view/oocihm.lac_reel_t3423/347.

351 LAC, RG33-62, Agents of a Foreign Power fonds, Reel T-3423, Exhibit 20PP, Telegram in Col. Zabotin's handwriting, no. 266, To the Director, 27.8.45, 566, https://heritage.canadiana.ca/view/oocihm.lac_reel_t3423/566.

352 LAC, RG33-62, Agents of a Foreign Power fonds, Reel T-1369, Smith testimony, 2925, https://heritage.canadiana.ca/view/oocihm.lac_reel_t1369/966.
353 LAC, RG33-62, Agents of a Foreign Power fonds, Reel T-1369, Smith testimony, 2925–6, https://heritage.canadiana.ca/view/oocihm.lac_reel_t1369/966.
354 LAC, RG33-62, Agents of a Foreign Power fonds, Reel T-1369, Smith testimony, 2926, https://heritage.canadiana.ca/view/oocihm.lac_reel_t1369/967.
355 LAC, RG33-62, Agents of a Foreign Power fonds, Reel T-1369, Smith testimony, 2963, https://heritage.canadiana.ca/view/oocihm.lac_reel_t1369/1004.
356 LAC, RG33-62, Agents of a Foreign Power fonds, Reel T-1369, Smith testimony, 2963, https://heritage.canadiana.ca/view/oocihm.lac_reel_t1369/1004.
357 LAC, RG33-62, Agents of a Foreign Power fonds, Reel T-3423, Exhibit 18D, File marked "Badeau," Assignment N, 25.8.45, 345, https://heritage.canadiana.ca/view/oocihm.lac_reel_t3423/345.
358 LAC, RG33-62, Agents of a Foreign Power fonds, Reel T-3423, Exhibit 18D, File marked "Badeau," Course of Meetings, 18.8.45, 347, https://heritage.canadiana.ca/view/oocihm.lac_reel_t3423/347.
359 Andrew, *Defend the Realm*, 342; Angela Gendron, "Looking Back at the Gouzenko Defection," *International Journal of Intelligence and CounterIntelligence* 0, no. 0 (2022): 9, https://doi.org/10.1080/08850607.2022.2080982.
360 LAC, RG33-62, Agents of a Foreign Power fonds, Reel T-1369, Smith testimony, 3033, https://heritage.canadiana.ca/view/oocihm.lac_reel_t1369/1075.
361 LAC, RG33-62, Agents of a Foreign Power fonds, Reel T-1369, Smith testimony, 3036–7, https://heritage.canadiana.ca/view/oocihm.lac_reel_t1369/1078.
362 "Didn't Know Russians, Smith Says in Defence," *Globe & Mail*, 21 December 1946, 7.
363 On the trial, see "Didn't Know Russians, Smith Says in Defense," *Globe & Mail*, 21 December 1946, 7; "Durnford Smith's 5-Year Sentence May Be Appealed," *Globe & Mail*, 28 December 1946, 13.
364 Rex v. Smith [1947] O.R. 378-395, Ontario Court of Appeal, 24 April 1947, https://www.canlii.org/en/on/onca/doc/1947/1947canlii110/1947canlii110.pdf.
365 LAC, RG33-62, Agents of a Foreign Power fonds, Reel T-3423, Exhibit 22A, Page out of Notebook in Col. Zabotin's handwriting, Second Group,

Polland, 643, https://heritage.canadiana.ca/view/oocihm.lac_reel_t3423/643.

366 As the flight training schools associated with the British Commonwealth Air Training Plan spread across Canada, updated maps of their locations were produced. LAC, RG33-62, Agents of a Foreign Power fonds, Reel T-1369, Group Captain H.R. Stewart (Stewart) testimony, 3445, https://heritage.canadiana.ca/view/oocihm.lac_reel_t1369/1495.

367 LAC, RG33-62, Agents of a Foreign Power fonds, Reel T-1369, Commission counsel Fauteux, 3444–5, https://heritage.canadiana.ca/view/oocihm.lac_reel_t1369/1411.

368 LAC, RG33-62, Agents of a Foreign Power fonds, Reel T-3423, Exhibit 22A, Page out of Notebook in Col. Zabotin's handwriting, Second Group, Polland, 643, https://heritage.canadiana.ca/view/oocihm.lac_reel_t3423/643.

369 LAC, RG33-62, Agents of a Foreign Power fonds, Reel T-1368, Gouzenko testimony, 146, https://heritage.canadiana.ca/view/oocihm.lac_reel_t1368/207.

370 The *Third Interim Report* makes Poland a resident of Toronto, but the documents to support this claim are not included in the LAC archive of the inquiry, and we have not been able to establish that Fred Poland resided in Toronto in 1942. TNA, KV 2/1423, 183A (attached), Documents Relating to the Proceedings of the Royal Commission, Third Interim Report, 9. However, Lovell's Montreal Directory indicates that "F.W. Poland, RCAF" resided at Apt. 2, 1220 Fort Street in Montreal in 1940 and was still there in 1942. Lowell's Montreal Directory, 1942 (Montreal: John Lovell & Son, 1942), 1983, 2038.

371 LAC, RG33-62, Agents of a Foreign Power fonds, Reel T-1368, Shugar testimony, 1924, http://heritage.canadiana.ca/view/oocihm.lac_reel_t1368/1997.

372 LAC, RG33-62, Agents of a Foreign Power fonds, Reel T-1368, Lunan testimony, 1242, https://heritage.canadiana.ca/view/oocihm.lac_reel_t1368/1303.

373 LAC, RG33-62, Agents of a Foreign Power fonds, Reel T-1369, Smith testimony, 2816–7, https://heritage.canadiana.ca/view/oocihm.lac_reel_t1369/857.

374 LAC, RG33-62, Agents of a Foreign Power fonds, Reel T-1369, Gerson testimony, 2287, https://heritage.canadiana.ca/view/oocihm.lac_reel_t1369/306.

375 LAC, RG33-62, Agents of a Foreign Power fonds, Reel T-1368, Boyer testimony, 1760–1, https://heritage.canadiana.ca/view/oocihm.lac_reel_t1368/1833.

376 LAC, RG33-62, Agents of a Foreign Power fonds, Reel T-1369, Group Captain H.R. Stewart testimony (Stewart testimony), 3427, https://heritage.canadiana.ca/view/oocihm.lac_reel_t1369/1477.

377 LAC, RG33-62, Agents of a Foreign Power fonds, Reel T-1369, Stewart testimony, 3421–2, https://heritage.canadiana.ca/view/oocihm.lac_reel_t1369/1471.

378 CJIC was composed of the directors of intelligence from each branch of the Canadian armed services, a representative from External Affairs, and one from the RCMP. C.P. Stacey, *Arms, Men, and Governments*, 128, https://www.canada.ca/content/dam/themes/defence/caf/militaryhistory/dhh/official/book-1970-policies-ww2-en.pdf.

379 Wesley Wark, "The Evolution of Military Intelligence in Canada," *Armed Forces & Society* 16, no. 1 (1989): 87. See also Maria A. Robson, "The Third Eye: Canada's Development of Autonomous Signals Intelligence to Contribute to Five Eyes Intelligence Sharing," *Intelligence and National Security* 35, no. 7 (2020), 959–60, https://doi.org/10.1080/02684527.2020.1768477.

380 LAC, RG33-62, Agents of a Foreign Power fonds, Reel T-1369, Stewart testimony, 3426–7, https://heritage.canadiana.ca/view/oocihm.lac_reel_t1369/1476.

381 Warren Baldwin, "Russian Secret Police Operating in Canada," *Globe & Mail*, 30 March 1946, 1.

382 LAC, RG33-62, Agents of a Foreign Power fonds, Reel T-1369, Stewart testimony, 3436–7, https://heritage.canadiana.ca/view/oocihm.lac_reel_t1369/1486. For this document, see LAC, RG33-62, Agents of a Foreign Power fonds, Reel T-3432, Exhibit 423, Calendar pad for the year 1946 found in office desk of F.W. Poland, 352–3, https://heritage.canadiana.ca/view/oocihm.lac_reel_t3432/352.

383 "Link with Pavlov Purely Social, Poland Testifies," *Globe & Mail*, 15 January 1947, 3.

384 Norman Altstedter, "Member of Parliament Involved in Spy Ring," *Western Star*, 29 March 1946, 1.

385 "Only One Name of Spy Suspects Still Unrevealed," *Globe & Mail*, 25 March 1946, 25.

386 TNA, KV 2/1422, MacDonald to Sargent, no. 425, 23.3.46, s. 158A.

387 *The Report of the Royal Commission (Final Report)*, 654, https://publications.gc.ca/site/eng/9.699909/publication.html. The Criminal Code sections are 652 and 664.

388 In the Matter of a Reference as to the Validity of the Regulations in relation to Chemicals Enacted by the Governor General in Council of Canada on the 10th Day of July, 1941, P.C. 4996, and of an Order of the

Controller of Chemicals, dated the 16th Day of January, 1942, made pursuant thereto, 3, 13, https://canlii.ca/t/1nmzg.

389 LAC, Diaries of WLMK, 28 March 1946, 3–4.

390 LAC, RG33-62, Agents of a Foreign Power fonds, Reel T-1369, Commissioner Kellock, 3694, https://heritage.canadiana.ca/view/oocihm.lac_reel_t1369/1749.

391 LAC, RG33-62, Agents of a Foreign Power fonds, Reel T-1369, Royden Hughes testimony, 3695, https://heritage.canadiana.ca/view/oocihm.lac_reel_t1369/1750.

392 LAC, RG33-62, Agents of a Foreign Power fonds, Reel T-1369, Commissioner Kellock, 3698, https://heritage.canadiana.ca/view/oocihm.lac_reel_t1369/1753.

393 LAC, Diaries of WLMK, 28 March 1946, 3–4.

394 LAC, RG33-62, Agents of a Foreign Power fonds, Reel T-1369, Hughes testimony, 3698, https://heritage.canadiana.ca/view/oocihm.lac_reel_t1369/1753.

395 LAC, RG33-62, Agents of a Foreign Power fonds, Reel T-1369, Commissioner Kellock, 3699, https://heritage.canadiana.ca/view/oocihm.lac_reel_t1369/1754.

396 LAC, RG33-62, Agents of a Foreign Power fonds, Reel T-1369, Commissioner Taschereau, 3732, https://heritage.canadiana.ca/view/oocihm.lac_reel_t1369/1787.

397 LAC, RG33-62, Agents of a Foreign Power fonds, Reel T-1369, Hughes testimony, 3732–3, https://heritage.canadiana.ca/view/oocihm.lac_reel_t1369/1787.

398 LAC, RG33-62, Agents of a Foreign Power fonds, Reel T-1369, Commissioner Kellock, 3735, https://heritage.canadiana.ca/view/oocihm.lac_reel_t1369/1790.

399 LAC, RG33-62, Agents of a Foreign Power fonds, Reel T-1369, Hughes testimony, 3735–6, https://heritage.canadiana.ca/view/oocihm.lac_reel_t1369/1790.

400 LAC, RG33-62, Agents of a Foreign Power fonds, Reel T-1369, 3737, https://heritage.canadiana.ca/view/oocihm.lac_reel_t1369/1792.

401 LAC, RG33-62, Agents of a Foreign Power fonds, Reel T-1369, F.W. Poland testimony, 3735, https://heritage.canadiana.ca/view/oocihm.lac_reel_t1369/1790.

402 *The Report of the Royal Commission (Final Report)*, 169, https://publications.gc.ca/site/eng/9.699909/publication.html.

403 "Testifies Moscow Wanted 'Polland' to Stay in Ring," *Globe & Mail*, 14 February 1947, 3.

404 "Halperin's Wife Is Granted Writ of habeas corpus," *Globe & Mail*, 27 March 1946, 4.

405 LAC, RG33-62, Agents of a Foreign Power fonds, Reel T-1369, Senator Arthur Roebuck (Roebuck) testimony, 3700, https://heritage.canadiana.ca/view/oocihm.lac_reel_t1369/1705.
406 LAC, RG33-62, Agents of a Foreign Power fonds, Reel T-1369, Commissioner Kellock, 3703, https://heritage.canadiana.ca/view/oocihm.lac_reel_t1369/1758.
407 LAC, RG33-62, Agents of a Foreign Power fonds, Reel T-1369, Commissioner Kellock, 3709, https://heritage.canadiana.ca/view/oocihm.lac_reel_t1369/1764. Halperin's military file 380A has not been archived with the records of the inquiry.
408 LAC, RG33-62, Agents of a Foreign Power fonds, Reel T-1369, Halperin testimony, 3709–10, https://heritage.canadiana.ca/view/oocihm.lac_reel_t1369/1765.
409 LAC, RG33-62, Agents of a Foreign Power fonds, Reel T-1369, Steenburgh testimony, 3069, https://heritage.canadiana.ca/view/oocihm.lac_reel_t1369/1111.
410 LAC, RG33-62, Agents of a Foreign Power fonds, Reel T-1369, Steenburgh testimony, 3070, https://heritage.canadiana.ca/view/oocihm.lac_reel_t1369/1112.
411 LAC, RG33-62, Agents of a Foreign Power fonds, Reel T-1369, Col. William van Steenburgh (Steenburgh) testimony, 3119–22, https://heritage.canadiana.ca/view/oocihm.lac_reel_t1369/1774; Canadian Army Routine orders nos. 4278 to 4280, LAC, RG33-62, Agents of a Foreign Power fonds, Reel T-3432, Exhibit 388A, Can. Army Routine Orders 4278–80; Instructions to Army Personnel dealing with classified matter, 398, https://heritage.canadiana.ca/view/oocihm.lac_reel_t3431/398.
412 LAC, RG33-62, Agents of a Foreign Power fonds, Reel T-1369, Halperin testimony, 3722–3, https://heritage.canadiana.ca/view/oocihm.lac_reel_t1369/1777.
413 LAC, RG33-62, Agents of a Foreign Power fonds, Reel T-1369, Halperin testimony, 3723–4, https://heritage.canadiana.ca/view/oocihm.lac_reel_t1369/1778.
414 LAC, RG33-62, Agents of a Foreign Power fonds, Reel T-1369, Halperin testimony, 3726, https://heritage.canadiana.ca/view/oocihm.lac_reel_t1369/1781.
415 LAC, RG33-62, Agents of a Foreign Power fonds, Reel T-1369, Halperin testimony, 3727, https://heritage.canadiana.ca/view/oocihm.lac_reel_t1369/1782.
416 LAC, RG33-62, Agents of a Foreign Power fonds, Reel T-1369, Commissioner Kellock, 3728, https://heritage.canadiana.ca/view/oocihm.lac_reel_t1369/1783.

417 LAC, RG33-62, Agents of a Foreign Power fonds, Reel T-1369, Halperin testimony, 3730, https://heritage.canadiana.ca/view/oocihm.lac_reel_t1369/1785.
418 LAC, RG33-62, Agents of a Foreign Power fonds, Reel T-1369, Halperin testimony, 3740, https://heritage.canadiana.ca/view/oocihm.lac_reel_t1369/1795.
419 LAC, RG33-62, Agents of a Foreign Power fonds, Reel T-1369, Halperin testimony, 3743, https://heritage.canadiana.ca/view/oocihm.lac_reel_t1369/1798.
420 LAC, RG33-62, Agents of a Foreign Power fonds, Reel T-1369, Commissioner Kellock, 3745, https://heritage.canadiana.ca/view/oocihm.lac_reel_t1369/1800.
421 LAC, RG33-62, Agents of a Foreign Power fonds, Reel T-1369, Halpern testimony, 3746, https://heritage.canadiana.ca/view/oocihm.lac_reel_t1369/1801.
422 LAC, RG33-62, Agents of a Foreign Power fonds, Reel T-3423, Exhibit 17E, Organizational Letter of 18.4.45, "Bacon's Report," 301–2, https://heritage.canadiana.ca/view/oocihm.lac_reel_t3423/301.
423 LAC, RG33-62, Agents of a Foreign Power fonds, Reel T-3423, Exhibit 17B, Scheme of the Group "Research," 318, https://heritage.canadiana.ca/view/oocihm.lac_reel_t3423/318
424 LAC, RG33-62, Agents of a Foreign Power fonds, Reel T-3423, Exhibit 17E, File marked "Back," Organizational Letter of 18.4.45, 323, https://heritage.canadiana.ca/view/oocihm.lac_reel_t3423/323.
425 LAC, RG33-62, Agents of a Foreign Power fonds, Reel T-3423, Exhibit 17B, Scheme of the Group "Research," 318, https://heritage.canadiana.ca/view/oocihm.lac_reel_t3423/318.
426 LAC, RG33-62, Agents of a Foreign Power fonds, Reel T-3423, Exhibit 17D, Organizational Letter Ottawa, 28 March, 321, https://heritage.canadiana.ca/view/oocihm.lac_reel_t3423/321.
427 LAC, RG33-62, Agents of a Foreign Power fonds, Reel T-1369, Steenburgh testimony, 3082–4, https://heritage.canadiana.ca/view/oocihm.lac_reel_t1369/1124.
428 LAC, RG33-62, Agents fond of a Foreign Power s, Reel T-1369, Steenburgh testimony, 3092, https://heritage.canadiana.ca/view/oocihm.lac_reel_t1369/1134.
429 LAC, RG33-62, Agents of a Foreign Power fonds, Reel T-3423, Exhibit 17E, Organizational Letter of 18.4.45, Bacon's Report, 324, https://heritage.canadiana.ca/view/oocihm.lac_reel_t3423/324.
430 LAC, RG33-62, Agents of a Foreign Power fonds, Reel T-1369, Steenburgh testimony, 3084–5, 3087, 3090, https://heritage.canadiana.ca/view/oocihm.lac_reel_t1369/1126.

431 LAC, RG33-62, Agents of a Foreign Power fonds, Reel T-1369, 3761–3, https://heritage.canadiana.ca/view/oocihm.lac_reel_t1369/1816.
432 LAC, RG33-62, Agents of a Foreign Power fonds, Reel T-3423, Exhibit 17G, Assignment Number 1, Given to Back's Group (Research) given 8.6.45, 305, https://heritage.canadiana.ca/view/oocihm.lac_reel_t3423/305.
433 LAC, RG33-62, Agents of a Foreign Power fonds, Reel T-3423, Exhibit 17F, Organizational Letter 5.7.45, 303, https://heritage.canadiana.ca/view/oocihm.lac_reel_t3423/303.
434 LAC, RG33-62, Agents of a Foreign Power fonds, Reel T-3424, Exhibit 32A, Back's Group, Material no. 1, 16–17 (pages 1–2), https://heritage.canadiana.ca/view/oocihm.lac_reel_t3424/16.
435 LAC, RG33-62, Agents of a Foreign Power fonds, Reel T-3423, Exhibit 17J, Assignment Number 2, 315, https://heritage.canadiana.ca/view/oocihm.lac_reel_t3423/315. The date 6.8.45 does not appear on the translation. See the original in Russian at LAC, RG33-62, Agents of a Foreign Power fonds, Reel T-3423, Exhibit 17J, Assignment Number 2, 316, https://heritage.canadiana.ca/view/oocihm.lac_reel_t3423/316.
436 On Lt. Linney's account of his conversation with Halperin, see LAC, RG33-62, Agents of a Foreign Power fonds, Reel T-1369, Henry J. Linney testimony, 3139–51, https://heritage.canadiana.ca/view/oocihm.lac_reel_t1369/1181.
437 LAC, RG33-62, Agents of a Foreign Power fonds, Reel T-1369, Steenburgh testimony, 3099, https://heritage.canadiana.ca/view/oocihm.lac_reel_t1369/1141.
438 LAC, RG33-62, Agents of a Foreign Power fonds, Reel T-1369, Halperin testimony, 3749, https://heritage.canadiana.ca/view/oocihm.lac_reel_t1369/1804.
439 LAC, RG33-62, Agents of a Foreign Power fonds, Reel T-1369, Halperin testimony, 3770, https://heritage.canadiana.ca/view/oocihm.lac_reel_t1369/1825.
440 Fauteux did not mention the document by title. He simply referred to Exhibit 389. For the title, see LAC, RG33-62, Agents of a Foreign Power fonds, Reel T-3431, Exhibit 389, 708, https://heritage.canadiana.ca/view/oocihm.lac_reel_t3431/708.
441 LAC, RG33-62, Agents of a Foreign Power fonds, Reel T-1369, Halperin testimony, 3772, https://heritage.canadiana.ca/view/oocihm.lac_reel_t1369/1827.
442 LAC, RG33-62, Agents of a Foreign Power fonds, Reel T-1369, Steenburgh testimony, 3098–9, https://heritage.canadiana.ca/view/oocihm.lac_reel_t1369/1140.

443 LAC, RG33-62, Agents of a Foreign Power fonds, Reel T-1369, Steenburgh testimony, 3100, https://heritage.canadiana.ca/view/oocihm.lac_reel_t1369/1142.
444 LAC, RG33-62, Agents of a Foreign Power fonds, Reel T-1369, Halperin testimony, 3774, https://heritage.canadiana.ca/view/oocihm.lac_reel_t1369/1829.
445 LAC, RG33-62, Agents of a Foreign Power fonds, Reel T-1369, Halperin testimony, 3775, https://heritage.canadiana.ca/view/oocihm.lac_reel_t1369/1830.
446 LAC, RG33-62, Agents of a Foreign Power fonds, Reel T-1369, Halperin testimony, 3780, https://heritage.canadiana.ca/view/oocihm.lac_reel_t1369/1835.
447 LAC, RG33-62, Agents of a Foreign Power fonds, Reel T-1369, Halperin testimony, 3780, https://heritage.canadiana.ca/view/oocihm.lac_reel_t1369/1835.
448 LAC, RG33-62, Agents of a Foreign Power fonds, Reel T-1369, Halperin testimony, 3781–2, https://heritage.canadiana.ca/view/oocihm.lac_reel_t1369/1836.
449 LAC, RG33-62, Agents of a Foreign Power fonds, Reel T-1369, Halperin testimony, 3782, https://heritage.canadiana.ca/view/oocihm.lac_reel_t1369/1837.
450 LAC, RG33-62, Agents of a Foreign Power fonds, Reel T-1369, Halperin testimony, 3783, https://heritage.canadiana.ca/view/oocihm.lac_reel_t1369/1838.
451 LAC, RG33-62, Agents of a Foreign Power fonds, Reel T-1369, Halperin testimony, 3784, https://heritage.canadiana.ca/view/oocihm.lac_reel_t1369/1839.
452 LAC, RG33-62, Agents of a Foreign Power fonds, Reel T-1369, Halperin testimony, 3785, https://heritage.canadiana.ca/view/oocihm.lac_reel_t1369/1840.
453 LAC, RG33-62, Agents of a Foreign Power fonds, Reel T-1369, Commission counsel Fauteux, 3786, https://heritage.canadiana.ca/view/oocihm.lac_reel_t1369/1841.
454 LAC, RG33-62, Agents of a Foreign Power fonds, Reel T-1369, Halperin testimony, 3787, https://heritage.canadiana.ca/view/oocihm.lac_reel_t1369/1842.
455 LAC, RG33-62, Agents of a Foreign Power fonds, Reel T-1369, Commissioner Taschereau, 3788, https://heritage.canadiana.ca/view/oocihm.lac_reel_t1369/1843.
456 LAC, RG33-62, Agents of a Foreign Power fonds, Reel T-1369, Commissioner Taschereau, 3789, https://heritage.canadiana.ca/view/oocihm.lac_reel_t1369/1844.

457 LAC, RG33-62, Agents of a Foreign Power fonds, Reel T-1369, Commissioner Taschereau, 3790, https://heritage.canadiana.ca/view/oocihm.lac_reel_t1369/1845.

458 LAC, RG33-62, Agents of a Foreign Power fonds, Reel T-1369, Steenburgh testimony, 3137, https://heritage.canadiana.ca/view/oocihm.lac_reel_t1369/1179.

459 TNA, KV 2/1423, Holmes to Addison, 2 April 1946, s. 183A, Third Interim Report (attached), 5.

460 "Orders Halperin to Stand Trial, Releases Shugar," *Globe & Mail*, 26 April 1946, 1.

461 "Lunan Sentenced Contempt Charge," *Medicine Hat Daily News*, 4 March 1947, 1.

462 "Halperin is Acquitted on Espionage Charges," *Globe & Mail*, 5 March 1947, 8.

463 Gordon Lunan, *The Making of a Spy* (Montreal: R. Davies, 1995), 145.

Chapter 12: Loose Ends

1 "Spy Suspects List Now 15," *Globe & Mail*, 30 March 1946, 3.

2 Kenneth L. Cragg, "Five More in Spy Case, Picked Up 43 Days Ago, Given Remands Bail," *Globe & Mail*, 30 March 1943, 3.

3 The Canadian Press account of the *Third Interim Report* appeared in the *Globe & Mail*. See "5 New Names in Third Spy Report," *Globe & Mail*, 30 March 1946, 8.

4 Warren Baldwin, "Russian Secret Police Operating in Canada," *Globe & Mail*, 30 March 1946, 1.

5 "The Wrong Admitted," *Globe & Mail*, 3 April 1946.

6 TNA, KV 2 1422, Malcolm MacDonald to Sargent, no. 435, 26 March 1946, s. 162A.

7 "Spy Informer Criminal Says Russ. Embassy," *Winnipeg Free Press*, 5 April 1946, 7.

8 See "Vsevolod Merkulov" in John Earl Haynes, *Index and Concordance to Alexander Vassiliev's Notebooks and Soviet Cables Deciphered by the National Security Agency's Venona Project*, revised 11/1/2014, 273, https://www.wilsoncenter.org/article/venona-project-and-vassiliev-notebooks-index-and-concordance.

9 This directive was sent to NKVD Residents in Algiers, Copenhagen, The Hague, Havana, Mexico City, New York, Washington, Brussels, Budapest, Prague, Paris, Zagreb, and four "unidentified lanes." Internal evidence suggests that the directive was first issued just after press disclosure of the Gouzenko affair in mid-February. National Security Agency (NSA), Washington, DC, 1996–97, Venona Decrypts, Moscow to Canberra, no. 76,

7 April 1946, Reissue Moscow's Observations on Guzenko [*sic*] Defection and Instructions to Residents for Tightening Security (1946), Release 5, vol. 2, 206–7, Ref. No.: 3/NBF/T261 (of 3/11/1952), https://www.nsa.gov/Helpful-Links/NSA-FOIA/Declassification-Transparency-Initiatives/Historical-Releases/Venona/smdsearch14707/guzenko/.

10 Apparently, via Sir William Stephenson, Kim Philby learned of Bentley's betrayal and warned Moscow via London station. Gorsky was ordered to cease contact with his network of agents and return to Moscow. Allen Weinstein and Alexander Vassiliev, *The Haunted Wood: Soviet Espionage in America: The Stalin Era* (New York: Random House, 1999), 103–7. In early December 1945, Philby also gave Moscow the names of forty-one Americans working for Moscow exposed by Bentley. Wilson Center, Vassiliev Notebooks, White Notebook, no. 2, 4.12.25 Bob from London – "S's" information, 33, https://digitalarchive.wilsoncenter.org/document/vassiliev-white-notebook-2.

11 Weinstein and Vassiliev, *The Haunted Wood*, 287–9.

12 Novikov was an ally of V.M. Molotov, long serving Soviet foreign minister and a collaborator with Molotov on the "Novikov telegram." V.M. Zubok and Konstantin Pleshakov, *Inside the Kremlin's Cold War: From Stalin to Khrushchev* (Cambridge, MA: Harvard University Press, 1996), 101– 3.

13 Wilson Center, Vassiliev Notebooks, Black Notebook, "Letter from Grigory to C.," File 43173 v. 2, 25 March 1946, 58–9, https://digitalarchive.wilsoncenter.org/document/vassiliev-black-notebook. On Novikov in Washington, see Jonathan Haslem, *Near and Distant Neighbors: A New History of Soviet intelligence* (Oxford: Oxford University Press, 2015), 150–1.

14 Wilson Center, Vassiliev Notebooks, Black Notebook, "Letter from Grigory to C.," File 43173 v. 2, 25 March 1946, 59, https://digitalarchive.wilsoncenter.org/document/vassiliev-black-notebook.

15 Wilson Center, Vassiliev Notebooks, Black Notebook, "Letter from Grigory to C.," File 43173 v. 2, 25 March 1946, 58–9, https://digitalarchive.wilsoncenter.org/document/vassiliev-black-notebook.

16 Weinstein and Vassiliev, *The Haunted Wood*, 287–9.

17 LAC, RG33-62, Agents of a Foreign Power fonds, Reel T-3424, Exhibit 34A, Two sheets draft telegram by Lt. Col. Motinov submitted to Col. Zabotin, 44–5, https://heritage.canadiana.ca/view/oocihm.lac_reel_t3424/44.

18 LAC, RG33-62, Agents of a Foreign Power fonds, Reel T-1370, Gouzenko testimony, 5073, https://heritage.canadiana.ca/view/oocihm.lac_reel_t1370/1245.

19 LAC, RG33-62, Agents of a Foreign Power fonds, Reel T-3424, Exhibit 35A, Two sheets draft telegram by Lt. Col. Motinov submitted to Col. Zabotin, 54, https://heritage.canadiana.ca/view/oocihm.lac_reel_t3424/54.

20 LAC, RG33-62, Agents of a Foreign Power fonds, Reel T-1368, Gouzenko testimony, 305, https://heritage.canadiana.ca/view/oocihm.lac_reel_t1368/354. Gregori Tounkin was first secretary in the Soviet embassy. LAC, RG33-62, Agents of a Foreign Power fonds, Reel T-3433, Exhibit 545, "Identity cards issued to Officers of the USSR Mission in Canada," 116, https://heritage.canadiana.ca/view/oocihm.lac_reel_t3433/116.

21 LAC, RG33-62, Agents of a Foreign Power fonds, Reel T-3424, Exhibit 34A, Two sheets draft telegram by Lt. Col. Motinov submitted to Col. Zabotin, 44–5, https://heritage.canadiana.ca/view/oocihm.lac_reel_t3424/44.

22 LAC, RG33-62, Agents of a Foreign Power fonds, Reel T-1368, Gouzenko testimony, 305, https://heritage.canadiana.ca/view/oocihm.lac_reel_t1368/354.

23 LAC, RG33-62, Agents of a Foreign Power fonds, Reel T-1368, Gouzenko testimony, 305–6, https://heritage.canadiana.ca/view/oocihm.lac_reel_t1368/354. See also Taschereau later citing Gouzenko, LAC, RG33-62, Agents of a Foreign Power fonds, Reel T-1370, Taschereau, 3937, https://heritage.canadiana.ca/view/oocihm.lac_reel_t1370/81.

24 There was a potential for Samuel Saul (S.S.) Burman to have been confused with Sol Berman "ins agent Crown Life." Sol Berman's office was located at 1117 St. Catherine Street W and his residence at apartment 21, 1045 St. Viatur Avenue. S.S. Burman, who resided at apartment 20, 5174 Cote des Neiges Rd., was employed by North American Life with offices at 660 St. Catherine Street W. LAC, RG33-62, Agents of a Foreign Power fonds, Reel T-1370, Burman testimony, 3866, 3870, https://heritage.canadiana.ca/view/oocihm.lac_reel_t1370/14. See Berman, Sol, and Burman, S.S., in *Lowell's Montreal Directory*, 1943 (Montreal: John Lovell & Son, 1943), 717, 818.

25 "Who Runs the 'Y'?," *The YMHA Beacon*, 30 August 1935; "'Y' Urban Camp Opens with Record Program – Vigorous Activity," *YMHA Beacon*, 15 July 1938; "M. Horowitz Is New Scout Master," *YMHA Beacon*, 1 December 1938; "Skiers Plan Fine Program, *YMHA Beacon*, 23 December 1939; "Attention 'Y' Skiers," *YMHA Beacon*, 22 November 1940, 3. "Thorough Canvas for 1942 Combined [Jewish] Appeal," *Canadian Jewish Chronicle*," 21 April 1942, 11.

26 TNA, KV 2/1428, "Soviet Espionage in Canada,"45.

27 LAC, RG33-62, Agents of a Foreign Power fonds, Reel T-1370, S.S Burman testimony, 3924–5, https://heritage.canadiana.ca/view/oocihm.lac_reel_t1370/67.

28 LAC, RG33-62, Agents of a Foreign Power fonds, Reel T-1370, Burman testimony, 3923–4, https://heritage.canadiana.ca/view/oocihm.lac_reel_t1370/67.

29 LAC, RG33-62, Agents of a Foreign Power fonds, Reel T-1370, Burman testimony, 3925, https://heritage.canadiana.ca/view/oocihm.lac_reel_t1370/69.
30 "Regulations – II," *Montreal Gazette*, 31 July 1942, 8.
31 S.S. Burman, "Flagrant Bit of Sophistry?" *Montreal Gazette*, 3 August 1942, 8.
32 Samuel Burman obituary, *Globe & Mail*, 25 March 1997, 10; LAC, RG33-62, Agents of a Foreign Power fonds, Reel T-1369, Burman testimony, 3870, https://heritage.canadiana.ca/view/oocihm.lac_reel_t1370/14.
33 Dr. David Borys, historian of the Civil Affairs branch, is not aware of any security checks performed on individuals accepted for service in Civil Affairs. E-mail message to Tom Mitchell, 20 November 2023.
34 David A. Borys, *Civilians at the Sharpe End: First Canadian Army Civil Affairs in Northwest Europe* (Montreal & Kingston: McGill-Queen's University Press, 2021), 4.
35 LAC, RG33-62, Agents of a Foreign Power fonds, Reel T-1369, Burman testimony, 3872, https://heritage.canadiana.ca/view/oocihm.lac_reel_t1370/16.
36 LAC, RG33-62, Agents of a Foreign Power fonds, Reel T-1369, Burman testimony, 3873, https://heritage.canadiana.ca/view/oocihm.lac_reel_t1370/17.
37 Borys, *Civilians at the Sharpe End*, 50.
38 LAC, RG33-62, Agents of a Foreign Power fonds, Reel T-1369, Burman testimony, 3873, https://heritage.canadiana.ca/view/oocihm.lac_reel_t1370/17.
39 LAC, RG33-62, Agents of a Foreign Power fonds, Reel T-1370, Gouzenko testimony, 5073, https://heritage.canadiana.ca/view/oocihm.lac_reel_t1370/1245.
40 Keith Jeffery, *The Secret History of MI6: 1909–1949* (New York: Penguin, 2010), 553.
41 LAC, RG33-62, Agents of a Foreign Power fonds, Reel T-3423, Exhibit 23B, Incoming telegram in the handwriting of Lieut. Koulakov, Director to Grant, no. 11273, 11.8.45, 660, https://heritage.canadiana.ca/view/oocihm.lac_reel_t3423/660.
42 LAC, RG33-62, Agents of a Foreign Power fonds, Reel T-3434, RG19, Subpoena, Samuel Saul Berman, 29 March 1946, 105, https://heritage.canadiana.ca/view/oocihm.lac_reel_t3434/105.
43 LAC, RG33-62, Agents of a Foreign Power fonds, Reel T-1369, Burman testimony, 3872, https://heritage.canadiana.ca/view/oocihm.lac_reel_t1370/16.
44 LAC, RG33-62, Agents of a Foreign Power fonds, Reel T-3424, Exhibit 34A, Two sheets draft telegram by Lt. Col. Motinov submitted to Col. Zabotin, 44–5, https://heritage.canadiana.ca/view/oocihm.lac_reel_t3424/44.

45 LAC, RG33-62, Agents of a Foreign Power fonds, Reel T-1369, Burman testimony, 3877–8, https://heritage.canadiana.ca/view/oocihm.lac_reel_t1370/21.

46 LAC, RG33-62, Agents of a Foreign Power fonds, Reel T-1369, Burman testimony, 3904, https://heritage.canadiana.ca/view/oocihm.lac_reel_t1370/48.

47 LAC, RG33-62, Agents of a Foreign Power fonds, Reel T-1369, Burman testimony, 3874, https://heritage.canadiana.ca/view/oocihm.lac_reel_t1370/18.

48 LAC, RG33-62, Agents of a Foreign Power fonds, Reel T-1369, Burman testimony, 3874, https://heritage.canadiana.ca/view/oocihm.lac_reel_t1370/18.

49 LAC, RG33-62, Agents of a Foreign Power fonds, Reel T-1369, Burman testimony, 3875, https://heritage.canadiana.ca/view/oocihm.lac_reel_t1370/19.

50 LAC, RG33-62, Agents of a Foreign Power fonds, Reel T-1369, Burman testimony, 3876–7, https://heritage.canadiana.ca/view/oocihm.lac_reel_t1370/20.

51 LAC, RG33-62, Agents of a Foreign Power fonds, Reel T-1369, Burman testimony, 3907–8, https://heritage.canadiana.ca/view/oocihm.lac_reel_t1370/51.

52 LAC, RG33-62, Agents of a Foreign Power fonds, Reel T-3424, Exhibit 34A, Two sheets draft telegram by Lt. Col. Motinov submitted to Col. Zabotin, 44–5, https://heritage.canadiana.ca/view/oocihm.lac_reel_t3424/45.

53 LAC, RG33-62, Agents of a Foreign Power fonds, Reel T-1369, Burman testimony, 3909, https://heritage.canadiana.ca/view/oocihm.lac_reel_t1370/53.

54 LAC, RG33-62, Agents of a Foreign Power fonds, Reel T-1369, Burman testimony, 3909–10, https://heritage.canadiana.ca/view/oocihm.lac_reel_t1370/53.

55 LAC, RG33-62, Agents of a Foreign Power fonds, Reel T-1369, Burman testimony, 3881, 3385, https://heritage.canadiana.ca/view/oocihm.lac_reel_t1370/25.

56 LAC, RG33-62, Agents of a Foreign Power fonds, Reel T-1369, Burman testimony, 3911, https://heritage.canadiana.ca/view/oocihm.lac_reel_t1370/55.

57 LAC, RG33-62, Agents of a Foreign Power fonds, Reel T-1369, Burman testimony, 3899–3903, https://heritage.canadiana.ca/view/oocihm.lac_reel_t1370/43.

58 LAC, RG33-62, Agents of a Foreign Power fonds, Reel T-1369, Burman testimony, 3913–14, https://heritage.canadiana.ca/view/oocihm.lac_reel_t1370/57.

59 *The Report of the Royal Commission* (*Final Report*), 373, https://publications.gc.ca/site/eng/9.699909/publication.html.
60 LAC, RG33-62, Agents of a Foreign Power fonds, Reel T-3423, Exhibit 22A, Page out of Notebook in Col. Zabotin's handwriting, Second Group, 4. Surensen, 643, https://heritage.canadiana.ca/view/oocihm.lac_reel_t3423/643.
61 LAC, RG33-62, Agents of a Foreign Power fonds, Reel T-3423, Exhibit 25cc, Page out of Notebook in Col. Zabotin's handwriting, Surensen, 778, https://heritage.canadiana.ca/view/oocihm.lac_reel_t3423/778.
62 LAC, RG33-62, Agents of a Foreign Power fonds, Reel T-1370, Sorensen testimony, 4009, 4025, https://heritage.canadiana.ca/view/oocihm.lac_reel_t1370/152, https://heritage.canadiana.ca/view/oocihm.lac_reel_t1370/168.
63 TNA, KV 2/1423, MacDonald to Sargent, no. 501, 9 April 1946, s. 189a.
64 LAC, RG33-62, Agents of a Foreign Power fonds, Reel T-1370, Lt. Commander George Tottenham testimony (Tottenham testimony), 4963–4, https://heritage.canadiana.ca/view/oocihm.lac_reel_t1370/1136; LAC, RG33-62, Agents of a Foreign Power fonds, Reel T-1370, Sorensen testimony, 4018, https://heritage.canadiana.ca/view/oocihm.lac_reel_t1370/161.
65 LAC, RG33-62, Agents of a Foreign Power fonds, Reel T-1370, Sorensen testimony, 4018–19, https://heritage.canadiana.ca/view/oocihm.lac_reel_t1370/161.
66 LAC, RG33-62, Agents of a Foreign Power fonds, Reel T-1370, Tottenham testimony, 4791–2, https://heritage.canadiana.ca/view/oocihm.lac_reel_t1370/1166.
67 LAC, RG33-62, Agents of a Foreign Power fonds, Reel T-1370, Tottenham testimony, 4972–4, https://heritage.canadiana.ca/view/oocihm.lac_reel_t1370/1144.
68 LAC, RG33-62, Agents of a Foreign Power fonds, Reel T-1370, Sorensen testimony, 5244, https://heritage.canadiana.ca/view/oocihm.lac_reel_t1370/1418.
69 LAC, RG33-62, Agents of a Foreign Power fonds, Reel T-1370, Sorensen testimony, 4018, https://heritage.canadiana.ca/view/oocihm.lac_reel_t1370/161.
70 LAC, RG33-62, Agents of a Foreign Power fonds, Reel T-1370, Sorensen testimony, 4026, https://heritage.canadiana.ca/view/oocihm.lac_reel_t1370/169.
71 LAC, RG33-62, Agents of a Foreign Power fonds, Reel T-1370, Sorensen testimony, 4018, https://heritage.canadiana.ca/view/oocihm.lac_reel_t1370/161.
72 Tyler Wentzell, *Not for King or Country: Edward Cecil-Smith, the Communist Party of Canada, and the Spanish Civil War* (Toronto: University of Toronto Press, 2020), 103–9.

73 LAC, RG33-62, Agents of a Foreign Power fonds, Reel T-1370, Sorensen testimony, 4012, https://heritage.canadiana.ca/view/oocihm.lac_reel_t1370/155.

74 "Canadian Doctor Due in Madrid This Week," *New Commonwealth*, 31 October 1936, 1. On the committee, see "Montrealers Aid Spanish," *New Commonwealth*, 31 October 1936, 1. In 1966 when Communist leader Tim Buck commemorated Bethune's "Blood Transfusion Unit" in Spain, he celebrated Dr. Bethune, Hazen Size, Ted Allan, and later Alan May and Dr. Henne, but he made no mention of Henning Sorensen. Tim Buck, "Soldiers of Democracy," *Marxist Quarterly* 18 (1966): 15.

75 "Commonwealth Reporter Has Arrived in Spain," *New Commonwealth*, 17 October 1936, 1.

76 LAC, RG33-62, Agents of a Foreign Power fonds, Reel T-1370, Sorensen testimony, 4012–13, https://heritage.canadiana.ca/view/oocihm.lac_reel_t1370/155.

77 LAC, RG33-62, Agents of a Foreign Power fonds, Reel T-1370, Sorensen testimony, 5247, https://heritage.canadiana.ca/view/oocihm.lac_reel_t1370/1421.

78 LAC, RG33-62, Agents of a Foreign Power fonds, Reel T-1370, Sorensen testimony, 5247–8, https://heritage.canadiana.ca/view/oocihm.lac_reel_t1370/1421.

79 See Henning Sorensen to the Central Committee of the Communist Party of Spain, Valencia, 4 August 1937, LAC [Moscow Archives], Comintern fonds, MG1-K3, fonds 539, file list 3, file 732, as cited in Roderick Stewart and Sharon Stewart, *Phoenix: The Life of Norman Bethune* (Montreal & Kingston: McGill-Queen's University Press, 2011), 412n10.

80 LAC, RG33-62, Agents of a Foreign Power fonds, Reel T-1370, Sorensen testimony, 4015, https://heritage.canadiana.ca/view/oocihm.lac_reel_t1370/158.

81 For these dates, see *Canada Declassified*, CSIS, The Feather Bed File (Feather Bed), vol. 1, 48, https://declassified.library.utoronto.ca/exhibits/show/featherbed/volume-1.

82 Stewart & Stewart, *Phoenix*, 412n10.

83 Hugh Thomas, *Armed Truce: The Beginnings of the Cold War 1945–46* (New York: Atheneum, 1967), 607n16. See also Alexander Foote, *Handbook for Spies* (Garden City: Doubleday, 1949), 9–16.

84 Michael Petrou, *Renegades: Canadians in the Spanish Civil War* (Vancouver: UBC Press, 2008), 41–2. On Bethune's project, see Ted Farah, "Canadian Trio Provide Blood Conserve Life," *Brandon Daily Sun*, 17 July 1937, 5; "Spain Grateful for Blood-Gift from Canadians," *Brandon Daily Sun*, 17 September 1937, 6.

85 Michael Cope, "Castro Still Eyes Other Latin Fields," *St. Petersburg Times*, 20 March 1962, 11. On Cope, see Michael Cope, "Cubans Flock to Churches," *Windsor Star*, 27 March 1962, 9.
86 See section IV.2, "Surensen," in *The Report of the Royal Commission* (*Final Report*), 527–32, https://publications.gc.ca/site/eng/9.699909/publication.html.
87 *The Report of the Royal Commission* (*Final Report*), 532, https://publications.gc.ca/site/eng/9.699909/publication.html.
88 TNA, KV 2/1635, Ignacy Samuel Witczak, "Extract from first report on information derived from CORBY," Copy no. 1, Issue no. 3, 30.10.45, s. 1A.
89 TNA/KV 2/1422, MacDonald to Sargent, 5 March 1946, TOP SECRET, no. 299, 5 March 1946, s. 106A.
90 On the complexities of getting from Canada to the war, see Wentzell, *Not for King or Country*, 103–9.
91 LAC, RG33-62, Agents of a Foreign Power fonds, Reel T-1370, Ignacy Witczak (Witczak) testimony, 4067, https://heritage.canadiana.ca/view/oocihm.lac_reel_t1370/211.
92 LAC, RG33-62, Agents of a Foreign Power fonds, Reel T-1370, Witczak testimony, 4067, https://heritage.canadiana.ca/view/oocihm.lac_reel_t1370/211.
93 LAC, RG33-62, Agents of a Foreign Power fonds, Reel T-1370, Witczak testimony, 4068, https://heritage.canadiana.ca/view/oocihm.lac_reel_t1370/212.
94 LAC, RG33-62, Agents of a Foreign Power fonds, Reel T-1370, Witczak testimony, 4077, https://heritage.canadiana.ca/view/oocihm.lac_reel_t1370/221.
95 LAC, RG33-62, Agents of a Foreign Power fonds, Reel T-1370, Gouzenko testimony, 5011, https://heritage.canadiana.ca/view/oocihm.lac_reel_t1370/1184.
96 TNA, KV 2/1619, Dübendorfer, Rachel, & Boettcher, Paul, "Extract from M.I.5. Report of S's Interview with Foote – Sunday Afternoon, 20 July 1947 mentioning DUEBENDORFER," s. 14D.
97 David Levy "The Sad Tale of Fred Rose, Stalin's Man in the True North," *International Journal of Intelligence and CounterIntelligence* 25, no. 2 (2012), 354–5.
98 On Tilton and Dozenberg, see Raymond W. Leonard, *Secret Soldiers of the Revolution: Soviet Military Intelligence, 1918–1933* (Westport, CT: Greenwood, 1999), 111–12.
99 On the career of "Harry I," see "Ernest Weiss," in Nigel West, *Historical Dictionary of British Intelligence*, 2nd ed. (New York: Rowman & Littlefield, 2014), 626–7.

100 On the supply of Canadian passports to Soviet agents operating in Europe, see Herbert Romerstein and Eric Breindel, *The Venona Secrets: Exposing Soviet Espionage and America's Traitors* (Washington, DC: Regnery, 2000), 123.
101 LAC, RG33-62, Agents of a Foreign Power fonds, Reel T-1368, Gouzenko testimony, 104, https://heritage.canadiana.ca/view/oocihm.lac_reel_t1368/165.
102 LAC, RG33-62, Agents of a Foreign Power fonds, Reel T-1370, Gouzenko testimony, 5008, https://heritage.canadiana.ca/view/oocihm.lac_reel_t1370/1181.
103 LAC, RG33-62, Agents of a Foreign Power fonds, Reel T-3423, Exhibit 19F, File marked "Frank," Sam Carr, 402, https://heritage.canadiana.ca/view/oocihm.lac_reel_t3423/402. Gouzenko testified that this note was in Motinov's script. LAC, RG33-62, Agents of a Foreign Power fonds, Reel T-1368, 108–9, https://heritage.canadiana.ca/view/oocihm.lac_reel_t1368/169.
104 LAC, RG33-62, Agents of a Foreign Power fonds, Reel T-1368, Gouzenko testimony, 184, https://heritage.canadiana.ca/view/oocihm.lac_reel_t1368/245.
105 LAC, RG33-62, Agents of a Foreign Power fonds, Reel T-1370, Gouzenko testimony, 4998–9, https://heritage.canadiana.ca/view/oocihm.lac_reel_t1370/1171.
106 LAC, RG33-62, Agents of a Foreign Power fonds, Reel T-1370, Gouzenko testimony, 5000, https://heritage.canadiana.ca/view/oocihm.lac_reel_t1370/1173.
107 LAC, RG33-62, Agents of a Foreign Power fonds, Reel T-1370, Gouzenko testimony, 5006–7, https://heritage.canadiana.ca/view/oocihm.lac_reel_t1370/1179.
108 LAC, RG33-62, Agents of a Foreign Power fonds, Reel T-1370, Gouzenko testimony, 5006, https://heritage.canadiana.ca/view/oocihm.lac_reel_t1370/1179.
109 LAC, RG33-62, Agents of a Foreign Power fonds, Reel T-3423, Exhibit 19G, File marked "Frank," Assignment Given, 1.8.45, 414, https://heritage.canadiana.ca/view/oocihm.lac_reel_t3423/414.
110 LAC, RG33-62, Agents of a Foreign Power fonds, Reel T-3423, Exhibit 19H, File marked "Frank," Assignment Given 16-8-45, 416, https://heritage.canadiana.ca/view/oocihm.lac_reel_t3423/416.
111 LAC, RG33-62, Agents of a Foreign Power fonds, Reel T-3423, Exhibit 19E, File marked Frank, "Course of Meetings," 15.6.45., 422, https://heritage.canadiana.ca/view/oocihm.lac_reel_t3423/422.
112 LAC, RG33-62, Agents of a Foreign Power fonds, Reel T-3423, Exhibit 19E, File marked Frank, "Course of Meetings," 15.6.45., 422, https://heritage.canadiana.ca/view/oocihm.lac_reel_t3423/422.

113 LAC, RG33-62, Agents of a Foreign Power fonds, Reel T-1370, Dr. Henry Harris (Harris) testimony, 5992, https://heritage.canadiana.ca/view/oocihm.lac_reel_t1370/1968.
114 LAC, RG33-62, Agents of a Foreign Power fonds, Reel T-1370, Harris testimony, 5992–3, https://heritage.canadiana.ca/view/oocihm.lac_reel_t1370/1968.
115 LAC, RG33-62, Agents of a Foreign Power fonds, Reel T-1370, Harris testimony, 5994, https://heritage.canadiana.ca/view/oocihm.lac_reel_t1370/1970.
116 LAC, RG33-62, Agents of a Foreign Power fonds, Reel T-1370, Harris testimony, 6006, https://heritage.canadiana.ca/view/oocihm.lac_reel_t1370/1982.
117 LAC, RG33-62, Agents of a Foreign Power fonds, Reel T-1370, Harris testimony, 6016, https://heritage.canadiana.ca/view/oocihm.lac_reel_t1370/1992.
118 "Spies Forged Passports, Royal Commission Says," *Globe & Mail*, 16 July 1946, 18.
119 "Grants $5,000 Bail for Harris Appeal in Espionage Case," *Globe & Mail*, 28 January 1947, 3.
120 Statutes of Canada, 1939, c. 49, Official Secrets Act (Ottawa: King's Printer, 1939), 449–58.
121 "Judge Refuses Dismissal Plea for Henry Harris," *Globe & Mail*, 25 January 1947, 3.
122 "Grants $5,000 Bail for Harris Appeal in Espionage Case," *Globe & Mail*, 28 January 1947, 3.
123 Rex v. Harris, 1947 CanLII 78 (ON CA), https://canlii.ca/t/g19pt.
124 LAC, RG33-62, Agents of a Foreign Power fonds, Reel T-3432, Exhibit 453, "Soboloff Declaration," 573, https://heritage.canadiana.ca/view/oocihm.lac_reel_t3432/573; LAC, RG33-62, Agents of a Foreign Power fonds, Reel T-1370, Dr. John Soboloff (Soboloff) testimony, 4079–80, https://heritage.canadiana.ca/view/oocihm.lac_reel_t1370/223.
125 LAC, RG33-62, Agents of a Foreign Power fonds, Reel T-1370, Soboloff testimony, 4089, https://heritage.canadiana.ca/view/oocihm.lac_reel_t1370/233.
126 "Endorsing Passport Said 'Gross Stupidity,' Soboloff Fined $500," *Globe & Mail*, 14 September 1946, 5.
127 LAC, RG33-62, Agents of a Foreign Power fonds, Reel T-1370, Cooper testimony, 4242, https://heritage.canadiana.ca/view/oocihm.lac_reel_t1370/391.
128 LAC, RG33-62, Agents of a Foreign Power fonds, Reel T-1370, Cooper testimony, 4246, https://heritage.canadiana.ca/view/oocihm.lac_reel_t1370/395.

129 LAC, RG33-62, Agents of a Foreign Power fonds, Reel T-1370, Mrs. Adrienne Souliere testimony, 4659, 4664–5, https://heritage.canadiana.ca/view/oocihm.lac_reel_t1370/817.
130 LAC, RG33-62, Agents of a Foreign Power fonds, Reel T-1370, W.M. Pappin (Pappin) testimony, 4810–1, https://heritage.canadiana.ca/view/oocihm.lac_reel_t1370/969.
131 *The Report of the Royal Commission* (*Final Report*), 563, https://publications.gc.ca/site/eng/9.699909/publication.html.
132 "Jury Will Try Passport Clerk in Spy Ring Case," *Globe & Mail*, 18 September 1946, 3; Douglas How, "Pappin Acquitted of Charges Based on False Passport," *Globe & Mail*, 19 October 1946, 7.
133 "Jury Will Try Passport Clerk in Spy Ring Case," *Globe & Mail*, 18 September 1946, 3.
134 Douglas How, "Pappin Acquitted of Charges Based on False Passport, *Globe & Mail*, 19 October 1946, 7.
135 How, "Pappin Acquitted," *Globe & Mail*, 19 October 1946, 7.
136 How, "Pappin Acquitted," *Globe & Mail*, 19 October 1946, 7.
137 LAC, RG33-62, Agents of a Foreign Power fonds, Reel T-3423, Exhibit 23DD, Incoming telegram in the handwriting of Lieut. Koulakov, no. 11436, To Grant, in reply to 227, 14.8.45, 688, https://heritage.canadiana.ca/view/oocihm.lac_reel_t3423/688.
138 LAC, RG33-62, Agents of a Foreign Power fonds, Reel T-1370, 4124, https://heritage.canadiana.ca/view/oocihm.lac_reel_t1370/273.
139 For Canadian reaction to Carr's arrest, see "Reds Disown Sam Carr; May Get Toronto Trial," *Globe & Mail*, 28 January 1949, 1.
140 TNA, KV 2, 1633, V2, Sam Carr, "Sam Carr Committed for Trial," *The Times*, 2 March 1949, s. 115a.
141 "Sam Carr Reaches End of Journey in Freedom Bid," *Globe & Mail*, 28 September 1949, 13.
142 Gouzenko, judging the handwriting, said that the sentence was written by Rogov as part of his administration of the Carr network. Rogov made the note because the arrangement predated his arrival in Canada and had been made when Sergei Koudriavtsev was putting the Rose and Carr network together in late 1942 or early 1943. See "Eric calls through Skelton." LAC, RG33-62, Agents of a Foreign Power fonds, Reel T-3423, Exhibit 19B-F [*sic*], Miscellaneous, Sam, 425, https://heritage.canadiana.ca/view/oocihm.lac_reel_t3423/425. On Dr. Henry Harris see TNA KV 2/1428, Soviet Espionage in Canada, 30–1.
143 TNA, KV 2/1896, Freda Linton, Extract from first report on information from "CORBY" RE THE Organization of the NKVD and of the Russian C.P. Central Committee within the Soviet embassy in Ottawa, mentioning Freda LINTON, undated, s. 1z.

144 TNA, KV 2/1896, Freda Linton, Extract from Royal Canadian Mounted Police Report re. Soviet espionage in Canada – "Corby" case, November 45, s. 1az.
145 TNA, KV 2/1571, Grace Marsh, Extract from telegram from NEW YORK dated 3.3.46. re RCMP interrogation at ROCKCLIFFE, s. 6a.
146 TNA, KV 2/ 1645, Hermina Rabinowitz, Extract from telegram from New York, mentioning RABINOWITZ (RABINOWITCH), 19.9.45, s. 2a.
147 LAC, RG33-62, Agents of a Foreign Power fonds, Reel T-3423, Exhibit 22A, Page out of notebook in Col. Zabotin's handwriting, Second Group, 2. ERNST, 642–43, https://heritage.canadiana.ca/view/oocihm.lac_reel_t3423/642.
148 In addition to being prime minister, Mackenzie King also retained responsibility for External Relations.
149 LAC, Diaries of Mackenzie King 20 February 1946, 2.
150 LAC, Diaries of Mackenzie King 20 February 1946, 2.
151 There is no record in the Kellock-Taschereau inquiry fonds to indicate that Skelton received a subpoena to testify before the inquiry. For the list of those who were served with a subpoena see LAC, RG33-62, Agents of a Foreign Power fonds, Reel T-3434, 100–1, https://heritage.canadiana.ca/view/oocihm.lac_reel_t3434/100.
152 Terry Crowley, *Marriage of Minds: Isabel and Oscar Skelton Reinventing Canada* (Toronto: University of Toronto Press), 177.
153 Crowley, *Marriage of Minds*, 229. On Skelton's personal life and attributes see Norman Hillmer, *O.D. Skelton: A Portrait of Canadian Ambition* (Toronto: University of Toronto Press, 2015), 30 *passim*.
154 On Skelton's entry into the Bank of Canada and his professional activities within the Canadian state see J.L. Granatstein, *The Ottawa Men: The Civil Service Mandarins 1935–1957* (Toronto: University of Toronto Press, 1982), 55 *passim*, 253.
155 See the testimony of Dean G. Marble, secretary of the Bank of Canada, LAC, RG33-62, Agents of a Foreign Power fonds, Reel T-1369, Marble testimony, 2595–6, https://heritage.canadiana.ca/view/oocihm.lac_reel_t1369/615; LC, RG33-62, Agents of a Foreign Power fonds, Reel T-3430, Exhibit 274A, "Agatha Chapman, Application for position Bank of Canada," 677, https://heritage.canadiana.ca/view/oocihm.lac_reel_t3430/677.
156 LAC, RG33-62, Agents of a Foreign Power fonds, Reel T-1370, Skelton testimony, 4685, https://heritage.canadiana.ca/view/oocihm.lac_reel_t1370/843.
157 Gregory S. Kealey, *Workers and Canadian History* (Montreal & Kingston: McGill Queen's University Press, 1995), 49.
158 Weisbord, *The Strangest Dream*, 126.

159 Crowley, *Marriage of Minds*, 254–5. Skelton and Green had been married in New York. Skelton had no grounds for divorcing his wife, and she did not divorce him. When she remarried in 1957, Green Skelton referred to herself as Mrs. Kathleen Green Skelton, and in her wedding announcement she was described as the "widow" of Alex Skelton. "Mrs. Skelton Engaged to Richard A. Herbert," *St Louis Post-Dispatch*, 4 June 1957, 4D.
160 Terry Crowley, *Marriage of Minds*, 229.
161 Terry Crowley, *Marriage of Minds*, 229.
162 LAC, RG33-62, Agents of a Foreign Power fonds, Reel T-1368, Willsher testimony, 771, https://heritage.canadiana.ca/view/oocihm.lac_reel_t1368/831.
163 Terry Crowley, email message to Tom Mitchell, 18 November 2022. Janet Naomi Turner Skelton died in 1994 shortly after an interview with Crowley.
164 Terry Crowley, email message to Tom Mitchell, 18 November 2022.
165 *Submission of the Central Committee, Communist Party to the Royal Commission on Dominion-Provincial Relations* (Toronto: Communist Party of Canada, 1938). For Buck's presentation of the *Submission* see Mary Louise Janigan, "The Art of Sharing: The Richer Provinces Versus the Poorer Provinces since Confederation," PhD dissertation, York University, 2017, 240–1, http://hdl.handle.net/10315/34499.
166 Norman Penner explains that he received this information "from one of the top three leaders of the CPC of that period." Penner, *Canadian Communism: The Stalin Years and Beyond* (Toronto: Methuen, 1988), 159n 57.
167 Terry Crowley, *Marriage of Minds*, 255.
168 See Stanley Jackson's petition to Senate for a divorce from Janet Naomi Turner in Senate Journals, 19th Parliament, 2nd Session, Vol. 81, May 13, 1941, 95. S.C. (Local and Private Acts) 1941, An Act for the relief of Stanley Jackson, c. 59, 49.
169 When Ferns arrived back in North America in 1940 after several years at Cambridge University, he recalled, "I was still very much a Marxist and I had no idea of repudiating the Communist party even though I disagreed with its line on the war and supported the war policies of the Canadian government." H.S. Ferns, *Reading from Left to Right: One Man's Political History* (Toronto: University of Toronto Press, 1983), 89, 191.
170 LAC, RG33-62, Agents of a Foreign Power fonds, Reel T-1370, Skelton testimony, 4686, https://heritage.canadiana.ca/view/oocihm.lac_reel_t1370/844.
171 LAC, RG33-62, Agents of a Foreign Power fonds, Reel T-1369, Skelton testimony, 4685, https://heritage.canadiana.ca/view/oocihm.lac_reel_t1370/843.

172 LAC, RG33-62, Agents of a Foreign Power fonds, Reel T-1370, Skelton testimony, 4686, https://heritage.canadiana.ca/view/oocihm.lac_reel_t1370/844.
173 LAC, RG33-62, Agents of a Foreign Power fonds, Reel T-1370, Skelton testimony, 4687, https://heritage.canadiana.ca/view/oocihm.lac_reel_t1370/845.
174 LAC, RG33-62, Agents of a Foreign Power fonds, Reel T-1370, Skelton testimony, 4686, https://heritage.canadiana.ca/view/oocihm.lac_reel_t1370/844.
175 *The Report of the Royal Commission (Final Report)*, 548, https://publications.gc.ca/site/eng/9.699909/publication.html.
176 Weisbord, *The Strangest Dream*, 173.
177 On British interest in the "Rote Kapelle," see Declan O'Reilly, "Interrogating the Gestapo: SS-*Sturmbannführer* Horst Kopkow, the *Rote Kapelle* and Post-war British Security Interests," *Journal of Intelligence History* 22, no. 2 (2023): 192–215, https://doi.org/10.1080/16161262.2022.2116861.
178 In formal terms, the commissioners were directed to "inquire into and report upon which public officials and other persons in positions of trust or otherwise have communicated, directly or indirectly, secret and confidential information … to the agents of a Foreign Power." For a certified copy of PC 411, see LAC, RG33-62, Agents of a Foreign Power fonds, T-3423, Exhibit 1, PC 411, 2–5, https://heritage.canadiana.ca/view/oocihm.lac_reel_t3423/104.
179 TNA, KV 2/1422, Sargent to MacDonald, no. 522, 7 March 1946, Top Secret, s. 117A.
180 TNA, KV 2 1422, no. 300, MacDonald to Sargent, 5 March 1946, Top Secret, s. 106A.
181 TNA, KV 2/1634, no. 539, Following for Hollis from RCMP, 24 April 1946, s. 19a.
182 LAC, RG33-62, Agents of a Foreign Power fonds, Reel T-3433, Exhibit 558, Arnold Smith, External Affairs to E.K. Williams and Gerald Fauteux, Counsel to Royal Commission of Inquiry, 17 May 1946, 195, https://heritage.canadiana.ca/view/oocihm.lac_reel_t3433/195.
183 For the subpoena, see LAC, RG33-62, Agents of a Foreign Power fonds, Reel T-3434, In the Matter of an Inquiry under Part I, 149–50, https://heritage.canadiana.ca/view/oocihm.lac_reel_t3434/149.
184 For her MI5 file, see TNA, KV 2/1634, "Hermina Rabinowitch." For a brief biographical account of Rabinowitch, see *The Rote Kapelle: The CIA's History of Soviet Intelligence and Espionage Networks in Western Europe, 1936–1945* (Washington, DC: University Publications of America, 1979), 332–4.

185 In July 1946, a near fifty-page account of her testimony before the commissioners appeared in the final report of the inquiry. *The Report of the Royal Commission* (*Final Report*), 565–613, https://publications.gc.ca/site/eng/9.699909/publication.html. Earlier in May 1946, Rabinowitch had been denied entry to the US; in late August the Department of Immigration and Naturalization imposed a permanent ban on her entry. "US Bars ILO Aide Miss Rabinowitch, *New York Times*, 30 August 1946, 6.

186 On Abramson, see TNA, KV3/350, The Case of the Rote Kapelle, Part III (A-L), "Abramson, Alexander," A1–A2.

187 TNA, KV 2/1634, Hermina Rabinowitz, FBI report of an interview of Irene Grunberg, 10 January 1948, 17.

188 Robert W. Pringle, *Historical Dictionary of Russian and Soviet Intelligence*, 2nd ed. (New York: Rowman & Littlefield, 2015), 254–55. For biographical accounts of Red Orchestra personnel, see TNA, KV3/350, "The Case of the Rote Kapelle," Part III (A–L).

189 TNA, KV 2/1634, Hermina Rabinowitz, Extract from Top Secret and personal letter from S.I.S mentioning RABINOWITSCH, 24 September 1945, s. 10A. For a comprehensive account of the "Rote Drei," see *The Rote Kapelle: The CIA's History*, 165–224. See also Timothy P. Mulligan, "Spies, Ciphers and 'Zitadelle': Intelligence and the Battle of Kursk, 1943," *Journal of Contemporary History* 22, no. 2 (1987): 235–60.

190 *The Rote Kapelle: The CIA's History*, 165.

191 On these developments, see TNA/KV 2/1648, Rado, Alexander. Rado, Helene, Re: Alexander Rado (Rote Kapelle), 4 April 1951, 19–21; and a further note from FLICKE, 6 April 1951, 22–3.

192 Rabinowitch testified that she subsequently destroyed the cable. LAC, RG33-62, Agents of a Foreign Power fonds, Reel T-1370, 5337, https://heritage.canadiana.ca/view/oocihm.lac_reel_t1370/1513. On Gregori Tounkin, see LAC, RG33-62, Agents of a Foreign Power fonds, Reel T-3433, Exhibit 545, "Identity cards issued to Officers of the USSR Mission in Canada," 116, https://heritage.canadiana.ca/view/oocihm.lac_reel_t3433/116.

193 LAC, RG33-62, Agents of a Foreign Power fonds, Reel T-1370, Rabinowitch testimony, 5337, https://heritage.canadiana.ca/view/oocihm.lac_reel_t1370/1513.

194 LAC, RG33-62, Agents of a Foreign Power fonds, Reel T-1370, Rabinowitch testimony, 5423, https://heritage.canadiana.ca/view/oocihm.lac_reel_t1370/1599.

195 LAC, RG33-62, Agents of a Foreign Power fonds, Reel T-1370, Rabinowitch testimony, 5427, https://heritage.canadiana.ca/view/oocihm.lac_reel_t1370/1603.

196 LAC, RG33-62, Agents of a Foreign Power fonds, Reel T-1370, Rabinowitch testimony, 5429, https://heritage.canadiana.ca/view/oocihm.lac_reel_t1370/1609.
197 TNA, KV 2/1634, Extract from Foote's comments on Canadian Royal Commission Report mentioning Rabinowitch, 8 August 1947, s. 35y. See also Foote, *Handbook for Spies*, 257–266. In an appendix to that publication Foote provided an extended commentary on Rabinowitch's complicated relationship with "Rote Drei." For Foote's MI5 file, see TNA, KV 2/1015, "Alexander Allen Foote."
198 TNA, KV 2/1427, Corby Case (Vol. IV), [The Swiss Group], "HERMINA," 36.
199 Open code used plain text to create a seemingly innocuous message, but one that gave a secret sense if one knew the secret equivalents of the words. National Security Agency, *Basic Cryptologic Glossary* (Washington, DC, 1955), 24.
200 TNA,KV 2/1427, Corby Case (Vol. IV), [The Swiss Group], "HERMINA," 32–3.
201 On Foote's mistaken account of "Lucy" and the real "Lucy," see *The Rote Kapelle: The CIA's History*, 214.
202 LAC, RG33-62, Agents of a Foreign Power fonds, Reel T-1370, Rabinowitch testimony, 5338, https://heritage.canadiana.ca/view/oocihm.lac_reel_t1370/1514.
203 TNA/KV 2/1427, Corby Case (Vol. IV), [The Swiss Group], "HERMINA," 33.
204 TNA/KV 2/1427, Corby Case (Vol. IV), [The Swiss Group], "HERMINA," 33.
205 TNA/KV 2/1427, Corby Case (Vol. IV), [The Swiss Group], "HERMINA," 34.
206 TNA, KV 2/1427, Corby Case (Vol. IV), [The Swiss Group], "HERMINA," 38; *The Rote Kapelle: The CIA's History*, 230.
207 TNA, KV 2/1427, Corby Case (Vol. IV), [The Swiss Group], 39.
208 TNA, KV 2/1427, Corby Case (Vol. IV), [The Swiss Group], 39.
209 TNA, KV 2/1427, Corby Case (Vol. IV), [The Swiss Group], 39.
210 TNA, KV 2/1427, Corby Case (Vol. IV), [The Swiss Group], Enclosed a Short memorandum ..., 40; TNA, KV 2/1634, Hermina Rabinowitch, copy of summary of information filed in the personalities index of The Case of the Roti [*sic*] Kapelle re Rabinowitch, 1–3, s. 39b.
211 TNA, KV 2/1427, Corby Case (Vol. IV), [The Swiss Group], 31 July 1944, LEON met HERMINA, 39.
212 LAC, RG33-62, Agents of a Foreign Power fonds, Reel T-1370, Rabinowitch testimony, 5331, https://heritage.canadiana.ca/view/oocihm.lac_reel_t1370/1507.

213 LAC, RG33-62, Agents of a Foreign Power fonds, Reel T-1370, Rabinowitch testimony, 5341–2, https://heritage.canadiana.ca/view/oocihm.lac_reel_t1370/1517.
214 LAC, RG33-62, Agents of a Foreign Power fonds, Reel T-1370, Rabinowitch testimony, 5332, https://heritage.canadiana.ca/view/oocihm.lac_reel_t1370/1508.
215 TNA, KV 2/1634, Hermina Rabinowitch, Switzerland/USSR Counter Espionage Canada Case, Interrogation of Abramson, 29 April 1947, no. 4267, s. 28B.
216 LAC, RG33-62, Agents of a Foreign Power fonds, Reel T-1370, Rabinowitch testimony, 5360, https://heritage.canadiana.ca/view/oocihm.lac_reel_t1370/1536.
217 LAC, RG33-62, Agents of a Foreign Power fonds, Reel T-1370, Rabinowitch testimony, 5361, https://heritage.canadiana.ca/view/oocihm.lac_reel_t1370/1537.
218 LAC, RG33-62, Agents of a Foreign Power fonds, Reel T-1370, Rabinowitch testimony, 5362, https://heritage.canadiana.ca/view/oocihm.lac_reel_t1370/1538.
219 MI 5 referred to it as the Helbein Watch Company.
220 LAC, RG33-62, Agents of a Foreign Power fonds, Reel T-1370, Rabinowitch testimony, 5366, https://heritage.canadiana.ca/view/oocihm.lac_reel_t1370/1542.
221 LAC, RG33-62, Agents of a Foreign Power fonds, Reel T-1370, Rabinowitch testimony, 5368, https://heritage.canadiana.ca/view/oocihm.lac_reel_t1370/1544.
222 LAC, RG33-62, Agents of a Foreign Power fonds, Reel T-1370, Rabinowitch testimony, 5380, https://heritage.canadiana.ca/view/oocihm.lac_reel_t1370/1556.
223 For the letter, see LAC, RG33-62, Agents of a Foreign Power fonds, Reel T-3424, Exhibit 40, Dear Hermina, 87–8, https://heritage.canadiana.ca/view/oocihm.lac_reel_t3424/87.
224 LAC, RG33-62, Agents of a Foreign Power fonds, Reel T-1370, Rabinowitch testimony, 5455–6, https://heritage.canadiana.ca/view/oocihm.lac_reel_t1370/1631.
225 LAC, RG33-62, Agents of a Foreign Power fonds, Reel T-1370, Rabinowitch testimony, 5458, https://heritage.canadiana.ca/view/oocihm.lac_reel_t1370/1633.
226 LAC, RG33-62, Agents of a Foreign Power fonds, Reel T-1370, Gouzenko testimony, 247, 249–50, https://heritage.canadiana.ca/view/oocihm.lac_reel_t1368/308.
227 LAC, RG33-62, Agents of a Foreign Power fonds, Reel T-1370, Rabinowitch testimony, 5489, https://heritage.canadiana.ca/view/oocihm.lac_reel_t1370/1665.

228 LAC, RG33-62, Agents of a Foreign Power fonds, Reel T-1370, Rabinowitch testimony, 5490, https://heritage.canadiana.ca/view/oocihm.lac_reel_t1370/1666.
229 LAC, RG33-62, Agents of a Foreign Power fonds, Reel T-1370, Rabinowitch testimony, 5490, https://heritage.canadiana.ca/view/oocihm.lac_reel_t1370/1666.
230 LAC, RG33-62, Agents of a Foreign Power fonds, Reel T-1370, Rabinowitch testimony, 5491, https://heritage.canadiana.ca/view/oocihm.lac_reel_t1370/1667.
231 LAC, RG33-62, Agents of a Foreign Power fonds, Reel T-1370, Rabinowitch testimony, 5527, https://heritage.canadiana.ca/view/oocihm.lac_reel_t1370/1703.
232 TNA, KV 2/1634, Hermina Rabinowitch, Copy of summary of information filed in the personalities index of The case of the Roti [*sic*] Kapelle re Rabinowitch, R.2, s. 39b.
233 LAC, RG33-62, Agents of a Foreign Power fonds, Reel T-1370, Rabinowitch testimony, 5527, https://heritage.canadiana.ca/view/oocihm.lac_reel_t1370/1703.
234 TNA, KV 2, 1634-2, Hermina Rabinowitch, 8 October 1946, Hermina Rabinowitch, with aliases William Helbein, with aliases, s. 22a.
235 TNA, KV 2/1619, Dübendorfer, Rachel & Boettcher, Paul, Extract from report forwarded by S.I.S. re interrogation of Mrs Bethe HELBEIN, member of Rote Drie, Soviet espionage organization in Switzerland, 7 July 1947, s. 14b.
236 TNA, KV 2/1634, Hermina Rabinowitch, 8 October 1946, Hermina Rabinowitch, with aliases William Helbein, with aliases, s. 22a.
237 TNA, KV 2/1634, Hermina Rabinowitch, Switzerland/USSR Counter Espionage Canada Case, Interrogation of Abramson, 29 April 1947, no. 4267, s. 28B.
238 TNA, KV 2/1634, Hermina Rabinowitch, Switzerland/USSR Counter Espionage Canada Case, Interrogation of Abramson, 29 April 1947, No 4267, s. 28B.
239 TNA, KV 2/1634, Hermina Rabinowitch, Copy of summary of information filed in the personalities index of The case of the Roti [*sic*] Kapelle, re Rabinowitch, 3, s. 39b.
240 LAC, RG33-62, Agents of a Foreign Power fonds, Reel T-1370, Rabinowitch testimony, 5513, https://heritage.canadiana.ca/view/oocihm.lac_reel_t1370/1689.
241 TNA, KV 2/1427, Corby Case (Vol. IV) [The Swiss Group], 31.7.44, LEON met HERMINA, 39.
242 LAC, RG33-62, Agents of a Foreign Power fonds, Reel T-1370, Rabinowitch testimony, 5519, https://heritage.canadiana.ca/view/oocihm.lac_reel_t1370/1695.

243 "Miss Rabinowitch Quit ILO on Request," *New York Times*, 1 September 1946, 27.

244 TNA, KV 2/1634, Hermina Rabinowitch, Hermina (Germina) or Helina RABINOWITCH, Stateless formerly Lithuanian, 22 January 1951, MI5 report to Immigration Branch, s. 44a; TNA, KV 2/1634, Hermina Rabinowitz, RCMP to MI6, s. 26A, 24 February 1947. In France, British intelligence services placed her under surveillance. TNA, KV 2/1634, Hermina Rabinowitz, Michael Serpell to Roger Hollis, S. 29 A, 12 May 1947. While she worked in French-occupied Baden-Baden to recruit German workers for France, an S.I.S. report disclosed that "[e]fforts are being made to have her removed from her post … and have her deported from the French zone." TNA, KV 2/1634, Hermina Rabinowitz, "Extract from S.I.S Report re EQUAL IN SWITZERLAND, 28 November 1947, s. 36. As late as 1951, MI5 still had Rabinowitch on its radar: C.W. Hinchley-Cooke urged C.B.J. Ruck of Britain's Home Office (Immigration) to recommend that Rabinowitch "be refused leave to land, if and when she attempts to visit the U.K.; and that similarly any application for a U.K. visa … be refused." TNA, KV 2/1634, no. 539, Brigadier W.E Hinchley Cooke (MI5) to C.P.J. Ruck, Home Office, 22 January 1951, s. 44a.

Chapter 13: The Final Report

1 LAC, Diaries of WLMK, 12 July 1946, 3.

2 LAC, Diaries of WLMK, 12 July 1946, 3.

3 LAC, RG33-62, Agents of a Foreign Power fonds, Reel T-3433, Exhibit 543, Precise Showing the History of the Establishment of the USSR Diplomatic Mission in Canada, 82–7, https://heritage.canadiana.ca/view/oocihm.lac_reel_t3433/82

4 TNA, KV 2/1421, MacDonald to Cadogan, no. 921, 21.12.45, s. 50a. A note at the bottom of the cable indicated that "Kim Philby telephoned this over on 17/12/45." See also TNA, KV 2/1426, Holmes to Cadogan, no. 956, 4.1.46, s. 105A.

5 TNA, KV 2/1426, MacDonald to Cadogan, no. 83, 1.2.46, s. 14b.

6 TNA, KV 2/1421, MacDonald to Cadogan, no. 92, 4.2.46, s. 55A.

7 TNA, KV 2/1421, MacDonald to Cadogan, no. 88, 2.2.46, s. 54a. See also "Ottawa Request Frees Mystery Red Officer Held Here as Drunk," *Globe & Mail*, 19 February 1946, 1.

8 TNA, KV 2/1422, William Stephenson to Sir Stewart Menzies, no. 432, 25.3.46, s. 160A.

9 "Memorandum from the Government of Canada to Embassy Soviet Union, Ottawa July 12, 1946," in Donald M. Page, ed., *Documents of*

External Affairs, vol. 12, 1946 (Ottawa: Minister of Supply and Services, 1977), 2058–9.

10 LAC, Diaries of WLMK, 12 July 1946, 3–4.

11 "Memorandum from Embassy Soviet Union to Government of Canada, Ottawa, July 15, 1946,"in Page, *Documents of External Affairs*, vol. 12, 2059–60.

12 LAC, Diaries of WLMK, 22 February 1946, 5.

13 Smith composed "the first ninety-five pages of the report, dealing with the general pattern of Soviet espionage methods. His name does not appear in the report because he hoped to return as a diplomat to the Soviet Union – which he did, as ambassador in Khruschev's time." Clyde Sanger, *Malcolm MacDonald*, 462n15. For Smith's role in the preparation of the report, see also Reginald Whitaker and Gary Marcuse, *Cold War Canada: The Making of a National Security State, 19451957* (Toronto: University of Toronto Press, 1994), 82–3, 118–26.

14 John Hilliker and Barry Donald, *Canada's Department of External Affairs: The Early Years, 1909–1946*, vol 1. (Montreal & Kingston: McGill-Queen's University Press, 1990) 315.

15 Mark Kristmanson, *Plateaus of Freedom: Nationality, Culture, and State Security in Canada 1940–1960* (Toronto: University of Toronto Press, 2003), 275n81.

16 W.L.M. King in House of Commons, *Debates*, 15 July 1946, 3440.

17 W.L.M. King in House of Commons, *Debates*, 15 July 1946, 3438.

18 W.L.M. King in House of Commons, *Debates*, 15 July 1946, 3439.

19 "Brais & Campbell, Royal Bank Building, 360 St. James St. West, Montreal, March 12, 1946, to E.K. Williams, G.H Fauteux, Justice Building, Ottawa (Secret and Confidential)" in Hon. W.L.M. King in House of Commons, *Debates*, 15 March 1946, 6–7.

20 W.L.M. King in House of Commons, *Debates*, 15 July 1946, 3439; TNA, KV 2/1423, For Hollis from the RCMP, Nos. 61, 62, 20.7.46, ss. 234A, 235A.

21 Freda Linton, an employee of the International Labour Organization and the National Film Board, was identified by Gouzenko as an associate of Fred Rose and Raymond Boyer, for whom she served as a link to Sokolov in the early Montreal-based GRU network. She had been subpoenaed to appear before the inquiry but was believed to have left Canada with Sam Carr in April 1946. TNA, KV 2/1423, 1896, Freda Linton, "Extract from first report on information from 'Corby,'" undated, s. 1Z. For Linton and Carr, see TNA, KV 2, 1633, Sam Carr, France/Canada, Sam Carr in France, no. 5762, 29 September 194 (*sic*), s. 101a.

22 W.L.M. King in House of Commons, *Debates*, 15 July 1946, 3439

23 W.L.M. King in House of Commons, *Debates*, 15 July 1946, 3439.

24 *The Report of the Royal Commission* (*Final Report*), 692, https://publications.gc.ca/site/eng/9.699909/publication.html.

25 Wilfrid Eggleston, "Canadian Espionage Report Will Be Best Seller This Year," *Saturday Night*, 27 July 1946, 8.
26 LAC, RG33-62, Agents of a Foreign Power fonds, Reel T-3433, "Mark McClung to Cloutier," King's Printer, 6 July 1946, 919, https://heritage.canadiana.ca/view/oocihm.lac_reel_t3433/919.
27 LAC, RG33-62, Agents of a Foreign Power fonds, Reel T-3433, "Mark McClung, Memorandum to Mr. Heeney re Selling Price to the Public of *The Report of the Royal Commission* on Espionage,"13 July 1946, 913. A note in script appears at the top of the Inquiry file copy that reads "Similar memorandum sent to Mr. Robertson." https://heritage.canadiana.ca/view/oocihm.lac_reel_t3433/913.
28 LAC, RG33-62, Agents of a Foreign Power fonds, Reel T-3433, "Mark McClung to A.M. Hill, Privy Council Office," 8 July 1946, 918, https://heritage.canadiana.ca/view/oocihm.lac_reel_t3433/918.
29 See for example Douglas How, "Several Spy Rings in Canada Steered by Russian Agents," *Saskatoon Star-Phoenix*, 15 July 1946, 1; Ottawa (CP), "Report Charges Fifth Column," *Regina Leader-Post*, 15 July 1946, 1; and Ottawa (CP), "Soviet Fifth Column in Canada Charged," *Winnipeg Tribune*, 15 July 1946, 1.
30 Douglas How, "Igor Gouzenko," *Maclean's*, 15 December 1946, 46.
31 F.C. Mears, "Parallel Networks to Zabotin's Bared in Royal Probe Report," *Montreal Gazette*, 16 July 1946, 1.
32 William Baldwin, "Royal Inquiry Reveals L-P Party Spied for Moscow – Parallel Rings in Operation," *Globe & Mail*, 1.
33 V.J. Mackie, "Parallel Spy Systems Operated in Canada," *Regina Leader-Post*, 16 July 1946, 1.
34 "Communist Party Main Source of Recruits for Spy Network Here," *Montreal Gazette*, 16 July 1946, 1.
35 "Énorme travail clandestine de Moscou," *La Press*, 16 July 1946, 1; "Les 5[ES] Colonnes de L'OGPU au Canada," *La Patrie*, 16 July 1946, 1; "L'espionnage soviétique opère en permanence en notre pays," *Le Soleil*, 16 July 1946, 1.
36 "Le Parti Communiste Canadien était a la base de l'espionnage" *L'Action catholique*, 16 July 1946, 1.
37 "Les cellules Communistes sont actives au Canada," *L'Action catholique*, 16 July 1946, 1.
38 Roger Duhamel, "Notre Cinquième Colonne," *La Patrie*, 16 July 1946, 8.
39 A.A. MacIntosh, "Mission from Moscow," *Globe & Mail*, 17 July 1946, 6.
40 Gerald Carlyle Allison "The Comintern in Canada," *Winnipeg Tribune*, 16 July 1946, 6.
41 Grant Dexter, "The Attack on Freedom," *Winnipeg Free Press*, 18 July 1946. Dexter may have been assisted by Bruce Hutchinson, his co-editor.

42 Ottawa (CP), "Soviet 'Fifth Column' in Canada, Report Reveals," *Winnipeg Free Press*, 16 July 1946, 1.
43 *National Affairs Monthly* was a monthly periodical issued by the National Committee of the Labour Progressive Party beginning in April 1944. https://bac-lac.on.worldcat.org/oclc/13418936?lang=en&q=national%20affairs%20monthly.
44 British-born Leslie Morris joined the Winnipeg branch of the Workers' Party of Canada when he was seventeen, serving as national secretary of the Young Workers League and as editor of the *Worker*, the *Daily Clarion*, and the *Canadian Tribune*. In intra-party struggles, Morris remained a reliable Stalinist, and in 1962 he succeeded Tim Buck as leader of the Communist Party of Canada. "Leslie Morris Communist Leader in Party 41 Years," *Globe & Mail*, 14 November 1964, 44.
45 Jonathan Sperber, *Karl Marx: A Nineteenth-Century Life* (New York: Liveright, 2013), 280; "The Trial of the Communists at Cologne," *The Peoples' Paper: The Champion of Political Justice and Universal Right*, 27 November 1852, 1.
46 "The Civil War in France: Alleged Organization of the Paris Revolution in London," *Supplement to the Nottinghamshire Guardian*, 7 April 1871. On Marx's involvement in the Commune, see Sperber, *Marx: A Nineteenth:Century Life*, 376–83.
47 Sean McMeekin, "Was Lenin a German Agent?" *New York Times*, 19 June 2017.
48 Christopher Andrew, *Defend the Realm: The Authorized History of MI5* (New York: Alfred Knopf, 2009), 154–6.
49 L.M., "The 'Espionage Report,'" *National Affairs Monthly*, 3, no. 8 (August 1946), 227–8.
50 LAC, RG33-62, Agents of a Foreign Power fonds, Reel T-3434, "Ambassador to Secretary of State for External Affairs," WA-2919, 23 July 1946, 1, 577, https://heritage.canadiana.ca/view/oocihm.lac_reel_t3434/577.
51 LAC, RG33-62, Agents of a Foreign Power fonds, Reel T-3434, "Ambassador to Secretary of State for External Affairs, WA-2919, 23 July 1946, 2, 577, https://heritage.canadiana.ca/view/oocihm.lac_reel_t3434/578.
52 LAC, RG33-62, Agents of a Foreign Power fonds, Reel T-3434, Ambassador to Secretary of State for External Affairs," 23 July 1946, 3-4, WA-2919, 577, https://heritage.canadiana.ca/view/oocihm.lac_reel_t3434/579.
53 LAC, RG33-62, Agents of a Foreign Power fonds, Reel T-3434, Ambassador to Secretary of State for External Affairs," 23 July 1946, 3-4, WA-2919, 579, https://heritage.canadiana.ca/view/oocihm.lac_reel_t3434/579.
54 "Official Secrets Act Charges: Civil Servant Remanded," *The Times*, 4 February 1950, 6.

55 On Donovan, see Douglas Waller, *Wild Bill Donovan: The Spy Master Who Created the OSS and Modern American Espionage* (New York: Simon and Shuster, 2011).

56 LAC, RG33-62, Agents of a Foreign Power fonds, Reel T-3434, Ambassador to Secretary of State for External Affairs," 23 July 1946, 3-4, WA-2919, 580, https://heritage.canadiana.ca/view/oocihm.lac_reel_t3434/583. On the OSS, see Patrick K. O'Donnell, *Operatives, Spies, and Saboteurs: The Unknown Story of the Men and Women of World War II's* OSS (New York: Free Press, 2004).

57 TNA, KV 2/1419, S.T. Wood to Sir Percy Sillitoe, 18 July 1946, s. 13B.

58 TNA, KV 2/1419, Sir Percy Sillitoe to Commissioner S.T. Wood, 30 July 1946, s. 15e.

59 TNA, KV 2/1419, F.J. Mead to Sir Percy Sillitoe, 30 July 1946, s. 16x. Later, the idea of publishing an "abbreviated version" was proposed by a member of the House of Commons (9 April 1948) to the British government, but the government responded that "it would be inappropriate for the United Kingdom Government to publish an abbreviated version of a publication issued by another Commonwealth Government." TNA, KV 2/1419, "Extract from Hansard," 9 April 1948, s. 80c.

60 TNA, KV 2/1419, Igor Gouzenko, R. H. Hollis to Sir Alexander Maxwell, 29 July 1946, s. 14 e.

61 TNA/KV 2/Igor Gouzenko, "Sir Percy Sillitoe to H.F. Cartmel-Robinson, Acting Governor, Northern Rhodesia," 28 January 1947, s. 58A.

62 Sir Ernest Graham-Little in House of Commons (Britain), *Debates*, 8 October 1946.

63 Sir Ernest Graham-Little, letter to the *Daily Mail*, 15 November 1946, as quoted in F.A. Voigt, "A Royal Commission," *The Nineteenth Century and After* 140, no. 838 (December 1946), 302n2.

64 Of these totals 9,071 copies had been distributed in Canada and 2,680 copies had been sent abroad. Unpublished Sessional Papers, 3rd Session of the 20th Parliament, 30 January 1947–17 July 1947, no. 208c, RG14, D2, Volume 517.

65 James McCook, "Espionage Report Widely Circulated," *Regina Leader Post*, 29 April 1948, 6.

66 See for example "Russian Spies in Canada," *Belfast Newsletter*, 16 July 1946, 2; "Fifth Column in Canada," *The Scotsman*, 16 July 1946, 5; "Fifth Column: Russia and Spy Ring in Canada," *Staffordshire Evening Sentinel*, 16 July 1946, 1; "Russia Had Its Own Fifth Column in Canada," *Lanarkshire Daily Record*, 16 July 1946, 3.

67 For an account of Moscow's staged approach to securing its dominance in Central and Eastern Europe post-1945, see R.N. Carew Hunt, *The Theory and Practice of Communism: An Introduction* (London: Geoffrey Bles, 1950),

225–33; and Hugh Seton-Watson, *The East European Revolution* (New York: Frederick A. Praeger, 1951), 167–71.

68 Reuters News Agency, "Nunn May Gave Uranium to Russians," *Birmingham Gazette*, 16 July 1945, 1.

69 TNA, KV 2/1423, From a Correspondent, "Espionage in Canada: Widespread and Highly Organized System," *The Times*, 3 September 1946, s. 243A.

70 TNA/KV 2/1423, David Zaslavsky, "A Sorry Finale to a Shameful Comedy," *Pravda*, 2, s. 240a.

71 TNA/KV 2/1423, Zaslavsky, "A Sorry Finale to a Shameful Comedy," *Pravda*, 1, s. 240a.

72 TNA/KV 2/1423, Zaslavsky, "A Sorry Finale to a Shameful Comedy," *Pravda* 2, s. 240a.

73 TNA/KV 2/1423, Zaslavsky, "A Sorry Finale to a Shameful Comedy," *Pravda*, 5, s. 240a.

74 TNA/KV 2/1423, Zaslavsky, "A Sorry Finale to a Shameful Comedy," *Pravda*, 5, s. 240a.

75 TNA/KV 2/1423, Zaslavsky, "A Sorry Finale to a Shameful Comedy," *Pravda*, 3, s. 240a.

76 TNA/KV 2/1423, Zaslavsky, "A Sorry Finale to a Shameful Comedy," *Pravda*, 4, s. 240a.

77 TNA/KV 2/1423, Zaslavsky, "A Sorry Finale to a Shameful Comedy," *Pravda*, 5, s. 240a

78 Canadian Communists also implied that the RCMP and particularly its Soviet specialist John Leopold were behind the conspiracy against Moscow. During a meeting in September 1946 to protest the treatment of Fred Rose, A.A. MacLeod asserted that "Gouzenko's documents were the 'genuine' documents Inspector Leopold had been preparing for a long, long, time before he met Gouzenko." "Spy Scare Called a 'Colossal Fraud,'" *Canadian Tribune*, 14 September 1946, 2. On Leopold, see Steve Hewitt, "Royal Canadian Mounted Spy: The Secret Life of John Leopold/Jack Esselwein," *Intelligence and National Security* 15, no. 1 (2008), 144–68, https://doi.org/10.1080/02684520008432590.

79 *Soviet Monitor* was a London-based TASS news service that issued daily bulletins of Soviet news in English.

80 David Zaslavsky, "Friendship Survived the Lies," *Canadian Tribune*, 17 August 1946, 7. Earlier on 10 September the *Tribune* had published a summary of Zaslavsky's Moscow Radio talk. "Spy Probe Deliberate Attack on Liberties is Soviet View," *Canadian Tribune*, 10 August 1946, 2.

81 TNA, KV 2/1423, Alexander Clutterbuck to Under Secretary of State for Dominion Affairs, no. 346, 17 August 1946, s. 244, 1–2.

82 TNA, KV 2/1423, Alexander Clutterbuck to Under Secretary of State for Dominion Affairs, no. 346, 17 August 1946, s. 368A, Appendix I Memorandum, 3.

83 TNA, KV 2/1423, Alexander Clutterbuck to Under Secretary of State for Dominion Affairs, no. 346, 17 August 1946, s. 368A, Appendix I, Memorandum, 2.
84 TNA, KV 2/1423, Alexander Clutterbuck to Under Secretary of State for Dominion Affairs, no. 346, 17 August 1946, s. 368A, Appendix I Memorandum, 5.
85 TNA, KV 2/1423, Alexander Clutterbuck to Under Secretary of State for Dominion Affairs, no. 346, 17 August 1946, s. 368A, Appendix I Memorandum, 7–8.
86 Hugh Wilford, "The Information Research Department: Britain's Secret Cold War Weapon Revealed," *Review of International Studies* 24 (1998): 355.
87 Wesley Wark, "Coming in From the Cold: British Propaganda and Red Army Defectors, 1945–1952," *International History Review* 9, no. 1 (1987): 48–50.
88 Hugh Wilford, "The Information Research Department," 355–6.
89 Wilford, "The Information Research Department," 358–60; Giselle Gwinnett, "Attlee, Bevin, and Political Warfare: Labour's Secret Anti-Communist Campaign in Europe, 1948–51," *International History Review* 39, no. 3 (2017): 426–9.
90 Philip Deery, "Confronting the Cominform: George Orwell and the Cold War Offensive of the Information Research Department, 1948–50," *Labour History* 73 (1997): 219–25.
91 See *The Report of the Royal Commission* (*Final Report*), "Section XI – Law and Procedure," 649–84, https://publications.gc.ca/site/eng/9.699909/publication.html. It appears from inquiry records that aside from the introductory ninety pages composed by Arnold Smith, the remaining chapters were composed by commission counsel for approval by Kellock and Taschereau. See for example correspondence between "Commission counsel" and Commissioner Taschereau contained in the inquiry records. LAC, RG33-62, Agents of a Foreign Power fonds, Reel T-3433, "Dear Mr. Commissioner from Commission Counsel," 4 July 1946, 946; "Robert Taschereau to illegible," 6 July 1946, 947, https://heritage.canadiana.ca/view/oocihm.lac_reel_t3433/946.
92 *The Report of the Royal Commission* (*Final Report*), 650,. https://publications.gc.ca/site/eng/9.699909/publication.html.
93 Rt. Hon. Earnest Lapointe in House of Commons, *Debates,* 30 May 1939, 4718. When the 1920 amendments were considered in the British parliament, the attorney-general added another amendment that the amended Official Secrets Act not apply to Canada because Ottawa was considering its own legislation on the subject. Martin Friedland, *National Security: The Legal Dimensions* (Ottawa: Commission of Inquiry Concerning Certain Activities of the Royal Canadian Mounted Police, 1980), 33.

94 For an account of the origin and passage of the British acts, see Friedland, *National Security: The Legal Dimensions*, 7, 31–3; Canada, *Report of the Royal Commission on Security* (abridged) (Ottawa: Information Canada, 1969) 74–9; and Canada, Privy Council Office. *Commission of Inquiry Concerning Certain Activities of the Royal Canadian Mounted Police – First Report – Security and Information* (Ottawa: Queen's Printer, 1980), 1–39. For commentary on the passage of the British versions of the Official Secrets Act, see G.T. Williams, *Not in the Public Interest* (London: Hutchinson, 1965), 15–39; Ann Rogers, *Secrecy and Power in the British State: A History of the Official Secrets Act* (London: Pluto, 1997), 17–23, 30–2; Rosamund Thomas, *Espionage and Secrecy: The Official Secrets Acts 1911–1989 of the United Kingdom* (London: Routledge, 1991), 3–24.

95 A.A. Heaps in House of Commons, *Debates*, 30 May 1939, 4719.

96 Parliament's consideration from second reading through committee consideration and third reading of the bill takes up seven pages of Hansard. See House of Commons, *Debates*, 30 May 1939, 4718–25.

97 Arthur Meighen in *Debates of the Senate*, 31 May 1939, 552-3.

98 Consideration of the bill took up four pages of Hansard. *Debates of the Senate*, 31 May 1939, 552–5.

99 *The Report of the Royal Commission* (*Final Report*), 689, https://publications.gc.ca/site/eng/9.699909/publication.html.

100 Canada, *Report of the Royal Commission on Security*, 75.

101 Canada, Privy Council Office, *Commission of Inquiry Concerning Certain Activities of the Royal Canadian Mounted Police*, 37.

102 *The Report of the Royal Commission* (*Final Report*), 654, https://publications.gc.ca/site/eng/9.699909/publication.html.

103 *The Report of the Royal Commission* (*Final Report*), 654, https://publications.gc.ca/site/eng/9.699909/publication.html.

104 *The Report of the Royal Commission* (*Final Report*), 654, https://publications.gc.ca/site/eng/9.699909/publication.html.

105 Official Secrets Act s. 10, 455.

106 *The Report of the Royal Commission* (*Final Report*), 655, https://publications.gc.ca/site/eng/9.699909/publication.html.

107 Friedland, *National Security: The Legal Dimensions*, 48.

108 *The Report of the Royal Commission* (*Final Report*), 656, https://publications.gc.ca/site/eng/9.699909/publication.html.

109 *The Report of the Royal Commission* (*Final Report*), 650, https://publications.gc.ca/site/eng/9.699909/publication.html.

110 *The Report of the Royal Commission* (*Final Report*), 661–2, https://publications.gc.ca/site/eng/9.699909/publication.html.

111 Official Secrets Act, s. 3(2), 451.

112 Official Secrets Act, s. 3(3), 451.

113 *The Report of the Royal Commission* (*Final Report*), 651, https://publications.gc.ca/site/eng/9.699909/publication.html.
114 Official Secrets Act, s. 9, 455.
115 *The Report of the Royal Commission* (*Final Report*), 672, 674, https://publications.gc.ca/site/eng/9.699909/publication.html.
116 *The Report of the Royal Commission* (*Final Report*), 672, https://publications.gc.ca/site/eng/9.699909/publication.html. The commissioners cited The King v. Walker, 1939 S.C.R. 214; Reg. v. Coote, L.R4 Privy Council 599 to support this point.
117 *The Report of the Royal Commission* (*Final Report*), 672–3, https://publications.gc.ca/site/eng/9.699909/publication.html.
118 *The Report of the Royal Commission* (*Final Report*), 675, https://publications.gc.ca/site/eng/9.699909/publication.html.
119 Commissioners of inquiry have no direct authority to enforce a subpoena. John D. Richard, "Judicial Review in Canada," *Duquesne Law Review* 45, no. 3 (2007): 501.
120 For a list of subpoenas issued by the inquiry, see LAC, RG33-62, Agents of a Foreign Power fonds, R.C. 19, Subpoenas & Orders Served and Correspondence relating thereto, Reel T-3434, 100–160, https://heritage.canadiana.ca/view/oocihm.lac_reel_t3434/100.
121 Wesley Wark, "Intelligence Requirements and Anti-Terrorism Legislation," in *The Security of Freedom: Essays on Canada's Anti-Terrorism Bill*, ed. Ronald J. Daniels, Kent Roach, and Patrick Macklem (Toronto: University of Toronto Press, 2001), 289.
122 Wark, "Intelligence Requirements," 290.
123 *The Report of the Royal Commission* (*Final Report*), 662, https://publications.gc.ca/site/eng/9.699909/publication.html.
124 *The Report of the Royal Commission* (*Final Report*), 676, https://publications.gc.ca/site/eng/9.699909/publication.html.
125 The existence of "apprehended war" was proclaimed 1 September 1939 through PC 2477; the existence of a state of war was proclaimed 10 September 1939 through PC 2626. For these documents, see Proclamations and Orders-in-Council Passed Under the Authority of the War Measures Act, R.S.C., chap. 206, vol. 1 (Ottawa: King's Printer, 1940), 19, 52.
126 "Report of Committee on Civil Liberties," *Canadian Bar Review* 22 (1944): 601.
127 "Bar Questions Peace Controls," *Globe & Mail*, 31 August 1945, 3.
128 Samuel Freedman, KC, "The Twenty-Eighth Annual Meeting," *Canadian Bar Review* 24 (1946): 697.
129 Grant Dexter, "Lawyers and Liberty," *Winnipeg Free Press*, 28 August 1946.
130 "Evidence of Mazerall to Royal Commission Produced Against Him," *Globe & Mail*, 21 May 1946, 3.

131 "Jurist Is Guest at Bar Dinner," *Winnipeg Free Press*, 29 August 1946, 8. On Fillmore, see "W.P. Fillmore," *Winnipeg Free Press*, 4 May 1978, 55.

132 The *Globe & Mail* published the complete text of the report. "Civil Liberties Should Be Inviolate," *Globe & Mail*, 31 August 1946, 6.

133 *The 1946 Yearbook of the Canadian Bar Association and the Minutes of Proceedings of the Twenty-Eighth Annual Meeting Winnipeg August 28th, 29th, and 30th, 1946* (Ottawa: National Printers, 1947), 143.

134 *1946 Yearbook of the Canadian Bar Association*, 141–2.

135 *1946 Yearbook of the Canadian Bar Association*, 142.

136 *1946 Yearbook of the Canadian Bar Association*, 142–3.

137 *1946 Yearbook of the Canadian Bar Association*, 144.

138 *1946 Yearbook of the Canadian Bar Association*, 144.

139 *1946 Yearbook of the Canadian Bar Association*, 145.

140 For *Fortnightly Review* criticisms of the King government during the war, see Eric M. Adams, "The Idea of Constitutional Rights and the Transformation of Canadian Constitutional Law, 1930–1960," unpublished PhD diss., University of Toronto, 2009, 101–7. "Outside the arena of property rights, Chitty's concern for civil liberties varied erratically: freedoms of speech, thought, and association ranked well below freedom of contract and commerce in his hierarchy of liberties." Adams, "The Idea of Constitutional Rights," 105

141 *1946 Yearbook of the Canadian Bar Association*, 147.

142 *1946 Yearbook of the Canadian Bar Association*, 150.

143 *1946 Yearbook of the Canadian Bar Association*, 145–6.

144 *1946 Yearbook of the Canadian Bar Association*, 151.

145 *1946 Yearbook of the Canadian Bar Association*, 152.

146 *1946 Yearbook of the Canadian Bar Association*, 151–2.

147 *1946 Yearbook of the Canadian Bar Association*, 155.

148 *1946 Yearbook of the Canadian Bar Association*, 155.

149 B.K. Sandwell, "Bar Association Utters Clarion Call for Renewal of Liberties," *Saturday Night*, 17 September 1946, 17; "Trumpet with Uncertain Sound," *Globe & Mail*, 2 September 1946, 6.

Epilogue

1 Douglas How, "Pappin Acquitted on Charges Based on False Passport," *Globe & Mail*, 19 October 1946, 7.

2 Douglas How, "Eric Adams Acquitted of Conspiracy Charge," *Globe & Mail*, 23 October 1946, 1.

3 "Nightingale Acquitted of Russian Spy Charge," *Globe & Mail*, 8 November 1946, 17.

4 "Agatha Chapman Wins Acquittal in Espionage Case," *Globe & Mail*, 28 November 1946, 10.
5 TNA, KV 2/14234, P.A. Clutterbuck, High Commissioner to Canada to Viscount Addison, K.G., Secretary of State for Dominion Affairs, no. 454, 25 November 1946, s. 247a, 2.
6 TNA, KV 2/14234, P.A. Clutterbuck, High Commissioner to Canada to Viscount Addison, K.G., Secretary of State for Dominion Affairs, no. 454, 25 November 1946, s. 247a, 4.
7 TNA, KV 2/1424, P.A. Clutterbuck, High Commissioner to Canada to Viscount Addison, K.G., Secretary of State for Dominion Affairs, no. 454, 25 November 1946, s. 247a, 5.
8 TNA, KV 2/1424, P.A. Clutterbuck, High Commissioner to Canada to Viscount Addison, K.G., Secretary of State for Dominion Affairs, no. 454, 25 November 1946, s. 247a, 6.
9 See "Repercussions of Spy Acquittals in Parliament," *Globe & Mail*, 12 December 1946, 7.
10 John Diefenbaker in House of Commons, *Debates*, 7 February 1947, 209.
11 TNA, KV 2/1424, P.A. Clutterbuck, High Commissioner to Canada to Viscount Addison, K.G., Secretary of State for Dominion Affairs, no. 129, 29 April 1947, s. 254A, 3. The Civil Liberties Association of Manitoba demanded that the government "repudiate" the contents of the addendum and withdraw the entire report from circulation. "Prof. Lower Makes Civil Liberties Plea," *Winnipeg Free Press*, 1 April 1947, 1.
12 John Diefenbaker in House of Commons, *Debates*, 17 May 1947, 3156.
13 J.L. Ilsley in House of Commons, *Debates*, 19 May 1947, 3219–20.
14 On Roy Kellock's possible role in the addenda debate, see Ross Lambertson, *Repression and Resistance: Canadian Human Rights Activists* (Toronto: University of Toronto Press, 2005), 190–1.
15 *The Report of the Royal Commission* (*Final Report*), 683, https://publications.gc.ca/site/eng/9.699909/publication.html.
16 *The Report of the Royal Commission* (*Final Report*), "Section XI – Law and Procedure," 684, https://publications.gc.ca/site/eng/9.699909/publication.html.
17 *The Report of the Royal Commission* (*Final Report*), 683, https://publications.gc.ca/site/eng/9.699909/publication.html.
18 Kent Roach, "The Administrative Law Scholarship of D.M. Gordon," *McGill Law Journal* 34, no. 1 (January 1989): 2. On the state of Canadian administrative law c. 1945, see F.R. Scott, "Administrative Law: 1923–1947," *Canadian Bar Review* 26, no. 1 (1948): 268–85.
19 D.M. Gordon, "Administrative Tribunals and the Courts," *Law Quarterly Review* 49, no. 1 (1933): 94.

20 Re Ashby et al. [1934] O.R. 42 Ontario Court of Appeal May 18, 1934; Re Ashby et al., 1934 CanLII 87 (ON CA), https://canlii.ca/t/g1j90.
21 *The Report of the Royal Commission* (*Final Report*), 683, https://publications.gc.ca/site/eng/9.699909/publication.html.
22 Stephen Goudge and Heather MacIvor, *Commissions of Inquiry* (Toronto: LexisNexis Canada, 2019), 86.
23 For a summary of "grounds for judicial review" of inquiries operating, as did the Kellock-Taschereau inquiry, under the federal Inquiries Act, see Goudge and MacIvor, *Commissions of Inquiry*, 87–95.
24 On this theme, see *Report on Public Inquiries* (Toronto: Ontario Law Reform Commission, 1992), 137; B.L. Strayer, "In the Beginning ...: The Origins of Section 15 of the Charter," *Journal of Law and Equality* 5, no. 1 (2006): 15; Ramsay Cook, "Canadian Freedom in Wartime, 1939–45," in *His Own Man: Essays in Honour of Arthur Reginald Marsden Lower*, ed. W.H. Heick and Roger Graham (Montreal & Kingston: McGill-Queen's University Press, 2014), 37–53; Ross Lambertson, *Activists in the Age of Rights: The Struggle for Human Rights in Canada*, PhD diss., University of Victoria, 1998, 152–230, 302–77, 453–4.
25 Goudge and MacIvor, *Commissions of Inquiry*, 72.
26 Goudge and MacIvor, *Commissions of Inquiry*, 73.
27 Lawrence Aronsen, "'Peace, Order and Good Government' During the Cold War: The Origins and Organization of Canada's Internal Security Program," *Intelligence and National Security* 1, no. 3 (1986): 363; Wesley Wark, "The Evolution of Military Intelligence in Canada," *Armed Forces & Society* 16, no. 1 (1989): 87.
28 Wark, "Evolution of Military Intelligence," 88.
29 Wark, "Evolution of Military Intelligence," 90. For an account of the transition within the RCMP from the Intelligence Branch to the Special Branch and the move from a primary focus on counter-subversive work to counter-espionage with the creation of B Branch in 1948, see John Sawatsky, *Men in the Shadows: The RCMP Security Service* (Toronto: Doubleday Canada, 1980), 96–103.
30 *The Report of the Royal Commission* (*Final Report*), 689, https://publications.gc.ca/site/eng/9.699909/publication.html.
31 Public Archives of Canada, RG2, Series 18, Privy Council Records vol. 103, file s-100-D, N.A. Robertson, "Interdepartmental Committee on Security," 18 April 1946 (Security Panel Document no. 1), as quoted in Reginald Whitaker, "Origins of the Canadian Government's Internal Security System, 1946–1952," *Canadian Historical Review* 65, no. 2 (1984): 158n7.
32 On RCMP domestic security arrangements before 1945, see Larry Hannant, *The Infernal Machine: Investigating the Loyalty of Canada's Citizens* (Toronto: University of Toronto Press, 1995).

33 On the origins of Feather Bed, see John Sawatsky, *For Services Rendered: Leslie James Bennett and the RCMP Security Service* (Markham, ON: Penguin, 1983), 253–5.

34 *Canada Declassified*, CSIS, Feather Bed, vol. 5, RCMP Commissioner R.H. Simmonds to the Honourable Allan Lawrence, Solicitor General of Canada, 28 December 1979, 3, 5, https://declassified.library.utoronto.ca/exhibits/show/featherbed/volume-5. For the chronological development of Feather Bed, see *Canada Declassified*, CSIS, Feather Bed, vol. 6, "Feather Bed," 19 November 1979, 85–9, https://declassified.library.utoronto.ca/exhibits/show/featherbed/volume-6.

35 *Canada Declassified*, CSIS, Feather Bed, vol. 6, "Feather Bed," Appendix A, 115, https://declassified.library.utoronto.ca/exhibits/show/featherbed/volume-6.

36 For the file, see *Canada Declassified*, CSIS, Feather Bed, https://declassified.library.utoronto.ca/exhibits/show/featherbed/introduction.

37 Jim Bronskill, "RCMP's Cold War Mole Hunt Included Several Top Diplomats," *Toronto Star*, 23 March 2012, A12.

38 *Canada Declassified*, CSIS, Feather Bed, "Feather Bed Section," vol. 1, 17, https://declassified.library.utoronto.ca/exhibits/show/featherbed/volume-1; *Canada Declassified*, CSIS, Feather Bed, Feather Bed Concept, vol. 3, 97–103, https://declassified.library.utoronto.ca/exhibits/show/featherbed/volume-3.

39 *Canada Declassified*, CSIS, Feather Bed, vol. 1, 105–30, https://declassified.library.utoronto.ca/exhibits/show/featherbed/volume-1. For an account of this pathology from a Canadian perspective, see Reg Whitaker, "Spies Who Might Have Been: Canada and the Myth of Cold War Counterintelligence," *Intelligence and National Security* 12, no. 4 (1997): 25–43, https://doi.org/10.1080/02684529708432447, and Reg Whitaker, "Cold War Alchemy: How America, Britain and Canada Transformed Espionage Into Subversion," *Intelligence and National Security* 15, no. 2 (2000): 177–210, https://doi.org/10.1080/02684520008432607.

40 *Canada Declassified*, Feather Bed, vol. 1, From Communism to Soviet Spy: A Study in the Motivation of Some Soviet Agents, 105–32.

41 *Canada Declassified*, CSIS, Feather Bed, "Feather Bed Section," vol. 1, 17, https://declassified.library.utoronto.ca/exhibits/show/featherbed/volume-1.

42 *Canada Declassified*, CSIS, Feather Bed, vol. 1, Top Secret, To the DSI Re: Suspected Underground Members, Etc., 67. A separate investigation, based on the suspicion that the security service itself had a mole (it did, but the mole wasn't the investigated employee), resulted in the investigation of Leslie James Bennett, who in the late 1960s had been responsible for RCMP's Russian Desk, "B" Ops, Counter-espionage. Bennett was put

under surveillance (Operation Gridiron), interrogated, and removed from the service. David Levy, "In the Wilderness of Counterintelligence: CIA, the Force, and the Leslie James Bennett Matter," *International Journal of Intelligence and Counterintelligence* 32, no. 4 (2019): 790–804, https://doi.org/10.1080/08850607.2019.1606661.

43 Carl Mollins, "Robert Broughton Bryce," *Canadian Encyclopedia*, https://www.thecanadianencyclopedia.ca/en/article/robert-bryce-obituary.

44 *Canada Declassified*, CSIS, Feather Bed, vol. 5, Top Secret, Robert Broughton Bryce, 54, https://declassified.library.utoronto.ca/exhibits/show/featherbed/volume-5.

45 *Canada Declassified*, CSIS, Feather Bed, vol. 5, Top Secret, Robert Broughton Bryce, 54, https://declassified.library.utoronto.ca/exhibits/show/featherbed/volume-5.

46 *Canada Declassified*, CSIS, Feather Bed, vol. 1, 76, https://declassified.library.utoronto.ca/exhibits/show/featherbed/volume-1.

47 *Canada Declassified*, CSIS, Feather Bed, vol. 5, Top Secret, Robert Broughton Bryce, 53, https://declassified.library.utoronto.ca/exhibits/show/featherbed/volume-5.

48 *Canada Declassified*, CSIS, Feather Bed, vol. 5, Top Secret, Robert Broughton Bryce, 54, https://declassified.library.utoronto.ca/exhibits/show/featherbed/volume-5. As noted earlier, Agatha Chapman appears to have been hired by Alex Skeleton, though because Skelton reported to Bryce, the latter probably approved Chapman's hiring.

49 Bronskill, "RCMP's Cold War Mole Hunt," A12.

50 Peter Hennessy and Gail Brownfeld, "Britain's Cold War Security Purge: The Origin of Positive Vetting," *Historical Journal* 25, no. 4 (1982): 966.

51 TNA, CAB 79-52-6, Meeting with Directors of Intelligence, The Spread of Communism Throughout the World and the Extent of Its Direction from Moscow, JIC (46)70(O)(Final) (Limited Circulation), Appendix B, 90–105.

52 TNA, CAB 81-134, J.I.C. (66) 101, November 18, 1946, The Spread of Communism Throughout the World, as quoted in Daniel W.B. Lomas, "Labour Ministers, Intelligence And Domestic Anti-Communism, 1945–1951," *Journal of Intelligence History* 12, no. 2 (2013): 120, https://doi.org/10.1080/16161262.2013.794569.

53 TNA, CAB 79-52-6, Meeting with Directors of Intelligence, The Spread of Communism Throughout the World and the Extent of Its Direction from Moscow, JIC (46)70(O)(Final) (Limited Circulation), 54.

54 Philip Deery, "'The Secret Battalion': Communism in Britain During the Cold War: Communism in Britain During the Cold War," *Contemporary British History* 13, no. 4 (1999): 16.

55 Deery, "The Secret Battalion," 17.

56 Deery, "The Secret Battalion," 16–17.

57 Hennessy and Brownfeld, "Britain's Cold War Security Purge," 966.

58 American historian K.A. Cuordileone points to David Caute, *The Great Fear: The Anti-Communist Purge under Truman and Eisenhower* (New York: Simon & Shuster, 1978); Richard M. Fried, *Nightmare in Red: The McCarthy Era in Perspective* (New York: Oxford University Press, 1990); and Ellen Schrecker, *Many Are the Crimes: McCarthyism in America* (Boston: Little, Brown, 1998) as representative of this historical current. Cuordileone, "The Torment of Secrecy: Reckoning with American Communism and Anticommunism after Venona," *Diplomatic History* 35, no. 4 (2011): 624.

59 Wilson Center, Vassiliev Notebooks, Black Notebook, 2009, Plan of measures for the 1st Department, 1st Directorate of the KI to improve intelligence work in the USA. Approved by S. Savchenko 16.03.50, 81. https://digitalarchive.wilsoncenter.org/document/vassiliev-black-notebook.

60 Wilson Center, Vassiliev Notebooks, Black Notebook, 2009, Plan of measures for the 1st Department, 1st Directorate of the KI to improve intelligence work in the USA. Approved by S. Savchenko 16.03.50, 81, https://digitalarchive.wilsoncenter.org/document/vassiliev-black-notebook.

61 Milstein's account of the commission provides no date for his appearance before the inquiry but Vladislav Zubok, based on his interview with Milstein in 1990, concludes that the inquiry took place in the "fall of 1945," a date that seems too early. V.M. Zubok and Konstantin Pleshakov, *Inside the Kremlin's Cold War: From Stalin to Khrushchev* (Cambridge, MA: Harvard University Press, 1996), 146, 312n32. See also Vladislav M. Zubok, *A Failed Empire: The Soviet Union in the Cold War from Stalin to Gorbachev* (Chapel Hill: University of North Carolina Press, 2009), 359.

62 *Vozhd*, "A leader, one who is in supreme authority: applied esp. to the Russian statesman Joseph Stalin (1879–1953)." *Oxford English Dictionary*, s.v. vozhd (*n.*), July 2023, https://doi.org/10.1093/OED/7100438251.

63 Yoram Gorlizki and Oleg Khlevniuk, *Cold Peace: Stalin and the Soviet Ruling Circle, 1945–1953* (New York: Oxford University Press, 2004), 7.

64 Roy Aleksandrovich Medvedev and Zhores Medvedev, *The Unknown Stalin: His Life, Death and Legacy* (Woodstock, NY: Overlook, 2004), 237. Following Stalin's death in 1953, Merkulov was executed with Beria and others for conspiring "to grab power and to liquidate the Soviet worker-peasant regime with a view of restoring capitalism." Richard R. Kasischke, "Beria, Aides Confess as Traitors: Moscow," *Globe & Mail*, 17 December 1953, 1. For their execution, see Richard R. Kasischke, "7 Executed after Secret Trial: Russians Shoot Beria," *Globe & Mail*, 24 December 1953, 1.

65 Gorlizki and Khlevniuk, *Cold Peace*, 29, 180n57.

66 On Vladmir Pavlovich Burdin (Bourdine), see Oleg Lyalin, FBI, 106, https://archive.org/details/OlegLyalin/1366648-0-File1-EBF_15/page/n105/mode/2up?q=bourdine.

67 Christopher Andrew and Vasili Mitrokhin, *The Mitrokhin Archive: The KGB in Europe and the West* (London: Allen Lane, 1999), 181.

68 Andrew and Mitrokhin, *The Mitrokhin Archive*, 181.

69 Andrew and Mitrokhin, *The Mitrokhin Archive*, 218–20.

70 On Golitsyn's turbulent career as a Soviet defector, see "Anatoli Golitsyn," in West, ed., *Historical Dictionary of International Intelligence*, 2nd ed. (New York: Rowman & Littlefield, 2015), 135–6.

71 Andrew and Mitrokhin, *The Mitrokhin Archive*, 477.

72 Andrew and Mitrokhin, *The Mitrokhin Archive*, 478. For an account of the "Thirteenth Department" of the KGB Intelligence Directorate (First Chief Directorate), see National Archives (Washington), 29 December 1975 — *104-10021-10115*. XAA2-23414. 29 Fob 64. 0. Item Prepared for the Warren Commission by SR/CI/RESEARCH entitled "Soviet Use of Assassination and Kidnapping." National Archives, 104-10021-10115.pdf.

73 The remainder were KGB defectors: Anatoli Golitsyn, Pyotr Deryabin, Yuri Rastvorov, Vladimir and Evdokia Petrov, Reino Hayhanen, Nikolai Khokhlov, and Bogdan Stashinsky. Andrew and Mitrokhin, *The Mitrokhin Archive*, 478. See also Kevin P. Riehle, "The 'KGB Wanted List' and the Evolving Soviet Pursuit of Defectors," *Journal of Cold War Studies* 26, 3 (2024): 37–60.

74 See Truman Library, "The Long Telegram," https://www.trumanlibraryinstitute.org/kennan/.

75 On the origins of the Cominform as a replacement for the Comintern, see D. Healey, "The Cominform and World Communism," *International Affairs* 24, no. 3 (1948): 339–49.

76 R.N. Carew Hunt, *The Theory and Practice of Communism: An Introduction* (London: Geoffrey Bles, 1950), 225–6.

Index

Abbott, Douglas: PC 6444, 16
Adams, Eric: against self-incrimination, 188; Agatha Chapman, 198; Bank of Canada, 186; Communism, 191; correspondence, 190–1; education and career, 186; "Ernst," 186; External Trade Advisory Committee, 186; famine in Russia, 192; George Luxton, 194; history of Canada, 194–5; industrial advances in Russia, 193; John P. Humphrey, 192; Kathleen Willsher, 188, 195–6, 199; library, 191; Main Examining Committee, 190; Soviet journalism, 192; Soviet Union, 192–4; Wilgress correspondence, 189
Adamson, Florence: Janet Skelton, 247
Ahearn, John G.: Eric Adams, 188
anti-Semitism, 114
Arcand, Adrian, 96
atomic bomb, 3, 10, 13, 19, 46, 55, 57, 81, 95, 128, 177
Attlee, Clement: Alan Nunn May, 19; Attlee/King Plan, 20, 21; Cabinet Committee on Subversive Activities, 278; Information Research Department (IRD), 265; inquiry sub judice, 105; pressed to act, 20; "purge procedure," 278
Avery, Donald: Raymond Boyer, 141
Aylen, Aldous: Durnford Smith, 211, 212

Beament, A.W.: addendum controversy, 274; counsel, David Shugar, 100, 154, 157; Inquiries Act, 269
Benning, Scotland: appeals conviction, 207; associates, 201; J.C. Dobie, 204–5; "Foster," 163, 200, 203; Munitions and Supply, 200, 201; Nikolay Zheveinov, 163, 200; prosecution, 207–8; Section 13 Communist, 209; transition to Communism, 202–3, 209
Bercuson, David, 113
Bevin, Ernest, 19; Attlee/King Plan, 20; Information Research Department (IRD), 265
Bolshakov, Ivan: Alan Nunn May, 142, 143; American troop movements, 236; cable traffic, 93; David Shugar, 145; First Interim Report, 108; fradulent passport, 245; identified, 93; intelligence

priorities, 108, 143; manufacturing illegals, 243; Nikolai Zabotin, 143, 145, 243, 245; "technological questions," 166; "The Director," 142; "Witczak" passport, 245
Boyer, Raymond, 245; "a new set of heroes," 129; anti-war activities, 132; associates, 138; Communism, 129; Communist Party, 134; Dr. Otto Maass, 134; education and career, 128–9; Fred Rose, 130; Friends of the Soviet Union, 129; international RDX committee, 136; motivation to spy, 141–2; National Conference on Civil Liberties, 130–2; National Research Council, 136; Official Secrets Act, 136, 140; "Professor," 138; RCMP interrogation, 64; RDX, 139; RDX research, 134–6; Reuben Ginsberg, 125; "Section 13" Communist, 129; Stanley Ryerson, 129, 132, 134, 141; war service, 133
Bracken, John, 19; "enemies of the state," 175; John Locke, 175; King's methods, 173; safety of the state, 173; "Star chamber" methods, 175
British commissions of inquiry: Balfour Committee, 32; legal controversy, 31–2; prerogative powers, 31; Tribunals of Inquiry Act, 32
British Security Coordination, 11; HYDRA, 10
Bromley, T.E., 20
Bryce, Robert: Agatha Chapman, 277; employed at Sun Life, 277; External Trade Advisory Committee, 189; Operation Feather Bed, 277; Wilgress correspondence, 189
Burdin, Vladimir, 279
Burman, Samuel Saul: associates, 237; "Berman," 234; Civil Affairs officer, 235; Communist Party, 235; Friends of the Soviet Union, 234; RCMP, 234
Butler, Neville, 20
Byrnes, James: First Interim Report, 105–6; Soviet relations, 24, 95

Canada: "Lesovia," 162; Aid to Russia Fund, 137; Anglo Soviet Accord, 137; financial aid to Britain, 105; Mutual Aid Board, 200; relationship with the USSR, 136–7; "Salute to Russia" rally, 137; Soviet diplomatic initiative, 136
Canada Evidence Act: Mackenzie King, 172; Ned Mazerall, 79; Part I, Sec 5(2), self-incrimination, 33–4, 178, 188, 268; Read / Varcoe Plan, 16
Canadian Bar Association: Canada Evidence Act, 271; Civil Liberties Committee Report, 269–72; F.P. Fillmore, 271; Inquiries Act, 270–1; J.T. Haig, 272; John MacLean, 271; President's Dinner attendees, 270; R.M. Wiles Chitty, 271; safety of the state, 271; W.B. Scott, 272; War Measures Act, 270
Canadian commissions of inquiry: administrative law, 32–5; administrative tribunals, 158; British inquiries, 15, 31–2; D.M. Gordon, 275; differ from judicial tribunals, 34; Inquiries Act 1846, 15, 32; limits of coercion, 32–5; natural justice, 34; *Re Ashby* (1934), 275
Carr, Sam: David Shugar, 46, 63, 144–5; "Frank," 245; John Soboloff,

244; Koudriavtsev network, 121, 138; opposition to war effort, 121; recruiting agents, 144; "Sam," 46; Vassili Rogov, 143; "Walter," 120, 122; "Witczak" passport, 242
Chapman, Agatha: acquitted at trial, 273; Communism, 197–8; culpability, 198–9; employed at Sun Life, 197; Eric Adams, 198; Fred Rose, 76; Friends of the Soviet Union, 197; Irene Kon, 197; Louis Kon, 197; Montreal Civil Liberties Union, 197–8; study group, 73, 122, 198, 201; transition to Communism, 197–8
Childs, Marquis, 56
Churchill, Winston, 280; Fulton, Missouri speech, 108; *New York Times*, 109
civil liberties: Canadian Bar Association, 270–1; H.P. Hill, 100; John Diefenbaker, 183–4; Kellock-Taschereau Royal Commission, 184; Ottawa Journal, 101; PC 6444, 231; Redmond Quain, 100; Second World War, 181; the National Conference on Civil Liberties, 131; wartime jurisprudence, 29
Civil Liberties Union: Agatha Chapman, 197; fifth column, 131; Gordon Lunan, 89; Henning Sorenson, 239; Raymond Boyer, 129; S.S. Burman, 235; Scotland Benning, 203
Clutterbuck, Alexander, 20; acquittals, 273; addendum controversy, 274; Canadian courts, 273; Final Report, 264
Cold War: Amy Knight, 5; George Orwell, 54; historical accounts, 5
Coldwell, M.J.: civil liberties, 170; Defence of Canada Regulations, 176; Fred Rose, 173
Coleman, E.H., 133
Combat, 95
Comintern: dissolution, 46; Sam Carr, 138; Soviet influence, 71
Communist Party of Canada: Agatha Chapman, 198; Alexander Skelton, 247; declared illegal, 121; Feather Bed, 277; Fred Rose, 79, 137; Henning Sorensen, 240; Janet Turner Skelton, 247; Matt Nightingale, 118, 122; Moscow's party line, 73; National Conference on Civil Liberties, 131; Raymond Boyer, 134; Sam Carr, 46, 121, 122; Scotland Benning, 209; Section 13 members, 89, 129, 138, 198, 209; the "corporation," 118; WWII, 129
Corby Committee: E.K. Williams, 30; membership, 7
Council of Foreign Ministers, 7, 24
Criminal Code: confessions, 15; conspiracy, 83; conspiracy provisions, 36; Defence of Canada Regulations, 16; detention provisions, 222, 266, 267; E.K. Williams, 36; Emma Woikin, 71; Gordon Lunan, 107; Harold Gerson, 173; hearsay evidence, 15, 83; Henry Harris, 243; Kathleen Willsher, 107; Matt Nightingale, 173; Ned Mazerall, 83; Official Secrets Act, 83; Raymond Boyer, 172; Read / Varcoe Plan, 15, 180; Section 668, 266

Defence of Canada Regulations, 183; Alan Nunn May, 8; civil liberties, 275; Communist Party of Canada, 12, 121; fascism, 96; legal custody,

17; Montreal Civil Liberties Conference, 130; Read / Varcoe Plan, 16; rights of the detained, 16
Diefenbaker, John: addendum controversy, 274; "Bill of Rights," 184; British colonialism, 183; Defence of Canada Regulations, 183; Magna Charta, 184; PC 6444, 183–4
Dies, Martin: Dies Committee, 95
Dolbin, Grigory: NKVD Rezident, Washington, 233, 234
Drew, George: conditions in the Soviet Union, 78
Dutt, R. Palme, 202
Dwyer, Peter, 11

Eid, Leif, 56
Evans, Jean-Paul, 11

Fauteux, Gérald: defending the inquiry, 99; First Interim Report, 102
fifth column, 12, 48, 56, 131, 132, 134, 176, 179, 259, 261
Fitin, P.M.: Chief of NKVD foreign intelligence, 10
Fitzpatrick, Sheila: fellow traveller's tale, 194
Foote, Alexander: Canadian GRU operation, 81; GRU operative, 251; interprets Dübendorfer letter, 252
Forsey Eugene, 89, 197
Foster, Cedric, 56
Fuchs, Klaus, 86

Gerson, Harold, 245; anti-Semitism, 164; associates, 164; Cliff Harvison, 167–8; consulting office, 167; evidence against, 159; Fred Rose, 164; "Grant's Mailing List," 165–7; "Gray," 159, 166, 167; Maj. Sokolov, 163; Munitions and Supply, 160; Proceedings of the Ordnance Board, 161; Schlein family, 162–3; Scotland Benning, 165
Golitsyn, Anatoliy, 279
Gouzenko, Igor, 283; Alan Nunn May, 14, 86; co-conspirator, 15; code name "Corby," 8; Comintern, 44; "Debouz," 46; defection, 4, 7; "Elli" or "Ellie," 46; "Ernst," 46; "Foster," 46; "Gray," 46; "Green," 46; Gregory Dolbin, 233–4; GRU cipher clerk, 44; GRU nomenclature, 44; GRU personnel, 44; GRU security measures, 47; hearsay evidence, 15, 41; "Leader," 46; Mikhail Milstein, 3; "Nora," 46; "political statement," 47; "Professor," 46; Red Army, 7; "Sam," 46; "special action" against, 279; Vsevolod Merkulov, 232–3; Western cryptanalysts, 70
GRU DOCUMENTARY REFERENCE: "Badeau," 215; "Berman," 234; Doruforth [*sic*] Smith "Badeau," 81; Durnford Smith, 216; "Ernst," 190; "Foster," 200; Gordon Lunan "Back," 81; "Gray," 138; "Green," 138; Hermina Rabinowitch, 251–2; Isidor [*sic*] Halperin "Bacon," 81; Mat [*sic*] Nantigale ("Squadron Leader"), 118, 124; Ned Mazerall ("Bagley"), 81; "Nora," 67; "Polland," 220; "Primrose," 61; Raymond Boyer, 138; "Skelton," 246; "Surensen," 238
GRU INTELLIGENCE PRIORITIES: communications British High Commission, 109; communications Department of External Affairs, 109;

electro-projector of the "V" bomb, 109; explosives and chemical materials, 108; locations of American troops, 109; microwave radar intelligence, 210; NRC personnel and research, 109; passports for spies, 242; production of atomic bomb, 109, 142; records Department of Munitions and Supply, 199; status American Army in Europe, 143; strategic centres, 199; uranium-235, uranium processing, 109; "Witczak" passport, 242

GRU PERSONNEL: Feodor Kuznetsov, 3; Georgi Gourshkov ("Chester"), 44; Gregory Popov, 256; Igor Gouzenko, 7; Ivan Bolshakov, 93; Ivan Bolshakov ("Director"), 108; Ivan Ilichev, 3; Mikhail Milstein, 3; Nikolay Zheveinov, 44; Pavel Mikhailov ("Molier"), 137; Pavel N. Angelov ("Baxter"), 44; Petr Motinov ("Lamont"), 44; Sergei Gousev ("Henri"), 44; Sergei M. Koudriavtsev ("Leon"), 43, 44; Vassili Rogov ("Brent" aka "Jan"), 44; Vsevolod Sokolov ("Davy" of "Davie"), 43, 44

GRU TRADECRAFT: agent recruitment, 73, 143–4, 243; agents warned, 11, 21, 241–2; Canadian operation, 81, 279; code-names, 14; Communist Party functionaties, 141; conspiracy, 14; "cut-outs," 245–6; dubok, 125; Koudriavtsev network, 137–8; manufacturing "illegals," 242–3; Radio library lists, 218; recall of agents, 241; "Research Group," 82; Sokolov network, 163; study groups, 73; telegram traffic, 142; toilet tank cover, 67

Gusev, Feodor: Soviet ambassador to Britain, 70; Soviet ambassador to Canada, 137

habeas corpus: A.A. McIntosh, 101; Davie Fulton, 183; denied, 11, 100, 101; E.K. Williams, 36, 40; Fred Poland, 63, 222; Israel Halperin, 224; John Bracken, 173; John Diefenbaker, 183; Justice Lyman Duff, 181; Louis St. Laurent, 18, 180; M.J. Coldwell, 173; Official Secrets Act, 19, 38; Re George Edwin Gray (1918), 18

Halperin, Israel: acquitted at trial, 230; ambivalent spy, 85, 228; atomic bomb, 86; "Bacon's" report, 226–7; Col. William van Steenburgh, 225, 227, 230; education military career, 225; *habeas corpus*, 224; uranium-235, 227; variable times (VT) fuse, 85; V-bomb, 228

Harold Laski, 73, 202

Harris, Henry: convicted, 243; conviction quashed, 243; "Witzak" passport, 243

Hollis, Roger, 20, 250; coordinates with RCMP, 14; lead MI5 Gouzenko investigator, 11; objects to Philby's soothing Gouzenko report, 55

Holmes, Stephen: Alan Nunn May, 103; Corby Committee, 8; Gestapo methods, 101; Gordon Lunan, 91; PC 6444, 101; release First Interim Report, 104

Hoover, J. Edgar: F.B.I. Director, 14, 23, 39, 55, 282

Howe, C.D.: PC 6444, 16; RDX, 140; war effort, 199–200
Howe, Douglas: Final Report, 259
Hughes, Royden: Fred Poland, 223–4

Ilsley, J.L.: addendum controversy, 274; First Interim Report, 102; PC 6444, 16
Inquiries Act, 158; Canadian Bar Association, 270–1; "law governing the inquiry," 52; legal challenges, 32; Louis St. Laurent, 179–81; origin, 32; Part I, Sec (4) (5), coercive powers, 15, 32; Part II Departmental Inquiries, 25; Part III, Sec (12), legal counsel, 35; Part III, Sec (13), statement of charge, 157, 168; PC 411, 40; PC 6444, 17; RCMP interrogations, 148; Read/Varcoe Plan, 16; self-incrimination, 33

Jackson, Janet Turner, 247
Jackson, Stanley, 247

Kardash, William: Matt Nightingale case, 127
Kellock, Roy, 37
Kellock-Taschereau Royal Commission PROCESS: addendum controversy, 274; civil liberties, 51–2, 275–6; confessions, 41; detentions, 52–3; Drew Pearson, 50; evidence, 43; ground-breaking investigation, 186; *habeas corpus*, 182; *habeas corpus* hearing, 222; hearsay evidence, 15; in camera, 42; political interference, 102; procedures, 99–100; progress of the inquiry, 185–6; RCMP interrogations, 60–4; Read/Varcoe Plan, 14–15; Rote Kapelle, 249–50; subpoena, 120; supporting cast, 43; use of testimony, 41–2; wartime constitutionalism, 52; world reaction to arrests, 53–8
Kellock-Taschereau Royal Commission QUESTIONING: A. J. Lawrence (Scotland Benning), 201; Adrien Cambron (Raymond Boyer), 135–6; Agatha Chapman, 198; Alexander Skelton, 246–8; Cliff Harvison (Harold Gerson), 167–8; David Shugar, 145–55; Dean Marble (Eric Adams), 190; Durnford Smith, 211–15, 213–15, 215–17, 219; Emma Woikin, 64–71, 71; Eric Adams, 187–8, 189, 190–1, 191, 195–6; F.E. Beamish (David Shugar), 156–7; Fred Poland, 222–4, 224; G.M. Fawcett (Matt Nightingale), 117–18, 118, 125; Gordon Lunan, 80–91; H.P. Hill (Scotland Benning), 206; H.R. Malley (Harold Gerson), 159–61, 165–7; H.R. Stewart (Fred Poland), 221; Harold Gerson, 160–8; Henning Sorensen, 238–9, 240; Henry Harris, 243; Hermina Rabinowitch, 251–4; Ignacy Witzak, 241; Igor Gouzenko, 44–7, 47, 155; Israel Halperin, 225–6, 229–30; J.C. Dobie (Scotland Benning), 204–5; Kathleen Willsher, 73–6, 75–6; Lesslie Reille Thompson (Eric Adams), 190; Matt Nightingale, 116–27; Ned Mazerall, 76–9; R.O. King (David Shugar), 157; Raymond Boyer, 133–41; Robert Bryce (Eric Adams), 189; Royden Hughes (Fred Poland), 223–4; Samuel Saul Burman, 236–7, 237;

Scotland Benning, 202–3, 203, 204–6, 206; Stanislas Daley (Emma Woikin), 70; Stanley Comach (David Shugar), 156; William van Steenburgh (Israel Halperin), 227, 230

Kellock-Taschereau Royal Commission REPORT FINAL: Alexander Clutterbuck, 264; authorship, 257; British access limited, 262; British MPs want copies, 262; British press reaction, 263; Canada editorial reaction, 260; Canada press reaction, 259–60; Communist critique, 260–1; law and procedure, 99–100; Nikolai Belokhvostikov, 256–7; Percy Sillitoe requests copies, 262; sale price, 259; Soviet reaction, 263–4; US editorial commentary, 261; US press reaction, 261–2

Kellock-Taschereau Royal Commission REPORT FIRST INTERIM: arrests, 107; Churchill "Iron Curtain" speech, 108; King's 15 February statement, 108–9; *New York Times*, 110; press France, 112; press Great Britain, 112–13; press United States, 110–12; response to Moscow, 102; response to press criticism, 104

Kellock-Taschereau Royal Commission REPORT SECOND INTERIM: arrests, 170; King defends inquiry, 172; press reaction Canada, 177–8; press reaction United States, 174–5

Kellock-Taschereau Royal Commission REPORT THIRD INTERIM: arrests, 231; Israel Halperin, 230; reaction from Moscow, 231–2

Kellock-Taschereau Royal Commission STATUTORY: Inquiries Act, 150, 168, 224, 268, 269; judicial review, 207–9; legal status of inquiry, 274–5; liberal state, 42; Official Secrets Act, 41, 103, 201, 207, 230, 240, 265, 266, 267; PC 411, 39–40, 40–1; PC 6444, 50–1, 99; Re George Edwin Gray, 18–19; terms of reference, 42–3; War Measures Act, 6, 18–19

Kennan, George: "Long Telegram," 113, 280

Keynes, John Maynard, 74; Anglo-Canadian negotiations, 205

King, Mackenzie GOUZENKO CRISIS: Attlee / King Plan, 20, 21; consults Clement Attlee, 13; consults Harry Truman, 13; Departmental inquiry, 25–6; E.K. Williams, 27; international implications, 7; London and Washington, 19–20; Nikolai Belokhvostikov, 53; PC 5991, 8–10; PC 6444, 16–17, 17; policy of inaction, 13; political career, 49; pressed to act, 20; Re George Edwin Gray, 18–19; Read / Varcoe Plan, 16; ready to act, 39; Royal Commission, 16; "true world patriot," 49; Washington Plan, 21–3, 24

King, Mackenzie INQUIRY: 15 February statement, 53–4; communications strategy, 99; critical of inquiry, 102, 185; eager to rescind PC 6444, 223, 231; European reaction to 15 February statement, 54–5; Final Report, 258–9; Final Report distribution, 259; First Interim Report, 108–9; free the suspects, 185; Inquiries

Act, Part III, Sec (13), 172; inquiry process, 40; John Locke, 174, 176; Moscow attacks, 96; PC 411, 39–40; regrets PC 6444, 169; Russian Charge d'Affaires, 53; Second Interim Report, 171–2; the "safety of the state," 173–4; "sub judice" no longer, 102; US reaction to 15 February statement, 55–8
Knight, Amy, 5, 6, 39, 71, 209
Kon, Irene, 197
Koudriavtsev, Sergei: constructs GRU Toronto network, 121; GRU networks before Zabotin, 137; Hermina Rabinowitch, 252, 254, 255; "Leon," 43, 44; meets David Shugar, 151; recruits Sam Carr, 138; "Skelton," 248; Vassili Rogov takes over passport project, 246
Kreshin, Boris: NKVD operative London, 10

Labor Progressive Party (LPP): Soviet outpost, 71–2
Larocque, H: Pan-Canadian Union, 131
Leopold, John, 43, 263
Liddell, Guy, 20, 111; arrest of Nunn May, 19; cooperation with Ottawa, 14; Kim Philby, 10; Moscow speaks, 93
Linton, Freda, 245, 259
Locke, John: "beasts of prey," 36; Cicero's De Legibus, 173; "common enemy," 36; Crown prerogative, 40, 42, 174; dangerous creatures, 28–9; salus populi suprema lex esto, 6, 173, 271
Lozovsky, Solomon: Soviet Deputy Commissar of Foreign Affairs, 92
Lubyanka Square: NKVD Headquarters, 4, 58
Lunan, Gordon: arrested, 53; associates, 89–90; Canadian Information Service, 80; Communist Party, 88–9; Durnford Smith, 84; GRU assignment, 81; GRU tradecraft, 82; Hazen Size, 89; ideological motivation, 64; Israel Halperin, 84–6; linchpin for prosecution, 79; money from Moscow, 88; morality of spying, 89–90; Ned Mazerall, 88; RCMP interrogation, 62; recruited, 80; refuses to testify, 230; self-justification, 90; Vassili Rogov, 81, 84

MacDonald, Malcolm: action plan, 21; Agatha Chapman, 61; Alexander Cadogan, 8, 20, 39, 42; arrests, 52; "Corby" Committee, 8; Drew Pearson, 50; Emma Woikin, 64; Fred Rose and Parliament, 175; Fred Rose implicated, 139; GRU tactics, 141; *habeas corpus*, 221–2; Henning Sorensen, 238; "Ignacy Witczak," 241; Matt Nightingale, 127; Ned Mazerall, 79; on failure to act, 20; Orme Sargent, 139; press reaction, 54; Rabinowitch investigation, 250; Raymond Boyer, 64; RCMP interrogations, 60–4; trials in camera, 107; Wilgress correspondence, 189; "Witczak" investigation, 250
Macleod, A.A., 131
Magna Charta, 101, 178, 181
Marsh, Grace: "Galya," 245
Martin, Paul: "British system," 184
Massey, Vincent, 54, 94

Mayrand, Leon: Comintern, 71–2; Moscow speaks, 92
Mazerall, Ned: "Badgley," 76; Canada Evidence Act Sec (5) (2), 79; confession, 79; Criminal Code, 83; education and career, 76; Fred Rose, 76; Gordon Lunan, 77, 88–9; groupthink pressures, 78; guilty of conspiracy, 79; implicates Durnford Smith, 77; money for spying, 77; motivation for spying, 78; oaths of allegiance, 76; RCMP interrogation, 62; recruited, 77; study groups, 76–7
McDougall, Judge A.G., Carlton County: acquits W.M. Pappin, 245; evidence against Halperin inadmissable, 230; Gordon Lunan testimony, 41; hearsay evidence, 159; "presumptions" Official Secrets Act, 243
McIntosh, A. A.: Alan Nunn May, 110; Communism as a religion, 260; First Interim Report, 109; John Diefenbaker, 184; John Locke, 110; totalitarian methods, 231; totalitarian procedure, 110; totalitarian state, 100
McRuer, J.C., Chief Justice Ontario High Court: attends CBA Annual meeting, 270; Benning conviction quashed, 207; Gordon Lunan convicted, 91; *habeas corpus*, 222, 224; Ned Mazerall convicted, 79; Scotland Benning convicted, 207
Menzies, Stewart: Ignacy Witczak, 21; Kim Philby, 10
Merkulov, Vsevolod: Gouzenko and Bentley, 24; Gouzenko debacle, 232–3; Malenkov inquiry, 278; Merkulov's fate, 278–9; People's Commissar of State Security (NKVD), 24; Stalin on his failures, 278–9
Mikhailov, Pavel ("Molier"): Canadian GRU networks, 137; GRU rezident New York, 254
Milstein, Mikhail: assessment of the West, 48; deputy director GRU, 3; Emma Woikin recruitment, 65; summoned to Lubyanka Square, 58; suspicions about Gouzenko, 3; "The Stutterer," 58; "Witczak" passport, 242
Morris, Leslie: Final Report Communist critique, 260–1
Morton, W.L.: "a gauche proceeding," 128
Moscow: 20 February statement, 58–9; Gouzenko crisis, 96; party line, 73; response to 20 February statement, 94–5, 95–6, 96–8
Motinov, Petr: Alan Nunn May, 87; "Berman," 235; draft telegrams, 234; "Gray's" relatives, 162; "Grant's Mailing List," 46; radiation poisoning, 87; Zabotin's secretary, 162

National Council for Canadian-Soviet Friendship, 137
National Emergency Transitional Powers Act, 40; PC 6444, 169
Neilsen, Dorise: Agatha Chapman, 198; Igor Gouzenko, 231
New York Times: First Interim Report, 110
Nightingale, Matt: acquitted at trial, 273–4; associates, 119–20; Communist activities, 121–2; education and career, 116; fourth meeting with Rogov, 125; GRU documents, 118; GRU requests, 125; "Leader," 46; leaves study

group, 122; oath of secrecy, 120; RCAF clearance certificate, 119; RCAF documents, 118–19; RCAF duties, 117–18; RCMP interrogation, 61, 116; Sam Carr, 120; Vassili Rogov, 122–7; "Walter," 126

NKVD: archives, 115; Boris Kreshin, 10; Canadian network, 44; couriers, 47; David Shugar, 151; Elizabeth Bentley, 23–4; fake "Ignacy Witczak," 241; Final Report, 263; Fred Poland, 62, 220, 221; Georgi Gourshkov, 145; Gouzenko defection, 7, 10–11; Grigory Dolbin, 233–4; Hermina Rabinowitch, 252; Ignacy Witczak passport, 241; Konstantin Volkov, 4; Merkulov directive on Gouzenko crisis, 232–3; Merkulov reports on Gouzenko Bentley crisis, 24; Operation Feather Bed, 276; P.M. Fitin, Chief of NKVD foreign intelligence, 10; passports, 242; relations with GRU, 138; Third Interim Report, 231; "Thirteenth Department," 279; Vitali Pavlov, 53; Vladimir Burdin, 279

Nunn May, Alan, 61; arrest, 103–5; atomic bomb, 86, 87; British Official Secrets Act, 104; deathbed admissions, 87; "facts given by Alex," 143; GRU agent, 14; Norman Veal, 87; October rendezvous, 17; Pavel Angelov, 86; PC 5991, 8–10; "Primrose," 61; proximity shells, 87; sometimes "Alek or Alec," 86

O'Leary, Grattan: Mackenzie King, 171–2

Official Secrets Act POLITICAL: A.A. Heaps, 265; Arthur Meighen, 266; civil liberties, 209; foreign conspiracies, 208–9; Read / Varcoe Plan, 14, 15

Official Secrets Act PROSECUTION: David Shugar, conspiracy to offend, 155, 159; Durnford Smith, conspiracy to offend, 220; Eric Adams, conspiracy to offend, 199; Fred Poland, conspiracy to offend, 224; Gordon Lunan, 91; Harold Gerson, 168; Henry Harris, conspiracy to offend, 243; inquiry questioning, 83; Israel Halperin, conspiracy to offend, 230; Kathleen Willsher, 76; Matt Nightingale, 127; Ned Mazerall, conspiracy to offend, 79; PC 411, 41; PC 6444, 36; Raymond Boyer, 132; relation to Criminal Code, 243; route to convictions, 13; Sam Carr, conspiracy to offend, 120; Scotland Benning, 207–8; wartime jurisprudence, 207

Official Secrets Act STATUTORY: British Official Secrets Act, 14, 18, 265; Canadian courts, 266; Communist Party of Canada, 195; confession of guilt, 82–3; conspiracy, 41; direct evidence, 14; employees of British government, 53; MacDonald Commission, 266; National Research Council security, 136; PC 6444, 51; Sec (10), detention provisions, 150, 182, 222; Sec (3) (2), presumptions, 243–4; Sec (3), circumstances of the case, 158; Sec 14, arrest of Fred Rose, 170; Sec 14, indictable offence, 170; Sec 3(2)(4), guilt by association,

273; Sec 3(2)(4), reverse onus clauses, 72, 208; Sec 3(2), known character, 80, 207; Sec 3(2), special provisions, 72, 146; Sec 3(4), agent of a foreign power, 203, 208; wartime jurisprudence, 89
Operation Feather Bed, 276, 277, 279, 283; ideological spies, 276

Pavlov, Vitali, NKVD Rezident, 138; Fred Poland, 62; Hazen Size, 151; Hermina Rabinowitch, 252; packing to leave, 257; Third Interim Report, 231
Pearson, Drew: Gouzenko crisis, 39; PC 411, 39–40; PC 6444, 49–50; Russian spy rings, 56
Pearson, Lester: James Brynes, 105; Washington Plan, 24
Philby, Kim, 283; Alan Nunn May, 18; Corby Committee, 10; Elizabeth Bentley, 23; false summary, 55; Gouzenko's defection, 10–11; Guy Liddell, 10; Konstantin Volkov, 4, 18; MI6 double agent, 10; Washington Plan, 21–3
Poland, Fred: acquitted at trial, 224; associates, 221; duties at RCAF, 221; Gouzenko on "Polland," 220; GRU agent "Polland," 220; *habeas corpus*, 221; NKVD, 62, 221; *Re George Edwin Gray*, 222; "Second Group," 220; Vitali Pavlov, 62, 221
Power, Chubby: Magna Charta, 183

Rabinowitch, Hermina: "cut-out," 254; education and career, 250; exile, 255; justification, 251–2; Lithuanian citizenhip, 250; Rachel Dübendorfer, 250–2; "Rote Kapelle" ("Red Orchestra"), 249–51; Sergei Koudriavtsev, 252, 254, 255
RCMP: Alan Nunn May, 9; arrests, 52–3; communism, 12; coordination with MI5, 14; Departmental inquiry, 25; dossiers, 43; E.K. Williams, 150; Fred Rose, 139, 171; Gouzenko's defection, 4, 96; Gouzenko's documents, 29; Hermina Rabinowitch, 250; Ignacy Witczak, 241; interrogations, 60–4, 148; John Leopold, 43, 263; John Soboloff, 244; Kellock-Taschereau royal commission, 153; King / Attlee Plan, 20; Montreal CLU, 132; PC 6444, 17; Samuel Saul Burman, 234; Security Panel, 276; Soviet Espionage in Canada, 21
Read, J. E.: Canadian Bar Association, 270; Read / Varcoe Plan, 14
Reid, Escott: on Communists, 36
Robertson, Norman: Alan Nunn May arrest, 103; Alexander Cadogan, 8; arrest of Fred Rose, 170; arrest of Gordon Lunan, 53; British scientists, 8; Commission counsel, 102; "Corby" Committee, 7; Final Report, 257; Grace Shugar, 101; PC 5991, 8; Read / Varcoe Plan, 177; safeguards Gouzenko, 7; "Security Panel," 276; to press King to act, 20; Washington Plan, 21
Robertson, Ontario Chief Justice R.S.: on Benning's appeal, 207–9
Roebuck, Arthur: Israel Halperin, 225, 226, 228
Rogov, Vassili, 108; David Shugar, 144–5, 155; Durnford Smith, 210, 216–17, 219; Gordon Lunan, 81, 84, 87, 88, 91; GRU tradecraft,

82; Matt Nightingale, 61, 122–7; Nikolai Zabotin, 47, 86; "Witczak" passport, 242
Rose, Fred: "Burman" contacts with GRU, 237; Agatha Chapman, 76; arrested, 170–1; bail, 171; Departmental inquiry, 25; Gordon Lunan, 62, 80; Kathleen Willsher, 61, 73; Koudriavtsev network, 137; Ned Mazerall, 62; Sololov network, 44
Ryerson, Stanley: Alexander Skelton, 247; "change of mind," 141; Section 13 Communists, 132; study group, 129

Sandwell, B.K.: Canadian Bar Association, 272
Sargent, Orme: Alexander Cadogan, 104; arrest Alan Nunn May, 104; Soviet Union, 68
Schiller, Charles, 32
Semichastny, Vladimir: assassination of Gouzenko," 279
Shugar, David: "Prometheus," 144; associates, 151; attends study group, 77; Communism, 146–7; F.E. Beamish, 156–7; Nicolai Zabotin, 151; NKVD, 151; objections to inquiry, 147–8; R.O. King, 157; RCMP interrogation, 149; Research Enterprises, 146; Royal Canadian Navy, 146; Sam Carr, 144, 151–4; Second Interim Report, 155; Sergei Koudriavtsev, 151; suspect, 148
Size, Hazen: David Shugar, 151; Gordon Lunan, 89; Henning Sorensen, 240
Skelton, Alexander: Communist Party, 247; domestic circumstances, 247–8; education, career, character, 246; Eric Adams, 246; Kathleen Green, 247; Mackenzie King, 246; O.D. Skelton, 246; "Skelton," 248–9; Stanley Ryerson, 247
Smith, Arnold, 43; Final Report, 257; Hermina Rabinowitch, 250; Soviet critic, 113
Smith, Arthur: Canada Evidence Act, 178; King's Gouzenko policy, 178–9; safety of the state, 178; the common law, 178
Smith, Durnford: assignments, 216–17; associates, 211; atomic bomb, 86; "Badeau's" GRU file, 215; British Official Secrets Act, 218; convicted and jailed, 220; Gordon Lunan, 211, 213; motivation, 219; Ned Mazerall, 210; Radio library, 217; recruitment, 210; Vassili Rogov, 216–17, 219
Soboloff, John: "Ignacy Witczak," 244; Mackenzie King, 259
Sorensen, Henning: Communist, 239–40; Communist Party of Spain, 239; employed at Sun Life, 239; GRU "Surensen," 238; Naval Intelligence, 238; Sam Carr, 239; Spanish Civil War, 239
St. Laurent, Louis: anti-Communism, 12; Canada Evidence Act, Part I, Sec (5), 5(2), 180; criminal prosecution, 179–80; *habeas corpus*, 180; Inquiries Act, 179–81, 180; Inquiries Act, Part I, Sec (4), 180; PC 6444, 40, 50; Re George Edwin Gray, 18–19, 181; safety of the people, 179; trials in camera, 107
Stalin, Joseph: atomic bomb, 87; Gouzenko and Bentley crisis,

24; Gouzenko's fate, 58; King's Gouzenko statement, 24; Merkulov's failures, 278–9; orders inquiry, 278; war with the West, 142; Washington Plan, 24; WWII as imperialist and unjust, 129
Stephenson, Sir John, 20
Stephenson, William: First Interim Report, 104–5; Gregory Popov, 256; J.Edgar Hoover, 39
Stimson, Henry: atomic energy, 3
Stoddard, Lothrop, 56
Strike, Glenn, Police Magistrate: orders Shugar released, 155; orders trial of Israel Halperin, 230; remands Lunan, Willsher, Woikin, and Mazerall, 107

Taschereau, Robert, 37
The Parliamentary Papers Act, 103
Thompson, Dorothy: Churchill's Fulton speech, 111; Moscow speaks, 97–8
Thompson, John: Canada Evidence Act, 33; Inquiries Act, 33
Tottenham, Lt. Commander, Naval Intelligence: Henny Sorensen, 238; Henny Sorenson, 238
Truman, Harry: Commission on Employee Loyalty, 278; declines joint action, 24; Hiroshima, 3; opposes immediate arrests, 13; Washington Plan, 23

Varcoe, Frederick Percy: Read / Varcoe Plan, 14
Venona: Gouzenko, 70; Red scare, 278; Soviet spying, 73, 115, 141
Volkov, Konstantin: NKDV defector, 4, 18, 48, 281, 283
Vyshinsky, Andrey: attacks King, 93

Wadsworth, A. P.: First Interim Report, 112
War Measures Act, 19; E.K. Williams, 38; Gouzenko crisis, 6; *habeas corpus*, 222, 224; invocation, 175, 270; John Diefenbaker, 184; Louis St. Laurent, 179; Lyman Duff on limits, 181; M.J. Coldwell, 176; October Crisis, 175; PC 6444, 16, 100; Re George Edwin Gray, 18–19, 18; Read / Varcoe Plan, 14; rescinded, 40; secret orders, 40; Section 3 on proclamation, 175; Section 6, 18; Transitional Powers Act, 40; wartime jurisprudence, 181
Wark, Wesley: security threats, 268–9
Weisbord, Merrily, 249; Bardic tradition, 132; Raymond Boyer, 132; Scotland Benning, 209; Section 13 Communists, 89
Wilfrid Eggleston: Final Report, 259
Wilgress, Dana, 46, 61, 71, 98, 189; First Interim Report, 113–14; Moscow speaks, 93–4
Williams, E.K.: advises on Gouzenko, 27; American investigation, 37; defending the inquiry, 99; First Interim Report, 102; Gouzenko's evidence, 30; *habeas corpus*, 36; inquiry experience, 29; judicial review, 37; Kafkaesque theatre, 35; native tongue, 27–9; PC 6444, 40; Read / Varcoe Plan, 30–1; trials in camera, 107
Willsher, Kathleen: Agatha Chapman, 71, 74; Anglo-Canadian negotiations, 74–5; arrest, 53; British High Commission, 74; Communism, 72; confessions, 61;

"Elli" or "Ellie," 46; Eric Adams, 73; Fred Rose, 73–4; Inquiries Act, 75; loyalty, 75; Official Secrets Act, 75; Wilgress correspondence, 189
Winnipeg Free Press: Canadian Bar Association, 270; First Interim Report, 109; Second Interim Report, 177
Witczak, Ignacy, 21, 240; Adrienne Soulière, 244; Albert Cooper, 245; C. Clancy, 245; Emma Woikin, 244; fake "Ignacy Witczak," 21; J.J. Robinette, 245; Mackenzie-Papineau Battalion, 241; passport, 241; Sam Carr, 245; W. M. Pappin, 244, 245
Woikin, Emma: Adrienne Soulière, 244; Amy Knight, 70; confesses to RCMP, 60; confession, 67; GRU agent "Nora," 65; Ignacy Witczak passport, 244; June Callwood, 66; life before Ottawa, 64; motivation, 66; Named Doukhobor, 66; recruitment, 65; Stanislas Daley, 70; transcriptions, 67–70; value of transcriptions, 70; warned, 11
Wood, Stuart: arrests, 21; criminal conspiracy, 12–13; Gouzenko crisis, 11; Soviet Espionage in Canada, 21
Wrong, Hume: "Corby" Committee, 7; Final Report, 257; Gordon Lunan, 53; Read / Varcoe Plan, 14–15, 39; Washington Plan, 21
Zabotin, Nikolai: agent recruitment, 157; Alan Nunn May, 86, 142; code name "Grant," 43, 142; David Shugar, 145; developing Emma Woikin, 65; Durnford Smith cargo, 218; "Ernst," 190; "Foster," 200; Gouzenko recalled, 3; "Grant's Mailing List," 43, 46, 67, 75, 165, 189, 190, 204–5, 206; "Gray," 165, 166, 167; GRU subordinates, 44; handwritten notes, 43; intelligence on atomic bomb, 3, 87; Ivan Bolshakov, 143, 145, 167, 218; Koudriavtsev's network, 137; Matt Nightingale, 118, 120, 124; "Nora's" summaries, 67; Order of the Red Banner, 87; Order of the Red Star, 87; "Polland," 220; "The Professor," 139; punished for Gouzenko debacle, 58; relations with "the Director," 47, 93, 102; Sergei Koudriavtsev, 151, 248, 254; Sokolov network, 163; telegram re. "Gray's" relatives, 162; telegrams Ottawa and Moscow, 44, 142; the "Second Group (Ottawa Toronto), 190; tradecraft, 44, 47, 163; Vassili Rogov, 47; Zabotin's safe, 118, 159, 161, 216
Zarubin, Georgy: James Byrnes, 95; Soviet Ambassador, 25
Zaslavsky, David: Soviet reaction Final Report, 263–4
Zinoviev letter, 94

PUBLICATIONS OF THE OSGOODE SOCIETY FOR CANADIAN LEGAL HISTORY

2026 Earl Cherniak, *In the Courts: A Counsel's Memoir*
David Berg, *There Is No Place for Sympathy Here: On Trial in the Belcher Islands*
Colin Campbell and Robert Raizenne, *A History of Canadian Income Tax Volume 3: Tax Reform and the Modern Act*
Patricia I. McMahon and Robert Bothwell, *In the Shadow of the Manhattan Project: Radium, Fraud, and Secrecy at Eldorado*
Tom Mitchell and Reinhold Kramer *"P.S. Burn After Reading": The Kellock-Taschereau Commission and Soviet Espionage in Canada*
Ian Radforth, *Making a Killing: Murder and Life Insurance in 1890s Ontario*

2025 Robert Sharpe, *My Life in the Law: Lawyer, Scholar, Judge*
Eric M. Adams and Jordan Stanger-Ross, *Challenging Exile: Japanese Canadians and the Wartime Constitution*
Carolyn Strange, *Fatal Confession: A Girl's Murder, a Man's Execution, and the Fitton Case*
Jim Phillips, *I Did Not Commit Adultery: Marital Conflict and the Law in Ontario in the 1870s*

2024 Adam Dodek, *Heenan Blaikie: The Making and Unmaking of a Great Canadian Law Firm*
Colin Campbell and Robert Raizenne, *A History of Canadian Income Tax Volume II, 1948–71*
Wayne Sumner, *Prairie Justice: The Hanging of Mike Hack*
Ian Radforth, *Deadly Swindle: An 1890 Murder in Backwoods Ontario That Gripped the World*

2023 Lori Chambers and Joan Sangster, eds., *Essays in the History of Canadian Law Volume XII: New Perspectives on Gender and the Law*
C. Ian Kyer, *The Ontario Bond Scandal of 1924 Re-examined*
Jonathan Swainger, *The Notorious Georges: Crime and Community in British Columbia's Northern Interior, 1909–25*

2022 Jim Phillips, Philip Girard, and R. Blake Brown, *A History of Law in Canada Volume II: Law for the New Dominion, 1867–1914*
J. Barry Wright, Susan Binnie, and Eric Tucker, eds., *Canadian State Trials Volume V: World War, Cold War and Challenges to Sovereignty, 1939–1990*
Constance Backhouse, *Reckoning with Racism: Police, Judges and the RDS Case*

2021 Daniel Rûck *The Laws and the Land: The Settler Colonial Invasion of Kahnawà:ke in Nineteenth-Century Canada*
Lyndsay Campbell, *Truth and Privilege: Libel Law in Massachusetts and Nova Scotia, 1820–1840*

Martine Valois, Ian Greene, Craig Forcese, and Peter McCormick, eds. *The Federal Court of Appeal and the Federal Court: Fifty Years of History*
Colin Campbell and Robert Raizenne, *A History of Canadian Income Tax Volume I: The Income War Tax Act 1917–1948*

2020 Heidi Bohaker, *Doodem and Council Fire: Anishinaabe Governance through Alliance*
Carolyn Strange, *The Death Penalty and Sex Murder in Canadian History*

2019 Harry Arthurs, *Connecting the Dots: The Life of an Academic Lawyer*
Eric Reiter, *Wounded Feelings: Litigating Emotions in Quebec, 1870–1950*

2018 Philip Girard, Jim Phillips, and Blake Brown, *A History of Law in Canada Volume 1: Beginnings to 1866*
Suzanne Chiodo, *The Class Actions Controversy: The Origins and Development of the Ontario Class Proceedings Act*

2017 Constance Backhouse, *Claire L'Heureux-Dube: A Life*
Dennis G. Molinaro, *An Exceptional Law: Section 98 and the Emergency State, 1919–1936*

2016 Lori Chambers, *A Legal History of Adoption in Ontario, 1921–2015*
Bradley Miller, *Boarderline Crime: Fugitive Criminals and the Challenge of the Boarder, 1819–1914*
James Muir, *Law, Debt, and Merchant Power: The Civil Courts of Eighteenth-Century Halifax*

2015 Barry Wright, Eric Tucker, and Susan Binnie, eds., *Canadian State Trials Volume IV: Security, Dissent and the Limits of Toleration in War and Peace, 1914–1939*
David Fraser, *"Honorary Protestants": The Jewish School Question in Montreal, 1867–1997*
C. Ian Kyer, *A Thirty Years' War: The Failed Public /Private Partnership that Spurred the Creation of The Toronto Transit Commission, 1891–1921*

2014 Christopher Moore, *The Court of Appeal for Ontario: Defining the Right of Appeal, 1792–2013*
Dominique Clément, *Equality Deferred: Sex Discrimination and British Columbia's Human Rights State, 1953–84*
Paul Craven, *Petty Justice: Low Law and the Sessions System in Charlotte County, New Brunswick, 1785–1867*
Thomas Telfer, *Ruin and Redemption: The Struggle for a Canadian Bankruptcy Law, 1867–1919*

2013 Roy McMurtry, *Memoirs and Reflections*
Charlotte Gray, *The Massey Murder: A Maid, Her Master and the Trial That Shocked a Nation*
C. Ian Kyer, *Lawyers, Families, and Businesses: The Shaping of a Bay Street Law Firm, Faskens 1863–1963*
G. Blaine Baker and Donald Fyson, eds., *Essays in the History of Canadian Law Volume 11: Quebec and the Canadas*

2012 R. Blake Brown, *Arming and Disarming: A History of Gun Control in Canada*
Eric Tucker, James Muir, and Bruce Ziff, eds., *Property on Trial: Canadian Cases in Context*
Shelley A.M. Gavigan, *Hunger, Horses, and Government Men: Criminal Law on the Aboriginal Plains, 1870–1905*
Barrington Walker, ed., *The African Canadian Legal Odyssey: Historical Essays*

2011 Robert J. Sharpe, *The Lazier Murder: Prince Edward County, 1884*
Philip Girard, *Lawyers and Legal Culture in British North America: Beamish Murdoch of Halifax*
John McLaren, *Dewigged, Bothered, and Bewildered: British Colonial Judges on Trial*
Lesley Erickson, *Westward Bound: Sex, Violence, the Law, and the Making of a Settler Society*

2010 Judy Fudge and Eric Tucker, eds., *Work on Trial: Canadian Labour Law Struggles*
Christopher Moore, *The British Columbia Court of Appeal: The First Hundred Years*
Frederick Vaughan, *Viscount Haldane: The Wicked Step-father of the Canadian Constitution*
Barrington Walker, *Race on Trial: Black Defendants in Ontario's Criminal Courts, 1850–1950*

2009 William Kaplan, *Canadian Maverick: The Life and Times of Ivan C. Rand*
R. Blake Brown, *A Trying Question: The Jury in Nineteenth-Century Canada*
Barry Wright and Susan Binnie, eds., *Canadian State Trials Volume 3: Political Trials and Security Measures, 1840–1914*
Robert J. Sharpe, *The Last Day, the Last Hour: The Currie Libel Trial*

2008 Constance Backhouse, *Carnal Crimes: Sexual Assault Law in Canada, 1900–1975*
Jim Phillips, R. Roy McMurtry, and John Saywell, eds., *Essays in the History of Canadian Law Volume 10: A Tribute to Peter N. Oliver*
Gregory Taylor, *The Law of the Land: Canada's Receptions of the Torrens System*
Hamar Foster, Benjamin Berger, and A.R. Buck, eds., *The Grand Experiment: Law and Legal Culture in British Settler Societies*

2007 Robert Sharpe and Patricia McMahon, *The Persons Case: The Origins and Legacy of the Fight for Legal Personhood*
Lori Chambers, *Misconceptions: Unmarried Motherhood and the Ontario Children of Unmarried Parents Act, 1921–1969*
Jonathan Swainger, ed., *The Alberta Supreme Court at 100: History and Authority*
Martin Friedland, *My Life in Crime and Other Academic Adventures*

2006 Donald Fyson, *Magistrates, Police and People: Everyday Criminal Justice in Quebec and Lower Canada, 1764–1837*
Dale Brawn, *The Court of Queen's Bench of Manitoba 1870–1950: A Biographical History*
R.C.B. Risk, *A History of Canadian Legal Thought: Collected Essays*, edited and introduced by G. Blaine Baker and Jim Phillips
2005 Philip Girard, *Bora Laskin: Bringing Law to Life*
Christopher English, ed., *Essays in the History of Canadian Law Volume 9: Two Islands, Newfoundland and Prince Edward Island*
Fred Kaufman, *Searching for Justice: An Autobiography*
2004 John D. Honsberger, *Osgoode Hall: An Illustrated History*
Frederick Vaughan, *Aggressive in Pursuit: The Life of Justice Emmett Hall*
Constance Backhouse and Nancy Backhouse, *The Heiress versus the Establishment: Mrs. Campbell's Campaign for Legal Justice*
Philip Girard, Jim Phillips, and Barry Cahill, eds., *The Supreme Court of Nova Scotia, 1754–2004: From Imperial Bastion to Provincial Oracle*
2003 Robert Sharpe and Kent Roach, *Brian Dickson: A Judge's Journey*
George Finlayson, *John J. Robinette: Peerless Mentor*
Peter Oliver, *The Conventional Man: The Diaries of Ontario Chief Justice Robert A. Harrison, 1856–1878*
Jerry Bannister, *The Rule of the Admirals: Law, Custom and Naval Government in Newfoundland, 1699–1832*
2002 John T. Saywell, *The Law Makers: Judicial Power and the Shaping of Canadian Federalism*
David Murray, *Colonial Justice: Justice, Morality and Crime in the Niagara District, 1791–1849*
F. Murray Greenwood and Barry Wright, eds., *Canadian State Trials Volume 2: Rebellion and Invasion in the Canadas, 1837–1839*
Patrick Brode, *Courted and Abandoned: Seduction in Canadian Law*
2001 Ellen Anderson, *Judging Bertha Wilson: Law as Large as Life*
Judy Fudge and Eric Tucker, *Labour before the Law: Collective Action in Canada, 1900–1948*
Laurel Sefton MacDowell, *Renegade Lawyer: The Life of J.L. Cohen*
2000 Barry Cahill, *"The Thousandth Man": A Biography of James McGregor Stewart*
A.B. McKillop, *The Spinster and the Prophet: Florence Deeks, H.G. Wells, and the Mystery of the Purloined Past*
Beverley Boissery and F. Murray Greenwood, *Uncertain Justice: Canadian Women and Capital Punishment*
Bruce Ziff, *Unforeseen Legacies: Reuben Wells Leonard and the Leonard Foundation Trust*

1999 Constance Backhouse, *Colour-Coded: A Legal History of Racism in Canada, 1900–1950*
G. Blaine Baker and Jim Phillips, eds., *Essays in the History of Canadian Law Volume 8: In Honour of R.C.B. Risk*
Richard W. Pound, *Chief Justice W.R. Jackett: By the Law of the Land*
David Vanek, *Fulfilment: Memoirs of a Criminal Court Judge*

1998 Sidney Harring, *White Man's Law: Native People in Nineteenth-Century Canadian Jurisprudence*
Peter Oliver, *"Terror to Evil-Doers": Prisons and Punishments in Nineteenth-Century Ontario*

1997 James W. St. G. Walker, *"Race," Rights and the Law in the Supreme Court of Canada: Historical Case Studies*
Lori Chambers, *Married Women and Property Law in Victorian Ontario*
Patrick Brode, *Casual Slaughters and Accidental Judgments: Canadian War Crimes and Prosecutions, 1944–1948*
Ian Bushnell, *The Federal Court of Canada: A History, 1875–1992*

1996 Carol Wilton, ed., *Essays in the History of Canadian Law Volume 7: Inside the Law – Canadian Law Firms in Historical Perspective*
William Kaplan, *Bad Judgment: The Case of Mr. Justice Leo A. Landreville*
Murray Greenwood and Barry Wright, eds., *Canadian State Trials Volume 1: Law, Politics and Security Measures, 1608–1837*

1995 David Williams, *Just Lawyers: Seven Portraits*
Hamar Foster and John McLaren, eds., *Essays in the History of Canadian Law Volume 6: British Columbia and the Yukon*
W.H. Morrow, ed., *Northern Justice: The Memoirs of Mr. Justice William G. Morrow*
Beverley Boissery, *A Deep Sense of Wrong: The Treason, Trials and Transportation to New South Wales of Lower Canadian Rebels after the 1838 Rebellion*

1994 Patrick Boyer, *A Passion for Justice: The Legacy of James Chalmers McRuer*
Charles Pullen, *The Life and Times of Arthur Maloney: The Last of the Tribunes*
Jim Phillips, Tina Loo, and Susan Lewthwaite, eds., *Essays in the History of Canadian Law Volume 5: Crime and Criminal Justice*
Brian Young, *The Politics of Codification: The Lower Canadian Civil Code of 1866*

1993 Greg Marquis, *Policing Canada's Century: A History of the Canadian Association of Chiefs of Police*
Murray Greenwood, *Legacies of Fear: Law and Politics in Quebec in the Era of the French Revolution*

1992 Brendan O'Brien, *Speedy Justice: The Tragic Last Voyage of His Majesty's Vessel* Speedy
Robert Fraser, ed., *Provincial Justice: Upper Canadian Legal Portraits from the Dictionary of Canadian Biography*

1991 Constance Backhouse, *Petticoats and Prejudice: Women and Law in Nineteenth-Century Canada*

1990 Philip Girard and Jim Phillips, eds., *Essays in the History of Canadian Law Volume 3: Nova Scotia*
Carol Wilton, ed., *Essays in the History of Canadian Law Volume 4: Beyond the Law – Lawyers and Business in Canada 1830–1930*

1989 Desmond Brown, *The Genesis of the Canadian Criminal Code of 1892*
Patrick Brode, *The Odyssey of John Anderson*

1988 Robert Sharpe, *The Last Day, the Last Hour: The Currie Libel Trial*
John D. Arnup, *Middleton: The Beloved Judge*

1987 C. Ian Kyer and Jerome Bickenbach, *The Fiercest Debate: Cecil A. Wright, the Benchers and Legal Education in Ontario, 1923–1957*

1986 Paul Romney, *Mr. Attorney: The Attorney General for Ontario in Court, Cabinet and Legislature, 1791–1899*
Martin Friedland, *The Case of Valentine Shortis: A True Story of Crime and Politics in Canada*

1985 James Snell and Frederick Vaughan, *The Supreme Court of Canada: History of the Institution*

1984 Patrick Brode, *Sir John Beverley Robinson: Bone and Sinew of the Compact*
David Williams, *Duff: A Life in the Law*

1983 David H. Flaherty, ed., *Essays in the History of Canadian Law Volume 2*

1982 Marion MacRae and Anthony Adamson, *Cornerstones of Order: Courthouses and Town Halls of Ontario, 1784–1914*

1981 David H. Flaherty, ed., *Essays in the History of Canadian Law Volume 1*

FSC
www.fsc.org
MIX
Papier | Fördert gute Waldnutzung
FSC® C083411

Kolibri 360 GmbH
Ferdinand-Jühlke-Straße 7
99095 Erfurt, Deutschland
produktsicherheit@kolibri360.de